W9-BVS-854

◆ *Inventing Eastern Europe* ◆

CARTE GÉNÉRALE

la France et l'Empire, la Pologne et la Russie.

◆ *Inventing Eastern Europe* ◆

The Map of Civilization on the
Mind of the Enlightenment

Larry Wolff

Stanford University Press / *Stanford, California* ◆ *1994*

Stanford University Press
Stanford, California

© 1994 by the Board of Trustees of the
Leland Stanford Junior University

Printed in the United States of America

CIP data are at the end of the book

Stanford University Press publications are distributed
exclusively by Stanford University Press within the United
States, Canada, and Mexico; they are distributed exclusively by
Cambridge University Press throughout the rest of the world.

Frontispiece: "Carte Générale: la France et l'Empire, la Pologne
et la Russie," from Chappe d'Auteroche, *Voyage en Siberie*, Paris,
1768, Volume IV. This was a "General Map," as the title
proclaimed, and included the mapping of the traveler's itinerary
from west to east, above the heads of the allegorical figures who
illustrated the significance of that directional displacement;
France and the Holy Roman Empire appear in association as
classically garbed goddesses, facing the figures of Poland and
Russia, also in association, as allegorical savages; such was the
philosophical deployment of the concept of "civilization" in
distinguishing between Western Europe and Eastern Europe.
(By permission of the Houghton Library, Harvard University.)

◆

For my parents, Robert and Renee Wolff

And in memory of my grandparents,
Lucy and Martin Stier
Esther and Joseph Wolff

Acknowledgments

As I worked on this project, and came to realize how intimidatingly broad was the scope of the problem I set out to address, I have had good reason to appreciate the guidance, assistance, and encouragement that I have received over many years from my professors, my colleagues, my friends, and my family. I also owe a great debt to scholars I never knew, whose work, some of it completed long before I was born, guided me as I attempted to put together the pieces of a very challenging puzzle. The reference notes at the end seem not quite enough to express the extent of my appreciation for those whose research has made it possible for me to try to pull together the material from several historical fields, and especially to try to bridge the historiographical gap between Eastern Europe and Western Europe in the interest of a study of their complementary relation in intellectual history. While I am eager to give credit for the assistance I have received, I also take full responsibility for the arguments of the book, the more so since they may appear controversial to some. The question of how the Enlightenment came to think of Europe as being divided into east and west is, I think, an urgent one for both historical and political reasons, and I hope that my thesis will provoke further critical discussion of the issue. I am aware that the scope of the historical question has led me to trespass into other people's fields of expertise, and I hope that my arguments may be challenged, clarified, and revised by those who feel, as I do, that the question of the Enlightenment and Eastern Europe is of great importance.

My deepest academic debt is to the professor who so wisely guided my graduate education at Stanford, Wayne Vucinich, Uncle Wayne. It was he who encouraged me to study Eastern Europe together with Western Europe, who guided my doctoral dissertation on Poland and the Vatican, and who showed me by his example the academic subtlety, sensitivity, and integrity which the subject of Eastern Europe deserves from historians. I owe an even older academic debt to Wiktor Weintraub, with whom I studied Polish language, literature, and intellectual history as an under-graduate at Harvard. The books that he gave me to read then, including Boy's *Znaszli ten kraj?* and Miłosz's *Rodzinna Europa*, stimulated me to start thinking about issues of Western Europe and Eastern Europe. I had the benefit of his advice in the earliest stages of this project, and, after his death in 1988, I greatly missed him and his guidance. The subject of my book reaches back yet another generation, to the professors of my profes-sors, picking up on the work of Robert Kerner about eighteenth-century Bohemia, and that of Stanisław Kot about the discussion of Poland in the political literature of Western Europe.

From my graduate education at Stanford there are two more professors, Gordon Wright and Gordon Craig, who helped to give me the academic preparation I needed to approach a subject like this one. In particular, Gordon Wright suggested that I read Chabod's *Storia dell'idea d'Europa*, and Gordon Craig started me thinking about what Eastern Europe looked like from the perspective of Vienna, in the period spanned by the policies of Prince Eugene and Prince Kaunitz. In view of my connection to Stan-ford, I am especially pleased that this book is being published by Stanford University Press, and am grateful to Norris Pope for his editorial guidance. I am also grateful to William Abrahams and Dorrit Cohn for the excellent advice they give me about the publication of my manuscript.

I have received financial support for this project from Boston College, and from the American Council of Learned Societies. I have been pre-senting pieces of my work at conferences for the last several years, and am especially grateful to Alex Pettit who encouraged me to talk about Vol-taire at the Eighteenth Century Studies conference in Seattle in 1991, and to Susan Suleiman who invited me to speak at the Center for Literary and Cultural Studies at Harvard in 1992. I was thinking through the issues of this project at the Cornell conference on France and Poland in 1988, and on that occasion Alain Guery kindly gave me the benefit of his work on the physiocrats and Poland; I also thank Michael Wilson for helping me to digest the intellectual fruits of that conference.

Many scholars have responded to my project with interesting criticism and valuable advice. I am deeply grateful to Gaetano Platania for his help with Boscovich, and to Marylina Żółtowska Weintraub for her help with Marat. Peter Stansky helped me locate Lady Craven as the Margravine of

Ansbach. Dena Goodman cautioned me not to underestimate Mme Geof-frin. Simon Schama encouraged me to be brave about taking on Gibbon. Robert Darnton kindly responded to my request for assistance with Carra in Moldavia. Anthony Cross answered my call for help, and took the time to set me straight about Joseph Marshall. Stephen Greenblatt and Antoni Mączak both gave me some very valuable suggestions about writing on travelers and travel literature. Jerzy Jedlicki kindly permitted me to read his manuscript on Poland in Europe.

I owe a special debt of gratitude to Leslie Choquette, not only for help-ing me with the marquis de Sade, but also for critically reading the first draft of my manuscript. I am also grateful to Kathy Ann Miller for reading the introduction in the middle of a hurricane. Maria Tatar has assisted, ad-vised, and encouraged me at every step of this project, and I have benefited tremendously from her inspirational sense of balance, whether between history and literature, or between sanity and scholarship; she also showed me that it is indeed possible to write a third book—and without losing all your friends. My work on travelers owes much to my friendship with Paul Marx, my co-teacher in History and Literature at Harvard in the 1980s; his intellectual enthusiasm stirred my own interest in travel literature. I have missed him badly since his death in 1989.

My colleagues in the history department at Boston College have been terrifically encouraging from start to finish on this project. I am particularly grateful to Tom Perry for our discussions of Mozart, to Robin Fleming for her suggestions about the Scythians, and to Paul Breines for helpful hints about Herder and Hegel. Two of my graduate students, Hugh Guilder-son and Nick Rowe, have also stimulated me to think through important eighteenth-century issues in my book. I am grateful to the O'Neill Library at Boston College, under the supremely excellent librarianship of Mary Cronin, for putting up with my barrage of requests, and getting me books I never thought I'd be able to obtain in Boston.

Jim Cronin is a great man and a great friend, and his friendship has not only helped me to write this book, but helped me to enjoy writing it. His advice has been so smart, his encouragement so enthusiastic, his example so inspirational, that he has given me a whole new standard of academic collegiality. His insight into the psychology of scholarship and the politics of academia, and his appreciation of all the different kinds of fun that come with being a history professor, have changed my life.

Perri Klass, once again as so many times before, has not only put up with my spiritual imbalance and my not altogether easygoing preoccupa-tion in the throes of the scholarly enterprise, but has given me just the right advice about every aspect of the whole project, from the first staking out of the scope of the subject, to the final and fussiest details of format. This book has been vastly improved by her suggestions, wherever I was wise enough to take them, and it was she who found the Polish angle on Louisa May Alcott. She (Perri Klass not Louisa May Alcott) has lived with me and with my interest in Eastern Europe for a very long time now, and has even camped in a tent outside Cracow. She sent me back to Eastern Europe, when I was too dumb to see that it was time for me to go, and she sent along the perfect companion for that trip, Professor Nicholas Francia, the secret heir to the throne of Brazovia in Loveswept Romance #239, *The Prince and the Patriot*. However, it is she (Perri Klass and not Professor Nicholas Francia) who is my role model, as well as my favorite writer, and my own true love. Together we have managed to put together a household in which many things do not get done, but books like this one do get written, and eventually even the children's lunchboxes do get packed. The children have been good sports about inventing Eastern Europe; Orlando was in on the whole project from the beginning, while Josephine was born in 1989, Eastern Europe's *annus mirabilis*. They have enhanced my work as only they know how.

My greatest, broadest, and oldest debt is to my parents, and this book is dedicated to them. It is also dedicated to the memory of my grandparents, who gave me some sense of personal connection to Eastern Europe.

In addition to my personal debts of gratitude, there are some debts of scholarship that have gone very deep in the course of my work on this project. I have depended upon the academic expertise of others to make up for my own limitations as I looked for comprehensive answers to a rather broadly framed question. In particular, I have found myself very much engaged with, involved in, and dependent on the researches of French scholars of past generations. The French philosophes were the central figures in the Enlightenment's invention of Eastern Europe, and French scholars, going back to the beginning of the twentieth century, have played the leading role in studying the significance of those eighteenth-century figures and forces. I am very much indebted to the work of Abel Mansuy on the Slavs and French literature, Marietta Martin on Mme Geoffrin, Alice Chevalier on Rulhière, Ambroise Jobert on the physiocrats, and above all the brilliant studies of Albert Lortholary on Russia and the Enlightenment, and Jean Fabre on Poland and the Enlightenment. I also acknowledge a great debt to more recent scholarship from Eastern Europe, and especially to the work of the Polish historian Emanuel Rostworowski and the Hungarian historian Béla Köpeczi, who have produced invaluable studies on the connection between France and their respective nations in the eighteenth century. Finally, only the superb scholarship in England and America, over the last generation, has made it possible for me to presume to take on titanic topics, like the one which stands at the center of this book, the relation between Voltaire and Catherine. I would never have found my bearings without constant reference to the work on Voltaire by Theodore Besterman, Peter Gay, and Carolyn Wilberger, while I was even more dependent in writing about Catherine on the work of Isabel de Madariaga, John Alexander, and David Ransel. I also acknowledge my comprehensive indebtedness to the work of M. S. Anderson on England and Russia, and that of P. J. Marshall and Glyndwr Williams on England and the rest of the world in the eighteenth century. I must reiterate here that none of these scholars is in any way responsible for my ideas and arguments, and that in fact I have sometimes even used their excellent work in ways that run somewhat against the grain of their own interpretations.

I have been very fortunate to be writing this book in these years when the question of Eastern Europe has received urgent and thoughtful attention in every forum of the academic world. Especially since the revolutions of 1989, an array of extremely insightful writers have commented at length on Eastern Europe's place in contemporary Europe, and I have followed that discussion with the greatest interest—in particular, the reflections of Timothy Garton Ash, Tony Judt, Jacques Rupnik, Daniel Chirot, Gale Stokes, Krishan Kumar, Milan Kundera, Josef Skvorecky, Stanisław Barańczak, Adam Michnik, and Czesław Miłosz. They have all participated in the rethinking of the idea of Eastern Europe in recent years, and it would have been impossible to pursue the eighteenth-century question that occupied me without taking into account the dramatic interest of current affairs and current debates. While I hope that my eighteenth-century concerns will illuminate the issues from a new angle, I am also well aware that the development of my own ideas and arguments owes more than a little, both in agreement and in dissent, to the insights of others, who have responded with solemn commitment and profound erudition to the most recent history of Eastern Europe.

I feel that I owe a more unconventional acknowledgment to the subjects of my work, the philosophes of the Enlightenment. It was of course their passionate interest in Eastern Europe which stimulated my interest in their interest. However, I am aware that my book may seem to take them to task for the nature of their interest, which, even at its most sympathetic, was politically inflected by aspects of Orientalism, standards of "civilization," and the implicit presumptions of hegemonic discourse. I am aware that there is also every indication of presumption in my own application of the critical tools of my time to the great minds of the Enlightenment, and I definitely feel a certain consciousness of my own intellectual puniness in the greater scheme of the centuries. This seems all the more important to acknowledge, inasmuch as the philosophes of the Enlightenment have been and remain among my intellectual heroes; their interest in Eastern Europe, however inflected, has seemed to me both astonishing and admirable, as evidence of the intellectual curiosity, boldness, and brilliance which they brought to every aspect of their world and which, I believe, largely created the modern world of ideas that we mentally inhabit. For that reason those ideas become our subjects and targets in intellectual history, and the idea of Eastern Europe has been for some years my own academic preoccupation.

The man who is most on my mind is Voltaire. He is one of my heroes, and there are few figures in intellectual history whose minds I admire more. Yet, in making him the subject of analysis and the center of discussion in large parts of this book, I am aware that I have cast his views in a critical, sometimes even ironic, light. Peter Gay tactfully observed, in *Voltaire's Politics*, that "the correspondence with Catherine shows him at his least admirable." I have taken that correspondence, and analyzed it at length as a crucial document of the Enlightenment's perspective on Eastern Europe. In short, I have taken my hero, and showed him from the angle at which he appears least admirable. Of course I do not believe in ghosts, any more than Voltaire did, but it is all too easy for me, as a passionate admirer of the wit of Voltaire, to imagine the devastating ease with which he would mock and dismiss my academic impertinences. I find this disconcerting, especially since my last book on Freud's Vienna was almost as analytically critical of another of my intellectual heroes. Take me then as an intellectual historian who seems to nourish a not untroubled relation to the minds he most admires. I humbly acknowledge that the extraordinary intellectual enterprise of the Enlightenment, even inventing Eastern Europe, defined the terms and terrain on which I now pursue my later and lesser efforts at intellectual history.

L.W.

Contents

◆ *Inventing Eastern Europe* ◆

Introduction

"From Stettin in the Baltic to Trieste in the Adriatic, an iron curtain has descended across the Continent," announced Winston Churchill in 1946, from Fulton, Missouri, deep in the heart of a different continent. It was to be his most stupendously successful rhetorical coinage, that iron curtain, dividing Europe in two, into Western Europe and Eastern Europe. For almost the next half century it stood as a crucial structural boundary, in the mind and on the map. The map of Europe, with its many countries and cultures, was mentally marked with Churchill's iron curtain, an ideological bisection of the continent during the Cold War. "A shadow has fallen upon the scenes so lately lighted by the Allied victory," Churchill observed, and that shadow too was cast upon the map, darkening the lands behind the iron curtain. In the shadow it was possible to imagine vaguely whatever was unhappy or unpleasant, unsettling or alarming, and yet it was also possible not to look too closely, permitted even to look away—for who could see through an iron curtain and discern the shapes enveloped in shadow?

The lands behind the iron curtain were identified geographically by Churchill as "these Eastern States of Europe." They were joined together now "in what I must call the Soviet sphere," all of them states in which Communist parties were seeking to assume "totalitarian control." Yet the line from Stettin to Trieste, delimiting that Soviet sphere, was not one of absolute geographical determinism, and Churchill admitted one exception: "Athens alone—Greece with its immortal glories—is free." As for the rest of the Eastern states, on the one hand Churchill recognized that "the safety of the world requires a new unity in Europe, from which no nation should be permanently outcast." On the other hand, there was also reason to accept, approve, even enforce the increasingly apparent separation. "In front of the iron curtain which lies across Europe are other causes for anxiety," said Churchill, and from the very first he had no directional doubts about which lands were "in front"—he named Italy and France—and which were consigned to behind. He was anxious about political infiltration, about ideological contamination, for even in Western Europe "Communist parties or fifth columns constitute a growing challenge to Christian civilization."[1] Throughout the Cold War the iron curtain would be envisioned as a barrier of quarantine, separating the light of Christian civilization from whatever lurked in the shadows, and such a conception was all the more justification for not looking too closely at the lands behind.

Churchill's Fulton speech proved to be prophetic, and his figure of speech was cast in iron as a geopolitical fact of international relations. In the next generation, however, diplomatic historians of the Cold War, like Walter LaFeber and Daniel Yergin, would wonder whether this was in part a work of self-fulfilling prophecy, whether the provocation of the speech at Fulton actually contributed to the crystallization of ideological spheres in Europe, hastening the hardening of lines. Churchill himself, when he published his memoirs, showed that he was a far from entirely innocent observer of what befell the Eastern states of Europe, that he had been eager to play a part in drawing the line and hanging the curtain. Not even two years before he went to Fulton, Missouri, accompanied by Harry Truman, to warn against the Soviet shadow, he was in Moscow with Joseph Stalin in 1944, proposing percentages for postwar influence in those same Eastern states. Jotting on a piece of paper, he offered Stalin 90 percent in Romania, 75 percent in Bulgaria, 50 percent in Hungary and Yugoslavia, but only 10 percent in Greece—with its "immortal glories." Churchill then suggested that they burn the paper, but Stalin told him he could keep it.

In 1989 there was a revolution in Eastern Europe, or rather a series of related revolutions in the different Eastern states, which toppled and replaced the Communist governments whose history dated back to the postwar years. Political revolution brought democratic elections, an opening to market capitalism, the lifting of restrictions on travel, the withdrawal of Soviet troops, and eventually in 1991 the dissolution of the Warsaw Pact. It was the Warsaw Pact, facing its counterpart of NATO in Western Europe, which since the 1950s had given military structure to the division of Europe, organizing the continent into confrontational blocs engaged in the Cold War. The revolutionary collapse of communism in Eastern Europe and the end of the Cold War rendered meaningless the conventional terms that formulated the sharp separation of Europe into opposing halves: Churchill's iron curtain, the Soviet sphere, the ominous shadow. The division of Europe suddenly appeared to be over, erased, abolished, the halves all at once reunited as one continent. Such was the thunderbolt of revolution. I was in Poland in 1988, along with a party of other American professors, meeting with Polish professors to discuss the knotty and uncertain significance of Soviet *glasnost* for Eastern Europe. All our combined academic expertise produced a wealth of reflections, analyses, paradoxes, predictions, and pronouncements, but not an inkling of the revolution that was about to strike in the following year. Neither I nor anyone else had the faintest notion of what the opaque future was hiding just out of sight; no one guessed that the significance of *glasnost* would prove so tremendous that in a year the very idea of Eastern Europe, as a distinct geopolitical entity for focused academic analysis, would have become dubious and equivocal.

The revolution of 1989 in Eastern Europe has largely invalidated the perspective of half a century, compelling the reconsideration of Europe as a whole. The maps on the wall have always showed a continent of many colors, the puzzle pieces of many states; the dark line of the iron curtain, supplying the light and shadow in front and behind, was drawn on the maps in the mind. Those maps must be adjusted, adapted, reconceived, but their structures are deeply rooted and powerfully compelling. In the 1990s Italians are worriedly deporting Albanian refugees: *Albanesi, no grazie!* reads the graffiti on the wall. Germans are greeting visitors from Poland with thuggish violence and neo-Nazi demonstrations, while tourists from Eastern Europe are being arbitrarily stopped and searched in Paris shops, under suspicion of shoplifting. Statesmen, who once enthusiastically anticipated the unity of Europe, are looking away from the siege of Sarajevo, wishing perhaps that it were happening on some other continent. Alienation is in part a matter of economic disparity, the wealth of Western Europe facing the poverty of Eastern Europe, but such disparity is inevitably clothed in the complex windings of cultural prejudice. The iron curtain is gone, and yet the shadow persists.

The shadow persists, because the idea of Eastern Europe remains, even without the iron curtain. This is not only because the intellectual structures of half a century are slow to efface themselves, but above all because that idea of Eastern Europe is much older than the Cold War. Churchill's oratorical image of the iron curtain was powerful and persuasive, and its success was in part on account of its apparent aptness in describing the contemporary emergence of a Soviet sphere as the international cataclysm of the historical moment. Yet its aptness and prescience also concealed a part of what made Churchill's imagery so powerful, the traces of an intellectual history that invented the idea of Eastern Europe long before. Churchill's demarcation of a boundary line "from Stettin in the Baltic to Trieste in the Adriatic" followed a line that was drawn and invested with meaning over two centuries, dating back to the age of his most famous ancestor, the warrior duke of Marlborough. The "iron curtain" seamlessly fit the earlier tracing, and it was almost forgotten, or neglected, or suppressed, that an older epoch in the history of ideas first divided the continent, creating the disunion of Western Europe and Eastern Europe.

The distinction is older than Churchill and the Cold War, but it is by no means a matter of time immemorial, undiscoverably ancient. It was not a natural distinction, or even an innocent one, for it was produced as a work of cultural creation, of intellectual artifice, of ideological self-interest and self-promotion. Churchill might remove himself to Fulton, Missouri, to produce a semblance of external perspective, discerning from a distance the division of Europe. The original division, however, happened at home. It was Western Europe that invented Eastern Europe as its complementary other half in the eighteenth century, the age of Enlightenment. It was also the Enlightenment, with its intellectual centers in Western Europe, that cultivated and appropriated to itself the new notion of "civilization," an eighteenth-century neologism, and civilization discovered its complement, within the same continent, in shadowed lands of backwardness, even barbarism. Such was the invention of Eastern Europe. It has flourished as an idea of extraordinary potency since the eighteenth century, neatly dovetailing in our own times with the rhetoric and realities of the Cold War, but also certain to outlive the collapse of Communism, surviving in the public culture and its mental maps. One may begin to understand and confront the idea of Eastern Europe by exploring the intricate historical process that left it embedded and encoded in our culture.

In the Renaissance the fundamental conceptual division of Europe was between the South and the North. The city states of Italy were the almost unquestioned centers of art and learning, of painting and sculpture, rhetoric and philosophy, not to mention finance and trade. The Italian humanists did not hesitate to proclaim a perspective of cultural condescension, most dramatically expressed in Machiavelli's famous "Exhortation to Liberate Italy from the Barbarians," the last chapter of *The Prince*. He was looking back to the landmark event of his generation, for every Florentine and most Italians, the invasion of Italy in 1494 by Charles VIII, the king of France, which inaugurated a period of "barbarian" invasions from the north, presaging the end of the *quattrocento*, the most glorious age of the Italian Renaissance. Even more traumatic was the great disaster of the next generation, the sack of Rome in 1527 by the German soldiers of the Holy Roman Emperor, Charles V. The Italian Renaissance saw itself battered by the blows of northern barbarians, and classically conscious humanists could look back a thousand years, from the sack of Rome by Germans in 1527, to the sack of Rome by the Goths in 476, to reinforce their directional perspective on the lands of barbarism. Ancient Romans and Renaissance Italians alike read Tacitus on the Germans to discover people who performed human sacrifices, wore wild animal skins, and generally lacked the refinements of culture: "When not engaged in warfare they spend a certain amount of time in hunting, but much more in idleness, thinking of nothing else but sleeping and eating."[2] Tacitus knew of other barbarians further to the east, such as the Sarmatians and the Dacians, but his chief concern was the Germans to the north, and this classical perspective was marvelously suited to the Italians of the Renaissance. Indeed, Machiavelli seized upon the perspective of ancient Rome with the same splendid verve and rhetorical opportunism that Churchill demonstrated in exploiting the perspective of the Enlightenment for the foundation of the iron curtain.

The polarization of Europe between Italy and the northern barbarians, so obvious to the ancient Romans, so convenient to the Renaissance Italians, survived into the eighteenth century as a rhetorical form. William Coxe, publishing in 1785 his *Travels into Poland, Russia, Sweden, and Denmark,* could still sum them up as "my travels through the Northern kingdoms of Europe."[3] Yet this geographical perspective had begun to appear seriously anachronistic, and it was the intellectual work of the Enlightenment to bring about that modern reorientation of the continent which produced Western Europe and Eastern Europe. Poland and Russia would be mentally detached from Sweden and Denmark, and associated instead with Hungary and Bohemia, the Balkan lands of Ottoman Europe, and even the Crimea on the Black Sea.

From the age of the Renaissance to the age of the Enlightenment, Europe's centers of culture and finance had shifted from the treasures and treasuries of Rome, Florence, and Venice to the now more dynamically important cities of Paris, London, and Amsterdam. Voltaire's perspective on Europe from eighteenth-century Paris was altogether geographically different from that of Machiavelli in sixteenth-century Florence. It was Voltaire who led the way as the philosophes of the Enlightenment articulated and elaborated their own perspective on the continent, gazing from west to east, instead of from south to north. In so doing, they perpetrated a conceptual reorientation of Europe, which they bequeathed to us so that we now see Europe as they did; or, rather, we have passively inherited the Europe that they actively reconceived. Just as the new centers of the Enlightenment superseded the old centers of the Renaissance, the old lands of barbarism and backwardness in the north were correspondingly displaced to the east. The Enlightenment had to invent Western Europe and Eastern Europe together, as complementary concepts, defining each other by opposition and adjacency.

Travelers were essential to this work of orientation, eighteenth-century travelers from Western Europe to Eastern Europe. The lands of Eastern Europe were sufficiently unfamiliar in the eighteenth century, still such unusual destinations, that each traveler carried a mental map to be freely annotated, embellished, refined, or refolded along the way. The operations of mental mapping were above all association and comparison: association among the lands of Eastern Europe, intellectually combining them into a coherent whole, and comparison with the lands of Western Europe, establishing the developmental division of the continent. This book will begin with a traveler, the count de Ségur, one of the French heroes of the American Revolutionary War, entering Eastern Europe on his way to St. Petersburg in the winter of 1784–85 to serve as French ambassador to the court of Catherine the Great. When he passed from Prussia into Poland— roughly where the iron curtain would descend two centuries later—he was powerfully conscious of crossing an extremely significant border. He felt he had "left Europe entirely," and furthermore had "moved back ten centuries." This book will end with another traveler returning to Western Europe, an American, John Ledyard, who had traveled around the world with Captain Cook, and in 1788 was returning from a solo expedition to Siberia, which ended in his arrest by order of Catherine. Traveling west across the Russian empire, then through Poland, he did not consider himself to be back in Europe until he reached the Prussian border. There, between Poland and Prussia, Ledyard located "the great barrier of Asiatic & European manners," and he "leapt" across with gushing enthusiasm: "Once more welcome Europe to my warmest embraces."[4] It is hardly necessary to consult an atlas to see that Ségur, when he felt he had "left Europe entirely," was nowhere near the boundary of Europe, and that Ledyard, traveling in the other direction, was all at once welcoming and embracing Europe in sheer defiance of the fact that he had already been traveling in Europe for more than a thousand miles.

Ledyard had a name for such freely constructed geographical sentiment; he called it "Philosophic Geography." Such was the Enlightenment's subordination of geography to its own philosophical values, its investment of the map with subtleties that eluded the stricter standards of scientific cartography. Ségur had a name for the space that he discovered when he seemed to leave Europe but still remained in Europe; eventually he located himself in "the east of Europe," which in French, as *l'orient de l'Europe*, offered also the potently evocative possibility of "the Orient of Europe." As late as the eve of World War I, French scholarship still alternated between two seemingly similar terms, *l'Europe orientale* (Eastern Europe) and *l'Orient européen* (the European Orient).[5] Edward Said's *Orientalism* has proposed that the Orient was constructed by the Occident "as its contrasting image, idea, personality, experience," an image of otherness, while Orientalism served as "a

Western style for dominating, restructuring, and having authority over the Orient."[6] The idea of Eastern Europe was entangled with evolving Orientalism, for while Philosophic Geography casually excluded Eastern Europe from Europe, implicitly shifting it into Asia, scientific cartography seemed to contradict such fanciful construction. There was room for ambiguity. The geographical border between Europe and Asia was not unanimously fixed in the eighteenth century, located sometimes at the Don, sometimes farther east at the Volga, and sometimes, as today, at the Urals.

Such uncertainty encouraged the construction of Eastern Europe as a paradox of simultaneous inclusion and exclusion, Europe but not Europe. Eastern Europe defined Western Europe by contrast, as the Orient defined the Occident, but was also made to mediate between Europe and the Orient. One might describe the invention of Eastern Europe as an intellectual project of demi-Orientalization. This was a process that could also work the other way. Martin Bernal's *Black Athena* has proposed that purposeful Hellenism purged our understanding of ancient Greece of its African and Asian influences. It also helped to exempt modern Greece from inclusion in the idea of Eastern Europe, and Churchill still celebrated the salvation of its "immortal glories" from the shadow of the iron curtain in the twentieth century. The parallel intellectual processes of Orientalism and Hellenism, both dating back to the eighteenth century, created important points of reference and influential parameters for the evolution of the idea of Eastern Europe. Interestingly, the idea of Europe as a whole came into cultural focus at the same time that the continent was conceived in halves. The Italian historian Federico Chabod, looking toward European unity after World War II, argued that the idea of Europe emerged with a coherent character and secular philosophical significance in the age of Enlightenment. Chabod placed special emphasis on the writings of Montesquieu, on the opposition between Europe and the Orient in the *Persian Letters*, and between European liberty and Asiatic despotism in the *Spirit of the Laws*.[7] Those oppositions, however, allowed for an intermediary cultural space, in which the idea of Eastern Europe evolved.

Philosophic Geography was a free-spirited sport, so much so that it was not actually necessary to travel to Eastern Europe in order to participate in its intellectual discovery. Some would make the voyage, with portentous anticipation and international publicity. Madame Geoffrin left the philosophes of her Paris salon to visit the king of Poland in 1766, and Diderot made his way to St. Petersburg in 1773 to pay his respects to Catherine the Great. Yet no one wrote more authoritatively and enthusiastically about Russia than Voltaire, who never traveled east of Berlin, and no one was engaged more passionately and creatively on behalf of Poland than Rousseau, who never went east of Switzerland. Mozart made the voyage between Western Europe and Eastern Europe, crossing the border at a point of intimate and intricate proximity, between Vienna and Prague. In fact Prague is north of Vienna, and just slightly to the west, but for Mozart, as for us in the twentieth century, it was a voyage into Eastern Europe nevertheless, into Slavic Bohemia. He marked the border crossing in the Mozartian mode, by adopting new identities for himself, his family, and his friends, expressed in pseudo-Oriental nonsense names: "I am Punktititi. My wife is Schabla Pumfa. Hofer is Rozka Pumpa. Stadler is Notschibikitschibi."[8] The curtain between Vienna and Prague went up on this frivolous operatic comedy long before it descended in its iron incarnation.

Whether fanciful or philosophical, in a spirit of imaginative extravagance or of earnest erudition, the study of Eastern Europe, like Orientalism, was a style of intellectual mastery, integrating knowledge and power, perpetrating domination and subordination. As in the case of the Orient, so also with Eastern Europe, intellectual discovery and mastery could not be entirely separated from the possibility of real conquest. France's eighteenth-century experts on Eastern Europe ended up in Napoleon's regime and academy, and the Enlightenment's discovery of Eastern Europe soon pointed the way to conquest and domination. Napoleon's creation of the Grand Duchy of Warsaw in 1807, his annexation of the Adriatic provinces of Illyria in 1809, and finally his invasion of Russia in 1812 put Philosophic Geography at the service of military mapping. It was not to be the last time that armies of Western Europe sought to establish an empire in Eastern Europe.

Immanuel Wallerstein, in his economic history of the "Origins of the European World-Economy," assigns to the sixteenth century the emergence of a capitalist "core" in Western Europe, exercising its economic hegemony over a "periphery" in Eastern Europe (and Hispanic America), creating a "complementary divergence" out of an initially minimal economic disparity.[9] As Western Europe's "periphery," Eastern Europe's essential economic role was the export of grain, cultivated by coerced labor with the establishment of a post-medieval "second serfdom." Yet, Wallerstein's argument is based almost exclusively on the case of Poland, whose economy was indeed significantly and dependently based on the Baltic export of wheat from Gdańsk to Amsterdam. He recognizes clearly that not all of modern Eastern Europe participated even in the periphery of the European world economy in the sixteenth century: "Russia outside, but Poland inside. Hungary inside, but the Ottoman Empire outside."[10] The identification of Eastern Europe as economic periphery involves, to a certain extent, taking the culturally constructed unity of the eighteenth century and projecting it backward to organize an earlier economic model. In fact, social and economic factors were far from fully determining Western Europe's associative construction of Eastern Europe.

The historical issues of core and periphery that Wallerstein raised in the 1970s focused the further study of Eastern Europe, and in 1985 an international academic conference convened at Bellagio to discuss the "Origins of Backwardness in Eastern Europe." Eric Hobsbawm compared the cases of Switzerland and Albania, superficially similar in terrain and resources yet dramatically different in their economic fates. Robert Brenner argued that "the problem of backwardness in Eastern Europe is a question badly posed," inasmuch as "historically speaking, non-development is the rule rather than the exception," and therefore the real question should be that of Western Europe's exceptional capitalist development. The conference recognized that "Eastern Europe is by no means a single entity," that different parts became "economic adjuncts" of Western Europe at different times and were "backward in many different ways." [11] The issues of backwardness and development in Eastern Europe were broached and defined in the eighteenth century, not essentially as economic issues, and they continue to frame our conception of these lands. It was Eastern Europe's ambiguous location, within Europe but not fully European, that called for such notions as backwardness and development to mediate between the poles of civilization and barbarism. In fact, Eastern Europe in the eighteenth century provided Western Europe with its first model of underdevelopment, a concept that we now apply all over the globe.

The very idea of an international conference of academic experts, meeting at Bellagio under the auspices of the Rockefeller Foundation, to discuss "the problem of backwardness in Eastern Europe" is profoundly consistent with the Enlightenment's approach to the same problem. At Ferney, across the Alps from Bellagio, Voltaire applied his own genius for twenty years to an ongoing one-man expert symposium on backwardness in Eastern Europe. In Paris the physiocrats met regularly at the salon of the elder Mirabeau to discuss the problem's specifically economic aspects. In fact, the Paris salon sent a physiocrat to Poland in 1774 with great fanfare, just as the Harvard economics department sent a professor to Poland in 1989. The revolution of 1989 has certainly dramatized the issue of "backwardness" in Eastern Europe, as new governments seek to clear away the economic debris of communism and enter the world economy of market capitalism. The recourse to expert advice and economic assistance from abroad will certainly be construed as the ultimate vindication of our own economic success and the backwardness of Eastern Europe. As the European Community prepared to constitute itself as an economic union, "the Europe of 1992," a special bank, the European Bank for Reconstruction and Development, was created to deal with the special problems of Eastern Europe. In the Europe of the 1990s Eastern Europe will continue to occupy an ambiguous space between inclusion and exclusion, both in economic affairs and in cultural recognition.

The philosophes of the Enlightenment explored and exploited this ambiguity, fitting it into a scheme of backwardness and development, making it into a defining characteristic that combined different lands under the sign of Eastern Europe. Already in the Renaissance it was possible to apply such a scheme to Poland, and Erasmus wrote in 1523 "to congratulate a people who, though formerly ill regarded as barbarian, now so blossoms in letters, laws, customs, religion, and in whatever else may spare it the reproach of uncouthness, that it can vie with the most distinguished and praised of nations."[12] For Erasmus the rise from barbarism had nothing to do with economic development. Montaigne in the sixteenth century accepted all men as his compatriots and would "embrace a Pole as Frenchman," though perhaps such vaunted cosmopolitanism implied as much condescension as Erasmus's congratulations. When a French prince became king of Poland in 1573, only to abandon the crown the next year to return to France as Henri III, the French poet in his entourage, Philippe Desportes, wrote a sarcastic "Farewell to Poland." It was farewell to ice and snow, bad manners, and "barbaric people."[13]

In the first half of the sixteenth century Rabelais mentioned in association "Muscovites, Indians, Persians, and Troglodytes," suggesting that Russia was part of an Oriental and even mythological domain.[14] After the English naval explorer Richard Chancellor discovered the Arctic sea passage to Russia in the 1550s and the trading Muscovy Company was established, accounts of Russia became a more serious concern. They were included in Richard Hakluyt's Elizabethan collection *Principal Navigations, Voyages, and Discoveries of the English Nation*, along with accounts of the New World in America. In 1600 a French mercenary soldier, Captain Jacques Margeret, entered the military service of the Russian tsar, Boris Godunov, and ended up publishing the most serious seventeenth-century French account of Russia. The Russians were identified as "those formerly called Scythians," in general "a thoroughly rude and barbarous people." Russia was furthermore reported replete with mythological wonders of natural history, including a rooted animal-plant: "The sheep eats the grass around itself and then dies. They are the size of a lamb, with curly wool. Some of the hides are completely white, others a little spotted. I have seen several of these hides."[15] While Captain Margeret was in Russia, another adventurous soldier, Captain John Smith, crossed the continent from England to Ottoman Europe on an expedition that was summed up as "his Service and Stratagems of war in Hungaria, Transilvania, Wallachia, and Moldavia, against the Turks and Tartars." He was taken prisoner by the Crimean Tartars in 1603, as he would be again in Virginia in 1607, by the American Indians of the Powhatan Confederacy, to be saved by the thirteen-year-old Pocahontas. He saved himself from slavery among the Crimean Tartars—by murdering his master—and then traveled through Russia, the Ukraine, and Poland, which were summed up simply as "Countries rather to be pitied, than envied." His experience as a prisoner and slave among the Tartars left him in a position to report that Tartary was indescribable: "Now you are to understand, Tartary and Scythia are all one; but so large and spacious, few or none could ever perfectly describe it; nor all the several kinds of those most barbarous people that inhabit it."[16] The Scythians were known from Herodotus as barbarians from the perspective of ancient Greece; when Europeans leaped back beyond the Germans of Tacitus to seize upon the Scythians of Herodotus, the orientation of barbarism shifted from the north to the east. The designation of Scythians was extended in the eighteenth century to cover all of Eastern Europe, until Herder appropriated another identification from among the barbarians of ancient history, and gave Eastern Europe its modern identity as the domain of the Slavs.

The most influential account of Russia in the seventeenth century was written by Adam Olearius, who traveled in the 1630s with a German mission from the court of Holstein, seeking to negotiate the commercial concession to establish trade with Persia through Russia. Such a mission suggested Russia's economic significance as well as its relation to the Orient, but the Olearius account, first published in German in 1647, and constantly republished throughout the century in German, French, Dutch, English, and Italian, evaluated Russia according to generally non-economic standards. Olearius related of the Russians that "their skin is of the same color as that of other Europeans." Such an observation suggested how little his readers were presumed to know about Russia. "When you observe the spirit, the mores, and the way of life of the Russians," Olearius wrote, at a time when very few had had such an opportunity, "you are bound to number them among the barbarians." He went on to censure them on largely moral grounds for using "vile and loathsome words," for lacking "good manners"—"these people fart and belch noisily"—for "lusts of the flesh and fornication" as well as "the vile depravity we call sodomy," committed even with horses. There was perhaps a hint of economic consideration in his judgment that the Russians were "fit only for slavery" and had to be "driven to work with cudgels and whips."[17] The Enlightenment would reconceive Russia in a redemptive spirit that envisioned an emergence from barbarism, an improvement of manners. The possibility of such redemption might be glimpsed in the *Brief History of Moscovia*, written by John Milton, probably in the 1630s. The future poet of *Paradise Lost* and *Paradise Regained* explained that he was interested in Russia "as being the most northern Region of Europe reputed civil."[18] The Enlightenment would rediscover Russia as an eastern region of the continent, and would align its reputation, philosophically and geographically, with the other lands of Eastern Europe.

On March 23, 1772, James Boswell found Samuel Johnson "busy, preparing a fourth edition of his folio Dictionary." They discussed a certain contemporary neologism that Johnson excluded from the dictionary as improper English: "He would not admit *civilization*, but only *civility*. With great deference to him, I thought *civilization*, from *to civilize*, better in the sense opposed to *barbarity*." That same day there was also a discussion of etymologies and language families, and Johnson observed that "the Bohemian language was true Sclavonick." When someone noted some resemblance to German, Johnson replied, "Why, Sir, to be sure, such parts of Sclavonia as confine with Germany, will borrow German words; and such parts as confine with Tartary will borrow Tartar words."[19] Looking back on that day, more than two centuries later, one can see two ideas simultaneously under evolution: the idea of civilization, conceived as the opposite of barbarism, and the idea of Eastern Europe, conceived as "Sclavonia." Boswell and Johnson treated them as two separate problems, related only inasmuch as they both concerned the dictionary, but one can see with historical hindsight that their relation was far more intimate. The new idea of civilization was the crucial and indispensable point of reference that made possible the consolidation and articulation of the inchoate idea of Eastern Europe in the eighteenth century.

Dr. Johnson's dictionary proudly insisted on the now virtually archaic definition of "civilization" as a purely legal term, the making of criminal process into civil process. Yet in the 1770s other dictionaries in both France and England were already admitting the new meaning of the word: in the Jesuits' *Dictionary of Trevoux* in Paris in 1771, in John Ash's *New and Complete Dictionary of the English Language* in London in 1775. The first prominent deployment of the new word has been traced to the elder Mirabeau and his physiocratic circle, where there was also an active interest in Eastern Europe. Beginning with his extremely successful *Ami des hommes* in 1756, Mirabeau used the word in both economic and cultural contexts, associating civilization with the increase of wealth and the refinement of manners. He was also, however, sensitive to "false civilization," especially with reference to the ambitions of Peter the Great in Russia. Another physiocrat, the abbé Baudeau, who actually traveled to Poland and Russia, wrote of stages and degrees of civilization, of the "progress" of civilization in Russia especially, and added an important twist to the new notion by qualifying it as "European civilization." The French Revolution, as interpreted by the French philosophes, further related the idea of civilization to a model of development. Volney envisioned the progress of civilization as the "imitation" of one vanguard nation, and Condorcet wondered whether someday all nations would achieve "the state of civilization reached by the most enlightened, most free, most unprejudiced peoples, such as the French and the Anglo-Americans." Auguste Comte, early in the nineteenth century, was still following the Philosophic Geography of the Enlightenment when he employed "civilization" as a measure of the coherence of "Western Europe."[20]

Eastern Europe was located not at the antipode of civilization, not down in the depths of barbarism, but rather on the developmental scale that measured the distance between civilization and barbarism. Ségur in the late eighteenth century saw St. Petersburg as a confused combination of "the age of barbarism and that of civilization, the tenth and the eighteenth centuries, the manners of Asia and those of Europe, coarse Scythians and polished Europeans."[21] Eastern Europe was essentially in between, and by the nineteenth century these polar oppositions acquired the force of fixed formulas. Balzac, in the *Comédie humaine*, casually summed up all of Eastern Europe from the perspective of Paris, in a passing reference that employed precisely the same terms: "The inhabitants of the Ukraine, Russia, the plains of the Danube, in short, the Slav peoples, are a link between Europe and Asia, between civilization and barbarism."[22]

I first started to think about writing this book ten years ago, when I was spending a year doing research in the Vatican Secret Archive for a study of Poland and the Vatican in the eighteenth century. I read the dispatches of Rome's apostolic nuncios in Warsaw. In 1783, after seven years in Warsaw, the nuncio Giovanni Archetti was preparing for a delicate and momentous diplomatic mission to St. Petersburg, to the court of Catherine. One of the many things on his mind at this important juncture in his career as an ecclesiastical diplomat was the fact that when he arrived in St. Petersburg he would be expected to kiss Catherine's hand. He was afraid that the pope in Rome would strongly disapprove, out of concern that the kiss would compromise the absolute independence of Roman Catholicism. There was some irony in the fact that Rome would worry about such trivialities of court etiquette in what was, after all, already the decade of the French Revolution. There was also humor in such preoccupation with merely kissing the hand of the tsarina, when her sexual excesses were already a legend in her own lifetime. Most interesting to me was the way in which Archetti justified in advance, in a dispatch to Rome, the kiss that he was resolved to bestow. From his experience in Poland he claimed to possess a special understanding of "these northern countries," thus associating Poland and Russia. There was, he observed, a gap between "more cultivated nations" and "those nations becoming cultivated at a later date." The latter nations, "the northern countries," practiced an exaggerated etiquette, kissing hands, for instance, in an attempt to equal "the more genteel nations."[23] Archetti's magnificent condescension suggested that, as far as he was concerned, there was little likelihood of such equality being achieved. However, his scale of cultivation—more or less, sooner or later—demonstrated a sophisticated and modern conception of backwardness and development. All that was lacking was the word "civilization"—and the reorientation that would recognize northern countries as eastern countries. Archetti, an Italian, still held to the Renaissance perspective. Catherine was also capable of condescension; she later described Archetti as a "good child," and she gave him a fur coat.

Archetti claimed that it was the less cultivated nations that made more of a fuss about courtesy, and yet it was he himself who had seized upon a detail of etiquette and dramatized its significance to construct a mental mapping of Europe. Norbert Elias has proposed that the idea of civilization developed from that of civility, as a culminating moment in the history of manners. The construct of civilization was so fundamental an aspect of identity, for those who claimed to possess it, that it found its most satisfying modern expression as a standard for others—for other classes, for other nations. It was when I read Archetti, summing up the northern countries as less cultivated, less genteel, that I began to think about the mapping of civilization within Europe. I thought about the way that his condescensions almost anticipated those of our own times—almost but not quite—and I wondered whether he spoke from the threshold of a great continental reorientation. I began to think about how people came to conceive of Europe as divided between east and west.

I thought about Archetti and Catherine's hand some years ago when I was somewhere behind the iron curtain, in Eastern Europe. I went to an apartment in the middle of the night to visit someone I didn't know very well, to get from him some messages and materials I had agreed to stow in my luggage on the train and carry back across the iron curtain. As I left, he kissed me three times, ritually alternating cheeks—Slavic style, as he said. I couldn't help thinking about Archetti and the way that details of manners sometimes seize upon the imagination and seem to represent worlds of difference. There are such details that have ended up mentally entangled with my whole experience of Eastern Europe, of encounters with underground political life, of hushed conversations and uneasy border crossings.

That Eastern Europe has ceased to exist since 1989, along with the iron curtain. Either we will find new associations to mark its difference, or we will rediscover old ones from before the Cold War. Or else we may take the extraordinary revolution of 1989 as an incitement and opportunity to reconsider our mental mapping of Europe. In 1990 the American Academy of Arts and Sciences marked the occasion with an issue of *Daedalus* entitled "Eastern Europe . . . Central Europe . . . Europe," which seemed to suggest the slippage of signifiers as Europe semiotically shifted and reshaped itself in all our minds. The lead essay in the collection, by Timothy Garton Ash, the English writer who became Western Europe's most insightful analyst of Eastern Europe during the fateful decade of the 1980s, was punctuated with a question mark: "Mitteleuropa?" That question mark hearkened back to another essay by the same writer, published before the revolution of 1989: "Does Central Europe Exist?" This was a delicate and thorny issue of mental mapping, for the idea of *Mitteleuropa* first made its mark in 1915, during World War I, when Friedrich Naumann published in Berlin a book with that title and without any question mark. Naumann's *Mitteleuropa* described a domain marked out for German economic and cultural hegemony, including lands more conventionally located in Eastern Europe. The idea of *Mitteleuropa*, and also those of *Osteuropa* and *Ostraum*, then played an important ideological role during World War II, as Hitler sought to carry out a program of vast conquest and terrible enslavement in Eastern Europe, beginning with the occupations of Czechoslovakia and Poland in 1939, culminating in the invasions of Yugoslavia and Russia in 1941. There was some irony in the fact that in the 1980s the idea of Central Europe was rediscovered by intellectuals in Poland, Czechoslovakia, and Hungary, as well as in Western Europe—and promoted as an ideological antidote to the iron curtain. The question of whether Central Europe existed therefore hinged on the distinction between intellectual construction and geopolitical reality, and Central Europe was only an idea: "It does not yet exist. Eastern Europe exists—that part of Europe militarily controlled by the Soviet Union."[24] Yet Eastern Europe also began as only an idea, and now, since 1989, it has become an idea once again, no longer under the military control of the Soviet Union. Eastern Europe, however, remains an extremely powerful idea, deeply embedded in the history of two centuries, so influential in its political consequences that its intellectual origins are barely recognized, hidden in historical camouflage.

Russia may resign its military domination of Eastern Europe, but it cannot banish the idea of Eastern Europe, for it did not invent or impose that idea. The idea of Eastern Europe was invented in Western Europe in the age of Enlightenment, and Russia was included in that idea. Russia was subjected to the same process of discovery, alignment, condescension, and intellectual mastery, was located and identified by the same formulas: between Europe and Asia, between civilization and barbarism. The advocates of Central Europe today are committed to shattering intellectually the oppressive idea of Eastern Europe, to redeeming the Czech Republic and Hungary, maybe Poland, even perhaps Slovenia. Yet the rubric of Eastern Europe may still be invoked to perpetuate the exclusion of the rest, to preserve the distinction that nourishes our own identity. Mikhail Gorbachev, the man who brought down the iron curtain and ended the Cold War, also demonstrated the most profound understanding of the division of Europe. "We are Europeans," he declared in *Perestroika* in 1987, envisioning a "common home" that stretched from the Atlantic to the Urals, noting the "artificiality" of the blocs, the "archaic nature" of the iron curtain. He challenged those in the West who would exclude the Soviet Union from Europe, and equate Europe with Western Europe.[25] That exclusion, and that equation, were in fact the axioms underlying two centuries of intellectual history, the history of "civilization" in Europe, the invention of Eastern Europe.

Chapter One

Entering Eastern Europe:
Eighteenth-Century Travelers
on the Frontier

"These Demi-Savage Figures"

In 1784 Count Louis-Philippe de Ségur left France for Russia, appointed as minister plenipotentiary and envoy *extraordinaire* of Louis XVI to the court of Catherine II at St. Petersburg. Ségur was only 31 and owed his posting to the fact that his father was the French minister of war. The young man went by way of Berlin and received a royal audience at Potsdam with the already old and famous Frederick. The king observed aloud that Ségur was wearing the decoration of Cincinnatus, the mark of his military service under George Washington in the American Revolutionary War. "How could you for so long forget the delights of Paris," asked Frederick sarcastically, "in a land where civilization is just beginning?" Such condescension toward America was typical of eighteenth-century assumptions about the locus of civilization, and both men, the Parisian and the Berliner, had to be aware that the comment carried a double significance, for the present posting to St. Petersburg as well as past service in America. In Russia, too, by enlightened consensus, civilization was just beginning in the eighteenth century, and Ségur would have many opportunities to reflect upon that in the five years that followed. It was a matter of reflection that interested him, though, the stages and progress of civilization in backward places, and he was willing to sacrifice delights and encounter inconveniences the better to learn about lands that excited only sarcasm in Frederick. "What route do you take to go to Petersburg, the shortest?" asked the king. The shortest and most convenient route would have been by sea. The most direct land route would have followed the Baltic coast. "No sire," said Ségur. "I want to pass by Warsaw to see Poland." To which Frederick replied, "It's a curious land."[1]

Both Ségur's curiosity to see Poland and Frederick's sense of its curiousness were features of an evolving eighteenth-century interest that applied to Russia as well as Poland. For Ségur they were linked in the same voyage by land, emphasizing their regional contiguity for him and for other eighteenth-century travelers. In the seventeenth century, commercial connections by sea—the Arctic passage from England to Archangel, the Baltic cruise from Holland to Gdańsk—masked the relation of Poland and Russia to each other. Nineteenth-century railroad travel would fully enforce that geographical relation, making tracks from Warsaw to St. Petersburg, from Warsaw to Moscow, but Ségur's eighteenth-century curiosity cost him more time and trouble. Frederick pretended to encourage him with some ironic reflections on what made Poland curious: "a free land where the nation is enslaved, a republic with a king, a vast country almost without population." The Poles were keen warriors but their armies undisciplined. Polish men were brave and *chevaleresque*, but Polish women seemed to have more firmness of character, even heroism. Thus Frederick concluded on a note of mockery, "The women are truly the men."[2] Contradiction and paradox were the rhetorical forms in which he elaborated upon the curiousness of Poland, its nonsensical disordering and inversion of eighteenth-century ideas about society, politics, demography, even chivalry and gender. Nonsense was the adjunct of anarchy, and anarchy had provided Frederick with a pretext in 1772 for proposing the partition of Poland and acquiring a portion for Prussia.

It is remarkable that Frederick, who obviously intended to be clever in his summing up and putting down of Poland, could not claim to understand it better, did not seek to define and explain its implied inadequacy. The comprehension of Poland was, paradoxically, a matter of outlining its incomprehensibility, presenting its paradoxical contrasts, unresolved. Ségur had no political designs on Poland, even claimed to detest the partition of 1772 as an act of injustice, but his voyager's curiosity inspired travel observations in Poland remarkably similar in rhetorical form to those that Frederick employed without leaving Berlin. Furthermore, the same style of characterization by contradictions continued to serve Ségur in Russia as well as in Poland. Such formulas, pronounced by the Prussian king or the French diplomat and applied to Poland or to Russia, marked the eighteenth-century discovery of Eastern Europe. The curiousness of Eastern Europe, that is, its difference from Western Europe, its backwardness, was formulated as an intellectual problem of unresolved contrasts.

When a traveler of the twentieth century looks back at Ségur's trip from Germany into Poland, it seems clear that he left Western Europe and entered Eastern Europe. Ségur could not explain it so neatly, though, since in the eighteenth century the whole idea of Eastern Europe was not yet fixed, was still evolving, was taking shape in the minds and words of travelers like himself. What was remarkable about his account of this passage, the 500 miles from Berlin to Warsaw, was how powerfully he felt that he was crossing a border of great significance, even without possessing the modern distinction between Western Europe and Eastern Europe to explain that transition.

In traversing the eastern part of the estates of the king of Prussia, it seems that one leaves the theatre where there reigns a nature embellished by the efforts of art and a perfected civilization. The eye is already saddened by arid sands, by vast forests.

But when one enters Poland, one believes one has left Europe entirely, and the gaze is struck by a new spectacle: an immense country almost totally covered with fir trees always green, but always sad, interrupted at long intervals by some cultivated plains, like islands scattered on the ocean; a poor population, enslaved; dirty villages; cottages little different from savage huts; everything makes one think one has been moved back ten centuries, and that one finds oneself amid hordes of Huns, Scythians, Veneti, Slavs, and Sarmatians.[3]

Clearly Ségur experienced this as much more than the mere passage from one kingdom to the next. He had passed beyond perfected civilization, had left Europe entirely, had even traveled in time and passed out of the eighteenth century. In fact, though he specified ten centuries, a thousand years, and could say of Poland that "there the feudal centuries live again," he seemed to pass out of history altogether into a world of prehistoric huts and hordes, the barbarians who "crushed beneath their weight the last debris of the Roman empire."[4] His own sensibility was allowed full play in governing his observations, the traveler's eye imparting sadness even to the trees. Ségur had told Frederick he only wanted "to see Poland," but his gaze was far from passive, engaging and transforming the landscape that art and civilization had not embellished. He left behind a "theatre" only to discover "a new spectacle." The new spectacle was Eastern Europe, but he could not yet name it. Where was he traveling? It was not Europe, he believed, but neither was it Asia, the Orient. It was some intermediary geographical space, with no precise location in time or history, where the inversions of nature were such that even his travel by land turned into an "ocean" voyage. In spite of his overland intentions, Ségur was at sea.

"Everything is contrast in this land," observed Ségur, echoing the formula of Frederick, "deserts and palaces, the slavery of the peasants and the turbulent liberty of the nobles." Poland was an "inconceivable mélange of ancient centuries and modern centuries, of monarchical spirit and republican spirit, of feudal pride and equality, of poverty and riches." The traveler's eye picked out the contrasts and combined the elements of observation into that inconceivable mélange. In the chateaux there were "a great number of servants and horses but almost no furniture, Oriental luxury but no commodities of life." Wealth in grain contrasted with a scarcity of money and almost no commerce, "except by an active crowd of avid Jews." The Polish "passion for war" contrasted with an "aversion to discipline."[5] Ségur, like Frederick, followed the formula of contrast and contradiction that rendered Poland as a curious land of nonsense and paradox, a land of luxury without furniture.

"Such was Poland and such the reflections that occupied me," wrote Ségur of his journey, "when emerging from the solitude of a vast forest of cypresses and pines, where one could have believed oneself at the extremity of the world, Warsaw offered itself to my gaze." Like Columbus he had left Europe entirely behind, took to the ocean, and found himself at the extremity of the world. Poland seemed to encourage in him a hyperbolic sensibility, which confused the significance of his discovery, for if he had announced, more modestly, "the extremity of Europe," he would have come much closer to the label that eluded him. The appearance of Warsaw occurred as an apparently unexpected interruption of the reflections that occupied Ségur, the reality of Poland intruding upon his thoughts of Poland. The relation of the two, reality and reflections, was suggested by the passivity with which Warsaw "offered itself" to his gaze, and the alacrity with which that gaze set about its analytical work: "Upon entering I remarked there more of those singular contrasts: magnificent mansions and mean houses, palaces and hovels." Further, "to complete the tableau," Ségur described his own place of lodging in the city, "a sort of palace of which one half shined with noble elegance while the other was only a mass of debris and ruins, the sad remains of a fire."[6]

One cannot help becoming suspicious of this gaze with which Ségur set out innocently "to see Poland." Warsaw had to offer itself up to the gaze as some sort of helpless victim, a sacrifice, to those irrepressible analytic energies that left the city in ruins, that is, the intellectual ruins of its internal contradictions. One thinks of Michel Foucault, who philosophized historically about the gaze that made vision into knowledge and knowledge into power, the gaze of classical analysis. It was the birthright of Ségur, a Frenchman in the age of Enlightenment, but somehow the whole operation of analysis seemed to go awry in Eastern Europe. Instead of discovering in the elements an understanding of the object they composed, Ségur's analysis, like Frederick's, rendered its object all the more incomprehensible, even ridiculous. Coming from Frederick, in a tone of frank sarcasm, such analysis was easily recognizable as an act of intellectual aggression, the accompaniment to partition. Frederick's gaze upon the map of Poland inspired in him thoughts of territorial dismemberment, just as the idea of Poland provoked rhetorical analysis. Warsaw, eventually, would "offer itself" to Prussia in the final partition of 1795. The gaze of Ségur meant neither conquest nor partition, but it was the gaze of intellectual mastery, posing as puzzlement, with which Western Europe discovered Eastern Europe.

Contradictions nested within contradictions. The divided palace where Ségur stayed, half elegance and half debris, was located within a divided city, half palaces and half hovels. By the same token Warsaw as a whole brought out the larger contradictions of all Poland. Ségur observed, "Art, spirit, grace, literature, all the charm of social life, rivaling in Warsaw the sociability of Vienna, London, and Paris; but, in the provinces, manners still Sarmatian."[7] Poland contained within itself the conflict between civilization and the barbaric horde, but at the same time Ségur marked points on the map to suggest an even larger contrast, a rivalry, between different parts of the European continent. Vienna, London, and Paris were the capitals of that Europe which Ségur left behind upon entering Poland, the capitals of Western Europe.

In Warsaw Ségur was strongly advised to put off his departure for St. Petersburg, since the snows of the winter of 1784–85 were already falling. He would not wait, but later wished that he had. Ségur could make progress through the snow only in a light sleigh, and so had to deposit his luggage along the way, somewhere between Bialystock and Riga. Later he learned it was all lost in a fire. In one of the typical paradoxes of Eastern Europe, "snow and fire united to inflict upon me this punishment."[8] In the last stretch of the voyage, from Riga to St. Petersburg, unburdened of baggage, Ségur in his sleigh was left to his reflections. He was thinking about how cold he was, and also about Peter the Great, who triumphed over nature by applying "upon this eternal ice the fecund warmth of civilization." The application of heat to eternal ice was another paradox, like the combination of fire and snow, but Peter's "triumphing over nature" was already a cliché of the Enlightenment when Voltaire wrote his biographical tribute in the previous generation. The sight of St. Petersburg itself interrupted Ségur's reflections, and he was ready with another conventional observation to greet the city "where once one saw nothing but vast, uncultivated, and fetid marshes." No eighteenth-century visitor could see St. Petersburg without also seeing at the same time, and even smelling, those fetid marshes, which one no longer saw. In Eastern Europe the gaze was capable of manifold superimpositions, making a "mélange" of centuries and landscapes.

Ségur was hardly the first Frenchman to come to St. Petersburg. He recalled Diderot's famous visit to Catherine ten years before. He knew that "enough voyagers and authors of dictionaries have described and detailed the palaces, temples, numerous canals, rich edifices" of the city he called "this capital of the North." He nevertheless thought it worth recording his less touristic impressions of the city, and, with the coming of spring and the melting of the snows, he described a city whose eastern features were far more emphatic than its northern situation. The format of his impressions was identical to that which served for Poland and Warsaw.

The aspect of Petersburg strikes the spirit with a double astonishment; there are united the age of barbarism and that of civilization, the tenth and the eighteenth centuries, the manners of Asia and those of Europe, coarse Scythians and polished Europeans, a brilliant, proud nobility, and a people plunged in servitude.

On the one hand, elegant fashions, magnificent costumes, sumptuous feasts, splendid fêtes, and theatres the equal of those that embellish and animate the select societies of Paris and London; on the other hand merchants in Asiatic costume, coachmen, domestics, peasants dressed in sheepskins, wearing long beards and fur caps, long skin gloves without fingers, and hatchets hanging at a broad leather belt.

This clothing, and the thick bands of wool around their feet and legs that form a kind of coarse buskin, bring to life before your eyes those Scythians, Dacians, Roxolans, Goths, once the terror of the Roman world. All these demi-savage figures that one has seen in Rome on the bas-reliefs of Trajan's column seem to be reborn and become animated before your gaze.[9]

Inevitably, the eyes of Ségur, his rampant gaze, became *your* eyes, *your* gaze, the gaze of all travelers to St. Petersburg, even those who traveled only vicariously by reading the memoirs of Ségur. Those memoirs were not published until many years later, in 1824, when Ségur was an old man in the nineteenth century, but he remembered that the Scythians had come to life for him, and so he brought them to life for *you*.

Clearly Poland and Russia, in the eyes of Ségur, belonged to the very same sphere of mélange where continents and centuries, barbarism and civilization, mingled in fantastic improbability. The confusion of its elements was itself an obstacle to giving that sphere a name. Even the savages were demi-savages, in contradiction with themselves. Yet these impressions of Russia were in certain respects more vivid and more explicit than those of Poland. Barbarian peoples of the ancient world simply came to life, marched right off a column that was carved in the second century, and stepped out of stone relief into three dimensions. Furthermore, though Ségur already claimed to have left Europe upon entering Poland, in Russia he explicitly recognized the alternative to Europe as Asia. A cautious reference to "Oriental luxury" in Poland gave way to emphatic impressions of Asiatic manners and costumes in St. Petersburg, "this capital of the North." When Ségur traveled from Warsaw to St. Petersburg, the direction was ambiguously northeast, perhaps even more north than east. He felt as if he had left Europe, but he knew he had not entered Asia in geographical fact. He had discovered a realm in between. In fact, the Russian empire spanned both continents, and eighteenth-century maps carefully distinguished between "Russia in Europe" and "Russia in Asia." St. Petersburg was unquestionably in the former moiety, but Ségur's penetrating gaze had discovered a certain cultural permeability in the continental frontier. The consequent confusion, allied to the analogous confusion of centuries, would make it possible for Eastern Europe to emerge, to come to life before the eyes of Western Europe, in the curious space between civilization and barbarism.

"At the moment when I arrived in Petersburg," wrote Ségur (and that moment was on March 10, 1785), "there remained in that capital, under the exterior forms of European civilization, many vestiges of anterior times." The complex truth, the pentimento of centuries, was thus a matter of the traveler's expert discernment, the penetration of exterior forms. "It was only after some examination," Ségur found, "that one could make this distinction; superficially this difference was not perceptible (*sensible*); after a half-century everyone had become accustomed to copying foreigners, to dress, and lodge, and furnish, and eat, and meet, and greet, and do the honors of a ball or a dinner, just like the French, the English, and the Germans."[10] In this case Ségur was obviously speaking not of the Scythians in their sheepskins but rather of the elegant elite of St. Petersburg, they of the sumptuous feasts and splendid fêtes. The criteria by which Ségur judged their imitation of foreigners were those of contemporary "civility," one measure of "civilization" in Western Europe, that is, in France, England, and Germany. These issues of eating, meeting, and greeting have been studied by Norbert Elias in *The History of Manners*, who found in them the key to how the social elite in those countries defined itself as an elite with regard to the rest of society. Ségur, himself a grand aristocrat, was putting the code of civility to new use here, making it a measure of distinction between different peoples in different lands. Warsaw might rival Vienna, London, and Paris, while Russians might imitate the elites of France, England, and Germany, but the "examination" of the gaze would discern the superficially imperceptible difference between exterior forms and anterior times.

"Only conversation," claimed Ségur, "and the knowledge of some interior details, marked the separation of the antique Muscovite from the modern Russian."[11] Just so an aristocrat in eighteenth-century France might have claimed to recognize a well-mannered bourgeois. The personal encounters of the traveler, in conversation—where Ségur preserved the advantage of conversing in his own language, French—brought out the interior details that escaped the eye. Civility might be a matter of rules and surfaces in the ancien regime, available to the imitative outsider, but the discovery of Eastern Europe insisted upon a more modern distinction based on fundamental character. The Russians were "marked," and Ségur would not allow them to evade their identity.

His recognition of the "antique Muscovite," even in St. Petersburg, referred back to the state of Muscovy, which antedated Peter and Petersburg. It was only natural that a visit to Moscow itself should confirm the formula already elaborated in St. Petersburg, and before that in Poland. In June 1785 he accompanied Catherine to Moscow, "this mélange of the cabins of the people, the rich houses of the merchants, the magnificent palaces of a proud and numerous nobility, this turbulent population representing at the same time opposing manners, different centuries, savage peoples and civilized peoples, European societies and Asiatic bazaars."[12] From Moscow the "eastern" aspect of Russia, its position between Europe and Asia, was all the more evident, effacing the conventional identification of Russia and the North. Ségur, however, was also aware that the Moscow he once knew was no longer there, that "the flames devoured the greater part of it."[13] For in the time that elapsed between Ségur's Russian travel and the writing of his Russian memoirs, the French armies of Napoleon had been to Moscow in triumph, left it in flames, and returned to France in defeat.

Ségur himself left Russia in 1789, after the outbreak of the revolution in France. At first he continued in the diplomatic service as a citizen noble, for his credentials as a friend of liberty were strong, his order of Cincinnatus, his service in the American Revolutionary War. Eventually, like so many other nobles, he was arrested, along with his father, and both were almost victims of the guillotine. Ségur survived, however, and went on to a new and extremely successful career in public service under Napoleon, as counselor, as senator, as grand master of ceremonies. It was only after Waterloo that he was excluded from public life and found the leisure to write his memoirs. For the most part they were written with the immediacy of the traveler's moment, probably from his notes and papers of that time, but nevertheless a generation had passed since he was in Russia. Sometimes that gap was made explicit in the memoirs, and especially when he contemplated Moscow:

I will speak little of Moscow: this name recalls too sombre memories. Besides, the description of this grand and beautiful capital has been given a hundred times: there are few of our families in which there is not a warrior covered with glory and wounds, whose recitals have made known to them the palaces, the gardens, the temples, the hovels, the shacks, the fields, the Kremlin, the Chinese quarter, the gilt steeples, that presented to our eyes, in Moscow, the bizarre image of several groups of palaces or chateaux surrounded each by its villages.[14]

The traveler's eyes joined with the eyes of the Napoleonic veterans, "our eyes," each glorious warrior with his own recital of the mélange that was Moscow. There was indeed a connection between the curious traveler's intellectual conquest, his analytical gaze, and the real power of conquest by arms. In fact, Ségur's son Philippe-Paul participated in Napoleon's Russian campaign and wrote a vivid account of it that served as one of Tolstoy's references for writing *War and Peace.*

When Ségur went to Russia as minister plenipotentiary, his chief ministerial business was the negotiation of a commercial treaty to allow France a share in the Russian trade that England then dominated. There was an element of economic imperialism in this, but even Ségur did not consider it very important diplomatic business. "My role seemed to have to limit itself to that of observer," he admitted, "attentive in a court over which we have no influence." [15] Yet the attentiveness of the observer could never be politically innocent. Russia and Poland both offered themselves to the eyes of Ségur, and the armies of Napoleon would take up that offer in the next generation. The eighteenth-century travelers who discovered Eastern Europe, between civilization and barbarism, between Europe and Asia, helped focus upon its contradictions the gaze of Western Europe.

"Peculiar to Poland"

William Coxe was also 31, like Ségur, when he made a similar trip through Poland to Russia. Coxe traveled in 1778–79, and Ségur came soon after in the winter of 1784–85, so the convergence in their nearly contemporary English and French observations suggests the evolution of a common perspective among travelers from Western Europe. Ségur was the scion of a great family of the French aristocracy, while Coxe was merely the dependent and employee of an equally grand English family. He was the son of a court physician, was educated at Eton and Cambridge, and became an Anglican clergyman and then the tutor of a six-year-old Churchill at Blenheim. In 1775 he was assigned to a new pupil, the teenage nephew of the duke of Marlborough, and charged with escorting and tutoring the boy through an exceptionally ambitious and educational five-year Grand Tour of Europe. Coxe took charge of teaching languages, geography, history, mathematics, poetry, music, and drawing, while the traveling party also included a certain Captain Floyd, whom Coxe hated, responsible for the boy's physical training in riding, shooting, swimming, tennis, fencing, and dancing. The boy's mother wrote to Coxe about yet another educational curriculum, hoping that her son would "fall desperately in love with a woman of fashion who is clever, and who likes him enough to teach him to endeavour to please her, and yet keep him at his proper distance." [16] The educational program was thus quite comprehensive. Coxe himself was seriously committed to the old-fashioned pedagogical purpose of the Grand Tour in the making of an English gentleman, but he was also ambitious enough to extend the traditional itinerary. Poland and Russia were his great innovations, as well as Sweden and Denmark. Columbus was looking for India when he discovered America. Coxe, like Ségur, set out toward the end of the eighteenth century to see the lands of "the North," a long-established geographical concept, and ended up discovering Eastern Europe.

In 1738 Thomas Nugent, in appreciation of "that noble and ancient custom of traveling," of its capacity "to form the complete gentleman," published an account that outlined the conventional Englishman's traveling domain: *The Grand Tour; Or, A Journey through the Netherlands, Germany, Italy and France.*[17] The formula of the title remained valid for a second edition in 1756. Coxe took his charge to all those places, but when it came to authoring an account of the trip, he recognized that readers would be most interested in the lands outside the usual tour. In 1784, the same year that Ségur set out for Poland and Russia, Coxe published *Travels into Poland, Russia, Sweden, and Denmark,* a book that went into several English editions before the end of the century as well as a French translation. This was an important aspect of the eighteenth-century discovery of Eastern Europe, an increase in knowledge of lands that were hitherto little known and rarely visited.

"We entered Poland," reported Coxe, dating this to July 24, 1778, and then "pursued our journey to Cracow through the territories which the house of Austria secured to itself in the late partition."[18] In other words, they were not really in the state of Poland. This land had belonged to the Habsburg empire since 1772, yet for Coxe the sense of entering Poland was sufficiently distinct to be dated precisely, and the impressions that marked this entry were duly recorded. "The roads were bad, the villages few and wretched beyond description," wrote Coxe, "the hovels all built of wood seemed full of filth and misery, and everything wore the appearance of extreme poverty." There followed another border crossing, the actual political border, at the Vistula just outside Cracow. There was a bridge, "at one end of which was an Austrian soldier, and at the other a Polish sentinel." Cracow was summed up as "a curious old town," and the first of its curiosities was that it was "once almost the center of the Polish dominions, but is now a frontier town." This idea of an unfixed border was joined to a sense of historical vagary. Cracow was a city of houses "once richly furnished and well inhabited, but most of them now either untenanted, or in a state of melancholy decay." It appeared as "a great capital in ruins," suggesting a temporal contrast between "original splendour" and "ruined grandeur."[19]

"I never saw a road so barren of interesting scenes as that from Cracow to Warsaw," wrote Coxe. "There is not a single object throughout the whole tract which can for a moment draw the attention of the most inquisitive traveler." The land was flat, the road was empty of other travelers, and there were few houses outside of occasional villages "whose miserable appearance corresponded to the wretchedness of the country around them." These villages were no more than "assemblages of huts," and of these "the only places of reception for travellers were hovels, belonging to Jews, totally destitute of furniture." The huts and hovels, the presence of Jews and absence of furniture, were all part of Ségur's experience as well. Coxe entered those hovels and invited his readers to enter with him.

Our only bed was straw thrown upon the ground, and we thought ourselves happy when we could procure it clean. Even we, who were by no means delicate, and who had long been accustomed to put up with all inconveniences, found ourselves distressed in this land of desolation. Though in most countries we made a point of suspending our journey during night, in order that no scene might escape our observation; yet we here even preferred continuing our route without intermission to the penance we endured in these receptacles of filth and penury: and we have reason to believe that the darkness of the night deprived us of nothing but the sight of gloomy forests, indifferent crops of corn, and objects of human misery. The natives were poorer, humbler, and more miserable than any people we had yet observed in the course of our travels: wherever we stopped, they flocked around us in crowds; and, asking for charity, used the most abject gestures.[20]

This entrance into Eastern Europe was a progress of poverty and misery, distress and desolation, and Coxe's impressions were obviously influenced by the fact that there were no comfortable accommodations to be had for travelers like himself.

His account, in this regard, almost immediately established a conventional wisdom on Poland, otherwise little known to English travelers. When Lady Elizabeth Craven went to Poland in 1785, the year after Coxe published his *Travels*, she already cited him: "I shall refer you to Mr. Coxe's book for the accommodations I met with on the road and confine my descriptions to agreeable circumstances."[21] Coxe exercised no such discretion, and not only wrote about "these receptacles of filth and penury" but also spoke of them conversationally. When he was later a guest at one of the grandest palaces in Poland, that of the Branicki in Bialystock, "the conversation turned upon our mode of traveling through a country so poor and wretched, and so deficient in comfortable accommodations." Coxe shocked the company of Polish nobles by telling them he slept "upon straw, when we can get it," and righteously informed the Countess Branicka that this was the way "to become acquainted with the domestic oeconomy of the peasant, by partaking of their accommodations, and by relying on them for the supply of our wants."[22] Inconvenience was the price that he paid to achieve the pedagogical purpose of his tour, to study the deficiencies of Poland, and to teach them to his pupil, to his readers in England, and even to the Poles themselves.

Sadness was the emotional key of Ségur's entry into Poland, and melancholy prevailed in his first impressions of St. Petersburg, "a double melancholy," both at the sight of the Gulf of Finland and at the thought of Russian despotism. Coxe found melancholy already in Warsaw, and it governed his elaboration of the city's contrasts according to the same formula favored by Ségur.

The whole town has a melancholy appearance, exhibiting that strong contrast of wealth and poverty, luxury and distress, which pervades every part of this unhappy country. The streets are spacious, but ill-paved; the churches and public buildings are large and magnificent; the palaces of the nobility are numerous and splendid; but the greatest part of the houses, particularly in the suburbs, are mean and ill-constructed wooden hovels.[23]

While Ségur made the northeastern trip from Warsaw to St. Petersburg, Coxe was making the more distinctly eastern journey to Moscow, which gave him the opportunity to see Poland's eastern domain, the Grand Duchy of Lithuania. There Grodno was summed up in the same useful formula of contrasts: "a mixture of wretched hovels, falling houses, and ruined palaces, with magnificent gateways, remains of its ancient splendour." He visited a cloth factory in Grodno, only recently established, and, coming himself from a country whose cloth industry led the world, he could manifest an interested condescension: "These manufactures are still in their infancy."[24]

In Grodno Coxe met with the French naturalist Jean-Emmanuel Gilibert, who was preparing to write a natural history of Lithuania, of its animals, minerals, and vegetables. Coxe noted "the infant state of natural knowledge in this country"—parallel to its infant state of manufactures—and seemed to take for granted that it was best left in the hands of someone from France. In Lithuania Coxe saw a bison, an animal that especially interested him, and cited the theory of Peter Simon Pallas, a German naturalist studying the natural history of Russia, that "this species of the wild-ox, which was formerly very common in Europe, exists no where in that continent, but in these Lithuanian forests, in some parts of the Carpathian mountains, and perhaps in the Caucasus."[25] In other words, the bison suggested the possibility of a natural history of Eastern Europe, with rare species surviving at the extremities of the continent.

Even more interesting were the characteristic varieties of the human species in Eastern Europe, and Coxe found, "In our route through Lithuania we could not avoid being struck with the swarms of Jews, who, though very numerous in every part of Poland, seem to have fixed their headquarters in this duchy." Ségur too had noticed in Poland "an active crowd of avid Jews." The idea of the Jews of Eastern Europe is perfectly familiar to the twentieth century, receiving its most emphatic formulation with their near extermination, but in the eighteenth century the Jews of Eastern Europe awaited discovery along with Eastern Europe itself. Coxe himself was reasonably composed on the subject of the Jews when he first entered Poland at Cracow. There he visited the tomb of "Esther the fair Jewess," supposed to have been the mistress of Casimir the Great in the fourteenth century. Coxe commented on "the industry of those extraordinary people," and reported that the Jews of Poland had "engrossed all the commerce of the country." On the road to Warsaw Coxe entered their "hovels." Traveling east from Bialystock there were crowds of beggars surrounding Coxe's carriage, while "Jews made their appearance without end." In Lithuania there were "swarms," and the traveler, in particular, encountered them at every turn: "If you ask for an interpreter, they bring you a Jew; if you come to an inn, the landlord is a Jew; if you want post-horses, a Jew procures them, and a Jew drives them." Traveling east from Minsk, through present-day Belarus, Coxe took shelter from a night storm in a barn, and there saw that "several figures, in full black robes and with long beards, were employed in stirring a large cauldron." The traveler in the age of Enlightenment, however, refused to entertain "a belief in witchcraft, or a little superstition," and "upon nearer inspection, we recognized in them our old friends the Jews, preparing their and our evening repast."[26] After seeing such swarms, after seeing Jews "without end," Coxe could claim a contemptuous familiarity with these "old friends." His descriptions, however, became increasingly troubled, from the tomb of the fair Jewess at Cracow to the scary scene around the cauldron near Minsk. As he demonstrated his own enlightenment in dismissing superstition, he suggested to his readers the disturbingly unenlightened character of Eastern Europe and its Jews.

It was in observing the people of Poland that Coxe, like Ségur, claimed to be leaving Europe behind: "The Poles, in their features, look, customs, dress, and general appearance, resemble Asiatics rather than Europeans; and they are unquestionably descended from Tartar ancestors." One key consideration was the way they wore their hair: they "shave their heads, leaving only a circle of hair upon the crown." Coxe cited a German authority on antiquity who believed that "the manner in which the Poles wear their hair is, perhaps, one of the most antient tokens of their origin," considering that "so early as the fifth century some nations, who were comprehended under the name of Scythians, had the same custom."[27] In exploring the Asiatic aspect of Eastern Europe, it was not enough to look back to a Tartar origin; for Coxe, as for Ségur, the crucial identification was with those ancient barbarians, the Scythians. In Russia they seemed to have come to life from the reliefs of Trajan's column, wearing their sheepskins; in Poland they could be recognized by the hairstyle they had maintained for more than a thousand years.

This interest in the hair of the Poles recurred in Coxe's final pages on the trip through Poland, in which he identified a disease supposedly originating in the hair.

Before I close my account of Poland, I shall just cursorily mention, that in our progress through this country we could not fail observing several persons with matted or clotted, hair, which constitutes a disorder called Plica Polonica: it receives that denomination because it is considered as peculiar to Poland; although it is not unfrequent in Hungary, Tartary, and several adjacent nations.[28]

Locating this disease in Poland, Hungary, Tartary, and adjacent nations, Coxe sketched out a domain that was recognizably Eastern Europe. It was very similar, in fact, to that of the bison in Lithuania, the Carpathians, and the Caucasus. The expert on natural history in Lithuania was French, the expert on the antique origins of the Poles was German, and the authority on plica polonica was also a foreigner, "an ingenious Swiss physician long resident in Poland." His treatise in French described "an acrid viscous humour penetrating into the hair, which is tubular," and "then exudes either from its sides or extremities, and clots the whole together, either in separate folds, or in one undistinguished mass." The symptoms included "itchings, swellings, eruptions, ulcers, intermitting fevers, pains in the head, languor, lowness of spirits, rheumatism, gout, and sometimes even convulsions, palsy, and madness." When the hair absorbs the pathogen, and clots, the symptoms subside, but when the head is then shaved, there is a relapse of symptoms until new hair grows to clot again. "This disorder is thought hereditary; and is proved to be contagious when in a virulent state."[29]

The supposed hereditary and contagious nature of plica polonica rendered it especially comprehensible as a regional sickness, both geographically and demographically, pertaining to "adjacent" lands and peoples, a characteristic pathology of Eastern Europe. Its occurrence in both Poland and Tartary was unsurprising if the Poles were supposed to be "descended from Tartar ancestors." The clotting of the hair in plica polonica, which could not even be shaved away, made the disease immediately perceptible to the observer, and for one such as Coxe, with his special erudition on Polish origins, this had to be associated with the Scythian style of Polish barbering. Polish bodies betrayed the stigmata of disease and barbarism. In fact, in enumerating the possible causes of plica polonica, Coxe specifically linked illness to backwardness. He cited, first, "the Polish air, which is rendered insalubrious by numerous woods and morasses"; second, the water, for "although Poland is not deficient in good springs, yet the common people usually drink that which is nearest at hand, taken indiscriminately from rivers, lakes, and stagnant pools"; and, third, "the gross inattention of the natives to cleanliness." Of these explanations, the first was one of geographical determinism, while the second, and especially the third, put the blame on the "indiscriminateness" and "inattention" of the Poles themselves. Indeed, the issue of cleanliness, raised here at the end of Coxe's Polish travels, capped an account that had taken note of "filth and misery" from the very beginning. Some of the same issues were raised by other eighteenth-century travelers and experts with regard to the incidence of plague in southeastern Europe, within the Ottoman empire. Coxe compared the social preconditions of plica polonica to those of leprosy, inasmuch as it "still prevails among a people ignorant in medicine, and inattentive to check its progress; but is rarely known in those countries, where proper precautions are taken to prevent its spreading."[30] The locus of plica polonica was one mapping of Eastern Europe as a domain of ignorance and backwardness.

"Nearer the Civilized Parts of Europe"

The crossing from Poland into Russia was as geographically confusing as the entry into Poland a month before, again on account of the partition. On August 18 "we crossed the Berczyna, which has been erroneously laid down by some modern geographers, as forming the new boundary between Russia and Poland," but then two days later "we entered Russia at the small village of Tolitzin, which in 1772 belonged to Poland."[31] If the political consequences of partition tended to confuse the border of Poland and Russia and make those lands appear to the traveler as part of the same zone, the resemblance of languages further defined that zonal unity. Coxe's interpreter was neither a Pole nor a Russian but a Bohemian servant, and a note to the reader explained that "the Bohemian and Russian languages are both dialects of the Sclavonian tongue." When Coxe sought to register the differences between Poland and Russia upon crossing the border, he observed that "the most striking contrast arises from the method of wearing their hair: the Russians, instead of shaving their heads, let their hair hang over the eye-brows and ears, and cut it short round the neck."[32] This emphatic attention to hair, in Russia as in Poland, revealed again the traveler's determination to discover visible marks and signs by which to distinguish alien peoples.

On the road from Smolensk to Moscow, those signs told Coxe that he was moving toward the Orient. One night the party stayed in a "tolerable hut" where "our hostess was a true Asiatic figure." This was determined from her clothes: "she was dressed in a blue garment without sleeves, which descended to the ankles, and was tied round the waist with a red sash; she wore a white piece of linen wrapped round her head like a turban, ear-rings, and necklace of variegated beads; her sandals were fastened with blue strings, which were also tied round the ankles, in order to keep up the coarse linen wrappers that served for stockings." The coarseness of clothing was related to the coarseness of the people themselves when Coxe concluded that "the Russian peasants appear in general a large coarse hardy race." They wore either "a coarse robe of drugget" to below the knee, or else a sheepskin. Like the Asiatic hostess, they wore "cloth wrapped around the leg instead of stockings," and their sandals were of bark. Ségur also noted in Russia the sheepskins and hatchets hanging at the belt, marking "demi-savage figures." For Coxe the hatchets were more than items of apparel, signaling not just a savage appearance but also a primitive level of civilization. He marveled that these Russian peasants built their houses, that is, their huts, "solely with the assistance of the hatchet," because they were "unacquainted with the use of the saw."[33]

As in Poland, Coxe had the opportunity to see these huts from the inside, inasmuch as they offered the only accommodations to the traveler. In some he was awakened by chickens, and in one, "a party of hogs, at four in the morning, roused me by grunting close to my ear." In the same room were sleeping his two companions and their servants, on straw; "three Russians, with long beards, and coarse sackcloth shirts and trowsers" on the floor; three women on a bench; and "four sprawling children almost naked" on top of the stove. On a later occasion Coxe even hinted at sexual impropriety in such primitive sleeping arrangements, mixing "men, women, and children, promiscuously, without discrimination of sex or condition, and frequently almost in a state of nature." There was also, he complained, "a suffocating smell."[34]

Towns along the way were registered with disappointment according to a particular formula: "At some distance the number of spires and domes rising above the trees, which conceal the contiguous hovels, would lead a traveller unacquainted with the country to expect a large city, where he will only find a collection of wooden huts."[35] This was clearly related to the formula of contrasts—between the impressive church spires and domes, on the one hand, and the humble huts and hovels, on the other—but by an interesting twist the juxtaposition became a matter of deception and illusion. What is striking about this observation in 1778 is how precisely it anticipated the legend of Russian illusion attached to Catherine's voyage to the Crimea in 1787, the legend of the "Potemkin village." Coxe applied the formula of illusory splendors and disappointed expectations even to Moscow itself:

The approach to Moscow was first announced at the distance of six miles by some spires over-topping an eminence at the extremity of the broad avenue cut through the forest; about two or three miles further we ascended a height, from whence a superb prospect of the vast city burst upon our sight. It stretched in the form of a crescent to a prodigious extent; while innumerable churches, towers, gilded spires and domes, white, red, and green buildings, glittering in the sun, formed a splendid appearance, yet strangely contrasted by an intermixture of wooden hovels.[36]

For all Moscow's vastness, for all its prodigious extent, when the traveler shielded his dazzled gaze from the glittering gilded spires, he looked down at hovels and recognized that even Moscow was a sort of Potemkin village, a city of illusionary distraction. Coxe was "all astonishment at the immensity and variety of Moscow," for "a city so irregular, so uncommon, so extraordinary, and so contrasted never before claimed my attention." Its contrasts made it sometimes difficult to recognize as a city at all, "for some parts of this vast city have the appearance of a sequestered desert, other quarters, of a populous town; some of a contemptible village, others of a great capital."[37] This was the traveler's mastery: to be able to see Moscow, at his discretion, as "a contemptible village."

A larger opposition was identified as the framework for these urban contradictions, explaining them in terms of the idea of Eastern Europe: "Moscow may be considered as a town built upon the Asiatic model, but gradually becoming more and more European; exhibiting a motley mixture of discordant architecture."[38] The discovery of Eastern Europe could be envisioned as a reclamation, focusing more and more attention on lands that were becoming more and more European. Discordance and motley were valuable aesthetic additions to the vocabulary of contrast and contradiction, and to get around Moscow, Coxe and company hired a carriage with "six horses of different colours." The coachman had a "long beard and sheep-skin robe," while the postillions were "in a coarse drugget garb." They carried with them plenty of hay, so that the horses could eat whenever the carriage stopped, while "with them were intermixed different parties of coachmen and postillions, who at the same time gratified the calls of hunger upon a repast ready prepared like that of their cattle, and which too required as little ceremony in serving up." While the coachman ate with the cattle, Coxe himself was visiting palaces, built "in the true style of Asiatic grandeur" and, most important, built with the axe: "The greater part of the timber employed in the construction of these vast edifices was fashioned with the axe. Though I often saw the carpenters at work, I never once perceived a saw in their hands."[39] Wherever he turned, Coxe consistently observed the characteristic displacements of Eastern Europe, for the palaces spoke of Asia in their style, and hearkened back to primitive times in their fashioning. Coxe's coachman with his beard and sheepskin, like the carpenter with his hatchet, matched Ségur's Russian-Scythian prototype.

It was not even necessary to invoke imaginary Scythians in Moscow, for there one could discover real and contemporary peoples from the far-flung provinces of the Russian empire, from the most distant frontiers of Europe, from the Urals or the Caucasus. While dining with Count Alexei Orlov, Catherine's naval commander, Coxe's attention was focused in fascination upon the train of dependents who gathered around Orlov:

In this train was an Armenian, recently arrived from Mount Caucasus, who, agreeably to the custom of his country, inhabited a tent pitched in the garden, and covered with felt. His dress consisted of a long loose robe tied with a sash, large breeches, and boots: his hair was cut, in the manner of the Tartars, in a circular form; his arms were a poignard, and a bow of buffalo's horn strung with the sinews of the same animal. He was extremely attached to his master; and when first presented, voluntarily took an oath of fealty, and swore, in the true language of Eastern hyperbole, to attack all the count's enemies; offering, as a proof of sincerity, to cut off his own ears; he also wished that all the sickness, which at any time threatened his master, might be transferred to himself . . . he danced a Calmuc dance, which consisted in straining every muscle, and writhing the body into various contortions without stirring from the spot: he beckoned us into the garden, took great pleasure in showing us his tent and his arms; and shot several arrows to an extraordinary height. We were struck with the unartificial character of this Armenian, who seemed like a wild-man just beginning to be civilized.[40]

This was Eastern Europe at its most extreme, geographically and anthropologically, yet available to the traveler in the garden of a palace in Moscow. That artificiality was apparently not enough to undermine Coxe's appreciation of the Armenian's "unartificial character." There were elements of similarity to images of the American Indian—the tent, the bow of buffalo horn and sinew—but the Kalmuck dance and Tartar haircut placed the Armenian clearly in the context of Eastern Europe. The circular haircut, in fact, was Coxe's link between Poland and Tartary. If he attributed to the Armenian a "language of Eastern hyberbole," it was also true that he himself employed a language of Western condescension, summing up the essential idea of Eastern Europe in the figure of the "wild-man just beginning to be civilized."

The traveler discovering Eastern Europe could actually recapitulate in the course of his travels this process of "beginning to be civilized." He could observe it not only in an individual wild man but also in the broadest canvas of landscape and society. Coxe set out from Moscow to St. Petersburg in September, traveling to the northwest. He passed herdsmen who "resembled, in dress and manners, a rambling horde of Tartars." He entered houses where people prostrated themselves before painted icons "of a saint coarsely daubed on wood, which frequently resembles more a Calmuc idol, than a human head." Sometimes people even prostrated themselves before Coxe, who remarked that "we were often struck at receiving this kind of eastern homage."[41] It was the Tartar and Kalmuck "resemblances" on the road to St. Petersburg, the same perceived in the Armenian in Moscow, that made nonsense out of any precise geographical interpretation of the traveler's experience. Just as reminders of the Scythians or Sarmatians of long ago defied the conventions of time and history, so resemblances to the Tartars and Kalmucks defied geography to create a more loosely structured anthropological zone of carelessly classified primitive people.

The country through which the traveler passed "was for some way almost a continued bog," and the road tended to sink into the ground and made "the motion of the carriage a continual concussion." Russia failed the simplest test of civilization in the working of the wheel: "The bad roads having shattered our new wheel, which was awkwardly put together, and already discovered symptoms of premature decay, we stopped to repair: but the repairs were as treacherous as the original fabric; for before the end of the stage, it again broke." Such "mechanical" failings made the journey from Moscow to St. Petersburg into a "visible" progress from barbarism toward civilization, illustrating for the traveler the course of development that awaited the Russian peasants with their hatchets and the Armenian wild man with his buffalo bow.

The backwardness of the Russian peasants in the mechanical arts, when compared with those of the other European nations, is visible to a superficial observer. As we approached Petersburgh, and nearer the civilized parts of Europe, the villagers were better furnished with the conveniences of life, and further advanced in the knowledge of the necessary arts. . . . The planks were less frequently hewn with the axe, and saw-pits, which we had long considered as objects of curiosity, often occurred: the cottages were more spacious and convenient, provided with larger windows, and generally had chimnies; they were also more amply stored with household furniture. . . . Still, however, their progress towards civilization is very inconsiderable, and many instances of the grossest barbarism fell under our observation.[42]

The presence of furniture and the use of the axe were important indexes, especially inasmuch as they rendered the state of civilization directly visible to the traveler, even to "the superficial observer." Ségur, in St. Petersburg itself, found that the "exterior forms of European civilization" masked superficially imperceptible vestiges, but Coxe, still on the road to St. Petersburg, claimed to recognize even the exterior forms of "the grossest barbarism." In fact, his observations implicitly organized a spectrum of relative civilization, a model of development, from the grossest barbarism through simple backwardness, drawing nearer to, making progress toward, civilization itself. The Russian "progress towards civilization" was reflected in his own "progress" toward St. Petersburg, a journey to the northwest. Russia's degree of civilization was measured in comparison to that of "other European nations," specified as "the civilized parts of Europe." Thus the map of civilization in Europe was marked on the mind of the Enlightenment.

Novgorod momentarily raised the traveler's expectations, for "that town, at a small distance, exhibited a most magnificent appearance." It proved another Potemkin village, where "our expectations were by no means realized," and Coxe responded to it exactly as he had to Cracow and Warsaw: "No place ever filled me with more melancholy ideas of fallen grandeur." At Novgorod Coxe had to give up his carriage altogether, "shattered by the bad roads," and continued toward St. Petersburg in a Russian cart, a kibitka, that he found extremely uncomfortable. "The country we passed through was ill calculated to alleviate our sufferings," he wrote, "by transferring our attention from ourselves to the surrounding objects." It was a "dreary extent," through forest of "gloomy uniformity." Then

"Intérieur d'une habitation Russe pendant la nuit," the interior of a Russian habitation at night, from Chappe d'Auteroche, *Voyage en Siberie; fait par ordre du Roi en 1761; contenant les moeurs, les usages des Russes*, Paris, 1768, Volume I; travelers found evidence of backwardness both in the exterior forms of "huts" or "hovels," and in the interior scenes of domestic life; Coxe in Russia complained of "a suffocating smell," and found that sleeping arrangements combined "men, women, and children, promiscuously, without discrimination of sex or condition, and frequently almost in a state of nature." (By permission of the Houghton Library, Harvard University.)

"suddenly" he saw cultivated land, "the country began to be enlivened by houses," the road improved in quality comparable "to the finest turnpikes of England," and at the end of an avenue of trees there was "a view of Petersburgh, the object of our wishes, and the termination of our labours."[43] The destination, civilization, appeared in sight.

Coxe's first reflections on St. Petersburg concerned its very recent creation: "In walking about this metropolis I was filled with astonishment on reflecting, that so late as the beginning of this century, the ground on which Petersburgh now stands was a morass occupied by a few fishermen's huts." Peter's removal of his court from the old capital at Moscow to the new capital at St. Petersburg was for Coxe entirely analogous to the journey that he himself had just completed. The czar had sought the "internal improvement" of Russia "by approaching the capital to the more civilized parts of Europe," in order "to promote his plans for the civilization of his subjects."[44] The traveler's experience could recapitulate not only the progress of any individual "wild-man" but also that of Russia as a whole. The risk, with civilization measured against a directional course, was that "if the court should repair to Moscow, and maintain a fainter connection with the European powers before an essential reformation in the manners of the people takes place, Russia would soon relapse into her original barbarism." Civilization, once endowed with a sense of geographical direction, became reversible for Coxe. St. Petersburg itself was topographically precarious, newly built upon a "morass" in a "low and marshy situation," and it was "subject to inundations," even the possibility of "total submersion."[45]

For the time being, the mansions of St. Petersburg were furnished, according to Coxe, "as elegantly as those at Paris or London." He saw ladies who wore, "according to the fashion of the winter of 1778 at Paris and London, lofty head-dresses." Those cities were made to serve as standards of comparison for St. Petersburg, as once again Coxe found the exterior signs of civilization, as of backwardness and barbarism, in the styling of the hair. At court, however, he claimed to discern "traces of the Asiatic pomp, blended with European refinement."[46] Coxe was in Eastern Europe after all.

This was even more apparent the minute he looked below the court and nobility to "the common people at work." He was impressed by the way they were "seemingly unaffected by the frost," even when "their beards were incrusted with clotted ice." Their sheepskin garments seemed well adapted to the cold, and bare necks were "well guarded by the beard." Coxe was surprised to see women washing clothes on the Neva by cutting holes in the ice "with a hatchet." With the sheepskins, the beards, and the hatchets, the characteristic picture was complete. Coxe watched coachmen and servants, waiting outside in the cold for their masters, making fires to keep from freezing to death. This scene was recorded as a picture: "I was much amused with contemplating the picturesque groups of Russians, with their Asiatic dress and long beards, assembled round the fire."[47]

The picturesque was partly a question of costume, as Coxe also discovered at court masquerades. There "natives of inferior rank appeared in their own provincial clothes," making "an exhibition of the several dresses actually used by the different inhabitants of the Russian empire." He saw "a greater variety of motley figures, than the wildest fancy ever invented in the masquerades of other countries." In Moscow "motley" was a matter of "discordant architecture" in a city between Asia and Europe. In St. Petersburg it was a matter of costume, suggesting to Coxe the idea of Eastern Europe as "the wildest fancy ever invented in the masquerades of other countries"—in those of England and France, perhaps. Eastern Europe could be something fantastic, as well as humorous, and above all something "invented," invented by Western Europe. Its picturesque qualities, however, went beyond architecture and costume to the fundamental issue of race. Here too was motley: "A traveller who frequents the houses of the Russian nobility will be struck with the variety of complexions and faces which are observable among the retainers and servants; Russians, Fins, Laplanders, Georgians, Circassians, Poles, Tartars, and Calmucs."[48] The traveler discovered Eastern Europe not only in the anthropological details of costume and hairstyle, but also in the racial distinctions of facial feature and skin complexion. Even in St. Petersburg, approaching "the more civilized parts of Europe," one had only to look away from the ladies of fashion to their servants, to see that Eastern Europe was a motley aggregation of primitive peoples.

"Places Utterly Unknown Amongst Us"

On January 16, 1717, Lady Mary Wortley Montagu wrote to her sister apprehensively, on the eve of leaving Vienna and beginning her journey toward Constantinople, where her husband was to be the English ambassador. "I am now, dear Sister," she wrote, "to take leave of you for a long time and of Vienna for ever, designing to morrow to begin my Journey through Hungary in spite of the excessive Cold and deep snows which are enough to damp a greater Courage than I am mistriss of." The weighty emotion of this epistolary farewell—even with its casual spelling—suggested the significance of the border she was about to cross, the need to "take leave" as she entered a domain where even correspondence became uncertain. Lady Mary's departure from Vienna and entry into Hungary at the beginning of the eighteenth century were analogous, in the portentous sense of drama, to Ségur's departure from Berlin and entry into Poland at the end of the century. She too was foregoing the most convenient route, the sea voyage from England to Constantinople, and she said she was taking leave of

Vienna forever because she had no intention of returning overland, even at the invitation of the Habsburg emperor and empress: "Their imperial majesties invited me to take Vienna in my road back, but I have no thoughts of enduring over again so great a fatigue." This was merely the fatigue of anticipation, for she had not yet set out. Traveling east from Vienna, like traveling east from Berlin, was a matter for apprehension in the eighteenth century. "Adieu, Dear Sister," she wrote. "If I survive my Journey you shall hear from me again." She was particularly concerned when she thought "of the fatigue my poor infant must suffer," for she was traveling with her son, not quite four years old.[49]

Lady Mary's fears could not be ascribed to the remoteness of England or any special daintiness on the part of the English aristocracy, for such fears were most pronounced among the Viennese themselves, whose proximity to Hungary heightened their consciousness of Eastern Europe as an abyss. "The Ladys of my acquaintance have so much goodness for me, they cry whenever they see me, since I am determin'd to undertake this Journey," she wrote. "Allmost every body I see frights me with some new difficulty." Even Prince Eugene of Savoy, whose military exploits took place precisely on the route of her journey, cautioned her against "desart plains cover'd with Snow, where the cold is so violent many have been kill'd by it." She recognized his expertise: "I own these Terrors have made a very deep impression on my mind because I beleive he tells me things truly as they are, and no body can be better inform'd of them." It was Prince Eugene whose military victories during the last two decades of the seventeenth century had brought about the Habsburg liberation of Hungary from the Ottoman empire, and in 1717 he was again masterminding a campaign against Turkey that would culminate in his most celebrated triumph, the conquest of Belgrade. Lady Mary claimed to be impressed by his warnings, but when she wrote from Vienna to Alexander Pope, she made something of a joke out of the "terrors" of Eastern Europe:

I think I ought to bid Adeiu to my freinds with the same Solemnity as if I was going to mount a breach, at least if I am to beleive the Information of the people here, who denounce all sort of Terrors to me. . . . I am threaten'd at the same time with being froze to death, bury'd in the Snow, and taken by the Tartars who ravage that part of Hungary I am to passe. 'Tis true we shall have a considerable Escorte, so that possibly I may be diverted with a new Scene by finding my selfe in the midst of a Battle. How my Adventures will conclude I leave entirely to Providence; if comically, you shall hear of 'em.[50]

The envisioning of displaced Tartars on the route to Constantinople, as later for Coxe on the route to St. Petersburg, was proof of the imaginative unity of the traveler's Eastern Europe. In the eighteenth century the name of Tartary designated a vague and vast geographical space—from the Crimea to Siberia—and some travelers would really go there, but the Tartars were a people whose name added a dash of barbarism to journeys over an even vaguer and vaster domain. They were a feature of every traveler's experience of Eastern Europe.

For Lady Mary entering Eastern Europe was like going to war, mounting the breach, and in fact the lands through which she traveled were in a war zone at that time. Yet she could not take the terrors of war seriously enough to give up hope of being "diverted with a new Scene," and above all of finding "Adventures" whose anticipated outcome lay undetermined between tragedy and comedy. This was to be a key to the traveler's Eastern Europe throughout the eighteenth century, a domain of adventure, an itinerary beyond the conventional Grand Tour. When Lady Mary wrote to Pope on January 16, 1717, she already seemed to anticipate a comic outcome; by the time this series of "Turkish Embassy Letters" was published in 1763, the year after her death, the dramatic suspense of the epistolary cycle was merely literary. Lady Mary wrote to her sister on January 30 from Peterwaradin, site of Prince Eugene's victory the previous year: "At length (dear Sister) I am safely arriv'd with all my family in good health at Peterwaradin, having suffer'd little from the rigour of the Season (against which we were well provided by Furs) and found every where (by the care of sending before) such tolerable Accomodation, I can hardly forbear laughing when I recollect all the frightfull ideas that were given me of this Journey."[51] It was the triumph of Western Europe's sense of humor, following fast upon Prince Eugene's triumph by arms. The same joke was reenacted and retold more than a century later, in 1839, when John Paget published his traveler's account of Hungary and gave the same cue to laughter: "The reader would certainly laugh, as I have often done since, did I tell him one half the foolish tales the good Viennese told us of the country we were about to visit. No roads! no inns! no police!" Paget went well armed, but had "no occasion to shoot anything more formidable than a partridge or a hare."[52]

This was the humor of knowledge and mastery, finding Hungary unformidable. Lady Mary moved immediately from laughter to pedagogy, reporting to her sister her daily itinerary through "a Country entirely unknown to you, and very little pass'd even by the Hungarians themselves." This was the characteristic presumption that inspired eighteenth-century knowledge of Eastern Europe, to know it better than did the people who lived there. Lady Mary reported traveling through "the finest plains in the world, as even as if they were pav'd, and extreme fruitfull, but for the most part desert and uncultivated, laid waste by the long war between the Turk and the Emperour"—and also by the recent Habsburg persecution of Protestants. She conceived of Hungary as the victim of devastation by both Habsburgs and Ottomans; her English Protestantism prevented her from taking automatically the side of the Catholic reconquest, and thus helped her to see Hungary as a land enmeshed between Europe and the Orient. Her own emotional response was identical to that of Coxe in Warsaw and Ségur in St. Petersburg: "Nothing can be more melancholy than travelling through Hungary, refflecting on the former flourishing state of that Kingdom and seeing such a noble spot of earth allmost uninhabited."[53] She had discovered not only the emotional key but also the eighteenth-century economic conception of Eastern Europe: fine and fruitful land that was uncultivated and uninhabited.

Towns Lady Mary found "quite ruin'd," and country "very much over-grown with wood, and so little frequented tis incredible what vast numbers of wild Fowl we saw." This betokened provisions in "great Abundance," including also wild boar and venison. As for the less plentiful human inhabitants of Hungary, "their dress is very primitive, being only a plain sheep's skin without other dressing than being dry'd in the Sun, and a cap and boots of the same stuff." The sheepskin was the uniform by which travelers recognized the peasants of Eastern Europe, and Lady Mary also observed, for contrast, a grand Hungarian lady "in a Gown of Scarlet velvet, lin'd and fac'd with Sables."[54]

Lady Mary was shown the battlefield of Mohacs, where in 1527 the victory of Suleiman the Magnificent made most of Hungary an Ottoman province, but then she passed through "the feilds of Carlowitz, where the last great Victory was obtain by Prince Eugene over the Turks." She witnessed "the marks of the Glorious bloody day," indeed, "the Skulls and Carcases of unbury'd Men, Horses and Camels," and "I could not look without horror on such numbers of mangled humane bodys," without feeling "the Injustice of War."[55] The consciousness of the traveler in Hungary was intimately involved in the recent reconquest, even, as in the case of Lady Mary, when horror of war outweighed any possible partisan celebration. To envision the rolling back of the border between the Habsburg empire and the Ottoman empire was the precondition for discovering and identifying the lands of Eastern Europe whose possession lay in the balance. The English physician Edward Brown traveled through Hungary in 1669, a half century before Lady Mary, and when he published his "brief account of some Travels in Hungaria, Servia, Bulgaria (etc.)" in London in 1673, he wrote of Hungary as the Ottomans' "farthest intrusion into the Western parts of Europe." This explicit reference to Western Europe still left Eastern Europe as something vague and implicit. Brown only knew that entering Hungary, "a man seems to take leave of our World . . . and, before he cometh to Buda, seems to enter upon a new stage of world, quite different from that of these Western Countrys."[56] Hungary, by the end of the seventeenth century, was the point of access into Eastern Europe where the idea of conquest and redemption could be most explicitly observed, for its evidence was as graphic as skulls and carcasses. The crucial eighteenth-century ideological development would be the interpretation of that idea, not in terms of the distinction between Islam and Christianity, but rather the distinction between primitive backwardness and enlightened civilization.

Lady Mary was in Belgrade only six months before it fell to Prince Eugene in 1717, perhaps his most celebrated triumph, though relatively short-lived in effect since the city was surrendered to the Ottomans again twenty years later. The victory of 1717, however, and even the surrender of 1739, were important for publicizing the idea of Belgrade, with Serbia, as a detachable part of Ottoman Europe, in the same frontier zone as Hungary, the frontier of Europe. For Lady Mary in 1717 Belgrade was still decisively the Orient, and her most interesting encounter there, of which she wrote enthusiastically to Pope, was with her host Achmet-Beg, who "explain'd to me many peices of Arabian poetry." She admired the poems for their expressions of love: "I am so much pleas'd with them, I realy beleive I should learn to read Arabic if I was to stay here a few months."[57] Belgrade in 1717 could still seem an obvious place for the study of Arabic. Though Lady Mary had, in fact, encountered Serbs on her journey, she did not particularly associate them with Belgrade or even Serbia. She called them "Rascians," after the clan chieftaincy of Raska that antedated the medieval Serbian state. This backward projection, apparently innocent of rhetorical purpose, nevertheless paralleled the designation of Sarmatians and Scythians elsewhere in Eastern Europe. Sure enough, when Lady Mary first observed the Rascians at Budapest, they were living in "little Houses, or rather huts," resembling "odd fashion'd thatch'd Tents," consisting of "one hovel above and another under ground." She had a distinct idea of Serbia as a land—"the desart Woods of Servia are the common refuge of Theeves"—but did not associate the "Rascians" with that land or those thieves. She told Pope the Rascians were "a race of Creatures, who are very numerous all over Hungary," looked like "Vagabond Gypsies," belonged to the Greek Church, and lived in "extreme Ignorance."[58]

Just as her experience of Belgrade, studying Arabic poetry, was unrelated to her observation of the Serbs, so her stop at Sofia had nothing to do with the Bulgarians. Her great adventure in Sofia was strictly Oriental, a visit to the Turkish baths, to be received with "obliging civility" by ladies "in plain English, stark naked." She declined their invitations to undress herself, but recommended the subject as one for English painting, "so many fine Women naked in different postures." The nineteenth-century French artist Jean Ingres did in fact copy in a notebook this passage from the French translation of the "Turkish Embassy Letters" for his painting of *The Turkish Bath*. As for "the peasants of Bulgaria," they were described less alluringly as observed by the side of the road: "Their Houses are nothing but little Huts rais'd of Dirt bak'd in the Sun." While the women in the baths at Sofia were admired for "skins shineingly white," the peasant women of Bulgaria wore "a great variety of colour'd Glass beads" and were "not ugly but of tawny Complexions."[59] Here in Bulgaria Lady Mary raised the same racial issue of complexion that Coxe would discover among the servants of St. Petersburg. It was not the Oriental Turks whose skin was darker, but rather the subject peoples of Eastern Europe.

On April 1 Lady Mary announced her arrival in Adrianople, modern Edirne, "having now gone through all the Turkish dominions in Europe," finding that "all I see is so new to me, it is like a fresh scene of an opera every day." She requested news of "what passes on your side of the globe." To another correspondent she wrote, "I am now got into a new World where every thing I see appears to me a change of Scene." To the Princess of Wales, she boasted, "I have now, Madame, past a Journey that has not been undertaken by any Christian since the Time of the Greek Emperours, and I shall not regret all the fatigues I have suffer'd in it if it gives me an opertunity of Amuseing your Royal Highness by an Account of places utterly unknown amongst us."[60] Adrianople appeared as the Orient, 150 miles west of Constantinople, with the sultan himself temporarily in residence there. The journey, however, with its changing scenes and unknown places, its operatic possibilities, its approach to a new world, was through Eastern Europe.

In Adrianople Lady Mary could don her Turkish costume to visit the bazaar or the great mosque, admire the special beauty of Turkish ladies, and declare herself "pritty far gone in Oriental learning."[61] So in Belgrade, Sofia, and Adrianople, without even reaching Constantinople, she appreciated the Orient, while Eastern Europe manifested itself incidentally along the way in dirt huts and tawny complexions. During the course of the eighteenth century the emphasis would shift: the peoples of Eastern Europe would come into cultural focus along with the political idea of driving the Ottomans out of Europe altogether. By the end of the nineteenth century, Lady Mary's route had become that of the Orient Express, traveling not *through* the Orient but *to* the Orient at Constantinople. In fact, where Lady Mary enjoyed Ottoman civility along the way, Agatha Christie could travel to and from the Orient without ever leaving the familiar comforts of the Calais coach. By then Eastern Europe had been discovered, explored, reclaimed, and even liberated, but it could still be watched from the traveler's window.

"The More or Less of Civilization"

It was on the way to Constantinople, and on the way to St. Petersburg, that eighteenth-century travelers discovered Eastern Europe. In the 1770s

Jean-Louis Carra, not yet a revolutionary but just another traveler of the ancien régime, formulated the connection between Constantinople and St. Petersburg as two opposite and isolated "extremities," aligned along the unexplored "circumference" of Europe: "Having arrived at the two extremities of Europe, I encountered only two cities on the circumference of the continent, Constantinople and Petersburg, where France has some isolated relations of commerce and policy." These were the great destinations, the capital of the Orient and the capital of the North, but travelers inevitably observed the lands and peoples along the routes. Lady Mary was far from oblivious in 1717, and never doubted her correspondents' interest in places "utterly unknown amongst us." For the full measure of the eighteenth-century gaze upon Eastern Europe, however, one may look to the roughly similar "Voyage to Constantinople" of Charles-Marie, marquis de Salaberry, who traveled in the winter of 1790–91 and published his account in Paris in 1799. Salaberry was the somewhat younger contemporary of Ségur, and was only 24 when he left revolutionary Paris as an émigré in 1790, traveling to the east. His father remained in France, to die on the guillotine in the Terror, and Charles-Marie would return as a counterrevolutionary fighting in the Vendée. The publication of his "Voyage to Constantinople" in 1799 coincided meaningfully with Napoleon's campaign against the Ottoman empire, evidence again of the alliance between travel and conquest. Salaberry, however, was no Bonapartist, and did not return to public life until the Bourbon Restoration, when he entered the chamber of deputies as an "ultra among ultras," demanding the death penalty for possession of the tricolor.[62] Ségur in 1784 traveled to Eastern Europe as an ambassador of the ancien régime, confident in his condescension toward backward lands and peoples, while Salaberry in 1790 traveled as an émigré from an ancien régime in ruins, clinging in bitterness to a sense of his own superior civilization.

Salaberry's first experience of Hungary was the Habsburg coronation of Leopold II in Pressburg, which was, to his taste, *magnifique*. The Hungarian noblemen, mounted on their horses, were noted in a flight of fantasy as "the centaurs of fable." Salaberry was extremely interested in the nature of the border that he crossed, in passing from Austria to Hungary, and interpreted it in notably modern terms, as a matter of character: "If nature has brought the Hungarians near to the Austrians in situation, it has separated them all the more by character." This was immediately evident to the traveler—"when one leaves Austria on the eastern side ('du côté de l'orient')." The Hungarian character was judged as childish in its "love of liberty," while the diet and constitution were deemed "the dangerous toys (*joujoux*) of angry children." The Hungarians could thus be identified by the childishness of their political discussion and their "extreme prejudice in favor of their country which is, according to them, the first country of the world." Salaberry invited his readers to recognize the people of Hungary by such talk: "If you hear men or women speaking thus, young people or old, these are Hungarians."[63]

In 1790 Salaberry had in mind Hungarian resistance to Habsburg authority. From his monarchist perspective, political constitutionalism in Hungary appeared as a matter of infantilism, of immaturity, of retarded development. This fit well enough with Salaberry's discovery of the "Tartar origin of the inhabitants." The road to Buda passed through villages where the houses resembled "the huts of savages," and through countryside "as fertile as it was uncultivated."[64] These were the more generally recognizable marks of Eastern Europe.

The Hungarians thought Buda was "the first city of the world," and this reminded Salaberry of Voltaire's castle Thunder-ten-tronckh, so much admired by Candide because he had never seen any other. This reference to the world of philosophical fable set the stage for Salaberry's Eastern Europe, a domain in which nothing was quite taken seriously. In Budapest, a century after its reconquest, he still hoped to have his first glimpse of the Orient, but was disappointed to see only "churches that used to be mosques." He also saw a natural history "cabinet" that contained a hare with two heads.[65] Other travelers to Buda and Pest in the 1790s left more detailed accounts of the attractions, and both the German natural historian Joachim von Hoffmannsegg and the English geologist Robert Townson were impressed by the city's animal fights. Hoffmannsegg saw bears, wolves, boars, and even a tiger in the arena, while Townson commented ironically on "this polite and humane amusement." Salaberry claimed to have visited the thermal baths of Buda, but it was Townson who related the experience in terms of comedy and impropriety: "I saw young men and maidens, old men and children, some in a state of nature, others with a fig-leaf covering, flouncing about like fish in spawning-time."[66]

Another Habsburg-Ottoman war was coming to an end in 1790, so that Salaberry, like Lady Mary traveling across Hungary 75 years before, found a "theatre" of recent war and testified to "the devastation of the most flourishing lands." By the light of the moon—"un superbe clair de lune"—he inspected the traces of war, lines of retrenchment. Some villages were nothing more than a "spectacle of desolation," inhabited by a few *misérables* who resembled "wandering ghosts among the tombs."[67]

Salaberry's attention to the human landscape afforded him opportunities for new observations of "character" as he passed from Hungary to Wallachia, on the way to Bucharest. If in Hungary he deduced the national character from political conversations with the gentry, in Wallachia his first encounters with the population were of a different nature. Peasants and horses were arbitrarily conscripted by corvée to drag his carriage along the extremely bad roads: "This was for me an occasion to observe the character of these good Wallachians." He was struck by the way they spurred each other on with "terrible cries," and admitted, "I have never loved these howls that seem to bring man closer to the animals." He declared himself touched with compassion for "these poor Wallachians." He noted the striking contrast between their "pusillanimity" and their appearance: "this savage figure, this hatchet that hangs at the belt, this dirty sheepskin, which however, thrown over the left side and attached at the breast, recalls the Roman garment!" [68] In Romania, as in Russia, the same savage figure, with the same sheepskin and hatchet, impressed the traveler to Eastern Europe. Townson and Hoffmannsegg found that sheepskin in Hungary as well. The former gave as standard peasant garb "a wide coat, made out of sheepskins, which is thrown loose over the shoulders," while the latter noted a "sleeveless sheepskin jacket." [69]

Salaberry knew that Wallachia and Moldavia once formed the Roman province of Dacia, and recognized that the inhabitants still spoke a Roman language, "although corrupted." His account of the history of the provinces stressed the invasions of Slavs and then Tartars. The former arrived in "hordes," and the latter as a "torrent." Beyond the dirty sheepskins and the corrupted language Salaberry did not see much to remind him of Roman civilization. The contemporary government of Phanariot Greek princes, subject to Ottoman sovereignty, he treated with a table of "Greeks, Wallachians, or Moldavians strangled or decapitated in this century on account of the two principalities." The princely intrigues and exactions had turned their lands into "deserts." [70]

One night in Wallachia Salaberry stopped at a cabin in the woods, where he saw "a woman all in tatters" with "an old blanket that moved from time to time," so that there seemed to be "little cats" underneath. This woman watched hungrily while Salaberry ate, and so he gave her a chicken wing. She immediately took out from under the blanket "a little child, completely naked," and fed the chicken to the child. To Salaberry it appeared remarkable that such a woman, in Wallachia, should turn out to be not only a mother but even a devoted mother who fed her child before herself. He thought of a funny story he had once read about the Hottentots in Africa, about one who was offered whiskey and insisted that all the members of his family taste it before he did himself. [71] Most travelers located Eastern Europe between Europe and Asia, but the imaginative nature of all but the most strictly geographical associations meant that they could also invoke Africa if they felt they had traveled very far from home.

In Bucharest Salaberry met a nobleman, a boyar, "an original whom I promised myself to remember," for his story more clearly situated Romania in Eastern Europe and established its relation to Western Europe.

He had been at Spa with a Russian officer, something unusual for the boyars whom the princes do not permit to leave the country. I found him more unhappy than the blind from birth; for Spa and Bucharest are assuredly the day and the night. He spoke to me of his mistress he left there, and to make a worthy eulogy for her, he said to me: She was beautiful as the moon.[72]

This story perfectly suited Salaberry, since it evaded the question of whether revolutionary Paris remained the center of civilization, pointing to Spa instead, where aristocrats went to take the waters in the eighteenth century, where émigrés found refuge after 1789. Eastern Europe, by contrast, was the land of the blind, of the night, of childishly simple lunar imagery. Russians and Wallachians were blessedly "blind from birth," because they had never seen Western Europe. Those few who had seen civilization, and lost it, would suffer in remembering it always, like a beautiful mistress. Bucharest, like Budapest, was the world of castle Thunder-ten-tronckh, the finest in the world until one saw anyplace else.

At Budapest Salaberry already felt a "great eagerness to go visit the first monuments I encountered of Turkish religion, arts, and manners." In Wallachia he claimed to find "a first sample of Oriental manners," especially with regard to women's costume. The assumed presence of these Oriental elements, and the "eagerness" of the traveler to discern them, gave Eastern Europe its eastern character, from St. Petersburg to Constantinople. At Sistova on the Danube, where Ottoman-Habsburg peace negotiations were even then under way, Salaberry saw his first camel and found it "grotesque." Seventy-five years before, Lady Mary reported her first sighting of camels as something "extraordinary," though she thought they were "ugly Creatures."[73] They were heralds of the Orient, already to be seen in Eastern Europe. Salaberry was to be no sentimental Orientalist, far less so than Lady Mary with her Arabic poetry and Turkish costume. He crossed the Balkan mountains, riding from Sistova to Constantinople, expecting the worst from plague, thieves, and both Russian and Ottoman armies. On the other side of the mountains he found a beautiful country of orchards, vineyards, and roses, "the Ghulistan of Europe," a taste of Persia.[74]

Just as Lady Mary studied Arabic poetry starting in Belgrade, so Salaberry was thinking of Persian poetry after crossing the Balkans. However, the rose gardens could not distract him from an increasingly unpleasant consciousness of "Turkish manners." It attended his progress, becoming more intense as he drew ever nearer to Constantinople: "At each step, one has in this land the image of the most disgusting uncleanliness (*malpropreté*)." Here was something emphatic, appropriate for publication in 1799, when Napoleon was making war on the Turks. "They live amid garbage," wrote Salaberry, "breathing the miasma of plague, for which it is unnecessary to seek the cause any further than in their frightful negligence."[75] In Adrianople Lady Mary went to see the great mosque, one of the sixteenth-century masterpieces of Sinan: "I was dress'd in my Turkish habit and admitted without Scruple." The mosque, she thought, was "the noblest building I ever saw." Salaberry, however, went to visit on a Friday, was refused entrance, and went away cursing "the imams, the believers, and the prophet." His only consolation was to learn later at Constantinople that all mosques look alike.[76] His hostility to Turkish manners in Constantinople expressed itself in repeated references to pederasty.

Salaberry's prejudice against the Orient seemed to develop on the road, "at each step," as he traveled through Eastern Europe. Oddly, he even cultivated a parallel prejudice against Russia on the same trip, though it was not on his itinerary. Russia was often discussed, however, "in the lands I traversed," and he added to his account a postcript "On the Russians," to declare that they were comparable to the Turks for ferocity, indiscipline, ignorance, superstition, and fanaticism—with even a mention of *mal-propreté*. Theirs was but an "affected (*pretendue*) civilization."[77] The voyages to St. Petersburg and to Constantinople were intimately related as passages through Eastern Europe, so much so that they could even be superimposed, and traveled together at the same time.

At Constantinople Salaberry was very much aware of having come to the end of Europe: "this position in Europe, at six-hundred steps from Asia."[78] On the day that he actually crossed the Bosphorus to set foot on the continent of Asia, he allowed himself appropriately weighty reflections, rhetorically formulated: "How can an arm of sea, a quarter of a league, cause the change I experience in my thoughts? or rather how does it make such a great difference between two parts of the universe so near and so dissimilar?" Ségur imagined he was leaving Europe when he entered Poland, but Salaberry really was leaving Europe when he ferried across the straits. "When I regard Europe which I have just quitted, and Asia which I see at my feet, my eyes and my spirit are struck with a completely new admiration." Indeed, he vanquished his previous distaste to admire momentarily the grandeur of great Asians like Zoroaster, Moses, Jesus, and even Mohammed. Less pompously rhetorical, almost touchingly sentimental, was his reflection on Europe: "Six hundred steps of sea have broken the thread that nine hundred leagues of land did not break, the thread that holds me to my land, to Europe, to my century."[79] Salaberry was a man who had given up France, his home, and did not know when or how he would be able to return, so the thread was important to him. Following the thread, he would someday be able to find his way back. He had given up France, but he had found Europe instead, and learned that Europe was of extraordinary extent. On his "Voyage to Constantinople" he had traveled through Hungary and Wallachia, seen centaurs and Hottentots, but it was Europe still.

In Constantinople Salaberry concluded that Europe possessed a moral unity based on "the resemblance of passions, of tastes, of manners, of faults, of habits, or of vices." The Turks he excluded from this unity as beyond "any idea of comparison." Their contempt for Europeans was, in itself, evidence of their moral inferiority, for they could not conceal it. Salaberry admitted that all peoples (even the French, perhaps) may feel superior to others, "but the more or less of civilization hides or reveals this universal fault."[80] Truly, no one could know better than Salaberry, after his voyage through Eastern Europe, that everyone is guilty of condescension. That voyage taught him that the unity of Europe rested on resemblances and comparisons, which he summed up so devastatingly as "the more or less of civilization"—"le plus ou moins de civilisation." The phrase expressed the eighteenth century's enlightened understanding of the relation between Western Europe and Eastern Europe. In his very first impression of Constantinople, however, with his voyage right behind him, his phrasing was even more vivid: "This land here gives to Europe the air of those works of steel, of which the worker has neglected to polish the extremity."[81] The civilization of Europe, "more or less," was a matter of polish, and Salaberry had followed its thread to the very end, to the unpolished extremity.

Chapter Two

Possessing Eastern Europe: Sexuality, Slavery, and Corporal Punishment

"After the Beating"

Casanova's arrival in St. Petersburg was remembered with perfect precision of timing in those notorious memoirs that have been so often suspected of embroidery upon the factual truth. He left Riga by carriage on December 15, 1764, and traveled for 60 hours straight to reach his destination on the morning of December 18:

I arrived in St. Petersburg just when the first rays of the sun were gilding the horizon. As we were exactly at the winter solstice, and I saw the sun appear, at the end of a vast plain, at precisely twenty-four minutes after nine o'clock, I can assure my reader that the longest night in that latitude lasts eighteen hours and three quarters.[1]

The long nights of winter were a function of the city's northern latitude, but Casanova, seeing the sunrise, arrived in Russia looking to the east. His first experience of St. Petersburg was a masked ball at court, which lasted for another 60 hours, and there he immediately found traces of the lands he had left behind. Conversation was in German, the dances were French, and Casanova soon recognized, behind their masks, not only Catherine and Gregory Orlov, but also a fellow Venetian and an old love from Paris.

"The History of My Life" is famously the history of Casanova's sexual adventures, but the changing scenes of his travels sometimes strongly influenced the quality of those adventures, and this was never more true than in Russia. It began with a dinner party outside Petersburg, including an Italian castrato, Luini, and his diva "mistress," La Colonna; a French merchant's wife who seemed to Casanova "the most beautiful woman in Petersburg"; a Venetian woman who had had doings with Casanova twenty years before, until her brother tried to murder him in the Piazza San Marco; and one Russian officer, related to the Orlovs. After dinner the castrato went hunting, so Casanova and the Russian officer, not up to such manly sport, went for a walk just to see what game could be caught.

I point out to him a peasant girl whose beauty was surprising; he sees her, he agrees, we walk toward her, and she runs away to a hut, which she enters; we enter it too, we see her father, her mother, and the whole family, and she herself in a corner of the room, like a rabbit afraid that the dogs it saw would devour it.[2]

Casanova was hunting after all, and the "hut" where he ran his prey to ground linked his hunt to so many other eighteenth-century accounts of Eastern Europe.

For fifteen minutes the officer spoke to the father in Russian, so that Casanova only understood that their subject was the girl—"for her father calls her and I see her come forward obediently and submissively and stand before the two of them." The officer then explained to Casanova that the father insisted on 100 rubles for the girl, since she was thirteen and a virgin. Casanova asked the officer to explain the situation:

"Suppose I were willing to give the hundred rubles?"
"Then you would have her in your service, and you would have the right to go to bed with her."
"And if she did not want it?"
"Oh, that never happens. You would have the right to beat her."
"Then suppose that she is willing. I ask you if, after enjoying her and finding her to my liking, I could go on keeping her."
"You become her master, I tell you, and you can even have her arrested if she runs away, unless she gives you back the hundred rubles you paid for her."
"And if I keep her with me, how much a month must I give her?"
"Not a copper. Only food and drink, and letting her go to the bath every Saturday so that she can go to church on Sunday."
"And when I leave Petersburg can I make her go with me?"
"Not unless you obtain permission and give security. Though she has become your slave, she is still first of all the slave of the Empress."
"Excellent. Arrange it for me. I will give the hundred rubles, and I will take her with me, and I assure you I will not treat her as a slave; but I put myself in your hands, for I should not want to be cheated."[3]

Here was Casanova, legendary master of the sexual systematics of the ancien regime, learning like a beginner to operate in a new domain. The key to the new code was a word that obviously made Casanova a little uncomfortable. The word was slavery.

It was a word that was frequently used by travelers to describe the harsh character of serfdom and peasant life in Russia, in Poland, and in Ottoman Europe. This was one unifying aspect in the emerging idea of Eastern Europe, based on certain socioeconomic similarities. In twentieth-century textbooks the distinction is taken for granted: "From the sixteenth to the eighteenth century, in Eastern Europe in contrast to what happened in the West, the peasant mass increasingly lost its freedom."[4] In the eighteenth century, however, the whole idea of "Eastern Europe" in contrast to "the West" was not the given framework of analysis, but rather what had to be pieced together by the accumulation of perspectives and resemblances.

Casanova was no student of socioeconomic structures, and treated his acquisition of the Russian girl more as a matter of sexual custom than feudal oppression, but he understood enough to draw back from the crucial word, to insist that he would not treat the girl as a slave. This new form of sexual opportunity appeared to Casanova as an Oriental aspect of Russia, for the next morning when he went to pay his 100 rubles, his officer friend offered to arrange for "a seraglio of as many girls as I could want." At the hut the girl's father awaited the imminent sale with thanks to St. Nicholas "for the good fortune he has sent him," and Casanova was then invited to check the girl's virginity. "My upbringing made me reluctant to insult her by examining her," he wrote, uncomfortable again, but nevertheless: "I sat down and, taking her between my thighs, I explored her with my hand and found that she was intact; but to tell the truth I would not have called her a liar even if I had found her maidenhead gone."[5] So he said, but the day before he had been worried about being cheated. His repeated equivocations showed a certain unease with regard to the embarrassing easiness of adventure under these circumstances. Nevertheless, his clinical description of the "exploration" was obviously titillating to him and was provided for his readers as an introduction to the pornography of possession. The money was paid to the father, who gave it to the girl, who passed it finally to her mother. The deal was done.

Casanova's first act of ownership was to give the girl a name, as if she had none before, and the name he chose, by which she attained her dubious immortality in his memoirs, made her neatly into a token of Eastern Europe, as conceived by the Enlightenment in Western Europe. He called her Zaire. Voltaire's *Zaire* was one of his most successful tragedies from its first performances at the Comédie-Française in 1732. The heroine Zaire was the Christian slave of the sultan of Jerusalem, the scene was the seraglio, and the drama followed their doomed love for each other; in the fifth act he stabbed her to death in mistaken jealousy. Casanova unhesitatingly appropriated the Orientalism of the Enlightenment in naming Zaire and thus, invoking the romance of the harem, found a formula to assuage his uneasiness at discovering slavery in Europe.

The reference to Voltaire came all the more easily to Casanova, inasmuch as then, in the 1760s, the philosopher himself was extremely interested in Catherine's Russia, and Russia reciprocated with an interest in Voltaire. In 1764 Catherine founded the first Russian school for girls, "Le Couvent des Demoiselles Nobles," or Smolny Institute, and in 1771 the Russian *demoiselles* gave a performance of Voltaire's *Zaire*.[6] "In those days Russians with pretensions to literature," according to Casanova, "knew, read, and praised only Voltaire, and after reading all that Voltaire had published, believed that they were as learned as their idol." The relation of the Enlightenment to Eastern Europe was such that even an interest in Voltaire could be interpreted as a superficiality of civilization. Casanova actually wrote down his memoirs 25 years later, in Bohemia, and looked back on a Russia of long ago: "Such were the Russians in those days; but I have been told, and I believe it, that they are profound today."[7]

Casanova took home Zaire, "dressed as she was in coarse cloth," and "stayed at home for four days, never leaving her until I saw her dressed in the French style." It was also presumably the period in which he took full sexual possession of his property, but that, uncharacteristically for Casanova, was elided and replaced by the report that he was making her over "in the French style." The rococo seductions that were his literary trademark when memorializing his adventures were altogether irrelevant to the case when the girl was thirteen and his purchased slave. He could hardly have exclaimed, as in Venice, "Oh, how sweet they are! those denials of a loving mistress, who delays the happy moment only for the sake of enjoying its delights better!" If in embarrassment he withheld the report of his first sexual requirements of his slave, his substitution was the perfect piece of special pleading. He was dressing her, introducing her to fashion and civilization. Having dressed her in private, however, he proceeded to undress her in public, taking her to the Russian baths "to bathe with her in company with thirty or forty other people, both men and women and all stark naked." It gave Casanova the literary opportunity he sought to describe the naked Zaire to his readers: "Her breasts were not yet developed, she was in her thirteenth year; nowhere did she show the indubitable imprint of puberty. Snow white as she was, her black hair made her whiteness even more brilliant."[8]

Casanova compared Zaire to a statue of Psyche in the Villa Borghese at Rome, but he may also have been thinking of Pygmalion's Galatea, for no sooner had he dressed her "in the French style" than he began to teach her Italian, and after three months she spoke "very badly, but well enough to tell me whatever she wanted to." He, of course, did not learn Russian, for "the pleasure I took in hearing her talk to me in Venetian was inconceivable."[9] Casanova had made slavery into an experiment in civilizing Eastern Europe. The elements of language and style that travelers like Coxe and Ségur would later observe as evidence of superficial civilization in St. Petersburg were taught in private tutorial to a peasant slave girl, four days of advice on French dress followed by three months of Italian language lessons. Casanova had only to give her readings by Voltaire in order to put the finishing touch on her superficiality, but that he could not do, for she herself was already a character from Voltaire, had received her identity from him and from Casanova.

"She began to love me," reported Casanova, smugly, "then to be jealous; once she came very near to killing me." He insisted that, "but for her accursed jealousy, which was a daily burden to me, and the blind faith she had in what the cards which she consulted every day told her, I should never have left her."[10] Violence, superstition, irrational and uncontrollable passion: these were the marks of her primitive character barely concealed by French fashion and Venetian dialect. Such attributes gradually and conveniently blurred for Casanova the basis of their relationship, the 100 rubles, her slavery. She had a right to be jealous, if a slave could be considered to have that right. Furthermore, his account of his infidelities to her, and of her jealous reactions, suggest something distinctive in the modulation of his sexuality in Russia.

The most dramatic occasion began with his paying a visit and leaving Zaire at home, "being sure that I should find there some young officers, who would have annoyed me too much by flirting with Zaire in their language." He did in fact meet Russian officers, two brothers, both lieutenants. The younger was "blond and pretty as a girl," and "he lavished such pretty attentions on me during dinner that I really thought he was a girl in men's clothing." The officer's name was Lunin, and after dinner Casanova asked if he really was perhaps a girl, "but Lunin, jealous of the superiority of his sex, immediately displayed his, and, curious to know if I would remain indifferent to his beauty, he laid hold on me, and thinking himself convinced that he had pleased me, put himself in a position to make himself and me happy." At that point a jealous Frenchwoman intervened, and ended up calling them both rude names.

The struggle made me laugh; but not having been indifferent to it I saw no reason to pretend that I was. I told the wench that she had no right to interfere in our business, which Lunin took to be a declaration in his favor on my part. Lunin displayed all his treasures, even those of his white bosom. . . . The young Russian and I gave each other tokens of the fondest friendship, and we swore that it should be eternal.[11]

Nothing was eternal with Casanova, of course, but this casual homosexual interlude was at least unusual in his career of notoriously heterosexual libertinage.

The man-to-man tokens and oaths of friendship stood, on the one hand, in emphatic contrast with Casanova's master-slave relation to Zaire. Lunin and Zaire, however, were also remarkably similar in their appeal to Casanova as sexual objects: Zaire possessed the body of a boy, no breasts, no marks of female puberty, while Lunin could be mistaken for a girl. In Venice, by contrast, Casanova would pick out a girl for her "most magnificent bosom," and immediately felt "the ardent fire of amorous desires." [12] In Russia Casanova entered a new world of new codes and could improvise upon his own sexuality, indulge in confusions and inversions of his sexual legend. It was true that the Orient also spelled pederasty for Salaberry in the next generation (though he seemed unable to enjoy it, as Casanova did), and perhaps the Oriental identification of Zaire was keyed to not only her condition of slavery but also her ambiguous prepubescent gender.

After Casanova and Lunin exchanged tokens, they rejoined the company for a more general orgy, though "I and my new friend alone appeared to keep our heads, calmly watching the encounters which quickly succeeded one another." The two lovers parted at dawn, and Casanova returned home to Zaire, who was awake and awaiting him.

I arrive at my lodging, I enter my room, and by the purest chance I avoid a bottle which Zaire has thrown at my head and which would have killed me if it had struck me on the temple. It grazed my face. I see her throw herself down in a fury and beat her head on the floor; I run to her, I seize her, I ask her what is the matter with her, and, convinced that she has gone mad, I think of calling for help. . . . She points to a square of twenty-five cards, in which she makes me read in symbols the whole of the debauch which had kept me out all night. She shows me the wench, the bed, the encounters, and even my sins against nature. I saw nothing; but she imagined that she saw everything.[13]

Casanova declared himself ready to get rid of her, but eventually, after she went down on her knees and begged to be forgiven for her fit, he took her in his arms and "gave her unmistakable tokens of the return of my affection." He did make her promise to give up reading cards.

Casanova's disapproval of Zaire's superstition was tempered by an apparent readiness to concede, at least to his readers, that her cards spoke truly, even unto the sins against nature. In general, regarding religion rather than cards, he declared the Russians to be "the most superstitious of Christians," especially in their devotion to St. Nicholas, whose image was in every house. "The person who enters bows first to the image, then to the master; if the image by some chance is not there, the Russian, after looking all over the room for it, is nonplussed, does not know what to say, and loses his head."[14] In the case of Zaire, superstition served as an incitement to jealousy and violence, but Casanova claimed to possess the one efficacious remedy for the frenzy of the girl:

It was pure jealousy and I feared the consequences, which consisted in ill-humor, tears, and fits of despair, which had more than once driven me to beat her; it was the best way to convince her that I loved her. After the beating she became affectionate little by little, and peace was made with the rites of love.[15]

These beatings were clearly connected to his sexuality and her slavery. The first time he considered the possibility of buying her, he had been told that he would have "the right to beat her" if she refused to sleep with him. This right of ownership he preferred to reconceive as a proof of love and an excitement to sex, justified not by the conditions of Russian slavery but rather by the commotions of Russian character. He beat Zaire to civilize her; he also dressed her in French clothes and taught her to speak Italian.

Casanova did not hesitate to generalize from his treatment of Zaire, to prescribe for the character of Russian servants in general.

Three things in particular had made the girl love me. The first was that I often took her to Ekaterinhof to see her family, where I always left a ruble; the second was that I had her eat with me when I invited people to dinner; the third was that I had beaten her two or three times when she had tried to keep me from going out.

Strange necessity for a master in Russia: when the occasion arises, he has to beat his servant! Words have no effect; nothing but stirrup leathers produce one. The servant, whose soul is only that of a slave, reflects after the beating, and says: "My master has not dismissed me, he would not have beaten me if he did not love me, so I ought to be attached to him."[16]

When Casanova first came to St. Petersburg, he claimed, he had no such intentions: "Being fond of my Cossack, who spoke French, I wanted to attach him to me by kindness, chastising him only with words when he drank himself senseless on spirits." A friend, however, laughed at Casanova for such softheartedness and warned him that only beatings would meet the case. Casanova soon conceded that his friend was right.[17] Servants were slaves in Russia not because of socioeconomic circumstances but rather because they possessed the souls of slaves, and Casanova did not hesitate to imagine the slave's point of view, the appreciation of a good beating, in phrases also adaptable to his erotic fantasies.

The pleasuring sexuality of Casanova was usually altogether distinct from that of Sade in the next generation. In Russia, however, the Venetian libertine found himself exploring more unusual currents in his erotic depths. Sade himself, writing the *History of Juliette* in the 1790s, introduced the fictional figure of Minski the Muscovite, an ogre of sadism who brutalized and cannibalized a whole harem of sexual slaves. Later, Catherine too appeared in the novel to preside over intricately arranged sadistic orgies in

St. Petersburg. The Frenchman who enjoyed these scenes with Catherine was then banished by her to Siberia, where he discovered, in the company of a Hungarian and a Pole, new levels of delight in sodomy and flagellation. They escaped from Siberia together (after raping and devouring a fifteen-year-old boy): "From Astrakhan we moved toward Tiflis, killing, pillaging, fucking, ravaging all that crossed our path." [18] This was Sade's Eastern Europe, and while he mastered other regions of the world in similar fashion, here the pace and intensity of sexual violence were especially savage.

"On Their Knees Before Me"

When Casanova arrived in St. Petersburg in winter, the nights lasted nineteen hours, but by the end of May it was always day, the white nights of the northern summer. "People say it is beautiful," wrote Casanova, "but it annoyed me." So he set off with Zaire to visit Moscow. When they stopped at Novgorod on the way, one of the horses refused to eat, and Casanova described the scene that ensued:

Its master began haranguing it in the gentlest of tones, giving it looks of affection and esteem calculated to inspire the animal with sentiments which would persuade it to eat. After thus haranguing it, he kissed the horse, took its head in his hands and put it in the manger; but it was useless. The man then began to weep, but in such a way that I was dying to laugh, for I saw that he hoped to soften the horse's heart by his tears. After weeping his fill, he again kisses the beast and again puts its head in the manger; but again to no purpose. At that the Russian, in a towering rage at such obstinacy in his beast, swears vengeance. He leads it out of the stable, ties the poor creature to a post, takes a big stick, and beats it with all his strength for a good quarter of an hour. When he can go on no longer he takes it back to the stable, puts its head in the trough, whereupon the horse eats with ravenous appetite, and the coachman laughs, jumps up and down, and cuts a thousand happy capers. My astonishment was extreme. I thought that such a thing could happen only in Russia, where the stick has such virtue that it performs miracles.[19]

Casanova's interest, his amusement, his astonishment, reflected the fact that he was watching a parallel and parody of his own relationship with Zaire, the counterpoint of kissing and beating. That too could only happen in Russia. Casanova had heard that in the reign of Peter, the tsar took a stick to the generals, the generals beat the colonels, the colonels the majors, and so on down through the captains and lieutenants. Casanova, of course, had some personal experience of Russian lieutenants. As one who beat his own Russian slave, Casanova too celebrated the "miracle" of the stick, and, writing his memoirs, looked back with nostalgia to the Russia of 1765: "I am told that today blows are not as much in fashion in Russia as they were at that time. The Russians, unfortunately, are beginning to become

French."[20] The implicit regret suggested that much as he enjoyed dressing Zaire in French fashions, he would not have wanted French manners and morals to rule against his beatings.

The hierarchy of beating that linked the throne to the stable was one which Casanova did not hesitate to label as "despotism," the political form that accompanied a society of slavery and corporal punishment. He had been warned when he came to St. Petersburg that if he did not beat his servants, they would eventually beat him, and it was in the presence of Catherine herself that he learned what happens under despotism when a horse kicks back.

One morning I saw the Empress dressed in men's clothing to go riding. Her Grand Equerry, Prince Repnin, was holding the bridle of the horse she was to mount, when the horse suddenly gave the Grand Equerry such a kick that it broke his ankle. The Empress, with a look of astonishment, ordered the disappearance of the horse and announced that death would be the punishment of anyone who dared in future to bring the offending animal before her eyes.[21]

Catherine exercised her despotic authority through a system of hierarchy so strict that even foreigners were assigned military ranks, which Casanova found amusing. He claimed that he himself was recognized as a general, while his fellow Italian the castrato Luini was only a lieutenant-colonel, and the painter Torelli a mere captain. It was a joke for these artists and adventurers to assume the roles of ranked subjects, for they could always end the game and leave the country. Russians, however, were absolutely subject to the tsarina, and Casanova had been warned, from the day he first saw Zaire, that his possession of her would always be qualified by the fact that she remained "first of all the slave of the Empress." He would not be able to take her out of Russia with him, and his adventure in sexual possession could never be more than an interlude in Russia.

Casanova could take Zaire to Moscow, though, pompously proclaiming that "those who have not seen Moscow cannot say that they have seen Russia, and those who have known Russians only in Petersburg do not know the Russians." This was apparently a received opinion, permitting the presumptuous traveler to claim to "know the Russians." More characteristic of Casanova was another sort of knowledgeable comparison: "I found the women prettier in Moscow than in Petersburg." His principal interest in Moscow, however, was going to dinner with Zaire. He came with letters of introduction that promptly produced invitations: "They all invited me to dinner with my dear girl." This was Pygmalion's opportunity to show off his creation:

Zaire, instructed in the role she was to play, was enchanted to show me that she deserved the distinction I was conferring on her. Pretty as a little angel, wherever I took her she was the delight of the company, who did not care to inquire if she was my daughter, my mistress, or my servant.[22]

What exactly was her role, however, if she could be daughter, mistress, or servant? The thrill of Moscow, for Casanova and for Zaire, was that no one knew exactly what she was, while in St. Petersburg too many people knew that she was a piece of purchased property. The distinction he conferred on her was the possibility of pretending not to be a slave, while he pretended not to be a slaveowner.

Their romance could hardly survive the fall from pretense that accompanied the return to St. Petersburg, and Casanova immediately began to think about leaving her.

Zaire would have wished me never to leave Moscow. Being with me at every hour of the day and the night, she had become so much in love that I was distressed when I thought of the moment when I should have to leave her. The day after my arrival I took her to Ekaterinhof, where she showed her father all the little presents I had given her telling him in great detail all the honors she had received as my daughter, which made the good man laugh heartily.[23]

Her father's laughter shattered the game, reminding them that here everyone knew the truth. He, after all, had bargained for and received the 100 rubles. He knew whose daughter she was, and whose she was not.

By the fall of 1765 Casanova was ready to go. He had hoped to obtain a position at the Russian court, but Catherine, though she strolled with him in the Summer Garden and listened to his thoughts on adopting the Gregorian calendar for Russia, did not make him any offers.[24] He boasted of his ideal arrangement with Zaire, of "how little my happiness, and hers, cost me," of the economic sense of sexual slavery. However, as well as the private scenes that marred their relations, there was also another cause for discontentment in St. Petersburg.

I was thought happy, I liked to appear so, and I was not happy. From the time of my imprisonment [in Venice] I had become subject to internal hemorrhoids which troubled me three or four times a year, but at Petersburg it became serious. An intolerable pain in the rectum, which returned every day, made me melancholy and wretched.[25]

A surgeon conducted a meticulous examination of Casanova's anus, in a scene that strangely paralleled Casanova's own examination of Zaire's virginity. The surgeon declared the case inoperable, but assured Casanova that his complaint was quite common in St. Petersburg, indeed "throughout the province in which the excellent water of the Neva was drunk."[26] His hemorrhoids were thus peculiarly Russian and therefore a reason to leave Russia as soon as possible.

At last it was time to take leave of Zaire. He was worried about "all the grief which her tears would cause me," but she was interested in less sentimental issues attendant upon their separation.

Knowing that I must leave and that, not being Russian, I could not take her with me, she was concerned about what was to become of her. She would belong to the man to whom I should give her passport, and she was very curious to know who he would be. I spent the whole day and the night with her, giving her tokens of my affection and of the grief I felt at being obliged to part from her.[27]

Once again, almost for the last time, it was their discussion of the terms of her slavery that aroused his erotic attentions. Those terms even imparted a pornographic effect to the memoirs, for its readers remained in sexual suspense: who would become her next master? Casanova had someone in mind, an Italian architect Rinaldi, then 70 years old, who was eager to get the girl next, even for 200 rubles. Casanova said he would not sell her against her will, and made Rinaldi come declare himself to the girl as a lover, just as if she were not a slave. The old architect, after 40 years in Russia, could address the girl in Russian, but she made a point of answering him in Italian, insisting that she had no preference in the matter, that it was entirely up to Casanova.

Later Zaire raised the subject with her master. "It seems to me," she said, "I am worth much more, since you are leaving me all that you have given me and since I can make myself understood in Italian." Casanova replied, "I don't want it said that I made a profit on you, and the more so because I have already decided to make you a present of the hundred rubles I shall receive upon giving him your passport." She insisted upon speaking as a slave, calculating her value; he refused to accept frankly his possession of her, denying any interest in profit. She next proposed that he simply return her to her father: "If Signor Rinaldi loves me, you have only to tell him to come to see me at my father's house. He speaks Russian too, they will agree on a price, and I will not object."[28] Casanova agreed, took her to bed, and brought her back to her father the next morning, back to where he had found her. She was no longer a virgin, but her value had increased in other ways, as she herself suggested.

Casanova was pleased with this resolution of the affair, and especially with his reception at Zaire's home: "I saw her whole family on their knees before me, addressing me in terms which are due only to the divinity." Zaire's situation was less divine, for in that "hovel" he could see that "what they called a bed was only a big straw mattress on which the whole family slept together."[29] This was the world of the Russian peasantry that Coxe would later discover by the side of the road, and Coxe too would experience the satisfaction of seeing Russian peasants prostrate themselves before him, as before their Kalmuck idols. Casanova accepted the family's prostrations and went his way, relieved to have gotten out of the slave trade and also to be rid of Zaire. He really could have taken her out of Russia, he explained to his readers, just by paying a security deposit. He would not do it, though, precisely because he loved her: "I loved her, and it would have been I who became her slave."[30] Thus he reconceived their relation, invoking a sentimental language of slavery that confused, inverted, and undermined the socioeconomic significance of the word. He had, at any rate, already begun a liaison with a French actress, and set out with her from St. Petersburg on the way to Warsaw.

Casanova was in Poland from the fall of 1765 to the summer of 1766, and was interested enough in the political situation created by Russian interference in Poland to write later a long book about it, *History of the Turbulences of Poland*. It was a turbulent time for him, too, for he first became involved in the rivalry between two Italian dancers in Warsaw, one a former lover, and then, on account of the dancers, fought a pistol duel with a powerful Polish noble of the Branicki family. Though both parties survived, Casanova became persona non grata in Warsaw and had to give up his hope of becoming the king's private secretary. Stanisław August had received his crown in 1764 as Catherine's protégé in Poland, and he was no more interested than she was in assigning Casanova a permanent post at court. Just as Madame Geoffrin was making her triumphant arrival in Warsaw as the muse of the Paris Enlightenment, "maman" to Stanisław August, Casanova had to flee from Warsaw and Poland in some fear for his life. Not surprisingly, he was unimpressed by the level of civilization in Poland and expressed himself in the same terms as Ségur: "The Poles, though generally polite enough nowadays, still keep a good deal of their old nature; they are still Sarmatians or Dacians."[31] His references to ancient barbarians were hardly fastidious, and so he carelessly associated and confused the Poles of the Vistula with the Romanians of the Danube. It was thus that the idea of Eastern Europe emerged from eighteenth-century epithets of ancient history.

For Casanova, however, the crucial connection between Russia and Poland was inevitably a matter of sexual conditions. In Poland he stayed for a week at Pulawy, the grand palace estate of the Czartoryski family. There he described a scene that had to evoke for him and for his readers a most powerful feeling of déjà vu.

At Pulawy a peasant girl who came into my room pleased me, and she ran away crying out one morning when I tried to do something with her; the caretaker came running, asking me coldly why I did not go about it in the straightforward way if the girl pleased me.

"What is the straightforward way?"

"Talk to her father, who is here, and ask him amicably if he will sell you her maidenhead."

"I do not speak Polish, make the bargain yourself."

"Gladly. Will you give him fifty florins?"

"You are jesting. If she is a maiden, and gentle as a lamb, I will give him a hundred."[32]

The frightened girl, the perplexed libertine, the dialogue of instruction, the native intermediary, even the round number of a hundred, all made this adventure identical to Casanova's discovery of Zaire in Russia. In fact, conditions of serfdom could be as harsh in Poland as in Russia, and travelers frequently remarked upon the "slavery" of the peasants. Casanova could have started all over again in Poland with a new Zaire, new lessons in Italian, and a new course of beatings.

This time, however, he was cheated: he paid his money, and then the girl disappeared, "ran away like a thief."[33] She herself was the property that she stole from him. Casanova was offered other girls in substitution, but he declined, insisting indignantly on the one he had lost. Perhaps his heart was not in it, this time around, his spirit not up to facing the embarrassing ambivalence that came with owning a slave. Travelers from Western Europe in the eighteenth century perpetrated and advanced a sort of conquest as they traveled. Casanova, his century's most celebrated general in sexual conquest, had already tasted the aphrodisiac power of mastery and fantasy that gave even sex a special character in Eastern Europe.

"Sometimes Cruel, Sometimes Bizarre"

Among his first impressions of Poland, Ségur observed "a poor population, enslaved." It was one of the indications that he was leaving Europe. In St. Petersburg his "melancholy" came from the contemplation of "a despotism without limits," from seeing nothing but "a master and slaves."[34] For him, for Casanova, for many observers of Eastern Europe, the social "slavery" of the peasantry was both explained and obscured by reference to the political "slavery" of all Russians under Catherine's "despotism."

Slavery was, above all, a measure of civilization in Russia, of its relative absence, and Ségur considered its consequences with a comparative eye. He saw "the Russian people vegetating in slavery" but nevertheless enjoying a certain protection from starvation that made them more secure than some "civilized (*policés*) peoples," even allowing the latter to be "a thousand times happier because they are free." Ségur disapproved of slavery, but was not so sure it was wrong for Russia, for less civilized people: "The lords, in Russia, have over their serfs an authority of right almost without limits, but it is fair to say that in fact almost all of them used this power with extreme moderation; by the gradual softening (*adoucissement*) of manners, the slavery of the peasant may become more and more like what was formerly (*autrefois*) in Europe the servitude of the soil."³⁵ No revolution, no liberation, was necessary, if Russian slavery was indeed close enough to European servitude so that the softening of manners could eventually close the gap. Here was a recognition that Russia was indeed a part of Europe, a model of relative civilization across the continent, of gradual development by less civilized peoples. Russia was not consigned to eternal vegetation, but was offered the hope of becoming more like the rest of Europe—not contemporary Europe, of course, but the feudal Europe of *autrefois*.

There was something circular in Ségur's logic of development, for while the softening of manners might alter the nature of slavery, manners themselves were a measure of civilization, and the advance of civilization was obstructed by the existence of slavery.

The real cause of this slowness of civilization is the slavery of the people. The serf, supported by no pride, excited by no amour-propre, lowered almost to the level of the animals, knows only limited and physical needs; he does not raise his desire beyond that which is strictly necessary to support his sad existence and to pay his master the tribute imposed upon him.³⁶

First vegetables, now animals, the peasants of Russia had no incentive to civilize themselves, and so Ségur could only look to the masters, with their commendable "moderation." The peasants were slaves, he admitted, but "they are treated with softness." During five years in Russia he never heard of an instance of "tyranny and cruelty."³⁷ This tribute to the Russian feudal nobility was but the echo of that beneficent enlightenment that justified the supreme despotism of Catherine in the eyes of Western Europe.

If Ségur applied the standard of feudal Europe to measure the backwardness of slavery in Russia, he could also invoke the despotism of Russia as a condemnation of contemporary Europe. "All foreigners, in their recitals," wrote Ségur, in his own recital, "have painted with vivid colors the sad effects of the despotic government of the Russians, and yet it is fair to admit that in this epoch we do not completely have the right to declaim thus against arbitrary power." Was there not, *chez nous*, the Bastille? Ségur urged the traveler to take heed:

The moral of this is that a traveler, before criticizing with too much bitterness the abuses that strike him in the places he passes through, must prudently turn around and look behind him, to see if he has not left, in his own country, abuses equally deplorable or ridiculous as those which shock him elsewhere. In scoffing at others, think, you, Prussians, about Spandau; Austrians, about Mongatsch (in Hungary) and Olmutz; Romans, about the Castel Sant'Angelo; Spaniards, about the Inquisition; Dutchmen, about Batavia; Frenchmen, about Cayenne and the Bastille; even you, Englishmen, about the tyrannical impressment of sailors; all of you, finally, about this trade in Negroes which, after so many revolutions, to the shame of humanity, is still so difficult to abolish completely.³⁸

In this peroration Ségur appeared as a soldier of liberty, wearing his decoration of Cincinnatus. The terms of his vocative address enumerated the
"more civilized peoples" of Western Europe: Prussians, Austrians, Italians,
Spaniards, the Dutch, the French, the English. Monatsch in Hungary and
Olmutz in Moravia were only the sites of Austrian infamy, much as Batavia
(on Java) and Cayenne (in Guiana) were for the Dutch and the French.
It was Russia that provoked the traveler "to turn around and look behind
him," to discover Western Europe and its shortcomings.

Those shortcomings, however, did not make Russia the equal of other
countries but rather, in spite of Ségur's indignant liberalism, affirmed an
inequality of civilization. Western Europe might offer a standard of civilization by which to measure the backwardness of Russia, but in this case
Russia reciprocally offered a standard of backwardness for measuring the
"more civilized peoples." It was in their resemblance to Russia that they
appeared relatively less so, in their notorious dungeons of despotism like
the Bastille, and above all in their perpetration of slavery, the black slave
trade. Here, implicitly, Ségur set slavery in Russia in an international context. It might perhaps be capable of gradually approaching the standard of
European serfdom, but it was also related, most emphatically in name, to
that slavery which was "the shame of humanity." Russian peasants could
be bought and sold like black Africans. Casanova was fascinated to discover that he could buy a slave girl in Russia, and enjoyed imagining his
ownership as an exotic Oriental experience, but in the eighteenth century
white men were buying slaves all over the world. Interestingly, Ségur's
own mother was from Haiti, of a rich French Creole land-owning, and
presumably slave-owning, family.

Ségur claimed to believe that Russian lords were gentle masters, but, as
the diplomatic representative of France, he came up against the issue of
corporal punishment on the unusual occasions when Frenchmen were subjected to it. In one case, a French cook came to Ségur, in pain and anger,
"eyes red and full of tears." For no reason that he could understand, the
cook had just received 100 strokes of the whip at the order of a powerful
Russian lord. Ségur was determined to obtain "reparation," for "I will not
suffer that one should treat thus my compatriots whom it is my duty to protect." The "ridiculous denouement" followed when it was discovered that
the Frenchman was beaten my mistake because he had been confused with
a Russian cook who had run off and perhaps stolen something. Thus it
came about that there fell "upon the back of a poor French cook, the blow
destined for that of a Russian cook and deserter."[39] Certainly Ségur had no
quarrel with the "destiny" of the Russian, and when he mused upon the
effects "sometimes cruel, sometimes bizarre" of seigniorial power in Russia, he was thinking mostly of its exceptional misapplication to foreigners.
Ségur related another story, not only ridiculous but "a little mad," of a for-

eigner, a banker, who was informed that Catherine had ordered him to be taxidermically stuffed. Fortunately, it emerged in time that she was actually thinking of a pet dog, who had just died, and happened to have the same name as the banker. Catherine herself found the scene "burlesque" and was pleased to resolve such a "ridiculous enigma." Ségur agreed that the situation was "without doubt funny (*plaisant*)," but also demonstrated "the fate of men who can believe themselves obliged to obey an absolute will, however absurd its object may be."[40] Thus it was that the consequences of despotism, social and political, were rendered as comedy, burlesque, absurdity, in cases that accidentally involved visitors from Western Europe.

In Kiev in 1787, Ségur hoped he would have the opportunity to present to Catherine the marquis de Lafayette, his old Cincinnatus comrade from the American Revolution. Lafayette, however, was detained in Paris, awaiting the assembly of notables, an anticipatory rumbling of the French Revolution to come. Instead, Ségur found himself in Kiev much occupied with another Frenchman who sought asylum with him in fleeing the service of a Russian general. He had entered the general's service in St. Petersburg and accompanied him to his estates. There, "far from the capital, the modern Russian disappeared, the Muscovite showed himself fully; he treats his people like slaves." He beat them for any reason at all and was following the Frenchman to Kiev to carry out an "exemplary punishment" of the deserter. Ségur in St. Petersburg had been fascinated to discern the "interior details" by which the "modern Russian" just barely failed to mask "the antique Muscovite." In Kiev he now had the opportunity to confront that Muscovite face to face, unmasked. He told the general that, as French minister, "I will not suffer that a Frenchman should be thus oppressed." Ségur was not sorry to relate that years later that Russian general was killed by one of his own oppressed peasants, his head cracked open with a hatchet.[41] A hatchet, of course, was always an emblem of the primitiveness of the Russian peasantry in the eyes of eighteenth-century observers.

Ségur was outraged when Frenchmen were treated like Russian peasants, and there were also French women in Russia who were treated like Casanova's Zaire. Ségur related the story of Marie-Félicité Le Riche, neither felicitous nor rich but "pretty and sensitive," whose father came to Russia to run a factory. The factory failed, she entered domestic service in St. Petersburg, and there she underwent the eighteenth-century experience of Richardson's Pamela, resisting the more and more insistent seductions of an enamored Russian officer, "the vile seducer." In the end he raped her, and she went mad. Ségur saw her two years later in a hospice, still insane. "Such a painful spectacle will never be effaced in my memory," he declared, and he kept with him, for the rest of his life, a sketch of the girl, "which often reminds me of the touching Marie and her misfortunes." His sense of spectacle, his acquisition of an artistic souvenir, even his prurient narration of the story of "the touching Marie" and her "vile seducer," showed a sense of its novelistic form. The plot, according to Ségur, developed from an incongruous confusion, the treatment of a French woman like a Russian peasant. He moralized on "the danger, in a country where servitude is established, pursuing even persons, born foreigners and free, but obscure, who find themselves by unhappy circumstances reduced to the state of domestic service, and may be unexpectedly confused with the most oppressed slaves."[42] In a land of slavery one could be mistaken for a slave, especially in Russia, where slavery was a matter of class rather than race, not so obviously clear as black and white.

It was at Kaffa in the Crimea, with Catherine and Potemkin, that Ségur's Russian experience came closest to Casanova's. Under Ottoman sovereignty from the fifteenth century, annexed by Russia only four years before, in 1783, the Crimea was Eastern Europe at its most Oriental. In order "to give a just idea of the manners of a land where servitude exists," Ségur related the story of what happened to him at Kaffa:

Suddenly a young woman offered herself to my eyes, dressed *à l'asiatique*; her stature, her step, her eyes, her brow, her mouth, all these traits presented to me finally, with an inconceivable resemblance, the perfect image of my wife.

The surprise renders me immobile; I doubt if I am awake; I believe for a moment that madame de Ségur has come from France to find me, and that someone enjoyed keeping it from me and arranging this unexpected meeting: the imagination is quick, and I was in the land of illusion.[43]

Ségur was far from home and presumably missed his wife very much. His conjugal homesickness may have welcomed, even assisted the illusion. Yet the "inconceivable resemblance" was a reminder that however far from home he might be, truly on the farthest frontier of Europe, he was in Europe nevertheless. The exotic ethnology of Eastern Europe could still set before his eyes "the perfect image" of Mme de Ségur.

Potemkin, master of illusion, was watching Ségur, who was watching the perfect image. When the woman was gone, Ségur confided in Potemkin, and a dialogue ensued:

"The resemblance is it so perfect?" he said to me.

"Complete and unbelievable," I replied to him.

"Eh bien, *batushka* (mon petit père)," he resumed, laughing, "this young Circassian belongs to a man who will let me dispose of her; and, when you will be at Petersburg, I will make of her a present to you."

"I thank you," I said, in my turn. "I do not accept, and I believe that such a proof of sentiment would seem very strange to madame de Ségur."[44]

This dialogue was uncannily similar to that of Casanova with his friend the Russian officer twenty years before, after their first glimpse of Zaire, though here the girl was a gift instead of a purchase, and the part of the Russian officer was taken by the most powerful man in Russia. The similarity suggests that a dialogue such as this one followed a form of eighteenth-century fantasy about Eastern Europe, which both Casanova and Ségur passed on to the nineteenth century in their memoirs.

The Circassians came from the Caucasus mountains, from the frontier between Europe and Asia. Slavery was important in Circassian society even into modern times, and Ségur's Circassian woman was apparently a slave if she could be promised as a gift. The tragedy of Marie-Félicité was that she had been "confused with the most oppressed slaves," but now, because of an inconceivable and unbelievable resemblance between a woman in Western Europe and another in Eastern Europe, Ségur had confused his own wife with a slave. In declining the gift, on the delicately ironic grounds that his wife would find it "very strange," he asserted the superiority of civilization in Western Europe even more emphatically than Casanova had in accepting a similar proposition. In fact, the adventure of travel in Eastern Europe, and the titillation experienced by readers of such travels, lay partly in the mere possibility of such possession. Readers might fantasize that they accepted with Casanova or declined with Ségur, but the two fantasies were closely related.

Ségur soon found that Potemkin had taken Oriental offense at the refusal of his gift. He accused the Frenchman of "false delicacy," and Ségur had to promise to accept any other gift Potemkin proposed.

He gave me a young Kalmuck child named Nagun: he was the most original little Chinese figure that one could envision. I took care of him for some time; I had him learn to read; but when I returned to France, the countess de Cobenzl [wife of the Austrian ambassador in St. Petersburg] whom he greatly amused, pressed me so spiritedly to cede him to her, that I consented. I have still in my home the portrait of that little Tartar.[45]

So Ségur acquired a slave after all, a little boy, perhaps the age of his own son in France. The boy already came with an exotic name and a distinct ethnology, Kalmuck, that Ségur could carelessly interpret according to his inclination as Tartar or Chinese. The Kalmucks were a Mongol nomadic people who migrated to Eastern Europe in the seventeenth and eighteenth centuries, to an area west of the Volga River and north of the Caspian Sea. In the twentieth century they came to constitute a republic of the Union of Soviet Socialist Republics, though in 1944 Stalin sought to transport them all back to Central Asia as punishment for alleged anti-Soviet activity.

Ségur's boy Nagun was brought to St. Petersburg and passed on to the wife of the Austrian ambassador, just as Casanova's Zaire was passed on to an Italian architect. Both slaves had increased in value, for just as Casanova taught Zaire to speak Italian, Ségur taught Nagun to read. The memoirs did not specify what language, but that was only because there could be no doubt: it had to be French. Ségur took back with him to France only a portrait of the boy, and he kept it as a souvenir, just as he kept the sketch of Marie-Félicité. She was a French girl who came to Petersburg and was there abused, as if "confused" with a Russian slave; the boy was a slave, taken to Petersburg by Potemkin for Ségur, and allowed to acquire certain skills and manners in amusing and confusing imitation of French civilization.

In 1789, when Ségur was back in St. Petersburg with his boy slave, another distinguished foreigner in the Russian capital found himself at the center of a sensational sexual scandal. John Paul Jones, the great naval hero of the American Revolutionary War, came to Russia the year before, having been invited to take command of Catherine's Black Sea fleet and fight against the Ottomans. He did so, victoriously, in 1788, but then the following year in St. Petersburg was charged with raping a young dairy girl. Her age was variously given as fourteen, twelve, and even ten. At Catherine's indication of displeasure, Petersburg society shunned the admiral, and almost his only friend remaining was none other than Ségur, his brother in the order of Cincinnatus. Jones told Ségur that the girl had made indecent overtures to him in his house, that he had rebuffed her, and that she then ran out into the street crying rape.[46] Ségur saw to it that Jones's side of the story was put before Catherine, who cut off the court-martial proceedings. Jones's career in the Russian navy was over, however, and he left the country soon after.

Ségur's account of the case cleared Jones's posthumous reputation in Europe and America through the nineteenth century, but the twentieth-century historian Samuel Eliot Morison has rather revised the verdict of gentlemanly innocence. Morison quoted Jones's testimony to the Russian police that he had often "played" with the girl, that she had been quite willing "to do all that a man would want of her," and that he had given her money every time. He protested only that he had never actually had intercourse with her, and that he had thought her older than she turned out to be.[47] John Paul Jones, like Casanova, was well known as a lover of women, of adult women, and like Casanova he found himself in Russia taking an interest in sex with a prepubescent girl. For him too Eastern Europe became the domain for exploring sexual fantasy, though instead of acquiring a slave he fulfilled his fantasies as a patron of child prostitution. Interestingly, Jones had begun his naval career in the 1760s on a ship carrying slaves from Africa to Jamaica, and then renounced forever that "abominable trade."[48] He could have had a slave in St. Petersburg in 1789, as Ségur did, as Casanova did before, but he had known the reality of slavery and was apparently not susceptible to the fantasy.

Jones died in Paris in 1792, in the middle of the French Revolution. As a hero of the American Revolution, he received an official funeral in France, public recognition that contrasted with the total isolation and exclusion he had experienced in St. Petersburg in 1789 at the moment of his disgrace. Ségur, indulging in his sense of Russia's paradoxical contradictions, thought of Jones and marveled at the transformation by which "a great capital became for him a desert."[49] Ségur himself left Russia in 1789, soon after receiving the news of the fall of the Bastille, which roused some enthusiasm in St. Petersburg: "Frenchmen, Russians, Danes, Germans, English, Dutch, everyone, in the streets, congratulated and embraced each other, as if they had been delivered from a too heavy chain that weighed upon them." It was as if St. Petersburg were part of Europe after all. Catherine had no such illusions and no such enthusiasm when Ségur came to take leave of her. "You would do better to remain with me," she said, "and not to go looking for storms of which you can not perhaps predict the full extent." She warned him against his own "penchant for the new philosophy and for liberty."[50] Ségur, whatever his commitment to liberty and enlightened philosophy, made a gift of his personal slave as a preparation for departure, and brought back to France a portrait of the Kalmuck boy as a souvenir. He did not have any picture by which to remember the Circassian girl at Kaffa, but he did not need one, for he would always be able to contemplate her "perfect image." He would see her every time he looked at his wife.

"To Know the Moldavians"

With the peace of Carlowitz in 1699 Hungary became a part of the Habsburg empire, lost forever to the Ottomans. During the first decade of the eighteenth century the prince of Transylvania, Ferenc Rakoczi, led a great Hungarian rising against the Habsburgs for independence, and was finally defeated and driven out of Hungary in 1711. The Baron François de Tott was the child of one of his adherents, born a Hungarian in exile in 1733 and brought up in France as a Frenchman of the Enlightenment. Tott was a military man, an artillery officer, and ended up providing unofficial French military counsel to the Ottoman sultan, whose army was badly in need of reform. In the 1770s Tott trained engineers in Constantinople, gave advice on artillery, and taught trigonometry in the new naval school of mathematics.[51] As a man of the Enlightenment, he supposedly taught the Turks to build cannons by reference to the Encyclopedia of Diderot.

Tott's memoirs, written in French and published in Amsterdam in 1785, boasted of 23 years of personal experience in the Ottoman empire. He decried the "false notions" propagated in all past accounts and singled out that of Lady Mary Wortley Montagu, the best known, as the worst offender. Her "Turkish Embassy Letters" were a "jumble of reveries" and "absurd contradictions." He proposed to offer his own account not to "those who love to dream," but rather "to those who want to be instructed." In a philosophical "preliminary discourse" he began his memoirs by addressing the eighteenth-century issue, so important to Montesquieu and even Rousseau, of government and climate. Tott rejected the connection, with its implicit ordering of civilization on a north-south axis, and proposed instead a less predictable domain of "despotism, sometimes under the torrid zone, sometimes toward the polar circle," influencing "that variety of manners which today differentiates the nations, to the point of having altered so visibly the natural and primitive resemblance of all human societies."[52] Thus he defined the space from polar Petersburg to torrid Turkey, and prepared to examine the "variety of manners" that characterized the lands in between.

Tott told of his journey through Eastern Europe on the way to Constantinople for his major military work. He left Paris in 1767 and went first to Vienna, then proceeded to Warsaw to see Poland and traveled south into the Ukraine. He crossed the Dniester River, which marked the border between the Polish-Lithuanian Commonwealth and the Ottoman empire, and he continued through Moldavia and Bessarabia to the Crimea, the easternmost point of his voyage. Tott appreciated the unity of this passage through Eastern Europe, beginning with his entry into Poland: "All that the shortage of provisions, the lack of horses, and the bad will of the people made me experience of difficulties in Poland, prepared me to support patiently those that remained to overcome in order to arrive at the term of my voyage."[53] From Poland and the Ukraine, through Moldavia and Bessarabia to the Crimea, this was a route with its own distinctive "difficulties."

It was on account of these difficulties that Tott, like others who traveled as official or unofficial envoys to the sultan, was met by a "mikmandar" or "tchoadar" when he crossed the border into Ottoman Moldavia. The mikmandar, in this case named Ali-Aga, took responsibility for horses, provisions, and accommodations. His assignment was the coercion of the local population for the convenience of the traveler.

To this effect he established us in a good enough village, in which the poor inhabitants were constrained right away to bring provisions. A family promptly dislodged made place for us, and two sheep slaughtered, roasted, eaten, without payment, together with several blows distributed unnecessarily, began to put me in a mood against my conductor.[54]

This was a typical experience of eighteenth-century travelers in the Ottoman empire, and therefore, presumably, a recurring and unpleasant experience of eighteenth-century villagers forced to accommodate those travelers. To cross the Prut River, Ali-Aga used his whip to assemble 300 Moldavian peasants for the construction of a raft, and then, waving his whip, assured Tott that the peasants would all hang if even a pin of the luggage was lost in the crossing.[55] At roughly the same time, in the 1760s, Casanova was learning about the necessity of beating the servants in Russia. Twenty years later in Wallachia, adjoining Moldavia, Salaberry would hear the animal howls of the peasants in their sheepskins when they were conscripted by corvée to drag his carriage along. Throughout the domain of Eastern Europe, travelers observed the susceptibility of the peasantry to forced labor and brutal beatings. It was the sign of their slavery.

Tott reported in his memoirs a complete dialogue between himself and the mikmandar Ali-Aga on the treatment of the Moldavians. Philosophical dialogue was a literary form much favored by the Enlightenment, brilliantly exploited by such giants as Voltaire and Diderot. Casanova employed informal conversational dialogue when presenting his pedagogical initiation into the terms of slavery in Russia and Poland, and Tott treated a similar theme with a more literary structure and philosophical moral. The dialogue began with Tott's enlightened objection to so much corporal abuse.

Le Baron: Your dexterity in the passage of the Prut, and the good food that you provide for us, would leave me nothing to desire, my dear Ali-Aga, if you would beat less these unfortunate Moldavians, or if you would beat them only when they disobey you.

Ali-Aga: What does it matter to them, if it's before or after, when it is necessary to beat them; isn't it better to finish instead of wasting time?

Le Baron: Wasting time! Is it then a good use of time to beat without reason these unfortunates, whose good will, strength, and submission execute the impossible?

Ali-Aga: Monsieur, how is it that you speak Turkish, you have lived in Constantinople, you know the Greeks, and yet you do not know that the Moldavians won't do anything until they've been bludgeoned (*assommés*)?[56]

Tott complained that "the morsels that you procure for me, with blows of the baton, stick in my throat," and he asked that he be allowed to pay for his food.

His sentiment was very close to that of Lady Mary in the same situation fifty years before, much as he may have despised her letters. Traveling through Serbia, she was horrified to realize that her escort of Ottoman janissaries, under their leader the Aga, were cruelly exploiting the local population on her behalf. She wrote of her dismay to the Princess of Wales:

I saw here a new Occasion for my compassion, the wretches that had provided 20 Waggons for our Baggage from Belgrade hither for a certain hire, being all sent back without payment, some of their Horses lam'd and others kill'd without any satisfaction made for 'em. The poor fellows came round the House weeping and tearing their Hair and beards in the most pitifull manner without getting any thing but drubs from the insolent Soldeirs. I cannot express to your Royal Highness how much I was mov'd at this Scene. I would have paid them the money out of my own pocket with all my Heart, but it had been only giving so much to the Aga, who would have taken it from them without any remorse.[57]

Tott also wanted to pay, for his civilized conscience troubled him, the morsels stuck in his throat. He told Ali-Aga, "Be tranquil, I will pay so well that I will get everything of the best, and more surely than you could procure it yourself." Ali-Aga said it would not work: "You won't have any bread, I tell you; I know the Moldavians, they want to be beaten."

Tott insisted that he would renounce the sultan's defrayal of his expenses, and that the peasants in turn "will renounce being beaten, provided that someone pays them." So Ali-Aga agreed to the experiment.

Ali-Aga: You want it, I consent; it seems to me that you need to have this experience in order to know the Moldavians; but when you have known them, remember it's not fair that I should go to bed without supper; and when your money or your eloquence has failed, you will think it good, no doubt, that I use my method.

Le Baron: So be it, and, since we are in agreement, it is only necessary, when we arrive at the village where we must sleep, that I find the village elder, so that I may treat amicably with him for our provisions.[58]

The traveler of the Enlightenment mastered Eastern Europe by learning to know it, and the whole point of the experiment, and the dialogue, was Tott's learning "to know the Moldavians." Similarly, Casanova insisted a visit to Moscow was necessary to "know the Russians." That knowledge, of course, was not for the traveler alone but also for the readers in Western Europe, not "those who love to dream" but "those who want to be instructed."

At last Tott was face to face with the village elder, and addressed him in Turkish. Tott was legitimately proud of his linguistic achievement, and thought that earlier travelers like Lady Mary had written nonsense because they never learned the language. Now he was eloquent: "Here, take some money, my friend, to buy provisions of which we have need; I have always loved the Moldavians, and I can not suffer that they should be maltreated, so I count on you to procure promptly for me a lamb and some bread; keep the rest of the money to drink my health." It must have been beautifully spoken, but the Moldavian elder, unfortunately, made signs to the effect that he did not understand Turkish. So Tott tried the same speech in Greek. The Moldavian did not understand Greek either. The baron had had his opportunity to show off his languages, but he had made no progress toward dinner. Now the Moldavian communicated by signs, "making gestures to express that there was nothing in the village, that people were dying of hunger." Tott turned to Ali-Aga, blaming his guide for taking them to such a poor village where there was no food, but Ali-Aga was unperturbed: "To prove to you that I know better than you the Moldavians, let me speak to this one." He further guaranteed that "if you don't have the most excellent supper in a quarter of an hour, you may return to me all the blows that I will give to him."[59]

With the whip concealed under his clothes, Ali-Aga approached "nonchalantly" the Moldavian elder and patted him amicably on the shoulder: "Hello, my friend, how are you? Well, speak then; don't you recognize Ali-Aga, your friend? come on, then speak." The Moldavian still did not understand. Ali-Aga continued, "What, my friend, seriously you don't know Turkish?" Then he knocked the Moldavian to the ground and kicked him a few times: "Take that, scoundrel, that's to teach you Turkish." In fact, the Moldavian started speaking Turkish: "Why do you beat me? Don't you know that we are poor people, and that our princes barely leave us the air that we breathe?" Ali-Aga ignored his appeal and turned to Tott: "Eh bien, Monsieur, you see that I am a good language teacher, he is already speaking delightful Turkish. At least we can actually chat, that's something." Next Ali-Aga took out his whip and began the beating: "Ah, scoundrel of an infidel, you have nothing! Well, I am going to make you rich, just as I have taught you Turkish." Provisions were supplied within the quarter of an hour. Tott conceded defeat: "After this example, how not to admit that the recipe of Ali was worth more than mine, how not to be cured of my stubborn humanity?"[60]

Tott had wagered for the soul of Eastern Europe, and he had lost. The optimism of the Enlightenment, its faith in human nature, had failed the test of Eastern Europe, and Tott allowed himself a dispensation from his "stubborn humanity." Casanova and Ségur in Russia similarly sloughed off any scruples about slavery, whether as personal possession or as the brutal subjection of the entire peasant class. Tott like Casanova learned that there were people who had to be beaten, even wanted to be beaten. In Eastern Europe the traveler from Western Europe had to learn to moderate his sentiments of humanity, according to "that variety of manners which today differentiates the nations." The moral seemed a weighty one, but the form of its presentation, the dialogue between "Le Baron" and "Ali-Aga," opening out to become a three-character playlet with the addition of "Le Moldave," was arranged as a literary entertainment. It was even, undeniably, a comedy.

Ali-Aga was a comic caricature of a villain, with his jokes about "teaching Turkish" and his smug confidence that he knew the Moldavians better than Tott did. He bears some relation to other comic Oriental villains of the eighteenth century, perhaps Osmin the Turk in Mozart's "Abduction from the Seraglio." The "mikmandar" or "tchoadar," on whom travelers were so dependent, was not a lovable figure in eighteenth-century travel literature, from Lady Mary Wortley Montagu to Lady Elizabeth Craven. Lady Craven, returning from Constantinople to Vienna in 1786, was furious at "my abominable Tchouadar," blaming him for delays, and especially furious when he took the hot water intended for her morning chocolate to make his Turkish coffee.[61] Tott's Turk, however, was vindicated as the winner of the wager, who truly "knew" the Moldavians. As for the Moldavian himself, he testified to the poverty of his people, extortionately exploited by the hospodar princes, themselves the vassal appointments of the sultan. Yet he too appeared as a figure of fun, pretending not to know Turkish, carrying on in a mock dumbshow of comic gestures. Tott also played a comic role, the butt of his own joke, naive in his faith in human nature, learning his lesson about the Moldavians. Yet even as he conveniently discarded his "stubborn humanity," he established the civilized superiority of Western Europe, for Ali-Aga, in contrast, had no humanity to discard. The three characters of the drama represented Western Europe, Eastern Europe, and the Orient. Western Europe ended by acquiescing, even appreciating, the kicking and beating of Eastern Europe, and this lesson in inhumanity was so brutal that perhaps it could only be presented as comedy.

"The Manners of the Natives"

The traveler in Eastern Europe found himself casually implicated in the brutality of oppression and slavery just by the conditions of travel, just in the arrangement of food, lodgings, transport, and security. This was as true in the Russian empire as in the Ottoman empire. In 1778 Coxe and his party planned a day trip from Moscow to visit the monastery of the Holy Trinity, but "obstacles continually occur in foreign countries, unforeseen by those who are not sufficiently acquainted with the manners of the natives," and so the trip took three days instead of one. The problem was that though they had been officially authorized to take the horses of the post for their outing, at a token price of hire, they soon learned that "a stranger, unless accompanied with a Russian soldier to quicken the expedition of those who furnish the post, must meet with infinite delays."[62] No one was eager to turn over horses to them, in spite of the official order they brandished. Starting at five in the morning, they were delayed nine hours setting out, and then they only managed to travel four miles of the 40 to the monastery before their drivers refused to take them any further.

In vain we produced the order for horses; they contended that it authorized us only to take them from village to village, and on the strength of that construction returned without further ceremony to Moscow. Two hours more were employed, and much broken Russian spoken by our Bohemian interpreter, before we were able to prevail on the inhabitants to supply us with horses, and were again deposited in a village about the distance of three miles; where all the old process of altercation, threats, and promises, was renewed. In this manner we continued wrangling and proceeding from village to village, which were thickly scattered in this part of the country, until near midnight.[63]

This was comedy again, a comedy of transport in Russia that followed the form of Tott's comedy of provisions in Moldavia ten years before. There was even the same farce of intentionally misunderstood language, the Bohemian hopelessly trying to achieve communication based on the presumed resemblance of Czech and Russian. The real proof of the comedy, however, was in the happy ending, and this one ended exactly as Tott's did in Moldavia.

On the second day, halfway to the monastery, they were met by a Russian sergeant, sent by a Russian prince to rescue them, and after that there were no more problems with horses.

We had, indeed, a successful agent in our friend the sergeant; for the peasants, who were beginning to wrangle, and make their usual altercations, were instantly dispersed by his cudgel, whose eloquence was more persuasive than the most pathetic remonstrances. The boors were certainly accustomed to this species of rhetoric; for they bore it patiently, and with perfect good-humour; and, the moment they were seated on the box, began whistling and singing their national songs as usual.[64]

The sergeant played the same role as the mikmandar in the Ottoman empire, and Coxe admitted that "the experience of the preceding day taught us the value of this military attendant."[65] He had learned the same lesson as Tott and could view the beating of the drivers with the same equanimity, speaking ironically of the cudgel's "eloquence," noting the cheerful "good-humour" with which they almost welcomed their beating. Indeed, it made them whistle and sing.

When Coxe eventually left Moscow on the longer journey to St. Petersburg, he remembered his lesson in Russian transport and reminded his readers.

Indeed, as I have before remarked, it is absolutely necessary for a foreigner, who wishes to travel with expedition, not only to provide himself with a passport, but also to procure a Russian soldier, who instead of attending to the arguments of the peasants, or waiting for the slow mediation of the post-master, summarily decides the business by the powerful interposition of his cudgel.[66]

The lesson was a matter not just of transport but also, as Coxe himself first suggested, of enlightening "those who are not sufficiently acquainted with the manners of the natives." Coxe's readers were being offered the benefit of his acquired knowledge of the Russians, like Tott's of the Moldavians, and especially of these peoples' affinity for corporal abuse. The second mention of cudgeling in Coxe's account was directly followed by another mention of "the propensity of the natives to singing," for "even the peasants who acted in the capacity of coachmen and postilions, were no sooner mounted than they began to warble an air."[67] One would almost suppose that they were beaten to make them sing rather than to make them drive.

Coxe knew why he could not obtain horses without a soldier: "the price

"Supplice du Grand Knout," from Chappe d'Auteroche, *Voyage en Siberie; fait par ordre du Roi en 1761; contenant les moeurs, les usages des Russes*, Paris, 1768, Volume I; corporal punishment with the knout illustrates "the customs and usages of the Russians," as discovered by the eighteenth-century traveler; the role of the Russian spectators, included in the print, appeared as further evidence of barbarism, while the beaten body of the subject was also exposed to the gaze of the interested, enlightened public in France. (By permission of the Houghton Library, Harvard University.)

"Supplice du Knout Ordinaire," from Chappe d'Auteroche, *Voyage en Siberie*, Volume I; in which the gaze of the Russian spectators in the print, meeting the gaze of the French readers outside the print, creates a pornography of barbarism in the encounter between Eastern Europe and Western Europe; the Russian knout was also described in detail in Sade's *Juliette*. (By permission of the Houghton Library, Harvard University.)

for the hire of horses being inconsiderable, the owners can employ them in other services to greater advantage."[68] Tott, however, went to considerable literary lengths to establish his willingness to pay, so that the resort to the whip could not be interpreted as a matter of stinginess. Other travelers were quite frank about enjoying the financial advantage of tapping into a socioeconomic system that allowed no security of property to the peasantry. Traveling in Hungary in 1794, Hoffmannsegg was pleased to be able to save money: "Every village was obliged to make horses available to the travelers if the latter can produce a warrant issued by the authorities. So if you are acquainted with an official with authority and can obtain a warrant from him, you can travel very cheaply."[69]

If violence was employed for the convenience of travelers, it was easiest to accept when administered by others, like the Turkish mikmandar or the Russian sergeant. The traveler could then reassure himself that this violence was natural to social relations in these lands and simply reflected "the manners of the natives." Salaberry, traveling from Hungary toward Wallachia in 1791, prepared to spend a night at Lugosh, near Timisoara.

At Lugosh we sent our travel order to the commissioner of the county, who sent it to the judge of the district. The latter was at a ball, and only arrived two hours later. The commissioner had him given some blows of the baton, the judge did the same to the pandour, the pandour to the peasants, who gave them to their horses. *Voilà*, the calculation made, there were at least fifty blows of the baton distributed at Lugosh for our sake (*à notre occasion*).[70]

Here the travelers felt sufficiently uncompromised by the beatings, for which they were the mere "occasion," that they could enjoy the proceeding as sheer slapstick. The number of blows, which Salaberry calculated—*voilà*—seemed almost to be taken as mock tribute to the travelers' importance. A little further along on his route Salaberry saw a Wallachian boyar give a beating to the servant who was supposed to prepare the travelers' room, light their fire, and bring the straw for their bed. The French marquis reported without a trace of outrage on the effect of the beating: "The slave was neither sadder nor prompter, because here that is only the manner of demanding things."[71] Salaberry's Wallachians were like Tott's Moldavians, and the beating barely required any explanation once Salaberry knew enough about Eastern Europe to call the servant a slave.

The application of corporal punishment, by travelers themselves like Casanova with Zaire, by official chaperones like Tott's mikmandar and Coxe's sergeant, and by local masters like the Wallachian boyar, was interpreted as a dramatic demonstration of slavery in Eastern Europe. Coxe, however, also had a special interest in prisons and penal systems and therefore devoted detailed attention to corporal punishment as an instrument of public law and order. Catherine's predecessor, the Empress Elizabeth, abolished the death penalty in Russia, while Catherine herself abolished torture, and these were hailed as signs of legal enlightenment by such as Voltaire in France and William Blackstone in England. Coxe, however, was not alone in somewhat begrudging such recognition to Russia, and he contributed to the founding of a long-lived discourse on condemnation to hard labor and transportation to Siberia: "The most benevolent person will probably entertain no extraordinary veneration for this boasted abolition of capital punishment, when he reflects, that though the criminal laws of Russia do not literally sentence malefactors to death, they still consign many to that doom through the medium of punishments, in some circumstances almost assuredly, if not professedly, fatal, which mock with the hopes of life, but in reality protract the horrors of death."[72] Such reflections required little adaptation to bear repetition in the nineteenth and twentieth centuries.

Less modern, however, was the scrupulous description of a public beating in St. Petersburg, which made the "knoot" or "knout" into an emblem of Russian barbarism. The story began as an event from a day in the life of a tourist:

One morning, as I strolled through the streets of Petersburgh, near the marketplace, I observed a large crowd of people, and on inquiring the cause of this concourse, was informed, that the multitude was assembled to see a felon, who had been convicted of murder, receive the knoot. Although I naturally shuddered at the idea of being a spectator of the agonies of a fellow-creature, yet curiosity overcame my feelings. I penetrated through the crowd, and ascended the roof of a wooden house; from whence I had a distinct view of the dreadful operation.[73]

The suppression of his natural shudder was related to the adjustment by which other travelers put aside the scruples of "stubborn humanity" in a society of slavery and a culture of corporal abuse. The curious reader was also invited to appreciate the view, which was sharply focused, in graphic detail and micrometric calibration.

The executioner held in his hand the knoot: this instrument is a hard thong, about the thickness of a crown-piece, and three quarters of an inch broad, and tied to a thick plaited whip, which is connected, by means of an iron ring, with a small piece of leather fastened to a short wooden handle.

The executioner . . . struck the flat end of the thong on the naked back of the criminal in a perpendicular line, reaching six or seven inches from the collar towards the waist. He began with the right shoulder, and continued his strokes parallel to each other quite to the left shoulder; nor ceased till he had inflicted 333 lashes, the number prescribed by the sentence.[74]

Coxe added that in conclusion the criminal's nostrils were torn with pincers and his face branded; at last he was ready to be sent to the mines of Siberia.

The vaguely imaginable "horrors" of Siberia were not a part of the view from the roof and could never be measured and reported with the same scientific exactitude as the application of the knout. Foucault has described the reformation of punishment in the eighteenth century from the spectacular execution of the would-be regicide Damiens in 1757, in which pincers played a prominent part, to a more "enlightened" and "modern" penitential discipline of supervised cells and meticulous timetables. What Coxe witnessed in St. Petersburg was a public penal spectacle of the ancien régime, but the enlightened eye with which he described it, his traveler's gaze, analyzed the beating scientifically according to what Foucault has called the "microphysics" of power: the thickness of the thong, the perpendicularity of the stripes, the counting up to 333. The civilization of Western Europe, watching from the roof, announced its mastery over the barbarism of Eastern Europe, as surely as over the beaten body of a slave.

Coxe was slightly self-conscious about the graphic precision with which he entertained his readers, and offered an uneasy self-justification: "As several authors have erroneously described the punishment of the knoot, I have been thus particular in relating what fell under my observation." All the same, it is hard not to attribute a certain prurience to Coxe when he offered the criminal's naked back to his readers as brutally as Casanova invited his reader to finger, along with him, the virginity of a newly purchased slave. Zaire, however, stood right between Casanova's thighs for that examination, while Coxe made his observations on the knout from up on the roof. How could he know that the thong was "the thickness of a crown-piece, and three quarters of an inch broad"? A note in his book promised the reader that these were truly "the exact dimensions" of the knout, for he "procured" one in Russia, "which is now in my possession." One must imagine Coxe writing his account, putting down his pen to take the knout in one hand and a measuring tape in the other:

Length of the thong 2 feet; breadth of the top ¼ inch; at the bottom 1/2.—Thickness 1/8.—Length of the platted whip 2 feet.—Circumference of ditto 2 and ½ inches.—Diameter of the ring 1 inch and ⅜.—Length of the leather spring 1 inch and ½.—Length of the handle 1 foot, 2 and ½ inches.—Length of the whole 5 feet 5 inches and ⅜.—Weight 11 ounces.[75]

The knout was meticulously measured. The information was relegated to a footnote, but Coxe insisted on including it in his book, for perhaps some reader would find it as interesting as he did.

The book was published in 1784, the same year that the marquis de Sade was transferred from a dungeon at Vincennes to a cell in the Bastille. In the *History of Juliette* Sade had his hero acquire the habit of flagellation in Siberia, reporting that "this habit is so compelling that its addicts are unable to do without whipping." Sade also presented Catherine herself, knout in hand, and described that instrument in a sadistic footnote that almost seemed to parody the footnote of Coxe:

This whip is fashioned from a bull's pizzle; to it are attached three thongs of moose hide. A single stroke draws blood: these instruments are of incomparable utility to those who cherish, either actively or passively, the pleasures of flagellation. To increase their effectiveness, steel tips may be fitted to the thongs; it then becomes possible to remove flesh virtually without effort; one hundred strokes applied by a vigorous arm will kill anyone. One such whip, more or less studded, is in the possession of every voluptuous Russian.[76]

And one such whip remained in the possession of the English clergyman William Coxe. Ségur brought back to Paris the sketch of a French girl who had been raped in Russia and the portrait of a Kalmuck boy who had been his personal slave. Coxe took home from Eastern Europe a less sentimental souvenir.

"Poor Abject Slaves!"

"The personal service in which the lower ranks of Poland are kept, is a mere slavery," wrote Joseph Marshall, in a travel account of 1772, "such a despotism as the planters in the West-Indies use over their African slaves. Compared with this, the oppressed state of the Russian peasants is an absolute freedom." Yet Marshall also thought the peasants in Russia were "very near on the same rank, as the blacks in our sugar colonies." Indeed, he supposed that before the enlightened reign of Catherine "they were greater slaves than even in Poland."[77] It was a fine point, the question of where in Eastern Europe conditions of slavery were most oppressive, but Marshall stated clearly what others only implied, that peasant slavery in Eastern Europe was the same condition as black slavery in the Western hemisphere.

Marshall's account of his travels around Europe, including Russia, the Ukraine, and Poland, constitutes an unusual, though not unique case in the travel literature of the eighteenth century, since he himself was a figure of perfect obscurity, and it has been suggested that he never traveled anywhere at all. John Parkinson, who traveled to Russia in the 1790s, heard in Stockholm "some good stories" about Marshall, who "has published travels through various parts of Europe without having once crossed the channel."[78] If indeed Marshall's travels were a fraud and a fiction, his case clearly suggests that Eastern Europe offered fertile soil to the inventive imagination. Soil, in fact, was his chief preoccupation, for he presented himself as an English landowner with an interest in scientific agricultural improvement, touring Europe to make comparative observations. For that reason he attended to the condition of the peasantry in Russia, though his comments were conventional enough to have come out of other travelers' accounts. In one unusual touch, he claimed to have brought back to Northamptonshire as a souvenir not a knout but an extremely large potato of the Ukraine, measured at the size of a quart bottle, which he hoped would seed and flourish in English soil.

Marshall wrote of traveling through Russia by commandeering horses; he was equipped with "a military order to be supplied by the peasants," and accompanied by five soldiers, "each armed with a broad sword, a pair of pistols and a carbine." This was a guarantee of safety as well as of horses, but Marshall was disturbed to see that his soldiers were eager to beat the peasants they encountered: "I curbed this licentiousness, which gave me a clear idea of the government of Russia." He declared the government to be "the most absolute in Europe" and found that "all ranks are equally slaves to the Empress, not subjects." There was evidence of this in the penal system, for even "the greatest nobility are liable to suffer the knout, that is to be whipped to death," while other punishments included "cutting out tongues, hanging up by the ribs, and many other efforts of barbarity, which show the cruelty of despotism."[79] Thus he created a chain of associations from slavery and corporal punishment to barbarism and despotism. The connection between slavery and despotism was most famously formulated in the age of Enlightenment by Montesquieu in 1748 in *The Spirit of the Laws*: "In despotic countries, where they are already in a state of political servitude, civil slavery is more tolerable than in other governments," for "the condition of a slave is hardly more burdensome than that of a subject." Marshall accepted this association of slavery and despotism, and indulging in the kind of political taxonomy which Montesquieu practiced, he began to list "countries of pure despotism, like Russia, Turkey, Persia &c."[80] In this scheme both slavery and despotism in Russia acquired that Oriental character so often invoked in Eastern Europe.

Marshall speculated upon the socioeconomic significance of slavery for the demography of Russia, making comparisons to "the most western countries of Europe." Russia was "better peopled than I expected," refuting "the common ideas of this country being all a desart," but nevertheless it was "very badly peopled." Such concern, taken together with Marshall's all-consuming interest in agriculture, identified him as an eighteenth-century physiocrat. Population was the key to agricultural cultivation, which was the source of the only meaningful economic power and prosperity. He wrote of Russia's enormous size, a vastness he thought would "surprise" people in "the western part of Europe," and saw only one way to people such an expanse: "Liberty must be diffused, all slavery of the lower ranks broken through, and every man allowed to become a farmer that pleases."[81] This was not a humanitarian passion, but an economic priority.

Marshall believed that the Russian peasants were "so habituated to slavery" that it would be impossible to bring about any general liberation.

Instead, he forecast a future of virtually mechanical demographic migration within Eastern Europe. Of Poland, where society was then disrupted by the crisis that would soon lead to partition, Marshall observed that "because the Polish nobles treat all the peasants as slaves in the utmost extent of the word: when, therefore, a scene of trouble and confusion comes, they are sure to take the first opportunity to desert."[82] Marshall claimed to be struck by the number of Poles in Prussian Silesia, there "escaping the miseries of Poland." He imagined that Poland must be "amazingly depopulated," calculating fantastically a loss of "several millions of people" and supposing that the country would be left "a mere desart." Interestingly, when he wrote of Bohemia, which as part of the Holy Roman Empire he treated under "Travels through Germany," he stipulated that the peasants were "treated in a wretched manner" and "in every respect resemble nearly those of Poland, than whom they are not favoured more." Bohemia, Poland, and Russia thus comprised together a domain of wretched social oppression, of slavery like that of the West Indies. Those slaves were island-bound, but the peasants of Eastern Europe, thought Marshall, would move magnetically in whatever direction offered a marginal improvement of status. If Catherine could attract them to flee both "the disorders in Poland and the oppressions in Turkey," she could hope to achieve a physiocratic empire of productive farmers, and everywhere else "mere desart."[83]

William Richardson was in Russia for four years, from 1768 to 1772, including the years that Marshall claimed to be there. Richardson accompanied Charles, Lord Cathcart, England's ambassador extraordinary to Catherine, and served both as Cathcart's secretary and as tutor to his sons in St. Petersburg.[84] He spent the rest of his life as professor of humanity at the University of Glasgow, and his *Anecdotes of the Russian Empire*, published in London in 1784, were adorned with professorial quotations from the classics. He quoted Virgil to evoke the cold of Russian winter, associating the Russians with the ancient Scythians, and Tacitus on the ancient Germans as "quite applicable to the Russians," representing the barbarism of the peasants with their skins, beards, and hatchets.[85] On the Baltic passage to St. Petersburg in 1768, at the entrance to the Gulf of Finland, Richardson saw "an uncouth, black, and disagreeable island; the first specimen of the Russian dominions." In 1772, from the moment he set foot in a British homebound man of war at Kronstadt harbor, he felt his "heart throb" and "tears start," experienced "ineffable rapture" as he "leaned over the side of the ship, and thought of Britain."[86] The passage from Western Europe to Eastern Europe, and vice versa, was thus quite abrupt by the Baltic Sea, and one missed the transition of entering Poland and leaving Europe, the opportunity to wonder whether slavery was more abject in Poland than Russia, or in Russia than Poland. Richardson, however, with his head in the classics and his heart in England, resembled Marshall in his keen eye for the conditions of slavery in Russia and his readiness to speculate on its significance.

In June of 1769 Richardson was pleased to be able to see the transit of Venus, but he also looked down to the earth to consider "The State of Agriculture in Russia." He could not match Marshall's obsession with the subject, but felt qualified to judge the Russian plough, on account of its size, "indeed, a ridiculous object." He also allowed himself the generalization that "agriculture is still in its infancy in Russia, on account of the slavery of the peasants." Infancy was one way of expressing the idea of backwardness, and Richardson would describe the Russians, generally, as "bearded children." The peasants—"bearded boors"—were "even infantine in their amusements."[87] The association between backwardness and slavery was important for establishing the relative distinction of civilization in Western Europe and Eastern Europe; it complemented the association of slavery and despotism, which quite broadly encompassed both Eastern Europe and the Orient. From a political point of view Richardson too classified Russia as "a great oriental empire," influenced by Peter to "some resemblance to other European states" but still in danger of "relapse into its former oriental condition." In comparing social structures, however, Richardson did not oppose the Orient to Europe, but rather Russian slavery to "the feudal system, as it arose in the west of Europe."[88]

Richardson had much more to say on "The Slavery of the Russian Peasants," prefacing his discussion with a declaration of perspective:

It is impossible for a native of Britain, giving an account of this country to an Englishman, not to express such feelings and reflections as a comparison between the British government, and that of other nations, must naturally suggest.

The peasants in Russia, that is to say, the greatest part of the subjects of this empire, are in a state of abject slavery; and are reckoned the property of the nobles to whom they belong, as much as their dogs and horses.[89]

The abjectness of slavery in Eastern Europe was thus defined by direct comparison with Western Europe. Richardson explained that a peasant in Russia could own no property, inasmuch as everything "may be seized by his master." He could be bought and sold, or even given "in exchange for a dog or a horse." These were the signs of slavery, and there was another: "The owner may also inflict on his slaves whatever punishment he pleases." Richardson told of a woman at Moscow who was said to have killed more than 70 of her slaves by "scourging" and "other barbarous punishments," making it "a matter of amusement to contrive such modes of punishment as were whimsical and unusual." Another woman used her Kalmuck slaves for "whimsical services," though more benign, teaching them to read as Ségur taught his Kalmuck slave, and having them "read by her bed-side till she falls asleep; and continue reading or talking, without intermission, all the time she is asleep."[90] If Russian "amusements" were thus either barbaric, whimsical, or infantine, it should be noted that Richardson's own amusement was the relation of Russian manners. In one letter, for instance, he expected that Russian education would "afford some amusement" to an old Etonian, while in another he promised an English clergyman "some allusions to the manners of the country, that will make you smile."[91]

Like Coxe, Richardson had witnessed a public knouting in a crowd so thick that he could not actually see the victim: "a scourge rose at intervals above the heads of the people; at intervals were heard the repeated strokes; and every stroke was followed by the low suppressed groan of extenuated anguish."[92] It would be difficult to say whether these suggestive sound effects were more or less prurient than Coxe's readiness to put the criminal's naked back directly in his readers' line of vision. Richardson took his observations of brutality as a cue to reflection on the relation between slavery and the national character of the Russians.

Exposed to corporal punishment, and put on the footing of irrational animals, how can they possess that spirit and elevation of sentiment which distinguish the natives of a free state? Treated with so much inhumanity, how can they be humane? I am confident, that most of the defects which appear in their national character, are in consequence of the despotism of the Russian government.[93]

Slavery and despotism thus retarded not only agricultural but also sentimental development in Russia. William Richardson's appeal to "elevation of sentiment" suggested some sort of spiritual kinship to Samuel Richardson, whose *Pamela* and *Clarissa* had created a sentimental revolution in eighteenth-century England and even France. William Richardson was unusual among travelers and commentators in making much of the fact that Russian peasants could be forced to marry by their masters:

Marriages of this sort must produce little happiness; neither husband nor wife are very studious of conjugal fidelity: hence the lower classes are as profligate as can possibly be conceived; and, in such circumstances, we cannot expect that they will have much care of their children.[94]

For Richardson sentiment too became a measure of civilization.

In his "Reflections on the Effects of Despotism" he developed this theme, beginning with an allusion to Lucretius and the articulation of a British perspective:

There is some satisfaction in recollecting, that while other nations groan under the yoke of bondage, the natives of our happy islands enjoy more real freedom than any nation that does now, or ever did, exist. In other respects, it is no very pleasing exercise to witness the depression and sufferings of the human race; to contemplate the miseries and manners of slaves! Poor abject slaves![95]

Every traveler from Western Europe was capable of deriving "some satisfaction" of this sort from the contemplation of Eastern Europe, which served to define the superior civilization of the visitor. Richardson pursued his sentimental analysis of Russian slavery:

Poor abject slaves! who are not allowed the rights of men—hardly those of ir-rational creatures! who must toil, undergo hardship, and suffer the most grievous suffering. . . . From the hour of their birth they are in the power of a rapacious chief, who may sell, scourge, or employ them in any labour he pleases. They have no property—no home—nothing that their proud superior may not seize, and claim as his own. The horse and the bull may chuse their loves, according to their own inclination; a privilege not allowed to the Russians. They no sooner arrive at the age of puberty, than they are often compelled to marry whatsoever female their proprietor chuses, in order, by a continued progeny of slaves, to preserve or aug-ment, his revenue. In such families, no conjugal happiness,—no paternal or filial affection can ever exist. Where the husband and wife hate each other, or are in-different, there can be little fidelity; the husband takes little care of the child; the mother is not always affectionate; the poor guiltless infant is thus neglected. . . . Those who survive become little better than savage. In their early years, no tender affection softened or humanized their hearts.[96]

The concluding emphasis on "the poor guiltless infant" lacking "tender affection" in "early years" ingeniously summed up the evils of slavery by invoking the sentimental mystique of childhood, so recently stimulated by the writings of Rousseau. Inadequacy of sentiment became an issue of civilization when it left the child "savage," not even "humanized."

While Marshall compared the Russian peasants to "the blacks in our sugar colonies," Richardson proposed for comparison the Incas of Peru. Inspired by "the scenes of oppression I too often behold," he wrote a poem about slavery: "Twas thus th' Iberian *humaniz'd* the guiltless tribes who roam'd Peruvian forests."[97] The word was italicized for ironic effect. Richardson really believed that slaves were rendered inhuman: "Those poor unhappy men, who are bought and sold, who are beaten, loaded with fetters, and valued no higher than a dog, treated with unabating rigour, become inhuman."[98] They did not necessarily feel the effects of their sentimental deprivation, these unloving parents and spouses. Their condition was described to bring tears to the eyes of Richardson's readers in England, who better appreciated the importance of conjugal and filial affection. When Harriet Beecher Stowe wrote about the evils of slavery in *Uncle Tom's Cabin* in the nineteenth century, she roused the conscience of her age by playing upon similar themes: the separation of husbands and wives, of parents and children.

From his "Reflections on the Effects of Despotism," Richardson moved next to "National Character of the Russians." Their weakness was not in lacking altogether an emotional life, for he admitted, "They have lively feelings." The problem was that they could not employ "reason" to form "general rules of conduct"—such as conjugal or filial commitment—and thus regulate "variable and shifting emotions." This was "extreme sensibility, unsubdued or ungoverned by reason," manifesting itself in excesses of passion and deceit, of violence and despondency. The Russians "seldom look back on the past, or anticipate the future," and this was what made them into "bearded children; the creatures of the present hour." There could never be a "great revolution" in Russia without some "steady foreigner" to "take advantage of their temporary transports," while "irregular sensibility" could best be "corrected" in the army by "the strictest discipline." [99]

Any true transformation of this character, however, could only come about when the Russians "have entire security for their persons and possessions"—that is, when slavery was abolished. "Immortal would be the glory of that sovereign who would restore above twenty millions of men to the rights of intelligent and rational beings," wrote Richardson, but he did not advise Catherine to make that bid for immortality. Liberation would have to be a long and slow process lest it "let loose on mankind so many robbers and spoilers." Richardson insisted that "before slaves can receive freedom in full possession, they must be taught to know, relish, and use its blessings." The Enlightenment in general was subject to ambivalence on the subject of slavery, wherever it occurred, and in his hesitation over emancipation Richardson was only typical of the times. "I quit such Utopian speculations," he concluded, "and will only express my wishes, that the small portion of the human race who enjoy real freedom, may preserve and make a proper use of it." Again the traveler who discovered slavery in Eastern Europe had learned from it to appreciate the superiority of his own civilization. Richardson left Russia in 1772, persuaded that if it were possible "to teach them to act from fixed principles," the Russians might someday become "a respectable people." [100]

Coxe's book of travels was published in 1784, the same year as Richardson's. When Coxe came to evaluate "the present state of civilization in the Russian empire," he declared himself much disappointed in the expectations raised by Peter's reforms:

For though a nation, compared with itself at a former period, may have made a rapid progress towards improvement; yet, as the exaggerated accounts which I had heard and read of the great civilization diffused throughout the whole empire, led me to expect a more polished state of manners, I must own I was astonished at the barbarism in which the bulk of the people still continue.[101]

The standard of "manners" made it possible to envision a sliding scale of civilization, a scale of "progress towards improvement" in which a nation might be measured against its own past as well as against other nations. "The civilization of a numerous and widely dispersed people," wrote Coxe, "is not the work of a moment, and can only be affected by a gradual and almost insensible progress." [102]

Civilization was a quality that the traveler had to be able to discover upon inspection, and one of the most famous details of Peter's legend was his campaign against the Russian beard. Coxe was one of many who remarked upon the beards of the Russians, and what made them so remarkable was the supposition that Peter had had them all shaved away long ago: "notwithstanding the rigorous edicts issued by Peter I the far greater number still wear beards; being scarcely less attached to that patriarchal custom than their ancestors." The indicated conclusion was that "the peasants, who form the bulk of the nation, are still almost as deficient in the arts as before the reign of Peter." Manners might exist in all different degrees of polish throughout society, but the peasantry revealed its lack of civilization even more fundamentally by its technological deficiency in "the arts"—the Scythian hatchet, the ridiculously tiny plough. Indeed, the peasants were equated with their primitive tools when Coxe described them as "the private property of the landholders, as much as implements of agriculture, or herds of cattle." [103]

Just as Richardson considered slavery the obstacle to any improvement in the Russian national character, Coxe was equally emphatic in regarding slavery as the single most important factor retarding the advance of civilization.

It may be perceived, that though proceeding towards civilization, they are still far removed from that state; that a general improvement cannot take place while the greater part continue in absolute vassalage; nor can any effectual change be introduced in the national manners, until the people enjoy full security in their persons and property.[104]

The concluding phrase was so close to Richardson's as to suggest the consensus that had come about by 1784 on the issue of slavery and civilization in Eastern Europe. There was always a suggestion of self-congratulation when the traveler rhetorically posed the crucial question, along with William Coxe: "How then can a country be said to be civilized, in which domestic slavery still exists?" [105]

Chapter Three

Imagining Eastern Europe: Fiction, Fantasy, and Vicarious Voyages

"These Frontiers of Europe"

Like so many other great ideas in the age of Enlightenment, that of Eastern Europe may be said to have begun with Voltaire. His famous fascination with Russia was formalized in the extremely uncritical *History of the Russian Empire Under Peter the Great*, published in two volumes in 1759 and 1763. Then, in the 1760s and 1770s, the correspondence of mutual adulation between Voltaire and Catherine helped the philosopher to envision the tsarina as the greatest patroness of the Enlightenment. Voltaire, however, had already made his map of Eastern Europe much earlier in his long career. In 1731 his enormously successful *History of Charles XII* followed the Swedish king on a campaign of conquest, describing lands that were only just being recognized as conceptually related, Poland and Russia, the Ukraine and the Crimea. The book went into several translations and many editions throughout the eighteenth century. Voltaire, encouraging his readers to follow with him the trail of the bold campaigner through little-known lands, became the Enlightenment's first traveler to Eastern Europe.

The voyage was historical, for Charles had set out in 1700, when Voltaire was six, and died in 1718, the year that Voltaire assumed his pen name and began to make it famous. The voyage was also, considered as a traveler's account, entirely vicarious and vividly imaginary. Voltaire, for all his interest in Russia and later devotion to Catherine, never in his life traveled farther east than Berlin, where he visited Frederick. Yet, Voltaire's *Charles XII* was powerfully influential in mapping Eastern Europe on the mind of the Enlightenment, and demonstrated that the philosophes could explore that domain with no more cumbersome traveling apparatus than a curious imagination. By the same token, real travelers to Eastern Europe brought along and gave free rein to their imaginative and philosophical preconceptions, so that the image that emerged from their accounts was often conditioned by an element of fantasy. Eastern Europe was constructed by the combined conceptions of travelers in the imagination and imaginative travelers.

Charles crossed the Baltic from Sweden in 1700 and proceeded to defeat Peter the Great in the battle of Narva. Voltaire therefore started his survey of Eastern Europe with "very curious particularities" about Russia. He began by locating it geographically for his readers and then evaluated its level of civilization:

Muscovy, or Russia, embraces the north of Asia and that of Europe, and from the frontiers of China it extends for the space of fifteen-hundred leagues to the borders of Poland and Sweden. But this immense land was scarcely known to Europe before the Tsar Peter. The Muscovites were less civilized than the Mexicans when they were discovered by Cortes; all born slaves of masters as barbaric as themselves, they were stagnating in ignorance, in need of all the arts, and in insensibility of these needs, which smothered all industry.[1]

Voltaire emphasized Russia's position on two continents, Europe and Asia. Its European part he always assigned, according to the prevailing convention, to the north of Europe, though Peter's conquests had taken him almost to the Black Sea by the end of the seventeenth century. Voltaire could define the geography of Russia in different terms in the same work, "from the limits of the Caspian Sea to those of the Baltic Sea," remarking that "this great part of the continent still has vast deserts."[2] This great part of the continent, however, if it extended from the Caspian to the Baltic, could only be the eastern part. In 1731 Voltaire was already toying with alternatives to the conventional division of Europe into north and south.

Voltaire obviously knew that a part of Russia was in Europe, but still he could write paradoxically of Russia being "scarcely known to Europe." Thus he suggested the possibility of a double Europe, one Europe that "knew" things, as Tott learned to "know" the Moldavians, and the other Europe that waited to become "known." That other Europe was Eastern Europe, and Voltaire equated the condition of "scarcely known" with that of being "less civilized." His analogy to Cortés and the Mexicans, like that of Richardson to the Peruvians, awaiting discovery by the Iberians in order to be "humaniz'd," suggested the dark side of the "discovery" of Eastern Europe. Voltaire himself, following Charles, would become the philosophical Cortés of Eastern Europe, discovering it and making it known to his public of enlightened readers.

After the battle of Narva, Voltaire followed Charles into Poland, whose crown was bestowed upon the Swedish king's Polish client, Stanisław Leszczyński. The latter, when later driven from Poland, would settle in Western Europe as the duke of Lorraine, give his daughter in marriage to Louis XV as queen of France, and become himself a patron of the Enlightenment, sometimes of Voltaire. Here was a chain of descent from Charles, the patron of Leszczyński, who would become the patron of Voltaire; this was the personal link between the Swedish king and the French philosopher, who both sought to master Eastern Europe. Poland for Voltaire was not even located on contemporary maps but instead was identified as a "part of ancient Sarmatia." He described the Poles in the Sejm, the parliament: "sabre in hand, like the ancient Sarmatians." He affected to "see" them himself and show them to his readers: "One sees still in the Polish soldiers the character of the ancient Sarmatians, their ancestors, as little discipline, the same fury to attack."[3] In fact, Polish nobles often proclaimed themselves Sarmatian as an expression of caste and cultural pride, but this was quite different in spirit from Voltaire's deployment of the label. His projection of the Poles into ancient history, his absolute identification of them with their ancient "ancestors," served as a literary device for relegating Poland anthropologically to a lower level of civilization.

After Russia and Poland, Charles proceeded to "sink himself (*s'enfoncer*) in the Ukraine." It was a fateful military descent for Charles, who would meet defeat at Poltava, but it was an important intellectual breakthrough for Voltaire. This sinking into the Ukraine brought him to a land even less known than Poland and Russia, assumed to be less civilized for that very reason, and above all a land that "sank" to the south on the map of Europe. When Voltaire followed Charles into the Ukraine, the book could no longer pretend to be about "the North" of Europe. The Ukraine was introduced by Voltaire as the "land of the Cossacks, situated between Little Tartary, Poland, and Muscovy," and that grouping of lands could only make sense as Eastern Europe. The Ukraine was repeatedly explained by reference to its neighboring lands, politically vulnerable because "surrounded by Muscovy, the [Ottoman] states of the Grand Seigneur, Poland," agriculturally backward because "ravaged" by Tartars and Moldavians, "all brigand peoples."[4]

The Ukraine, according to Voltaire, was an "unknown land," unknown in the same paradoxical sense as Russia before Peter, assigned to the same double register, a land of Europe unknown to Europe. Voltaire sought to render it known by locating it among its neighbors: Poland, Russia, Moldavia, Tartary, Turkey. In seeking to define one term, he ended up outlining "this great part of the continent." The method was that of Voltaire's Swedish contemporary Charles Linnaeus, the great natural historian of the Enlightenment, who in his *Systema Naturae* of 1735 identified individual species by presenting them in tables of related species. Foucault has suggested this method as the essence of eighteenth-century epistemology, that "all designation must be accomplished by means of a certain relation to all other possible designations."[5] Such a method, when it came to designating geographical spaces, demanded of Voltaire a mental rearrangement of the map of Europe, a table of relations that replaced the north-south axis with an east-west axis. He brought into alignment the lands where Charles XII pursued his dreams of conquest, lands that tempted foreign armies and native brigands, lands that awaited discovery by adventurous travelers and far-away philosophers. The alignment made sense from the French perspective, because these lands appeared as related in backwardness.

Charles marched his army to the "eastern extremity of the Ukraine," to the eastern extremity of Europe itself, where Voltaire discovered the Zaporozhian Cossacks, "the strangest people who are on the earth." The Zaporozhians were identified as "a pack of ancient Russians, Poles, and Tartars." Their religion was "a sort of Christianity," their economy was based on "brigandage" of course, and their political system involved electing a chief and then cutting his throat. Strangest of all, however, was their method of reproducing their numbers: "They do not suffer any women among them, but go and carry off all the children for twenty or thirty leagues around, to raise according to their own manners (*moeurs*)."[6] This extravagant conception was also deeply Linnaean in its implications, inasmuch as Linnaeus looked to sexual reproduction as a key to defining individual species. Voltaire imagined the Zaporozhians as a people who did not sexually reproduce, a strange and unnatural miscellany of ancient peoples. Yet they possessed something to pass on to the children they abducted: *moeurs*, that is, manners or customs. Voltaire conceded that even cutthroat brigands could be said to have manners, however strange, however primitive. It was the concept by which he would evaluate all of world history in his *Essay on Manners* of 1756, and when he wrote his *Charles XII* manners already suggested a standard for measuring different levels of civilization.

Charles passed through the Ukraine during "the memorable winter of 1709, still more terrible on these frontiers of Europe than we experienced it in France." Voltaire was aware that his history was pioneering the "frontiers of Europe," the eastern frontiers, and equally aware that the Ukraine, for all its strangeness, was so much a part of Europe as to partake of the same memorable winter that "we" experienced in France. A common continental experience linked the Zaporozhians to Voltaire himself; he remembered the winter of 1709, when he was fifteen years old. For Charles the Ukraine was an "unknown land," as it certainly was for the young Voltaire, but Charles was actually there in 1709, and because it was unknown he could not know his way. "Charles advanced in these lost lands (*pays perdus*), uncertain of his route," wrote Voltaire in a dazzling bit of wordplay.[7] Charles himself was obviously the one who was lost, but Voltaire cleverly engineered the literary reversal by which the Ukraine was lost instead, *pays perdus*. These were the lost lands of Eastern Europe, which awaited the discovery of Charles the conqueror and Voltaire the philosopher. Voltaire could declare these lands to be lost and allow himself the satisfaction of discovering them, analyzing them, classifying them, and putting them on the map in their proper relation to Western Europe.

Charles was defeated by Peter at Poltava and escaped still farther to the south, completing the traversal of Eastern Europe that took him from the Baltic toward the Black Sea. He found refuge as the guest, really the prisoner, of the Ottoman sultan, at Bender on the Dniester River, between Tartary and Moldavia. Voltaire presented the Crimea: once a commercial center of the ancient Greeks, then of the medieval Genoese, now only ruins amid "desolation and barbarism." The Tartars were brigands and yet hospitable to Charles XII: "The Scythians, their ancestors, transmitted to them this inviolable respect for hospitality."[8] Like Voltaire's Pole-Sarmatian, his Tartar-Scythian remained a barbarian of the ancient world. It was such a successful formula that, 50 years later, travelers like Coxe and Ségur would discover Scythians all over Eastern Europe.

The sultan relocated Charles from Bender to Demotica in Thrace, near Adrianople. He was still in Europe, and never reached the Orient; he returned to Sweden in 1714. Before Poltava it seemed to Voltaire that Charles might have tumbled the empires of Turkey and Persia, and if he had done so, Voltaire's history would have had to become a work of Orientalism to follow its hero.[9] Instead, his last stop was with Charles "at Demotica, buried in inaction and in oblivion (*l'oubli*)." The reader would have been rightly uncertain whether it was Charles or Demotica lost in oblivion, and Voltaire followed ambiguity with paradox: "He was believed dead in all of Europe." This could not be true, for Charles was in Demotica, and Demotica was in Europe. The *oubli* seemed to touch even Voltaire when he forgot this geographical fact. Eastern Europe remained lost even after it was discovered, but Demotica, after Charles and Voltaire, could not be completely forgotten. In 1791, when Salaberry was making the last leg of his voyage, from Adrianople to Constantinople, he passed by Demotica and remembered that Charles XII had been there.[10]

Charles was able to conquer Eastern Europe with his troops by instilling "discipline to render them invincible." Peter was able to stop Charles at Poltava because the tsar possessed the same key: "discipline was established among his troops." Foucault has suggested that "discipline" was the dark secret of enlightened civilization in the eighteenth century, "a whole set of instruments, techniques, procedures" for the most effective application of power. Voltaire repeatedly invoked discipline in explaining the successes of Charles and Peter in Eastern Europe. Polish soldiers possessed "as little discipline" as the ancient Sarmatians. Peter proposed "to discipline the Cossacks" in the Ukraine.[11] The peoples of Eastern Europe awaited not only discovery but also discipline, and Charles and Peter were the masters of discipline who sought to harness the energy that was wasted in brigandage. Charles tried and failed, but Peter and his successors, from Catherine to Stalin, would have somewhat more success in dominating Eastern Europe. Voltaire's *Charles XII* surveyed the lands and peoples of Eastern Europe, and articulated their relation of backwardness to Western Europe, their relation of resemblance to each other, and their relation of identity to their own ancient ancestors. These relations constituted the philosophical foundation for the eighteenth-century construction of Eastern Europe. "I have shown here a general survey of natural bodies," wrote Linnaeus in the *Systema Naturae*, "so that the curious reader with the help of this, as it were, geographical table knows where to direct his journey in these vast kingdoms."[12] Voltaire offered a similar opportunity to readers and travelers who might want to journey in kingdoms other than the animal, vegetable, and mineral. The formulas of his imaginative voyage would recur throughout the century in the accounts of travelers who actually went to Eastern Europe, even those who sought to rebut or revise his verdicts. At the same time, the curious readers and armchair travelers of the ancien régime in Western Europe confidently defined their own level of enlightened civilization when they imagined Eastern Europe with Voltaire as their guide.

"The Ruder and More Unmannerly Nations"

In 1751 Gotthold Ephraim Lessing, then a young and little-known journalist, wrote in Berlin a review of a book *Polonia litterata* that had just been published in Breslau, written by a Pole in Latin, on contemporary Polish literature. Lessing reported that Stanisław Poniatowski (father of the future king of Poland) was publishing his comments on Voltaire's *History of Charles XII*. Lessing also particularly mentioned a forthcoming Polish translation of Voltaire's *Zaire*. In addition to remarking upon such responses to the French Enlightenment, Lessing also noted in Poland a current Latin literature (including the book under review), and a readiness among Polish writers "to emulate (*nacheifern*) strongly other lands in the restoration of their own language." Above all, the publication of *Polonia litterata* would "earn the attention of the curious all the more for the fact that it makes better known to us the present condition of learning in a realm which all too many still believe to be in deep barbarism."[13] Lessing, who would eventually be celebrated as one of the giants of the German Enlightenment, thus showed an early, broad-minded interest in Poland, a willingness to see it as other than barbaric, but most worthy of commendation when engaged in the emulation of other lands. This was the classic conception of Eastern Europe in the age of Enlightenment, standing somewhere between barbarism and civilization, evaluated with respect to a standard set in Western Europe.

In 1758 Lessing sketched out an idea for a play that he never completed, *The Horoscope*, set in Podolia, a province of the Ukraine, which was part of the Commonwealth of Poland and Lithuania.[14] By then Lessing was already a well-known playwright, noted since 1755 as the author of *Miss Sara Sampson*, a pioneering bourgeois tragedy conceived without the conventional noble and mythological heroes of neoclassical drama. *The Horoscope* was not a bourgeois tragedy; its heroes were emphatically of the nobility. It was, however, set in fifteenth-century Podolia, far from the England of *Miss Sara Sampson*, and the noble protagonists were Poles and Tartars. Contemplating a less modern drama, by his own standard of modernity, Lessing looked for an appropriate setting and found it in the Ukraine. By the same token, the horoscope that gave the play its title, an Oedipal forecast that Lukas Opalinski would one day murder his father Petrus Opalinski, Palatine of Podolia, required a setting where a superstitious faith in prophecies and horoscopes could drive the drama along. The Ukraine was the quintessential geographical expression of Eastern Europe, because, as Voltaire had discovered when he followed Charles XII, it was so clearly not the North and not the Orient. It could only be Eastern Europe.

The plot concerned Anna Massalska of Lvov, who had been carried off (*weggeschleppt*) by Tartars, and had then fallen in love with one of them, Zuzi. When Anna was rescued by the Opalinski heroes, father and son, they both promptly fell in love with her, thus moving toward their Oedipal destiny. Zuzi meanwhile followed her, pretending to be a Pole, and was recognized as a Tartar only by his compatriot Amru. The one character from Western Europe was the doctor at the Opalinski palace, an Englishman named Connor, representing science in a land of superstition. Though in his review of 1751 Lessing dissociated himself from those who believed Poland to be a land of "deep barbarism," there is little in the extant fragment of *The Horoscope* to suggest otherwise. The frontier struggle between Poles and Tartars, with reciprocal taking and retaking of prisoners, seemed to set them on the same level. The Poles were at least endowed with plausible Polish family names, like Opalinski and Massalska, while the Tartars received such whimsical epithets as "Zuzi" and "Amru." The love of Anna

Massalska and Zuzi did not seem to require any particular condescension on her part, and their romantic union was obstructed by the warfare of their two peoples, not by any gap of civilization between them. Indeed, Zuzi was able to pass himself off as a Pole in the Opalinski palace. Poles and Tartars both belonged to Eastern Europe, just where Voltaire had found them and left them in the previous generation, labeling them as Sarmatians and Scythians, respectively. Like adjoining species on a Linnaean table, the Poles and Tartars of Lessing's drama were zoologically related but not supposed to mate.

In 1732 Voltaire's *Zaire* explored the tragedy of love between a Christian woman and a Moslem sultan in medieval Jerusalem, while in 1779 Lessing himself, in *Nathan the Wise*, would triumphantly dramatize the love of a Jewish woman and a Christian crusader, again in Jerusalem. Yet in *The Horoscope*, without making a clear distinction between different religions, an enlightened playwright like Lessing could not work through the dramatical tensions of star-crossed lovers, or star-crossed parents and children. *The Horoscope* of 1758 remained only the fragmentary sketch for a neoclassical tragedy of superstition and violence on the frontiers of Europe, Oedipus in the Ukraine. Herder in 1769 seemed to follow a similar impulse when, considering the "wild peoples" of Eastern Europe, he prophesied that "the Ukraine will become a new Greece."[15] It was this unstable position between wildness and barbarism on the one hand, and emulation and civilization on the other, that made Eastern Europe with its ambivalent associations a less workable dramatic setting for Lessing than Oriental Jerusalem.

In 1760 Voltaire produced a brief dialogue in verse, which also underlined the potential importance of Eastern Europe in the imaginative literature of the Enlightenment. It was entitled "The Russian in Paris" and was explained as a "little poem in alexandrine verse, composed in Paris, in the month of May 1760, by M. Ivan Alethof, secretary of the Russian embassy." This fictitious figure was identified in an introductory paragraph: "All the world knows that M. Alethof, having learned French at Archangel, of which he was a native, cultivated belles-lettres with an unbelievable ardor, and made still more unbelievable progress." The little poem appeared chronologically right in between the two large volumes of Voltaire's *Peter the Great*. These volumes were frankly the work of a Frenchman on Russia, while the poem pioneered the fictional device of an invented Russian persona and perspective. The dialogue was between two figures, "Le Parisien" and "Le Russe," and the former began by welcoming the visitor with a poetic tribute to Peter the Great, who "caused arts, manners, and laws to be born" in Russia, while the latter replied that he had come to Paris "to enlighten myself, to learn from you." The Russian's self-presentation matched the formulas of the Enlightenment, which was hardly surprising since Voltaire had helped to invent those formulas for defining Russia and the Russians:

> I come to form myself on the shores of the Seine;
> It is a coarse Scythian voyaging to Athens
> Who conjures you here, timid and curious,
> To dissipate the night that covers still his eyes.
>
> (Je viens pour me former sur les bords de la Seine;
> C'est un Scythe grossier voyageant dans Athène
> Qui vous conjure ici, timide et curieux,
> De dissiper la nuit qui couvre encor ses yeux.) [16]

To such a humble petition, from the self-styled Scythian, the Athenian-Parisian replied by wondering, "what can you learn on the shores of the Occident?" For France was no longer the land of Molière, and had fallen so low as to admire Rousseau; the Russian, if he wished to enlighten himself here, would have to wait for reason to return to Paris. The literary device of the invented Russian perspective thus became a vehicle of cultural criticism to belabor the French.

The largest eighteenth-century literary venture to employ this device in juxtaposing Eastern Europe and Western Europe was the *Polish Letters*, a novel by Jean-Paul Marat, probably written in the 1770s. Marat's principal model was obviously Montesquieu's *Persian Letters* of 1721. Just as Lessing experimented with a dramatic setting in Eastern Europe as an alternative to the Orient, Marat attempted an analogous displacement in substituting a Polish for a Persian perspective in his fiction. Montesquieu virtually inaugurated the Enlightenment by inventing Usbek, a Persian traveler to France, and critically analyzing French society, religion, and civilization from the perspective of the Oriental eye. It was a deeply influential masterpiece, and the formula naturally appealed to the young Marat, who hated the ancien régime far more than Montesquieu ever could have. He chose to invent a Polish traveler to Western Europe, to France, England, Holland, and Switzerland, and took him through two ponderous volumes of unoriginal reflections that would not be published until the twentieth century, and only then as a curiosity. The future revolutionary and "Friend of the People," destined to die in his bath in 1793, was an aspiring philosopher and scientist of the Enlightenment. He published a two-volume *Philosophical Essay on Man* in 1773, and *The Chains of Slavery* in 1774, before putting his pen to science in works on optics and electricity, as well as improvising a suspiciously marvelous cure for tuberculosis. His interest in Poland found expression not only in the *Polish Letters* but also in a romantic epistolary novel with a Polish setting, *Adventures of the Young Count Potowski*; this too was unpublished in Marat's lifetime, though it anticipated the triumph of Polish romance in French literature in the 1780s, with the *Loves of the Chevalier de Faublas* by Jean-Baptiste Louvet du Coudray.

In the *Polish Letters*, Marat assumed the identity and perspective of a Polish nobleman in order to formulate his criticisms of the ancien régime. The letters were attributed to "Kamia," writing to his friend "Shava" in Cracow. Changes in the manuscript show that Marat fussed over the name of his Polish hero, finally settling on "Kamia" instead of "Puski," which itself had replaced the original "Sobieski." Such vaguely Oriental designations as Kamia and Shava were not far in spirit from Lessing's Tartars, Zuzi and Amru. Montesquieu's *Persian Letters* included not only reports from France but also sensational letters from Persia that told the story of the hero's harem in Isfahan, his wives and eunuch slaves. Montesquieu was enthusiastically committed to creating a Moslem Persian perspective. Marat, however, included hardly any letters from Poland; there were no reports from the hero's home, no accounts of his Polish background, and very little detail to distinguish his Polish perspective from that of an unoriginal, disaffected French philosophe like Marat himself. Marat was aware of his work's inadequacy in this respect, and offered a figleaf of justification from Kamia to Shava: "You will perhaps be surprised that I have not compared our own country with others; but I have purposely avoided the parallel. A man can hardly be a disinterested judge where his own country is concerned."[17] The real reasons were presumably several: that Marat was a bad writer, that he knew little of Poland, and finally that the perspective of Eastern Europe was more subtly difficult to distinguish from that of Western Europe than was the Orient of Montesquieu.

Marat's Polish hero subscribed to Western Europe's general conception of itself, announcing in his first letter his intention to "travel through the civilized countries of Europe." As for Eastern Europe, his denunciation of the falsity of French politeness was framed from the perspective of "the ruder and more unmannerly nations." There were moments when Kamia's comments on the French seemed to parody those of travelers to Eastern Europe, when he regretted that "a people who are so favored in all respects by Nature" should be so frivolous and depraved, that so many were poor in spite of fertile soil and fine climate.[18] Early on, Kamia gave up his Polish clothes and found a French tailor, though he claimed to find French fashions "ridiculous," especially in being too tight, "a sort of fetters." Kamia exclaimed, "What a difference between this and the noble, easy dress of the Poles!" Thus attired, Kamia appeared outwardly, as in his letters, indistinguishable as a Pole.

When Kamia left France for England and Holland, his perspective drew even closer to that of a Frenchman of the Enlightenment. He found the English "cold, dull, sober" and admired only their government, based on "power wisely limited." He observed immediately that the Englishman "thinks his own nation superior to every other in the world" but, after observing the English, repudiated "this strange madness of looking upon them as perfect beings!"[19] In Holland Kamia found that "the Dutchman has a repulsive manner" and "knows nothing of the amenities or conventions of society." This was the perspective of French civilization, as was Kamia's censuring of Dutch commerce: "These people think only of money, speak only of money, love only money."[20]

Thus Marat employed his Pole as a foil to the false values of Western Europe, and though the *Polish Letters* were not to be published, the device that Marat handled so unsuccessfully was to become a triumphant convention of nineteenth-century literature. After the Kościuszko insurrection of 1794, after the risings against Russia of 1830 and 1863, the figure of the émigré Pole was to become a hero of romantic appeal, in fiction at least. From the century's beginning in 1803, with the publication of *Thaddeus of Warsaw* by Miss Jane Porter, the first of that book's many editions, the type of the Polish hero in Western Europe was established. Count Thaddeus Sobieski, bearing the surname that Marat had discarded, and a Christian name that inevitably associated him with Kościuszko, appeared as the only true nobleman in English aristocratic society, and won the infatuated hearts of the author, the heroine, and the readers. In 1847 Balzac introduced into his *Comédie humaine* Count Wenceslas Steinbock, rescued from suicide by the malevolent Cousin Bette. The suicide note testified to national despair and quoted Kościuszko, Finis Poloniae! In 1872 George Eliot in *Middlemarch* introduced Will Ladislaw, descendant of a Polish émigré grandfather, perhaps even of Miss Porter's Thaddeus of Warsaw. Eliot found Will the only man worthy to marry her most spiritually magnificent heroine Dorothea, who in fact ends the novel as "Mrs. Ladislaw." The year before, in 1871, Louisa May Alcott published a personal reminiscence and literary confession. She remembered how six years before in Paris she had befriended a Polish youth who had fought against Russia in 1863: "the best and dearest of all my flock of boys was my Polish boy, Ladislaw Wisniewski—two hiccoughs and a sneeze will give you the name perfectly."[21] She just called him "Laddie," though, and in 1868 in *Little Women* she changed his name again, to Laurie, and made him into a fictional friend for Jo.

Marat's Polish hero never made it to America, but ended up spending most of the second volume of the *Polish Letters* in the mountains of Switzerland, receiving instruction from a hermit who introduced him to philosophical skepticism. Kamia learned that all morality was relative, varying from China to Rome, from France to ancient Greece, from Constantinople to India. Even the prohibition against incest, suggested Marat subversively with Sade, has "no foundation in Nature." Every man saw the same object from different points of view: "the Chinaman, the Tartar, the African, the European." If morality was alarmingly variant, society and government were depressingly similar throughout the world. The skeptic made no difference between Western Europe and Eastern Europe when he observed that "in Greece, Italy, Poland, England, and France, you will see millions of men slaves under the name of helot, serf, or villain." Even the difference between Europe and the Orient disappeared when "entire nations in Asia, Africa, and Europe are slaves to the cupidity of a single man!" Kamia was distressed by these teachings and wondered, "Why did I wish to leave my home?" Then he encountered a wiser philosopher, who reassured him with the news that all morality could be summed up in a simple maxim: "Be obedient to the laws of your country."[22] Discovering that Kamia was a Polish prince incognito, this unsubversive philosopher sent him home to make use of what he had learned on his travels.

The constitution of your country is very faulty; it is a remnant of barbarism which shames humanity. When the people are groaning under so hard a yoke, how very fortunate for them to get a good and enlightened prince. . . . By the gentleness of your government let your subjects find themselves free, their hideous chains of slavery being broken.[23]

Marat's Polish traveler in Western Europe learned to appreciate the barbarism of his own country, and to remedy it by exercising enlightened authority.

No doubt, condemning the "hideous chains of slavery" in Poland also concealed a denunciation of society in France, for as Rousseau had observed in the *Social Contract*, men were "everywhere in chains." Marat even warned at the end of the *Polish Letters* of a coming "tempest" that would destroy tyrannical government and bring down "violence on the devoted heads of the ministers."[24] Yet the revolutionary Marat, who would one day celebrate the gathering of heads at the guillotine, could comfortably prescribe for Eastern Europe the gentle government of an enlightened prince. Voltaire imagined an Eastern Europe in need of discipline and domination, by Charles or by Peter, and Marat thought Poland was fit for princes to rule. The backwardness of Eastern Europe justified fantasies of authority in Western Europe, even on the part of those who were most subversive at home.

"With a Wolf Face to Face"

Eastern Europe was most fully revealed as a realm of fantasy in *The Travels and Surprising Adventures of Baron Munchausen*, by Rudolf Erich Raspe. These fictional "travels" were published in England in 1785, the year after the publication of Coxe's and Richardson's travel accounts, and became a great success in German translation as well in 1786. Raspe, like his apocryphal hero, was himself a German, but, born in Hanover, he took advantage of the Hanoverian dynastic connection between Germany and England to pursue his shady career between them. He was educated at Göttingen, and it was there, supposedly, that he made the acquaintance and heard the tales of the phenomenal Munchausen. As custodian of the gem collection at Kassel from 1767, Raspe had such a fine opportunity to steal gems that he had to flee to England in 1775. There Baron Munchausen was born and sent upon his first traveling adventure: "I set off from Rome on a journey to Russia, in the midst of winter, from a just notion that frost and snow must of course mend the roads, which every traveller had described as uncommonly bad through the northern parts of Germany, Poland, Courland and Livonia."[25] From the beginning, Munchausen and Raspe showed themselves familiar with the travel literature on Eastern Europe, upon which they worked their fantastic embroidery. The book was first published just as Ségur was completing exactly the same overland itinerary.

Baron Munchausen's entry into Eastern Europe was marked by the sight of "a poor old man" who was lying "on a bleak common in Poland, lying on the road, helpless, shivering, and hardly having wherewithal to cover his nakedness." This was the last conventionally observed encounter with Eastern Europe on the route to St. Petersburg, and also one of the last to involve a human being. For Munchausen, Eastern Europe was a realm of fantastic adventures with savage beasts, whose wildness he triumphantly tamed in a parable of conquest and civilization. As he drove his horse-drawn sledge "into the interior parts of Russia," there suddenly appeared "a terrible wolf, making after me with all the speed of winter hunger." The baron's escape, with the wolf almost upon him, demonstrated the invincible mastery of the traveler to Eastern Europe:

Mechanically I laid myself down flat in the sledge, and let my horse run for our safety. What I wished, but hardly hoped or expected, happened immediately after. The wolf did not mind me in the least, but took a leap over me, and falling furiously on the horse, began instantly to tear and devour the hind-part of the poor animal, which ran the faster for his pain and terror. Thus unnoticed and safe myself, I lifted my head slyly up, and with horror I beheld that the wolf had ate his way into the horse's body; it was not long before he had fairly forced himself into it, when I took my advantage, and fell upon him with the butt-end of my whip. This unexpected attack in his rear frightened him so much, that he leaped forward with all his might: the horse's carcase dropped on the ground, but in his place the wolf was in the harness, and I on my part whipping him continually: we both arrived in full career safe to St. Petersburg, contrary to our respective expectations, and very much to the astonishment of the spectators.[26]

Unquestionably, this was the harness of discipline, the taming of savagery by the traveler from Western Europe, ultimately acclaimed as spectacle.

The spectators in St. Petersburg, however, saw only the wolf in harness, the stunt achieved, without witnessing the brutal intimacy of the taming process. Readers in England, who came to this scene the year after reading Coxe, would have found the whipping of the wolf painfully familiar, remembering that the beating of men was a hallmark of Russian slave society. The use of the "butt-end" of the whip, however, for "an unexpected attack in his rear," made the taming of the wolf into an act of anal rape. It was a sexual triumph over savagery, consummated with the whip, perpetrated with humorous brutality. For Sade also, in the *History of Juliette*, Eastern Europe was preeminently an arena of reiterated anal rape, though Sade's heroes and heroines found such arenas elsewhere as well.

In St. Petersburg Baron Munchausen moved in "the politer circles" and hinted at sexual conquests of a more polite nature than his rape of the wolf. He was waiting in the capital to obtain a commission in the Russian army and passed his time in fantastic feats of hunting. When he came upon "a fine black fox, whose valuable skin it would have been a pity to tear by ball or shot," he nailed it to a tree, reached for his whip, and "fairly flogged him out of his fine skin."[27] Another encounter with a Russian wolf was even more penetratingly intimate:

A frightful wolf rushed upon me so suddenly, and so close, that I could do nothing but follow mechanical instinct, and thrust my fist into his open mouth. For safety's sake I pushed on and on, till my arm was fairly in up to the shoulder. How should I disengage myself? I was not much pleased with my awkward situation—with a wolf face to face; our ogling was not of the most pleasant kind. If I withdrew my arm, then the animal would fly the more furiously upon me; that I saw in his flaming eyes. In short, I laid hold of his tail, turned him inside out like a glove, and flung him to the ground, where I left him.[28]

Again the language conveyed an experience of extremely nasty rape, from the first mechanical instinct, to the thrusting of the fist, and the pushing on and on beyond hope of disengagement. The baron, however, found even more explosive satisfaction with a bear, this time in Poland.

What do you say of this, for example? Daylight and powder were spent one day in a Polish forest. When I was going home a terrible bear made up to me in great speed, with open mouth, ready to fall upon me; all my pockets were searched in an instant for powder and ball, but in vain; I found nothing but two spare flints: one I flung with all my might into the monster's open jaws, down his throat. It gave him pain and made him turn about, so that I could level the second at his back-door, which, indeed, I did with wonderful success; for it flew in, met the first flint in the stomach, struck fire, and blew up the bear with a terrible explosion.[29]

Violated "down his throat" and then "at his back-door," the bear suffered both oral and anal assault, but this time the baron certainly ruined the pelt.

Later in his adventures Munchausen would have the opportunity to send thousands of bearskins to the Russian empress, and she must have appreciated the sexual implications of such a gift, for she responded with thanks and an invitation to "share the honours of her bed and crown." The baron declined "in the politest terms." In Sade's *Juliette*, "politeness" indicated the opposite course: "All manners of enjoyment were desired by Catherine, and you will of course understand that I refused her none of them: her ass especially, the fairest ass I'd seen in my life, caused me no end of sweetest comforts and cheer."[30] Together with Catherine, Sade's hero then went on to sexual exploits of the most savage and sadistic nature, not so dissimilar to those practiced by Munchausen upon the animals of Eastern Europe. Sade's fantasies, however, required human victims.

The baron's handling of wild animals was not necessarily fatal. While visiting an estate in Lithuania he saw a horse that no one dared mount.

In one leap I was on his back, took him by surprise, and worked him quite into gentleness and obedience, with the best display of horsemanship I was master of. Fully to show this to the ladies, and save them unnecessary trouble, I forced him to leap in at one of the open windows of the tea-room, walked round several times, pace, trot, and gallop, and at last made him mount the tea-table, there to repeat his lessons in a pretty style of miniature which was exceedingly pleasing to the ladies, for he performed them amazingly well, and did not break either cup or saucer.[31]

By his horsemanship Baron Munchausen reconciled the contrasts of Eastern Europe, savagery and civility, the wild horse upon the tea-table. Naturally the horse was offered to him as a gift, and so he rode a Lithuanian horse into battle with the Russian army against the Turks. The first volume of Baron Munchausen's *Travels and Surprising Adventures*, which made his reputation, thus established his truly incredible prowess, as soldier as well as huntsman and horseman, across the lands of Eastern Europe.

The idea of horsemanship, with its suggestion of civilization by taming and harnessing, was also essential to artistic images of Eastern Europe in the 1780s. In the Paris Salon of 1781 Jacques-Louis David showed his painting *Count Potocki*, of a Polish nobleman astride a perfectly poised, intensely muscled horse, head bent in submission beneath a dramatic mane. A foreleg is held aloft from the ground so still, with such obvious discipline, that there would be no need to fear for any nearby cups and saucers. In 1782, for the centennial of Peter's accession, Catherine unveiled in St. Petersburg the bronze equestrian statue of Peter executed by the French sculptor Etienne-Maurice Falconet. Falconet was a protégé of Madame de Pompadour in France, and after her death went to Russia in 1766 to enjoy the patronage of Catherine. He was working on the statue of Peter already in 1770, when Richardson saw the designs and pronounced them "allegorical." Peter, on his horse, upon a rock pedestal, represented "the difficulties surmounted by Peter in his great labour of reforming the Russians."[32] In the nineteenth century Pushkin's poem "The Bronze Horseman" would give the statue a place in Russian culture, but in the eighteenth century it was distinctly the work of a Frenchman, an envisioning of Russia from the perspective of the Enlightenment. David's Polish horseman and Falconet's Russian horseman consolidated the artistic and allegorical convention that was then preposterously adapted in literary form when Baron Munchausen made such a spectacular display of his horsemanship on the tea-table in Lithuania.

Baron Munchausen fought gloriously against the Turks, as he himself attested. When the enemy fled, "the swiftness of my Lithuanian enabled me to be foremost in the pursuit." Eventually, however, he was taken prisoner and sold as a slave in Turkey. The idea for this adventure may even have been borrowed from the travel literature, for Coxe's book was published the year before and included an account of his meeting with George Brown, an Irish émigré in Russia, who had really fought in the same campaign as the fictional Munchausen and really was taken prisoner and sold into slavery. Brown was ransomed by the French ambassador in Constantinople, and he returned to Russia to become eventually Catherine's governor-general in Riga. Munchausen, of course, could escape from slavery in a more picturesque fashion. While tending the sultan's apiary he lost a bee, which was attacked by two bears. The baron threw a silver hatchet at the bears, but "by an unlucky turn of my arm, it flew upwards, and continued rising till it reached the moon." He climbed up a beanstalk to the moon to retrieve his hatchet.[33] From Russia he passed to Turkey, from Turkey to the moon, thus establishing a hierarchy of remoteness. Amazing adventures could occur in Eastern Europe, especially because it was so close to the Orient, and not much further from outer space.

Baron Munchausen would later return to Constantinople as a favorite of the sultan, and Raspe then explicitly inserted his hero into the context of contemporary travel literature by establishing a mock rivalry with Baron de Tott. Tott's memoirs were in fact published at the same time as Munchausen's travels. Tott, as the sultan's artillery engineer, supposedly succeeded in firing the largest cannon in the world, but Munchausen "was determined not to be outdone by a Frenchman" and boasted of his own exploits in Turkey with that same extremely large, and ridiculously phallic, cannon. Raspe freely invented an origin for the "swaggering, bouncing Tott," making him the illegitimate offspring of Pope Clement XIV and the proprietress of an oyster stand in Rome.[34] Raspe thus appropriated Tott as a semifictional character to set beside Munchausen, tangling them both in the yarns of a travel literature that was always, as fiction or nonfiction, susceptible to elements of fantasy. The other model that Raspe proposed for Munchausen and his travels was Swift's Gulliver, and the seventh English edition of 1793 was even published under the title *Gulliver Revived*.

If the first volume of 1785 was focused on adventures in Eastern Europe, the central feature of the second volume was a voyage to Africa. Its publication in 1792, during the French Revolution, allowed for a finale in which Munchausen did battle against Voltaire, Rousseau, and Beelzebub, "three horrible spectres," in order to rescue Marie Antoinette after reading Edmund Burke. Earlier, in the heart of Africa, where Munchausen was "introducing the arts and sciences of Europe," he discovered some interesting ancient inscriptions that showed the Africans to be "descended from some of the inhabitants of the moon." Raspe included a sample of the inscription, with a scholarly reference for specialists ("Vide Otrckocsus de Orig. Hung.") and a brief explanation:

These characters I have submitted to the inspection of a celebrated antiquarian, and it will be proved to the satisfaction of every one in his next volume, what an immediate intercourse there must have been between the inhabitants of the moon and the ancient Scythians, which Scythians did not by any means inhabit a part of Russia, but the central part of Africa, as I can abundantly prove to my very learned and laborious friend. The above words, written in our characters, are Sregnah dna skoohtop; that is, The Scythians are of heavenly origin.[35]

This playful bit of nonsense seemed to parody the contemporary impulse to find the Scythians at the origin of any backward people, here whimsically displaced from Voltaire's Tartary and Ségur's Russia. The cryptic reference to *Orig. Hung.* allusively related the Scythians to Hungary as well. Munchausen made the same association between Eastern Europe and Africa that had occasionally occurred to other travelers, and emphasized the remoteness of both with another connection to the men on the moon.

Munchausen also found his way back to Eastern Europe by way of the wilds of North America. There the baron suffered the indignity of scalping at the hands of American "savages," but after traveling through "this prodigious wilderness" he found himself on the frontier of Russia, at the castle of "the Nareskin Roskimowmowsky." The name itself was obviously intended as comedy, and the Russian Roskimowmowsky did his fighting with the fitting assistance of a wild bear. Munchausen had to vanquish them both in combat, and in a manner that emphasized the association between beast and barbarian:

An enormous bear at the same time attacked me, but I ran my hand still retaining the hilt of my broken sword down his throat, and tore up his tongue by the roots. I then seized his carcase by the hind-legs, and whirling it over my head, gave the Nareskin such a blow with his own bear as evidently stunned him. I repeated my blows, knocking the bear's head against the Nareskin's head, until, by one happy blow, I got his head into the bear's jaws, and the creature being still somewhat alive and convulsive, the teeth closed upon him like nutcrackers.[36]

Thus the triumphant traveler turned the savagery of Eastern Europe against itself.

Before going on to save Marie Antoinette, Munchausen made one last visit to St. Petersburg, where he married the tsarina, brought about peace between Russia and Turkey, and dispatched a team of Russian and Turkish workers to build an important canal.

I now proceeded to the Isthmus of Suez, at the head of a million of Russian pioneers, and there united my forces with a million of Turks, armed with shovels and pickaxes. They did not come to cut each other's throats, but for their mutual interest to facilitate commerce and civilization, and pour all the wealth of India by a new channel into Europe.[37]

Thus the cause of civilization, and the connection of Asia to Europe, both so essential to the idea of Eastern Europe, were appropriately advanced by Munchausen, who mobilized the labor of millions of slaves.

"I Am Punkitititi"

The employment of nonsense in the rendering of Eastern Europe, the fabrication of Tartar names or Scythian inscriptions, was fundamental to the fact that the Slavic languages, let alone Hungarian, were usually incomprehensible to writers or travelers from Western Europe. The most ambiguous border between Western Europe and Eastern Europe was marked by the eighteenth-century genius who could make even nonsense into something sublime, by Wolfgang Amadeus Mozart on the way from Vienna to Prague. One of the most obvious ironies of the division of Europe in the twentieth century is the fact that Prague, as any map of Europe will show, lies to the northwest of Vienna but is nevertheless regarded as one of the capitals of Eastern Europe. The reasons for this seemingly misguided designation have been geopolitical in the twentieth century, from the decisions of Versailles to those of Yalta, reinforced by the emphatic nineteenth-century nationalist distinction between Germans and Slavs. In the eighteenth century Bohemia was often regarded as a principality of Germany, that is, of the Holy Roman Empire, though there was also a recognition that the Habsburgs wore the crown of St. Wenceslas analogously to that of St. Stephen in Hungary. Bohemia as a province, and Prague as a city, possessed mixed populations of Germans and Czechs, and even when Bohemia was considered as a part of Germany, there was an increasing awareness in the eighteenth century that the Bohemians were not necessarily Germans. Coxe appreciated the Slavic nature of Bohemia when he employed a Bohemian as his interpreter in Russia. Mozart, who loved Prague and was loved in Prague, probably more than in Vienna, also understood that the northwestern passage into Bohemia brought him into a Slavic, and in that respect alien, domain.

In January 1787 Mozart made his first trip to Prague, there to conduct

The Marriage of Figaro, which had not been received altogether warmly at its Viennese premiere in 1786. On January 15 he wrote from Prague to a friend in Vienna, Gottfried von Jaquin, "I must sincerely confess to you, that (although I enjoy here all possible courtesies and honors, and Prague is in fact a very pretty and pleasant place) I still very much long to be back in Vienna." After this perhaps perfunctory expression of homesickness, Mozart gave an extraordinary account of his journey to Prague, addressing Jaquin thus:

Now farewell dearest friend, dearest Hikkiti Horky! That is your name, so you will know it; we have all of us on our trip invented names ("auf unserer Reise Namen erfunden"); they follow here. I am Punkititi.—My wife is Schabla Pumfa. Hofer is Rozka Pumpa. Stadler is Notschibikitschibi. Joseph my servant is Saga-darata. Goukerl my dog is Schomanntzky—Madame Quallenberg is Runzifunzi.—Mademoiselle Crux Ps: Ramlo is Schurimuri. Freistädtler is Goulimauli. Have the kindness to communicate to the last-mentioned his name.[38]

It was just the sort of silliness that would eventually contribute to the Mozart legend, but it was also the comical expression of alienation that attended the imaginative eighteenth-century traveler to Eastern Europe. Mozart, born in Salzburg, resident in Vienna, a German by native tongue, was not at home in Slavic Bohemia where the language he heard around him sounded like nonsense. In fact, Mozart was a cosmopolitan European who could understand the language almost anywhere his musical career might take him: to Italy, to France, all over Germany. He did not understand Czech. Ignorance of the language was an inconvenience for travelers, but it also offered a sort of imaginative liberation, and Mozart seized the opportunity to create new identities for everyone in his party and even for his friends at home. He freely employed the elements of pseudo-Slavic and pseudo-Oriental sounds that others had drawn upon, though Mozart's amalgams were more extravagantly silly: Punkititi himself, Hikkiti Horky, Runzifunzi, Goulimauli, Notschibikitschibi. These were worthy (and roughly contemporary) companions to Raspe's Nareskin Roskimow-mowsky. Marat's hero corresponded with "Shava" of Cracow, but Mozart built on the same base with greater brio when he christened his own beloved Constanze "Schabla Pumfa."

During this visit to Prague Mozart conducted not only *Figaro* but also the D-major symphony that would come to be known as the "Prague Symphony." He gave a piano recital that was later, in the early nineteenth century, remembered as an occasion of near-orgiastic appreciation:

In conclusion Mozart fantasized at the piano for a good half hour, and thus heightened to the highest the enthusiasm of the delighted Bohemians, so of course with the stormy applause rendered to him he felt compelled to sit down at the piano once again. The stream of this new fantasia had an even more violent effect with the result that he was stormed by the enflamed audience for a third time. . . . A loud voice from the parterre arose with the words "From Figaro!" whereupon Mozart introduced the motif of the favorite aria "Non piu andrai farfallone" and played a dozen of the most interesting and artistic variations extempore, so that this remarkable artistic exhibition ended with the most intoxicated jubilation, which for him was certainly the most glorious of his life, and the most delightful for the rapturously drunk Bohemians.[39]

This was a reminiscence from the perspective of a later Romantic age, and it participated in an already evolving Mozart legend, but certain features of the account were suggestive of the eighteenth-century composer's experience in Eastern Europe. There was Mozart's own indulgence in "fantasia," a liberation from the constraints of classical form, and a related freedom of extemporization. Above all, however, the Bohemians themselves, in this account, appeared not only as paragons of musical appreciation but also as enflamed, intoxicated, enraptured, their emotional susceptibilities at the mercy of this masterful performer who played upon his audience even as he played upon the pianoforte. Mozart's "triumph" in Prague was as much a part of the legend as Prague's devotion to Mozart.

The musical reputation of Bohemia antedated the arrival of Mozart. Charles Burney, the English organist and author of the *General History of Music*, labeled Bohemia the "conservatory of Europe" in 1771, for the quantity of Bohemian musicians. The philosophe Friedrich Melchior von Grimm—patron of Mozart, friend of Diderot, correspondent of Catherine —founded in 1753 the *Correspondance Littéraire* as an international newsletter on French culture; he published in that same year a pamphlet on "The Little Prophet of Bohemian Broda." Grimm's little prophet was a fiddler who was supernaturally transported across Europe from Bohemia to Paris as an oracular spokesman for the true spirit of music against the false taste of French opera. He was a prophet of decadence and doom, the decline of civilization in France:

And far-off peoples will see the masterpieces of your fathers; and they will see them in their theatres and will admire them without making mention of you; for your glory will be passed, and you will be in relation to your fathers what the Greeks of today are in relation to the ancient ones, that is, a barbarous and stupid people. . . .

And I, Gabriel Joannes Nepomucenus Franciscus de Paula Waldstorch, called Waldstoerchel, student of philosophy and moral theology in the Greater College of the Reverend Jesuit Fathers, native of Boehmisch-Broda in Bohemia, I wept at the fate of that people, for I am tenderhearted by nature.[40]

Grimm intended this as an ironic reversal, the pity of Bohemia for France. The fictional fiddler from Bohemia might foresee a French descent into barbarism, but Hester Lynch Piozzi, in Prague in 1786, only months before Mozart, found that "here everything seems at least five centuries behind-hand."[41] This matched the language of other travelers elsewhere in Eastern Europe.

The young Mozart himself befriended an older Bohemian composer, Joseph Myslivetschek, known in the Italian musical world simply as "il Boemo," though surely Mozart, the future inventor of Notschibikitschibi, was not intimidated by an unfamiliar Czech name. Mozart may have been musically influenced by Myslivetschek, and perhaps also by Czech folk songs, like Haydn with his Hungarian themes.[42] The legend of Mozart's first visit to Prague in 1787, however, reversed the influence and had the composer endowing the folk music of Bohemia, in the person of a poor street musician, who was presented with a Mozart melody of his very own. This was not to be his greatest musical gift to Prague, however, nor even the D-major symphony, for he promised to return again and reward Prague's appreciation of *Figaro* with a brand new opera. It was to be *Don Giovanni*.

The return to Prague that autumn, with the new opera still not quite finished even at the last minute, took its place in the Mozart legend, fictionalized by the German Romantic poet Eduard Mörike in the 1855 novella *Mozart on the Way to Prague*. Mörike's Mozart was a character of touching sensitivity and childlike charm, stopping by the side of the road to exclaim to Constanze at the beauty of the forest: "You see, in my young days I traveled up and down half Europe, I saw the Alps and the ocean, all that is grandest and most beautiful in creation: and now, idiot that I am, I stand by chance in an ordinary fir-wood on the borders of Bohemia, lost in wonder and rapture that such a thing should really exist." It must have been rather different in fact, for the letter of January revealed that on the borders of Bohemia Mozart's "idiocy" did not take the form of rapture among the firs. Instead he assumed the identity of Punkititi and made Constanze into Schabla Pumfa. Interestingly, at least one twentieth-century German edition of Mozart's letters neatly edited the silly passage on new names right out of that letter, thus presenting a more earnest Mozart on the way to Prague.[43]

In 1787 Casanova was also in Bohemia, settled as a guest at the castle of Count Waldstein. The old adventurer went to Prague to make arrangements for the publication of his *Icosameron*, a fantasy fiction of incestuously married siblings who travel to the center of the earth to the land of the Megamicres. These were swimming creatures, two feet tall, "of every color imaginable except for black and white," communicating in a musical language of "harmonious singing."[44] Casanova may have been present at the premiere of *Don Giovanni*, and he would surely have recognized the reflection of his own career of conquests. In any event, the conquering hero of that occasion was Mozart himself, triumphing in Prague for the second time in the same year. Prague's enraptured reception of *Don Giovanni* is supposed to have provoked Mozart to the exclamation, "Meine Prager verstehen mich" (my Pragers understand me), and this then became the slogan of the ongoing legendry of Mozart's special relation to the city.[45] It meant that they appreciated his music, but surely Mozart, with his love of wordplay, also enjoyed the irony of the fact that they understood him, while he, from the moment he was among Czechs, did not understand them. They applauded Wolfgang Amadeus, little knowing that they were also applauding Punkitititi.

Mozart would have reason to remember that they understood him in Prague, for when *Don Giovanni* was produced in Vienna in 1788, it was distinctly less well received. The librettist Lorenzo Da Ponte recorded his shock:

And *Don Giovanni* did not please! And what did the Emperor say about that? "The opera is divine, maybe even better than *Figaro*, but it is no meal for the teeth of my Viennese."[46]

Joseph's casual imperial reference to "my Viennese"—whose taste he obviously presumed to know—was not so far from Mozart's allusion to "my Pragers." There was, after all, something suggestively imperial, even presumptuous, in the famous phrase, which made the people of Prague into Mozart's loyal and loving subjects.

Potemkin had hopes of bringing Mozart to St. Petersburg, and Mozart himself acquired a book entitled *Geographical and Topographical Travel Book Through All the States of the Austrian Monarchy, with the Travel Route to St. Petersburg Through Poland.* Such a voyage would surely have yielded new conquests, and perhaps new funny names as well.[47] In Bohemia Mozart's assumption of a new identity as Punkitititi did not make him any less of a visitor from Vienna, indeed emphasized his comic distance with a hint of condescension. Mozart might have seen himself as Punkitititi, but a volume of German poetry published in Prague in 1787 hailed him more earnestly as "the German Apollo" and apostrophized the composer: "Germany, your fatherland, holds out its hand to you."[48] The poem's invitation found its echo in Don Giovanni's seduction of the peasant girl Zerlina: "La ci darem la mano."

The imperial aspect of Mozart's relation to his Pragers came out all the more explicitly on his third and last visit to the city in the late summer of 1791, only months before his death. He came for the premiere of *La Clemenza di Tito*, on the clemency of the Roman Emperor Titus, which he wrote for the coronation of the Habsburg Emperor Leopold II as king of Bohemia. Another German visitor to Prague, Alexander von Kleist, kept a record of his journey to the coronation, published in Dresden the following year as "Fantasies on the Way to Prague." Kleist's fantasies, like Mozart's, involved the appropriation of a new identity. "Whether it was daydreaming (*Schwärmerei*) or proper human sentiment," wrote Kleist, who attended *La Clemenza di Tito*, "at that moment I wished to be Mozart rather than Leopold."[49] The emperor and the composer were identified with each other, both of them masters of Prague, arriving in triumph from Vienna, exciting the fantasies of other German visitors. Kleist made his devotion to Mozart into a matter of German pride, citing the special enthusiasm of "our German listeners." Leopold himself was not especially impressed by *La Clemenza di Tito*, while his consort the Empress Maria Louisa of Spain, after many years in Tuscany with Leopold, gave her own sort of recognition to the German quality of Mozart's Italian opera when she supposedly dismissed it with queenly vulgarity as *una porcheria tedesca*.[50]

Mozart's first biographer in 1798 was the Bohemian Franz Xaver Niemetschek, who portrayed a melancholy departure from Prague in 1791, Mozart with "a presentiment of his approaching death." Back in Vienna there were those who attributed his fatal illness to the unhealthful "Bohemian air," and even to Bohemian beer, but Niemetschek insisted that when death came in December, more tears were shed in Prague than in Vienna. The following year, in 1792, a Prague newspaper was already formulating mythologically the city's special "understanding" of Mozart: "Mozart seems to have composed for Bohemia; nowhere else is his music understood and executed better than in Prague."[51] His librettist Da Ponte returned to Prague in 1792 and saw performances there of the Mozart–Da Ponte collaborations: *Figaro, Don Giovanni*, and *Così fan tutte*. In his memoirs Da Ponte recalled "the enthusiasm of the Bohemians" for Mozart, their appreciation even of "the pieces least admired in other countries," and their ability to understand "perfectly" a genius whom other nations recognized only "after many, many performances."[52] Da Ponte's tribute to the taste of Bohemia was not without an element of ironic inversion, in the same spirit that allowed Grimm's little fictional fiddler of Bohemia to prophesy in Paris and denounce the falsity of French opera. Before leaving Bohemia, Da Ponte looked up his fellow Venetian Casanova, who owed him some money, but Casanova could not pay up. Mozart was dead, and Da Ponte, no longer in favor in Vienna, was uncertain where to seek his future. In 1792 Casanova strongly advised Da Ponte to go to London, which he did, and ended up concluding his long career in New York, teaching Italian at Columbia University. In 1791, however, Da Ponte was thinking of going to St. Petersburg.[53]

In 1794 Mozart's pupil Franz Xavier Süssmayr came to Prague. He had accompanied Mozart to Prague in 1791 for *La Clemenza di Tito* and was rumored to have written the recitatives for that opera while Mozart raced through the musical composition. It was Süssmayr who completed the requiem that Mozart left unfinished at his death, and his visit to Prague in

1794 became an occasion for celebrating the legend of Mozart in Bohemia. Süssmayr had composed a "Song of the Bohemians" on the occasion of the emperor's birthday. Leopold was dead, succeeded by his son Franz, but the rector of the university in Prague seemed to be still working out the coronation dilemma of 1791—whom to crown, Mozart or Leopold?—when he sought to reconcile Bohemia's love for Mozart and loyalty to the Habsburgs. Thus the rector welcomed Süssmayr:

> Through beautiful and overpowering music you enflame our hearts still more with love toward our adored monarchs. . . . Use still further your great talent always for the honor of God and for the glorification of our Emperor Franz, and if someday you should have the luck to attain the level of the immortal Mozart . . . do not forget that the Bohemians, this worthy nation, because of its loyalty to monarchs, because of its various beautiful actions expressed at such diverse opportunities, and above all because of its inborn genius for music, such a famous nation, I say, the Bohemians were those who knew best to treasure your talent.[54]

There was no danger of the uninspired Süssmayr attaining the level of his master, and Prague in 1794 was still celebrating Mozart in the person of his pupil. The rector's insistent interweaving of political loyalty to Vienna and the nation's appreciation of music, indeed his claim that music inspired political devotion, brought out the still significant aspect of "overpowering" mastery in Mozart's musical triumph at Prague.

In 1937, the 150th anniversary of *Don Giovanni* in Prague, Paul Nettl finished his book *Mozart in Bohemia*, piously hoping to restore the spirit of the past in which "Germans and Czechs together celebrated Mozart as 'their master' . . . that spirit of harmony and reconciliation."[55] The book was written in German and published in Prague in 1938, the year of Munich and the international abandonment of Bohemia to the mastery of Germany. In fact, the mutual celebration of Mozart, the German Apollo, by "Germans and Czechs together" was always asymmetrical in its implicit balance of power, and that asymmetry reflected the culturally constructed imbalance between Western Europe and Eastern Europe.

In 1794 in Prague, Süssmayr was present for the performance of his Italian opera *The Turk in Italy*. Eastern Europe, occupying a conceptual space between Asia and Europe, was particularly appropriate for the production of a work about the meeting of Orient and Occident. Mozart's German opera *The Abduction from the Seraglio*—the drama of Europeans in Turkey instead of Turks in Europe—was his first big operatic success in Vienna in 1782, and was received with equal enthusiasm in Prague in 1783. In the 1780s a Frenchman in Warsaw, Fraissinet de Larroque, wrote a comedy entitled *Two Frenchmen in the Ukraine*.[56] Lessing had already tried, and given up, writing a tragedy set in the Ukraine; perhaps comedy appeared as the more appropriate form.

The Abduction from the Seraglio offered a comic conception of the Orient, but to find Mozart's Eastern Europe in his work, to discover the spirit of Punkititi in his operatic oeuvre, one must look to *Così fan tutte*. First performed in Vienna in 1790, it was the last collaboration of Mozart and Da Ponte, the story of two men in Naples who experiment with the fidelity of two women of Ferrara by wooing them in disguise. The heroes disguise themselves as Albanians, and their lovers do not recognize them. When the gentlemen make their first appearance thus disguised, the ladies' maid Despina, who is in on the joke, expresses Mozart's and Da Ponte's amusement. Unnecessarily, the libretto notes that Despina sings *ridendo*, laughing.

> Che sembianze! che vestiti!
> Che figure! che mustacchi!
> Io non so se son valacchi,
> O se turchi son costor.
>
> (What appearances! what clothing!
> What figures! What moustaches!
> I don't know if they are Wallachians or Turks.) [57]

They are neither Turks nor Wallachians but Albanians, and the cheerful uncertainty of Despina perfectly matched the century's casual confusion of the diverse peoples of Eastern Europe and the Orient. Da Ponte's rhyming of "mustacchi" and "valacchi" suggested the facility of representing some such curious people upon the stage. The plot of the opera depends on the improbable premise that the ladies do not recognize their lovers in disguise, while allowing for the possibility that on some deeper level they really do, as they fall in love again, each with the other's lover. The intermediary position of Eastern Europe, between Europe and Asia, between civilization and barbarism, domain of fantasy and adventure, offered the key to an ambiguous staging between identity and disguise, between comedy and romance.

In the second act Despina appears disguised as a notary to execute a mock marriage between the newly formed couples:

> Quelle, dame ferraresi;
> Questi, nobili albanesi.
>
> (Those, the ladies of Ferrara;
> These the Albanian nobles.) [58]

To solemnly pronounce such a pairing between the "ferraresi" and "albanesi" was comedy in itself. The rhyming of the two terms suggested the balance of distance and identity between peoples of Western Europe and Eastern Europe, the latter sufficiently related to serve as a comic rhyme to the former. To prepare for the finale it was enough for the heroes to appear, according to the libretto, "without hat, without cloak, without moustaches," but still in the rest of their Albanian costumes—now the ladies could recognize them.[59]

To understand, however, why *Così fan tutte* offers Albanians, instead of Bohemians for instance, one must bear in mind that the libretto was written in Italian by Da Ponte, a Venetian. Albania lies on the east coast of the Adriatic Sea, and the Adriatic was the old empire of Venice. It was the Venetians who competed with the Ottomans for domination of Albania in the fifteenth century, and it would be the Italians who invaded and conquered Albania in 1939, making it a province of Mussolini's empire. In the eighteenth century Albania was still under Ottoman rule, but historically there was an imperial interest that made Albania appear from the perspective of Da Ponte's Venice analogous to Bohemia from the perspective of Mozart's Vienna. In fact, the Habsburgs purposefully developed Trieste, their port on the Adriatic, through the eighteenth century, and in 1790, the year of *Così fan tutte*, the armies of Vienna were fighting in southeastern Europe against the Ottomans. It was easy enough for Mozart to draw upon the same sense of comic delight that he experienced on the way to Prague and apply it to the preposterous mock Albanians of Da Ponte's libretto. After all, Mozart himself knew the fun of assuming a new and comic identity in Bohemia. The Albanian disguises of *Così fan tutte* were designed to appeal to the susceptible heroines of Ferrara, and at the same time to a musical public whose imagination would respond to the comedy and fantasy of Eastern Europe.

The public of Vienna was perfectly prepared to appreciate such a comedy, for the diverse peoples of the Habsburg empire were visibly represented there in the capital. Johann Pezzl, in his *Sketch of Vienna* in 1786, described the population of the city in a theatrical catalogue of exotic costumes.

Here you can often meet the Hungarian, striding stiffly, with his fur-lined dolman, his close-fitting trousers reaching almost to his ankles, and his long pigtail; or the round-headed Pole with his monkish haircut and flowing sleeves: both nations die in their boots.—Armenians, Wallachians and Moldavians, with their half-Oriental costumes, are not uncommon.—The Serbians with their twisted moustaches occupy a whole street. . . . The Polish Jews, all swathed in black, their faces bearded and their hair all twisted in knots, resemble scarecrows: a living satire of the Chosen Race.—Bohemian peasants with their long boots; Hungarian and Transylvanian waggoners with sheepskin greatcoats; Croats with black tubs balanced on their heads—they all provide entertaining accents in the general throng.[60]

This was Eastern Europe enacted as theater in the streets of Vienna, each foreign identity summed up in its "half-Oriental" costume: from Wallachians to Bohemians, from sheepskin coats to twisted moustaches. Mozart and Da Ponte in Vienna would also have encountered and appreciated these "entertaining accents" in the population, for as composer and librettist, after all, they were in the business of entertainment.

"In an Unknown Land, Disoriented"

Imaginary travels in Eastern Europe, like those of Baron Munchausen, were published alongside the real travels that they parodied, like those of Tott and Coxe. At the same time, real travelers like Mozart, and even Casanova, added to their accounts imaginative touches, exotic names, that effaced the borderline between fantasy and reality from the other direction. Voltaire's vicarious voyage across Eastern Europe, with Charles XII, served as an important literary model for later travelers, who wrote about Eastern Europe through a haze of cultural fantasies and literary effects. Voltaire's convention of an adventurer finding his way through "unknown lands" governed the very first journal entry of Alexandre-Maurice Blanc de Lanautte, count d'Hauterive, as he set out in 1785 from the French embassy in Constantinople to take up a position at the court of Moldavia.

When a secretary to the prince of Moldavia departs from Pera, and believes that he can voyage in Europe as in France, here is the first adventure of his voyage. In the evening he finds himself alone in an unknown land, disoriented (*désorienté*).[61]

Hauterive discovered his unknown land in Europe itself, indeed, upon entering Europe. For his voyage was the reverse of Salaberry's to Constantinople, and proved that one could discover Eastern Europe on the way to Europe as well as on the way to the Orient. Constantinople, for all its exoticism, was "known" at least, while in this case departure from the Orient resulted in punning "disorientation." Such disorientation was enhanced by the unexpected discovery of displaced peoples from within the domain of Eastern Europe. Eight days out of Constantinople, approaching Bulgaria, Hauterive encountered a colony of Jews, "transplanted from Poland by order of Mohammed IV who conquered Podolia." Eleven days out of Constantinople he met Tartars from the Crimea, established in Bulgaria since the annexation of their own land by Russia two years before.[62]

From the first week of his voyage Hauterive pronounced Eastern Europe to be philosophically disorienting as well, a challenge to the philosophy of the Enlightenment. When he saw thieves impaled by the side of the road, he refused to judge by the standards of Western Europe:

I hear from here our *philosophes* who cry out! Eh, let them leave their own homes some time! If M. de Beccaria had seen all the cutthroats of this land, he would be less disposed to be tender (*s'attendrir*).[63]

It was the same lesson that Tott had learned in Moldavia when he was "cured" of his "stubborn humanity." Cesare Beccaria's *Crimes and Punishments* was a sensation of the Enlightenment when it was published in 1764, but his arguments against torture, penal brutality, and capital punishment were rejected by Hauterive as irrelevant to an "unknown land," unknown to the Milanese Beccaria. Hauterive did not even soften when he learned that those impaled were not necessarily thieves, that when thefts occurred the Ottoman authorities were not too fastidious about whom they executed. In the Rhodope or Balkan mountains they would "look for some shepherd still part savage, having barely a human figure, incapable of speaking reason about anything." He would do: "The Bulgarian is hung."[64] Though Hauterive allowed that he was a "poor devil," his savagery, his inhuman appearance, his incapacity for reason rendered the tender standards of the Enlightenment irrelevant.

Hauterive himself, after a year in Constantinople, was on his way to serve for two years as French representative and enlightened adviser to the prince of Moldavia. He was 31 in 1785. Though educated by the Oratorians and sometimes designated as an abbé, Hauterive's religious affiliations were loose enough to be lightly shed with the coming of the French Revolution. He served as the French consul in New York, and later rose to the position of director of the National Archives in Paris under Napoleon.

"This Bulgaria, of which the name causes fear, is one of the most beautiful lands of Europe," wrote Hauterive. "One sees nowhere more beautiful plains, smoother, better graded slopes, and a landscape more suited to receive all the embellishments of cultivation (*culture*)." This Bulgaria was very much a literary discovery, from the frightful ring of its name to the artistically represented beauty of the landscape. Even the essence of Eastern Europe, its suitability to receive *culture*—which could mean cultivation and could also suggest civilization—was made into a matter of artistic embellishments. Hauterive had already observed that though buffalo, horses, cattle, sheep, and goats lived together "pell mell" in the villages, while grazing on the slopes "each species assembled and formed picturesque groups."[65] This eye for the "picturesque" would repeatedly prevail over less pleasant impressions of Bulgaria.

The very first Bulgarian village on Hauterive's route, nine days out of Constantinople, was Codgea-Torla, a name that Mozart would have enjoyed, but not a prosperous place: "One can imagine nothing more miserable than the aspect of this hamlet, the wretched property of the first horseman of the Grand Seigneur, who every year torments and torments in a thousand ways his unhappy vassals." The previous year they had tried to run away but were hunted down by their master "with thousands of baton blows." This was the syndrome of corporal abuse and feudal oppression observed all over Eastern Europe, but Hauterive did not linger over it. He proceeded immediately to the "singular" houses of the village with their beehive chimneys, the women at their multicolored embroidery, the little girls eager for coins to make into jewelry and save for their dowries.

On the whole, thought Hauterive, "they have a less unhappy air than our peasants," seeming "softer and more sociable." He learned that they lived together with their cows, buffalo, sheep, geese, and goats, and he thought that the villagers' agility, their eyes, and their physiognomy gave them "a little the air of goats," especially wearing their hairy bonnets. The next day he left Codgea-Torla and had the chance to look down upon another village on his route: "From high on the mountain, one sees at the bottom men, women, and children coming out, like an ant hill, assembling into troops, the most curious and most avid coming up to the voyagers, dancing and singing around the carriages."[66] Hauterive threw coins, and well he might have, for the ant hill perspective had made a triumph of the picturesque out of the misery of Bulgarian village life.

The next day, setting out from Karabounari, Hauterive appreciated more "magnificent tableaux of perspective," this time including a hunting scene:

Thirty beautiful dogs, white as the snow, light as the winds that blow in the plain, a hundred hunters on horses equally agile. . . . *Voilà*, the scene I enjoyed from high on the long hills that join the Rhodopes to the Balkans. In less than two minutes, they tracked down six hares who had run like arrows, amid the barkings of the pack and the cries of the hunters.[67]

The hunters turned out to be the Tartars from the Crimea, but the significance of the hare hunt in Hauterive's journal was that this "scene," which he so much "enjoyed," served as a literary revision of the story he had heard two days before about the brutal manhunt for the vassals of Codgea-Torla.

Beautiful perspectives overlaid unpleasant experiences, but they remained disturbingly intertwined. After passing by the hunt, Hauterive came to rest in "the most horrible hamlet of Bulgaria and the world," which was still "part of the perspective of that beautiful plain I just praised." The problem with the hamlet was, in a word, mud: "It was muddy like the bottom of a marsh; the streets, the fields, the houses are of mud; the inhabitants are ugly, dirty, and, I believe, sick, covered with bristles, tatters and lice." Yet, no sooner was the muddy village behind him than he faced the Balkans, witnessing "the perspective of black, immense, and dense forests," hoping for "something new to observe in the physical and moral character of the mountaineers."[68] He met an old man of 94 who measured his age by the memory of three wars between Russia and Turkey, back to the beginning of the century: "But the destiny of the two empires matters little to him, provided that he can outlive a Turk of the same age in the same village." This comic parable of the rival ancients suggested an ethnic life in the mountains of Eastern Europe, apart from, even irrelevant to, the dynamics of international politics. The mountains were "not excessively high, nor excessively painful to climb," though they were highly "recommendable to poets and to painters," thoroughly picturesque. "The travelers who traverse Bulgaria need only fear the cold, the winter, the thieves, and the wolves," he concluded.[69] With that ironic reassurance, he proceeded to invite his hypothetical readers to travel with him in Bulgaria:

Terrible roads conduct you to Schiali-Kavak; you rest, to creep for three more hours in the mud of a very beautiful, very large forest, in which you hear no other noise than that of the gun you fire from time to time, in order to warn those who are not hurrying enough and those who are hurrying too much . . . and *voilà*, that's how one passes the too famous Balkans.[70]

Hauterive insisted upon bringing *you* to Eastern Europe with him, in the mud, putting a gun in your hand, and encouraging you to fire it and discipline your party of guides and carriers to a steady pace. All the same, while *you* crossed the Balkans, Hauterive lay inside his carriage, "condemned to stomach aches, martyred by nausea."

Two weeks out of Constantinople, Hauterive's travel journal became more and more a collection of literary parables. Still undergoing his medical martyrdom, he presented a religious utopia in Bulgaria:

I passed thus without interest and in silence Chinguali, Kaiali, Erubialar, Kouchou-flar, Charvi, villages of half Turks, half Bulgarians, where Moslems and Christians live without hatred, even in alliance, and drink bad wine together, violating Ramadan and Lent . . . and are no less honest folk.[71]

The element of fantasy was all the more pronounced here in view of the fact that Hauterive had just declared himself confined to his carriage with nausea and could hardly have made a careful study of five villages on the route. The phrasing was obviously influenced by Voltaire, especially when the villagers "drink bad wine together, violating Ramadan and Lent," and such suggestions of *Candide, Zadig,* or even the *Philosophical Dictionary* gave the supposed travel journal an overpowering literary air.

Hauterive may have sometimes passed for an Oratorian abbé, but he was distinctly a worldly abbé of the Enlightenment, who looked benignly upon the peaceful coexistence and even commingling of the faiths.

The imams and priests always have the same indulgence for alliances between the faithful of the two religions. It is not at all rare to see turbans and images sheltered under the same roof, and the Koran and the Gospel one upon the other.[72]

Just as war between empires, between Russia and Turkey, was irrelevant to the rivalry of the two old men, so the war of religions was found similarly irrelevant to the heterogeneous ethnic communities of Bulgaria. Yet the more Hauterive sought to focus on the people themselves of Eastern Europe, the more those people appeared as a conventional literary construction of the Enlightenment, imagined more than observed. Hauterive attributed religious peace to "the ignorance and coarseness of a people without education and enlightenment," and, taking the part of an enlightened abbé, he administered philosophical absolution: "This religious scepticism, so peaceful and so docile, seemed to me infinitely pardonable." The people of Bulgaria were not, in fact, "always savages incapable of speaking reason about anything." This was exactly the phrase, verbatim, that Hauterive had employed a week before to describe the Bulgarian of the Balkans who was scapegoated and executed for theft. Having crossed the Balkans himself, Hauterive had come to appreciate civilization as a philosophically ambivalent condition, and concluded with the irony of Voltaire: "These unfortunates are thus very far from civilization, since they have none of the passions that prejudice elsewhere renders so common and so incurable."[73]

At the Danube, the border between Bulgaria and Wallachia, Hauterive reflected upon the presence of plague and then banished such reflections:

The neighborhood of Silistria is covered with cemeteries, tilled with recent graves; the environs have the air of a desert, and the imagination, adding to the sadness of their aspect, sees everywhere death surrounded by cadavers and the dying, and vomiting from its foul mouth the poisons of contagion. Amid the horror of this scene, I don't know how to render the effect produced on me by the sight of a kite that went up in the air and floated over the town as gaily as anything in the world. The idea of a troop of children running and romping around the cord reached my spirit immediately; their laughter, that I seemed to hear, dissipated the sad vision that obsessed me, and two thousand Bulgarians, Turks, Armenians, Christians, who came to see our flags, to hear our drums, and eat out of our hands for more than an hour, did not cause me any more terror, thanks to the kite.[74]

Hauterive's "imagination" was stimulated to take over from his observations, allowing him a vision of death and then a competing vision of happy children, which immediately prevailed. The next night in Wallachia, having crossed the Danube, Hauterive experienced the new "torment" of being "devoured by fleas" and triumphed over their assaults with another imaginative vision.

I saw myself in a moment pitted and covered with red points and round spots that ran into each other by their multiplicity and rather resembled those little scales that formed the shingled armor of the ancient Dacians, in whose country I had the misfortune to go to bed for the first time.[75]

These points and spots may have been torment, but at least they were not the marks of plague. Hauterive lost no time transforming the evidence of his vulnerability into a fantasy of armor, and, following the form of so many other travelers in Eastern Europe, he imagined himself not a contemporary Wallachian but an ancient Dacian. He continued to enjoy watching children at play "in the mud, nimble and naked, like little monkeys."[76]

Hauterive appreciated the similarity of Wallachia and Moldavia, though the eighteenth-century traveler could not yet express their connection under the rubric Romania: "The points at which the two states touch resemble each other perfectly; the same vicissitudes, the same misfortunes, the same history, have reduced the Wallachians and the Moldavians to the most absolute physical and moral uniformity." This "reduction" by "misfortune" was meant to express the same backward level of both, though Hauterive was not above enjoying in Moldavia the people's "extreme politeness at the sight of a man who has the air of pertaining to the prince."[77] Two days from his destination at Jassy he enjoyed a final fantasy of something more than politeness on the part of the population. He stayed in a house where an eighteen-year-old girl, at her embroidery, caught his attention: "Our duchesses do not embroider with a prettier hand." Hauterive ate and went to bed, experiencing "other desires," but resolving to respect the girl's virtue. That day's journal entry came to an end, and the next day's began without telling whether he had maintained his resolve.

Adieu, charming embroidress; the Moldavian who makes you happy will be very happy himself, if he finds you as beautiful as I do. . . . I give her a piece of money in leaving: she takes it, lowers her eyes, kisses my hand; as for me, I admire her like a madonna of Correggio.[78]

Hauterive's imagination, alternately gallant and pious, made the girl a duchess in the evening and a madonna in the morning, but the suggestive ellipsis, right before the piece of money changed hands, left uncertain what happened in the night. The imaginative Hauterive had found so much in Eastern Europe to exercise his sense of fantasy and literary form that he could certainly leave something to the imagination of others.

"The Warmest Imagination"

Lady Elizabeth Craven made the same journey as Hauterive in the following year, 1786. Setting out from Constantinople, she rejected the Belgrade route as overly infested with robbers: "I have consulted maps, and the best informed travellers here, and am assured I can go through Bulgaria, Wallachia, and Transylvania to Vienna with great ease and dispatch." Then, however, she received new warnings of "much greater risques in taking this new route, for that I should find heads stuck up on poles at every mile, those countries being much more infested with robbers and murderers than the other."[79] She decided not to believe it, but traveled nevertheless with "two most excellent little English pistols I wear at my girdle." She admitted, "Most women would be frightened with the journey I am taking; but I must get out of this country of Mahomet's now I am in it, and so I shall proceed chearfully and merrily." That she was a woman made her journey appear especially adventurous, in the making and in the telling. She played upon this in her travel account, in Bulgaria for instance:

Bulgaria is but little cultivated, and where I saw a Turk at work in the fields, he was armed with a gun. . . . Such a sight, and a wood I passed through, so little worn by travellers, that the trees and bushes tore off the door of my carriage, were circumstances that might have made any fine lady tremble.[80]

Thus the reader—any fine lady—was invited to tremble with her. In fact, she had a traveling companion, "Mademoiselle," a Frenchwoman with a little white dog, and both fine ladies had an official Turkish guide—"my abominable Tchouadar"—to make all arrangements.

The prince and princess of Wallachia importuned Lady Craven to stay for a year, perhaps thinking her an even finer catch than Hauterive, who was then staying in neighboring Moldavia—"but I assured them I should not stay four-and-twenty hours in Buccorest." All the same, she noted with pleased surprise that Wallachia was not quite the Orient: "The supper was served in a more European manner than I should have imagined; a table upon legs, and chairs to sit on, were things I did not expect." She took away with her "some very beautiful embroidered handkerchiefs" as a souvenir.[81] She admired the mountains and forests of Wallachia: "Nothing more wild or romantic can be conceived . . . but such scenery can scarcely compensate for the dreadful road." Indeed, though twenty peasants were carrying her carriage over the mountains, it nevertheless overturned and she found herself upon the ground, with Mademoiselle beside her crying over and over, "Je suis morte." With an English eye for agriculture, she admired the soil of Wallachia, "a rich black mould," and concluded, "This country may be called indeed a jewel ill set, what would it be under the hands of taste and industry." The metaphor of the "jewel ill set" neatly expressed Lady Craven's Eastern Europe, for it suggested the lack of polishing and finishing that made those lands almost, but not quite, a lady's prize. The Transylvanian Alps, or Southern Carpathians, ran along the border between Ottoman Wallachia and the Habsburg empire, "those enchanting mountains destined certainly for other purposes than harbouring oppressed subjects or fugitive murderers." She was relieved to see the Habsburg eagle, to enter Transylvania and "feel myself under the Imperial protection," and the old customs official told her she was "the first lady he had seen or heard of passing that frontier." She dramatized her account as a lady's adventure, from start to finish, discovering lands where visiting adventurers had been mostly men. The Emperor Joseph II was reviewing his regiments in Transylvania when Lady Craven crossed the border, and he "sent me word he should wait upon me, which he did." He was especially interested in the maps she had collected on her journey, which "seemed to please him very much."[82] In fact, Joseph would go to war with the Ottoman empire the very next year, in 1787, his last great adventure in foreign policy. He hoped to conquer Wallachia and Moldavia, so the maps and experiences of Lady Craven were of special interest in 1786. The jewel, even ill set, appeared desirable to an emperor. If the Habsburgs had reached Bucharest, they would have stayed for more than a day.

For Lady Craven, the journey from Constantinople to Vienna was only the last leg of a much longer voyage through Eastern Europe in 1786. She had separated from her husband in 1783, and while in Italy in 1785 determined to head north: "Now I am on the wing, I will see courts and people that few women have seen." Her itinerary took her from Vienna to Cracow and Warsaw, then St. Petersburg, the long voyage south to the Crimea, by boat on the Black Sea to Constantinople, and finally the return through Bulgaria and Wallachia to Vienna. This encompassed all three of the routes that defined Eastern Europe for the eighteenth-century traveler: first the trip through Poland to St. Petersburg, last the voyage to Constantinople through southeastern Europe (here accomplished in reverse), and, in between, the line that linked St. Petersburg to Constantinople and defined Eastern Europe along a north-south axis, the journey to the Crimea. That was to become the most celebrated itinerary of the decade when Catherine went to the Crimea the very next year, in 1787. The Emperor Joseph II would accompany her, perhaps prepared by Lady Craven's maps. Lady Craven could then count on the publicity of that doubly imperial voyage to add interest to the publication of her own travels in Dublin in 1789: *A Journey Through the Crimea to Constantinople*. With this book she was determined to show "where the real Lady Craven has been," for an impostor had been claiming to be she "in most of the inns in France, Switzerland, and England," passing "for the wife of my husband." [83] The account of her travels would thus clear her name of any scandal caused by "this insolent deception," establishing that the real Lady Craven was traveling around Eastern Europe, while the impostor (with Lord Craven, presumably) was making a more conventional tour of Western Europe. This scenario of the two ladies, each claiming the same name, each in her respective half of the continent, made Eastern Europe the domain of adventure and authenticity, while Western Europe became that of falseness and impropriety. The idea of "civilization" was ambivalent again; one jewel was ill set, but the other was a fake. Lady Craven's book was made up of letters, written along the way, from the author to the margrave of Brandenburg, Anspach, and Bayreuth. She addressed him as "dear brother," from "your affectionate sister," but in 1791, after Lord Craven died, with Eastern Europe behind her, the margrave ceased to be a brother and became her second husband.

Lady Craven received a foretaste of Eastern Europe in Vienna in December 1785, when she admired the uniforms of Hungarian and Polish officers in the Habsburg army, and expressed the opinion that "every nation ought to preserve the fashion of their country, and that there is no necessity for mankind to ape one another in dress." She traveled from Vienna to Cracow and found "melancholy proof" of Poland's political failure. "Had I been born a Polish nobleman," she reflected, in a moment of assumed identity, she would have renounced her privileges to save her country from partition. In Warsaw in January 1786 she learned that dwarves and servants were "the absolute property of the master." King Stanisław August spoke to her flatteringly of England, which "would make me prejudiced in favour of my own country, if I could love it better than I do; but the word comfort which is understood there only, has long stamped the value of it in my mind."[84] The inseparable ideals of comfort and civilization always conditioned the confident superiority of the traveler in Eastern Europe.

In St. Petersburg in February she felt all the more strongly that "the elegance which is produced by the cleanliness and order seen with us, is found no where out of England." She was offended by the conventionally observed contrasts of the Russian capital and invited the margrave and her readers to inspect: "You come into a drawing-room, where the floor is of the finest inlaid woods, through a staircase made of the coarsest wood in the rudest manner, and stinking dirt—The postillions wear sheep-skins."[85] She was equally disapproving of the refinements of the Russian nobility: "The fashion of the day is most ridiculous and improper for this climate; French gauzes and flowers were not intended for Russian beauties." The sight of Catherine herself, in Russian dress—"a very handsome one"— confirmed Lady Craven's conviction that each nation had to hold to its own fashion. She was also impressed by a "very superb" carnival ball given by Ségur in St. Petersburg.[86]

Her chief complaint about St. Petersburg betrayed the motive of her travels. It was the cold of winter, which "must congeal the warmest imagination." This was no place for poets and painters: "the flowers of fancy must fade and die, where spring is not to be found." Lady Craven traveled in Eastern Europe to feed her imagination and fancy, and if they could not flourish in St. Petersburg, she would have to move on. Sitting next to Potemkin at dinner reminded her that the Crimea, his personal charge, was now part of the Russian empire since 1783. It set her to wondering whether one day "an empire, which extends from the South to the North, will prefer basking in the rays of the sun," whether the capital could be transferred to the Crimea, and St. Petersburg "turned into storehouses."[87] This was the north-south axis that made it possible to envision Eastern Europe as the eastern part of the continent. Charles XII and Voltaire had discovered it almost haphazardly as they stumbled from victory and conquest to defeat and captivity, from Russia and Poland to the Ukraine and the Crimea. There would be nothing haphazard about Catherine's voyage to the Crimea in 1787, every station on the way dazzlingly prepared to greet the imperial party. In fact, the preparations were well under way in 1786, so Lady Craven was able to enjoy some of the accommodations that were being arranged for the empress.

That Lady Craven's "imagination" called her to the south, fancifully transferring the capital of the empire as well, was perfectly in keeping with the intellectual history of the decade. The year 1786 was also when Goethe set out from Weimar for Italy, nourishing his artistic imagination on the discovery of the south of Western Europe. He described himself as "drawn by an irresistible need," impelled upon "this long, solitary journey to the hub of the world," to Rome, where "all the dreams of my youth have come to life."[88] Lady Craven followed an analogous impulse to discover the south of Eastern Europe, along an axis parallel to Goethe's Italian journey. The intellectual consolidation of Europe into two halves, Western Europe and Eastern Europe, depended on the clarity of these axial connections, between Germany and Italy on the one hand, between the Baltic and the Black Sea on the other. Lady Craven's was a very different adventure, though, taking her not to the hub but rather to the end of the world, to the unknown land of the Crimea. That these were related impulses was suggested by the fact that Goethe in Italy in 1786 was finally able to finish his drama *Iphigenie in Tauris*. And what was Tauris but the ancient Crimea? Rescued by Artemis at the moment of Agamemnon's sacrifice, Iphigenie languished in the Crimea, "in solemn sacred bonds of slavery," proclaiming her alienation: "Here my spirit can not feel at home."[89]

Lady Craven was not likely to feel at home there, either, but imagination beckoned. She resisted warnings in St. Petersburg about the Crimea, that "the air is unwholesome, the waters poisonous, and that I shall certainly die if I go there." She knew that "a new acquired country, like a new beauty, finds detractors," and had heard at least one favorable account that made her think "I should not be sorry to purchase a Tartarian estate." In March she was on her way south, in Moscow already, and all the more excited about "that peninsula called the Tauride, which, from the climate and situation, I look upon to be a delicious country; and an acquisition to Russia which she should never relinquish." Lady Craven was confident that "the Tauride must naturally become a treasure to posterity."[90] Thus the Crimea became a treasure, just as Wallachia was a jewel, both designated in a language that casually made unknown lands into imperial prizes.

She paused at Poltava in the Ukraine to see the battlefield where Peter had subdued "the wild spirit of Charles the Twelfth," but her own indomitable spirit urged her on to the Crimea. Still on the road, she reviewed its reputation, the fame of its slave trade in Ottoman times—"the great market for the Circassians"—the ancient presence of the Scythians, then the Sarmatians. For once, almost by chance, this was historically accurate. The Scythians, whose potently charged name was fancifully associated with every corner of Eastern Europe in the eighteenth century, were probably really based around the Crimea until the fourth century B.C., when they were overcome by the Sarmatians. Lady Craven crossed the steppe—

"called Steps, I should call it desert"—and entered the land of the Tartars. She sent a servant ahead to a Tartar village, one "whose ridiculous fear through the whole journey have not a little amused me," and received a terrified report that the Tartars were "very ill black-looking people." She herself did not comment on their blackness, but "this village gave me no great opinion of Tartarian cleanliness, a more dirty miserable looking place I never saw." It was just a circle of huts, and in the context of the "majestic landscape" it gave her a not unpleasing idea of "the primitive state of the world." She brought civilization with her: "I stopped there and made tea." The perfect Englishwoman, she always traveled with "my tea equipage."[91]

Though this was Tartary, her sense of its ethnicity was rather varied, especially with regard to the military presence. She met a Russian general, a Cossack chief, and even a troop of Albanians. The Cossack admired her riding: "When I jumped down from my horse on returning home, he kissed the edge of my petticoat, and said something in his language which I did not comprehend, but the general told me he had paid me the highest compliment imaginable, viz. I was worthy of being a Cossack."[92] The circumstances of Eastern Europe, an incomprehensible language combined with an extravagant gesture of submission, promptly stimulated her sense of fantasy. Later she attended a Cossack feast, followed by an "entertainment," which she described:

After dinner from the windows, I saw a fine mock battle between the Cossacks; and I saw three Calmoucks, the ugliest fiercest looking men imaginable, with their eyes set in their head, inclining down to their nose, and uncommonly square jawbones. These Calmoucks are so dexterous with bows and arrows that one killed a goose at a hundred paces, and the other broke an egg at fifty.[93]

This land was at once an ethnological laboratory and a theatrical forum for Lady Craven; she examined jawbones as she watched fierce peoples enact their ferocity for her entertainment. Fifty years after Voltaire had narrated the battles of Charles XII, impressing upon the enlightened public the terrible strangeness of the Cossacks and the Tartars, Lady Craven could enjoy a mock battle on the same terrain. Like Voltaire, who spoke from no experience, she was full of praise for Tartar "hospitality."[94] In fact, the sense of mastery she enjoyed, as Cossacks hospitably kissed her petticoats, was the consequence of the actual conquest of the Crimea by another woman. In the following year Catherine would come to see it for herself.

At last Lady Craven reached the tip of the peninsula, the new Russian harbor and naval base at Sevastopol, from which she would soon embark for Constantinople. She gazed upon the harbor, focused on a huge ship named *Catherine's Glory*, and reflected that "all the fleets in Europe would be safe from storms or enemies in these creeks or harbours."[95] This peculiar, and distinctly imperialist, fantasy became less implausible with the course of history, for in the nineteenth century European ships and troops would really come to the Crimea, of all places, and the year-long siege of Sevastopol in the Crimean War would become a military legend. Like so many other fantasies of conquest that attended eighteenth-century travelers in Eastern Europe, this one too would one day be realized in an adventure of arms.

Sevastopol stimulated Lady Craven's imagination to an even more explicit vision of the future of the Crimea, which she imparted to the margrave in Anspach:

> Though I have not been absolutely all over this peninsula, I think I am perfectly acquainted with it, and though it is a new acquaintance to me, I sincerely wish it to be peopled by the industrious. . . . Can any rational being, dear Sir, see nature, without the least assistance from art, in all her grace and beauty, stretching out her liberal hand to industry, and not wish to do her justice? Yes, I confess, I wish to see a colony of honest English families here; establishing manufactures, such as England produces, and returning the produce of this country to ours.[96]

This was imperialism indeed. Lady Craven presumed upon her new knowledge of the Crimea, her "perfect" acquaintance, established in about a month, to spin out a fantasy of the Enlightenment certain to appeal to "any rational being," man or woman. The grace and beauty of nature were to be assisted by the art of manufacture and economic exploitation. "This is no visionary or poetical figure," insisted Lady Craven. "It is the honest wish of one who considers all mankind as one family."[97] Of course it was visionary, and she knew that her margrave, and all her readers, would think so, but perhaps it was a vision in which they too could participate. For all the economic implications of her vision, hers was most truly an imperialism of the imagination. She had set out for the Crimea in order to feed her imagination, like Goethe setting out for Italy on a parallel course, and her fantasies of Eastern Europe were the fruits of the voyage.

"The Image of Civilization"

In January 1787 Catherine the Great set out from St. Petersburg, hailed as the Cleopatra of the North, to voyage through her empire and visit the newly annexed Crimea, traversing Europe from the Baltic to the Black Sea. "From every side people assured me that my march would be bristly with obstacles and annoyances," she commented after it was over. "People wanted to frighten me with the fatigues of the route, the aridity of the deserts, the insalubrity of the climate." Just like Lady Craven, the tsarina herself was warned away from the Crimea, but the empire was hers, and, just like Lady Craven, Catherine became all the more eager for the adventure: "To oppose me is to excite me."[98] She brought with her, as official witnesses to her triumphal march, the representatives of Western Europe who attended her court, the ambassadors of England, Austria, and France. The last was the count de Ségur.

"This grand voyage whose announcement and anticipation so sharply excited our curiosity," wrote Ségur, "seemed to weigh upon us at the moment when we were about to undertake it; one would have said it was a presentiment of the long storms and terrible revolutions that would not be slow to follow." Perhaps the voyage to the Crimea distracted his attention from the developing political crisis in France, the coming of the French Revolution. Certainly one of his reasons for apprehension at the journey's beginning was that St. Petersburg seemed much closer to home than the Crimea, and he feared the interruption of correspondence that would cut him off from "news of my wife, my children, my father, my government." It was, in any event, his job to follow Catherine, and "our melancholy was but a light cloud" which "disappeared like a dream of the night."⁹⁹ The voyage would soon give him new dreams, and these would stand up to the light of day.

Ségur warned his readers that this would be no ordinary travelogue of the Enlightenment, that he himself did not expect "to see places and men in their natural state," any more than someone could expect to understand "the manners of our villages if he had only observed them at the Opera." Actually, one could attend an operatic representation of French village life even in Moscow, for William Coxe in 1778 had seen a performance of the pastoral opera *Le Devin du village*, by Jean-Jacques Rousseau, translated into Russian and performed in the Moscow Foundling Hospital. The voyage to the Crimea in 1787 would be an epic open-air performance, an operatic enterprise.

Illusion is almost always more attractive than reality, and certainly the magical tableau that was offered at every step to Catherine II, and that I will try to sketch, will be for many spirits more curious by its novelty than the rather more useful relations, in other respects, of some savants who have traveled through and observed philosophically this vast Russia, so recently emerged from the darkness (*ténèbres*) to become all at once so powerful and colossal from its first flight (*essor*) towards civilization.¹⁰⁰

Illusion would be the watchword of Ségur, as he sought to sketch the magical tableau of Russia, witnessed with Catherine. He knew that this was not a "philosophical" travel account, like those in which his philosophical century sought to discover Russia, but he also hinted that a fantastic account might even be more appropriate to Russia's fantastic flight from darkness toward civilization.

This voyage was also different from other travels because, though officially Catherine's court was traveling to see Russia, in fact the traveling

court itself became "the object of general curiosity," even "the true spectacle." The "reflections" that were so important to the eighteenth-century
traveler were here drowned out by "the perpetual noise of voluntary or
commanded acclamations" from the crowds gathered along the route. The
"general curiosity" of the Russian crowds was seconded by the broader
fascination of all Europe as it followed the press coverage of Catherine's
progress. The ambassadors reported to their courts, and Ségur's memoirs offered his own account as still "curious by its novelty" to readers of
the next generation. Ségur was proud to be a "witness" of "this extraordinary voyage which fixed the attention of Europe." No one was more
conscious of this than Catherine, and Ségur recalled that "we spoke of all
the conjectures that one would make in Europe about this voyage." As
in Voltaire's *Charles XII*, the Europe that observed and conjectured was
implicitly Western Europe. The travelers themselves felt almost as if they
had left Europe behind, indulging in fantasies of the Orient, and certain
that their voyage appeared utterly Oriental to those who followed it from
afar. Once Catherine had been joined by Joseph at Kherson, "we pretended
that everywhere people imagined that she and the emperor wanted to conquer Turkey, Persia, perhaps even India and Japan."[101] This was a highly
baroque complex, in which the travelers themselves were imagining what
Western Europe was imagining about their travels in Eastern Europe. Typically, those travels were immediately translated into fantasies of conquest
and especially fantasies of the Orient.

Setting out from St. Petersburg in January, the travelers were wrapped
in bear furs to protect them from the cold. The long winter nights of the
North were spectacularly, artificially illuminated:

> To dissipate the darkness (*ténèbres*), Oriental luxury did not let us lack for bright-
> ness: at very short distances, on both sides of the route, there were raised enormous
> pyres of firs, cypresses, birches, pines, that had been set aflame; so we traveled
> through a route of fires more brilliant than the rays of daylight. It was thus that the
> proud *autocratice* of the North, in the middle of the most somber nights, wished
> and commanded, *Let there be light.*[102]

It was the first of the voyage's magical, "Oriental" effects, flaming trees,
the triumph of day over night, metaphorically expressing Russia's emergence from the *ténèbres* into the light of civilization. Magic was no less
of a presence by natural daylight, when the snow-covered plains sparkled
with "the splendor of crystal and diamond." Though the cruise was not to
begin till they reached Kiev and the Dnieper, Ségur's imagination was prematurely transforming the wintry plain into "a frozen sea" and the sleighs
into "fleets of light boats." Peasants with icy beards gathered to watch the
travelers stop at specially prepared little palaces along the way, built "by
a sort of fairy magic (*féerie*)." There, among the cushions of divans, they
were immune to "the hardness of the climate and the poverty of the land,"

enjoying "exquisite wines" and "rare fruits," as well as the diversion that a charming woman always imparts to any circle, "*even when* she is a queen and a despot."[103]

Under such circumstances Catherine could confidently tease Ségur about Russia's image in France: "I bet, Monsieur le Comte, that at this moment your beautiful ladies, your elegant people and your savants of Paris, pity you deeply for voyaging in a land of bears, the home of barbarians, with a tedious tsarina."[104] Ségur tactfully reminded her of Voltaire's admiration for her, though Voltaire had been dead for almost ten years. Yet he knew that Catherine knew that "many people, especially in France and at Paris, still regard Russia as an Asiatic land, poor, plunged in ignorance, *ténèbres*, and barbarism," confusing "the new European Russia with the rustic and Asiatic Muscovy."[105] How could he fail to know it, when it was precisely that image of Russia that he himself would *still* be representing in his memoirs for the next generation? Yet Catherine and her French ambassador could banter about this on the way to the Crimea, because that voyage was no refutation but a bold dramatization of the French thesis on Eastern Europe. Catherine was German by origin, of course, and she too was susceptible to the idea of Russia's Oriental barbarism, which justified her enlightened despotism. Now she would embrace the Crimea, and with it the idea of an "Oriental" Eastern Europe. Her voyage, from the outset, was adorned with Oriental effects, and it was designed to express her power in a demonstration of mastery over bears and barbarians. If the imagination of Western Europe was ready to consume the Crimea, she would offer it up to the beautiful ladies of Paris even as she claimed it for herself.

At Smolensk the travelers already reached the Dnieper and began to think about the river's distant descent, and theirs, to the Black Sea. There was a grand ball for Catherine in Smolensk at which Ségur could observe, as in St. Petersburg, that "the surface (*superficie*) offers the image of civilization, but under this light peel the attentive observer still easily discovers the old Muscovy."[106] Civilization was not, apparently, one of the "rare fruits" to be peeled and consumed in Russia. Ségur found Smolensk "very picturesque," but one of the pictures that came to him, when he later wrote his memoirs, was that of the city in flames, surrendering to Napoleon, the bitter fruit of conquest. In February Catherine arrived at Kiev, where the whole party had to wait three months for spring, for the ice to melt, only then to embark upon the Dnieper. Ségur reported that the name of the city was of Sarmatian derivation, that it had been conquered by the Crimean Tartars, that it had once been part of Poland. Kiev was thus definitively of Eastern Europe, associated with so many of its elements, ancient and modern. Architecturally, it appeared as a "bizarre mélange of majestic ruins, of miserable hovels."[107]

Ethnically, Kiev appeared as no less of a mélange, for those who came to wait upon Catherine included "those famous Cossacks of the Don, richly dressed *à l'asiatique*—famous for their "indiscipline," among other things—and the Tartars, "once the dominators of Russia and now humbly submitted to the yoke of a woman." There were nomadic Kirghiz tribesmen and "those savage Kalmucks, the veritable image of those Huns whose deformity once inspired such terror in Europe." The terror of Eastern Europe was a thing of the past, now humbly reduced to submission, a colorful entertainment for the traveler. The familiar formula of contrast and mélange, which had served Ségur so well in St. Petersburg and Moscow, here acquired a headier air of the fantastic: "It was like a magic theatre where there seemed to be combined and confused antiquity and modern times, civilization and barbarism, finally the most piquant contrast of the most diverse and contrary manners, figures, and costumes." [108] This piquancy was a stimulus to fantasy so that Ségur lived in Kiev "like a Russian boyar," or, to make the fantasy more specifically Kievan, "like one of the descendants of Rurik and Vladimir." [109] He remembered once, on his way to Russia, having the chance to play the part of a Polish palatine, and predictably, when he got to the Crimea, he would easily assume the role of a pasha reclining upon his divan.

In Kiev the party was joined by the man who would become its most spirited member, the famously charming Charles-Joseph, prince de Ligne, whose irrepressible conversation would help keep alive the legend of the voyage all over Europe in the years to come. Originally from Brussels, his cultural and political allegiances lay sometimes with France, sometimes with the Habsburgs. He had passed some time in Poland and had even been briefly considered as a possible king, but now Catherine appealed to his fantasy not only with an invitation to the Crimea but also with a gift of land on the peninsula, at precisely the spot where Iphigenie was supposed to have served as the priestess of Artemis. Ségur was delighted to have him along on the voyage, and was confident that "by the vivacity of his imagination he would animate even the coldest society." In fact, when the prince appeared in Kiev, the "warmth" of his presence was marvelously effective: "From that moment we believed we felt that the rigors of somber winter were softening, and that the joyous spring would not wait long to be reborn." [110] The ice was melting, and on the first of May the boats took to the river.

Potemkin had been notably absent from the court company in Kiev, and he was rumored to be preparing a "brilliant spectacle" on the route along the river. Now at last they could inspect his handiwork from their boats, as they cruised by, and the Potemkin phenomenon was immediately evident.

Towns, villages, country houses, and sometimes rustic cabins were so ornamented and disguised by arches of triumph, by garlands of flowers, by elegant decorations of architecture, that their aspect completed the illusion to the point of transforming them, to our eyes, into superb cities, into palaces suddenly constructed, into gardens magically created. [111]

From the beginning this was a voyage of illusion, a word that constantly recurred in every descriptive account. There was an ideally illusionary perspective, in which the travelers regarded Russia from their boats, across water, without having the opportunity to peek behind the rococo facades of the spectacle. The prince de Ligne observed "the gauzes, the laces, the furbelows, the garlands," and cynically supposed they could have "come out of the fashionable shops on the rue Saint-Honoré."[112] It was rococo decoration, the style that had carried Madame Pompadour's Paris to the presidential pinnacle of taste and elegance, of civilization, and now it reconciled the jarring "contrasts" of Eastern Europe, by making rustic cabins into palaces, Potemkin villages into cities. These illusionary transformations pointed to the fundamental illusion that governed all others on Catherine's voyage to the Crimea: the illusion of civilization.

Before embarking at Kiev, Ségur had received news of the assembly of notables in France, whose meeting held out hope of political and financial reform. As the French ambassador, he accepted congratulations from all: "Happy days, that have never returned! What virtuous illusions surrounded us!"[113] Looking back in his memoirs, with retrospective knowledge of the Revolution and the Terror, Ségur could associate the illusions of 1787 that allowed people like himself to believe in civilized reformation in Western Europe and civilizing transformation in Eastern Europe.

The decorative spectacle on the Dnieper was not only architectural but also human, presenting the peoples upon whom civilization would work its own magical transformation. "The air resounded with the sounds of harmonious music from our boats," wrote Ségur. "The diverse costumes of the spectators along the shore constantly varied the rich and moving tableau." This was opera indeed, complete with costumes and music. The costumes, especially, "goaded our imagination." Everyone congratulated Catherine on having "softened the manners, lately still so rude and rough," of her subjects, and expressed high hopes for the "savage tribes that yet peopled the remote parts of her empire." Catherine imagined them in their tents, with their flocks, troubled by few needs and desires, and she wondered, "I don't know if in civilizing them, as I want to, whether I would spoil them." This was no more than affected Rousseauist sentimentalism, for when the party passed through the lands of the Zaporozhians, saluted by Voltaire 50 years before for their supreme strangeness and cutthroat brigandage, Ségur understood perfectly well how the sentimental tsarina brought civilization to the savages: "Catherine II, having finally destroyed this strange republic, established on its territory some regular Cossack regiments."[114] Just as Voltaire had envisioned, it was military discipline that brought the blessing of civilization—or was it perhaps the other way around? The diverse costumes that excited the imagination were picturesquely conceived uniforms, the uniforms of illusionary civilization, a part of the spectacle.

Ségur imagined a map in which "the antique hordes of Huns, Kirghiz, and Tartars" were cornered by civilization, limited in their brigandage to an ever shrinking domain: "For a long time they were, by their wandering life, by their invasions and ravages, the terror of the world; but this world, today civilized, peopled, armed, enlightened, has taken from them all possibility of conquest." This world was Europe, and Catherine's voyage to the Crimea spotlighted the last corner of Europe where those "antique hordes" held sway, where civilization and enlightenment were now ready to shut them out of Europe altogether, to "spoil" them, and enroll them in regiments. At Kremenchug the travelers were treated to the "spectacle" of military maneuvers, featuring "the Cossacks, lances in hand, giving out great cries." Kremenchug, "the name is not lyrical," wrote the prince de Ligne, though Mozart might have enjoyed it, and Potemkin as impresario was able to endow it with the poetry of Cossack cries. Ségur paid tribute to Potemkin's "imagination" as the voyage proceeded to the south: "He knew, by a kind of prodigy, to struggle against all obstacles, overcome nature, abridge distances, adorn misery, deceive the eye (*tromper l'oeil*) about the uniformity of sandy plains." Somehow the fleet only paused in "picturesque positions." Flocks and peasants "animated" and "vivified" the shores, while little boats approached the imperial fleet, full of boys and girls singing "rustic airs."[115] Potemkin's brilliant triumph over nature was a parody of the work of civilization, made into a matter of *trompe l'oeil*. Yet no one was deceived. Ségur knew that the Cossack cries and rustic airs were no more than sound effects, that the Potemkin villages were only facades. The legacy of this voyage would be a legend of Eastern Europe as a domain of illusion, but illusion that anyone in Western Europe could penetrate.

The count de Ségur and the prince de Ligne shared a boat and lived as roommates, their beds separated only by a light partition. The prince was always dazzling the count with the "vivacity of his imagination," and waking him up to recite impromptu poems and songs. The two men amused themselves with a mock correspondence, across the partition, as they cruised "through the land of the Cossacks, to go visit that of the Tartars."[116] There was certainly some spiritual resemblance here to Mozart on the way to Prague, that very same year, as the two representatives of French civilization on the Dnieper let their imaginations play upon unlyrical names and famously ferocious peoples. The prince de Ligne, at least, was known for the silliness of his sallies; Ségur found the prince's "frivolity" to be delightfully "piquant." Both gentlemen were further stimulated in their condescension by the heady companionship of crowns. They were delighted to be invited to *tutoyer* the tsarina, and the prince was especially tickled by the incongruous informality of the expression *ta majesté*. They enjoyed feeling sorry for the poor king of Poland, Stanisław August, who traveled to meet Catherine on the Dnieper and was given scant political attention by the woman who was once his lover. The prince de Ligne, who had once dreamed of becoming king of Poland himself, lost no time in circulating a *bon mot* of contempt for Stanisław August: "He spent three months and three million to see the empress for three hours."[117] Finally, when the Emperor Joseph II joined the imperial party at Kherson, he insisted on his customary incognito: "He absolutely wanted to be treated as a traveler, not as a monarch." The voyage created an illusionary carnival equality among travelers, emperor and empress, prince and count; they could all pretend to be only travelers in Eastern Europe, partly because they could also all pretend to be royalty in their fantasies of mastery. The incognito of Joseph assisted everyone's Oriental fantasies, for he became the Caliph Haroun al Rashid of the Arabian Nights. He strolled with Ségur in the evening, and marveled that they were "wandering in the desert of the Tartars." At the news of revolt in the Habsburg Netherlands, the prince de Ligne teased the emperor by suggesting that Tartars might make more loyal subjects than the Flemish.[118] The incongruity of the comparison between Western Europe and Eastern Europe gave this reflection the air of wit.

The travelers crossed the steppe, a green desert, a desert of the Orient according to Ségur, who knew that it stretched from Europe to the frontiers of China. For Ségur the steppe was above all a landscape that awaited civilization.

The part of the steppes where we found ourselves, upon which civilization seeks to extend its conquests and labors, resembles a plain canvas of which a painter is beginning to make a grand tableau, by placing there some hamlets, some groves, some cultivated fields; but this work, advancing slowly, will leave still, for more than a century, all the appearance of a desert.[119]

The idea of civilization as a conquering force in Eastern Europe was implicitly accepted by every traveler of the eighteenth century, but the voyage to the Crimea brought into focus the corollary idea of civilization as an artistic force, the slow accumulation of picturesque details. Though Potemkin could make only token efforts to decorate the immensity of the steppe, the travelers did appreciate the sight of Tartar nomads with their tents and camels, adding "a little life to this uniform landscape." They were even better entertained when he "made appear" 50 squadrons of Cossacks: "Their Asiatic and picturesque costumes, the celerity of their maneuvers, the agility of their horses, their races, their cries, their lances, made one momentarily forget the steppes."[120] This was staged and choreographed savagery, the grand opera of backwardness, a first decorative step toward civilization.

"From Illusions to Illusions"

"The peninsula of the Crimea," wrote Ségur, reflecting upon the long-anticipated arrival, "is surrounded on the east by the Sea of Azov, to the south and west by the Black Sea, and bounded on the north by the desert plains of ancient Scythia." For the eighteenth-century traveler to Eastern Europe the evocative idea of "ancient Scythia" could be as much of a geographic fact as the Black Sea, and this was really its correct location, north of the Crimea, more than 2,000 years before. The steppe was behind them, and all around were flowers and fruits, laurels and vines, not just as rococo ornamentation but also as the natural flora. The cold climate of the north had all at once given way to that of Italy, according to Ségur, the warmth of Venice and Naples. Goethe, on his parallel path in Western Europe, was actually in Naples just when Ségur reached the Crimea, his poetic imagination also at play upon the delights of Naples: "The many-coloured flowers and fruits in which Nature adorns herself seem to invite the people to decorate themselves and their belongings with as vivid colours as possible."[121] The travelers to the Crimea enjoyed a "representation of Vesuvius," which illuminated the landscape and turned night to day, courtesy of Potemkin, at around the same time that Goethe was watching the real Mount Vesuvius at Naples, actively erupting, its molten lava aglow in the night.[122] Eastern Europe became the fantastic, illusionary counterpart of Western Europe.

The Crimea appeared all fruits and flowers to Ségur, because the whole voyage, from the first garlands, had conditioned him to observe Eastern Europe in terms of the picturesque. In fact, before setting out, he had proved himself quite capable of taking a more hard-headed view of the Crimea's natural resources. When he pressed Potemkin to favor French trade against British predominance in Russia, he stressed especially Russia's "southern commerce." Ségur insisted to Potemkin that "only we could open outlets to the productions of that territory, immense but nearly a desert, which his sovereign charged him to people, civilize, enrich, and administer." They almost reached the point of concluding an unusual commercial convention between the provinces of southern Russia and those of southern France, Eastern Europe again finding a geographically analogous counterpart in Western Europe, the two quadrants linked in a vision of economic exploitation.[123] Like Lady Craven looking down at the harbor at Sevastopol and imagining the presence of British colonists and traders, Ségur in St. Petersburg looked way down to the Crimea and imagined French commerce as the agent of civilization.

When he was actually in the Crimea in 1787, however, his fantasies were far more whimsical. There was the prince de Ligne, at his side, wondering what "Europe" would think if the whole party of travelers, including Joseph and Catherine, was carried off by Tartars and delivered as prisoners to the sultan in Constantinople. The Orient was close by, just across the Black Sea, and the prince imagined an expedition "to leave Europe, if it is true that one can thus name that which we have seen, which resembles it so little."[124] The Crimea was Eastern Europe's point of least resemblance to "Europe," though in geographical fact it was entitled to the name. Ségur evaded that fact at Bakhchisaray, the former capital of the Crimean khanate before Russian annexation, where the travelers stayed in the palace of the former khan. At Bakhchisaray, "we could believe ourselves veritably transported to a town in Turkey or Persia, with the only difference that we had the leisure to examine everything without having to fear any of those humiliations to which Christians are forced to submit in the Orient." In the Crimea Eastern Europe became an illusionary Orient where Europeans held power, especially the power to observe and examine. They penetrated even into the harems of the palace, and did not stop at that: "The subject Moslems could refuse us nothing: so we entered the mosque during prayers." After such a display of courtesy, the visitors from enlightened civilization were naturally offended by the sight of whirling dervishes, "one of those spectacles that saddens human reason."[125]

Ségur created for himself an Oriental fantasy more to his taste, and remembered it in detail when he wrote his memoirs.

I remember that lying down upon my divan, overwhelmed by the extreme heat, enjoying however with delight the murmur of the water, the cool of the shade, and the perfume of the flowers, I abandoned myself to Oriental indolence, dreaming and vegetating as a true pasha; all at once I saw before me a little old man in a long robe, with a white beard, wearing on his bald head a red skullcap.

His aspect, his humble attitude, his Asiatic salute, rendered my illusion complete, and I could believe for some moments that I was a veritable Moslem prince, whose aga or bostangi came to take his sacred orders.

Since this slave spoke the Frankish language a little, that is to say, bad Italian, I learned from him that he was once the gardener of the khan Shahin-Girei. I took him for my guide.[126]

It was the almost magical appearance, "all at once," of a slave, which capped the other details of Oriental luxury and transformed Ségur, a mere count, into a prince. That the slave spoke some Italian—like Casanova's Zaire, after her lessons—made him too a reflection of the facing quadrant, the south of Western Europe. A voyage of illusion throughout thus culminated in the ultimate illusion of Eastern Europe: like Mozart on the way to Prague, Ségur assumed a new identity.

While the count was pretending to be a pasha in the palace of the Tartar khan, the prince de Ligne was informing his correspondents, with mischievous humor, that Ségur was really lodging in the room of the khan's black eunuch. If the prince amused himself by undermining his friend's fantasies, however, he was no less eager to give himself over to his own. His imagination was "fresh, pink, and round, like the cheeks of *madame la marquise*," wrote the prince from the Crimea to a French marquise, flatteringly perhaps. Residing in a palace—"our palace"—that was vaguely "Moorish, Arab, Chinese, and Turkish," he did not pretend to be anything so specific as a pasha. "I don't know anymore where I am," he recorded,

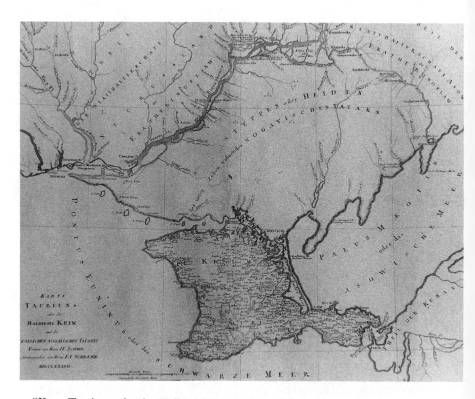

"Karte Tauriens oder der Halbinsel Krim" (Map of Tauride or the Crimean Peninsula), Vienna, 1787; published in the year of Catherine's triumphal visit to the Crimea, with the Habsburg Emperor Joseph II as her guest from Vienna, and also in the company of the count de Ségur and the prince de Ligne; here in the hitherto little-known southeastern corner of Europe (if one can call "Europe" that which, according to the prince, "resembles it so little") the map locates not only the Crimea, but also the adjacent "Steppes or Heaths of the tent-dwelling Nogay Tartars."

"or in what century I am." The prince's imagination was so fresh, so pink, so susceptible, that for him the Crimea raised the question of identity in its most general form. Located somewhere between Europe and the Orient, between civilization and barbarism, between true and false, Eastern Europe presented this dilemma, in some degree, to all of its eighteenth-century visitors. The prince de Ligne saw moving mountains that turned out to be the humps of dromedaries in the distance, and wondered if he was with the three kings on the way to Bethlehem. He saw young princes from the Caucasus on white horses, covered with silver, armed with bows and arrows, and thought he must have slipped into the ancient Persia of Cyrus the Great.[127] In a century of proverbial cosmopolitanism, the prince de Ligne was one of the truest stateless cosmopolitans, a condition that he better appreciated when he traveled in Russia: "I love my estate of foreigner everywhere, a Frenchman in Austria, an Austrian in France, and both one and the other in Russia; that's how to please yourself everywhere, and be nowhere dependent."[128] This independence was more than a matter of citizenship; in Eastern Europe the prince successfully cultivated a freedom of imagination and identity.

At Sevastopol Ségur admired the fortress and the fleet, and just outside the new city the travelers went to visit ancient ruins, where Iphigenia and Orestes "seemed to appear to our eyes." This was where the temple of Iphigenia at Tauride was supposed to have stood: "It was in the environs of this place, so rich in memories and illusions, that the empress had given land to the prince de Ligne; she could not have chosen anything better suited to the taste of that prince."[129] Ségur was right to suppose that the prince de Ligne was readier than anyone to own property in a land so rich in illusions.

The prince was visiting his new estate, at the site of Iphigenia's temple, sitting upon a Turkish carpet, writing to the marquise. He described himself "surrounded by Tartars who watch me write, and raise their eyes in admiration, as if I were another Mohammed." Around him were palms and olive trees, cherry, apricot, and peach trees, ornaments of "the most beautiful and most interesting place in the world." Goethe in Italy was tasting the figs and pears, admiring the lemon trees, and recognizing in Rome that "all the dreams of my youth have come to life." He was convinced that "in this place, whoever looks seriously about him and has eyes to see is bound to become a stronger character." Not so in the Crimea: the prince de Ligne declared himself "a new being" but, unlike Goethe, found no connections to his youth, no affirmations of his character. "I ask myself who I am, and by what chance I find myself here," he wrote, as the Tartars looked on, perhaps wondering the same thing about him. "I recapitulate the inconsistencies of my life." He found among the Tartars an Albanian who could speak a little Italian—like Mozart's "Albanians"—and through this interpreter the prince tried to ask the Tartars if they were happy and if they knew that they now belonged to him. "I bless the lazy ones (*les paresseux*)," he recorded, over and over again, enjoying a sense of beneficent mastery, not only as their prince but also as their prophet.[130]

He too was one of the lazy ones, upon his Turkish carpet, but his imagination was active: "What am I doing here then? Am I a Turkish prisoner? Have I been thrown upon this shore by a shipwreck?" Such fantasies seemed to him no more unlikely than the truth of his invitation from Catherine: "She proposes that I follow her into this enchanting land, to which she has given the name of Tauride, and, in recognition of my taste for Iphigenias, she gives me the site of the temple where the daughter of Agamemnon was priestess."[131] His "taste for Iphigenias" was obviously analogous to Casanova's "taste for Zaires." Iphigenia in Tauride was also held "in solemn, sacred bonds of slavery," and the prince de Ligne at Tauride could expect to discover among the Tartars of his estate someone to satisfy his taste; he would be able to name her according to his fantasy. When the prince fantasized about Iphigenia at Tauride he was probably thinking of Euripides' drama, but also perhaps of the recently acclaimed contemporary opera by Christoph Gluck. This operatic *Iphigénie en Tauride* was produced in Paris in 1779 and then in Vienna in 1781, when Joseph II welcomed to the Habsburg capital Catherine's son, Paul. The publication of Goethe's *Iphigenie in Tauris* in 1787 may have further conditioned public reception in Western Europe of the instant legend of Catherine's voyage to the Crimea.

The prince de Ligne toyed unconvincingly with the notion of staying and living on his estate at Tauride: "Blasé about almost everything that is known, why not establish myself here?" He would build himself a palace, create vineyards, and "convert the Muslim Tartars by making them drink wine." Such was his frivolous fantasy of bringing civilization to the Crimea, but it passed even as he was writing, pierced by the call to prayer from nearby minarets: "I feel with my left hand for the beard I do not have; I rest my right hand on my breast; I bless the lazy ones, and I take leave of them." His imaginary beard made him at home in Eastern Europe, and the feel of his own clean-shaven chin reminded him that this was not his home after all. So he took leave:

I gather my wits, which have been so scattered; I randomly assemble my incoherent thoughts. I look around me with compassion at these beautiful places, that I will never see again, and that have let me pass the most delicious day of my life.[132]

Far from strengthening the prince's character, if anything could, the Crimea scattered his wits, dissolved his mental coherence, and effaced his identity. This self-indulgence was conditioned by an idea of Eastern Europe as a domain of fantasy and illusion.

To look behind the veil of illusion in the Crimea was both disappointing and dangerous. The prince de Ligne and the count de Ségur got into trouble before leaving when the prince became too curious and presented a proposition to the count:

"What's the use," he said to me, "of passing through this vast garden if we don't let ourselves examine the flowers? Before leaving Tartary I must at least glimpse one Tartar woman without the veil, and I am quite resolved upon it. Would you like to accompany me in this enterprise?" [133]

They went hunting and found three women bathing in a stream at the edge of the woods: "But alas! what a disappointment, not one of them was young or pretty." The women became aware of the watchers and began to scream, and so the two bold adventurers found themselves being chased through the woods by Tartar men, who were waving daggers and throwing rocks. Catherine scolded them like children for their bad behavior, but she let them hide and peek from behind a screen when she granted an audience to a Tartar princess.[134] Just as Potemkin had scrupulously landscaped the views of the voyagers, so even an instance of voyeurism had to be staged for their satisfaction.

Yet the stage management and illusionism were supposed to be recognized and appreciated. "I know very well what is sleight of hand (*escamotage*)," wrote the prince de Ligne. He prided himself on having seen behind the facades, and pretended that it was Catherine who was supposed to be fooled by the Potemkin villages, "by towns without streets, streets without houses, and houses without roofs, doors, or windows." [135] The illusionary spectacle was designed to appeal to the imagination of the travelers, to flatter their sense of superior civilization, and finally to induce them to become themselves the inventors and publicists of the fantastic legend of Catherine's empire. "We are led from illusions to illusions," said the Emperor Joseph II, summing up the tour.[136]

The end of the voyage, for Ségur, was "to leave the rapid and varied action of the novel (*roman*), to return to the slow and serious march of history." If traveling in Eastern Europe meant living as a character in a novel, then it was hardly surprising that travelers rendered their accounts imaginatively, nor that the fictional Baron Munchausen could take his place among them. As for history, it was certainly true that the travelers to the Crimea, like so many other eighteenth-century travelers to Eastern Europe, had been fantastically cavalier in their imaginative indifference to historical centuries and circumstances. The prince de Ligne meandered from mythological Tauride to ancient Persia, and saw himself on the road to biblical Bethlehem. Ségur cast a regretful glance over his shoulder:

Coming out of the circle of fairyland, I would never again see, as in our triumphant and novelistic (*romanesque*) march, at each moment new objects of surprise:

fleets created suddenly, squadrons of Cossacks and Tartars hastening up from the depths of Asia, illuminated routes, mountains on fire, enchanted palaces, gardens created in one night, savage caverns, temples of Diana, delicious harems, nomadic tribes, camels and dromedaries wandering in the desert, hospodars of Wallachia, princes of the Caucasus, persecuted kings of Georgia, all offering their homage and addressing their prayers to the queen of the North.

It was necessary to return to the dry calculations of politics.[137]

Politics, like history, could only be a disappointment after fairyland. Certainly Ségur had throroughly appreciated the fairy message when he subordinated his marvelous memories to the presiding figure of Catherine, queen of the North. Yet on the way to the Crimea, she was really a queen *from* the north, and the fairy empire she visited, conjured up from "the depths of Asia," was extremely Oriental though entirely within Europe. It was the moment in the history of the eighteenth century that most dramatically presented the drama and dilemma of Eastern Europe.

Ségur saw himself turning away from "the Orient" just in time to receive from "the Occident" the first inklings of "a total revolution." The French Revolution appeared as "a subject of reflections, hopes, and fears, quite differently serious and profound from the sentiments inspired by that short and brilliant dream of the Tauride, by that chapter from the *Thousand-and-one Nights*, of which the illusion had just disappeared."[138] The coming of the French Revolution in Western Europe was politics and history indeed, while Eastern Europe appeared in contrast as an insubstantial empire of dreams and illusions. The prince de Ligne wrote a letter to his marquise from the Crimea in 1787, setting up the same opposition: "The subjects of this empire, whom one so often has the goodness to pity, don't care about your Estates General; they implore the philosophes not to enlighten them."[139] The frivolous prince fully understood, on the spot, that Eastern Europe could serve as a refuge from the march of the eighteenth century.

There was one last spectacle saved for one last stop on the journey back from the Crimea to St. Petersburg. The travelers stopped at Poltava in the Ukraine, where Peter had defeated Charles XII in 1709, where Voltaire had set up a literary signpost in 1731 to mark the discovery of Eastern Europe in his *History of Charles XII*. Ségur appreciated Poltava's importance, presenting it as a sort of inverted Potemkin village whose humble appearance belied its historic significance:

Poltava, a little town, badly fortified, very poorly peopled, offering to the gaze no edifice, no monument worthy to fix the attention, would only have been known to the erudite; but in 1709 a splendid victory and a great disaster, fixing upon it the attention of Europe, rendered it immortal.[140]

This was worthy of Voltaire himself, the suggestion of a double Europe, one that gave attention where it was due, the other upon which that attention might or might not become fixed. Ségur now came to Poltava to see what it had to "offer" to his "gaze." On this occasion the offerings were spectacular, for Potemkin, in one last grand gesture as impresario, staged the battle of Poltava for the edification of Catherine and her guests. Ségur described it as "an animated tableau, moving, living, in the end, almost a reality." Catherine fully appreciated this homage to Peter, and so "this grand and magnificent spectacle worthily crowned her voyage, as novelistic as it was historical." [141]

Ségur explained the battle's historical significance for Russia in accordance with the Enlightenment's conception of emerging civilization in Eastern Europe: "If Peter had succumbed, this vast empire would have returned perhaps forever into darkness and barbarism." It was a battle that "changed the destiny of the north and the east (*l'orient*) of Europe." [142] With that unobtrusive phrase—"the east of Europe" or "the Orient of Europe"—Ségur consummated the eighteenth-century discovery of Eastern Europe by giving it a name. Voltaire in 1731, even though he followed Charles XII south to Poltava, could not break with the conventional designation of Russia as a land of "the North." Ségur in 1787, who had traveled all the way to the Crimea and was on his way back to St. Petersburg, could not help appreciating that Russia was no longer in "the North," that there was in fact an "Orient of Europe"—complete with camels and harems—an Eastern Europe. A world-shaking political revolution was ready to begin in France, but in the Crimea and the Ukraine, amid illusions and spectacles, a momentous cultural revolution was completed that would change the map of Europe in the all-powerful "gaze" of the beholder. Western Europe had fixed its civilized attention upon Eastern Europe, and thus defined itself as well.

Coda: "The Charge of the Light Brigade"

In the 1820s Lord Byron sent his epic hero, Don Juan, into eighteenth-century Russia, there to captivate Catherine. Byron himself was delighted with the poetic comedy of Russian names, and jokingly celebrated the daunting rhythms and rhymes that challenged an English poet when he followed his muse to Eastern Europe.

> The Russians now were ready to attack;
> But oh, ye goddesses of war and glory!
> How shall I spell the name of each Cossaque
> Who were immortal could one tell their story?
> (Canto VII, Stanza XIV)

Byron was altogether ironic, as he dedicated his verse to "thousands of this new and polished nation,/ Whose names want nothing but pronunciation."

The notion of Russia as a "polished nation" took its irony from the phrases of Voltaire, but the comedy of names was closer to the spirit of Mozart and Baron Munchausen:

> Ending in 'ischskin', 'ousckin', 'iffskchy', 'ouski',
> Of whom we can insert but Rousamouski,
> Scherematoff and Chrematoff, Koklophti,
> Koclobski, Kourakin, and Mouskin Pouskin,
> All proper men of weapons, as e'er scoffed high
> Against a foe, or ran a sabre through skin.
> (Canto VII, Stanzas XVI, XVII)

The comic sensibility that rhymed "Mouskin Pouskin" with "sabre through skin" was bequeathed to Byron by the Enlightenment in its idea of Eastern Europe.

In the 1850s there were armies of English, French, and Italians who came to fight against Russia in the Crimean War, to fight for an Eastern Europe balanced between St. Petersburg and Constantinople. Lady Craven in 1786 insisted that her imperialist image of the Crimea was not a "poetical figure," but in 1855 Lord Tennyson provided the monument in verse to mark the Crimea as the scene of Western Europe's war against Eastern Europe:

> Plunged in the battery-smoke
> Right through the line they broke;
> Cossack and Russian
> Reeled from the sabre-stroke
> Shattered and sundered.
> Then they rode back, but not,
> Not the six hundred. . . .
>> When can their glory fade?
>> O the wild charge they made!
>> All the world wondered.
>> Honor the charge they made!
>> Honor the Light Brigade,
>> Noble six hundred!

Tennyson's "poetical figure" of the reeling Russian put Eastern Europe in its place for the Victorians, but the Crimea was not a new destination of the imagination for the public of Western Europe. Dating from Catherine's celebrated voyage, the peninsula possessed a mystique that survived the eighteenth century, and the domain of illusion became an arena of warfare and international relations in the nineteenth and twentieth centuries.

In the twentieth century the Crimea played again a fateful role in the history of Eastern Europe, for it was at Yalta in the Crimea, in 1945, that Roosevelt and Churchill came to meet with Stalin and negotiate the balance of the postwar world. There in the Crimea they wrestled over the future of Poland, and out of their impasse would develop the division of Europe by the Cold War which gave crude geopolitical force to the subtle cultural distinctions of the eighteenth century. Later in 1945 Truman, Attlee, and Stalin would meet at Potsdam and find themselves still unable to avoid diplomatically the division of Europe. Potsdam too was an important site for the eighteenth-century discovery of Eastern Europe, for it was there, at Frederick's court, that travelers like Ségur took leave of Europe and set out for Poland. Potsdam was the perfect point of departure, just as the Crimea was the ultimate destination for travelers to Eastern Europe in the eighteenth century, and, fittingly, Potsdam and Yalta would be names indelibly associated with the fate of Eastern Europe in the twentieth century. The veil of illusion became an iron curtain, but Eastern Europe could only be surrendered because it had long ago been imagined, discovered, claimed, and set apart.

Chapter Four

Mapping Eastern Europe: Political Geography and Cultural Cartography

"To Conclude European Geography"

In Voltaire's *Charles XII* he described a diplomatic encounter between the king of Sweden and the duke of Marlborough in 1707, two of the greatest soldiers of their age. Voltaire heard the story twenty years later in England from Sarah Churchill, the old duchess of Marlborough, and reported that the duke had happened to notice that Charles kept "on a table, a map of Muscovy." The map was the crucial clue to Charles's strategic intentions, immediately betraying to John Churchill that "the true design of the king of Sweden, and his sole ambition, was to dethrone the tsar after the king of Poland."[1] The map on the table represented a land to be conquered; in fact the map itself seemed to act as a stimulus and invitation to conquest. Yet when Charles was on his way to catastrophe at Poltava, crossing the "unknown land" of the Ukraine—"these lost lands"—he was, according to Voltaire, "uncertain of his route." His failure to conquer Russia, like his original intention, was thus partly a matter of mapping.

Voltaire's account was historically plausible, for at the beginning of the eighteenth century the lands of Eastern Europe were still incompletely mapped by comparison to the cartographical standard of Western Europe, and the mapping of Eastern Europe that took place during the course of that century, often carried out by foreign experts, was a fundamental part of the general discovery which produced and organized knowledge of "these lost lands." Indeed, Voltaire's history was itself a form of philosophical mapping, an encyclopedia of Eastern Europe with information ordered sequentially to follow the lands of Charles's itinerary; that itinerary, if traced upon a contemporary map, defined the domain of Eastern Europe. Maps provided a basic geographical framework for organizing other forms of knowledge, from natural history to national history, and furthermore made visually evident the emerging distinction between east and west. Eighteenth-century maps of Eastern Europe, published in the atlases of Western Europe, assured that Napoleon would have better maps of Russia than Charles XII, though no more ultimate success in conquest. In 1787, having traveled triumphantly with Catherine through the Ukraine and the Crimea, Ségur and all the other voyagers received as souvenirs a medallion with Catherine's profile on one side and a map of the voyage on the other. The map on the table had served as an invitation to conquest at the beginning of the eighteenth century; the map on the medallion, at the end of the century, could be carried home to Paris, London, and Vienna by the three traveling ambassadors. It was a token of the fact that the lost lands of Eastern Europe had been discovered, mapped, traveled, studied, and stamped, according to the enlightened standards of Western Europe.

In 1695 Nicolas Sanson, royal geographer to Louis XIV, published in Paris a "New Introduction to Geography, for the usage of Monseigneur le Dauphin, by which one may learn in little time and with facility geography, and the division of all the parts of the world." Sanson included a map of "The Estates of the Tsars," which was decorated with lots of little pictures of trees and showed fewer and fewer place names toward the eastern border of the map, which was also identified as the boundary between Europe and Asia.[2] The predominance of little trees made it that much easier to master this map "with facility," and reflected the still rudimentary mapping of Russia at the end of the seventeenth century. In the early eighteenth century it was Peter who sponsored surveying expeditions to create improved maps of Russia. These were the collaborative efforts of Russian and foreign mapmakers, and Peter was attentive to the publication of the resultant maps abroad as well as in Russia. The relation between Eastern Europe and Western Europe dictated that "putting Russia on the map" meant getting that map into the atlases that appeared in such cartographical centers as Amsterdam and Paris.[3]

Peter's mapping projects were naturally tuned to his foreign policy, and typically his military breakthrough to the Sea of Azov in 1696 was followed by a new map of Azov in 1701, engraved to the standard of Dutch professionalism by Adriaen Schoonebeck. In 1719 Peter created his own Cartographic Office, inaugurating a rocky Franco-Russian collaboration between Ivan Kirilov and Joseph-Nicolas Delisle, whose brother Guillaume was Premier Geographer at the Royal Academy of Sciences in Paris. Delisle insisted on scientific astronomical surveying in Russia, while Kirilov favored rivers over astronomical points of reference in the interest of more quickly achieving their aim, a complete atlas of Russia. The atlas eventually appeared in 1745, but, typically, Robert's *Atlas Universel*, published in Paris in 1757, already claimed superiority for its own map of European Russia, warning that the Russian atlas could be used only with "circumspection" due to carelessness at the borders.[4] Above all it was Russia's relentless eighteenth-century expansion that kept foreign cartographers continually active and made geography essential to accounts of contemporary international politics. In Paris in 1772, it was Jean-Baptiste d'Anville, author of atlases, secretary to the Duke of Orleans, and corresponding member of the Academy of Sciences in St. Petersburg, who published *L'Empire de Russie, son origine et ses accroissements*, "its origin and its increases."[5] That was the year of the first partition of Poland, and the empire of Russia enjoyed an additional increase.

The St. Petersburg Academy of Sciences sponsored several German scholars in expeditions that further extended geographical knowledge of Russia and built upon it with comprehensive studies in geology and natural history. Under Catherine the naturalist Peter Simon Pallas, born in Berlin, educated at Halle, Göttingen, Leyden, and London, with a special zoological interest in tapeworms, set out from St. Petersburg in 1768 to study Russia from end to end. Beginning with geography, he moved easily to the geology of the Urals and the ethnography of Siberia, cataloguing the fossils, flowers, and insects of Russia. Coxe paid tribute to the perfect fit between Catherine, who "perceived the deficiency of the topographical accounts, and anticipated the advantage of deputing learned men to visit the distant provinces of her extensive dominions," and Pallas, whose prodigious scientific energies were activated by "an irresistible desire to visit regions so little known."[6] Catherine traveled south to the Crimea in 1787, in fantastic magnificence, and Pallas then went south in 1793–94 to make and record those geographic and ethnographic observations that cleared away the clouds of Potemkin's illusions and established an absolute intellectual mastery through science. The researches of Pallas eliminated from the mythological map of Russia such wonders of natural history as the *boronets*, the "Scythian lamb" that grew on a stalk, mentioned by Mandeville in his medieval travels, accepted by Margeret in the seventeenth century, and still sought on the lower Volga by one English traveler as late as the 1730s.[7]

In Poland Stanisław August sponsored the French naturalist Jean-Emmanuel Gilibert, who left Lyon for Lithuania in the 1770s, to conduct Linnaean researches there, as Pallas did for Catherine in Russia. Coxe found

Gilibert at Grodno hard at work on his *Flora Lituanica*, roughly contemporary with the *Flora Russica* of Pallas. Like Pallas, Gilibert found special scientific satisfaction in charting an unexplored domain, "a land as virgin as Canada," which was so recently surrendered by France in 1763. Natural history, however, was subordinate to cartography in Poland, inasmuch as the making of maps and the compilation of an atlas, according to Jean Fabre, became for Stanisław August "one of the principal tasks of his reign."[8] The territorial losses that Poland suffered in the first partition became a stimulus to preserve an image of the complete Commonwealth in atlas form. The Jesuits, on the verge of papal suppression in 1773, provided local data for the atlas, but ultimately the project was in French hands, those of the cartographer Charles de Perthées and the engraver Jacques-Nicolas Tardieu. Determined to execute the project according to the most scientific standard of astronomical surveying, they worked slowly, beginning to print the first maps of the separate palatinates in 1783. In 1792, in the midst of simultaneous revolutions in France and Poland, Stanisław August worried that "our geographical work may be compromised." In 1794 he would not turn over the cartographical work in progress to Kościuszko for strategic planning in the military insurrection against Russia, supposedly exclaiming, "I would rather give my diamonds than my maps." Even after the final partition of Poland, its elimination from the geopolitical map of Europe, the king without a kingdom was still corresponding with Perthées and trying to supply from memory geographical details for the atlas.[9] While French cartography worked to keep up with Russian political expansion, it could also preserve the picture of Poland in defiance of Polish political extinction.

The lands of the Ukraine, those in the Polish Commonwealth as well as those in the Russian empire, were among the worst mapped and least generally known. Charles XII may have been "uncertain of his route" in 1709, but Joseph Marshall claimed to have been equally uncertain in 1769: "the country's being so extremely out of the way of all travellers, that not a person in a century goes to it, who takes notes of his observations with intention to lay them before the world." Though Marshall himself may not actually have gone, and may have taken his account from other people's books, still he affected to regret that "our writers of geography, who are every day publishing, copy each other in so slavish a manner, that a fact in 1578 is handed down to us as the only information we can have in 1769; a circumstance which reigns in all the books of general geography that I have seen." Though English travelers might be looking to Elizabethan guides, the French could refer to the *Description of the Ukraine* published by Guillaume Le Vasseur de Beauplan in Rouen in 1660. In 1772, Marshall wrote confidently about the geography of the Ukraine:

It has been supposed that the hemp and flax, coming to us from so northern a place as Petersburg, would grow in the midst of perpetual frosts and snows; but though we import it from latitude 60, yet it all grows in the Ukraine, which lies between latitude 47 and 52, and is besides as fine, mild a climate as any in Europe: this is the latitude of the south of France.[10]

Thus Marshall implicitly recognized the eastern nature of Eastern Europe, reporting that Russia was not all northern frosts and snows. It was a matter of latitudinal analogues, France and the Ukraine, like Italy and the Crimea. Yet the essence of Eastern Europe in the eighteenth century was still its resistance to precise geographical location and description. In 1769, for instance, the war between the Russian army and the Polish Confederation of Bar had already shifted the political border, three years before the formal partition, and Marshall was confused about "a province once Polish, and which all the maps I have lay down as a part of Poland," yet apparently now under Russian rule. He concluded that "the greatest changes happen in such remote parts of the world, without any thing of the matter being known."[11]

In the case of the Ukraine those lands that were transferred from Polish to Russian political sovereignty moved out of the geographical and scientific domain of Perthées and Gilibert, and into that of d'Anville and Pallas. As for the Crimea, annexed by Russia in 1783, while it awaited the coming of Catherine and then Pallas, there was already Lady Craven in 1786 to exclaim in a letter to Anspach, "I am in possession of several maps of this country drawn and coloured very well, which I shall have the honor of shewing you when I see you." Later in Hungary she showed them to Joseph II, who "sat two hours and a half looking over the maps and presents I have received," and she thought "the maps seemed to please him very much."[12]

The cartographical ambition of Western Europe to master Eastern Europe in the eighteenth century met its most serious resistance in the Ottoman empire. Here there was no Catherine or Stanisław August to welcome the scholarly ambassadors of science and enlightenment. With no assistance forthcoming from Constantinople, cartographers in Western Europe experienced academic frustration that was frankly expressed in Robert's *Atlas Universel* of 1757.

If in the detail of the different parts of Europe that one has traveled through to the present, we have had the satisfaction of receiving aid from the savants who have worked on their countries, we can not say that we have enjoyed such an advantage in the description that we have to make of the states submitted to Ottoman domination. We would have wished to be able to conclude (*terminer*) European geography with more success; but the approach to these states is difficult for enlightened people (*gens éclairés*), and does not permit one ever to hope for sufficient lights (*lumières*) to give something satisfying in geography; for the relations that voyagers give us are not of sufficient help to confirm the topographical detail of the lands that they have traveled through. It would be necessary for these voyagers to be instructed in mathematics.[13]

The close relation between mapmakers and travelers was emphasized here; the traveler was dependent upon the map, of course, but the cartographer was also dependent upon the voyager's observations. Cartography was clearly identified with the Enlightenment, the work of "enlightened people" seeking to cast light upon the darkest corner of the continent. Furthermore, the light of cartography was implicitly related to the light of civilization, for Eastern Europe was often described in the eighteenth century as emerging from darkness, *ténèbres*. Interestingly, the proclaimed determination to map Ottoman Europe in this period coincided with the emergence of the "Eastern Question" and its specific political agenda of driving the Turks out of Europe.

The world as a whole was far from fully mapped in 1757, the year of the *Atlas Universel*—the thrilling discovery of Tahiti, for instance, would not occur until 1767—but the limited ambition of mapping Europe seemed to be within sight. That atlas commented on the still increasing geographical appreciation "of Asia, of Africa, and even of Europe."[14] In the eastern half of the continent there was work to be done, and cartography was one of the arenas in which Western Europe focused its lights and sights upon Eastern Europe.

"Erased from the Map of the World"

While cartographers insisted upon their work as a matter of mathematics and astronomy, in fact there were far from objective forces at work in the making of maps. Armies and treaties, of course, rearranged the map of Europe, especially Eastern Europe, throughout the eighteenth century, but maps and atlases also possessed a power of presentation over the supposed facts of geography. Lady Craven boasted of maps "drawn and coloured very well," but neither drawing nor coloring was a precise science. Though printing could give a certain standardization to any given drawing, the coloring of printed maps in the eighteenth century, often done by hand, not necessarily by professional cartographers, added a casual element of artistic license to the maps' most visually evident representations. On a world map it was the colorist who made the far from fixed decision of where to divide the Eurasian land mass into Europe and Asia. On a continental map, the colorist determined which lands were to be represented as independent political entities, and even when the crayon conscientiously sought to follow the negotiated rearrangements of international relations, those too could be ambiguously subject to alternative interpretations. Indeed, the printed features of the map, the precise location of towns with respect to each other, with respect to rivers and coasts, to latitudes and longitudes, was highly variable in Eastern Europe, where cartography was still working toward definitive descriptions through the eighteenth century. Robert's *Atlas Universel* was further frustrated by an absence of uniformity in the generally problematic case of Turkey: "It is only necessary to compare the different maps that have been published of that empire to convince oneself, by the little resemblance they have among them, of the degree of confidence due to them."[15]

The expansion of Russia and contraction of Turkey required careful attention to changing boundaries, but two other cases in Eastern Europe posed more delicate dilemmas for the makers of maps: the case of Hungary at the beginning of the eighteenth century and that of Poland at the century's end. The Treaty of Carlowitz in 1699 recognized that Hungary had been liberated from the Ottoman empire (though Buda fell to the Habsburgs as early as 1686), and mapmakers should have then ceased to represent the lands of Hungary in the same colored bloc as the rest of Ottoman Europe. That they were slow to follow this fact was due not only to professional inertia, but also to the now pressing problem of how to dispose, cartographically, of the new Hungary. For Hungary was liberated from the Ottomans to be claimed and ruled by the Habsburgs, and from 1703 to 1711 an insurrection led by Ferenc Rakoczi vainly fought to realize a declaration of Hungarian independence. That eighteenth-century mapmakers in Paris were willing to accept that unachieved independence in coloring their maps was due partly to anti-Habsburg sentiment in France and partly to the incongruity of having to color Hungary as if it were part of the Holy Roman Empire of Germany. The *Atlas Universel* of 1757 was still apologetically defensive about an influential map of 1700 that had failed to separate Hungary from Ottoman Europe.

One would never have thought of reproaching the late Guillaume Delisle for having in 1700 let Hungary be enveloped in the estates of the Turk in Europe, for that skillful geographer well knew that it was not part of that empire. One must attribute these faults, or rather these light inadvertencies, which often are only picked out by caustic and unemployed spirits, to the great occupations that we have, and that do not permit us always to verify these maps, accordingly as they are colored.[16]

This particular inadvertency was still weighty enough to call for comment half a century later. The caustic comments of unemployed spirits in a philosophical and cartographical underground—men who might get to do some coloring, even if locked out of scientific mapmaking—only emphasized the power of the profession to represent the world to the public. The impulse to color Hungary as independent, neither Ottoman nor Habsburg, though flouting political reality, acquired cultural plausibility from the eighteenth-century idea of a domain between Europe and the Orient, the idea of Eastern Europe.

The partitions of Poland in 1772, 1793, and 1795 proved as problematic for mapmakers as the liberation of Hungary at the beginning of the century. Marshall claimed that by 1769 military movements had rendered the maps incorrect, for they told him he was in Poland (even if he was really in England) when the town in question had "a Russian garrison, Russian government, and, in a word, scarcely any thing Polish in it." The partition of 1772 was widely perceived as a matter of monarchs operating directly, and irregularly, upon the map, represented in a famous French cartoon, "The Royal Cake," which showed Catherine, Frederick, and Joseph fingering their respective claims upon a huge map of Poland unfolded among them.[17] Enlightened statecraft meant mathematical calculations of the balance of power in mutually negotiated aggrandizement, so that monarchs and statesmen had to become studious geographers.

The mapmakers' dilemma was to decide how quickly and how completely to follow the lead of the monarchs, and the issue became still more delicate after 1795, when the third partition eliminated Poland altogether. The partitioning powers might agree, as they did by secret treaty in 1797, that the very name of Poland "shall remain suppressed as from the present and forever," but such a covenant was hardly binding upon the mapmakers of Paris and Amsterdam.[18] In fact, the name of Poland could be left in print, even while recording the partition in the coloring of the map. Cartography, which identified Poland as a domain of conquest for purposes of partition, at the same time, paradoxically, rendered its parts culturally resistant to consumption and liquidation by inscribing them on the minds and maps of men. Thomas Jefferson wrote of "a country erased from the map of the world by the dissensions of its own citizens," but the idea of "erasure" did not really fit the printing and coloring procedures of eighteenth-century cartography. As Stanisław August had hoped, when he labored over his atlas project with Perthées and Tardieu, the scientific progress of geography was a cultural force for preservation against the depredations of diplomacy. The American press recognized this in 1797, regretting that Poland "will speedily only be remembered by the Historian, the Geographer, or the Newsmonger." [19]

While geographers faced political and cultural complications in representing the component parts of Eastern Europe, the concern "to conclude European geography" also focused attention on the border between Europe and Asia. At Constantinople this was perfectly clear, but the integrity of the Eurasian land mass allowed for a variety of lines—not necessarily the one that we recognize today, which runs south along the Urals to the north shore of the Caspian Sea. In Sanson's "New Introduction to Geography" of 1695, the introductory world map showed Muscovy as something distinct from Europe, therefore presumably in Asia. Yet the "Geographical Table" that followed on the next page, enumerating "The Divisions of the Terrestrial Globe," clearly specified that Muscovy was included in Europe. This dissonance between image and information was soon to be further confused, for next came a map of Europe that included Muscovy to the eastern border, and then a map of Asia that also included Muscovy to the western border. The dauphin could decide for himself.[20] In 1716 the "Almanach Royal" of Paris listed Poland, but not Muscovy, as a kingdom of Europe; in 1717 Muscovy was added to the list.[21] Indeed, it was a prerogative that Western Europe would come to exercise over Eastern Europe as a whole in the eighteenth century, the reservation of judgment as to whether it was in Asia or Europe, geographically and culturally.

The uncertainty over whether Muscovy was in Europe or Asia was obviously dependent upon an uncertainty of demarcation between the two continents. This became increasingly interesting as Eastern Europe came into focus, for its focus rested paradoxically upon fundamental confusion. The ancient geography of Ptolemy found the border between Europe and Asia at the Don River, known as the Tanais in the ancient world, flowing into the Sea of Azov, in turn connected to the Black Sea at the Kerch Strait. This was a conception of Europe considerably smaller than our own, based on a geographically known world of generally lesser dimension. It was in Renaissance Italy, already in the age of explorations, that a map of 1459 (the Mappamundi of Fra Mauro) proposed the Volga as an alternative border, thus extending Europe significantly from the Black Sea to the Caspian Sea, closer to our twentieth-century demarcation.[22] These two alternatives, clear enough along the rivers as they flowed into their respective seas, both left the border still uncertain to the north. Sigmund von Herberstein visited Russia as a Habsburg diplomat and published in Vienna in 1549 the best informed and most widely read sixteenth-century account of Russia. "If one draws a straight line from the mouth of the Tanais to its source," wrote Herberstein, speculatively, "the result is that Moscow is in Asia, not in Europe."[23] Herberstein's principal geographical source, supplementing his personal experience, was the *Treatise on the Two Sarmatias, Asian and European*, published in Cracow in 1517, in Latin, and then in many translations and editions through the sixteenth century. The Polish author Miechowita delimited "European Sarmatia" from the Vistula to the Don, and "Asian Sarmatia" from the Don to the Caspian Sea. Sarmatia was a name from ancient history, not contemporary geography, and, furthermore, rivers and seas made for uncertain continental boundaries as long as geographical knowledge itself was uncertain. Miechowita thought the Volga flowed into the Black Sea, not the Caspian; Herberstein corrected the error.[24]

For Peter, at the beginning of the eighteenth century, it became an issue of state policy and national identity to distinguish symmetrically between

Detail of "L'Europe," by Guillaume Delisle, Paris, 1700; based on the observations of the Royal Academy of Sciences; emphasizes the distinctions between Moscovie Europe & Moscovie Asiatique, between Turquie Europe & Turquie Asiatique; European Turkey and European Muscovy, together with Poland, form the geographical basis on the map of what will come to be seen as Eastern Europe over the course of the eighteenth century. The very restricted delimitation of Europe as a whole begins at the Don, and from there follows an irregular line roughly to the north. In 1757 Robert's *Atlas Universel* looked back at Delisle's map of 1700, and commented that "one would never have thought of reproaching the late Guillaume Delisle for having in 1700 let Hungary be enveloped in the estates of the Turk in Europe, for that skillful geographer well knew that it was not part of that empire," and there was no cause to carp at "these faults, or rather these light inadvertencies." (From the Harvard Map Collection, Harvard University.)

European Russia and Asian Russia, with the latter relegated to semicolonial status. Peter's geographical expert in these matters was Vasilii Tatishchev, and it was he who proposed the Urals as a continental boundary between the two moieties. That same boundary was suggested at around the same time by the Swede Philipp Johann von Strahlenberg, and Tatishchev and Strahlenberg, the Russian and the Swede, actually disputed over who had thought of the Urals first.[25] Strahlenberg regarded the continental demarcation as a pressing problem of contemporary geography, and was confident that he had the solution: "I must mention this much concerning the Boundaries between Europe and Asia; that whereas, in several new Maps, from an uncertainty where to place them, they have been wholly left out, I have shew'd them so plain in mine, that they will remain determin'd forever."[26] Yet, throughout the eighteenth century, the Urals remained only one of several plausibly accepted geographical demarcations between Europe and Asia. The German geographer Johann Georg Gmelin went far beyond the Urals, into Siberia, and located the continental boundary at the Yenisei in 1747.[27]

Maps of Europe, during the course of the century, allowed for an increasingly eastern extent, which also corresponded to advances in geographical knowledge. The Black Sea in the lower righthand corner suggested a more limited demarcation, at the Don, while the appearance of the Caspian Sea in that corner implied a broader Europe. A map of 1720 (by Homann, published in Nuremberg) showed Europe colored only to the Don, at the Sea of Azov. The Caspian Sea was excluded from the map, but, further north, the Russian empire extended liberally to the map's straight edge, leaving the border between Europe and Asia unspecified. A map of 1772 (by Desnos, published in Paris) allowed the northeastern shore of the Caspian to appear on the edge and, still without marking a precise border between continents, suggested that Europe might extend to the Urals.[28]

Where the continental border was explicitly marked, it was usually a question of coloring, nothing engraved, open to interpretation. A map of 1700 (by Guillaume Delisle, published in Paris) separated "Moscovie Europe" from "Moscovie Asiatique" with a colored border that ran north from the Don to the White Sea, around 40 degrees longitude, east of Greenwich, delimiting a very restricted Europe. A map of 1743 (by Hass, published in Nuremberg) extended the continent, by coloring to the Don in the south, but then all the way to Novaya Zemlya in the north, around 60 degrees longitude, thus creating a rough diagonal that cut across the longitudinal parallels.[29] The *Atlas Universel* of 1757 included a world map showing the full Eurasian mass, Europe with a colored border of green, Asia with a colored border of red, separated by a diagonal that ran from southwest to northeast.[30]

The diagonal border was a compromise between possible longitudinal borders, north from the Sea of Azov, north from the Caspian. At the same time the diagonal was culturally convenient, suggesting a less strictly ruled division between east and west, encouraging an ambiguous conception of Eastern Europe. In the eighteenth century Europe was discovered to possess unsuspected eastern depths, awaiting geographical exploration and appropriation, but Asia also remained intimately adjacent, the border both variable and permeable. In 1759, Voltaire's *Peter the Great* surveyed the provinces of the empire and warned that "there the limits of Europe and Asia are still confused," that "one no longer knows where Europe finishes and where Asia commences."[31] In 1787, in the Crimea, the prince de Ligne enjoyed the idea that Asia was close at hand, and a geographical tradition of consummate ambiguity supported his Oriental fantasies.

"The Germans and the Huns"

Geographical reorientation was driven by geopolitical change, and yet mapmakers could still interpret international relations in terms of cultural considerations. In 1696 Peter, age 24, came down the Don River with Russia's first fleet, his own creation; not till the next year would he travel to the shipyards of Holland and England, to contemplate the construction of a navy. In 1696, however, he had ships enough to conquer Azov, where the Don flowed into the sea, and a Dutch mapping of the region quickly followed. The Don was one of the conventional geographical borders between Europe and Asia, and Peter had made himself the master of that junction. Furthermore, in acquiring a southern outlet he dramatically challenged the idea of Russia as a northern land, thus suggesting its eastern aspect; Catherine would consummate this reconception by annexing and traveling to the Crimea. Actually, Peter lost Azov in 1713 after an unsuccessful war with Turkey, and it would be regained only by his successors after another war in 1739. Yet the conquest by Peter in 1696, and the map by Schoonebeck of 1701, had geographically established Azov, at the mouth of the Don, as an object of Europe's attention, either taken or to be taken. The half century of fluctuation between Ottoman and Russian sovereignty, of cession and retrocession, only enhanced the element of uncertainty inherent in the idea of Eastern Europe. The possible axes of Eastern Europe might include their endpoints, as at St. Petersburg, or might not include them, as at Constantinople. Azov, perhaps the point at which Europe and Asia met, perhaps not, could belong to the Orient, fortified against the Russian river, or become the outpost of Eastern Europe, a naval base upon the Turkish sea.

In 1699 the Treaty of Carlowitz recognized the conquest of Hungary by the Habsburgs after sixteen years of war against the Ottomans, dating from their unsuccessful siege of Vienna in 1683. The English traveler Edward

Brown was in Ottoman Hungary in 1669, and his Turkish guides had laughed at him for trying to orient himself according to his maps; even the Danube was drawn wrong.[32] Conquest would open the way to cartography after 1699, and also present the dilemma of how to represent Hungary's political affiliation on the map of Europe. The conquest of Hungary, like the conquest of Azov, marked a turning of the geopolitical balance of Europe, for the Ottoman empire was now in territorial recession. In 1684 Pope Innocent XI could still godfather for the Habsburgs a "Holy League" to crusade against the Turks, but in the eighteenth century such wars appeared increasingly as matters of secular power and policy. Furthermore, from the religiously indifferent perspective of the Enlightenment, the recession of Islam seemed less important than the recession of the Ottoman Orient, with its insufficient *lumières* and uncooperative attitude toward geography.

In 1676 Mme de Sévigné read about "the wars of Hungary" in a spirit of general interest in the Orient; she recommended to her daughter the book, "a little history of the viziers and the intrigues of the sultans and the seraglio, which may be read agreeably enough." In 1685, with the war of the Holy League under way, Jean de Vanel published in Paris a book about Hungary that would be repeatedly reissued into the eighteenth century. Vanel included a geographical description as well as rudimentary observations about national character: "The peoples of this kingdom, having more inclination for war than for business or the arts, care very little about the cleanliness of their lodgings." After the reconquest of Buda in 1686, a German traveler, Jacob Tollius, arrived in 1687 to find the city was "razed to the ground during the siege."[33] Hungary, after Carlowitz in 1699, awaited material reconstruction in the hands of the Habsburgs, and cultural reconstruction in the eyes of the Enlightenment.

In 1700 Charles XII crossed the Baltic and defeated Peter at Narva, an auspicious beginning for Sweden in the "Great Northern War." The war was to last for twenty years, ending with the Treaty of Nystad in 1721 whereby Sweden ceded to Russia the lands of Livonia, Estonia, and Ingria, the southeastern coast of the Baltic from Riga to St. Petersburg. This outcome of the Northern War, the withdrawal of Sweden to Scandinavia and Finland, helped to dissolve the whole idea of "the North" by neatly separating for the first time Sweden from Russia and Poland. Yet the geographical course of the war over its two decades, the range of its battlefields, even more emphatically undermined its "northern" designation, encouraging the conceptual realignment of Europe. A map by Sanson, published in Amsterdam in 1702, presented the "Theatre of the War of the Crowns of the North." The name of the "Ukraine" was printed at the border, indicating that it was just off the map, outside the theatre. Yet it was in the Ukraine at Poltava that the most famous and decisive battle of the war would be fought in 1709. When the Ottomans entered the war against Peter in the following year, he attacked them in Moldavia, was defeated on the Prut River, and ended up ceding the utterly non-northern Azov in 1713. In 1702 one might have planned to follow this war on a map of "the North," but well before its conclusion one would have had need of lower latitudes. In London in 1708 there was published a map by Hermann Moll that met the purpose: "A Map of Muscovy, Poland, Little Tartary, and ye Black Sea."[34] It was not a conventional association of lands, but the ambitions of Peter and Charles, and the progress of their Northern War, had rendered such a map both necessary and plausible, a map of Eastern Europe.

This was the map that Voltaire represented in prose when he wrote his *Charles XII* in 1731. The assumed Swedish perspective, that of an unequivocal northerner, rendered all the more apparent the geographical contradictions of the conventional "North" and the "Northern War." In fact, in 1730 in Stockholm, Strahlenberg published in German his book *Das nord- und östliche Theil von Europa und Asia*, including new information about Siberia. Here was the axis of Europe in rotation, the awkward identification of a "north- and eastern part." Strahlenberg had the opportunity to study his subject while serving under Charles XII, and then as a Russian prisoner of war. He admired "the wonderful ways of Providence, that though most arts are generally brought to decay by the fate of war, yet the science of geography is often increased and improved thereby." Furthermore, Strahlenberg explicitly related the providential advances of geography to a celebration of civilization, inspired by the discovery of uncivilized lands and peoples.

Every reader may not perhaps be equally diverted with this my description of these cold and in part desolate regions, where unpolished manners and ignorance, as well in religious as worldly affairs, ride triumphant, and deprive the natives of the true use of those blessings which nature has, in so liberal and extraordinary a manner, bestowed on some of these countries. When we, therefore, compare the brutish and wretched condition of these people, with the civilized state of Europe, where better and more prudent manners are cultivated, where arts and sciences flourish, where we have abundant means to come to a true knowledge of God and his worship, we have the greatest reason to praise the Divine Goodness, to rejoice at our own happy state, and to deplore the misery and blindness of these people.[35]

This opposition, between one domain of flourishing arts and sciences, and another of unpolished manners and blind ignorance, demonstrated that for Strahlenberg in 1730, as for Voltaire in 1731, the geographical discovery of Eastern Europe was ideologically inseparable from the axioms of civilization and enlightenment in Western Europe.

Strahlenberg's book was translated into English and published in London in 1736 as *An Historico-Geographical Description of the North and Eastern Parts of Europe and Asia*. The French translation, however, resisted the new conceptual orientation and appeared as *Description historique de l'empire russien* in Amsterdam in 1757, in time for Voltaire to consult it as he wrote his *Peter the Great*.[36] Eventually even a Frenchman, Ségur, would have to recognize the new formulation when he stood on the battlefield of Poltava in 1787 and contemplated "the destiny of the north and the east of Europe." The Ukraine, after all, was in the same latitudinal range as France, and the path from Paris to Poltava was due east.

In 1703, still early in the war, Peter began to build a fortress on the marshy delta of the Neva River, in Ingria, which he had just snatched from Sweden. There was to be a shipyard there by the Neva, on the Gulf of Finland, opening into the Baltic Sea; and then there was a town, which became Peter's new capital, St. Petersburg. The construction of a city where before there was only a swamp became a part of Peter's legend, eventually a metaphor for the building of civilization in Russia. Voltaire, writing his *Peter the Great*, insisted that in seventeenth-century Russia "almost everything was still to be done," the better to emphasize Peter's work of "creation."[37] Buda had to be rebuilt from the ground, but St. Petersburg was created from nothing. Thus Peter unilaterally inscribed a new name upon the map of Europe, his own name actually, and geographers all over Europe had to put that point upon their maps.

St. Petersburg and Azov, both with shipyards looking out to their respective seas, reflected Peter's preoccupation with coastal outlets and the development of naval power in Russia. Yet St. Petersburg and Azov were also intimately related to each other as opposite endpoints of a new geographical axis. No longer the old Muscovy that expanded outward from its central capital at Moscow, Peter's Russia extended from the Baltic to the Black Sea, an axis that emphasized the eastern character of Russia in Europe. Catherine would only fix the endpoints more firmly when she made Sevastopol into her harbor on the Black Sea in the 1780s and brought her guests there from St. Petersburg to admire *Catherine's Glory*. The new axis was still culturally confusing in the eighteenth century, and Coxe, on the northern road from Moscow to St. Petersburg, felt he was getting "nearer the civilized parts of Europe," while Ségur, traveling south on the Dnieper to the Crimea, obviously felt he was sailing to the Orient. This jumbling of north and south, east and west, meant that Eastern Europe in the eighteenth century was inevitably located between Europe and the Orient, no matter which way the compass was pointing.

In 1703, the same year that Peter moved to put St. Petersburg on the map, Ferenc Rakoczi inaugurated the insurrection against the Habsburgs that would bring Hungary forcefully to the attention of Western Europe, especially in France, and establish an image of Hungary for the eighteenth century. The Hungarian insurrection from 1703 to 1711 coincided not only with the Northern War, encouraging Rakoczi to seek assistance from Peter, but also with the War of the Spanish Succession, which pitted Bourbons against Habsburgs, and made the French and the Hungarians extremely interesting to each other. Rakoczi's manifesto of rebellion in 1703 was promptly sent to Paris for translation and publication. In 1703 there were also published a map of Hungary, by Guillaume Delisle, and another one in Amsterdam by Gerard Valck.[38] The Dutch followed the Hungarians far less favorably, for, by the Grand Alliance of 1701, Holland and England stood with the Habsburgs against France. The war over Spain thus guaranteed that the eyes of Europe were on the map of Hungary.

The Hungarian historian Bela Köpeczi has studied the outpouring of French attention to Hungary during these years, in pamphlets and the press, observing the central political irony by which Louis XIV, that paragon of monarchical absolutism, officially endorsed the Hungarian claim to independence and elective monarchy. In the *Gazette de Paris* the soldiers of Rakoczi were never "rebels," but at first "discontents," and after 1708, at the cue of Louis XIV, simply "confederates."[39] Eustache Le Noble produced a series of pamphlets in fable form, in the manner of La Fontaine, to publicize the Hungarian cause. In 1705 he versified *The Eagle, King of the Cranes*, with a Habsburg eagle and Hungarian cranes, and in 1706 he produced a *Fable of the Lion's Cavern*, in which Rakoczi was the wise fox resisting the Habsburg lion.[40] The leading intellectual antagonist of Le Noble was Nicolas Gueudeville, who wrote for the exiled French Huguenots in Holland, which was anyway in alliance with the Habsburgs. Guedeville did not write fables, but employed animal imagery that brought the debate even closer to natural history. Writing from the Hague in 1705, he labeled the Hungarians as "monsters of inhumanity," worse than the Lapiths or the Iroquois. Thus he suggested an equation between metaphorical "monsters" and primitive peoples, relevant to contemporary ideas about Eastern Europe. The language of natural history appeared again in 1706, when Gueudeville regretted that "the Germans have not yet won any solid advantage over the Hungarians." The problem was that "this rising resembles the body of an animal: when one cuts off some limb, the spirits rally and it is only more vigorous." There was an odd convergence of classification between Le Noble and Gueudeville, polemicizing over Hungary in 1707. The latter denounced "a nasty beast" of "barbarous zeal," and the former respectfully recognized "a strange beast," that is, "a people revolting for its liberty."[41]

The marquis de Bonnac, French envoy in Poland, channeled French soldiers into Hungary and claimed special knowledge of the beast that fought for its liberty. "It is necessary to have known the Hungarians or the Poles particularly," wrote Bonnac, "in order to know the profound roots that liberty has cast into their hearts." It was less a matter of bestiality than biology: "The children carry it in their hearts at birth, and suck it in with the milk of their mothers." The invocation of the maternal breast made Bonnac's image of Poland an anticipation of that of Rousseau in 1772. Bonnac himself saw Poland in revolt against its Saxon king, Augustus the Strong, ally of Peter the Great, and rallying to Stanisław Leszczyński, protégé of Charles XII. The French association of Hungary and Poland made a mapping of contemporary conflicts into regional relations. If the ideal of liberty linked Hungary to Poland, military tactics seemed to relate the Hungarians even more provocatively to the Tartars. Lieutenant General Pierre Des Alleur, representative of Louis XIV at the camp of Rakoczi, was teased in a letter from the maréchal Claude de Villars, who wondered "how a man trained in the infantry accommodates himself to this little war of the Tartars." Referring to the irregular military tactics of the insurgents, the maréchal of France was also making an ethnic distinction when he wrote of "the division between the Germans and the Huns." He could not know that in another war, 200 years later, the Germans themselves would be the Huns. Villars associated the Hungarians with the Huns of the past and with the Tartars of the present, envisioning Eastern Europe as a confusion of unassorted backward peoples. Le Noble in 1707 published in Paris a *History of Prince Rakoczi or the War of the Discontents*, explaining that there were few regular battles, "because the Hungarians make war on the run in the manner of the Tartars." Charles Ferriol, the French ambassador in Constantinople, observed the Hungarians from that vantage point and concluded in 1711, at the end of the insurrection, that no one could "reduce them to a discipline of which they were not capable."[42] Voltaire, with Charles XII, would discover that same inaptitude for discipline all over Eastern Europe.

A French geographical account of 1708 allowed that Hungary was "one of the most beautiful lands in the world." The Hungarians themselves, however, were explained in terms of an alien origin: "The nation that possesses this beautiful land came there from Tartary, where it belonged to the Huns, so celebrated for their ravages and their cruelties." In Paris in 1711, with Rakoczi on the point of final defeat, "invincible Hungary" was celebrated geographically for its past glory, bounded by "the Adriatic Sea on one side and the Black Sea on the other."[43] Those markers suggested one set of parameters for Eastern Europe, just as St. Petersburg and Azov defined an axis from the Baltic to the Black Sea. Hungary could no longer be taken as part of the Ottoman Orient, but its image could also resist the force of Habsburg arms by defining and claiming the space of Eastern Europe.

"A Singular and Unique Species"

In 1704, one year after the outbreak of the insurrection in Hungary, John Churchill, duke of Marlborough, joined forces with the Habsburg hero Prince Eugene of Savoy to defeat the French at the battle of Blenheim on the Danube. It was also a blow to the Hungarians, since a Habsburg victory could hardly be favorable to the prospects of their recent rising. In Churchill's England the logic of alliance weighed against sympathy for the Hungarian cause. Daniel Defoe thought the Hungarians should have been grateful to the Habsburgs for liberation from the Turks, though Jonathan Swift in *The Conduct of the Allies* of 1711 thought the Habsburgs should have settled with Hungary and fought harder against France. In Swift's view the Habsburg emperor "chose to sacrifice the whole alliance to his private passion, by entirely subduing and enslaving a miserable people."[44] In 1712, a year after the final defeat of the Hungarians, an English map was made by Hermann Moll and dedicated to "His Grace, John Duke of Marlborough, Prince of Mindelheim," for Churchill was now, for his victories, a prince of the Holy Roman Empire. The map showed him that empire, representing "Dominions Belonging to the House of Austria," that is, "A New Map of Germany, Hungary, Transylvania, and the Suisse." This was not just a new map, but a new mapping, this cartographical combination of Germany and Hungary, a celebration of the Habsburg triumph over Rakoczi, who himself had held the title of prince of Transylvania.

Yet this combination would never prevail on maps of Europe in the eighteenth century. A Dutch map by Zürner of 1712, made for Augustus, elector of Saxony and king of Poland, was no more sympathetic to Hungarian independence, but asserted the separateness of Eastern Europe by simply coloring Hungary as part of "Turcia-Europaea," Ottoman Europe. There Hungary formed part of a distinct yellow bloc, dramatically set off from the Holy Roman Empire in pink, but joined together with Croatia, Bosnia, Dalmatia, Transylvania, Wallachia, Moldavia, Bessarabia, Bulgaria, and Serbia. A map by Guillaume Delisle, published in Paris in 1724, used shaded borders to imply that Hungary was part of "Turquie d'Europe." A Dutch map by De Witt, published in Amsterdam in 1730, claiming to be "accuratissima," combined Hungary with Wallachia, Moldavia, and Bulgaria in Ottoman Europe.[45] To represent Hungary as part of the Ottoman empire after 1699 was hardly "accuratissima," indeed not even true, if truth was a matter of political sovereignty. The mapmakers of Europe recognized another truth of images and associations that sometimes overcame the supposed facts of the state system.

The compromise convention, however, throughout the eighteenth century, would be the representation of an independent Hungary, or rather the coloring of Hungary as a distinct entity, not affiliated with either the Habsburg or the Ottoman empire. This evasion of the political circumstances was conditioned by the period of the Rakoczi insurrection at the beginning of the century, when the political fate of Hungary was genuinely uncertain, when Hungarians were actually fighting for their independence.

On the map, the uncertainty of this interim period long survived the fairly definitive peace of Szatmar in 1711, when the principle of Habsburg hereditary rule triumphed along with Habsburg arms. An accident of contemporary geography further contributed to the importance of this period for the maps of the next generation. In 1706, with the insurrection in full swing, there was a solar eclipse, which was of great interest to scientific geographers who relied on astronomical calculations to make their terrestrial maps. The moment of the eclipse then became a cartographical point of reference, so that maps represented the world as it was in 1706. There was no scientific reason for this to affect the political coloring of maps, but coloring was no science, and Hungary's unresolved political condition of 1706 was perpetuated on the map through the representation of independence. In Nuremberg in 1720 Johann Homann published a map of "Europa Eclipsata," that is, the Europe of 1706, in which Hungary and Transylvania were colored distinctly green. In 1743 Johann Hass made a map of Europe, published by the heirs of Homann, still insisting on a distinct "Hungaria," which in this case included Moldavia, Wallachia, and Bulgaria as well; this map was reprinted in 1777.[46] Thus the independence of Hungary, a general cultural conviction that drew strength from issues of political ambiguity, was established and preserved on the map through a century of Habsburg rule. The political plausibility of Moll's map for Marlborough could not prevail over the powerful associations and impressions that created Eastern Europe.

While Hungary, Moldavia, Wallachia, and Bulgaria could be colored together on the map of Europe as adjacent lands, another association was less culturally and cartographically obvious, that between Hungary and Bohemia. In 1720 Henri Abraham Châtelain published in Amsterdam his *Atlas Historique*, promising not only new maps, but also "dissertations on the history of each state by M. Gueudeville." The latter was the same French émigré who spoke for the Habsburg perspective in Holland during the Rakoczi insurrection. Gueudeville, naturally, gave a history that suited his own political perspective: "The Hungarians were Scythians, cruel peoples, it is said, who lived only by blood." They were "barbarians" who received from the medieval Holy Roman Empire "the just chastisement for their brigandage and their ferocity."[47] Châtelain and Gueudeville, however, made their most powerful political statement in the organization of the atlas. The first part of the second volume covered "Germany, Prussia, Hungary, and Bohemia," close to the combination that Moll had prepared for Marlborough in the map of 1712. The historical and geographical discussion of those lands was then further divided so that Hungary and Bohemia were treated together.

First came a map of Hungary, then one of Bohemia; they could not form one map together, for they were not contiguous. That was what made the geographical pairing unusual. Next came a map of "different states and lands situated along the Danube," and here the two principals could appear together. This map was unusual inasmuch as it represented simultaneously "ancient and modern," inscribing together the names of Hungary and Pannonia, the Ukraine and Sarmatia, Bulgaria and Moesia, Wallachia and Dacia, Bohemia and Boiohemum. This was perfectly suited to constructing a map of Eastern Europe, between ancient and modern, and Bohemia too had to have an ancient equivalent, even if the Latin was awkward. The individual maps of Hungary and Bohemia each featured a "chronology of kings," which hinted at the correspondence between the two kingdoms. The Danube map, which united them, offered a "remark" of explanation: "As the kingdoms of Hungary and Bohemia, and the states of Silesia and Moravia, are regarded as hereditary states of the Emperor, so as not to return to this later, it has been judged appropriate to join them to the history of the Empire, and to give if possible at the same time the abridged description of the ancient peoples of these states."[48]

This link was further reinforced on the table that followed: "Genealogical Chart of the Kings of Hungary and of Bohemia and Summary of the Government of these Two Kingdoms." Side by side the two royal chronologies proceeded to 1526, when Louis Jagiellon, king of Hungary and Bohemia, died in battle against the Turks at Mohacs; most of Hungary became part of the Ottoman empire, but the Habsburgs inherited both crowns. After that the two royal chronologies coincided in the Habsburg family. Though the atlas was published in 1720, this chart was annotated with an anachronistic reference to the period of the Hungarian insurrection: "The whole kingdom being at present troubled, the majority of the estates follow the party of Prince Rakoczi, and the others have remained loyal to the emperor, which reduces this kingdom to a sad and very miserable state."[49] There followed the remark that "Bohemia, like Hungary, has also had its times of trouble and confusion," referring to "rebels" who were eventually crushed by the Habsburgs in the Thirty Years War. Hungary and Bohemia were joined together in the atlas as Habsburg crowns, those of St. Stephen and St. Wenceslas, as lands where trouble and confusion challenged imperial authority. By mapping and charting them together, Châtelain and Gueudeville made the fate of Bohemia in 1620, overwhelmed at the battle of the White Mountain, a prescription by analogy for Hungary in 1720.

Yet, the posing of this parallel, for the purpose of reducing Hungary to the status of Bohemia, also had the reciprocal effect of dramatizing the difference between Bohemia and the other lands of the Holy Roman Empire. Gueudeville clearly recognized this as a paradox of cartography:

This land, although included in the map of Germany, although a member of the Empire, does not cease to be a separate state. Its laws and customs are not the same as those of the Germanic corps; even its language is particular; and on both accounts, this state is of a singular and unique species within this vast region.[50]

The *Atlas Historique*, by insisting on the analogy with Hungary, ended up emphasizing the fact that Bohemia was not a German land. On the map of Bohemia there appeared the "remark" that "Bohemia once depended upon the Empire, but little by little became detached."[51] Though strongly endorsing the political reattachment of Bohemia, as well as Hungary, to the Habsburg monarchy, the Amsterdam atlas ended up formulating a new kind of "detachment" for Bohemia—"a singular and unique species"— based on customs and language. The opposition of Slavic and German was not explicitly invoked, only implied, for though it might have associated Bohemia with other lands of Eastern Europe, it would hardly have supported the comparison to Hungary.

Eighteenth-century geography served as the vehicle for every kind of observation and annotation, and the atlas map of Hungary was also inscribed with "remarks" on history, manners, and language. "Their language is almost completely particular," said the map about the Hungarians, echoing the remark on the preceding map of Bohemia. As for their manners (*moeurs*), these were "not very different from those of the Turks." The Hungarians were an "inconstant" and "bellicose" people, who "love passionately horses, the hunt, and good living, but do not love the Germans."[52] Even this was more nuanced than some earlier "geographical" observations, as in an *Introduction to Geography*, published in Paris in 1708, which reported of the Hungarians that "they love war and horses."[53]

Gueudeville, morever, recognized that Hungary, in spite of its allegedly Turkish manners, was no longer in the Ottoman empire. Hungary had been reclaimed by Europe, and he appraised its qualities in terms that seemed to anticipate visitors, or even colonists: good land for agriculture and pasturage but, on the other hand, unhealthy air and water, even an "abyss" whose "stink" was fatal to birds that flew overhead, like the entrance to hell. The most interesting geographical observation, however, concerned the abundance of fish in the rivers of Hungary. Gueudeville cited a contemporary opinion that fish was more nourishing than meat for contemplative people, because it thinned the blood, making the spirit more susceptible to the agitation of ideas. If so, then "Hungary is the health spot of the Republic of Letters ('Lieu de Santé de la Republique des Lettres'): all of us other little authors who, perhaps on account of thick blood, corrupt the public with our evil and disgusting works, would not do badly to retire there."[54] It was ironically intended, of course, a joke, and its humor depended partly on the obvious implausibility of Hungary, a land of Scythians, Tartars, and Huns, as a retreat for the intellectuals of Europe. At the same time such humor illustrated the easy appropriation of Hungary by those intellectuals as they claimed their share in the Habsburg conquest. They could, if they wished, retire to Hungary, which was thus annexed to the Republic of Letters as a sort of spa. The crude confidence of "all of us other little authors" belonged to the earliest generation of the Enlightenment, proud of its thick blood, unintimidated by those who denounced its "evil and disgusting works," an Enlightenment that flourished in the Holland of Bayle even before it came to France. The Enlightenment, from the beginning, needed another Europe against which to define its own sense of superior civilization. No one in the Republic of Letters actually intended to retire to Hungary and eat fish.

The political reconquest, geographical mastery, and intellectual appropriation of Hungary encouraged an imperialist eye to what remained of Ottoman Europe. The historian Karl Roider, in *Austria's Eastern Question 1700–1790*, has traced back to the very beginning of the eighteenth century an issue traditionally dated to the century's end. In 1715, only four years after the defeat of Rakoczi, the Habsburg resident in Constantinople was already hailing a new opportunity "to defeat the Turks"—"but also, God willing, to throw them completely out of Europe."[55] Throughout the eighteenth century this was to be a preoccupation and dilemma of policy in Vienna, drawing the attention of every other court and capital as well to those same lands of Ottoman Europe that might or might not be reclaimed and recovered from the Orient. Hungary, when it was not being charted beside Habsburg Bohemia, was still being mapped and colored together with Ottoman Wallachia and Moldavia. The paradox of "Turquie d'Europe," in Europe yet of the Orient, was essential to the emerging idea of Eastern Europe, and Habsburg ambitions, whatever the extent of military and political realization, contributed to the elaboration of that idea.

In 1717 Prince Eugene took Belgrade in the fog, a triumph publicized all over Europe. This was the redemption of a fortress of the Orient, a city where six months before Lady Mary Wortley Montagu studied Arabic poetry. It little mattered that Austria would have to surrender Belgrade again in 1739, for as in the case of Azov, likewise back and forth, the idea of Eastern Europe thrived upon this very uncertainty. After the fall of Belgrade, the Habsburg emperor thought of acquiring Moldavia and Wallachia, while the military experts of the Vienna Hofkriegsrat were planning to send soldiers to Sofia.[56] The ongoing War of the Spanish Succession ruled out such interesting advances for the moment, and the Habsburgs and Ottomans made peace at Passarowitz in 1718. The taking of Belgrade, however, following upon the reconquest and reduction of Hungary, made all of Ottoman Europe an object of ambition and imagination, and not only to Viennese statesmen. Mapmakers freely associated Hungary, Wallachia, Moldavia, and Bulgaria, in defiance of contemporary political borders, while the Republic of Letters was presumably ready to follow the Danube to the Black Sea, in quest of ever better fishing. Prince Eugene himself, for whom conquest was a military affair and empire a matter of administration, was actually hesitant in 1718 about extending the Habsburg empire deep into southeastern Serbia. He wrote to the emperor, "I do not find that Your Majesty would be well-served by the possession of these faraway places because their distance and difficult communication would cause more problems than advantages."[57] The possession of Eastern Europe, however, was not simply a matter of arms and administration; it was also a philosophical and geographical challenge. Statesmen might contemplate the Turks and aim "to throw them completely out of Europe," but geographers were simultaneously eager to master Ottoman Europe and thus "to conclude European geography."

"The Progress of Geography"

The international conflicts of the first two decades of the eighteenth century brought the map of Eastern Europe to the attention of Western Europe in focuses and forms that remained powerfully influential to the century's end. The Treaty of Carlowitz in 1699, the battle of Poltava in 1709, the peace of Szatmar in 1711, the fall of Belgrade in 1717, and the Treaty of Nystad in 1721 all developed the geopolitical issues of Russian expansion and Ottoman recession, and emphasized the uncertainty of sovereignty attending the Polish and Hungarian crowns. Stanisław Leszczyński, the protégé of Charles XII on the Polish throne between 1704 and 1709, could not politically survive his patron's defeat at Poltava. Augustus II, who was also elector of Saxony, regained the Polish crown in 1709, two years before the Habsburgs reestablished their hold on the Hungarian crown in 1711. Rakoczi took refuge in the Ottoman empire, settling on the Black Sea, though his memoirs were published posthumously in Paris. Leszczyński, after he lost his throne in Poland, found his refuge in France. In 1725 his daughter became queen of France, fated to be the long-suffering wife of the amorous Louis XV, while Leszczyński himself remained a king without a kingdom, a man who needed to find a place on the map. The territorial establishment of King Stanisław, father-in-law of the French crown, became a matter of international conflict and treaty in the 1730s in the War of the Polish Succession.

In 1731 Voltaire's *Charles XII* gave good publicity to the brief reign of Leszczyński in Poland twenty years before. In fact, Voltaire had used him as a first-hand source: "King Stanisław did me the honor of recounting what he said in Latin to the king of Sweden." Leszczyński also did Voltaire the honor of validating his account of Poland: "He has spoken of Poland and all the events which happened there, as if he had been an eye witness."[58] In 1733 Augustus II died, and the assembled Polish nobility elected Leszczyński to succeed him, for a second brief reign, lasting only six months. In the War of the Polish Succession, a Russian army drove out King Stanisław to establish Augustus III, the late king's legitimate son (among more than 300 illegitimate siblings). French military assistance reached Poland too late to preserve the throne for Leszczyński, but the peace of Vienna in 1738 finally settled his territorial fate by establishing him as duke of Lorraine and Bar, keeping only his title as king of Poland. The Bar of the ducal title referred to Bar-le-Duc in Lorraine, but there was also a Bar in Podolia, the Polish Ukraine, which in the next generation would become famously associated with resistance to Russia. The possibility of a dual reference underlined the anomaly of a shadow king of Poland who reigned in Lorraine, parodying the real king of Poland whose court was in Saxony. The map of Eastern Europe was subject to appropriation and reappropriation, in an increasingly ambiguous spirit that partook of pretense and fantasy, as well as politics and power.

Stanisław Leszczyński, king of Poland, established a court at Lunéville and an academy at Nancy where the philosophes of the Enlightenment all came to visit. It was at Lunéville that Voltaire lost the love of his life, the marquise du Châtelet, first in 1748 to another man, then in 1749 to death in childbirth. In 1749, Leszczyński published a book in France, *The Free Voice*, on liberty and the Polish constitution. In 1751 he wrote to defend the arts and sciences against the doubts of Rousseau's *Discourse*. In 1761 the abbé Gabriel-François Coyer, influenced by *The Free Voice*, published his highly successful *History of Jan Sobieski*, and in 1763 he was welcomed into the academy at Nancy.[59] This book was itself the major source for Louis Jaucourt when he wrote the article on Poland for the great Encyclopedia of the Enlightenment. Jaucourt completed the intellectual chain with an allusion in the Encyclopedia to someone "who shows us in a province of France what he would have been able to execute in a kingdom."[60] The Lorraine of Leszczyński was thus presented as a miniature model of Poland, mapped into Western Europe, illustrating the possibility of enlightened progress against the presumption of backwardness in Eastern Europe.

The academy of Nancy was not without its geographer. The Paris *Atlas Universel* of 1757 was the work of Robert, geographer to Louis XV, but also of Robert de Vaugondy, the son, who titled himself geographer to the king of Poland, duke of Lorraine and Bar, and belonged to the academy at Nancy. In progress since the 1740s, the atlas was self-consciously a work of the Enlightenment, following from the principle that "the sciences universally cultivated in our century have so much assisted the progress of geography."[61] The atlas map of Poland, composed by a French geographer who served a Polish king who ruled over a French province, was appropriately based on French models. The most important was the map of Poland by Nicolas Sanson from the late seventeenth century, which incorporated the map of the Ukraine by Beauplan. The atlas map, however, improved upon Sanson by taking into account a map of Lithuania, published in Nuremberg in 1749, the work of a Polish Jesuit. The whole atlas created by father and son, one as geographer to Louis XV, the other as geographer to Leszczyński, included among its subscribers the royal mistress Madame Pompadour, the foreign minister Choiseul, the secretary to the French embassy in Warsaw, and a half dozen men in the service of Augustus III, the elector of Saxony, the other king of Poland, the real one. French geography thus mediated between the two kings of Poland, the academy of Nancy providing the map of Poland for the government in Warsaw. Robert de Vaugondy also made a map of Europe (published in London in 1770), which offered a political annotation on Poland: "The Poles live under one Head who bears the Title and lives in the Splendor becoming a King, but his Power is so Circumscribed that, in Effect, he is no more than the Prime or Chief Regent of a Commonwealth."[62] This was a conventional eighteenth-century observation on the Polish constitution, but no one knew better than Robert de Vaugondy, "Member of the Academy of Nancy," that from 1738 until the death of Stanisław Leszczyński in 1766, when Lorraine finally reverted to French rule, there were in fact two "heads" of Poland, one even more titular than the other.

The Habsburg and Russian alliance against Leszczyński in the War of the Polish Succession from 1733 segued into allied war against the Ottomans from 1736. An emerging linkage in international affairs between the Ottoman empire and the Polish commonwealth, as objects of aggression, annexation, and domination, would help to consolidate by association the idea of Eastern Europe. In 1732 at the Hague, Luigi Ferdinando Marsigli published an Italian work on the military weakness of the Ottoman empire, suggesting that Islam could be driven back "to the extremities of Arabia." Prince Eugene died in 1736, however, and in 1739 the Habsburgs actually had to give up Belgrade. Though the Russians regained Azov, the war was more interesting for the grand ambitions it fostered than for the adjustments it achieved. In 1737 the Habsburg war office could imagine conquering almost all of Ottoman Europe, and even enumerated the lands that this conquest would comprise: "Such a border would place the kingdom of Serbia, the greatest part of the kingdom of Bulgaria, the kingdom of Macedonia, Turkish Dalmatia, the whole kingdom of Bosnia, the provinces of Albania, Epirus, Thessaly, Achaya, etc. under the dominion of the emperor." At the same time Russia revealed that its war aims included Wallachia, Moldavia, and the Crimea.[63] Military and diplomatic attention to these lands on the map of Europe underlined the inadequacy of contemporary cartography, and in London, for instance, it was impossible to obtain maps on which to follow the course of the Russian-Turkish war. Twenty years later the *Atlas Universel* still regretted its want of geographical details for the map of Turquie d'Europe: "Moldavia, Bulgaria, and the rest of Turkey have not been able to procure any for us."[64] The lands that the Habsburg and Russian statesmen coveted were precisely those that geographers sought to study; the two ambitions were inevitably related and arguably interdependent.

If Poland and Ottoman Europe were focuses of international affairs in the 1730s, the War of the Austrian Succession from 1740 to 1749, and the Seven Years' War from 1756 to 1763, dominated the middle decades of the century and refocused international attention. The struggle between Frederick the Great and Maria Theresa, which ran through these wars, started from his seizure of Silesia in 1740 and continued with her efforts to regain it. Silesia was actually a possession of the Bohemian crown, and came to the Habsburgs along with Bohemia in 1526; in successfully annexing it to Prussia, Frederick detached Silesia from the government of Vienna, the crown of Bohemia, and the idea of Eastern Europe. In fact, Silesia would one day rejoin Eastern Europe, assigned to Poland after the German defeat of 1945. The name of Silesia was identified with these wars from the moment of Frederick's attack in 1740, but almost as important was the international attention to Bohemia as a principal battleground. "It was upon Prague then that all Europe had its eyes," wrote none other than Voltaire; his account was published in 1752 in his *History of the War of 1741*, composed in his role of court historian to Louis XV.[65] The eyes of Voltaire were the eyes of the Enlightenment, but court and king also had an interest in such a history inasmuch as it was a French army that invaded and occupied Bohemia after Frederick took Silesia; one French commander was the father of Ségur. For Voltaire, writing about Bohemia, as in writing about Poland in the *History of Charles XII*, it was possible to be an "eye witness" from a distance.

In 1741 Prague fell to the French and Bavarians, and in 1742 Maria Theresa—recognized only as "queen of Hungary" by Voltaire, as in the writings of Frederick—sent her armies to recover Prague. Voltaire hinted at an element of barbarism in the queen of Hungary with her Hungarian troops, recounting that Maria Theresa commissioned "an amazon costume to enter Prague on horseback in triumph." Maria Theresa was certainly no amazon, but Voltaire's sympathies were with the French troops in the besieged city, which they would have to surrender before the end of 1742: "to find themselves thus, far from their fatherland, among a people whose language they did not understand, and by whom they were hated."[66] Voltaire's ear for the incomprehensible language, as he focused the eyes of Europe on Prague, made Bohemia seem even more alien. The French occupation and surrender of Prague in 1742, which caught Voltaire's attention and set him reading about Jan Hus and the religious history of Bohemia, was the first of several newsworthy assaults on the city in the following years.[67] Frederick himself took Prague, and gave it up again in 1744; at the beginning of the Seven Years' War in 1757 he won the battle of Prague, but then had to give up his siege of the citadel. These oscillations and occupations made Prague appear in these decades as an ultimate military object, like Belgrade and Azov in the first half of the century. If Azov on the Don was located on an ambiguous eastern border, and Belgrade on the Danube was the frontier fortress of a receding Ottoman Orient, Prague was to become and remain the westernmost point of Eastern Europe.

The posthumous publication of Rakoczi's memoirs in France in 1739 was related to the anti-Habsburg sentiment that followed the end of the War of the Polish Succession in 1738 and preceded the outbreak of the War of the Austrian Succession in 1740.[68] In the Seven Years' War, however, such sentiment had no place, for by the reversal of alliances in 1756 the French and the Habsburgs were suddenly allies against Prussia and England. France now counted on the loyalty of Maria Theresa's Hungarian soldiers, and the name of Rakoczi was an embarrassment of the past. The name of Peter the Great, however, acquired new luster in France, for Louis XV was now also fighting in alliance with Elizabeth, the Russian tsarina, Peter's daughter. It was only appropriate that Voltaire's first volume on Peter appeared in 1759, in the middle of the Seven Years' War.

Peter himself had once hoped to marry his daughter Elizabeth to Louis XV and make her queen of France. Instead, it was an ambassador of the French king in St. Petersburg who conspired in the plot that made Elizabeth tsarina in 1741. During her reign French culture came to Russia, French fashions and manners, the French language. There were actors and artists from France, a French doctor sent by Louis XV to attend to the tsarina, and even the geographer Joseph-Nicolas Delisle, who finally finished work on the long-awaited atlas of Russia, which appeared in 1745. Russia joined France and Austria in the Seven Years' War, attacking East Prussia in 1757. Voltaire's *Peter the Great* in 1759 gave an account of the Cossacks in the Russian army, which acquired contemporary relevance from the fact that they were fighting in alliance with the French: "They serve in the armies as irregular troops, and woe to anyone who falls into their hands."[69] Berlin was in the hands of the Cossacks in 1760; the Russian army had reached the frontier of Western Europe. Frederick wrote to Voltaire, unenthusiastic about the publication of *Peter the Great*:

Tell me, I pray you, what made you think of writing the history of the wolves and bears of Siberia? and what could you report of the tsar that is not found in the *Life of Charles XII*? I will not read the life of these barbarians; I even wish I could ignore the fact that they live in our hemisphere.[70]

The Russians were not just in Frederick's hemisphere; they were in Berlin. Frederick, in his *History of My Time*, first written in 1746 but revised for publication in 1775, attributed the power of the Russians to "the number of Tartars, Cossacks, and Kalmucks that they have in their armies." Russia's "neighbors" had every reason to fear these "vagabond hordes of pillagers and incendiaries."[71] These were the wolves and the bears.

The Seven Years' War suggested that Western Europe and Eastern Europe were geographically neighbors. In London in 1760 and 1761, Oliver Goldsmith published in *The Public Ledger* his "Chinese Letters," to be collected in 1762 as *The Citizen of the World*. Fum Hoam wrote to Lien Chi Altangi, "I cannot avoid beholding the Russian empire as the natural enemy of the more western parts of Europe." Goldsmith's Chinese correspondents declared Russia to be "at that period between refinement and barbarity, which seems most adapted to military achievement," threatening to "deluge the whole world with a barbarous inundation."[72] The tsarina died in 1762, and her successor, Peter III, withdrew from the war against Prussia, but not before London had learned a lesson in the geographical polarization of Europe between western parts and eastern parts.

"Those Barbarous Regions"

In 1762 James Porter, the English ambassador in Constantinople since 1746, gave up his post and returned to England. His grandson in the nineteenth century explained why Porter did not take the usual Mediterranean sea route in 1762: "As he had an extreme aversion to a sea voyage, he declined returning in the frigate which had brought out his successor, and undertook the journey to England by land—a task, of which we of the present generation, spoiled by the facilities afforded by good roads and railways, can scarcely form an adequate conception."[73] Just as the land route to Russia through Poland offered an unusual opportunity to the traveler, so the land route to and from Constantinople was interesting in proportion to its inconvenience. In 1762 Porter's itinerary was further complicated by the ongoing war, for by the reversal of alliances, Austria and England were no longer allies, as in the days of Prince Eugene and Lord Marlborough, but combatant enemies, and Porter could not follow the usual land route from Constantinople through Habsburg Hungary to Vienna. Instead he traveled with his wife, his two little children (a four-year-old girl and a two-year-old boy), and a small accompanying party through Bulgaria and Moldavia to Poland. From there they entered allied Prussia—on the way to Berlin they saw "villages burnt and in ruins, destroyed by the Russians"— and proceeded to Holland, then finally home to England.[74]

The inconveniences of travel could be taken with a sense of humor, and when plague in an Ottoman village forced the travelers to camp out in tents, Porter's wife found amusement in observing one member of the party. "Father Boscowitz," she recorded, "gave us a perfect comedy from the agitation he was in, and the trouble he took in placing his bed and all his comforts in the best possible order our situation would admit." More-over, when his baggage was delayed, "then his fidget and distress amused us much."[75] This was Ruggiero Giuseppe Boscovich, who, apart from his amusement value, was a Jesuit priest, a Copernican astronomer and New-tonian physicist of international reputation, and furthermore an eminent scientific geographer. He was born in 1711 in Dubrovnik, then Ragusa, with a Slavic surname, of a Serbian father and Italian mother, but he became definitively a man of Italian culture when he was sent to a Jesuit college in Rome at the age of fourteen. He became a professor of mathematics at the Collegio Romano in 1740 and took his final vows as a Jesuit in 1744. From his first publication on sunspots in 1736, he published a stream of scientific treatises, on aurora borealis, on gravity, on telescopes, on the sphericity of the earth, on the orbits of planets, on the division of fractions. In 1742 the pope requested his mathematical attention to the possible collapse of the dome of St. Peter's. In 1750 he turned down an invitation from the king of Portugal to participate in the mapping of Brazil and took on instead a geo-graphical project closer to home, the scientific mapping of the papal state. The peasants thought he was a sorcerer with his geodetic instruments. His account of this project was published in Latin in Rome in 1755, but in French in 1770 under a title that emphasized the important connection between the relevant disciplines: "Voyage astronomique et géografique." In 1760 he was in London, where he met Benjamin Franklin, was elected to the Royal Society, and published an epic poem in Latin on the eclipse of the sun. He left London for Constantinople, hoping to witness the tran-sit of Venus in 1761. On the way, he stopped at Nancy to be honored by Stanisław Leszczyński, patron of the Enlightenment.[76]

When Boscovich left Constantinople with the Porter family in 1762 his ultimate destination was St. Petersburg, for he had recently been elected to the Russian Academy of Sciences. Injury and illness on the road prevented him from making it to St. Petersburg, but he did travel through Bulgaria and Moldavia to Poland, through precisely those lands of Ottoman Europe whose inadequate mapping geographers lamented. Five years before, the *Atlas Universel* regretted that "the approach to these states is difficult for en-lightened people," remarking that travelers' reports were anyway unhelpful since "it would be necessary for these voyagers to be instructed in mathe-matics." Boscovich happened to be one of the most important mathema-ticians and astronomers in Europe. The English ambassador's wife might find him fussy, but cartography had little to hope of her.

Boscovich kept a travel journal in 1762, which was published in French translation in Lausanne in 1772, and then in the original Italian in 1784 with a preface by the author. The preface revealed that the needs of geography were on his mind, from the beginning, when he kept a journal on this voyage through little known lands.

I wrote the relation of this little part of my travels through lands so much less known ("paesi tanto meno conosciuti"), and in a very particular manner, noting . . . the places through which, or in the vicinity of which, one was passing, and the hours of departure and arrival at each, which served to rectify the map of that part of the Ottoman empire which, by order of the count de Vergennes, Zannoni designed at Versailles, as he himself attested to me. . . . It displeased me quite enough to not have with me any portable instrument that could accurately give me the precise geographical situation of the places themselves.[77]

Boscovich was in fact carrying around a few astronomical instruments, which made a great impression on the prince of Moldavia in Jassy, including "a little instrument which contains a mobile little mirror of metal, that I had made in London, and with which in a camera obscura I usually projected where I wished upon the wall the image of the sun, in order to show its spots and its eclipses." In spite of his later regrets about portable instruments and precise calculations, his journal showed him deeply involved in determining the latitude and longitude of Galati on the Danube. By observing the reflection of the horizon on the waters of the Danube at twelve o'clock noon, he came up with a latitude of 45 degrees and 23 minutes, "which is rather less than that which is found on various maps." He did less well with the longitude, for he would have needed to know "the place of the moon well determined on that day in some well known land (*paese cognito*)."[78] Thus the mapping of unknown Eastern Europe depended not only on the astronomer from Western Europe who happened to be visiting, but also on astronomical information reliably available only in Western Europe at that moment.

The distinction between "well known" and "less known" lands, scientifically and geographically, was fitted to a cultural differentiation between parts of Europe, and perfectly expressed the interest of Eastern Europe for the enlightened traveler.

I was enticed by the opportunity of seeing Bulgaria and Moldavia, lands too different from those which I had observed in the more cultivated part of Europe ("nella piu colta parte d'Europa"), through which a traveler can not pass without most serious inconveniences and dangers, excepting such an opportunity as this to put himself in the retinue of an ambassador assisted by the public authority.[79]

Thus the "less known lands" were set in opposition to "the more cultivated part of Europe," which clearly implied a reciprocal opposition between the well-known lands and a less cultivated part of Europe. Boscovich went so far as to speak of barbarism, in the context of regretting that he had not been able to bring back a more complete account:

The lack of appropriate instruments, ignorance of the language of the land through which one passed, though supplied in part by interpreters, and the rapid continuation of the voyage which did not permit us to stop except for a few days stay at the two ends and in the center of Moldavia, did not permit the observation on the spot and examination of a quantity of objects, which would have been essential for a more complete work ("un'opera piu compita") and more universally advantageous: yet this brief account will not be useless or boring, if only in presenting news of the manner in which one travels with a royal ambassador in those barbarous regions.[80]

The ignorance of Western Europe about Eastern Europe assumed the cultural backwardness of the latter, and Boscovich recognized as an ambition of the Enlightenment the compilation of a "more complete work" of knowledge on those barbarous regions. If his was not such an *opera*, it was at least, as Boscovich stated in the preface, an *operetta*.[81]

A map of the "Post-Roads of Europe" in 1758, completed by John Rocque, topographer to the prince of Wales, decorated with a picture of horse-drawn wagons carrying sacks of mail, showed two main roads to the east. One led southeast from Vienna, along the Danube to Buda and Belgrade, and on into the Ottoman empire; the other led northeast from Vienna to Warsaw.[82] Boscovich, who went from Constantinople to Warsaw, geometrically traversed these two conventional routes, and discovered the axis of Eastern Europe. Few travelers could fully appreciate the adjacency of its component lands as Boscovich did when he crossed the Dniester River at the border between Ottoman Moldavia and the Polish Ukraine. An English ambassador and his Dutch wife, traveling with an Italian astronomer, represented the parallel axis of Western Europe, from Rotterdam to Rome, which defined their cultural perspective.

Though Boscovich wished he had better instruments and more time to make geographical observations, in the absence of equipment his cartographical consciousness helped him to discover other approaches to mapping Eastern Europe. He professed ignorance of "the language of the land," but in fact, as an Italian of Dalmatian origin, he possessed a linguistic sensitivity to both Slavic and Romance tongues that enabled him to attempt in his journal a rudimentary ethnographic ordering of Bulgaria and Moldavia in the context of Eastern Europe. Furthermore, his ecclesiastical identity as a Jesuit rendered him aware of distinctions of religion in these lands, not just between Moslem and Christian, not just between Orthodox and Catholic, but also among different levels of religious knowledge and ignorance. Thus issues of language and religion, in the journal of Boscovich, enabled him to sketch a more modern sort of map based on unconventional keys. These have long since become essential to the mapping of Eastern Europe, where political borders were already highly unstable in the eighteenth century, and complex constellations of ethnography could be represented under new conventions of cartography.

The travelers left Constantinople on May 24, 1762. Two days later, Boscovich saw herds of horses driven by Tartars—"they had bows and arrows"—and soon after, he saw a caravan of camels moving toward Constantinople.[83] On May 30 the travelers came to a town where Boscovich observed that the inhabitants were "for the most part Turks" but included some Greeks. Assigned to lodge in a house that he found dirty and dark, he was struck by the fact that its owner was actually proud of it: "So much is due to education and the scarcity of ideas, and so true is it that everything among men is respective." Later he went to see the house of the local Orthodox priest and found it "incomparably more filthy."[84] Little wonder that Mrs. Porter found him fussy about accommodations, as he immediately discovered a different, "respective" standard of civilization for the journey ahead of him.

On June 1, one week out of Constantinople, the travelers passed more Tartars and horses on the road and came to the first Bulgarian village, Canara, in which they were to stay for the night. Boscovich found the houses to be poor but clean. Perhaps even more surprising was his discovery that he could understand the people of the village: "The language of the land is a dialect of the Slavic language, and that being also my own natural language of Ragusa, I could make myself understood by them, and understand something of what they were saying."[85] This was a rare, perhaps unique, occasion, that an eighteenth-century traveler to Eastern Europe, himself a scientist and scholar in Western Europe, a representative of enlightened civilization, should also, by the coincidence of his own Slavic origin, be able to recognize those he encountered as Slavs and explore that identity in simple conversation. Boscovich happened to be carrying an instrument for the ethnic and linguistic mapping of Eastern Europe, broadly focused in the assumption of one Slavic language with many dialects, and that instrument, highly portable, was nothing but his own childhood tongue.

Father Boscovich sought out the Bulgarian village priest, "a young man of twenty-five years, married, who already had children." The Greek Orthodox priesthood did not require celibacy, as Boscovich confirmed in this case, establishing a clear difference in ecclesiastical perspective between the young man and himself. "He was born in this village," wrote Boscovich, "and was ordained, to the extent that I seemed to be able to understand, at Constantinople." Mutual comprehension was uncertain, but Boscovich understood enough to conclude that the priest and the villagers were utterly ignorant:

His ignorance, and that of all these poor people, is incredible. They do not know anything of their religion except for the fasts and holidays, the sign of the cross, the cult of some image, of which one encounters now and then among them some quite horrid and ugly ones, and the name of a Christian. To the extent that I could discover that evening, speaking my language, and also having inquiries made in Turkish, which is commonly understood among them, they know neither the Pater Noster, nor the Credo, nor the essential mysteries of the religion.[86]

Boscovich made use of his Slavic vocabulary to ascertain the absolute difference between himself and the Bulgarians. The conventional Roman Catholic disapproval of Greek Orthodoxy was here unconventionally keyed to an ethnic identification of the Slavs, established by awkward communication in their own language. It was also that evening that Boscovich tripped on some stairs—"of the roughest wood and furthermore half ruined"—and injured his leg, causing an inflammation that plagued him for the rest of the voyage, and eventually forced him to stop in Poland and forego St. Petersburg.

"Such a Long Stretch of Uncultivated Barbarism"

On June 2 Boscovich came to a village called Faki, "of 88 houses, all of Bulgarian Christians." On June 4 he arrived at Karabunari, "an extremely large village of five to six hundred houses, Turkish and Bulgarian." On June 5 he passed through a Tartar village, Harmanli, which the sultan had assigned in Bulgaria to a Crimean prince. That day Boscovich also noted with interest the sight of "goats mixed with sheep in a flock." On June 6 he happened upon a fair at Carnabat, where there mingled "Turks, Greeks, Jews, carrying a thousand usual things." A Jew from Constantinople was selling mirrors, which might have interested Boscovich as reflectors for astronomical or geographical observation. His journal entries were already composing a complex ethnographic image of Bulgaria, a pattern of peoples even more interesting than the mixing of sheep and goats. On June 10 at Scialikavak, Boscovich reported 200 Bulgarian houses and 50 Turkish ones: "The Bulgarians told us that they live in optimal correspondence with the Turks; they also make mixed marriages." There were even Gypsies, who "played some instruments and made a little boy and girl dance."[87]

On June 13 at Jenibazar, "a mixed town of Turks and Christians," Boscovich counted 50 out of 300 houses as those of Christian Bulgarians, though he himself was lodged with a Wallachian family. Religious ignorance continued to prevail: "Examining various Christians of the place, I saw clearly that there too they had nothing of Christianity but the name and the baptism, not knowing anything but the sign of the cross, not even the Pater Noster, which is general in these unhappy lands." Ready to extend his generalization, he found himself on June 15 in Coslige, "a great place of 200 Christian houses and 300 Turkish ones." The travelers lodged in Christian houses, which were good enough, measured against "the usage of the Bulgarians and the misery of these lands." Boscovich was reading a book when an Orthodox priest approached: "I had in hand Suetonius, which I was reading then to distract myself." It was possible to communicate "with the help of my Slavic language," and Boscovich made use of the book as a prop for ascertaining the ignorance of his interlocutor:

Of Rome he had no knowledge, neither of the pope, nor of any religious controversy, and he asked me if there were priests in Rome. Of such ignorance I assured
myself also in employing more than one interpreter so as not to rely on what I
understood myself.[88]

Again, rough knowledge of the language became an instrument for ascertaining the ignorance of those Boscovich only half understood. The Orthodox priest further revealed his remove from civilization by wondering why
both Boscovich and Porter had no beards. "He asked me," reported the
Jesuit, "whether anyone had given me the order to shave it as a penance,
and he was astonished when he heard that this was the common usage of
our lands."[89] Thus Boscovich joined Italy and England in a common perspective, setting up an opposition between "the usage of the Bulgarians"
and "the common usage of our lands."

On June 19 the travelers came to Baltagikioi, "a village composed of two
groups of houses," one Turkish and the other Bulgarian. They spoke with
some of the Bulgarians, and learned "that their part was, and had been for
a while, healthy enough, that in the part of the Turks there had been some
mortality, and one supposed it was plague."[90] With some apprehension the
travelers proceeded, and on June 21 they reached the Danube, which separated Bulgaria from Moldavia. That border raised new issues of language,
ethnography, and geography.

Boscovich now encountered people who "spoke the Wallachian language, quite different from Bulgarian." While his Dalmatian childhood
gave him access to Bulgarian, he should have been equally capable of attempting the Romanian language of Wallachia and Moldavia, for Wallachian, he observed, was a "mixture (*miscuglio*) of various languages, mostly
of Italian and Latin." Boscovich had lived in Italy since he was fourteen
(he was now 51), and his Latin also had to be excellent, since he wrote
his scientific treatises in Latin, never mind his epic poem on the solar
eclipse. Boscovich, however, seemed to do less well with Romanian than
Bulgarian. Arriving in Pucen on June 29, he observed that the houses were
"little better than those of Bulgaria," and for further information he sought
out the local Orthodox priests: "Moldavians by nation, they speak only
the Moldavian language, so I could not understand them or make myself
understood." All he could do was analyze the elements of the *miscuglio*,
discovering in it not only Latin and Italian, but also "something of the
Slavic language and of Turkish." The same word governed his first impression, upon crossing the Danube, of the population in Moldavia, "a
mixture (*miscuglio*) of persons of so many different lands," and Boscovich
gave up the mathematical impulse by which in Bulgaria he analyzed villages into their ethnic components. He perceived the same confusion at the
highest levels of authority, puzzling over Moldavia's Turkish sovereignty

Detail of "L'Europe," by Robert de Vaugondy, geographer to the titular king of Poland, Stanisław Leszczyński; from the *Nouvel Atlas Portatif*, Paris 1762; the component lands of Eastern Europe include European Turkey and European Russia, whose respective domains even appear to overlap at "Petite Tartarie," as well as Poland, Hungary, and Bohemia, which is heavily outlined to mark its distinction from surrounding Germany. Robert de Vaugondy wrote the article on "Geography" in the *Encyclopedia*, declaring that the eighteenth century "must be regarded as the epoch of a general renewal of Geography in France; and, so to say, in all the other lands of Europe, to which it seems that this kingdom has given the key." (From the Harvard Map Collection, Harvard University.)

"Voyage of a Dane," dated 1744; the map of a personal voyage, showing the conventional traveler's Europe; the route ends at Vienna, and southeastern Europe appears unmapped, but illustrated with a scene of mountains and tents; the Dane travels from north to south, but the prominent directional finger points from east to west across the map. (From the Harvard Map Collection, Harvard University.)

and Greek prince, its Orthodox church subordinate to the patriarch in Constantinople, and its Catholic minority under the protection of Poland. Nevertheless, Boscovich found in his lodgings some reason to believe that in Moldavia he was coming a little closer to civilization. The travelers spent a night in a monastery on the way to Jassy, and though it seemed "poor in comparison to the buildings of the cultivated lands of Europe," it was "magnificent after the houses, or rather huts, of the villages of Bulgaria."[91] Boscovich believed that the uncultivated lands of Europe could be ordered on a scale that measured the relative absence of cultivation.

His Slavic background helped Boscovich to make those measurements, and at the Danube he made etymological observations that leaped over Moldavia to link Bulgaria with Poland. Learning that an Ottoman governor in Bulgaria was titled Ali-Aga Voivoda, he explained that "Voivoda is a Slavic word," and "in Poland the palatines call themselves Voivoda." On a little island in the Danube he found a village called Mocrova, and observed that "*mocro* in the Slavic language signifies *wet*." In Moldavia he noted the use of the Slavic word *miasto*, meaning town, "by which name cities are called there, and also in Poland." The town in question was Birlat, which Boscovich thought really no more than a village, but he reaffirmed his sense of a Polish connection by noting the presence of Jews: "they go around dressed as in Poland with certain long black habits." He also learned that the town had been ransacked and wrecked by Tartars a few years before.[92] Thus an ear for the Slavic word helped him sort out his impressions and create a sense of continuity in travel as he passed from Bulgaria through Moldavia to Poland.

Moldavia appeared "extremely beautiful" to Boscovich, but abandoned and uncultivated, "like a desert." Once the travelers saw a mounted man in the distance, but he fled at the sight of them, for fear that their Ottoman escort would appropriate his horse (which was exactly what would have happened). Boscovich learned that the Greek Phanariot princes of Moldavia paid for the post in Constantinople, and tried to make back the expenditure "by whatever way, stealing, extorting, despoiling" their subjects. He was sufficiently a man of the Enlightenment to exclaim against "an atrocious despotism" in an "oppressed land." However, he could not help being flattered when the prince, Gregory Calimachi, sent for him personally: "he said to me that he knew me already by reputation, and that he had much pleasure in hearing that I would be passing through Jassy." The prince honored his visiting celebrity by offering him coffee and sweets. "I was truly surprised," wrote Boscovich, "not expecting on any account such finesse in such a land," not supposing that a "man of letters" like himself would get a "distinguished reception in a land of ignorance and barbarism."[93] This was obviously a pleasant surprise, suggesting that Moldavia was linked to the Republic of Letters and recognized its leading lights.

This condition of second-class subscription to civilization was even more evident in Poland, as Boscovich experienced it. He was an honored guest in the Polish Ukraine of Stanisław Poniatowski, whose estates lay just across the Dniester from Ottoman Moldavia. His son Stanisław August was to be the next king of Poland, but Boscovich paid tribute to the father, "whose great genius is well known to all Europe." The source of that reputation was Voltaire's *Charles XII*, that bible of renown in matters of Eastern Europe, which described Poniatowski's military and diplomatic service to the Swedish king at the beginning of the century. Now Boscovich admired Poniatowski's model town of Zaleszczyk, staying in an unfinished palace in "an optimal apartment furnished according to the usage of the cultivated lands of Europe, where we entered and breathed freely again, after such a long stretch of uncultivated barbarism." Ottoman Europe was "uncultivated," but Poland was still not one of "the cultivated lands of Europe." Boscovich noted the presence of German colonists "to stimulate many arts and manufactures that are incredibly neglected in all of Poland." Clearly, Zaleszczyk represented to Boscovich only the possibility of development in Poland, and this possibility, even more than the clear-cut conviction of barbarism, was crucial to the idea of Eastern Europe in the eighteenth century. Still, when Boscovich reported that at dinner at the palace he found "all that there was of cultivated persons in the land," it was evident that he was not impressed.[94]

After the first fall on rough stairs in Bulgaria, Boscovich had limped across Eastern Europe, and by the time he reached Poland he was increasingly concerned: "My leg, getting worse and worse, had begun to form some black matter on the wound, which gave some suspicion of gangrene." Then in Zaleszczyk the absentminded professor fell in "a sort of big well," which played some part in the town's model manufactures. This caused a contusion of the thigh, on top of his old wound, and made it almost impossible to walk. He was rushed to the Jesuit college at Kamieniec, where he expected to find suitable medical treatment among his brothers.

My own, of whom I had known one in Rome, treated me with all possible attentions, but as no good doctor was there, being away, nor a good surgeon, I fell, to my great misfortune, into the hands of an extremely ignorant man, who completely ruined me, upsetting me also internally by inflaming all my blood, and causing me violent fevers.[95]

It was thus that Boscovich had to give up on St. Petersburg, and spent some time recuperating in Warsaw. The disappointed expectation of finding a good doctor in Kamieniec was only the conclusion of a voyage in which his own personal complaint, in addition to the constant rumors of plague, had made Eastern Europe appear as a domain of disease and disaster, medically unmitigated. "Yet there too," wrote Boscovich in Bulgaria, attempting to remain philosophical, "the sick may recover, and they may die, and one arrives at any age, like elsewhere."[96]

The last word on illness in Eastern Europe belonged to Mrs. Porter, who left poor gangrenous Boscovich "with indifference" at Zaleszczyk (in her account, "Salichick"), and went on from the Poniatowski estates to tour those of the Czartoryski family.

> Generally, when I alighted from the carriage, I found the hall of entrance filled with minor nobles, dependants, or vassals of the Prince—those well-dressed in the becoming Polish costume. As they advanced towards me, they bent on one knee, drawing my garment to their lips or foreheads, kissed it, and offered wishes for my prosperity. Among them, I occasionally discovered some with the plica, a complaint of the country. One symptom, I believe, is blood oozing from the root of the hair.[97]

The scene represented a powerful vision of Western Europe in relation to Eastern Europe. The Dutch woman stood, while Poles knelt to kiss the hem of her garment, an expression of courtesy that was easy to imagine as subordination. While they knelt before her, she took the opportunity to study their hair for the stigmatic symptoms of the plica polonica, which identified them as Poles more intimately than their "becoming Polish costume," and allowed her to diagnose their backwardness from the medical evidence; it was marked in blood. This was the gaze of Western Europe at its most penetrating and potent, the convergence of civilization and the clinic. Eventually Mrs. Porter came home to Holland: "I thought myself in Paradise, so happy was I to find myself in Holland—the cleanliness of everything around delighted me, and I was the more struck with this for having gone through so many months in a state of perfect contrast."[98]

Boscovich in Warsaw was a guest of the younger Poniatowski, the future king, and took a sufficient interest in Polish affairs to write an *Essai politique sur la Pologne*, published in Paris in 1764, the year of the royal election in Poland. By then Boscovich was back in Rome, publishing also in that year an engineering treatise on the draining of the Pontine Marshes. In that same year he moved to Milan, to found and direct a new astronomical observatory with the most modern instruments. Jealous academic colleagues intrigued against him and, with insinuations of excessive expenditure, forced him to resign in 1773. It was an unhappy year for Boscovich, for it also brought the papal suppression of the Jesuits, depriving him of his ecclesiastical order and identity, leaving him, in his own words, "almost an orphan."[99] He spent a decade in Paris, doing scientific work for the French navy, publishing the French translation of his poem (*Les Eclipses*) with a dedication to his new patron Louis XVI. He returned to Italy in 1782 to oversee the publication of his collected works, including the *Journal of a Voyage from Constantinople into Poland* in 1784.

That description of southeastern Europe represented a significant scientific advance over contemporary conceptions in the middle of the century. The Hass map of 1743, still reprinted in 1777, showed Bulgaria and Moldavia, as well as Wallachia and Serbia, all as components of a huge "Hungaria." A traveler's personal map of 1744, "The Voyage of a Dane," showed a European itinerary that went no further east than Vienna, while the unmapped southeastern corner was decorated with pictures of mountains and tents.[100] The account of Boscovich, with its emphases on linguistic and religious patterns of ethnicity, pointed toward a more sophisticated map of Eastern Europe.

It is possible that Boscovich himself was not unaffected by his sojourn. In 1768 in Milan he wrote with Slavic self-consciousness to the Habsburg governor of Lombardy to protest the misspelling (*stroppiatura*) of his name as "Boscovik" in the catalogue of the University of Pavia. As for an interest in peculiar peoples, in 1785 he wrote of the possibility of life on other planets:

The immense space between us and the stars is more inhabited than one might have believed. God knows how many things—and of what species, maybe also of a genus of moles without need of light—there are in those spaces immense to us, who esteem them so from our own immense littleness, but extremely capacious for so many beings of our size, and much greater than us.[101]

If the *Atlas Universel* envisioned Ottoman Europe as a dark land without the "lights" of enlightened geography, then its people were also "a genus of moles." By 1785 Boscovich was already suffering from mental disturbances, ranging from melancholy to obsessions, deliriums, and attempted suicide. He died in 1787. His name became part of his monument, as geographer and astronomer, assigned to name not a village in Bulgaria but rather a crater on the moon.

"In Asia and in Europe"

Boscovich himself recognized that his was but "a brief account" of a limited itinerary, and invoked the importance of achieving "a more complete work and more universally advantageous." This eighteenth-century impulse toward complete knowledge found its most celebrated expression in the Encyclopedia of Diderot and d'Alembert, of which the concluding volumes were being readied for publication at the same time that Boscovich was traveling through Eastern Europe. The premise of the Encyclopedia was that now, in the eighteenth century, the knowledge of all subjects from A to Z could be reformulated in the light of reason. The lands of Eastern Europe, generally stipulated as geographical subjects, were scattered alphabetically throughout the seventeen volumes of text, but, taken together, those articles constituted the state of enlightened knowledge about Eastern Europe in the middle of the century.

The first volume, which appeared in 1751, included among its A-subjects the "Agnus Scythicus," that Scythian lamb, part animal, part vegetable, one of the natural wonders of Russia, which the Encyclopedia critically considered and exploited as a vehicle for mocking the miracles of religion.[102] The lands of Eastern Europe themselves received extremely brief treatments in the second volume of 1752: two B subjects, Bohemia and Bulgaria. Each term was followed by a parenthetical abbreviation to specify the nature of the subject, in this case geography: "BOHEME, (Géog.) royaume de l'Europe," a kingdom of Europe. A short paragraph then named Prague as the capital, recognized the fertility of the soil, the wealth of the mines, and the success of glass manufactures. The conclusion summed up politics, character, and ethnicity: "This kingdom belongs to the house of Austria. The Bohemians are very industrious; their language is a dialect of Slavic (*l'Esclavon*)."[103] The entry on Bulgaria was just as short, but interesting for the fact that the subject was divided into two entries, both identified as geographical. There was, on the one hand, "BULGARIE, (la grande)," specified as a "province of Asia in Russian Tartary," and, on the other hand, "BULGARIE, (la petite)," which was a "land of Turkey in Europe."[104] By treating Bulgaria strictly as a geographical subject, the Encylopedia located it in Asia as well as Europe, though paradoxically the Asian part was ruled from Europe as part of the Russian empire, and the European part was ruled from the Orient as part of the Ottoman empire. Bulgaria, as a land of Eastern Europe, was geographically between Europe and Asia.

This strategy of geographical location came into its own in the much larger article on Hungary—"vast land in Asia and in Europe"—which appeared in the eighth volume of the Encyclopedia. Volumes VIII through XVII all appeared together in 1765, under the false imprint of a Swiss publisher, in an effort to circumvent and overwhelm the royal decree of 1759 that forbade publication in France. The long articles on Hungary, Poland, Russia, and Tartary, in volumes VIII, XII, XIV, and XV, respectively, possessed some unity of conception from the fact that they all came from the same pen, that of the eternal encyclopedist Louis, chevalier de Jaucourt. Voltaire, looking over the batch of volumes that appeared in 1765, commented that "the chevalier de Jaucourt did three-quarters of it." His part has been more modestly estimated at one-quarter of the entire Encyclopedia, still impressive enough. A Frenchman educated at Geneva, Leyden, and Cambridge, Jaucourt had touched the bases that constituted the enlightened perspective of Western Europe. His special interest in science and medicine did not prevent him from undertaking articles for the Encyclopedia on any and every subject, a willingness that was not unequivocally rewarded with respect by his fellow philosophes. Diderot, who owed him a quarter of the Encyclopedia, remarked, "The chevalier de Jaucourt?—Have no fear that he will get bored of grinding out articles; God made him for that." Grimm wrote in the same spirit: "A great number of articles of every sort, and the most essential, were abandoned to the chevalier de Jaucourt, a man of great zeal and indefatigable labor, but a merciless compiler, who did nothing but collect contributions from the best known books and often the most mediocre."[105] Such a method of compilation guaranteed that his articles would reflect conventional eighteenth-century enlightened opinion, that he was not indulging mere personal prejudice when he located Hungary "in Asia and in Europe."

In fact, this treatment of Hungary was precisely analogous to the Encyclopedia's division of Bulgaria, but developed in greater detail. In both cases, where modern geography showed a land on the map of Europe, albeit in Eastern Europe, the Encyclopedia invoked ancient geography to link that land to an Asian counterpart.

Asiatic Hungary, or great Hungary, was the ancient fatherland of the Huns or Hungarians, who passed into Europe during the decline of the empire: M. Delisle puts it to the east of Bulgaria in Asia. . . . Wallachia was to the south of Hungary; thus these three nations, the Bulgars, the Hungarians, and the Wallachians, were neighbors in Asia, as they are in Europe.[106]

Here the issue of adjacency, by which the neighboring lands of Eastern Europe were associated, was dramatized to suggest a sort of geographical destiny. If Hungary, Bulgaria, and Wallachia were sometimes colored together on the map of Europe, this was not only on account of the recent Oriental association that bound them together under Ottoman rule, but also because of a more distant ancestral connection in Asia itself. Ancient lands of Asia were neatly transposed onto the modern map of Europe, following peoples who "passed into Europe" and reconstituted their past geographical constellations.

Medieval Hungary was treated in terms of its geographical components, establishing further connections among the lands of Eastern Europe.

The Hungarian monarchy comprehended at the beginning of the fourteenth century Hungary proper, Transylvania, Moldavia, Wallachia, Croatia, Bosnia, Dalmatia, and Serbia; but the progress that she made in growth in those times resembled the sea, which sometimes swells and leaves its bed, to return there soon after. The success of Ottoman arms prodigiously diminished this monarchy, and entire provinces were detached, though, by the peace treaty of Passarowitz, the emperor recovered some parts of Wallachia, of Bulgaria, of Serbia, of Bosnia, and of Croatia.[107]

Eastern Europe appeared as a sea where shifting borders moved with the rising and ebbing tides. These were lands that ultimately evaded the competing claims of Europe and the Orient, lands that neither encyclopedist nor geographer could locate with fixed certainty.

Jaucourt could be quite mistaken in fact when he surrendered to conventional associations. "The language of Hungary is a dialect of Slavic," he reported, absolutely incorrectly, "and therefore it has some relation to the languages of Bohemia, Poland, and Russia."[108] Hungarian, of the Finno-Ugric linguistic group, has no relation whatsoever to Czech, Polish, or Russian, and the error testifies to the fallibility of the Encyclopedia, but even more to the irresistibility of the emerging idea of Eastern Europe. One land was enough to conjure up the entire domain. The Hungary of the Encyclopedia was geographically inseparable from Bulgaria and Wallachia, and also linguistically associated with Bohemia, Poland, and Russia.

The connection to Poland was further developed in points about politics and society: "Hungary once governed itself as Poland still does; it elected its kings in its diets." Furthermore, "the nobles had the same privileges as in Poland," especially over the peasants, for "the populace was slave, and still is."[109] Hungary and Poland were linked again in describing the fourteenth-century reign of Louis the Great who ended up ruling over both kingdoms: "His peoples gave him the name of Great, of which he was worthy; however he was almost unknown in Europe; he did not reign over men who knew how to transmit his glory to the nations." This opposition between Hungary and Poland on the one hand, and Europe on the other, rested on the dynamic of known and unknown lands, sustained by the Enlightenment throughout the century. Jaucourt aligned himself with already established enlightened perspectives when he quoted Voltaire on Hungary's inability to exploit its own resources.

In vain, says M. de Voltaire, nature has placed in this land mines of gold and silver, and the true treasures, grains and wines; in vain she has formed there robust men, well made, spiritual! One saw almost nothing more than a vast desert.[110]

It was appropriate that Jaucourt, who probably never *saw* Hungary, should have quoted Voltaire, who also never *saw* Hungary, to the effect that one *saw* nothing but desert. This was the eye of the Enlightenment at its most marvelously penetrating. The mention of wasted resources and untouched treasures might naturally raise the issue of more effective exploitation, and Jaucourt concluded with a gushing tribute to the Habsburg Maria Theresa, "queen of all hearts" and queen of Hungary. The French Encyclopedia, without mentioning the embarrassing name of Rakoczi, observed the spirit of the reversal of alliances of 1756 by welcoming Hungary into the Habsburg empire.[111]

The treatment of Poland in the Encyclopedia began with a short article on "geography," locating a "large kingdom of Europe," and then a long article on "history and government." Jaucourt promised that the "general tableau" of Poland—"the sketch of it which I am going to crayon"—would be "useful" in stimulating political and philosophical reflections, and referred the reader to his own basic source, the *History of Jan Sobieski* by Coyer.[112] This work was controversial because its sympathetic treatment of Poland's republican institutions, based on Leszczyński's manifesto of reform, appeared somewhat subversive in the monarchical France of Louis XV. Jaucourt, however, while drawing heavily on Coyer, and paying tribute to Leszczyński, made rather more critical political reflections. He admired "the grandeur of the spectacle" of the Polish parliamentary diet, which he probably never saw, but naturally disapproved of the veto, which, "if it produces good sometimes, causes still more evil." In general, he concluded, "this kingdom of the north of Europe uses so badly its liberty and the right to elect its kings, that it seems to want to console thereby those neighboring peoples who have lost both of these advantages." Jaucourt was still more scathing on the subject of Polish serfdom, comparing it to slavery in Asia. He conjured up an image of "naked children under the rigors of a frozen climate, pell-mell with the farm animals," and pitied the slave who could never say "my field, my children, my wife." Jaucourt wondered which would destroy Poland first, between "the height of slavery and the excess of liberty." [113]

The Poles, "when they were still Sarmatians," possessed an empire that extended from the Don to the Vistula, and the Black Sea to the Baltic, in sum, all of Eastern Europe, including even Bohemia. This Jaucourt attributed to "the savage instinct" of a "barbarian people." The Poles, however, failed to preserve the "heritage" of their Sarmatian ancestors and were, over the centuries, reduced to contemporary Poland. This idea of Poland as an ever shrinking domain, of Polish history as a process of reduction, suggested the geographical consequences of "history and government," and pointed toward the next generation, when Poland would be eliminated from the map altogether in the partitions. One wonders whether geography and government were treated in separate articles because it was already possible to conceive of Poland as a negative political example without a geographical base. Just as the Poles had lost the empire of the Sarmatians, they had not entirely preserved the ancient barbarian character: "The Poles resemble their Sarmatian ancestors less than the Tartars do theirs." The difference, however, was construed by Jaucourt, in the manner of Rousseau, as a change for the worse: "They have forgotten the simplicity and frugality of the Sarmatians their ancestors." He could not approve of the Poles adopting French fashions to be "mixed with Oriental magnificence." In a separate note on Poland's royal coronations, Jaucourt described them as he supposedly *saw* them: "One sees there Asiatic magnificence mixing with the taste of Europe." [114] It was just these possibilities of combination and confusion, between Europe and the Orient, between barbarism and civilization, that located Poland in Eastern Europe.

In the anticlerical spirit of the Encyclopedia, Poland's tenth-century conversion to Christianity was hardly represented as an alleviation of barbarism. Jaucourt evoked an age of conversion by torture in which those who ate meat during Lent were punished with the extraction of their teeth, and a fornicator was suspended by a nail driven through "the instrument of his crime." If Poland was later more religiously tolerant than elsewhere in Europe, becoming even "the paradise of the Jews," this was an incidental advantage of being more backward: "Poland however was barbarous longer than Spain, France, England, and Germany, which proves that demi-science is stormier than crude ignorance." This enumeration of lands created a contrast between Poland's barbarism and the dubious semi-civilization of Western Europe. Devout Catholicism in Poland offered further evidence of backwardness, inasmuch as "exaggerated devotion to the decrees of Rome," that is, "the blind obedience of the Poles," was attributed to "superstitious fear." [115]

Like Hungary, Poland was reproached for wasting its natural resources: "Nature has put in this state all that is needed to live, grains, honey, wax, fish, game; and all that is needed to become rich, grains, pastures, livestock, wools, leathers, salt mines, metals, minerals; however Europe has no poorer people." This conjunction of rich land and poor people represented a paradoxical failure in the relation between geography and society. Jaucourt expressed the absence of economic development in terms of a meaningless geography, in which lands were worth no more than the maps that rendered them as abstract representations:

The earth and the water, everything there calls for great commerce, and commerce does not show itself. So many streams and beautiful rivers, the Duna, the Bug, the Dniester, the Vistula, the Niemen, the Dnieper, serve only to figure in the geographical maps. It has been remarked for a long time that it would be easy to join by canals the northern ocean and the Black Sea, to join the commerce of the Orient and the Occident; but far from constructing some merchant vessels, Poland, which has been several times insulted by fleets, has not even thought of a little military marine.[116]

The rivers of Poland were no more than lines on the map, useless to the Poles themselves, but exciting to the imagination of geographers in Western Europe, who inevitably envisioned in Eastern Europe a meeting of the Orient and the Occident. Typically disorienting was the prospect of joining east and west by rivers that, fundamentally, flowed to the north or the south. Typically confusing was the elementary error by which the Encyclopedia allowed Poland access to the "northern ocean," when, in fact, Poland's northern coast was on the Baltic Sea. However much one insisted that Poland was a land of the North, it was nevertheless distinctly non-Arctic.

Jaucourt was perhaps confusing Poland and Russia, for it was only Russia that could conceivably connect the Black Sea to the Arctic Ocean, and the building of canals in Russia was also of interest to observers in Western Europe during the eighteenth century. Coxe's *Travels in Russia* included a "Plan of the Canal of Vishnei Voloshok which unites the Baltic and the Caspian," and also a "Plan of the Ladoga Canal," in progress, to connect the Arctic White Sea to the Baltic.[117] There was another long-standing project for a canal to link the rivers Don and Volga, ultimately envisioning connections from the Black Sea and the Caspian Sea to the Baltic. The Don-Volga project had been entrusted by Peter to John Perry, an English engineer. Throughout the century, such canal schemes for both Poland and Russia gave commercial meaning to the idea of Eastern Europe, mapping its emphatically eastern domain in terms of inland waterways, from the seas of the North to the seas of the South.

"This state, larger than France, counts only five million inhabitants," reported the Encyclopedia of Poland, but enlightened demography, like enlightened geography, could also be erroneous. In fact, the population was more like twelve million. The Encyclopedia insisted on a comprehensive picture of uncultivated resources and an undeveloped economy, the better to cultivate the idea of cultivation, to develop the idea of development. Jaucourt enumerated the negative cultural features of Poland: "It has no school of painting, no theatre; Architecture is in its infancy; History is treated there without taste; Mathematics little cultivated; sound Philosophy almost unknown." There remained, however, the hope of development according to foreign models: "Time matures everything; perhaps one day Poland will achieve that which has been perfected in other climates." Notions of immaturity and imperfection helped define the underdevelopment of Eastern Europe relative to Western Europe. Jaucourt left Hungary to Maria Theresa, and he concluded his article on Poland with the call for "a great king." He cited Coyer on the kind of king Poland needed: someone "who seeing around him fecund earth, beautiful rivers, the Baltic Sea and the Black Sea, would give vessels, manufactures, commerce, finances, and men to this kingdom," someone who, abolishing servitude, might bring to Poland "emulation, industry, arts, sciences, honor, and prosperity."[118] Such a king would act upon a vision of Poland's geographical situation and undertake a course of development that proceeded from the facts of geography to the facets of civilization.

"The Flesh of the Horse and the Milk of the Mare"

The article on Russia in volume XIV of the Encyclopedia was specified as a subject in "modern geography," and began by locating Russia on two continents: "vast land that forms a great empire, as much in Europe as in Asia." In spite of this suggestion of clear division, Jaucourt went on to suggest that Russia as a whole was both European and Asiatic, and in spite of the stipulation of "modern" geography, he almost immediately raised the subject of the ancient Slavs. Referring to the description of Russia in Voltaire's recently published first volume on Peter, Jaucourt quickly surveyed the provinces and identified Novgorod as the oldest establishment of the ancient Slavs. "But where did they come from, these Slavs," he wondered, plagiarizing Voltaire, "whose language spread in the northeast of Europe?" [119] Jaucourt and Voltaire did not know the answer, but it was significant that they located the contemporary Slavs "in the northeast of Europe," a step away from the conventional category of "the North," a step toward the modern idea of Eastern Europe.

An eastern emphasis was further evident in Jaucourt's explanation of Peter's importance, again closely following Voltaire: "Before the tsar Peter, the usages, clothing, and manners in Russia always had more of a resemblance to Asia than to Christian Europe." Jaucourt found a past resemblance in government between Russia and Turkey, comparing streltsi and janissaries, and thought the title of the tsars probably "derived rather from the shahs of Persia than from the caesars of Rome." [120] As for commerce, "the Russian nation is the only one that traffics by land with China," and, in the matter of public baths, "the usage is as frequent among the Russians as the Turks." It was Peter, however, who tilted Russia toward Europe:

Under the reign of Peter, the Russian people who valued Europe ("qui tient à l'Europe"), and who lived in the large cities, became civilized, commercial, curious about the arts and sciences, fond of spectacles and ingenious novelties. The great man who caused these changes was fortunately born in a time favorable to produce them. He introduced into his estates the arts that were completely perfected among his neighbors; and it came about that these arts made more progress in 50 years among his subjects, already disposed to taste them, than anywhere else in the space of three or four centuries; however they have not yet sunk such profound roots, that some interval of barbarism might not be able to ruin this beautiful edifice, undertaken in an empire depopulated and despotic, where nature never spreads its benign influences. [121]

In Russia becoming civilized meant choosing Europe, declaring an allegiance, not just on Peter's part, but also on the part of the Russian people. The arts and sciences of civilization awaited them, perfected by their neighbors. Eastern Europe, with such neighbors on the one hand, but with so many Asian influences and resemblances on the other, could either choose to advance toward civilization or risk relapsing into barbarism.

The most overwhelming eastern vector of influence upon Russia, viewed unequivocally as a force of barbarism, was that of Tartary and the Tartars. China, Persia, and Turkey could be recognized in the age of Enlightenment as possessing their own Oriental civilizations, but the Tartars received no such concession. If Russia belonged to the Tartar empire in the age of Batu Khan, Tartary belonged to the Russian empire in the age of Peter, but the relation, even reversed, still weighed in the balance between Europe and Asia, civilization and barbarism. Jaucourt's article on the persistent barbarism of the Tartars in volume XV was the necessary complement to his article on the developing civilization of the Russians in volume XIV. In this case the people took precedence over the land, with a long article on Tartars and a short note on Tartary, both construed as subjects in modern geography. Tartary was divided into three parts, based on political affiliation: Chinese, Russian, and independent. Subordinate notes identified Crimean Tartary and Little Tartary, which were sometimes used as interchangeable terms to cover the Crimean peninsula and the lands just north of the Black Sea, to be distinguished from Great Tartary, which, like the shadowy ancient realms of Great Bulgaria and Great Hungary, was located in Asia.[122]

Great Tartary could still be found on the map at the end of the seventeenth century. In Sanson's *New Introduction to Geography* of 1695, the world map showed "Moscovie" as a distinct entity, in between "Europe" to the west and "Grande Tartarie" to the east. "Petite Tartarie," however, appeared on the map of Europe, as part of "Turquie en Europe."[123] A map of Europe by Guillaume Delisle, published in Paris in 1700, already preferred to distinguish simply between "Moscovie Europe" and "Moscovie Asiatique," establishing a perfect parallel to "Turquie Europe" and "Turquie Asiatique." A Dutch map of Europe in 1712, by Zürner, inscribed on the border of the continent the name of Siberia, which, over the course of the century, tended to displace Great Tartary on the map of northern Asia.[124] In Stockholm in 1730 Strahlenberg's *North and Eastern Parts of Europe and Asia* promised a more particular description of "Russia, Siberia and Great Tartary." In Paris in 1768 Siberia was a special subject in its own right when the abbé Jean Chappe d'Auteroche published his *Voyage into Siberia*. If "Great Tartary" was becoming a less important geographical concept in the eighteenth century, "Little Tartary" or "Tartary Minor," including the Crimea, retained a place on not just any map, but on the map of Europe. Though under the formal sovereignty of Constantinople, it was often colored independently, as on the Zürner map of 1712. Eventually, just as Great Tartary would be passed on to modern geography as Siberia, Little Tartary would become the Crimea.

When Jaucourt was writing for the Encyclopedia, the geographical notion of Tartary was already far less interesting to him than the ethnographic idea of the Tartars. He summed them up as "peoples who inhabit almost all of the north of Asia," neglecting for the moment their presence in the south of Europe. He then proceeded to a riotously Linnaean subdivision of the Tartars into fifteen principal nations, which he discussed alphabetically. The Barabinskoi Tartars, for instance, were consigned to Great Tartary, but the Budziack Tartars were obviously residents of Europe, living on the west coast of the Black Sea, near the mouth of the Danube. The Kalmucks had "no fixed habitation, but only tents of felt, with which they camp and decamp in an instant," ranging from Mongolia to the Volga.[125]

The Tartars of the Crimea, according to Jaucourt, resembled the Kalmucks, "yet without being so ugly." They were small and square, with "a burnt complexion (*teint brûlé*), the half-open eyes of a pig (*yeux de porc*), the turn of the flat face, a quite small mouth, teeth white as ivory, and very little beard." It was an attempt at a racial characterization, and not a flattering one. To complete this alien image of the Crimean Tartars it remained only to report that "the flesh of the horse and the milk of the mare are their delicacies."[126] When Robert de Vaugondy published his roughly contemporary *New Portable Atlas* in Paris in 1762, one map, by skin color, showed that all of Europe was white, while another, by face type, showed that the inhabitants of Little Tartary, with "flat faces and oval eyes," were racially different from other Europeans.[127] Jaucourt, who borrowed freely from Buffon's *Natural History* on the "Varieties in the Human Species," was consistent with the conventions of the Enlightenment in using racial characteristics to suggest that the Crimean Tartars, though living in Europe, were an alien people of Asia.

The Circassian Tartars lived on the Caspian Sea around the mouth of the Volga, and it went unmentioned that they were therefore also arguably residents of Europe. They could be recognized as Tartars by "language, customs, inclinations, and even the exterior." Regarding that exterior, they were "quite ugly," though it was conceded that their women were very beautiful—as Ségur would one day discover. The men were also marked by circumcision, "and observe some other Moslem ceremonies." The Tartars of Daghestan lived around the Caspian and were given the distinction of being "the ugliest of all the Moslem Tartars." Their skin was "very burnt" (*fort basané*). The Mongol Tartars "occupy the most considerable part of Great Tartary," living east of the Kalmucks and extending all the way to the "Oriental Sea." The Nogai Tartars, who lived on the Volga and the Caspian, resembled the Tartars of Daghestan, "except, in an increase of deformity, they have a wrinkled face like an old woman." The Uzbek Tartars, alphabetically last in the survey, were located in Great Bukhara, "a vast province of Great Tartary."[128]

Commenting on the Tartars historically, in comparison with other barbarians, Jaucourt observed that while the Goths, who conquered the Roman empire, brought monarchy and liberty, the Tartars, wherever they conquered, brought only servitude and despotism. Nevertheless, the immensity of their conquests "confounds our imagination." It was "humiliating for human nature that these barbaric peoples should have subjugated almost all of our hemisphere," that "this people so nasty of face (*vilain*

de figure)" should have been "the ruler of the universe." Jaucourt was referring to the age of Genghis Khan, at whose court "one saw a mélange
of Tartar barbarism and Asiatic luxury" as well as "those ancient Scythian
chariots whose use still subsists even among the Tartars of the Crimea." If
the Tartars were confounding to Western Europe, a mélange of barbarism,
as Jaucourt "saw" it, he could sort them into an alphabetical classification,
Bashkirs to Uzbeks, related to each other by language, customs, inclinations, and (nasty) exteriors. That so many of these peoples lived in Europe,
that is, Eastern Europe, was a dilemma difficult to countenance. "This vast
reservoir of ignorant, strong, and bellicose men vomited its inundations
in almost all of our hemisphere," wrote Jaucourt. He reassured his readers
that today the Tartars were still fighting with bows and arrows, that civilization was safe: "The great emigrations of such peoples are no longer to
be feared; the polished nations are sheltered from the irruptions of these
barbarous nations." [129] In fact, however, it was not simply an issue of emigrations, inundations, and irruptions from without; for the Tartars were
also within Europe, along the Black Sea and the Caspian Sea, at the mouth
of the Danube, at the mouth of the Volga. In 1944 Stalin deported 250,000
Crimean Tartars, all of them, to Siberia and Central Asia; today they are
finally returning home, to the Crimea, to Europe.

It was Jaucourt who wrote the short article on the continent of Europe
for the Encyclopedia, published in volume VI, before he wrote up Hungary, Poland, Russia, or Tartary. The eastern border of the continent was
not geographically defined. Europe, though "the smallest of the four parts
of the world," was the most important "for its commerce, for its navigation, for its fertility, for the enlightenment and industry of its peoples,
for the knowledge of the Arts, the Sciences, the Professions, and, what is
most important, for Christianity." [130] In later entries Jaucourt wrote about
lands and peoples in Europe that appeared to him less impressive on these
counts, his criteria of civilization, so for those lands the enumerated graces
of Europe became a program for development instead of a declaration of
self-congratulation. Though Jaucourt was assigned all of these geographical subjects, which inevitably expanded the Europe of the Encyclopedia,
he was not the author of the article on Geography in volume VII. That was
written by Robert de Vaugondy, co-author with his father of the *Atlas Universel*, member of Stanisław Leszczyński's Academy at Nancy. The article
mentioned Boscovich and the scientific mapping of the papal states. It
mentioned Peter the Great, who brought "the Sciences" to Russia, including cartography; it mentioned Joseph Delisle, who came to Russia to work
on the atlas. "The beginning of our century," declared Robert, fully in
the spirit of the whole Encyclopedia, "must be regarded as the epoch of
a general renewal of Geography in France; and, so to say, in all the other
lands of Europe, to which it seems that this kingdom has given the key." [131]

Geography was one of the disciplines of mastery in the eighteenth century, ordering the relation of France and the other lands of Europe, of Europe and the other lands of the world. From atlas to encyclopedia, geography was essential to locating the lands of Eastern Europe, and mapping them on the mind of the Enlightenment.

Chapter Five

Addressing Eastern Europe, Part I: Voltaire's Russia

"The Great Gallop to Adrianople"

"Your majesty is obliged to direct armies," wrote Voltaire to Catherine in 1770, "in Wallachia, in Poland, in Bessarabia, in Georgia; and she still finds time to write to me." Yet the letters that passed between them in wartime were not exceptions to the rule of their correspondence, for, on the contrary, it was precisely in the years of Catherine's first long war against Turkey and Poland, from 1768 to 1774, that this extraordinary correspondence reached its highest pitch, an intensity of epistolary exchange that was never matched in time of peace. Catherine's ambitious Russian foreign policy of domination and conquest, in both Poland and Turkey, simultaneously, combined the northeastern and southeastern quadrants of Europe into one coherent domain of Eastern Europe, evident on the military maps of generals and statesmen, and in the mental maps of an enlightened public. Voltaire's letters in wartime offered Catherine the philosophical reflection of her military campaigns, in which Wallachia, Poland, Bessarabia, and Georgia were associated as building blocks of a reconceived European geography. "The spirit of M. d'Alembert and mine," wrote Voltaire to Catherine, still in 1770, evoking thus a collective mentality of the Enlightenment, "fly to the Dardanelles, to the Danube, to the Black Sea, to

Bender, into the Crimea, and especially to St. Petersburg."[1] This mental mapping of Eastern Europe was a work of the imagination, stimulated and enhanced by the epistolary form, which allowed him to stay at home at Ferney in Switzerland, while his words took wing and traversed Europe to arrive at St. Petersburg. As military movements mapped out the coherent domain of Eastern Europe from St. Petersburg to the Dardanelles, postal routes established both the geographical remoteness and intellectual accessibility of that domain, coded as the address of a letter posted eastward. When the "The Posts of Europe" were mapped in 1758, Russia was still excluded, and the route from Vienna appeared to end somewhere east of Warsaw.[2] By 1770 Voltaire could easily correspond with Catherine, but this postal connection, like any other, linked the correspondents while at the same time emphasizing the distance that separated their respective addresses.

This was not the first time that Voltaire traveled vicariously to Eastern Europe, for he had been there before with Charles XII, who camped, in fact, at Bender, when he was a guest among the Tartars. Voltaire's letters to Catherine acquired an extra intensity from the old philosopher's déjà vu, as he rediscovered the traces and places he had first explored when he wrote about Charles 40 years earlier. While Voltaire's *Charles XII* had obliged the historian to hide behind his hero, the better to assume an air of authenticity in the narrative account of lands and peoples, the epistolary form of the private letter gave free rein to the writer's geographical imagination. Both Voltaire and Catherine gave some publicity to their private correspondence, and after Voltaire's death in 1778, some of the letters were prepared for publication by Beaumarchais, entering into the public construction of Eastern Europe by the Enlightenment.

Those critics, ever since the eighteenth century, who have wondered disapprovingly why Voltaire chose to write the history of a conqueror like Charles have missed the significance of Voltaire's vicarious discovery of the lands and peoples of Eastern Europe. Voltaire's enthusiastic acclamation of Catherine's armies has given even more cause for critical disapproval, and hidden the significance of the epistolary excitement he experienced in returning with another conqueror to that same domain. "It's enough," he exulted, though in truth it was not enough for him, "that in so little time you should be absolute mistress of Moldavia, of Wallachia, of almost all of Bessarabia, of the two shores of the Black Sea, on one side toward Azov, on the other toward the Caucasus." Catherine read his letters and responded in 1771 to his geographical consciousness and enumeration of names.

Isn't it true that here are plenty of materials to correct and augment the geographical maps? In this war, one has heard named places which one never heard mentioned previously, and which the geographers said were deserts.[3]

Thus she articulated the intimate relation between geopolitical conquest and geographical knowledge of Eastern Europe in the eighteenth century. Voltaire's response assumed the same connection; since Catherine's armies had just entered the Crimea, he looked forward to a map of that land. "One has never had passable ones till now," he observed, and denounced the Turks for their geographical ignorance: "You possess a beautiful land, but you do not know it. My empress will cause you to know it."[4]

The geographical significance of this war, however, was not just in the attention it focused on individual places and names, but above all in their association and combination. The Russian war against Turkey and Poland, between 1768 and 1774, put almost all of Eastern Europe on the same military map, conceived as one vast war zone. Catherine would fight against Turkey and Poland again, toward the end of her reign, from 1787 to 1795, concluding with the final partition of Poland, and reinforcing the geopolitical and geographical messages of the earlier period. As the indisputable eminence of the Enlightenment, Voltaire in his letters formulated an idea of Eastern Europe to cover the ground of Catherine's campaigns. "I expect very humbly of destiny and of your genius," he wrote in 1773, "the unscrambling (*débrouillement*) of all this chaos in which the earth is plunged, from Danzig to the mouth of the Danube," the triumph of "light" (*lumière*) over "darkness" (*ténèbres*).[5] Voltaire made the mastery of Eastern Europe a point of the program of the Enlightenment, the unscrambling of lands that were scrambled just because he said they were. By the same intellectual authority, Eastern Europe was proclaimed a part of the earth plunged in chaos and darkness. What was truly original here, however, and perhaps inconceivable before this war, was the mental association of rivers that linked Gdańsk, at the mouth of the Vistula on the Baltic, to the mouth of the Danube on the Black Sea.

In the correspondence Voltaire pursued enlightened ideas about power and empire, celebrating Catherine as the "absolute mistress" of little known lands, and his formula for absolutism in Eastern Europe combined aspects of political theory and personal fantasy. Rousseau, writing about Poland, gave celebrated expression to a complementary discourse which, in defiance of Catherine and Voltaire, envisioned the liberation of Eastern Europe on the basis of national identity. Yet this too was prescribed by the Enlightenment from Western Europe, and, significantly, Rousseau gave his prescription the narrative form of an open letter to the Poles. The letter to Eastern Europe allowed the philosopher, Voltaire or Rousseau, to participate personally in a voyage of political discovery into unknown lands. "It seems to me that it is I who have passed the Danube," wrote Voltaire in 1773. "I mount the horse in my dreams, and I go the great gallop to Adrianople."[6]

"I Am Older than Your Empire"

Catherine wrote first to Voltaire in 1763, to thank him for the second volume of his *Peter the Great*. The completion of that work, taken together with the conclusion of the Seven Years' War in that year, marked the end of the first phase in the Enlightenment's discovery of Eastern Europe, and the opening of a new phase of even more dynamic interest, in international affairs and in cultural construction, focused above all on the fascinating figure of Catherine herself. She was a German princess who had come to Russia in 1744, at the age of fourteen, to marry the heir to the empire, grandson of Peter the Great. He succeeded Elizabeth in 1762 as Peter III, and was promptly displaced by Catherine in a completely effective coup; the deposed tsar was conveniently killed. So when Catherine wrote to Voltaire in the following year, she was 34 years old, tsarina for just a year, and still consolidating her political position at home and abroad. Voltaire, she knew, had been a figure of some significance in the previous reign, composing his history of Peter for Elizabeth, Peter's daughter, receiving materials in correspondence with Elizabeth's favorite, Ivan Shuvalov. Catherine thanked Voltaire for the volume on Peter in a phrase of perfunctory tribute, which may have been intended to apply to the author as well as the subject: "It is true that one can not be astounded enough at the genius of this great man."[7]

Catherine's letter of 1763 sought to establish a personal connection between herself and Voltaire. She had heard that Voltaire spoke flatteringly of her; in fact, he was a famous flatterer of crowned heads, and hers would soon be heaped higher than any other. Now she modestly warned him against praising her before she had shown herself worthy, after only a year on the throne, lest premature congratulation compromise the "reputation" of them both. She could not have more accurately identified in a word the currency of their future relationship, which was above all an association of two tremendous reputations, deployed at the highest levels of culture, politics, and international relations. His reputation was even grander than hers in 1763, for though she had staged one spectacular political coup, he had reigned over the Enlightenment in Europe for a whole generation. The year 1746, she wrote, was a turning point in her intellectual development, the year that, "by chance, your works fell into my hands," and "since then, I have not ceased to read them." She would wish to read other books equally good: "but where to find them?"[8]

Catherine, looking back in 1763, assigned a precise date to her discovery of Voltaire, one closely correlated to her arrival in Russia and her assumption of a Russian identity. She came in 1744, and that same year she underwent ceremonial conversion to Russian Orthodoxy, shedding even her name, Sophia, to become Catherine then and forever after. The next year, in

1745, she consummated this new Russian identity with her probably uncon-summated marriage. Then in 1746 she discovered Voltaire, and undercut her Russian persona by taking the part of a private subscriber to the French Enlightenment—or so she represented herself and her allegiances in 1763. The year 1746 was also significant for Voltaire and his relation to Russia, the year that he was elected to the Academy of Sciences in St. Petersburg as a foreign associate. The academy, however, was generally grudging about the assignment of Peter's life to Voltaire, and such academic pillars as the German Gerhard Müller and the Russian Mikhail Lomonosov were full of criticism of the resulting manuscript.[9] When Catherine's letter focused the memory of Voltaire on the year 1746, she reminded him that he too could be said to have come to Russia, as a foreigner, soon after she came herself. As grand duchess she faced personal and political frustrations at court, while as foreign associate he experienced intellectual tensions with the academy. The coup of 1762 brought Catherine political power, in defiance of dynastic legitimacy, while her correspondence with Voltaire, from 1763, worked over the heads of the academy to bring about his philosophical triumph in Russia as counselor and confidant of the tsarina.

In that first letter of 1763, Catherine did mention Rousseau, dismissively, to emphasize her allegiance to Voltaire. The year of Catherine's political coup in 1762 was also the year of Rousseau's intellectual coup, with the publication of both the *Social Contract* and *Emile*, announcing the arrival of a new generation of the Enlightenment with philosophical trumpets that even old Voltaire could not fail to hear as a challenge. Among the many radically original points of Rousseau, the *Social Contract* took issue with Voltaire on the subject of Russia.

Peter the Great had the talent of a copyist; he had no true genius, which is creative and makes everything from nothing. Some of the things he did were sound; most were misguided. He saw that his people was uncivilized, but he did not see that it was unready for government; he sought to civilize his subjects when he ought rather to have drilled them. He tried to turn them into Germans or Englishmen instead of making them Russians. He urged his subjects to be what they were not and so prevented them from becoming what they might have been. This is just how a French tutor trains his pupil to shine for a brief moment in his childhood and then grow up into a nonentity. The Russian empire would like to subjugate Europe and will find itself subjugated. The Tartars, its subjects or neighbors, will become its masters—and ours.[10]

Rousseau's view of Russia (which he never visited) was in certain respects consistent with the vision of Eastern Europe in Voltaire's *Charles XII*: uncivilized, undisciplined peoples, fundamentally different from the French, the English, and the Germans.

Voltaire's first volume on Peter in 1759 had declared its subject, in a spirit of shameless self-advertisement, "perhaps of all princes the one whose deeds most merit being transmitted to posterity." Voltaire pronounced almost biblically on the tsar's creative achievement: "Peter was born, and Russia was formed."[11] Rousseau obviously intended a challenge when he slipped into the *Social Contract* those derogatory remarks on Peter, denying him "any true genius," just as Voltaire's second volume was about to appear. When Catherine paid tribute to Peter's genius ("one cannot be astounded enough"), she allied herself with Voltaire against Rousseau, and promised that she would give the lie to Rousseau's "prophecy." That prophecy was the triumph of the Tartars, and philosophical feuding certainly conditioned Voltaire's epistolary enthusiasm for Catherine's wars, when she fought against the Poles, the Turks, and the Tartars after 1768. Inevitably, in the course of those campaigns, Rousseau became the champion of Poland. In 1783 Catherine annexed the Crimea, and in 1772, 1793, and 1795 she had her shares in the partitions of Poland. If, however, the tsarina was triumphant on the map, the competing visions of the two philosophers, Voltaire and Rousseau, both survived as the influential ideological poles that jointly defined the modern political conception of Eastern Europe.

On Voltaire's side the extant correspondence does not pick up until 1765, when he dedicated to Catherine his *Philosophy of History*, written in the pseudonymous persona of the "abbé Bazin," supposedly "edited" by the nephew of that alarmingly anticlerical cleric. The book of the abbé Bazin had not yet been burned in France, reported Voltaire to Catherine; in fact, "people believe that he wrote it in your estates, for truth comes from the north."[12] No one held more tenaciously to the rubric of "the north" than Voltaire, who himself emptied the concept of its significance in discovering Eastern Europe. He subtly negotiated the distance between Eastern Europe and Western Europe, with the invention of an alias, Bazin, who supposedly wrote in Catherine's estates, while Voltaire himself remained on his own estate at Ferney. Interestingly, in 1758 Voltaire had initially considered settling in Lorraine, as a subject of Leszczyński, titular king of Poland.[13] This illusionary establishment of Voltaire in Eastern Europe did not come to pass, and he found his quasi-extraterritorial refuge instead at Ferney, on the border between France and Switzerland, offering escape from enemies of the Enlightenment on either side.

"The nephew of Bazin told me," wrote Voltaire to Catherine, "that he had been very attached to Madame the Princess of Zerbst, mother of Your Majesty, and he said she was also very beautiful and full of spirit." In fact, Voltaire had met Catherine's mother, though the "attachment" of "the nephew" was certainly a polite exaggeration of whatever Voltaire himself may have felt upon that acquaintance. Indeed, the tribute to beauty and spirit, taken together with the suggestive condition of "very attached," even hinted at a romance between Voltaire's invented persona and Catherine's mother, which might make Catherine a sort of fictional child of the French Enlightenment. She seemed to pick up on this in her reply: "The attachment of the nephew Bazin to my late mother gives him a new degree of consideration with me (*chez moi*)." Did she mean to suggest that the nephew Bazin was in Russia with her after all? In Voltaire's next letter, he had Catherine with him at Ferney, or at least a medallion that "represented" her: "Most precious for me are the medallions that represent you. The features of your majesty recall those of the princess your mother."[14] Epistolary correspondence allowed for playful displacements in time and space, as the letters themselves moved over the map of Europe. Voltaire and Catherine used their letters to explore the possibilities of correspondence between Western Europe and Eastern Europe, and first they invented a relationship of their own, based on her encounter in St. Petersburg with his books, and his encounter in Paris with her mother.

The special significance of Catherine's mother in the correspondence was to emphasize that Catherine herself was a foreigner in Russia. In 1770 Voltaire, after meeting a Russian prince, wrote to Catherine to profess himself "enchanted by the extreme politeness of your subjects." He gave credit to her, and also to her mother: "You have brought (*apporté*) into your empire all the graces of madame the princess your mother, which you have embellished." Voltaire thus insisted that what Catherine brought to Russia, she brought from abroad. "I see always with a lot of pleasure," wrote Catherine in reply, "the memory you have of my mother."[15] It was a memory that served, in the correspondence with Voltaire, as a reminder of her own origin and identity.

Catherine's assumed Russian identity was already an issue in Voltaire's first letters of 1765: "Dare I, madame, say that I am a little angry that you should call yourself Catherine?" For Catherine was a saint's name, and he, for poetical purposes, would have preferred to address her as Juno, Minerva, or Venus. He seemed to subscribe to the conviction of the Enlightenment that any man or woman, from Catherine to Casanova, could come to Russia and improvise an identity as the prerogative of power. Catherine could assume the guise of a goddess, and Voltaire himself assumed an air of mythological venerability when he measured himself with a Russian ruler.

I am older, madame, than the city where you reign, and which you embellish. I even dare to add that I am older than your empire, in dating its new foundation from the creator Peter the Great, whose work you perfect.[16]

If Russia was a realm of creativity, where Catherine might perfect the work of Peter even as she embellished the graces of her mother, Voltaire also exercised and refined his intellectual program in applying its principles to the unfinished forms of Eastern Europe. Voltaire hailed Catherine as a goddess of the Enlightenment in Russia, and then took her as his muse, his inspiration to complete the symphonic trajectory of a lifelong philosophical enterprise. The *History of Charles XII* announced Voltaire's exciting discovery of Eastern Europe in 1731, and the *History of the Russian Empire Under Peter the Great*, with its two volumes in 1759 and 1763, made for a slow middle movement; then followed the fantastic finale in the philosopher's correspondence with Catherine from 1763 to his death in 1778.

"Unscrambling the Chaos"

The historian Albert Lortholary has described a "Russian mirage in France" in the eighteenth century, an illusionary image created and admired by the philosophes, moving from "the myth of Peter" to "the legend of Catherine."[17] The former myth dated from Peter's own visit to France in 1717, followed soon after by the eulogy of Bernard de Fontenelle, composed for the French Academy of Sciences, on the occasion of Peter's death in 1725. That myth then underwent further development, above all, in the writings of Voltaire, whose prominence and influence made Peter a primary political hero of the Enlightenment, though Rousseau in the *Social Contract* still preserved the plausibility of a dissident perspective. In 1759, the year of the first volume on Peter, the myth moved into another phase and genre, as Antoine Thomas found inspiration in Voltaire to begin writing an epic poem on Peter, a *Petreid* modeled on Virgil's *Aeneid*. With Voltaire's encouragement, Thomas devoted the rest of his life to this project, holding readings of the work in progress, but ending with an unfinished, unpublished manuscript at his death in 1785. The early cantos emphasized Peter's lessons in civilization on his travels in England, France, and Holland, and Thomas offered up in sometimes dreadful verse the already established platitudes of Peter's myth:

> Je vois le despotisme en tes heureuses mains,
> Etonné de servir au bonheur des humains. . . .
>
> (I see despotism in your fortunate hands,
> Surprised to be serving the happiness of humans. . . .)
>
> Et, du trop lent destin changeant l'ordre commun,
> Que dix siècles pressés viennent s'unir en un.
> (And, changing the common order of slow destiny,
> So that ten centuries rushed come together as one.)[18]

Enlightened despotism and accelerated progress were interdependent parts of Peter's myth, shaping the idea of Eastern Europe as a domain of backwardness.

Voltaire claimed to have seen Peter when the tsar came to Paris in 1717, but this claim did not emerge until 1759, when the first volume of Voltaire's

Peter the Great was about to appear. "When I saw him forty years ago, visiting the shops of Paris," recalled Voltaire, "neither he nor I suspected that one day I would be his historian."[19] While the young Voltaire may well have seen the tsar in 1717, the reminiscence was called into play, like his memory of Catherine's mother, to establish a personal connection in a literary engagement that generated the celebratory stuff of myth and legend. Others who recorded their impressions of Peter in Paris were wrestling with his relation to "barbarism" in Russia, like Marshal Villeroi, who thought "this supposedly barbarous prince is not at all so." Saint-Simon, however, tempered his general admiration by observing in Peter "a strong stamp of that ancient barbarism of his country," and snootily saluted "this monarch, who wished to raise himself and his country from barbarism."[20] The development of a barbarous land thus appeared to depend on the civilizing reforms of a barbarian prince. The prescription of enlightened absolutism for Eastern Europe finally evaded this dilemma, and prevailed triumphantly, when the ruler of the Russian empire was Catherine, who was not Russian at all.

In 1717 Peter visited the French Academy of Sciences and became an honorary associate, providing some much appreciated maps of Russia. At Peter's death in 1725, Fontenelle, as secretary of the Academy, presented a eulogy, just as two years later he would give the eulogy for Sir Isaac Newton. Eulogy was a function that suited Fontenelle, famous for his "Dialogues of the Dead," while the rhetorical discovery of Russia was equally appropriate to the author of reflections on the "Plurality of Worlds." His appreciation of Peter established the fundamental lines of the eighteenth-century myth, describing a process of development in which Russia itself was the tsar's blank canvas, civilization degree zero: "Everything was to be done ('tout était à faire') in Muscovy, and nothing to perfect." Peter had to "create a new nation." This thesis assumed a variation in levels of civilization, so that Russia could learn from "the wiser and more polite nations," soon to arrive "at their level (*niveau*)," at an accelerated pace, speeding up "the slow progress they had to undergo."[21] The programmatic power of these phrases was evident enough when Voltaire, in the 1750s, planning his own *Peter the Great*, merely modified the formulation of Fontenelle to express more clearly an idea of developmental scale in Russia before Peter: "almost everything was still to be done."[22]

When Peter first appeared as a character and historical problem in the writings of Voltaire, it was as the nemesis of Charles XII, his rival for the mastery of Eastern Europe. Through the 1730s, as that history triumphantly went through successive editions, Voltaire became somewhat abashed at his own enthusiasm for the spirit of conquest embodied in Charles. In an edition of 1739 he added material to build up the character of Peter as an alternative hero: "One man alone changed the greatest empire in the world." Yet the tsar lacked "humanity," according to Voltaire, who at that time still maintained some sense of critical balance concerning Peter: "Brutality in his pleasures, ferocity in his manners, and barbarism in his vengeances mixed with so many virtues. He civilized (*policait*) his peoples, but he was a savage." Peter personally executed criminals, and Voltaire remarked that "there are in Africa sovereigns who spill the blood of their subjects with their own hands, but these monarchs pass for barbarians." Voltaire even alluded to the condemnation and death of Peter's own son as a black mark against the record of "the good that he did his subjects."[23] In shifting his focus of interest from Charles to Peter, Voltaire developed a subtly modulated conception of mastery in Eastern Europe, mastery as a civilizing process rather than mere conquest. Peter also illustrated the issue of a native protagonist—a Russian, who could pass for an African, who could pass for a barbarian—as opposed to a foreign adventurer from Sweden, or a foreign princess from Germany.

In 1748 Montesquieu included a few remarks on Peter in *The Spirit of the Laws*, and Voltaire contributed a little bit more in his *Anecdotes on the Tsar Peter the Great*, an adumbration of the full-scale treatment to come. Montesquieu made Peter the principal subject of a section on "the natural means of changing the manners and customs of a nation." The legislation of custom was censured as unnatural, and Peter's mandatory trimming of beards and shortening of clothes were cited by Montesquieu as "instances of tyranny" and furthermore unnecessary to the purpose in Russia:

The facility and ease with which that nation has been polished plainly show that this prince had a worse opinion of his people than they deserved: and that they were not brutes, though he was pleased to call them so. The violent measures which he employed were needless; he would have attained his end as well by milder methods.[24]

Montesquieu subscribed to "the empire of climate" over customs and manners, creating a crucial distinction between Europe and Asia, and also between the North and the South in Europe itself. Political attention to climate clouded the emergence of Eastern Europe throughout the eighteenth century, yet Montesquieu, firmly committed to the notion of "the North," had no reservations about including Russia in Europe. Russia before Peter possessed manners "foreign to the climate," introduced by Tartar conquest; barbarism was but an anomaly. Therefore Peter was not polishing against the grain in "giving the manners and customs of Europe to a European nation."[25] Montesquieu, in conceiving of European lands without the manners of Europe, adumbrated an important new approach to the philosophical division of the continent.

Montesquieu wrote of the Russians from afar, deducing conclusions from a climate whose rigors he had never actually experienced. He was in Vienna in 1728, and considered an invitation to St. Petersburg; while he hesitated he wrote for a copy of Fontenelle's eulogy of Peter. In the end Montesquieu left Vienna only to go as far east as Hungary before turning back to Venice. "I wanted to see Hungary," he wrote, "because all the states of Europe were once as Hungary is now, and I wanted to see the manners of our fathers."[26] In Hungary, which he witnessed, as in Russia, which he imagined, he recognized Europe, but insisted on a gap of manners that could only be bridged by a theory of backwardness and development.

Voltaire's *Anecdotes* of 1748 followed a Russian refusal to supply him with the source materials for a full account of Peter's reign. He wrote to Elizabeth in 1745, proposing to write about her father, "to raise a monument to his glory in a language that is now spoken at almost all the courts of Europe."[27] The Russian Academy, however, still hesitated to entrust Peter's life to a foreigner. Voltaire, thus rejected by the Russians, was perhaps all the readier to differ from Montesquieu by insisting that they owed everything to Peter. "His people, before him," wrote Voltaire at the beginning of the *Anecdotes*, "were restricted to those first arts taught by necessity." In conclusion, this assumption of primitive people was emphasized with a mock mathematical calculation of the extreme improbability that one such as Peter should have appeared among barbarians to civilize them, "this genius so contrary to the genius of his nation." Voltaire compared Peter to Prometheus, while Montesquieu saw Peter's achievement as less titanic, inasmuch as the tsar was merely giving European manners to a European nation. For Voltaire the civilizing of Russia was much more explicitly a matter of importing arts across the continent: "At present there are in Petersburg French actors and Italian operas. Magnificence and even taste have in everything succeeded barbarism." Even the currency of the French language at the court of Elizabeth (like "almost all the courts of Europe") prevailed "accordingly (*à mesure*) as this land became civilized." Here was a measurable sense of developmental scale, and a model of development that Voltaire employed as generally applicable: "There are still vast climates in Africa where men have need of a tsar Peter."[28] Eastern Europe became the domain in which enlightened absolutism proved itself as political theory, as the formula for development and civilization.

At last in 1757, when France and Russia were allied in the Seven Years' War, St. Petersburg took up Voltaire on his long-standing interest in composing a full account of Peter. "You propose to me," he responded, "that which I have been desiring for thirty years; I could not better finish my career than in consecrating my last efforts and my last days to such a work." For Voltaire there thus appeared a consistency of preoccupation that dated back over decades, and when the first volume finally appeared two years later, it was without Voltaire's name, with the authorship simply attributed to "the author of the *History of Charles XII*."[29] Voltaire had twenty years to live, in spite of the rhetorical flourish about "last efforts" and "last days."

The exaggeration of his own senescence (Voltaire was 63 in 1757) suited his intention to decline on account of ill health Elizabeth's invitation to St. Petersburg for purposes of research.

This refusal guaranteed that the writing of the history was nested within a complex correspondence with Russia, principally with Ivan Shuvalov, Elizabeth's favorite, who also mediated Voltaire's receipt of the patronage of the tsarina and the criticism of the still resentful Russian Academy. Above all Shuvalov arranged for the shipping of source materials to Voltaire, so that Peter, that celebrated sojourner, was sent to Western Europe once again, to sit for his philosophical portrait.[30] From the start, the project on Peter was intended to establish its subject as a European one, written in French for the courts of Europe. Voltaire wrote to Shuvalov to remind him of that audience, rejecting a parochial perspective: "We are speaking of all of Europe, so we must not, neither you nor I, restrict our view to the steeples of Petersburg."[31] Voltaire had never seen the steeples of St. Petersburg, let alone ascended for the view, but in letters he could claim to participate in the perspective of his Russian correspondent—"neither you nor I"—the better to transcend its limitations for them both.

It was, above all, the authorship of Voltaire that made a book about Peter into a European event, and he was well aware of that: "I go to appear before all of Europe in giving this history." For this reason he resisted the pressures that reached him from Russia to render the work ever more flawlessly flattering. "Most people of letters in Europe reproach me already that I am going to do a panegyric, and play the role of a flatterer," he wrote to Shuvalov in 1758, the year before publication.[32] By the time both volumes were published in 1763, d'Alembert was writing privately that the work "makes one vomit by the baseness and platitude of its eulogies," and the prince de Ligne later claimed that Voltaire himself admitted to having been corrupted by gifts of fancy furs. The verdict of the twentieth century has hardly raised the book's standing; Peter Gay has called it "a collection of gross compliments disguised as history."[33]

While it was true that Voltaire was pressured by St. Petersburg during the years that he devoted to this project, from 1757 to 1763, the crucial dependency that kept him in correspondence was not a fondness for fox but rather his need for documentary source materials on Peter. Voltaire's foreign account of Peter was, to a considerable extent, based on other foreign accounts, most notably Strahlenberg's geographical work (published in German in Stockholm in 1730, published in French in Amsterdam in 1757, the year that Voltaire began his book), and John Perry's memoir of his years in Peter's service as a naval engineer (published in English in London in 1716, published in French in Paris in 1717, the year of Peter's visit to France). Still Voltaire counted on receiving Russian materials to advance his scholarship, and they did arrive, starting with maps in 1757, to be followed by translations of Russian memoirs with an excess of military detail. His scholarly work was "unscrambling (*débrouillant*) the chaos of the archives of Petersburg," just as Catherine's imperial mission was to be, as he saw it, the "unscrambling of all this chaos" in Eastern Europe, from Gdańsk to the mouth of the Danube.[34]

Selective archival assistance inevitably shaped the form and content of the work, but Russian correspondence also offered explicit guidelines and detailed criticism that rightly led Voltaire to fear that he was being cast in "the role of a flatterer." In 1758 he received from Lomonosov three pieces about Peter, one an "Apotheosis of Peter the Great," the second a "Parallel with Alexander the Great and Lycurgus," and the third a "Refutation against Certain Authors" who failed to do justice to Peter, especially Voltaire himself in his *Charles XII*. Such preliminary guidance from Lomonosov testified to the persistent resentment of the Petersburg Academy, which was certainly confirmed by Müller, when he responded to Voltaire's completed manuscript with hundreds of corrections, and gave especially fussy attention to the transliterated spelling of Russian names in French. Voltaire preempted the adoption of these proposed corrections by rushing his manuscript to press in Geneva in 1759, supposedly to get ahead of pirated versions in Hamburg and the Hague. Thus the irresistible enthusiasm of Western Europe, for Voltaire and for Peter, seemed to roll right over the last efforts of the Petersburg Academy to reclaim a role in the representation of the tsar. In the preface to the second volume of 1763 Voltaire made fun of the corrections he had received on the first volume. He had, for instance, in his description of primitive peoples in the Russian empire, mentioned the religious adoration of a sheepskin, and now he stood corrected: it was a bear fur. "A bear fur is still more adorable than a sheepskin," remarked Voltaire, sarcastically, "and one needs the hide of a donkey to weigh oneself down with such bagatelles."[35] Thus he turned academicians into asses, but in fact the "bagatelle" was more than an anthropological inexactitude. The sheepskin garment, which recurred in so much of eighteenth-century literature on Eastern Europe, was recognized as an emblem of backwardness, and it was perhaps no coincidence that Voltaire made the sheepskin into an object of totemic worship.

The most significant dilemma that emerged in correspondence over writing Peter's life concerned the fate of the tsarevich Alexis, Peter's son. "The sad end of the tsarevich embarrasses me a little," wrote Voltaire to Shuvalov in 1759, already thinking ahead to the second volume, and Müller had many corrections to make on Voltaire's version. To be sure, Voltaire was ready to justify Peter for condemning his son to death, and this justification followed directly from his conception of Peter and Russia, his conviction that "one man alone changed the greatest empire in the world." Alexis wanted to change Russia back again, "to plunge it again into the darkness" ("la replonger dans les ténèbres")—and so Peter had no choice but to "sacrifice his own son to the safety of his empire."[36] This was, thus far, the line of Lomonosov, but Voltaire had a touchy exchange with St. Petersburg over the convenient death of the tsarevich in prison. Voltaire was asked to accept that this was a natural death, caused perhaps by the shock of hearing his death sentence, but certainly not a killing at Peter's command. He ended up writing, with a hint of irony, that it was "very rare" for a young man to die just from the reading of a death sentence, but added that "the doctors admit the thing is possible."[37] Issues like the death of the tsarevich "embarrassed" Voltaire by recalling the thesis on Peter he himself had once proposed: "He civilized his peoples, but he was a savage." It was thus to evade his own formula that Voltaire declared in 1757, in a letter to Shuvalov, that he was not interested in writing about Peter's private life; the work would be not a life of Peter, but rather *The History of the Russian Empire Under Peter the Great*.[38]

From 1745 Voltaire conceived of such a work as a "monument" to Peter, and he came to compare it more specifically to a "statue," whose "beautiful effect" depended on an effacement of petty details and personal flaws. As in the classical sculpture of Phidias, these would be "eclipsed and annihilated before the great virtues that Peter owed only to himself, and before the heroic works that his virtues have operated."[39] It was to be a sort of sculpture of sculpture, inasmuch as Peter himself was a creator of heroic works; Russia was Peter's masterpiece, as Peter was to be Voltaire's. The monument was completed with the second volume of 1763, and in 1766 Falconet went to St. Petersburg to start on the real statue. Falconet's mounted bronze Peter was posed on a giant boulder of natural rock, suggesting, like Voltaire's monument, the relation between the heroic tsar and the raw material of Russia upon which his creative virtues operated.

In Voltaire's work the rock pedestal was the long "Description of Russia" that introduced the first volume, with its primitive peoples and their totemic sheepskins, or whatever, published just in time to become the basis of Jaucourt's article on Russia in volume XIV of the Encyclopedia. Voltaire described a domain where "the limits of Europe and Asia are still confused," where "Scythians, Huns, Massagetae, Slavs, Cimbrians, Getae, and Sarmatians are today the subjects of the tsars."[40] The first volume concluded with Peter's victory over Charles XII at Poltava, and though Voltaire had been there once before, in Charles's camp, now he knew better, and saw that civilization itself was at stake. If Peter lost, Russia would "fall back into chaos," and if he won, he would be able "to civilize (*policer*) a great part of the world."[41]

Carolyn Wilberger, writing about "Voltaire's Russia," has concluded that "Voltaire's optimism about Russia was limitless because it was an aspect of his overall optimism about civilization itself."[42] This was evident in his climactic account of Poltava as a triumph of civilization, but 1759, the year of the first volume, was also the year of *Candide*, in which optimism was mercilessly satirized, and providence revealed as a preposterous delusion. At this critical moment in Voltaire's intellectual development, conditioned by the ongoing brutalities of the Seven Years' War, he hilariously mocked the philosophical optimism of Dr. Pangloss, but was himself Pangloss in earnestly optimistic tribute to the advance of civilization in Peter's Russia. In *Candide* Europe became the battlefield of the primitive pillaging peoples of Eastern Europe, the Bulgars and the Avars, while in *Peter the Great* Europe offered the hope of civilization to Scythians, Huns, Slavs, and Sarmatians. The next year, in 1760, when Voltaire wrote his poem "The Russian in Paris," he seemed less certain: "What can you learn on the shores of the Occident?"[43]

Voltaire's history presented Peter as one who looked to "our part of Europe," who "wanted to introduce into his estates neither Turkish manners nor Persian, but ours." The first-person plural identified the perspective of Western Europe, "our part of Europe." Peter sought to introduce "the clothing of our nations," and Voltaire mapped out the implied domain of other nations when he noted the resemblance of Russian clothing to those of "the Pole, the Tartar, and the ancient Hungarian."[44] Neither the Orient of Turkey or Persia, nor "our part of Europe," this was clearly Eastern Europe, the lands and peoples in between. Voltaire's *Peter the Great* was negotiated in correspondence with Russia, and served as a sort of mirror (no iron curtain) in which readers could see their own reflections, admiring Peter as Peter admired our clothing, our manners, our part of Europe. The book's balance of power was evident from the fact that Voltaire described Peter's travels in Western Europe (even claimed to have seen him in Paris in 1717), but declined to make the reciprocal trip to St. Petersburg for the purpose of research. Created in correspondence, this work initiated a new and more important correspondence across the continent when Voltaire sent the second volume to Catherine in 1763.

"To Sup at Sofia"

"It seems to me," wrote Voltaire to Catherine in 1766, "that if that other great man Peter I, had established himself in a gentler climate than that of Lake Ladoga, if he had chosen Kiev, or some other more southern terrain, I would be actually at your feet, in spite of my age." For the rest of his life Voltaire would indulge in such epistolary fantasies of voyaging to visit Catherine. The alleged obstacle, the frigid northern climate of St. Petersburg, was in fact precisely what liberated his imagination to encounter Catherine all over Eastern Europe. "It is now to the star of the north that all eyes must turn," proclaimed Voltaire, in his next letter, and yet no one was more intent than he upon undermining the conventionally apostrophized northern nature of the Russian empire. His own eyes, like Catherine's ambitions, inevitably wandered from the north to the south, discovering a domain that was emphatically eastern. "If you want to make some miracles," he wrote in 1767, "just try to render your climate a little hotter." This was to be not a meteorological miracle but rather the geographical displacement of Russia itself: "When you have placed Russia at the thirtieth degree, instead of around the sixtieth, I will ask of you permission to come there and complete my life."[45] Even the measurements of scientific geography in Eastern Europe were altogether at the disposal of enlightened absolutism and whimsical philosophy. While a shift from 60 to 30 degrees latitude would have meant relocating St. Petersburg in the neighborhood of Cairo, a compromise at 45 degrees would have indicated the Crimea, where twenty years later, in 1787, Catherine was in fact attended by representatives of Western Europe like Ségur and the prince de Ligne. Long before that, in 1773, Diderot would establish that even the path to St. Petersburg was not beyond the endurance of an aging philosopher.

Catherine played to Voltaire's fantasies of Eastern Europe by reporting on travels of her own. She regretted that she could not miraculously change the climate of Russia, but promised to try for cleaner air in St. Petersburg by draining the surrounding marshes. Finally, she announced that she herself was about to tour Russia, along the Volga: "And at the moment perhaps that you least expect it, you will receive a letter dated from some shack (*bicoque*) in Asia." Catherine appealed to Voltaire's own idea of an empire where "the limits of Europe and Asia are still confused" to suggest that he might find himself, unexpectedly, in correspondence with Asia. She was true to her word, and two months later wrote to him from Kazan: "Here I am in Asia; I wanted to see it with my own eyes."[46] In fact, Kazan, on the eastern bank of the Volga, was only in Asia according to an elastic eighteenth-century geography, already giving way to the modern and unequivocal location of Kazan in Europe. If Catherine herself, on the spot, could indulge in a certain confusion about the limits of Europe and Asia, her faraway French correspondent could experience even more exquisitely that sense of geographical liminality. After all, his "Description of Russia" in *Peter the Great* conceded that beyond Azov "one no longer knows where Europe finishes and where Asia commences."[47]

Catherine aimed her letter explicitly at Voltaire's imagination when she wrote from Kazan of giving Russia uniform laws: "Imagine, I pray you, that they must serve for Europe and for Asia: and what a difference of climate, of people, of customs, even of ideas!" Voltaire responded too by referring to the preface of his *Peter the Great*, which began by wondering rhetorically, "Who would have said in 1700 that a magnificent and polite court would be established at the end of the Gulf of Finland?" Now, writing to Catherine about her legislative commission, he enlarged upon this vision. "I would not have guessed in 1700, that Reason, one day," wrote Voltaire (who was only six years old in 1700), "would come to Moscow, at the voice of a princess born in Germany, and that she would assemble in a great hall idolaters, Moslems, Greeks, Latins, Lutherans, who would all become her children." He emphasized her German origin, and declared that "in his heart" he too was her subject. He even imagined one of his own pseudonymous personae at the mouth of the Volga, on the frontier between Europe and Asia: "The late abbé Bazin often said that he was horribly afraid of the cold, but that if he weren't so old, he would go establish himself in the south of Astrakhan, to have the pleasure of living under your laws."[48] Voltaire's enthusiasm for Catherine's codification of laws followed naturally from the myth of Peter which he had codified himself; absolute power became an unequivocal force for civilization and enlightenment when applied to the backward lands and peoples of Eastern Europe. Peter Gay, in *Voltaire's Politics*, has suggested that Voltaire was most clearly an advocate of enlightened despotism in his conception of Catherine, on the principle that "benevolent autocracy may not be appropriate to Western countries, but it is appropriate to a country whose population is still close to primitive conditions."[49]

From 1768 Catherine was at war with Poland and Turkey, and Voltaire could aggressively envision the expansion of that domain, the consolidation of Eastern Europe under the reign of Reason, personified by a princess born in Germany.

On one side she forces the Poles to be tolerant and happy, in spite of the papal nuncio; and on the other side she seems to deal with the Moslems, in spite of Mohammed. If they make war on you, madame, there could well come about that which Peter the Great once had in view, which was to make Constantinople the capital of the Russian empire. These barbarians deserve to be punished by a heroine, for the lack of consideration they have shown till now for ladies. It is clear that people who neglect all the fine arts, and who shut up women, deserve to be exterminated. . . . I ask your majesty for permission to come and place myself at her feet, and to pass some days at her court, as soon as it shall be established at Constantinople; for I think very seriously that if ever the Turks should be chased from Europe, it will be by the Russians.[50]

Here was a modern formulation of the Eastern Question from the first philosopher of the Enlightenment. The Turks were to be chased from Europe on account of their barbarous customs and neglect for the arts; they deserved to be punished, even exterminated, so Europe might be reclaimed for civilization. Catherine had just made a powerful public demonstration of her faith in science and civilization by receiving inoculation against smallpox, and recommended reading *Candide* as a perfect painkiller. The happy ending of the tale brought everyone together at Constantinople, and Catherine responded enthusiastically to Voltaire's fantasy of visiting her there. She promised—"for your entry into Constantinople"—a Greek costume lined with "the richest skins of Siberia."[51] This fashion statement suggested that Greece was still implicated in the discovery and recovery of Eastern Europe, part of the same Eastern Question, though Hellenism would soon sort out the descendants of ancient civilization from those of ancient barbarism.

Voltaire in 1769 was more convinced than ever that the Turks had to be "relegated forever to Asia." While Catherine read his *Candide*, he read her *Instruction* to the legislative commission, now available in French translation, and pronounced her superior to Solon and Lycurgus. Voltaire held a reading of Catherine's *Instruction* at Ferney, and a six-foot, sixteen-year-old Swiss boy cried out, "My God, how I wish I were Russian!" Voltaire replied, "It depends only upon you to be that," and cited the example of Catherine's Swiss secretary François Pictet. He might as well have cited Catherine herself. The assumption of a Russian identity was a matter of will, or even whim, just as the traversing of Eastern Europe was the ultimate vicarious experience. In this case Voltaire was ready to send in his stead a sixteen-year-old substitute, as before he sent the fictitious abbé Bazin. The Swiss boy was young enough to endure the climatic rigors of Riga, to study German and Russian there, before proceeding to serve Catherine in St. Petersburg. Voltaire's vicarious voyage did not stop there: "If your majesty goes to establish herself at Constantinople, as I hope, he will quite quickly learn Greek; for it is absolutely necessary to chase from Europe the Turkish language, as well as all those who speak it."[52] Here Voltaire hinted at a more radically modern idea of Europe, defined linguistically, against an Asian domain of Oriental languages, at a time when Herder was already working toward a new emphasis on the relation between language and culture.

In 1769 Voltaire followed the progress of Catherine's armies, with his imagination anticipating them in every corner of Eastern Europe. In May he wondered whether "Azov is in your hands," whether "you are also mistress of Taganrog." Then shifting his epistolary focus to a different military arena, he envisioned her "on the road to Adrianople"—an object he deemed worthy of the "legislator of the north," though Adrianople was anything but northern. Voltaire himself assumed the part of the Emperor Joseph II, imagining that "if I were a young Emperor of the Romans, Bosnia and Serbia would see me soon, and I would then ask you to sup at Sofia or Philippopolis." Obviously Voltaire participated personally in fantasies of conquest when he made himself the master of Bosnia and Serbia, and prepared to encounter Catherine in Bulgaria—"after which we would share (*nous partagerions*) amiably." The verb *partager* was prominent here, three years before the partition of Poland, which supposedly shocked all of Europe, including Voltaire. There was no need to specify the particular lands to be shared or partitioned, for when Eastern Europe was on the table, from Azov to Adrianople, from Bulgaria to Bosnia, it was safe to assume that partition would find an appropriate object. The letter concluded with Voltaire engraving imaginary medals to Catherine as "Triomphatrice de l'empire ottoman, et pacificatrice de la Pologne."[53]

In September Catherine's triumphs at Azov and Taganrog were celebrated by Voltaire as "jewels" in her crown—"and I imagine that Moustapha will never disturb your coiffure." The sultan was always an object of comic derision in this correspondence, and that Moslem Turkey was allied with Catholic Poland against Catherine was, to Voltaire's mind, "worthy of Italian farce." In fact, it was the two correspondents who made the disputed domain of Eastern Europe into an arena of farce, as they made appointments to sup at Sofia. The peoples of Eastern Europe might figure in the comedy, as contested prizes of the sultan, the tsarina, and even the old philosopher: "Old though I may be, I am interested in those beautiful Circassian women who have given to your majesty an oath of fidelity, and who give without doubt the same oath to their lovers. Thank God, Moustapha will not touch them."[54] This was farce indeed.

Yet Voltaire might almost have been in earnest when he announced, in this same September letter, that he was ready at last to travel to St. Petersburg himself:

I will be, truly, seventy-seven years old, and I do not have the vigor of a Turk; but I do not see who could prevent me from coming, in the good weather, to salute the star of the north and curse the crescent. Our Madame Geoffrin made the voyage to Warsaw quite well, why should not I undertake that of St. Petersburg in the month of April? I will arrive in June, I will return in September; and if I should die on the road, I will put on my little tomb: Here lies the admirer of the august Catherine, who had the honor to die while going to present to her his profound respect.[55]

Madame Geoffrin went to Warsaw in 1766, and Voltaire's intention was perhaps also more distantly shadowed by the voyage of Descartes to Stockholm, where he died as the guest of Queen Christina in 1650. Catherine wanted no such fragile guests, and while she was willing to respond playfully to his proposed entry into Constantinople and the supper in Sofia, she promptly rejected his plan for St. Petersburg. She would not expose him to "such a long and painful voyage," for she would be "inconsolable" if his health were to suffer as a consequence: "neither I myself, nor all of Europe, would pardon me."[56]

Voltaire's epistolary appreciation of Eastern Europe now rose to new heights of fantasy. "Madame," he declared in October, "your imperial majesty gives me life in killing the Turks." He was ready to jump from his bed, "crying Allah, Catharina!" and even "Te Catharinam Laudamus, te dominam confitemur." He himself was her prophet: "The angel Gabriel informed me of the total rout of the Ottoman army, of the taking of Choczim, and showed me with his finger the road to Jassy." It was thus that the tsarina "avenged Europe." If then Catherine was to be acknowledged as *domina*, her domain in Europe was clearly indicated by the angel's finger, which pointed to the Ukraine and Moldavia, to the heart of Eastern Europe. In March 1770, with spring around the corner, Voltaire was not packing for St. Petersburg. Indeed, in a new excess of fancy, he expected to encounter not Catherine but Peter, "to whom I will soon pay court in the other world." The sultan might also be encountered in another world, the fictional world of Voltaire: "Could he not pass the carnival of 1771 at Venice with Candide?"[57] It was in Venice that Candide encountered no fewer than six deposed princes, including one sultan, two kings of Poland, and one tsar, Ivan VI. The last had reigned briefly over Russia as an infant in 1740 and 1741, and was conveniently killed in captivity in 1764, soon after Catherine's accession. As Catherine picked up the pieces of Eastern Europe, Voltaire prepared to welcome more monarchs to this carnival of the deposed and dispossessed.

In 1770 Voltaire followed the Danube, several steps ahead of Catherine's armies, to discover the lands of Eastern Europe along its banks.

I would still wish that the course of the Danube and the navigation of that river belonged to you, the length of Wallachia, of Moldavia, and even of Bessarabia. I don't know if I am asking too much, or if I am not asking enough: that will be for you to decide.[58]

In any event Voltaire himself felt free to propose, even while leaving to Catherine the final disposition of the Danubian lands. "I feared the Danube would be very difficult to traverse," he wrote, caught up in that campaign in September. "I certainly do not know enough about it even to dare examine whether your army can pass the Danube or not," he wrote in October. "It is for me only to make wishes." His wishes still anticipated her military achievements, leaving him wistful that "the race of the Turks are not yet chased from Europe." The same letter congratulated Catherine on fighting to achieve "the empire of the Orient," but what was the Oriental empire he envisioned along the Danube? If the Turks were chased from Europe, the lands that they would leave were obviously European. The next letter celebrated the fall of Bender to Catherine and wondered why she was not yet in Adrianople, two more towns that were indisputably in Europe, in Eastern Europe. He lay sick in bed at Ferney, and could only be restored by the news of her victories. In December, admitting that Catherine inspired in him a fanciful passion ("un peu romanesque"), he thought he would die of grief if she did not take Constantinople. Early in 1771, with his fancy (*mon imagination*) occupied only by the Danube, the Black Sea, Adrianople, and the Greek archipelago, he was ready "to have myself transported in a litter" to the Constantinople of Catherine's conquest.[59] Without leaving his bed Voltaire acquired an empire of his own in Eastern Europe.

"A New Universe Created"

Voltaire sponsored workshops for watchmakers at Ferney, and instead of arms he was sending shipments of Swiss watches to Catherine in 1771. He wrote that he wished he could establish a colony of watchmakers in Astrakhan, by the Volga, where previously he had settled the imaginary abbé Bazin. Catherine entered into the spirit of the fantasy by offering to come to visit Voltaire at Astrakhan, but suggesting that he consider Taganrog instead, on the Sea of Azov, where the climate was even lovelier and healthier. Peter, she assured him, had once considered establishing his capital at Taganrog, before settling on Petersburg.[60] Voltaire replied, "Then I will have myself carried in the litter to Taganrog." He intended to die there, neither *à la grecque* nor *à la romaine*, that is, without religious rites: "Your Majesty permits each man to embark for the other world according to his fantasy." When Voltaire really did die in Paris in 1778, the issue of his last rites became a public sensation; in 1771 he envisioned Eastern Europe as a domain of fantasy, offering an escape from that dilemma.

When Voltaire learned of Catherine's conquest of the Crimea, his fantasies found a new focus on the land of "the beautiful Iphigenie." He recalled that Apollo bestowed upon the Tartar Abaris a magic arrow to carry him from one end of the world to the other. Now Voltaire appropriated that magic as his own mythological booty from Catherine's conquest: "If I had that arrow, I would be today at Petersburg, instead of stupidly presenting, from the foot of the Alps, my profound respect and my inviolable attachment to the sovereign of Azov, of Kaffa, and of my heart." Catherine offered to send the khan of the Crimea to dance at the Comédie-Française, though Voltaire might also have welcomed him to Candide's carnival at Venice.[61] On New Year's Day 1772, Voltaire could imagine a coherent domain that extended from the Crimea to Poland, the lands of Catherine's triumphs, united in their superstitious backwardness. The Crimea was "the land where Iphigenie, acting as priestess, cut the throats of all foreigners in honor of a nasty wooden statue, quite similar to the miraculous Notre-Dame of Częstochowa." Two weeks later he hailed Catherine's presence in all of Eastern Europe, envisioned as an association of lands: "your spirit shared among the Crimea, Moldavia, Wallachia, Poland, Bulgaria."[62]

In 1769, Voltaire was ready to sup at Sofia with Catherine and partition Ottoman Europe, and now in 1772, as Russia, Prussia, and Austria prepared to take shares of Poland, he praised the partition as "noble" and "useful" work, the remedy for anarchy. He still pressed the complementary advance into Ottoman Europe, for now that Catherine had achieved

Detail of "Nuova carta geografica per servire alla storia della guerra presente tra la Russia e la Porta Ottomana," new map "to be of use for the history of the present war" between Russia and the Ottoman empire; map made in Paris, 1770; included in the *Storia della Ultima Guerra tra la Russia e la Porta Ottomana*, published in Venice in 1776; Catherine's wars focused attention on southeastern Europe and the geographical adjacency of Bulgaria, Wallachia, Moldavia, the Ukraine, the Crimea, and the Tartar territories, around the Black Sea and the Sea of Azov; on this map Poltava is marked with the year "1709" as the site of the Russian victory which first focused attention on this arena at the beginning of the century; a line (not shown) marks the "limits of Europe and Asia" along the Volga, indicating that the lands to that point do indeed belong to Europe. (By permission of the Houghton Library, Harvard University.)

"this great project" in Poland, she might manage "the other," and one day reign from "three capitals, Petersburg, Moscow, and Byzantium."⁶³ Voltaire envisioned the campaign against the Ottomans as a mock crusade, with elements of Italian farce to be sure, and he sent the scenario to St. Petersburg at the end of 1772:

> For four years I have been preaching this little crusade. Some idle spirits like me insist that the time approaches when Saint Maria Theresa, in concert with Saint Catherine, will fulfill my fervent prayers; they say that nothing would be easier than to take, in a campaign, Bosnia and Serbia, and to give you the upper hand at Adrianople. It would be a charming spectacle to see two empresses pull the ears of Moustapha, and send him back to Asia.
>
> Certainly, they say, since these two brave ladies understood each other so well to change the face of Poland, they will understand each other still better to change that of Turkey.
>
> Here is the time of great revolutions, here is a new universe created, from Archangel to the Borysthenes.⁶⁴

In fact, Catherine would celebrate the creation of a new empire in 1787 by sailing with Ségur down the Borysthenes, that is, the Dnieper. The language of new creations and great revolutions was very much that of Voltaire's *Peter the Great*, but what he envisioned in 1772 was more than a Russian empire, if less than a new universe, but certainly a prodigious part of Europe, from Archangel to Adrianople. The role of "idle spirits like me," the philosophes of the Enlightenment in Western Europe, was evident throughout, as prompters to the empresses, as preachers of the crusade, as audience to the spectacle. Voltaire wrote the script in 1773 for Catherine to address Maria Theresa—"my dear Marie"—and remind her that the Turks had twice besieged Vienna and that this was the moment to destroy them. To continue the campaign would be, for the empresses, "an amusement of three or four months at most, after which you would arrange things together, as you arranged things in Poland." Voltaire despaired that peace was coming too soon, with the Ottomans still in Europe, and he clung to the fantasy of himself (*c'est moi*) crossing the Danube, mounting in his dreams for "the grand gallop to Adrianople."⁶⁵

Maria Theresa was in fact reluctant, just as Voltaire suspected, to participate in the partition of Ottoman Europe. She regarded the partition of Catholic Poland as a dishonorable act, perhaps even a mortal sin, which she committed for reasons of state, and she regarded with similar distaste even the dismemberment of a Moslem empire. Furthermore, she regarded the lands of Ottoman Europe, like Bosnia and Serbia, as "unhealthy" and "depopulated," more likely to weaken than strengthen her empire. Kaunitz, who was more willing to consider proposed partitions, came to the same conclusion in 1771 about acquiring Wallachia and Moldavia, which would bring into the Habsburg empire the "wildest people."⁶⁶ Voltaire himself, for all his eagerness in 1773 to gallop to Adrianople in Thrace, had written disparagingly of that land in his *Essay on Manners* in 1756. "Our part of Europe," wrote Voltaire, "must have had in its manners and in its genius a character which was lacking in Thrace, where the Turks established the seat of their empire, or in Tartary from which they once emerged."[67] For Voltaire, however, the backwardness of Eastern Europe, as measured in its manners, was no obstacle to annexation, but rather the justification for imperial redemption in the name of civilization.

One of the warnings that Voltaire passed on to "my dear Marie" in 1773 was that if the Ottomans were not driven from Europe now, the baron de Tott—"who has a lot of genius"—would fortify them for the future. Tott's name had been regularly recurring in Voltaire's letters to Catherine since 1770: "I am a little afflicted, as a Frenchman, to hear said that there is a chevalier de Tott who is fortifying the Dardanelles."[68] Voltaire regarded Tott as a representative of France in Constantinople, and therefore not only an enemy of Catherine, but also a rival of his own for the mastery of Eastern Europe by the wisdom of Western Europe. Rousseau was a more fitting rival, a fellow philosopher, with antithetical views on Poland and Russia, but Tott was a troubling figure nevertheless precisely because he could engage in the battle for Eastern Europe in ways that Voltaire could not: as an officer, as an engineer, even as a traveler. Appropriately, when Tott later published his memoirs in 1785, he was immediately challenged as a rival by the fictional Baron Munchausen. Tott's presence in Constantinople provoked in Voltaire a sort of Homeric conception of the ongoing wars, in which Frenchmen were engaged like Olympians on either side. In 1771 Tott was ironically saluted as "protector of Moustapha and the Koran," while other Frenchmen were reported fighting against Catherine on behalf of the Confederation of Bar in Poland. One of these was a man of letters, Stanislas-Jean de Boufflers, from Lorraine, the son of the mistress of Stanisław Leszczyński. "I beg your majesty to take him prisoner of war," wrote Voltaire to Catherine, ironically. "He will amuse you a lot." Furthermore, "he will make songs for you; he will sketch you; he will paint you, but not so well as my colonists at Ferney paint you on their watches." Voltaire could not help seeing Frenchmen as ambassadors of the arts and sciences in Eastern Europe, even in opposition to his own partisan engagement. With Boufflers and Tott among Catherine's enemies, Voltaire declared himself even more extravagantly in her camp. She was "the first person of the universe," and he was confident that she would "humiliate Ottoman pride with one hand, and pacify Poland with the other." Though he could not build fortifications on the Dardanelles or fight against fanaticism in Poland, Voltaire hoped that he and his watchmakers at Ferney would "one day work for the vast empire of Russia."[69]

When Voltaire reflected on the fact that Frenchmen were fighting against Catherine while some Tartars were rallying to her side, he declared that "it

is the Tartars who are polite, and the French who have become Scythians."
As for Voltaire himself: "If I were younger I would make myself Russian."[70] The rhetorical reversal of the balance of civilization between Western Europe and Eastern Europe depended for its effect upon an implicitly
ironical amazement: Frenchmen as Scythians! Voltaire as a Russian!

Voltaire also recognized the limitations of his own role on Catherine's
behalf. "Madame," he wrote early in 1772, "I fear that your imperial majesty
may be quite weary of the letters of an old Swiss reasoner who cannot
serve you in anything, who only has for you a useless zeal, who cordially
detests Moustapha, who does not love at all the Polish confederates, and
who limits himself to crying, in his desert, to the trout of Lake Geneva:
Let us sing Catherine II." Though he could only cheer for her military
victories in letters from afar, correspondence could also serve as a medium
of cultural exchange for the sometimes trivial tokens of civilization. In
1772 Voltaire offered to edit Molière, to make the plays suitable for performance by the girls at the Smolny Institute in St. Petersburg. "This little
work will be an amusement for me," he wrote, "and will not harm my
health." He also thought he knew of an appropriate new play that concerned "two species (*espèces*) of Tartars," and promised to send it as soon as
it was published. Catherine replied that the girls were performing Voltaire's
Zaire. She graciously accepted his offer to bowdlerize the French classics
and, with just a hint of prurience, assured the old man that the young
girls made a pretty picture: "If you could see them, I am persuaded that
they would attract your approbation." Catherine was then entertaining as
a guest at her court a young Tartar prince from the Crimea, whose land she
had just conquered. He went with her on Sundays to see the performances
of the girls from the Institute. Lest Voltaire fear that she was letting "the
wolf among the fold," Catherine assured him that the prince in the audience was separated from the girls on stage by a double balustrade.[71] It was
a perfect mutual expression of their civilizing concerns that Voltaire was
purveying to Petersburg French drama about the Tartars, while Catherine
in Petersburg was introducing the Tartars to French drama as performed
by Russian girls.

In the spring of 1772 Catherine was sending seeds to Voltaire so that
he might plant Siberian cedars at Ferney. In May he planted the seeds and
remarked upon their displacement from Eastern Europe: "Those cedars
there will perhaps give shade one day to some Genevans; but at least they
will not have beneath their shade any rendezvous of Sarmatian confederates." Catherine was pleased to learn that he was planting, and reflected
upon their parallel pursuits in their respective domains.

You are seeding at Ferney; I am doing the same this spring at Tsarskoye Selo. This
name will seem to you perhaps a little hard to pronounce; however, it is a place that
I find delicious, because I am planting and seeding there. The baroness of Thunder-

ten-tronckh found her château quite the most beautiful of all possible châteaux. My cedars are already at the height of the little finger; what are yours? I now madly love English gardens.[72]

Catherine and Voltaire found a world that transcended the crucial disjunction between Ferney and Tsarskoye Selo, between Western Europe and Eastern Europe, that best of all possible worlds which Voltaire invented for Candide to cultivate his garden. The only reminder of that which separated the correspondents was a name "perhaps a little hard to pronounce." Voltaire picked up on her remark later that year, with a sarcasm about "Notre-Dame de Częstochowa, a name very difficult to pronounce."[73] The game was entirely gratuitous, since in letters of course no names needed to be pronounced. Yet the affirmation of mutual delicacy served to construct a sphere of impossible Slavic pronunciations, from Catherine's château in Russia to the monastery-fortress of her enemies in Poland.

"I asked your majesty for the cedars of Siberia," wrote Voltaire. "I dare ask of you now a comedy of Petersburg." It was perhaps an amateur work of her own that he was requesting, but in any event it would have to be sent in French translation, for he declared himself too old to learn Russian. At the end of 1772 he sent her another surrogate traveler, to visit Russia and learn Russian, a young man "who is one third German, one third Flemish, and one third Spanish, and who wanted to change these three thirds for a Russian totality." It was an equation that once again emphasized the distinction between Russia and Western Europe while proposing the possibility of transformation and transplantation. In 1773, however, the most important traveler to St. Petersburg was neither a young protégé nor a fictional persona of Voltaire, but his philosophical peer Denis Diderot. Voltaire wrote to Catherine that Diderot was "the happiest of Frenchmen, since he is going to your court." Yet the voyage was also deeply disturbing to Voltaire, inasmuch as it challenged the whole pretense on which his correspondence with Catherine flourished, the pretense that the philosophical and geographical curtain between Western Europe and Eastern Europe was impassable except by means of magic arrows and posted letters. Now Diderot was ready to face the reality of Russia, and Voltaire was left to formulate his epistolary poses and fantasies: "I limit myself to lifting my hands toward the star of the north."[74] For him there was to be no great gallop to Adrianople after all.

"My Reverie to Myself"

In 1762 Jacques-Henri Bernardin de Saint-Pierre arrived in St. Petersburg, only months after Catherine's coup d'état. On the Baltic boat with him were English, French, and Germans, eager to make their fortunes in

Russia as singers or dancers, even as hairdressers; they brought the arts of civilization to a land where those arts were supposedly in demand. This may seem odd company for Bernardin de Saint-Pierre, who many years later, in 1788, would become famous for celebrating the idyll of island love, far from civilization, in *Paul et Virginie*, but in 1762 he too was an adventurer seeking to make his fortune by investing in the advance of civilization in Russia. Indeed, one might even see Catherine herself as a foreign adventuress who hit the jackpot of fortune in Russia that very same year. Bernardin de Saint-Pierre wanted to establish "a little republic of Europeans" within her empire on the Aral Sea—more foreign adventurers—to mediate trade between Europe and Asia. Discouraged by the Russian government's reluctance to embrace his plan, he moved on to Poland in 1764 and ended up as one of the Frenchmen who embarrassed Voltaire by fighting for Poland against Catherine.[75]

The year that Bernardin de Saint-Pierre left Russia, 1764, was the year of Casanova's arrival, a far more frivolous adventurer. In St. Petersburg he found himself among French and Italian singers and dancers, including a few old flames, the same crowd from the boat that brought Bernardin de Saint-Pierre. Casanova also had hopes of making an impression on Catherine. In his memoirs he claimed to have strolled with the tsarina in the Summer Garden and to have conversed with her about calendars, urging her to adopt the Gregorian calendar in Russia. He wanted a job in her civil service—"though I did not myself know for what employment I might be fitted in a country which, furthermore, I did not like"—and when he was disappointed he too moved on to Poland in 1765.[76] The story of strolling with Catherine and counseling her to take enlightened measures was a perfect parable of the fantasy that tantalized both philosophers and adventurers of the Enlightenment with regard to Eastern Europe. It was a fantasy of influence, prescription, and power, easily adapted to an epistolary connection; Voltaire and Catherine planted parallel cedars in their respective gardens, though they would never stroll together in one or the other. Diderot's visit to Catherine in St. Petersburg offered the most convincing consummation of this fantasy. Baron Munchausen would play upon it preposterously, outdoing Casanova in claiming Catherine's favor: nothing less than an invitation "to share the honours of her bed and crown," which the baron politely declined.[77]

The philosophical refusal of Catherine was not a merely fictional property, but referred to at least one extremely celebrated case of an invitation (less extravagant than bed and crown) declined amid plentiful publicity. It was Jean d'Alembert, Diderot's collaborator in the creation of the Encyclopedia, whom Catherine invited in 1762 to come tutor her son and heir. Her letter of invitation was published by the French Academy as a tribute to the Enlightenment, and Thomas, at work on his epic of Peter, praised Catherine's epistolary style as something extraordinary "for the land of the ancient Tartars and Sarmatians." The refusal of d'Alembert was also much admired as an act of independence, though he himself explained his motives differently in a letter to Voltaire: "I am too subject to hemorrhoids."[78] Catherine had attributed the death of her murdered husband to "hemorrhoidal colic," so the demurral of d'Alembert was somewhat sarcastic. It was also true that in 1765 Casanova really did have troubles with hemorrhoids in St. Petersburg. When d'Alembert wrote to Catherine in 1772 on behalf of the Frenchmen taken prisoner in Poland, appealing for their freedom in the name of philosophy, she replied with cool disinterest. After ten years the refusal of d'Alembert really should have lost its sting, and anyway Catherine had before her the prospect of Diderot in 1773.

Diderot began to contemplate a voyage to Russia in 1765. It was the year that Casanova walked with Catherine in the gardens, the year that she received her first letters from Voltaire. It was in that year that Diderot, short of funds, thought of selling his library, and Catherine, hearing of this, not only made the purchase but also left the library to him for his lifetime, and even paid him an annual stipend for the custodianship of the books, which now belonged to her. Voltaire was thrilled with Catherine's inversion of the balance of civilization: "Would one have suspected fifty years ago that one day the Scythians would recompense so nobly in Paris the virtue, science, and philosophy so unworthily treated among us?" Such munificence, however, could be only inadequately appreciated in letters of gratitude to Russia: "If I do not make that voyage," Diderot agonized, "I will stand badly with myself, badly with her."[79] The library would travel to Petersburg after his death; he would have to make the trip himself while he was still alive. He hesitated, however, while celebrating her glory from afar, rallying the philosophes to her cause, purchasing books and pictures on her behalf to be packed off to Petersburg, sending his protégés to precede him.

Falconet went to Russia in 1766 to create Catherine's monument to Peter; he was in Petersburg to welcome Diderot in 1773, and stayed on after him until 1778. Catherine, writing to Mme Geoffrin in Paris, made it clear that the sculptor's service was contracted between herself and a higher philosophical party: "M. Diderot caused me to make the acquisition of a man who I believe has no equal; it is Falconet, and he is incessantly commencing the statue of Peter the Great."[80] Diderot sent her a less gratifying guest in 1767, the physiocrat Lemercier de la Rivière. This too was an explicitly arranged arrival, Diderot now writing to Falconet in St. Petersburg to recommend Lemercier to Catherine: "When the empress has this man, what use would be the Quesnays, the Mirabeaus, the Voltaires, the d'Alemberts, the Diderots?" Lemercier would even "console her for the loss of Montesquieu"—who died in 1755. Thus one philosophical economist, the author of one celebrated book, just published in 1767, might stand in for the entire Enlightenment of Western Europe, and especially for Diderot himself, who still had not made his voyage to Russia. The case of Lemercier, however, dramatically illustrated the awkwardness of bringing face to face an absolute monarch and an enlightened philosopher, especially in Eastern Europe, where fantasies of mastery and programs of civilization were anyone's prerogative. It was the year of the legislative commission, 1767, the year of Catherine's *Instruction*, but she found the late Montesquieu a less presumptuous philosophical guide than the live Lemercier. He was recently returned from serving as royal intendant of Martinique, and assumed the role of intendant of the Enlightenment in Russia. He revised the most successful phrase from Fontenelle's eulogy—"tout était à faire"— when he wrote to the abbé Raynal, another expert on the West Indies, and pronounced a summary verdict on Russia: "Everything remains to be done in that land; or to say it better still, everything remains to be undone and redone."[81]

Catherine hated Lemercier, and though he was on his way back to France in 1768, she did not forget him. In 1774 she wrote to Voltaire about Lemercier, "who supposed, six years ago, that we walked on four paws, and who very politely gave himself the trouble of coming from Martinique to stand us up on our hind feet." In 1787, on the way to the Crimea, she told Ségur that Lemercier "got it into his head that I had called him to help me govern the empire, to draw us out of the darkness of barbarism by the expansiveness of his lights." In 1788 the story was performed as comedy in the theater of the Hermitage in St. Petersburg; the drama was *Regimania*, with a caricature of Lemercier center stage. "I will certainly go to Russia," wrote Diderot to Falconet in 1768, after the debacle of Lemercier, "but I will not send anyone else there."[82] And still he waited, five more years.

The first volume of Diderot's Encyclopedia appeared in 1751, and the last volume was not published until 1772. With this work of a lifetime completed at last in Western Europe, he finally traveled to Russia, arriving in St. Petersburg in October 1773. From the perspective of Western Europe, the condescension was all on one side, and Thomas, for all his poetry on Peter, thought it was something extraordinary "to show a philosopher to an empress." General opinion, according to Thomas, disapproved of Diderot's voyage, regarding him as a "divinity" who should "never go out of his sanctuary." Diderot himself worried over the distance ahead of him, which would separate him from his friends by a "terrestrial demi-diameter." He feared that he would die like Descartes, far from home.[83] In fact Diderot stayed for six months, through the winter of 1773–74; he was sometimes sick, but he survived. In St. Petersburg he met regularly with Catherine for long conversations. Far from decorously posing "to show a philosopher to an empress," Diderot, according to Grimm, who was visiting at the same time, "takes her hand, seizes her arm, taps on the table, all as if he were in the middle of the synagogue of the rue Royale." So physically engaging was his conversation that Catherine supposedly had to put a little table between them to keep the philosopher from bruising her. Yet she praised the "inexhaustible imagination" of Diderot and ranked him "among the most extraordinary men who have ever existed."[84] What fed his imagination was Catherine herself, her sovereign power over Russia, and the significance of that power for applying philosophy to the work of civilization—at the distance of a demi-diameter, in Eastern Europe.

These were the very same stimulants that perfumed the pages of the letters between Catherine and Voltaire, around the margins and between the lines of their mutual congratulations. The extent to which Diderot was capable of raising these issues face to face, while taking her hand and tapping on the table, may be measured from the remarkable record of his memoranda to Catherine written during his stay in St. Petersburg. Diderot wrote expansive essays in epistolary form, that is, addressed to Catherine, though there was no need to post them, for he and she were so often together. These writings were a record not of what Diderot said to Catherine—though they were later published as "interviews" (*entretiens*)—but rather of what he wished to say, even perhaps of what he could not say directly. Catherine kept them to herself, and Diderot's notebook, bound in red morocco leather, preserved in Russia through the nineteenth century, was presented to Maurice Tourneux in 1882, and published in Paris in 1899.[85]

The "interview" that most clearly revealed the unusual nature of this literary form was significantly titled as "My Reverie to Myself, Denis the Philosophe." It was written in the narrative form of a letter, addressed to "Your Imperial Majesty," sometimes more directly to "Madame," and yet it retained for Diderot the air of a reflexive reverie, addressed to himself. Like Voltaire far away at Ferney, Diderot, even in St. Petersburg, even as he seized Catherine by the arm, could not break through the constraints of an inexhaustible imagination, which freed his fantasy even as it blocked his direct access. The barrier that separated philosophy and power, aligned with the curtain between Western Europe and Eastern Europe, meant that Diderot had traveled across a terrestrial demi-diameter to address himself. The competing claims of private fantasy and epistolary address were awkwardly combined from the start: "I take the liberty of addressing these reveries to Her Imperial Majesty." The whole notebook concluded with a plea for Catherine's indulgence toward these "reveries," which offered her "the spectacle of the efforts, as puerile as they are singular, of a speculator who takes it into his little head to govern a great empire."[86] If Diderot belittled his memoranda as mere reveries, deflecting their address from Catherine back to himself, it was precisely because their pretensions were so enormous. The daydreams of Diderot only just fell short of those of Baron Munchausen.

Diderot's visit was a personal pilgrimage of gratitude, but he was also commissioned by the French government to work for better relations with Russia. In "My Reverie to Myself" he affirmed the cultural connection between France and Russia, beginning with the cult of Catherine herself:

There is not one honest man, not a man in Paris who has a grain of spirit and light, who is not an admirer of Your Majesty. She has for her all the academies, all the philosophes, all the thinkers, all the men of letters, and they do not make a secret of this. People have celebrated her grandeur, her virtues, her genius, her goodness, the efforts that she makes to establish the sciences and arts in her land.[87]

Yet with all this celebration the French still appreciated Catherine inadequately, declared Diderot. He swept aside the formality of her imperial title and addressed her directly in the epistolary second person: "They believe they know you (*vous connaître*), my good compatriots!" Diderot promised to teach them to know her even better. Yet as the piece advanced toward its peroration, it was suddenly not Catherine whom Diderot addressed, but his compatriots themselves. He summoned them to a fantasy with Catherine as its object: "Ah! my friends! suppose this woman on the throne of France!" Yet no sooner had he rendered his friends her subjects in France than he proceeded to invite them all to Russia: "Just come pass a month in Petersburg. Come relieve yourselves of a long constraint that has degraded you; it is then that you will feel yourselves to be the men that you are!"[88] By the end of the century Diderot's personal reverie—which obviously did not exclude his compatriots—was the stuff of vaudeville performances, like "Allons en Russie" ("Let us go to Russia"), produced in Paris in 1802. Such a visit was declared to be not just "the fashion" but "the furor." The characters included an artist, an actress, a dancer, a hairdresser, and an author, all of whom hoped to find their fortunes in Russia.[89] Ten years later, in 1812, Napoleon would take up the refrain, "Allons en Russie!"

Diderot, in his reverie, claimed to have acquired a new soul at the Russian border, at Riga, and declared to his friends, "I have never known myself more free than when I inhabited the country you call that of slaves, and never more a slave than when I inhabited the country you call that of free men." He repeated this formulation almost exactly in a letter to Catherine from the Hague in 1774, where he had just arrived from Russia, and he told her that he had indeed, unfortunately, reassumed at Riga "the mean little pusillanimous soul that I had left there." That Diderot did not feel like a slave in Russia was hardly surprising, since he was not performing serf labor but, rather, conversing with the tsarina. The new soul of a free man, which he claimed to have found inside himself, was at the same time a bubble of intellectual extraterritoriality enclosing him, locking him into reverie with himself. When he sought to address himself to Catherine, he found himself addressing his friends in France instead, for it was really only to them that his Russian experience was relevant. They distinguished between free lands and slave lands; he only inverted the terms, drawing the same dual map with a different key. That he felt so free, in a supposed land of slaves, was partly because that land was experienced as a domain of mastery by visitors from Western Europe.

Diderot's spiritual metamorphosis at Riga initiated an ongoing Russian reverie, which found its literary expression in "My Reverie to Myself." That interview concluded in a mood of riotous international fantasy:

And then I admit I would be transported (*transporté*) with joy to see my nation united with Russia, a lot of Russians at Paris, and a lot of Frenchmen at Petersburg. No nation in Europe becomes French (*se francise*) more rapidly than Russia, both for language and for usages.[90]

The double meaning of "transported" underlined the fact that for Diderot the voyage to Russia was reflected in a self-induced spiritual transport that occurred inside himself, the same experience that allowed Voltaire to travel to Eastern Europe without ever leaving Ferney. Diderot's joyous fantasy of cultural exchange had something of the spirit of the vaudeville refrain—"Allons en Russie"—and though people moved in both directions, west to east and east to west, the arrow of cultural influence was still unequivocally aimed. In St. Petersburg Diderot celebrated Russia becoming French; if he envisioned one Europe, it was a French Europe. At the same time, his experience supervising Russian students in Paris, as a favor to Catherine, convinced him that Russians could also be corrupted by French vices, unless one could "subject them to a rigorous discipline."[91] Becoming French, becoming civilized, was a disciplinary project; becoming Russian, for Diderot as for Voltaire, was a matter of fantasy and reverie.

"To Execute a Plan of Civilization"

Diderot could converse with Catherine, take her hand, seize her arm, but when it came to discussing Russia he ended up talking to himself. His presence served passively "to show a philosopher to an empress," but he hesitated to assume a more active role for philosophy. In one of the interviews he presumed to make a precise recommendation, set among a thousand apologies for that presumption, and its very precision underlined the impossibility of philosophizing more expansively. Casanova recommended that Catherine change calendars; Diderot advised her to change capitals. The memorandum was entitled "Of the capital and of the true seat of an empire, by a blind man who judged colors." The epistemological conceit of the blind man, which always interested Diderot and the Enlightenment generally, here marked again the barriers between philosophy and power, and between Western Europe and Eastern Europe. Diderot began by mocking Lemercier and humbling himself:

I did not write from Riga to Petersburg, as did from Berlin to Moscow a French-man, a man of merit and probity, but a man who believed himself, a little ridicu-lously, authorized by his lights and the places he had occupied, to give himself importance: "Madame, wait: one will do nothing good before having heard me; he who knows how to administer an empire, it is I! (*c'est moi!*)" Even if the thing had been true, the tone was such as to make one laugh.[92]

Fifteen years before *Regimania* was staged at the Hermitage, Diderot was performing a private burlesque of Lemercier for Catherine's amusement. Yet it was Diderot who had recommended Lemercier to Catherine in 1767, and there were hints of that recommendation still to be found in the mockery of the interviews: "a man of merit and probity," after all. In his own presumption, qualified by intense self-consciousness and lavish dis-avowals, Diderot knew that he too might appear as "a speculator who takes it into his little head to govern a great empire." Excusing himself, he recognized that Catherine indulged him, "as she would permit one of her children to speak all the innocent foolishness that passed through its head."[93] Then he proceeded to suggest that she shift her government from Petersburg to Moscow.

This was just the sort of speculative manipulation of the map that West-ern Europe practiced upon Eastern Europe in the eighteenth century, and in fact for some years it had been Voltaire's favorite sport to consider dis-placements of Catherine's capital: to Kiev, to Azov, to Constantinople. The twentieth century has proved Diderot more on the mark, but in the eighteenth century both philosophers were exercising a presumptuousness that Catherine indulged because it was so obviously fanciful. Diderot ex-pressed concern about the manners (*moeurs*) of Petersburg, a "confused mass of all the nations of the world," which gave the city "the manners of Harlequin." Surely he meant the motley crew of artists, actresses, and hairdressers who were on the boat with Bernardin de Saint-Pierre; there may even have been Italian performers of the commedia dell'arte, including Harlequin himself. Certainly there was the occasional French philosopher, like Diderot. Yet these foreign presences could have been construed as the epiphenomena of civilization, and Diderot's distaste indicated a flickering of reserve about the whole hopeful program of the Enlightenment for East-ern Europe. Was he himself no more than Harlequin at Catherine's court? He swallowed his doubts and imagined that all would be well at Moscow: "Does Your Majesty want to light (*éclairer*) a vast apartment with one sole torch? Where should she place that torch so that all the surrounding space may be lit to the best advantage?"[94] At the center, of course, which meant Moscow—though he did not specify who held the torch of enlightenment, the tsarina or the philosopher. Neither did he consider that the dancers and hairdressers would inevitably follow the court to Moscow, drawn to the torch like moths around a flame.

Diderot's faith in Moscow was another matter of reverie, for he had never been there. "I missed the opportunity to go to Moscow, and I regret it a little," he later wrote. "Petersburg is only the court, a confused mass of palaces and cottages." In a typical eighteenth-century transposition, his own confusion was projected onto the city itself. "I hardly saw anything but the sovereign," he further conceded.[95] Yet if he saw only the sovereign, how could he speak to her of Russia, for what could he know? In the conclusion to the notebook of interviews he begged her indulgence for his "reveries," congratulating her on being "delivered" from the childish "stammering" of one "who calls himself a philosopher."[96] The philosopher's place in Eastern Europe was easier to establish at an epistolary remove. There was no stammering in Voltaire's epistolary relationship with Catherine, which certainly included much talk of travel but was sustained by the excitement of an ever-deferred consummation.

Diderot left St. Petersburg in March 1774, and, on the interesting assumption that a personal farewell would be too painful for them both, he took leave of Catherine by letter. All through his stay he had written letters to her, the so-called interviews, and now his departure would restore their relations to a more conventional correspondence.

All my life I will congratulate myself on the voyage to Petersburg. All my life I will remind myself of those moments when Your Majesty forgot the infinite distance which separated me from her, and did not disdain to lower herself to me, in order to conceal my smallness. I burn with the desire to converse with my compatriots ("entretenir mes compatriotes") about this.[97]

He was already jumping from his *entretiens* with Catherine into new *entretiens* with his fellow Frenchmen, a natural transition considering that even when he addressed Catherine he irresistibly slipped into addressing his compatriots: "Ah! my friends!" Since Diderot was alone when he wrote his farewell to Catherine, it was only natural that his reflections should take on a grammatically reflexive cast, congratulating himself, reminding himself. Though he wrote of Catherine condescending to forget the infinite distance between them, between an empress and a philosopher, he himself tended to forget the actual proximity between them as they resided in the same city for six months, meeting regularly, conversing at length. Up to the very moment of his departure, a spirit of epistolary reverie isolated him from Catherine and from Russia.

Diderot, returning to Western Europe, preferred not to emerge from his carriage, even to eat or sleep, all the way from St. Petersburg to the Hague. In Hamburg he sent regrets to Carl Philipp Emanuel Bach, in a note of introduction that also suggested the tentative resumption of a suspended identity:

I am a Frenchman; I am called Diderot. I enjoy some consideration in my land as a man of letters; I am the author of some pieces of theatre, among which the *Père de famille* will perhaps not be unknown to you. I am coming from Petersburg.[98]

Riga was behind him, and he was himself again, at home in Western Europe. In a letter to Catherine from the Hague, he reported on his trip, lots of cold and snow till Riga, followed by lovely weather after that. He gave her a generic formula for his conversations:

"Well then, did you have the honor of approaching Her Imperial Majesty?
"Most assuredly."
"Did you see her a lot?"
"A lot."
"Is she a great sovereign?"
"Very great."[99]

He appeared unable to respond in more than two words, and he excused himself to Catherine by pleading a failure of memory: "Ah! If I could remember all that the presence of Your Majesty made me feel!" The crucial experience of their personal interviews, face to face, which he had so recently resolved to remember all his life, was already eluding him as something left behind, at Riga perhaps—when he started to feel like a Frenchman, called Diderot, who enjoyed some consideration as a man of letters. He concluded the letter emotionally: "Again I wet your hands with my tears."[100] In fact, however, at worst he wet the page on which he wrote, and he had not even really wet her hand in farewell at St. Petersburg, since that too was accomplished in a letter.

Still at the Hague in September, just before his return to Paris in October, he wrote to congratulate Catherine on peace with the Ottomans in the Treaty of Kuchuk Kainarji: "What a peace! What a glorious peace!" Diderot, sounding just like Voltaire, exulted about "the point of the sword at the throat of the enemy," and declared himself as happy as "the best of your subjects." It was perhaps his way of reminding her and himself that he was not one of her subjects, even though he rejoiced "as a man, as a philosopher, and as a Russian." Like Voltaire he could assume a Russian identity when he wished, without becoming Catherine's subject, though when he introduced himself to Carl Philipp Emanuel Bach he was emphatically a Frenchman, coming home from St. Petersburg. Diderot hoped that the peace would last, so that Catherine could prove her genius beyond the glory of military triumphs: "Thanks to the progress of reason it is for other virtues than those of the Alexanders and Caesars that our admiration is reserved." Here was the Enlightenment resuming a more confident philosophical role, from the safe epistolary distance of Western Europe, the perspective of "our admiration." Diderot reminded Catherine of Peter's ambition for Russia, relating it reciprocally to the condition of France: "You have a young nation to form; we have an old one to rejuvenate." He predicted that when she had achieved a "degree of perfection" in her reform of Russia, the world would bear witness: "As once one visited Sparta, Egypt, and Greece, one will visit Russia." [101] Remarkably, Diderot wrote as if visits to Russia belonged to the utopian future, as if he had not just returned from Russia six months before. Even though he had been there himself, the notion of the voyage to Russia still remained for him, as for Voltaire, something imagined, projected, deferred, and ultimately fantastic.

In that same letter, Diderot promised to correct Jaucourt's article on Russia in a new edition of the Encyclopedia, to gratify Catherine, but he also hinted that Catherine herself was not immune to correction, for he was rereading her *Instruction*: "and I have had the insolence to reread it, pen in hand." [102] This self-conscious declaration of philosophical presumption was not followed by any critical commentary, and Catherine must have forgotten that "insolence" by the time she received, after Diderot's death in 1784, his books and papers which she had purchased in 1765. These included a manuscript entitled "Observations on the Instruction by the Empress of Russia," and the empress was not pleased to see it. "This piece," wrote Catherine irritably to Grimm, ever loyal, "is true babble (*babil*)." It was just the kind of expression Diderot himself employed to describe his childish cacklings and stammerings in the interviews. "He must have composed this after his return from here," concluded Catherine, "for he never spoke to me of it." [103] By the time she came to speak of Diderot to Ségur in 1787, it was obvious that her reading of his posthumous criticism had completely revised her memory of his visit. She claimed that in their interviews Diderot wanted everything "overturned" in Russia, "to substitute impracticable theories." She claimed that he did all the talking, so that "a witness who came upon us would have taken the two of us, him for a severe pedagogue, and me for his humble student." He lectured her on law, administration, politics, and economy. Finally, "speaking frankly," she put Diderot in his place:

Monsieur Diderot, I have heard with the greatest pleasure that which your brilliant spirit has inspired in you, but with all your great principles, which I understand very well, one would make beautiful books and bad works. You forget in all your plans of reform the difference between our two positions; you, you only work on paper, which bears everything; it is all smooth, supple, and opposes no obstacles, neither to your imagination nor to your pen; while I, poor empress, I work on human skin, which is quite otherwise irritable and ticklish.[104]

In 1787 that is what she told Ségur she had said to Diderot in 1774; no doubt it is what she wished she had said, after seeing what Diderot wrote about her *Instruction*. Yet, Diderot's own memoranda suggested that in St. Petersburg he never had the nerve to lecture Catherine about legislation or politics, that his boldest flight of fancy was advising her to move to Moscow. So Catherine's harangue was probably apocryphal, but it demonstrated how well she understood the philosophical impulse to "work" on Eastern Europe, its appeal as an abstract domain that "opposes no obstacles" to the imagination or the pen.

Diderot, pen in hand, just back from Russia in 1774, began by remarking that there was, in politics, no true sovereign but the nation, no true legislator but the people. He went on to pronounce that Catherine was a "despot," and to question whether her *Instruction* pointed toward a legal code under which she sincerely intended to "abdicate" her despotism. This was certainly an issue he wished he had raised in St. Petersburg—and never dared—so that now, writing only for himself, he conjured up the physical presence of the woman he had encountered so frequently and so recently, but would never see again:

> If in reading what I just wrote and in listening to her conscience, her heart quivers with joy, then she wants no more slaves; if she trembles, if her blood recedes, if she turns pale, then she has believed herself to be better than she was.[105]

This was the philosopher's fantasy, to tell the truth to the empress, to stir her conscience, to overwhelm her in an almost sexual triumph of the blood and leave her either quivering or trembling. Catherine, however, was not to read this until after Diderot's death, and her revenge was the speech to Ségur with which she claimed to have dismissed Diderot from the beginning. That their many personal interviews had to be completed afterward by fictional elaborations and revisions suggests the complex constraints upon their direct communication in St. Petersburg.

"Russia is a European state," declared Catherine in the *Instruction*; this was no simple statement of geographical fact, but a programmatic statement of policy that played upon the Enlightenment's discovery of Eastern Europe. "It little matters," commented Diderot, pen in hand, "whether it is Asiatic or European," and as for manners in general, they could only be judged as good or bad—"neither African, nor Asian, nor European." [106] Diderot rejected the conventional concept of characteristic continental influences, for the ambiguities of Eastern Europe defied the Asia-or-Europe dichotomy of Montesquieu. Catherine's *Instruction* remarked geographically that "the empire of Russia occupies an extent of 32 degrees in latitude and 165 in longitude"—the better to insist that such a vast empire required the rule of an absolute sovereign. Diderot, however, in his commentary, considered these measurements as a problem not of politics but rather of civilization: "To civilize all at once such an enormous country seems to me a project beyond human forces." He therefore made three recommendations, and the first, no surprise, was to move the government to Moscow. Second, he proposed the creation of a model district in the Russian empire where it might be possible "to execute a plan of civilization." This was the Enlightenment at work, making plans of civilization for districts that did not exist, and Diderot explained the hypothetical effects with a clarifying analogy: "This district would be, by its relation to the rest of the empire, what France is in Europe relative to the countries that surround it."[107] That Diderot cast France in this role, as the influential example of civilization in Europe, revealed the extent of his cultural engagement. He might pretend to make no distinctions among the manners of Africa, Asia, and Europe, but only because all three continents were governed by the same model of development with the same land of reference.

If Diderot's attention to Russia was less comprehensive than Voltaire's vision of Eastern Europe, Diderot was more philosophically ambitious in generalizing from his Russian observations to a universally applicable scheme of backwardness and development, governed by a plan of civilization. Diderot's third recommendation for Russia, after changing the capital and establishing a model district, was to establish a Swiss colony.[108] That was also Voltaire's fantasy, the watchmakers of Astrakhan, or Azov, elaborated in the course of his correspondence with Catherine.

"Your Old Russian of Ferney"

In November 1773, Voltaire wrote to Catherine about himself and Diderot, who was then in St. Petersburg, describing their role in Eastern Europe in contrast to the roles of Tott at Constantinople or Boufflers in Poland. "We do not get ourselves taken prisoner like fools; we do not meddle with artillery of which we understand nothing," explained Voltaire. "We are the lay missionaries who preach the cult of Saint Catherine, and we can boast that our church is quite universal." For Voltaire at Ferney the cult of Catherine always remained identical with the cause of the Enlightenment in Eastern Europe. Diderot, however, who went to St. Petersburg, came away with the compulsion to preach at least posthumously to Catherine herself. As "lay missionaries" their mission was ambiguously double: to worship Catherine in Western Europe, and to celebrate the advance of civilization in Eastern Europe. The former was a practical project of publicity that they could effectively execute as eminences in the Republic of Letters. The latter was more purely philosophical, conceived at a distance and elaborated in fantasy or even as farce. The cult of Catherine, wrote Voltaire, awaited her baptism in Constantinople, "in the presence of the prophet Grimm," while Maria Theresa, who established a commission of chastity to oversee morals in Vienna, might do the same in Bosnia and Serbia.[109]

Catherine was perhaps less fully receptive than usual to such playful insinuations at this particular period, for she was facing the gravest domestic crisis of her reign, the popular rebellion headed by the Cossack Pugachev, who claimed to be none other than her deposed and deceased husband Peter III. Diderot appeared to have been only minimally aware of this political upheaval in the provinces, which roughly coincided with his stay in St. Petersburg. Catherine, however, informed Voltaire by letter in January 1774 that a certain "highway robber" was pillaging the province of Orenburg, which she described as a land of Tartars and deported criminal elements, like those sent to populate the American colonies; those colonies were also on the brink of rebellion in 1774. As for Pugachev himself, Catherine assured Voltaire that "this freak of the human species does not disturb at all the pleasure I have in conversing with Diderot."[110] Voltaire's response in February was thoroughly typical, commencing with yet another imaginary voyage: "Madame, the letter of 19 January, with which your imperial majesty honored me, has transported me in spirit to Orenburg, and introduced me to M. Pugachev; it is apparently the chevalier de Tott who has had this farce performed." Again Eastern Europe was the domain of farce, in which the scenes were staged and characters invented by imaginative interlopers from Western Europe. Voltaire was much struck by Catherine's account of Orenburg, just south of the Ural mountains, and his spiritual transport brought him to the eastern frontier of the continent. In fact, the area of Pugachev's rebellion was basically between the Ural and Volga rivers, the geographical band that was still widely regarded as Asia in the eighteenth century, though it is Europe today. In 1774 Pugachev put to the torch the town of Kazan on the Volga, from which Catherine had saluted Voltaire—"here I am in Asia"—in 1767. Just as Diderot imagined a model district that would enlighten by its influence the rest of the Russian empire, so Voltaire imagined the province of Orenburg as the area of least enlightenment, a "barbaric land," conceived according to the same model of development. "Your rays cannot penetrate everywhere at the same time," he wrote to Catherine. "An empire of two thousand leagues in longitude only becomes civilized ('se police') in the long run."[111] Pugachev himself was dismissed as a mere puppet, a figment of Tott's imagination; for Voltaire the cultural geography of Eastern Europe was the key to understanding an insurrection against Catherine, and against civilization.

Voltaire wrote to Catherine that he hoped Diderot would consider stopping at Ferney on the way back from St. Petersburg to recount his encounters with Catherine: "If he does not come to the shore of Lake Geneva, I will go myself to be buried on the shore of Lake Ladoga."[112] In fact, he was jealous of Diderot's voyage in the flesh, and in August 1774 Voltaire's anxiety exploded in an epistolary protest against Catherine's "indifference" to him: "Your imperial majesty has given me up for Diderot, or Grimm, or some other favorite." He accused her of ingratitude, for he had "quarreled with all the Turks on your behalf, and yet again with M. le marquis de Pugachev." Voltaire resolved that he would "never love another empress in my life"—a safe bet, since he was 80 and had only four years to live. Still, he signed the letter "your old Russian of Ferney." Catherine graciously reassured him of her favor and friendship, accepting his continued devotion in the form that he offered it: "You are a good Russian." He replied, much mollified, that unfortunately he would not be among "the crowd of Europeans and Asians" who paid homage to her at St. Petersburg that year, though he begged permission to come "next year, or in two years, or in ten." Instead of going himself, he recommended another young Swiss engineer who wanted to enter her service, who could "survey the plan of Constantinople, and thwart (*contrecarrer*) the chevalier de Tott." The war was over, though, except in Voltaire's imagination; the Treaty of Kuchuk Kainarji was signed, as he certainly knew. The crisis in his correspondence with Catherine in 1774 was triggered not only by Diderot's voyage, but also by the waning of the war which had fired his geographical imagination to visionary fantasies of empire in Eastern Europe. The destinations of geography still glimmered in the correspondence, and mingled pathetically with Voltaire's frankly declared jealousy of his own protégé, the Swiss engineer: "Your majesty cannot prevent me from being jealous of all those who are twenty-five, who can go to the Neva and to the Bosphorus, who can serve you by head and by hand."[113] The idea of Eastern Europe, born from his head in Catherine's service, would outlive them both to influence the modern history of Europe over the next two centuries.

The final letters of the final years reinterpreted their now irrevocable geographical separation as a spiritual condition of Voltaire's religious reverence for the cult of St. Catherine. In a letter of 1775 he wrote that he had his portrait painted as he wrote in front of Catherine's portrait. This artistic "fantasy"—which united them on the same canvas—was to remind Catherine that there was one who adored her "as the quietists adore God." In the very last letter of 1777 he declared her recent code of reforms to be "the gospel of the universe," and hoped she still possessed the secret of driving the Turks from Europe. Addressing Eastern Europe, his final words carried him across the continent from Ferney to St. Petersburg, in the vocative voice of prayer: "I prostrate myself at your feet, and I cry in my agony: allah, allah, Catherine rezoul, allah."[114] The farce was finished. Voltaire's apotheosis of Catherine fed upon the cultural transpositions and geographical associations that formed the presiding fantasies of their passionately imaginative correspondence.

Chapter Six

Addressing Eastern Europe, Part II: Rousseau's Poland

"Brave Poles, Take Care"

"We are three, Diderot, d'Alembert, and I, who set up altars to you," wrote Voltaire to Catherine in December 1766. It was an impressive congregation, even if d'Alembert had already declined the ultimate invitation to worship in person, and Diderot not yet provided that perfect proof of his devotion. Still the cult was incomplete, the Enlightenment not unanimous, and in that same month Catherine's favorite, Gregory Orlov, wrote an insinuating letter of invitation to the most outstanding dissenter, Jean-Jacques Rousseau. Orlov, described by the Englishman George Macartney as colossal in stature but "totally unimproved by reading," was hardly one to weep over *La nouvelle Héloïse*, and he could not have summoned Rousseau to Russia unless Catherine was sponsoring the invitation. Politely, Orlov thanked Rousseau for "the instruction I have taken from your books, though they were not written for me," and invited the philosopher to come live on an estate of pastoral simplicity, near St. Petersburg, where "the inhabitants understand neither English nor French, still less Greek and Latin." Rousseau replied from England, declining the invitation in precisely the terms that Voltaire also employed to rule out any real voyage to Russia: "If I were less infirm, more active, younger, and if you were nearer to the sun. . . ."[1] The philosopher further pleaded that he was insufficiently sociable to make such a visit, no conversationalist, altogether solitary, and only interested in gardening.

When Rousseau wrote the *Social Contract* in 1762, he was already critical of Peter, and when he wrote about Poland ten years later at the time of the first partition, he became the declared enemy of Catherine. By 1778, the year that Voltaire and Rousseau both died, they left behind antithetical reputations for partisanship concerning Eastern Europe: Voltaire for Russia against Poland, Rousseau for Poland against Russia. Yet such a neat opposition was belied by the identical terms in which they evaded invitations, and Rousseau never went to Warsaw any more than Voltaire to St. Petersburg. Rather, Poland and Russia provided Rousseau and Voltaire respectively with alternative visions of Eastern Europe, the laboratory of ideological experimentation in which the Enlightenment explored political possibilities by performing theoretical operations within a hypothetical domain.

"If one does not thoroughly know the Nation for which one labors," cautioned Rousseau, at the very start of the *Considerations on the Government of Poland*, "the work one does for it, however excellent it may be in itself, will always fail in application, and more still when it concerns a nation already fully instituted, of which the tastes, the manners, the prejudices, and the vices are too rooted (*enracinés*) to be easily smothered (*étouffés*) by some new seeds (*semences*)."[2] In 1766 Rousseau declined to go to Russia because he was only interested in gardening; five years later, when he accepted an invitation to write about Poland without actually going there, he framed the philosophical problem in the language of the garden. In the *Social Contract*, he had censured Peter for having "urged his subjects to be what they were not and so prevented them from becoming what they might have been." He compared the Russian tsar to a French tutor, forcing the minds of his pupils, whatever their natural aptitudes and inclinations. Rousseau might also have made the analogy to classical French gardening, with its rigorously forced designs, finally challenged in the eighteenth century by the "natural" values of English taste. Rousseau's refuge at Ermonville was, of course, an English garden. Yet natural gardening was also a labor of design and cultivation, less obviously advertised, and Rousseau's respect for the "roots" of Poland—its tastes, manners, prejudices, and vices—could not hide the hand of the philosophical gardener. The work of political prescription that he undertook in the *Considerations*, he readily admitted, would be better entrusted to Poles, or at least to "someone who has studied well on the spot the Polish nation and those which neighbor it." He himself was only a foreigner, capable at most of "general views."[3] Yet it was precisely his perfect innocence and ignorance of the nation and its neighbors that enabled him to theorize imaginatively and formulate an alternative to

Voltaire's vision of Eastern Europe, while advancing "general views" on the political theory of patriotism.

Rousseau conceived the *Considerations* as a work not only about Poland, but also for Poland: "the Nation for which (*pour laquelle*) one labors." This phrase possessed a double sense of patronage and prescription; Poland commissioned the work, and the work itself made recommendations to Poland. Rousseau alluded to his commission in the first sentence of his work, which also identified the principal source: "The tableau of the government of Poland made by Count Wielhorski, and the reflections there appended, are instructive pieces for whoever (*quiconque*) would wish to form a regular plan for the recasting (*refonte*) of that government."[4] Rousseau himself was the particular *quiconque* in this case—yet Poland was presented as anyone's subject, generally inviting the ideas of whoever, of the enlightened public. In fact, these were years of remarkable public attention to Poland, from the rising of the Confederation of Bar against Russia in 1768 to the shock of the first partition in 1772. Not only did Voltaire and Rousseau take their respective public stands, in dramatic disagreement, but the period also inspired such uncharacteristic efforts as Marat's epistolary novel *Adventures of the Young Count Potowski* and Casanova's long, earnest *History of the Turbulences of Poland*.

Michal Wielhorski came to Paris in 1770 as the representative of the Confederation of Bar. There he hoped to translate the sympathy of Choiseul into more active support from the French government, but the Choiseul ministry fell from power at the end of that year, and Wielhorski's greatest diplomatic triumphs were among the philosophes of the Enlightenment. Wielhorski, ostensibly soliciting suggestions for constitutional reform in Poland, rallied intellectual support to the cause of the Confederation, won sympathy, and inspired manuscripts from the abbé Mably and from Rousseau himself. Mably's *Government and Laws of Poland* and Rousseau's *Considerations* were both written between 1770 and 1772, though neither was published at that time; Wielhorski's own account, which Rousseau acknowledged as the principal source for the *Considerations*, was published in French (in London) in 1775, updated to cite in its own support the sentiments of Rousseau. In fact, Rousseau's reliance on Wielhorski indicated simultaneously his degree of partisan engagement and of academic distance. To the considerable extent that the *Considerations* was based on Wielhorski's "tableau," Rousseau's recasting of the government of Poland was still further intellectually removed from its subject, from Poland itself.

Rousseau found the literary solution to the dilemma of distance by employing epistolary forms. He was a foreigner who knew nothing of Poland "on the spot," so rather than affecting the omniscience of an expert treatise throughout, the *Considerations* repeatedly revealed itself as an open letter to Poles in Poland. The intellectual gap that separated the author from his subject was represented in an epistolary space that separated Western Europe from Eastern Europe. "Brave Poles, take care," wrote Rousseau, suddenly introducing direct address into his introductory "State of the Question." From that moment the second person became a narrative option which expressed his philosophical relation to the subject of Poland as an epistolary relation to the Poles: "You love liberty, you are worthy of it; you have defended it against a powerful and cunning aggressor."[5] In its epistolary character as an open letter, addressed to an entire nation, the *Considerations* showed itself in form, as well as content, the antithesis and counterpart of Voltaire's private letters to one absolute sovereign, who was, of course, the very same "powerful and cunning aggressor" arraigned by Rousseau.

In Rousseau's review of Poland's political institutions he tended to recommend minor adjustments rather than major reforms, reluctant to smother rooted plants by scattering new seeds: "Correct, if possible, the abuses of your constitution, but do not despise that which has made you what you are." Thus Rousseau reformulated in the second person his criticism of Peter, who tried to make the Russians "what they were not." In his respect for Poland's constitution Rousseau would not even recommend the abolition of the *liberum veto*, which required parliamentary unanimity, though he judged the excessive employment of the veto "barbaric," and thought its abuse should be a capital crime. On the whole, though he had penned into the *Social Contract* an extremely powerful position for a "lawgiver," he responded rather modestly when Wielhorski offered him that role with respect to Poland. He recommended that changes be made only "with an extreme circumspection." For law had to govern "the hearts of the citizens," and the fundamental question Rousseau posed was "how then to move hearts, and make them love the country and its laws?"[6] It was in addressing this question that the *Considerations* transcended its commission as a critique of Polish government and made its contribution to the Enlightenment as an original work of political theory.

Rousseau first stated the problem of Poland in a set of conventional observations, familiar as formulas of the Enlightenment on Eastern Europe. Poland, Rousseau conceded, possessed "no economic order" and "no military discipline." Therefore, its only hope of survival against aggressive neighbors was—and here Rousseau exploded the conventional premise— "to establish the Republic in the heart of the Poles," that is, "the unique asylum where force can neither reach nor destroy it." Neighboring powers might "gobble you up" ("vous engloutissent"), Rousseau warned, but they would be unable to "digest" a land that lived in the heart. "Patriotic zeal" was the only reliable rampart of the republic, and he cited the exemplary spirit of the Confederation of Bar, not yet finally defeated as Rousseau was writing; the Confederation held out against the Russians at Częstochowa until 1772, the year of the partition. Yet neither imminent defeat nor even partition invalidated the political theory Rousseau proposed for the case of Poland, inasmuch as the Poland he envisioned was immune to operations of force, secure in the hearts of its people. "If you make it so that a Pole can never become a Russian, I answer you that Russia will never subjugate Poland."[7] This was an epistolary moment fraught with significance, between the "I" of the philosophe and the "you" of the nation; the former had already declared the latter "worthy" of liberty, and now guaranteed that liberty by reinterpreting its significance. This was also a revolutionary moment in intellectual history, for these were crucial phrases in the ideological articulation of modern nationalism. Rousseau apostrophized the Pole who could never become a Russian, the Pole who carried his country in his heart, and the next two centuries of European history would prove this prophetic vision.

In his *Charles XII* Voltaire sketched a "natural history" of Eastern Europe, a table of lands and peoples organized in the spirit of Linnaeus. Voltaire's table made Eastern Europe into an object of mastery for the conqueror and the philosophe alike. Forty years later Rousseau seized upon the same principles of natural history, but turned over the table by declaring the distinct species to be a classification of ultimate power rather than a sign of imminent subjection. Eastern Europe was the field of observation in which he discovered Poles who could not become Russians, and heralded their unmasterable identity as a defiant challenge to Voltaire's vision of civilization and empire.

Rousseau's natural history was not purely a matter of observing and classifying according to nature. The nation could be cultivated in its distinctness, which allowed a purpose to politics and a role for the political philosopher, like Rousseau, called in consultation. He recommended to Poland institutions designed to "form the genius, the character, the tastes, and the manners of a people; that make it itself and not another; that inspire in it that ardent of love of country founded on habits impossible to uproot." In fact, he had already begun from the premise that the nation possessed this distinctness of species, characterized by tastes, manners, prejudices, and vices "too rooted to be easily smothered." Rousseau's return to the issue of roots emphasized that national identity was dialectically formed between nature and cultivation, between botany and gardening. If it was urgent to cultivate, even inculcate a distinct identity, that was because there were antithetical forces that worked to efface that distinctness. "Today there are no more French, Germans, Spanish, or even English," he declared, perhaps prematurely. "There are only Europeans." Here the Europe he pejoratively invoked was evidently Western Europe, where "all have the same tastes, the same passions, the same manners." Poland, however, was challenged to refuse the mold: "Give another bent to the passions of the Poles; you will give to their souls a national physiognomy that will distinguish them from other peoples."[8] The "you" addressed by Rousseau was initially the "brave Poles" themselves, but here he implied the existence of an external agent at work upon Poland's national physiognomy. As surely as he assigned a supremely powerful position to the lawgiver in the *Social Contract* and the tutor in *Emile*, Rousseau also assumed such a presence in the Poland of his *Considerations*.

Yet the creation of national character was inevitably a work of detail, and Rousseau frankly acknowledged the obstacle of his own ignorance about Poland.

The succinct exposé of the manners of the Poles, which M. Wielhorski was good enough to communicate to me, does not suffice to acquaint me with their civil and domestic usages. But a great nation which has never mixed too much with its neighbors must have a lot which are its own, and which perhaps were becoming bastardized day by day by the general bent (*pente*) of Europe to take the tastes and manners of the French.[9]

The fastidiousness with which Rousseau looked to a nation "which has never mixed too much with its neighbors" not only conformed to his sense of species but also challenged the conventionally careless confusion and combination of the peoples of Eastern Europe. Voltaire observed similarities of dress among Poles, Russians, Tartars, and Hungarians, but Rousseau was determined to discover a unique national costume for Poland, preserved and protected from all foreign resemblances and influences, especially French. "Do exactly the contrary of that much admired tsar," ordered Rousseau, even as he himself issued edicts of apparel for Poland no less peremptory than those of Peter for Russia. "Let no Pole dare to appear at court dressed French style," wrote Rousseau of the Warsaw court he never visited.[10] Diderot, who did visit the court at St. Petersburg just after Rousseau wrote the *Considerations*, came away full of enthusiasm for the rapidity with which the Russian nation "becomes French." These antithetical sentiments suggest that what was at stake was not just costume but civilization, French style. Rousseau's challenge to the Enlightenment, dating back to the discourses, was his suspicion and rejection of civilization. Rousseau's construction of Eastern Europe associated Poland and Russia as lands that faced a portentous alternative, to accept or resist "the general bent of Europe."

The crucial recommendation of the *Considerations*, taking precedence over all thoughts of constitutional reform, was a system of national education.

It is education that must give to souls the national form, and so direct their opinions and tastes, that they may be patriots by inclination, by passion, by necessity.

A child, in opening its eyes, must see its country and till death must see nothing but that. Every true republican sucks with the milk of his mother the love of his country.[11]

With such observations as these Rousseau pioneered the intellectual origins of modern nationalism, and it was the case of Poland that served as stimulus to his political imagination. Rousseau himself, who never opened his eyes on the Polish landscape, defined and delimited the vision of every Polish soul, from infancy to death. While Voltaire corresponded with an absolute empress, presiding with her over the peoples of Eastern Europe, Rousseau penetrated to the people directly and dictated their identity. "A Frenchman, an Englishman, a Spaniard, an Italian, a Russian, are all virtually the same man," declared Rousseau, but a Pole "must be a Pole."[12] In appending the Russian to his catalogue of interchangeable Europeans he only reemphasized the perversity of Peter's program, while exaggerating its success, and implicitly warned that the Pole might find himself last on that list if he failed to follow Rousseau's injunction.

There was, however, another danger that Rousseau foresaw in the *Social Contract*, prophesying with regard to Russia: "The Tartars, its subjects or neighbors, will become its masters—and ours." Rousseau's Eastern Europe confronted a continental crisis, polarized between French tastes and manners on the one hand and Tartar inundations and devastations on the other. He did not explicitly formulate this as the conventional conflict between civilization and barbarism, between Europe and Asia, because he was not prepared to advocate either civilization or Europe. Instead he sought to resolve the dilemma by envisioning Eastern Europe as a crucible for the formation of national identity.

Voltaire's construction of Eastern Europe was above all an operation of mapping; he discovered and assembled its parts as he followed on the map the conquests of Charles and then Catherine. When Rousseau relocated Poland in the hearts of the Poles, he also liberated it from the constraints of cartography. In fact, Rousseau was no man for maps, dismissing them from the education of Emile as meaninglessly abstract representations. If Emile were to study maps, he would learn only "the names of cities, countries, and rivers of whose existence apart from the paper that we show him he has no notion."[13] Voltaire's correspondence with Catherine perfectly illustrated the syndrome Rousseau deplored, allowing the philosopher at Ferney to "fly to the Dardanelles, to the Danube, to the Black Sea, to Bender, into the Crimea, and especially to St. Petersburg." Poland's doom was to be its inscription on the maps of Voltaire and Catherine, their maps of conquest and partition. Rousseau's Poland, however, was safe from such inscription, secure in the hearts of its people; he had already removed Poland from the map twenty years before its annihilation. Because Rousseau understood, on the eve of the first partition, that Poland was menaced on the map, he found in Poland the point of departure for the political theory of national identity. Catherine might be mistress of the maps, but as far as Rousseau was concerned there were no real Russians. Poland might disappear from the maps and yet persist in its "national physiognomy." Poland was the point at which Rousseau inverted Voltaire's map of Eastern Europe.

Jean Starobinski has analyzed the life and works of Rousseau in terms of overcoming obstacles to "transparency," to the direct apprehension of intellectual and emotional truth. Rousseau's Poland was illuminated across an opaque curtain that separated him and his readers from Eastern Europe; in epistolary form the *Considerations* sought transparent access to the hearts of the Poles, assigning to them their Polish identity. His insight had in fact seized upon something essential in the Polish situation, the issue of national survival without political independence, but his imagery and ideology of patriotism had their greatest triumph among the revolutionary generation in France. Rousseau knew too little about Poland to be confident of having hit his mark, and concluded the *Considerations* with the same intellectual self-deprecation that Diderot demonstrated in his interviews with Catherine. "Perhaps all this is only a heap of chimeras," wrote Rousseau, who then labeled the so-called considerations as "my reveries."[14] As in the case of Diderot, a narrative of direct address revealed itself as reflexive reverie, personal fantasy. Poland, like Russia, equivocally accepted as part of Europe, challenged the Enlightenment to consider the viability of its political values and visions.

"To the End of the World"

"Won't you go to Poland with Mme Geoffrin?" wrote Voltaire to Jean-François Marmontel. It was just a joke, for Marmontel was no more likely to be going to Poland than Voltaire himself, and the mock challenge indicated the extent to which the voyage of Mme Geoffrin, who presided over the most celebrated salon of the Enlightenment in Paris, was a public event of compelling interest, permitting the philosophes to travel vicariously in her train. Grimm, who specialized in the intellectual gossip of the Enlightenment, declared that the visit of Mme Geoffrin in 1766 to Stanisław August, the king of Poland, was "a subject of conversation and curiosity for the public during the whole course of the summer." Grimm thought it showed "astonishing courage," the public spectacle of a "private person, going to the end of the world to enjoy the friendship of a great king."[15] Perhaps he himself took courage from her example when he traveled further still, some years later, to visit an even greater sovereign in St. Petersburg. Voltaire actually wrote from Ferney to Mme Geoffrin in Warsaw, at the end of the world, to regret that he could not make "the same voyage as you," but he declared her own to be "in France, a great epoch for all who think." In contrast, Mme Deffand, who ran a rival salon in Paris, could in her correspondence with Horace Walpole make mock of the traveler as "Mme Geoffrinska," as a character in the comedy of Eastern Europe.[16] Yet whether as comic curiosity or as epochal event, the journey of Mme Geoffrin to Poland in 1766 was certainly the most celebrated encounter of the Enlightenment with Eastern Europe until Diderot went to St. Petersburg in 1773. She was also the Enlightenment's most celebrated patron of Poland until Rousseau wrote his *Considerations* without undertaking her voyage.

Marie Thérèse Rodet, as Mme Geoffrin, was the wife of a wealthy bourgeois businessman in Paris, and she established in the 1750s a successful salon that included the most eminent of the philosophes. She entertained such founding fathers of the Enlightenment as Fontenelle and Montesquieu, as well as the editors of the Encyclopedia, Diderot and d'Alembert. Marmontel, himself a regular at her Wednesday evenings, reported that "she possessed no inkling either of art or of literature and had never read nor learned anything except at random," but she nevertheless "excelled in the art of presiding" and moderated the conversation of her guests by "setting limits to their liberty and reining them back in case of need by a word, a gesture, as if by an invisible thread."[17] Stanisław Poniatowski, the loyal follower of Charles XII, recommended his son to Mme Geoffrin in 1753 when the 21-year-old future king of Poland came to Paris for a six-month stay. She maternally adopted the young man—he addressed her as "maman" forever after—and he made a fine impression upon her philosophes for possessing those perfect French manners which Rousseau would later deplore as fatal for Poland. Fontenelle even asked if the young Pole knew "Polish as well as French."[18] In 1758 Mme Geoffrin entertained in Paris the visiting princess of Anhalt-Zerbst, Catherine's mother, who also made such a favorable impression on Voltaire. So when Catherine seized the throne of Russia in 1762, and then placed her lover on the throne of Poland in 1764, Mme Geoffrin found herself the confidante and correspondent of two reigning sovereigns. Both correspondences soon turned on the possibility of summoning Mme Geoffrin to Eastern Europe.

In September 1764 Stanisław August wrote from Warsaw to Mme Geoffrin, his "chère maman," to report proudly on his election as king of Poland:

I had the satisfaction of being proclaimed by the mouth of all the women as by that of all the men of my nation, present at this election; for the primate, in passing before their carriages, actually did them the courtesy of asking who they desired for king. Why were you not there? You would have named your son![19]

She was not there because she was not Polish, was not part of his nation, was in fact utterly Parisian; she was born in Paris in 1699, died in Paris in

1777, and rarely left Paris at all, except for her journey to Warsaw in 1766. Yet, from the moment of the election of Stanisław August in 1764, the correspondence raised the improbable fantasy of her presence in Poland, even as he lamented her actual absence.

Ma chère maman, will I then never see you again? Will I then enjoy no more of the sweetness, of the wisdom of your opinions (*vos avis*)? For from there where you are, you can give me maxims (*maximes*), but advice (*conseil*) is out of range (*hors de portée*).[20]

Stanisław August thus formulated for Mme Geoffrin, perhaps even as a warning, the political dilemma of the Enlightenment in Western Europe with respect to enlightened absolutism in Eastern Europe. For it was there that the philosophes envisioned a domain of political play, the lands of opportunity and experiment, where "everything was to be done." Yet all their wisdom was qualified by distance, "out of range." This was more than a matter of miles, as Diderot discovered when he actually went all the way to St. Petersburg in 1773 and felt himself as far as ever from philosophical impact. The context of correspondence was perfectly suited to the distinction of Stanisław August between general maxims, the prerogative of Paris, and specific advice, which he dismissed in advance as beyond the range of even the most celebrated salon of the city.

He made this point more explicit in a letter of October: "As it suits everyone at the beginning of a reign to confirm ancient treaties, I begin by authorizing you in the most authentic, the most solemn, the most immutable manner, to continue to give me your sincere opinions." Thus with the charm of affected pomp, he "authorized" the epistolary transmission of "opinions." Then he took into account the distance from Paris to Warsaw: "I further reserve to myself the right not always to conform exactly to your advice, because it is impossible that at this distance you should be always exactly instructed of the facts."[21] One of the most striking characteristics of the correspondence between Stanisław August and Mme Geoffrin was the self-consciousness with which their letters addressed the issue of epistolary advice across the continent of Europe, with its relevance for the role of enlightened absolutism in Eastern Europe, even though he was a monarch of modest authority, at times a mere puppet, and she was less a philosopher than a famous hostess.

Mme Geoffrin's first letter to the new king saluted him in the same spirit of casual blasphemy that Voltaire employed in his letters to Catherine: "My dear son, my dear king, my dear Stanislas-Auguste! there you are, three persons in one; you are my Trinity!" With the same mock religious fervor she proclaimed a vision of Poland's happy destiny: "I see Poland reborn from its ashes, and I see it, like the new Jerusalem, resplendent!" Just as he imagined her present in Poland, at his election, she claimed to see Poland, his Poland, in her imagination. Immediately she considered the possibility of a visit:

My heart rushes toward you, and my body longs to follow it. Here! my dear son, if you are as great a king as I desire and I hope, why should I not go to admire you as another Solomon? I do not wish to see that as impossible.[22]

The conditional tenses suggested that the voyage they dared to contemplate hovered on the horizon between possible and impossible, a challenge to their imaginations. For the moment it appeared as biblical allegory, with Warsaw as Jerusalem and Stanisław August as Solomon, but in crowning herself as the queen of Sheba Mme Geoffrin already foresaw that such a pilgrimage would become a public sensation. "When the queen of Sheba went to see Solomon she surely had a squire," wrote Voltaire to Marmontel two years later, casting the latter as the squire. "You would have a charming voyage!"[23]

Mme Geoffrin, as soon as she declared the voyage both desirable and possible, revealed her reasons with reference to the earlier letter: "Your Majesty is quite right to say that advice on everything is out of range, and maxims, even the most beautiful, are very common." She was not ready to restrict herself to mere maxims, and the way to Warsaw appeared as the solution to the dilemma he had posed. In the meantime, the first subject on which she wished to interrogate and advise him, that of the prospects for his marriage, was constrained, as foreseen, by epistolary distance and the need for discretion. He declined to respond to her urgent queries: "You are at five hundred leagues, and I am king, and who can guarantee me against the hazards to which this letter may be humanly exposed." The limits of epistolary communication brought him back to the idea of the voyage: "Ah, why can't you come to see me!" For the moment he could only suggest that their correspondence on this subject remain one-sided: "I can not tell you if I will marry and who I will espouse, but I would take very great pleasure in receiving from you all the different ideas, opinions, advice, divinations possible upon this subject." This was hardly correspondence at all, and though he gave her carte blanche to say whatever she wished, he relieved himself not only of any obligation to follow her advice but even of the courtesy to reply. The details of his letter told her nothing about his marriage but only about his carriage, which he was ordering from France through her. He wanted yellow upholstery inside, and a lantern for reading.[24] It was French taste as well as French philosophy that created the standard of civilization in the eighteenth century, measuring the distance between Western Europe and Eastern Europe, but Mme Geoffrin, and the Enlightenment in general, aspired to an influence that went beyond upholstery.

The king's concern about the discretion of correspondence was nevertheless legitimate, especially since his private epistolary relations with Mme

Geoffrin, like those of Catherine with Voltaire, were partly conceived as public relations, for the projection of an enlightened image in Western Europe. "All my friends were very impressed to see the first letter that Your Majesty wrote to me after his election," wrote Mme Geoffrin. "I read to them the first page; they were all enchanted by it, but the letter did not leave my hands." Thus she promised him both publicity and discretion, and the scene represented the complex interplay of public and private concerns that conditioned the correspondence. She was perhaps less meticulous about keeping both hands on her first letter from Catherine the year before, for that one actually ended up being published in a gazette, to the embarrassment of all parties. "I feared to write you a second time," wrote Catherine wryly, "lest you think me infatuated with the desire to shine by letters."[25]

When Stanisław August was elected to the Polish throne, Catherine, who had engineered the election, wrote to congratulate Mme Geoffrin on the success of "your son." Catherine piously attributed the election to Providence ("if he has become king, I don't know how"), and even outlined an influential role for Mme Geoffrin: "They say that your son conducts himself marvelously, and I am very glad of that; I leave the care of rectifying him in case of need to your maternal tenderness." Such a right of rectification was one that Catherine would allow no person in Paris to exercise upon herself, and in fact it was she who intended to rectify the behavior of Stanisław August if he failed to conform to the dictates of her Polish policy. Toward the end of 1764, when Mme Geoffrin was already imagining a visit to Warsaw, Catherine imagined her visiting St. Petersburg, and envisioned their encounter in a letter to Paris. There would be no Persian prostrations:

If you should enter into my room, I would say to you: "Madame, sit down, let us babble (*jasons*) at our ease." You would have an armchair vis-à-vis me, a table between us two.[26]

It was a fantasy of philosophy and power meeting on equal terms—if only to babble—though when Diderot came to St. Petersburg in 1773, the little table supposedly served to keep his hands off the empress. The armchair offered to Mme Geoffrin was that of any armchair traveler to Eastern Europe in the eighteenth century.

Stanisław August was in Paris as a young man when he met Mme Geoffrin, and his two lifelong regrets were never seeing Rome and never meeting Voltaire. Catherine had never been to Paris, as she admitted to Mme Geoffrin in ironic self-deprecation; the tsarina remained in Russia and affected surprise that "nine hundred leagues from here people are occupied with me." Peter went to Paris, but for Catherine the continental chasm of 900 leagues, across which she corresponded, was essential to her mystique in Western Europe. Her correspondents were invited to come to her, and

Mme Geoffrin was even informed—for Catherine affected to deprecate her own written French—that "if you would learn Russian, that would much accommodate me."[27] This was certainly intended ironically, for Mme Geoffrin was most unlikely to learn Russian, and in fact even her written French was not very good. Mme Geoffrin could not spell.

Mme Geoffrin's own letters to Catherine have not survived, but clearly she responded to the image of the table for two in St. Petersburg, for Catherine returned to it in a letter of the following spring. "I remember very well, madame," wrote the tsarina, "the place I gave you vis-à-vis me, the little table between us two." Catherine, however, solicited no opinions or advice about governing Russia. "People have false ideas about Russia among you (*chez vous*)," declared Catherine flatly, and in that "vous" she included "you yourself, madame, who are so instructed and so enlightened."[28] Catherine was more strict than Stanisław August in defining the limits of epistolary impact, and even a visit to St. Petersburg promised no more than an occasion of babbling. That was just how Diderot described his own interviews with Catherine in 1773, in modesty to be sure, but also in frustration at the failure of dialogue, the obstruction of the little table, the impossibility of an honest vis-à-vis.

In March 1765 Stanisław August began to consider more seriously the fantasy of a visit from Mme Geoffrin: "Could it be that you should think of realizing your voyage to Poland?" Still he clung to conditional tenses, but the voyage now seemed sufficiently realizable to arouse in him a certain ambivalence:

Ah! *ma chère maman!* could it be? could it be? But you well know I would wish already to occupy myself only with acting so that there would be beautiful roads, beautiful bridges, good lodgings, in short all that it would require to keep you from saying: "Ah! what a nasty (*vilain*) kingdom is the kingdom of my son!"[29]

Thus he attributed to her, in advance, the laments of every eighteenth-century traveler from Western Europe to Eastern Europe, while assuming for himself the project of someday closing that gap. The certainty of her condescension to his kingdom defined the respective roles of their correspondence, negotiating the relation between two individuals and between two separate spheres of Europe. In her reply to his letter, the voyage appeared for the first time as something settled and scheduled for the following year, no longer a conditional fantasy: "I will depart from Paris April 1, and I will go slowly, as long as the earth can carry me to the foot of your throne, and there I will die in your arms of joy, of pleasure, and of love." Yet she was not yet too far gone in ecstasy to take up the king on his expressed concern over her experience of Poland.

My dear son, I will find very beautiful all the roads that conduct me to this happiness; I will not judge them such as they are until I am leaving you; for then I well believe that they will appear quite ugly to me. I laughed in reading the exclamation that you pretend I will make, saying: "Ah! what a nasty kingdom is the kingdom of my son!" To be sure, I will not find it worthy of you.[30]

Like Rousseau, who presumed to declare the Poles "worthy" of liberty, Mme Geoffrin prepared to find them unworthy of an enlightened monarch. She laughed at the king's anticipation of her exclamation, but only because his guess, as she readily agreed, was right on the mark.

Indeed it was precisely such nastiness, such unworthiness as evidenced on every road, at every bridge, that made enlightened absolutism appear so compellingly appropriate in Eastern Europe. The Enlightenment in Western Europe staked out an empire of prescriptive influence, and Mme Geoffrin, in anticipation of Poland, even assumed a crown of her own. "Yes, yes, I will go like the queen of Sheba to admire your wisdom," she declared. "Since my son is king, I can well compare myself to a queen." Such was the imaginary coronation of Mme Geoffrin, who presided over philosophers in Paris on Wednesday evenings, holding the reins of invisible thread. Did she contemplate the forms of power and conquest? According to her daughter, Mme de la Ferté-Imbault, Mme Geoffrin possessed "the soul of Alexander."[31]

"Descending as if from a Planet"

Mme Geoffrin wrote to the king in May to observe that the voyage seemed "not impossible," to declare herself "neither fearful nor difficult about the delicacies of women," and to analyze what she saw as the fundamental urgency of her going to Poland.

It would be impossible for me to maintain with you a commerce of several years if my ideas about your spirit, about its range, about its nature, and about its faculties were not further renewed. . . . Insipidity will enter into our commerce if all I say to you has no longer any relation to all that you feel and all that surrounds you.[32]

The voyage then was necessitated by their correspondence, was but the means toward its continued vitality. The letter was the primary form of "commerce" connecting their separate spheres, but her personal presence in Poland, for a matter of months, would legitimize years of epistolary exchange. Without the voyage she would gradually cease to know her correspondent, and would know nothing of "all that surrounds you." What surrounded him was Poland; she wrote of his court and courtiers as "a lot of surroundings (*d'entours*) and of quite different species." The letter ended in a triple exclamation upon the standard of the correspondence: "Frankness, frankness, frankness!"[33] Like Rousseau, Mme Geoffrin was conscious of writing to Poland across a curtain of uncertain transparency.

The king was also apprehensive: "*Ma chère maman*, I would give treasures to be able every day of my life to pass one hour with you, and yet I fear the effect of the prodigious difference that you will find between what surrounds you there where you are, and what you will find here." Geographical distance measured "prodigious difference," an unbridgeable chasm:

> You certainly have a lot of experience, but you do not have that of such a considerable displacement; you have never, so to speak, left Paris, and you would come all at once as far as Poland (*jusqu'en Pologne*)! No, I will believe it only when I see it, and I admit that I fear almost as much as I desire to see you here.[34]

Correspondence could mediate prodigious difference, even "as far as Poland," but the displacement of travel was a breach of the barrier between separate surroundings. Caught between fear and desire, the king, in June 1765, a whole year in advance, recognized that such a displacement called for the most scrupulous rehearsal and arrangement:

> You will lodge in the palace where I reside, on the same floor with me. . . . You will dine and sup *chez vous* when you wish, or with me. . . . You will have a carriage at your orders. . . . When I know if you are coming by Vienna, Dresden, or Berlin, I will send ahead of you a man who knows French, German, and Polish.[35]

Mme Geoffrin's entry into Poland was elaborately anticipated from all possible angles, as the decisive moment of displacement, the moment that Ségur would experience twenty years later as a departure from Europe itself. The arrangements for Mme Geoffrin were intended to structure her experience in the face of "prodigious difference," and the rumors in the gazettes about her voyage included the speculation that in Warsaw she would find, constructed especially for her, a house whose plan and furnishing exactly duplicated her home in the rue Saint-Honoré. The notion of such symmetrical mimicry, dramatizing the difference between Western Europe and Eastern Europe, also exercised its fascination after the death of Voltaire in 1778, when Catherine considered constructing a replica of Ferney at Tsarskoye Selo to house the library of the late French philosopher.[36]

Mme Geoffrin, in June 1765, wanted to know which of the three routes into Poland proposed by the king would be "least bad," and whether the water of Warsaw was of good quality: "When I have good water, I ask for nothing else." At the same time she contemplated the refinements of travel as she continued with the commission for the king's own carriage, forwarding to Warsaw fabric scraps of yellow velvet so that he could make a final decision about the upholstery. She also offered to act as agent in acquiring for Poland the diamonds of Mme Pompadour, recently deceased, but the great subject of the summer was the possibility of her own personal displacement.

> All the world, that is to say my friends and my society, are such admirers of your friendship for me, that they all tell me I absolutely must go see you. I stiffen up,

purse my lips, and respond in the style of an oracle: Nothing is impossible. This idea of going to see you, my dear son, is so delicious for me, that there is no day that I do not make some arrangements, purchases, inquiries in that regard.[37]

The deliciousness of the project was greatly enhanced by the public interest in her "impossible" adventure. That summer Mme Geoffrin made little excursions outside Paris, "like those little birds who try to fly," and all her friends guessed, as she intended they should, that she was trying her wings for Warsaw.[38]

Immediately after declaring delicious the idea of Poland, Mme Geoffrin proceeded to apply the adjective adjacently on the map: "I have again received a delicious letter from over there, over there ('là-bas, là-bas'). Really, she is a charming woman." The woman could be none other than Catherine, whose charms Stanisław August well knew, and "là-bas, là-bas" was an expression that recurred in the correspondence to refer to Russia, the land beyond Poland. Stanisław August delineated Russia's relation to Poland even more obliquely in a letter to Mme Geoffrin, when he offered her "the news from farther on" ("les nouvelles de plus loin").[39] Poland was far, and Russia was farther. Neither Russia nor Catherine was named in the letters of Mme Geoffrin and Stanisław August, in a spirit of delicacy that followed from both sexual and political considerations. When he came to the throne, Stanisław August was still in love with Catherine, perhaps even cherished the hope that they would marry and unite their kingdoms, but she had moved on to other lovers and preferred to pull his puppetstrings at a distance from Petersburg. Now he wrote to Mme Geoffrin that he feared he would never again be able to love with such "plenitude of heart," such blind adoration:

But as it is very true that friendship gains at the expense of love, *maman* will take that which would have been for *là-bas, là-bas!* You are right, she is a charming woman! But it is far from here to *là-bas, là-bas!*[40]

Thus the king made over his romantic passion for Catherine into filial devotion for the much older woman in Paris, whom he now ardently awaited in Warsaw. Thereafter, though Catherine would continue to assert her predominance as his political patron in Petersburg, Mme Geoffrin might claim to have won his heart for the Enlightenment in Paris. Rousseau would improve upon her claim in speaking to the hearts of the Poles.

If the king was choosing between two women in 1765, Mme Geoffrin was choosing between two sovereigns, for she still corresponded with them both. As a gesture of priority she sent her letters from Catherine to Warsaw that summer, an epistolary betrayal, so that Stanisław August could read them. These presumably included the March letter of "the little table," and the "delicious letter" of June in which Catherine announced that she led "the life of a Kalmuck," always on the move, a life that would "make the ladies of Paris faint."[41] Mme Geoffrin, however, was preparing to leave Paris, and when Stanisław August sent back "your letters from *là-bas, là-bas*," he solemnly anticipated her visit. "That which friendship alone engages you to do is, so to speak, without example," he wrote, "for you come from Paris to Poland uniquely to be able to love me as deeply and still more usefully perhaps than you have till now." No one in Warsaw could advise him disinterestedly, but Mme Geoffrin, coming from Paris to Poland, "descending as if from a planet," would speak "without partiality." He met her triple invocation of frankness with a passionate triple injunction to come, come, come: "Oh! venez, venez, venez, ma chère maman!"[42] The voyage from Western Europe to Eastern Europe was hyperbolically acclaimed as an interplanetary displacement, and her presence in Poland was welcomed for its utility, its promise of impartial advice from the planet of the Enlightenment.

At New Year's 1766 Stanisław August wrote to Mme Geoffrin, worrying about Catherine's reaction to the intended voyage: "All that I imagine could happen is that *là-bas, là-bas* one could perhaps conceive some jealousy of what you do for me, and perhaps insinuate to you that one could quite wish you were doing still four hundred leagues more."[43] The grammatical conditionals were excruciating, reflecting the delicacy of triangular relations, but Mme Geoffrin was immune to Catherine's insinuations and invitations. Mme Geoffrin in 1766, the same year that Rousseau declined Orlov's invitation, would decisively reject Russia and discover Eastern Europe in Poland.

In January she declared, "I have no fear of bad roads." She resolved to place herself in the hands of the appointed trilingual guide: "I will close my eyes and think of nothing more than the delight I will have in seeing Your Majesty." The voyage to Warsaw was to be worked by blind faith, and she put aside her apprehensions from the beginning: "I will depart as if I were going to Chaillot, which is the village nearest to Paris." The departure took place at the end of May, and in early June she reached Vienna. She was given an imperial audience with Maria Theresa at Schönbrunn, where the visitor from Paris admired the prettiness of the empress's eleven-year-old daughter, Marie Antoinette, and promised to report favorably to France, where the child's marriage to the future king was already under consideration. It was in setting out from Vienna on the road to Warsaw that Mme Geoffrin truly traveled into Eastern Europe, like Lady Mary Wortley Montagu when she set out from Vienna on the road to Belgrade 50 years before. In Vienna she met her guide, provided by Stanisław August, along with the necessities of the trip: a bed, furniture, silverware. The king's letter to Vienna anticipated her imminent arrival in Warsaw, "in flesh and bone," and imagined that her presence there would seem a work of "fairy magic" (*féerie*).[44] The means of travel were hardly magical, for, just as when Catherine went to the Crimea twenty years later, any magical effects were produced by meticulous preparation. When Mme Geoffrin came to Poland in 1766, Stanisław August himself arranged all the practical details of her journey, and yet even he saw her voyage into Eastern Europe as something fantastic, the descent from a planet.

"The Unworthiness of the Poles"

"I arrived in Warsaw, as if I were getting out of my armchair," reported Mme Geoffrin to her daughter in Paris, thus assisting that same imagery of fairy travel, suggesting that she really did close her eyes in Vienna and open them to find herself in Warsaw. The king too, in greeting her, seemed to hail her arrival as a magician's conjuring trick, crying out: "Voilà maman!" She further described his "transports of joy" at seeing her, and her own beating heart and trembling limbs as he took her in his arms. "I do not speak of that which could flatter my amour-propre," she assured her daughter, but went on to announce her own "brilliant court" in Warsaw, with "old and young lords, the whole household of the king at my orders." With a remarkable lack of political perspicacity, she declared the king himself to be "adored by all who surround him." Her voyage was a sensation in Western Europe, and she was not above measuring the interest it aroused: "If people have spoken of my voyage in Paris, I assure you that people have spoken of it even more in Vienna." Mme Geoffrin wrote from Warsaw to her daughter in Paris, Mme de la Ferté-Imbault, and then lightly scolded her for showing around the letters—"because I believe you to be a little bit the cause of the uproar (*tintamarre*) which displeases me so." Far from displeased by the uproar, however, Mme Geoffrin gleefully encouraged the curiosity of Paris: "As my modesty does not permit me to say myself to what extent are my successes in all genres, upon my return to Paris I will do as in the great romances of chivalry; I will take a squire to recount them."[45] Poland might be at her feet—"at my orders"—but her triumph could only be consummated in Paris.

Her notion of taking a "squire" (*écuyer*) to tell her adventures matched precisely the role in which Voltaire had cast Marmontel: "When the queen of Sheba went to see Solomon she surely had a squire." Indeed, it was only natural to expect the philosophes, especially those of her own salon, to celebrate her voyage, and both Marmontel and Voltaire exchanged letters with Mme Geoffrin while she was in Warsaw. Marmontel began his letter to Warsaw with a reference to the abbé de Saint-Pierre and his *Project of Perpetual Peace* of 1713, the eighteenth-century charter for a league of nations to preserve the peace of Europe. The abbé, Marmontel reflected, must have hoped that "one day Truth would travel to the courts of Europe." Thus

Mme Geoffrin herself was apostrophized by implication as that allegorical traveler, and Marmontel, who not only attended her salon but actually
lived in her house, assigned an international significance to her pilgrimage
persona as Truth:

The good abbé supposed that not only would there be sovereigns good enough to
let themselves be touched, persuaded by her, but that these sovereigns would be
found even in the regions from which have come for so many centuries the scourges
of humanity and the source of those ravages which have desolated the universe.[46]

The visit of Mme Geoffrin to Stanisław August was a "happy presage"
of the future of Europe, in which "perpetual peace" would even embrace
those "regions" now reclaimed from the dark shadow of Tartar terror, the
lands of Eastern Europe. Such imagery clearly conditioned the public sensation surrounding the voyage of Mme Geoffrin, a woman of 67, of perfect bourgeois respectability and celebrated common sense, displaced to
those regions conventionally associated with the scourges and ravages of
humanity. Her mission as ambassador of the Enlightenment was to touch
and persuade the sovereign. Voltaire, writing to Warsaw, charged her to
be the "witness" of what might be achieved by an enlightened monarch.
This last letter was so little a purely private communication to Mme Geoffrin that the envelope instructed the king to open it if she had already left
Warsaw.[47]

The most public letter to Mme Geoffrin in Poland, however, was paradoxically one whose contents could barely be known. It came from the abbé
de Breteuil, whose handwriting was altogether illegible. Mme Geoffrin
reported back to Paris on the scratching (*griffonage*) of the letter:

To give to this beautiful piece all the celebrity that it merits, I laid it on the table, and
I cried: Hasten everyone, princes and princesses, palatins and palatines, castellans
and castellanes, starostes and starostines, finally, peoples, hasten: here are hieroglyphics to interpret, and ten ducats to the winner. All the estates arrived, and the
ducats remained mine.[48]

This was the Polish court of Mme Geoffrin, male and female, denominated
by ranks, at her orders. The joke was the indecipherability of the paper from
Paris, but this joke only exercised its full effect when Mme Geoffrin wrote
back to Paris with her account of the letter's reception in Poland. Copies of
her account circulated there, and, according to Grimm, everyone in Parisian society read it.[49] There were thus two related receptions, that of the
"hieroglyphics" by the Polish court in Warsaw, and that of Mme Geoffrin's
legible letter in the salons of Paris. The joke of the Frenchman's inability
to write became, at the same time, a joke of the Poles' inability to read,
their failure in the face of hieroglyphic mystery. Mme Geoffrin herself de-
ciphered the letter by relying on her "clairvoyant" heart. The hieroglyphic

letter, its reception, and the narration of that reception, taken together, constituted a sort of "writing lesson," like that described by Claude Lévi-Strauss in his account of the Nambikwara in Brazil in the twentieth century—later interpreted by Jacques Derrida as a key to the grammatology that originated in the age of Rousseau.[50] The power and prestige of the written word, the hieroglyphic sign, served Mme Geoffrin in a staging of mock mystification by which she contrived to present to Paris her own Polish court—"at my orders."

Yet her crucial connection to Poland, that is, her friendship with its king, rendered itself also uninterpretable during the period of her visit to Warsaw, for naturally their correspondence was interrupted as they lived for almost three months in the same palace. Though she was welcomed with "transports of joy," though she recommended the king to Voltaire as the very model of an enlightened monarch, something happened in Warsaw that left her deeply troubled. She departed in September, and when the king forwarded to Vienna Voltaire's letter, his own letter, for the first time in the correspondence, addressed her intimately as *tu*. She was, however, so bitter that when she replied she threw his intimacy back in his face: "I regard this *tu* as an illusion of Satan."[51] Not until two years later, in 1768, did she explode and express her resentments regarding the visit, but that letter was lost or destroyed, and only a subsequent reference remains.

The letter that Your Majesty calls the terrible letter was absolutely necessary for the relief of my heart; since my return from Poland I did everything possible to contain it, but it was so full that it spilled over: at present it is clear, and no more bitterness will enter there.[52]

This account of the missing "terrible letter" of 1768 is sufficient to suggest that her direct encounter with Stanisław August in Poland was no more successful than that of Diderot with Catherine in Russia. In 1772 Mme Geoffrin finally admitted in a letter to Mme Necker, famous for her own salon, that she had hated the journey to Poland six years before. It was just as the king had predicted before she set out, when he wished there were time to arrange for "beautiful roads, beautiful bridges, good lodgings," lest she think Poland "a nasty kingdom." Vividly Mme Geoffrin now recalled "roads that were not roads, going to bed in stables where it was necessary to evacuate the beasts to make a place, inedible bread, detestable water."[53] This was a far cry from "fairy magic," though no worse than the conventional complaints about travel in Eastern Europe. It was perhaps not just coincidental that Mme Geoffrin at last announced her objections to Poland in 1772, the same year that the kingdom was subjected to the ultimate insult of partition.

The memoirs of Stanisław August suggested some bad feeling between him and his guest over issues of taste in art and decoration. In Warsaw someone insinuated to Mme Geoffrin that the king spoke slightingly of her taste, and she was wounded and indignant. The king was then subjected to "the most turbulent scenes" by Mme Geoffrin—scenes that he found "sometimes even comic"—and the whole visit became for him more bother than pleasure. Furthermore, he worried about what she would say when she returned to Paris: "Her nature was so impetuous, and she was so little mistress of her tongue, that if she were irritated she could do real harm to the king with the foreign public." He allowed himself the last word in his memoirs, which she would never read, asserting for posterity that her "pretension" was indeed greater than her good taste.[54]

Such was the king's own retrospective account of what had gone wrong between them, but another perspective, that of his political enemy, Kajetan Sołtyk, bishop of Cracow, suggested that the tensions between Stanisław August and Mme Geoffrin were more broadly based than a mere matter of slighted taste and wounded vanity. In a letter from the end of August, a few weeks before she left Warsaw, the bishop observed that "the king must be already disgusted with Mme Geoffrin because she speaks the truth to him in everything." The bishop was no man of the Enlightenment, and yet his conception of Mme Geoffrin was not so far from that of Marmontel. Sołtyk saw Mme Geoffrin as a teller of displeasing truths, and Marmontel allegorized her as Truth itself. She had come to Warsaw fiercely determined upon "frankness, frankness, frankness," but direct confrontation between the Enlightenment and Eastern Europe could be disastrously awkward, lifted from the literary context of epistolary correspondence across the continent. Jean Fabre, writing about Stanisław August and the Enlightenment, has concluded that in the case of the king and Mme Geoffrin, "enchantment could not withstand presence."[55]

In July Mme Geoffrin wrote from Warsaw to d'Alembert, suggesting that she had come up against the limits of frankness: "It is a terrible condition to be king of Poland! I do not dare to tell him to what extent I find him unfortunate." His misfortune, apparently, was in the nature of his kingdom, and it was her grievances against Poland itself that she found herself unable to express freely and fully. She had predicted before she ever got to Poland that she would not find it "worthy" of her son, and, once there, she found it still less worthy of herself. She wrote to d'Alembert, "Everything that I have seen since I left my *penates* makes me thank God to be born French and a private citizen!"[56] This was the ultimate significance of the cultural construction of Eastern Europe in the eighteenth century, to define the condescending perspective of supposedly superior civilization in Western Europe. Mme Geoffrin traveled to Poland to discover that she was glad to be French. Her further relief in being only a private citizen, not a royal sovereign, might seem merely trite were it not for the fact that in traveling to Poland she had in fact assumed a crown, as the queen of

Sheba. D'Alembert received another letter from Eastern Europe that summer from someone who really was a royal sovereign. It was Catherine, who knew that Mme Geoffrin was in Warsaw and interpreted that voyage as a rejection of herself and St. Petersburg. She wrote coolly to d'Alembert in August, "I only learned of the voyage of Mme Geoffrin after her departure. I did not propose to her, and will never propose to her that she come here." The "rigor of the climate" would be too extreme. Mme Geoffrin, when she returned to Paris, would receive a last long letter from Catherine, boasting of her connections to Voltaire and Diderot as well as of the "acquisition" of Falconet for St. Petersburg.[57] Catherine could not easily forgive Mme Geoffrin for having chosen to discover her satisfaction at being French in Poland rather than in Russia.

Though Mme Geoffrin claimed to appreciate in the summer of 1766 the "terrible condition" of a Polish king, the real troubles of Stanisław August were only just beginning that autumn, after she left. At the Sejm of 1766 Catherine blocked his program of institutional reform for Poland and provoked an ongoing political crisis of Russian interference; this led to the rising in 1768 of the Confederation of Bar against the king and against Russia. Stanisław August was declared deposed, then kidnapped and almost murdered. He retained his crown only through the triumph of Russian troops and only to undergo the humiliation of seeing his kingdom partitioned in 1772. Rousseau, who endorsed the Confederation and despised Stanisław August for his relations with Russia, concluded in the *Considerations* that "he is today perhaps no more than unfortunate." Like Mme Geoffrin, Rousseau pitied the king of Poland, and, also like her, he allowed himself to try on the crown and imagine how it would fit—"if I were in his place."[58]

If Mme Geoffrin was troubled by her voyage to Poland, she nevertheless presented an appearance of perfect composure upon her return. Her account of the arrival in Warsaw—"as if I were getting out of my armchair"— was echoed in Grimm's account of her arrival in Paris: "as little fatigued as if she were returning from a promenade." Her voyage, he thought, was "something inconceivable," especially for a woman of her age.[59] The first letter that she received in Paris from Stanisław August, written on the ominous eve of the Sejm, reestablished the epistolary distance that rendered their relationship conceivable to Paris and supportable to her:

Ma chère maman! ah! *ma chère maman!* You are already quite far from here! So much the worse for me, but so much the better for you! You would not be able to bear my troubles in seeing them up close.[60]

While this seemed to hint at certain tensions that attended her visit, by the following spring the conventions and illusions of epistolary communication had surmounted any awkward memories of direct encounter. "*Ma chère maman*, you are five hundred leagues from me," wrote the king, "but friendship, this need of the soul, brings me close to you, and causes me to write to you as if I were speaking to you."[61] Correspondence restored the enchantment that had succumbed to presence.

By the beginning of 1767 Mme Geoffrin was back in the business of purveying civilization to Poland. She inquired whether it would be possible, given the uncertain political situation, for the famous French actress Mlle Clairon to appear on the stage in Warsaw. She arranged for Stanisław August to receive Grimm's *Correspondance Littéraire*, with its current cultural reports on the news of the Enlightenment. She forwarded to Warsaw a copy of Marmontel's *Belisarius*. Though she arranged for the king to receive a bust of Voltaire, she declined to send her own portrait, stiffly referring to herself in the third person:

Here is what Mme Geoffrin, living in the rue Saint-Honoré, replies on the subject of her portrait. She admits that in Warsaw, in one of those moments when she was transported by love for her king, she promised him to send the original of her portrait painted by Nattier; but upon her return home, feeling a little more *sang-froid*, she thought it was an impertinence to send her portrait to Poland.[62]

She feared it would appear "ridiculous," making such a fuss about her own portrait, and yet this objection might have been made about the whole voyage to Poland in the previous year. She established her address in the rue Saint-Honoré as if to insist that she would travel to Poland no more, not even as a painted image.

At the end of 1767 she acknowledged her trip to Poland as the only "extraordinary incident" of her carefully planned and thoroughly regulated life, with its weekly rhythm of Mondays for the artists and Wednesdays for the philosophers. She assured Stanisław August that the visit was a success after all:

It succeeded very well for me. I saw my king, I saw his surroundings, and finally I saw well what I saw, and I am content to have had the courage to have undertaken this voyage, and the happiness to have made it without any accident. Arriving home I took up again my genre of life.[63]

Mme Geoffrin's appreciation of Poland was encapsuled in the sphinxlike utterance "I saw well what I saw," but it was enough to proclaim her pride in the achievement of directly witnessed experience. By the beginning of 1768 she celebrated her own youthfulness of spirit by remarking that, in spite of "reason, wisdom, and reflection," her heart "would perhaps make her return again to Poland." In fact, Poland was now to become for her, as for Rousseau, a realm to which the heart held direct access. She spoke of Stanisław August with a visitor from Poland and was transported on the spot: "I could believe myself to be still in Warsaw."[64]

In 1769, as Stanisław August found himself in an increasingly disastrous political situation, Mme Geoffrin could not bear to contemplate Poland: "I have my head in a sack."[65] Yet she then produced, in her very next letter, the fantastic hypothetical of her having remained in Poland indefinitely: "It is certain that if I were still in Warsaw, all that which has happened would have happened still." His political enemies would have sought to discredit her friendship to annul any possible influence. The suggestion that she might have stayed in Warsaw was perhaps, after all, less fantastic than the notion that her presence there might have altered Poland's political fortunes, which she seemed to consider even in denying its probability. Mme Geoffrin did, however, presume to possess a perfect appreciation of Poland's tremendously complicated problems by virtue of her visit:

Friendship alone conducted me to your court, where I well saw what I could not see from as far as I am; but I have seen it so well, that I see at present, from where I am, everything that happens there.[66]

Though she had in fact left just before the crisis exploded at the Sejm of 1766, the experience of travel rendered Poland ever after transparent to her vision, even from the distant perspective of Paris, even with her head in a sack. Rousseau, of course, aspired to the same transparency of vision without ever having been to Poland at all. Such was the light of the Enlightenment, permitting the pellucid penetration of darker domains.

Mme Geoffrin preserved a photographic vision of Poland, developed in the summer session of 1766, presumed thereafter to be perfect even without the latest information. In 1770 she would not ask questions of Poles in Paris, "in the fear of learning new misfortunes." In fact, she informed the king, "I do not hear the name of Poland pronounced without shuddering."[67] Her horror at the name was consistent with a general geographical reserve in her correspondence with Stanisław August, in striking contrast to that of Voltaire and Catherine, who were relishing the names of places "which one never heard mentioned previously," names on the map of Eastern Europe. Stanisław August occasionally introduced such names into his letters, but Mme Geoffrin never responded with the slightest interest in the map, an indifference altogether fitting in one who traveled by closing her eyes and magically materializing in Warsaw. In 1768 the king wrote of the Confederation of Bar, its appearance "in Podolia, in the neighborhood of the Turks and the Tartars," just the sort of information Voltaire would have most appreciated. The king wrote to Mme Geoffrin that a French agent in the Crimea was encouraging the Ottomans to go to war against Russia.[68] He informed her that the peasants of the Ukraine were in revolt, perpetrating massacres, but such news was only incidental to the spirit of epistolary communion that dominated the correspondence.

I can not tell you, express to you, to what extent my heart is penetrated by you, by your friendship, and how much sometimes, and, for example, at this moment when I am writing to you, I would wish to chat with you. It seems to me sometimes that I see you, and leaving titles and passions at the door, we set ourselves to babbling at ease, naming each thing by its name, and making fun of all those important misfortunes one must respect.[69]

The king's near hallucinatory vision of Mme Geoffrin rivaled hers of Poland, but the confederates in Podolia, the peasants in the Ukraine, the agents in the Crimea were only shadows over his shoulder, which he escaped while writing to her and which she ignored, because she had seen Warsaw and that was enough. In 1772 Stanisław August located for her the last stronghold of the confederates, at Częstochowa, "a little fortress toward the frontiers of Silesia, famous for the sanctity of an image of the Virgin."[70]

Approaching her seventieth year, Mme Geoffrin announced to Stanisław August that she was preparing for death, "as I made my packets for my voyage to Poland, gaily." Poland thus served as a metaphorical anticipation of her final voyage. Yet, in 1770, when Stanisław August asked her to send some of the gaiety of Paris 500 leagues to Poland, she replied that she could not for she had none to spare. "I saw in Warsaw the germ of all your misfortunes," she insisted gloomily.[71] In 1773, after the partition, she was even more insistent on her foreknowledge, judging Poland harshly:

I admit to Your Majesty that the injustice, the folly, and the unworthiness (*l'indignité*) of the Poles has penetrated me with pain, but has not surprised me at all. I saw, during those two months that I was in Warsaw, the germ of everything that has hatched. I believe I let Your Majesty glimpse it, but I did not want to show it to him too clearly, because I saw little remedy, and I did not want to take away the hope that sustained him.[72]

Such was the eye of the seeress, in retrospect anyway. Poland was beyond philosophical assistance from Paris: "There is no advice, no opinions, no consolations, to give Your Majesty." She herself had nothing to say about Poland, reaffirming only that "when someone speaks about Poland I would like to have my head in a sack." As for Stanisław August, she suggested that he abdicate: "I would go to Rome." One last time she assumed the crown, only to show by her example how to despise and discard it. She suggested that he become a cardinal and enjoy a tranquil retirement. "I ask your pardon for this nonsense (*radotage*)," she wrote. "Your state puts me out of myself."[73] Diderot was in St. Petersburg just then, making written suggestions to Catherine and awkwardly, prophylactically, begging her pardon for speaking nonsense.

The voyage of Diderot to St. Petersburg entered into the correspondence of Mme Geoffrin and Stanisław August because the philosophe did

not stop in Warsaw. Just as Mme Geoffrin offended Catherine in being un-
willing to visit Russia after Poland, so Diderot offended Stanisław August
by passing through Poland without paying respects. Mme Geoffrin con-
soled the king in 1774, insisting that Diderot was anyway bad company,
too much "a man who dreams," recommending instead the company of
Grimm, who was quite willing to acquire another crowned acquaintance on
the way back from St. Petersburg.[74] The same letter contained news of the
new king of France, Louis XVI, and expressed the opinion that the Pari-
sians, unlike the Poles, knew how "to love their king." Here Mme Geoffrin
showed herself a poor prophetess, for if there was any contemporary king
who ended his reign more miserably than Stanisław August, it was surely
Louis XVI. While Paris celebrated the commencement of the new reign,
Mme Geoffrin awaited the return of Grimm: "It will be very sweet for
me to speak about Your Majesty." When she finally met with Grimm and
talked about Poland, there was bitterness as well as sweetness:

Alas, he tells me that he found no one except Your Majesty was sad in Warsaw. He
made me indignant in telling me that people are gay, that they dance and they sing
there; in sum, that Warsaw does not show at all the public calamities. A people so
insensitive is made to be subjugated.[75]

She had already censured the Poles for their "unworthiness," and now,
provoked by Grimm's malicious report, she finally confessed her conversion to Voltaire's perspective on the partition. The Poles were not only
unworthy but also "made to be subjugated." Rousseau was able to translate his commitment to Poland into a brilliant reconception of Eastern
Europe, based on national identity, immune to partition or subjugation.
Mme Geoffrin, in her correspondence with Stanisław August, was wedded
to the more conventional formula of enlightened absolutism, the collaboration of philosophy and power, ruling in backward lands of "roads that
were not roads" and "detestable water." After all, she herself had traveled to
Eastern Europe, hailed as allegorical Truth, and there she saw what she saw.

"The Last People in Europe"

The sensation of Mme Geoffrin's visit to Warsaw in 1766, followed immediately by the protracted Polish crisis that culminated in the partition
of 1772, focused an unprecedented level of foreign attention upon Poland
and its place in Eastern Europe. In 1765 Jaucourt's article on Poland in the
Encyclopedia had established a baseline of general knowledge and critical
judgment, and the following years after 1766 witnessed an explosion of
interest and abundance of writings on Poland, of which Rousseau's *Considerations* was only the most significant for general intellectual history. The
intensity of interest in Poland during this period was comparable to that of

interest in Hungary during the first decade of the century, and the analogy became even more striking after the rising of the Confederation of Bar against Russia in 1768. The war of the confederates against Catherine polarized foreign opinion, especially in France, in the same way the rising of Rakoczi against the Habsburgs had in 1703. Just as Rakoczi's manifesto had promptly appeared in French in Paris, so the manifesto of the Confederation of Bar was published in Paris in 1770 to justify Poland before foreign opinion. Finally, the attention to Hungary generated by the Rakoczi insurrection had the effect of inscribing that land on the map of Europe, more surely than Habsburg rule could ever efface, and similarly the sensation of Poland in the years preceding the first partition made a profound impression that defied cartographical instability. Rousseau in the *Considerations* could already envision Poland's nonexistence as a state, and could already see beyond that catastrophe to a transcendent inscription within a reconceived cartography. He hailed the Confederation of Bar with an urgent injunction: "It is necessary to engrave this great epoch in sacred characters on all Polish hearts."[76] Yet as Rousseau pretended to practice his artisanship upon the heart of Poland, the broader appeal of his *Considerations* was to his readers in Western Europe, to their minds, memories, and mental maps.

Rousseau's enthusiasm for the Confederation of Bar was a complementary response to Voltaire's contempt, which was in turn the natural corollary to his devotion to Catherine. Ideological tensions within the Enlightenment were exercised in the discovery of Poland or Russia as alternative faces of Eastern Europe. Voltaire's interest in Poland was indeed as old, if not as keen, as his interest in Russia, and his *Charles XII* virtually created as characters for the enlightened public both Stanisław Leszczyński and Stanisław Poniatowski, the father of Stanisław August. Leszczyński was later the host and patron to Voltaire at the court of Lorraine and even made another literary appearance, in *Candide*, among the six dethroned kings: "Providence gave me another realm in which I have done more good than all the kings of the Sarmatians were ever able to do on the banks of the Vistula." In 1761 Voltaire specified points of reference for measuring Poland's backwardness in a letter to the French diplomatic representative in Warsaw, Pierre Hennin: "I still give five hundred years to the Poles to make the fabrics of Lyon and the porcelain of Sèvres." Hennin had hoped to bring Voltaire over "to Poland's side" ("du côté de la Pologne")—demonstrating the extent to which Poland was already a partisan issue for the philosophes. The notion of counting centuries to determine development was related to the work of the marquis d'Argenson, *Considerations on the Ancient and Present Government of France*, which compared medieval France with contemporary Poland. The book was published in 1764, but Voltaire

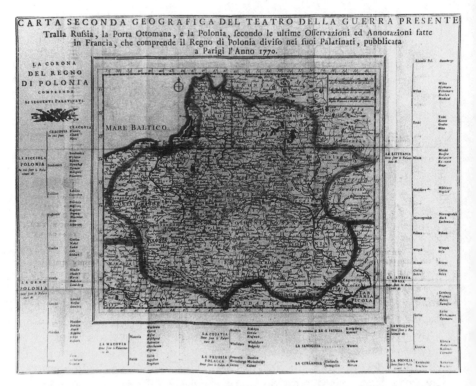

"Carta seconda geografica del teatro della guerra presente," map of "the theatre of the present war between Russia, the Ottoman Porte, and Poland, according to the latest observations and annotations made in France, which includes the kingdom of Poland divided into its palatinates, published in Paris in the year 1770," included in the *Storia della Ultima Guerra tra la Russia e la Porta Ottomana*, published in Venice in 1776; it was the "theatre of the present war," as followed by an audience in Paris or Venice, which associated the lands of Eastern Europe on the same international stage; Poland, on the verge of partition in 1770, stands heavily outlined on the map as the focus of attention abroad, adjacent to Moravia, Moldavia, and Moscovia, and analyzed into its palatinate parts and component places according to "observations and annotations made in France." (By permission of the Houghton Library, Harvard University.)

read the manuscript as early as 1739. It was to d'Argenson that Voltaire declared Poland, with its "miserable government," to be "a beautiful subject of harangue."[77] That was precisely the position of Poland after 1766, serving as a subject of harangue to the writers of the Enlightenment.

Catherine appreciated this perfectly when she made religious toleration into the pretext for Russian interference in Poland, and forwarded to Voltaire a variety of materials on the subject prepared in St. Petersburg. Throughout the 1760s Voltaire was engaged in combat against the "infamy" of intolerant Catholicism in France, as manifested in the cases of Calas, Sirven, and La Barre. The cause of the non-Catholic Dissidents in Poland was as congenial to him as it was convenient to Catherine, and in 1767 he produced a "Historical and Critical Essay on the Dissensions of the Churches of Poland," which appeared under the pseudonym of Joseph Bourdillon, an erudite professor. Such an essay against Catholicism in Poland followed naturally from the eighteenth-century press and pamphlet literature in Protestant England (and also in Prussia), which expressed outrage over Polish excesses, dating from the riots and executions at Thorn in 1724. The issue of Poland was implicitly expanded in Voltaire's essay by the linking of neighboring lands to construct Catherine's imperial domain: "Not only does she establish tolerance at home, but she has sought to cause it to be reborn among her neighbors." When he updated the ending to account for the partition of 1772, Voltaire concluded, "Such was the unscrambling of the Polish chaos."[78] This echoed the broader construction of Eastern Europe in Voltaire's comment to Catherine on "the unscrambling of all this chaos" from Gdańsk to the Danube.

Voltaire was not content to lecture about Poland without taking the opportunity to harangue the Poles themselves. In 1767, when Bourdillon had had his say, Voltaire wrote to Stanisław August, encouraging the king to embrace enlightened absolutism:

Sire, this Bourdillon imagines that Poland would be a lot richer, more populous, happier, if its serfs were emancipated, if they possessed the liberty of body and soul, if the remains of the Gothico-Slavonico-Romano-Sarmatian government were abolished one day by a prince who would not take the title of eldest son of the church, but that of eldest son of reason.[79]

The preposterousness of "Gothico-Slavonico-Romano-Sarmatian government" made reform appear all the more appropriate in Poland, while epistolary form, the letter to Eastern Europe, was the vector of enlightened influence. In 1768 Voltaire pitched his appeal to the Polish nation in a "Discourse to the Catholic Confederates of Kaminiec in Poland," attributed to a Prussian officer named Kaiserling. "Brave Poles," he addressed them, as Rousseau did a few years later, "would you wish to be today the slaves and satellites of theological Rome?" They dared to complain that

Catherine sent Russian troops into Poland, dared to ask by what right: "I respond to you that it is the right by which a neighbor brings water to the house of a neighbor that is burning." The Russian army was sent "to establish tolerance in Poland." Voltaire reminded the Poles that Catherine had purchased Diderot's library, and he contemptuously concluded, "My friends, begin by learning how to read, and then someone will buy libraries for you."[80] Like Rousseau's more sympathetic appeal to the brave Poles, Voltaire's was really intended for his readers in Western Europe, who were thus called to witness the phenomenon of philosophy preaching to Poland. The illusory nature of the ostensible audience was all the more evident in Voltaire's "Sermon of the Priest Chariteski, pronounced in the Church of Saint Toleranski, village of Lithuania," written in 1771. That this was aimed at the Parisian public and not the villagers of Lithuania was apparent from the fact that the sermon responded to the manifesto of the Confederation of Bar, which was published in Paris the previous year. "I have the honor to send your imperial majesty the translation of a Lithuanian sermon," wrote Voltaire to Catherine. "It is a modest response to the somewhat crude and ridiculous lies which the confederates of Poland have had printed in Paris." Voltaire was thus completely engaged in Catherine's campaign against Poland, so much so that in 1769 Stanisław August thought to open a diplomatic front at Ferney, and sent an agent to obtain Voltaire's intervention with Catherine on behalf of a negotiated peace in Poland.[81] Voltaire did not cooperate, either because he was too caught up in the excitement of Catherine's wars and conquests, or because he knew he could not influence her policy in Poland, only justify and celebrate it.

Voltaire's sermon of 1771 further indicated its audience in Western Europe by the mock Slavic names of Chariteski and Saint Toleranski, which transformed Poland's crisis into a comedy of Eastern Europe. This treatment of the Polish situation as literary entertainment was written at the same time as the *Adventures of the Young Count Potowski*, an epistolary novel in which the young Marat used contemporary Poland and the war of the confederates as background for a romance. The convergence of intellectual interests in Poland was striking at this time, from 1770 to 1772, as Mably and Rousseau penned their respective dissertations at the encouragement of Wielhorski, Voltaire wrote his satirical addresses from Ferney, and Marat composed a novel in England at Newcastle, where the future revolutionary was working as a veterinarian. While in the *Polish Letters* Marat presented a Pole's perspective on Western Europe, in the *Adventures* he imagined the Polish experience of Poland's political crisis as the great obstruction to the happy union of two young lovers. He employed Polish and pseudo-Polish names—Potowski, Poulawski, Ogiski, Sobieski—and the different characters expressed a variety of verdicts upon the Polish situation, ranging from enthusiasm to contempt for the Confederation of Bar, reflecting the divergence of opinion in Western Europe as well as in Poland itself.

The hero was horrified by the atrocities of civil war and foreign invasion, and eventually renounced the confederates as a "troop of barbarians." Yet, it was in dialogue with a displaced Frenchman that he received definitive instruction on the condition of his own country. Coyly, Marat represented the Pole as "moi" and the Frenchman as "lui":

Moi: But you seem to me well informed; I would also have pleasure in hearing what you think of the affairs of unhappy Poland.
Lui: You are lost, perhaps without resource; but whatever misfortune happens to you, you have only too well deserved it.
Moi: Explain yourself, please, for I do not understand you.
Lui: In the state of anarchy in which you live, how could some of you not be the victim of others, or the prey of your neighbors? Your government is the worst that could exist.[82]

This invented dialogue of harsh judgment between a Frenchman and a Pole was recorded in a fictional letter between two Poles, and was included in an epistolary romance about Poland written by a Frenchman in England. The layering of literary material thus preserved the priority of Western Europe. Though Marat's fiction of Polish affairs remained unpublished until 1847, Jean-Baptiste Louvet du Coudray wrote and published his *Loves of the Chevalier de Faublas* in the 1780s, with a Polish plot that looked back to the period of the Confederation of Bar. Louvet's romance of Lovzinski and Lodoiska was interesting enough to the French public to be reworked as a dramatic comedy, *Lodoiska and the Tartars*, and as an opera by Cherubini, both performed in revolutionary Paris in 1791.[83]

Voltaire drew upon the story of Stanisław August and the Confederation of Bar for his tragedy *The Laws of Minos*, written around the time of the first partition, set not in contemporary Poland but in ancient Crete. There an enlightened king lamented, "Thus fanaticism and sedition/ Always animate my sad nation."[84] The play was not produced, but an even less public literary event was the satirical poem about Poland that Frederick the Great composed in 1771 for Voltaire's amusement, "The War of the Confederates." Rousseau, Marat, and Frederick were all writing about the Polish crisis at exactly the same time, but if Rousseau was sympathetic and Marat ambivalent, Frederick was viciously contemptuous. He invoked the goddess of stupidity as an appropriate muse:

> Avec plaisir elle vit la Pologne
> La même encor qu'à la création
> Brute, stupide et sans instruction,
> Staroste, juif, serf, palatin ivrogne,
> Tous végétaux qui vivaient sans vergogne.
>
> With pleasure she saw Poland
> The same still as at the creation
> Crude, stupid, and without instruction

Starosta, Jew, serf, drunken palatine,
All vegetables who lived without shame.[85]

Beyond the rhyming of *Pologne* with *ivrogne* and *vergogne*, he constructed the conventional comedy of Eastern Europe out of "all that multitude of imbeciles whose names terminate in ski." Such comedy and contempt, however, from Frederick's poison pen, exposed the implicit relation between poetry and power that characterized the whole literature on Poland's crisis, as witnessed from Western Europe. For Frederick was about to hatch the scheme of partition, and Voltaire appreciated the analogy between poem and partition in 1772: "What you are actually doing quite equals your poem about the confederates. It is pleasant to destroy the people and to sing of them." Voltaire recognized these as related aptitudes, flattering Frederick that "never has anyone made a poem or taken a kingdom with such facility." In fact, Voltaire celebrated the partition itself as a work of imaginative genius, as if it were a poem: "It is supposed that it was you, sire, who imagined the partition of Poland, and I believe it, because there is some genius in that." As for Frederick, he began the fateful year of 1772 with a letter to Voltaire, saluting the Poles in plain prose as "the last people in Europe."[86] It was this implicit hierarchy of peoples, who were still Europeans in spite of insult and invasion, that ultimately structured the poetic and political values of Frederick's Eastern Europe.

"Economic Advice"

Such a ranking of peoples pointed to the possibility of development, and the most prominent eighteenth-century school of economic theory, the physiocrats, took a special interest in Poland during precisely these years of political crisis. As in our own times, after 1989, when Poland's disastrous economy became a test case for the efficacy of market capitalism, with foreign economics professors flying into Warsaw to lecture and pronounce, so two centuries earlier the proto-capitalist physiocrats seized upon Poland's eighteenth-century crisis as an opportunity to export and experiment with their own economic ideas. The doctrine was established by François Quesnay, author of the *Tableau économique* in 1758, proposing the priority of agricultural wealth over commerce, free trade in grain according to the slogan of laissez faire, and the institution of one single landowners' tax. When the physiocrats eyed Eastern Europe in the light of these ideas, they harbored ambitions for economic influence in both Poland and Russia. It was his physiocratic dissertation, *The Natural and Essential Order of Political Societies*, that brought Lemercier an invitation to St. Petersburg in 1767. In that same year the elder Mirabeau, father of the revolutionary, organized the physiocratic movement by establishing a regular Tuesday dinner at his own home, and by the end of the year he could boast in a letter to Rousseau that the salon had sent Lemercier to Russia "with some assistants we have given him, to plant there economic legislation."[87] Disappointment would follow, but clearly the arrogance of Lemercier was not altogether personal; he represented a whole school that held the same presumptions with regard to Eastern Europe.

The physiocratic enterprise in Poland also began in Mirabeau's Paris salon in 1767, with the appearance there of Ignacy Massalski, the bishop of Vilnius. He had come to France to evade the fraught political situation in Poland, a worldly churchman and a compulsive gambler with an interest in economics. He had excellent foreign connections, and in 1771 Mme Geoffrin arranged for his niece and nephew to be educated in France, while in 1779 Mirabeau helped arrange for the niece to marry none other than the prince de Ligne.[88] In 1767 Massalski was prepared to patronize the presence of the physiocrats in Poland, and a suitable candidate was found in the person of the abbé Nicolas Baudeau, who was promised a benefice in Lithuania. He too had authored a physiocratic text in 1767, the *First Introduction to Economic Philosophy*, in which he demonstrated a critical interest in the issues of despotism and slavery in Russia and Poland. Baudeau clearly understood economy as an issue of civilization in Eastern Europe: "What chimera more absurd than the idea of civilizing an empire while leaving in servitude of the soil all the workers of cultivation." Contemporary opinion viewed his voyage to Poland as a physiocratic "pendant" to the mission of Lemercier in Russia. The journal that Baudeau edited, *Éphémérides*, announcing his departure in 1768, declared that he "envisaged in Poland a career worthy of his love for humanity." In Poland he was awaited with some concern that "accustomed to the pleasures and commodities of Paris, he may find his sojourn in Poland, and still more in Lithuania, a little strange."[89]

Baudeau's chief interest in Poland, naturally, was grain, and it emerged that his economic program consisted chiefly in arranging the export of Polish grain to France. In fact, he measured Poland's agricultural wealth, in a report to *Éphémérides*, by estimating that the quantity wasted on bad beer and whiskey was enough to "nourish for three years the kingdom of France." Clearly, the interest of physiocracy in Poland's agriculture was not untinged by an element of colonial calculation, and if Poland appeared suitable to the theoretical ideal of a predominantly agricultural economy, that would be convenient for France as well as admirable in itself. Baudeau, however, arrived in Lithuania in the middle of a war, whose horrors Marat only imagined in Newcastle, but were in any event sufficient to obstruct the achievement of an agricultural utopia. After spending the winter in Lithuania, Baudeau traveled to St. Petersburg, where Lemercier had recently been sent packing. Baudeau, with some help from Falconet, had a poem presented to Catherine and hoped to interest her in a peace settlement for Poland, but she dismissed him as just a "poor little abbé." He was ordered out of Russia in 1769 for speaking against Frederick's intentions in Poland.[90] By the end of the summer he was back in France, having survived in Eastern Europe for less than a year.

It was quite enough experience for Baudeau to assume a mantle of authority in writing about Poland, and he proceeded to write *Letters on the Actual State of Poland and on the Origin of Its Misfortunes*, published serially in *Éphémérides* in 1770–71. Poland was found to be not only "without arts" and "without commerce" but even "without agriculture worthy of that name," for so much land lay fallow. Baudeau further published during the same years his *Economic Advice to the Enlightened Citizens of the Republic of Poland on the Manner of Collecting Public Revenue*. This followed the narrative form of an epistolary appeal, with the purpose of persuading the Poles that they were ripe for physiocracy. "The direct levy on the net product of the lands suits you more than any other people," he urged, staking out a claim for the physiocrats on the lands of Poland.[91]

Oddly, it was not only Baudeau, returning from Poland, who wrote as an expert upon Polish affairs, but also Lemercier, returning from Russia, who felt that he too had something to say about Poland. During these same years Lemercier wrote a work on "The Common Interest of the Poles, or Memoir on the Means of Pacifying Forever the Actual Troubles of Poland, in Perfecting Its Government and Conciliating Its True Interests with the True Interests of Other Peoples." He too addressed the Poles directly, in a spirit of political approval that resembled that of Rousseau, perhaps stimulated by the recent rejection experienced in Russia. "Noble Poles, the base of your government is admirable," Lemercier declared. "To perfect it you have but a few things to do." His suggestions were economic, referring collegially to the *Economic Advice* of Baudeau, and including the establishment of the "law of property" and of "liberty of commerce." Even Rousseau, in spite of his primarily political and cultural interests, did not refrain from writing about economic issues in the *Considerations*, and he too urged the priority of agriculture, vaguely resembling the physiocrats in his enthusiasm for limiting Poland to the land. In a spirit of utopian fantasy he counseled the Poles against finance, and even against money, addressing them directly with pretty condescension: "Cultivate well your fields, without caring about the rest."[92]

Clearly, a lot of intellectual talent in France was being invested in the problem of Poland around 1770, and this common focus of attention was arguably more important than divergences of political party and academic emphasis. Mably favored more radical political reform in Poland than Rousseau, including the eventual abolition of vetoes, confederations, and royal elections. Baudeau and Lemercier emphasized economic issues more than Rousseau and Mably. Yet all these French perspectives were united in the momentary devotion of their intellectual energies to Poland, in the irresistible impulse to write about Polish affairs and address the Poles. As the manuscripts circulated, as they came to be published in the 1770s and the 1780s, it was evident that the true audience was the enlightened public of Western Europe, and the true ideological agenda was that of the French Enlightenment. Poland was an intellectual opportunity—for Baudeau, briefly, the mirage of a worthy "career"—even more promising than Russia inasmuch as it appeared more accessible. To make a career in Russia, or of Russia, the essential condition was an audience or correspondence with Catherine, but the Poles could be addressed and advised more generally—brave Poles, noble Poles—and on any subject.

Physiocratic ambitions in Poland did not end immediately with the partition. The new Russian ambassador in Warsaw after 1772, Otto Magnus Stackelberg, became the most powerful man in Poland, dominating and humiliating Stanisław August, who compared him to the Roman proconsuls. Stackelberg was also, by conviction, a physiocrat; indeed, it was he who originally made the ill-fated discovery of Lemercier for Catherine in 1767. In 1773 he reported to St. Petersburg on his plans for Poland, which included free commerce, the guarantee of property, and "the establishment of a single tax upon the land, following the system of the economists."[93] So Catherine's all-powerful ambassador was enthusiastic, Stanisław August was sympathetic, and the head of the newly created Commission on National Education, arguably the first ministry of education in Europe, was none other than Massalski, the physiocratic bishop of Vilnius. Educational reform was the first principle of Rousseau's *Considerations*, but Rousseau was not Massalski's man, and it was Baudeau who was invited to return to Poland and participate in the work of the commission. Baudeau, however, after making some inquiries through Mme Geoffrin, decided that he had had enough experience of Poland, and declined the invitation. The opportunity then passed to another physiocrat, Pierre-Samuel Dupont de Nemours, who had collaborated with Baudeau in the editing of *Éphémérides*. Dupont was furthermore the first choice of the Polish prince Adam Czartoryski to undertake the private tutoring of Czartoryski's child.[94]

Dupont had some obligations at the German court of Baden, but the margrave Charles Frederick, himself physiocratically inclined, wrote to Mirabeau that Dupont should certainly go to Poland and seize the opportunity "to do an infinite good to a whole great nation." Dupont himself was no less presumptuous about the role of physiocracy when he delivered his farewell address to the Mirabeau salon in the spring of 1774. For the work of restoration in Poland, he declared to his fellow physiocrats, "your students have been chosen," demonstrating "that one proposes to be guided by your counsels, that one desires to be associated in some way with this academy." The impersonal "one" in need of counsel, in search of association, was Poland itself, and it was with reference to such a "one" that the Enlightenment assumed its own importance. "One has caused me to envision," orated Dupont, "the honor of creating a nation by public instruction." The formula of "creating a nation" was precisely that which French intellectuals applied to Peter in Russia, dating from Fontenelle's eulogy, but now the same creative work was to be undertaken in Poland by French intellectuals themselves. "My friends, my dear friends, shed some tears at my departure," exclaimed Dupont to the sentimental physiocrats, and he promised to uphold "the honor of having been your student," even if it meant giving his life for Poland. Someone would have to carry home his ashes, or else "my worn out body, as it will be after twelve years of the career that opens itself before me." At the moment of departure for Poland his conception of what awaited him became still more dramatic:

I go to Poland to swim in the void, nearly as Milton depicts Satan, struggling in space with efforts as prodigious as they are useless. I go into a land of intrigues, jealousies, cabals, despots, slaves, proud ones, inconstant ones, weak ones, and madmen.[95]

Here was Poland as hell itself, inhabited by demons of every variety, that is, by Poles, themselves just so many obstacles to Dupont's titanic work of "creating a nation."

"The famous and long awaited M. Dupont, finally, at last, has arrived with his wife and his children," announced a somewhat cynical ex-Jesuit in Warsaw in September. Dupont's formal position was that of secretary for foreign correspondence on the Commission, and he began by dismissing the plan for parish schools proposed by his own patron, Massalski. Dupont's confidence was a function of coming from Western Europe to Eastern Europe, and his faith in the intellectual preeminence of the former was evident in his plan for a Polish academy. Such an academy, he thought, should sponsor translations into Polish after querying other academies in Europe about which works were sufficiently meritorious. The Academy of Sciences in Paris would propose the classics of mathematics; the Royal Society of London would evaluate works on chemistry, electricity, and physics; the Economic Society of Bern would take care of practical agriculture. Finally, Mirabeau's physiocrats in Paris would handle morality, social economy, politics, public law, and "the rest." Thus England, Switzerland, and France formed a constellation of superior civilization, that of Western Europe, from which Poland might receive light, and the Paris of the physiocrats was the brightest star. Dupont further composed a curriculum for Polish students that culminated in reading the works of Quesnay and Mirabeau. The cynical ex-Jesuit attributed this curriculum to "the enflamed head of Dupont," and observed that "no professor here has undertaken to conform to this plan."[96]

In Poland, as elsewhere, such plans were easier to invent than to execute, and by October Dupont was deeply disillusioned on that account, writing to Baden that "we have been deceived." He even suggested that Baudeau exaggerated the possibilities of Poland "to send me to a job which he did not want." Schools in Poland, declared Dupont, in a sliding geographical metaphor, were "castles in Spain." Inevitably Dupont blamed the Poles, and formulated his grievance as an issue of civilization and savagery:

The people of Poland are still serf and savage; and what difficulties to take them out of the former condition which necessitates the latter! I have made on this point some memorandums, which one applauds today, which one will forget tomorrow, which one will consult and perhaps execute its ideas in a hundred years.[97]

Backwardness was measured in centuries, though one century was a modest handicap compared to the five that Voltaire stipulated for Poland to produce Sèvres porcelain.

The year 1774 was not only one of high hopes for the physiocrats in Poland but also that of their ultimate opportunity in France itself. With the accession of the young Louis XVI there rose to ministerial power the remarkable Anne-Robert Turgot, by conviction a physiocrat. His edict proclaiming freedom of commerce in grain was published with a preamble by none other than Dupont. Already as he was preparing to depart for Poland, Dupont was offered the French administrative position of intendant on the island of Mauritius in the Indian Ocean, east of Madagascar. He went to Poland instead. As soon as he was in Warsaw, however, Louis XVI ordered him to return to France to participate in the Turgot government, and Dupont obeyed, not unwillingly. His "worn out body" was returning home, not after the anticipated twelve-year struggle, but after only three months. On the road, from Germany, he wrote a letter to old Quesnay, then 80, in the last year of his life, and described the Polish experience as "torment," the anticipated return as "joy." Tutoring the four-year-old Czartoryski child was particularly "tedious"—though in fact the little prince was going to grow up to become one of the most influential Polish statesmen of the nineteenth century. Above all, Dupont expressed to Quesnay his satisfaction at returning to "the first nation of Europe," that is, to France: "For my dear Master, I am quite convinced by my eyes that the French are, were even in their misfortunes which have heated the bile of us all, the first nation of our continent."[98] Dupont's observations of Poland had persuaded him of the priority of France, like Mme Geoffrin, who returned from Warsaw happy to be French. From Frederick's contempt for the Poles as "the last people in Europe" to Dupont's conviction that France was first, the philosophical perspective of Western Europe on Poland established a hierarchy of nations, a measurement of backwardness, and a model of development.

In 1776 Adam Smith published *The Wealth of Nations* in London. He admired the physiocrats and followed them in favoring freedom of commerce, but in fact his economic theory of capitalism rendered physiocracy, with its limited agricultural emphasis, ultimately obsolete. A passing observation about Poland in *The Wealth of Nations* revealed his sense of economic hierarchy among the nations of Europe:

Poland, where the feudal system still continues to take place, is at this day as beggarly a country as it was before the discovery of America. The money price of corn, however, has risen; the real value of the precious metals has fallen in Poland, in the same manner as in other parts of Europe.[99]

For Smith Poland was backward and beggarly, but its prices and values proved that it was still part of Europe. When Smith sought to establish the economic level of Mexico and Peru, before the discovery of America, he asserted that "in arts, agriculture, and commerce, their inhabitants were much more ignorant than the Tartars of the Ukraine are at present."[100] Thus "the Tartars of the Ukraine" established the extreme point of reference for backwardness in Europe. Smith assumed that he himself was knowledgeable enough to pronounce upon the ignorance of "the Tartars of the Ukraine"—yet why not the Cossacks of the Ukraine, or the Tartars of the Crimea? In fact, it was in the casual slippage of categories, the combining of adjacent lands and peoples, that Smith demonstrated the irresistible ascent of the eighteenth-century idea of Eastern Europe.

"The Anarchy of Poland"

Poland merited only an incidental observation from Adam Smith, while Rousseau, Mably, Baudeau, Lemercier, and Marat all wrote entire manuscripts on Poland, and all at the same time; yet for none of them was the subject more than one interest among many in the context of a life's work. However, one Frenchman writing about Poland during these years was actually dedicating to the subject the best efforts and energies of his whole career, and that was Claude-Carloman de Rulhière, author of the *History of the Anarchy of Poland*. Rulhière began his researches in 1768, working for the ministry of foreign affairs under the auspices of Choiseul, whose policy was generally sympathetic to the Confederation of Bar. After 1770 Rulhière, like so many others, was in close contact with Wielhorski in Paris, finding in him a ready source of reports on contemporary Polish history. Rulhière composed a first draft of his manuscript during 1770–71, at the same time that Mably and Rousseau were writing, and in frequent communication with them both on the subject of Poland. Yet while others exploited that subject as the occasion for pronouncing their positions on general political and economic issues, Rulhière discovered in Poland his own vocation as a historian. He was not alone in finding the Polish crisis a stimulus to historical reflection, and Casanova too, who had not yet discovered his true vocation as an erotic memoirist, wrote a long Italian *History of the Turbulences of Poland*, published anonymously at Gorizia in 1774. Rulhière's even longer work remained incomplete, and was not published until the beginning of the nineteenth century. Even then its appearance was intensely controversial, but its quality as Western Europe's foremost history of Poland was recognized well into the century, culminating in a definitive edition of 1862.

Rulhière's career as an observer of Eastern Europe began exactly one century before that, not in Poland but in Russia, for he was present in St. Petersburg, attached to the French embassy, in 1762 at the time of Catherine's coup d'état. Five years later, back in Paris, he began to give salon readings of his manuscript of *Anecdotes of the Revolution in Russia*, which began thus:

> I was upon the spot, and an eye-witness of the Revolution, which hurled the grandson of Peter the Great from the throne of all the Russias, and placed a female stranger upon it. I have seen that princess, the very day she fled from the palace as a fugitive, forcing her husband to resign into her hands at once his life and his empire.[101]

The frankness of Rulhière's account was disturbing to Catherine, who sought through Diderot and Grimm to purchase the manuscript and suppress it. Those gentlemen further engaged the mediating services of Mme Geoffrin, who insulted Rulhière by proposing a substantial bribe; she herself was displeased by his frankness about the past intimacy between Catherine and Stanisław August. Mme Geoffrin could judge for herself, since she hosted a reading by Rulhière in her very own salon, after he read at the rival salon of Mme du Deffand. Even Diderot and Grimm attended readings, while denouncing the work as a "tissue of lies." Talleyrand's memoirs recalled that Rulhière's account became one of a number of salon favorites (another being *The Marriage of Figaro* by Beaumarchais) which one was "obliged to hear" whenever one went out to dinner. In 1776, on a diplomatic mission, Rulhière gave readings in Berlin and Vienna. Still, he promised he would not publish the *Anecdotes* in Catherine's lifetime, and she, though a little older, managed to outlive him. She died in 1796, and the book immediately appeared in French, and in English, German, and Dutch translations, all in 1797.[102]

Rulhière himself claimed that Catherine should not have been offended by his account, and even composed a flattering ode in an unsuccessful attempt at ingratiation, celebrating her in the standard formulas for changing deserts into provinces and submitting ancient Scythia to her laws. According to Rulhière, his purpose in recounting Catherine's accession to power was "to introduce into the recital of a terrible event all the circumstances,

sometimes humorous, which relate to the manners of the Russian Nation."
In depicting "the licentiousness of Russian manners" he had to recount
such "risible anecdotes" as would render gravity "ridiculous," and this imparted to the work its salon appeal as a comedy of manners. "The Russian
nation is indolent, gay, dissolute," wrote Rulhière, "and though the mild-
ness of the late reign had given some polish to the mind, and some decency
to manners, the time was not long passed since that barbarian court had
celebrated, by a festival, the nuptials of a buffoon with a goat." If he wrote
glibly about Russia, it was because his century had already accumulated a
set of formulas for treating the subject, creating the illusion that Russia
was easy to know: "Scarcely has one spent eight days in Russia than one can
already speak reasonably of the Russians: everything leaps to the eye." [103]

Rulhière's time in Petersburg could be measured in months, not in days,
but his experience of Warsaw in 1762 was a matter of hours, sleeping hours.
On the road to Russia, "I threw myself upon a bed fully dressed for three
hours in Warsaw." The rest of the journey through Poland was notable for
an absence of food due to the rigorous observation of Lent during Holy
Week: "a dreadful voyage to make in that season." [104] Beyond that rather
limited experience of sleep and hunger, when Choiseul in 1768 commissioned a piece about Poland, supposedly intended to educate the future
Louis XVI, Rulhière's chief qualifications for the job were his manuscript
about Russia and his reputation as an enemy of Catherine. For Choiseul
as a statesman, for Rulhière as a historian, Russian and Poland were intimately related alternatives. This intimacy was articulated from the very
first sentence of the work: "The Poles and the Russians are divisions of
that numerous people who, under the common name of Slovene or Slav,
spread twelve centuries ago in all the east of Europe (*l'orient de l'Europe*),
and whose language is spoken from the mountains of Macedonia and the
shores of the Adriatic gulf to the islands of the Glacial sea." [105] Thus, from
the beginning, this history of Poland was a history of "the east of Europe,"
the Orient of Europe, and the preamble went on to outline the whole
project, from the common Slavic origin, to the differentiation of Russians
and Poles on their respective political paths to despotism and republicanism, and finally to the contemporary history of Russia's designs on Poland's
independence.

The historian of Eastern Europe, according to Rulhière, had to overcome obstacles, inherent in the respective natures of Poland and Russia:

How to follow the thread of events across the stormy movements of anarchy? How
to paint without confusion an astounding multitude of personages. . . . How to
penetrate into those mysterious cabinets where, at the bosom of voluptuousness, a
despot presided over the destiny of so many peoples. . . . Long voyages undertaken
for the purpose of knowing myself almost all the courts, the sovereigns, and the
ministers I have to paint, my personal liaisons with the chiefs of the opposed fac-

tions, the communication of the most reliable memoirs, and innumerable relations sent from all lands to the ministry of France, authorize me to speak with certitude of most of the events, intrigues, and characters.[106]

Rulhière saw his research as a work of intellectual heroism, finding and following the thread to unravel anarchical confusion, lifting the veil and penetrating the mysteries that hid Eastern Europe from Western Europe. In 1770, at the height of his researches, Rulhière had a personal connection with Wielhorski as well as the patronage of Choiseul with access to the archives of the ministry of foreign affairs. That year Choiseul fell from power, though, and Rulhière lost his official position, but by then he had enough material to complete a first draft of his manuscript in 1771. In 1774 began the new reign of Louis XVI, and the new minister of foreign affairs, Vergennes, recommended to the king the reinstatement of Rulhière that he might continue working on his history of Poland. He was to finish it by explaining historically "a denouement so unexpected as the dismemberment of that republic."[107] Working for the ministry once more, Rulhière was sent in 1776 on a diplomatic mission to Vienna and Berlin, two cities that throughout the century served as points of departure for visits to Poland.

Rulhière, for all his claims to "long voyages undertaken," did not undertake the voyage into Poland in 1776. The reasons against it were forcefully put to him in a letter from Poland, where Mably had recently arrived to visit Wielhorski. Perhaps Mably felt that two French philosophes in Poland at once would be one too many, but in any event he wrote discouragingly to Rulhière in Vienna, "to warn the person who wrote the history of the last revolution of Russia that the Russians are here the masters." If Rulhière was determined to come, he should use a false name and prepare for the possibility of being arrested and deported to St. Petersburg. The Russians, however, were not the only reason to stay away, according to Mably. There was also the problem of Poland itself, which, by an association of lands, became the problem of Eastern Europe in general: "What a land, Poland! I would just as soon travel in Tartary!" Mably's conventional outrage at conditions of travel in Poland was quite equal to that of Mme Geoffrin. "To avoid sleeping on the ground, bring with you your bed," he warned Rulhière. "To avoid dying of hunger and thirst, carry with you provisions and even water, for the Poles are of a swinishness (*cochonnerie*) and laziness which extinguishes even the crudest industry."[108]

Such was the correspondence between two of France's most ardent friends of Poland, and Rulhière no doubt accepted the account, for he had already had the experience of going hungry in Poland in his rapid traversal during Holy Week in 1762, that "dreadful voyage." Mably left no stone unturned to dissuade Rulhière from coming, and passed from the issue of refreshments to that of research.

I do not know if in coming here you could get great lights for your work: there reign here the strangest prejudices and the most barbarous ignorance. You would see men who know neither their situation nor that of Europe.[109]

Nothing could have revealed more clearly the axioms of the French pre-occupation with Poland than this conviction that it was not worth going there even to study the land itself, since the Poles, in "barbarous igno-rance," understood neither themselves nor their situation. Rulhière was left to find his own "lights" on the subject in France, assured that Poland could best be appreciated and explained from a distance, though Mably offered to pass on his own observations, and even to write up an account—"if I have time for it."[110] Rulhière did not go to Poland, but he may have later consulted Mably's *Political Situation of Poland in 1776*.

Rulhière polished his manuscript, and by 1782 he was giving readings from it in the salons of Paris, including that of Mme Necker; he was persuaded that this work on Poland, like the other on Russia, could not be published, since it concerned too many living persons and sovereigns. If in 1770, at the beginning, Rulhière's chief consultant was Wielhorski, by the end of the decade he was working most closely with Leonard Thomas, a master of style and rhetorical eloquence, a figure from Mme Necker's salon. The literary values of Thomas, no doubt, helped to en-dow the manuscript with its salon appeal: "The painting of the town of Warsaw at the moment of the Diet has something picturesque and strik-ing which pleases the imagination." After forgoing the visit to Poland in 1776, Rulhière might labor in Paris over picturesque effects, appealing to the "imagination"—which so often participated in the Enlightenment's Eastern Europe. Thomas was bored by the *longueur* of one passage on the Cossacks, but appreciated them elsewhere: "What a horrible and profound impression is made by the painting of the massacres of the Ukraine!"[111]

The problem of assigning the Cossacks an appropriate role in the work, and likewise the Tartars, was consistent with Rulhière's purpose in writ-ing a history of "the east of Europe." For Rulhière's contemporary his-tory of Poland was also inevitably a history of Russia, and of other lands as well, while reciprocally those, like Voltaire, who approached Eastern Europe through Russia also discovered the rest implicitly comprised. Rul-hière's interest in the Tartars dated from reading the *Social Contract*, with its prophecy of their triumph over Russia, and he wrote to Rousseau in 1763, "It is true that the Tartars are terrible people, but are they to be feared to the extent that you believe?" In the tenth book of the *Anarchy of Poland*, Rulhière addressed that question in considering the Russian-Turkish war, inextricably bound to the fate of the Confederation of Bar. Working in the archives of the French ministry, he was able to consult the papers of French agents in Constantinople and the Crimea, like the baron de Tott

and Charles de Peyssonnel.[112] Even Casanova's history of Poland, chronicled year by year, included special sections on the "Origin of the Cossacks"
and "Tartars, Turks, Poles, Muscovites."[113]

Casanova was favorably impressed by Stanisław August in Warsaw, and
was probably especially interested in the figure of a king who ascended
his throne by way of Catherine's bed; the king appeared in Casanova's
history as "handsome and of virile presence." For Rulhière, however, as
for Rousseau, he was anything but a hero, and even his virility was subject to insinuations.[114] Rulhière's heroes were the confederates, especially
Casimir Pulaski, whom he knew in France after 1772. In fact, the historian
helped arrange with Benjamin Franklin for Pulaski to join the American
army in the Revolutionary War, and the Pole met his death at Savannah in
1779.[115] In 1783 Rulhière showed his manuscript to the young Talleyrand,
who thought Poland a "striking" subject to choose, agreeing that with its
republican constitution it was, along with newly independent America,
"the only land that merited a historian." Talleyrand thus understood how
Poland served the Enlightenment as an ideological opportunity, for Rulhière, for Rousseau, for the physiocrats, but felt the *Anarchy of Poland* was
still not philosophical enough. "I saw nowhere the people who compose
the kingdom," he wrote to Rulhière, indignantly. "One waits from page to
page for the philosophe to take the place of the historian." Certainly, the
manuscript, a success in the salons, was very much a work of the *ancien
régime*, though when Rulhière died in 1791 he was working on a history of
the French Revolution, unfolding all around him.[116]

At Rulhière's death there began a protracted struggle between his family
and the French government over the unpublished manuscript on Poland.
On both sides were ranged figures who had participated in the Enlightenment's involvement in Eastern Europe during the previous generation. The
government was represented by Pierre Hennin, who had written to Voltaire from Warsaw in 1761; the family consulted with Marmontel, who had
written to Mme Geoffrin in Warsaw in 1766. The case was overwhelmed
by the storm of the revolution, and Rulhière's brother lost his life in the
massacres of September 1792, but in 1805, under the empire of Napoleon,
the work was acquired by a Paris publisher. It was then edited in such a
way as to render it no longer anti-Russian, thus canceling its whole political perspective. The word "barbarian" was elided wherever it referred to
the Russians.[117] Such was the intimate relation of partisan alternatives—
for Russia or for Poland—merely a matter of editing, and the distinction
between civilization and barbarism was also subject to arbitrary elision
and revision. In 1806, however, the government suddenly seized the edited
manuscript, on the point of publication, to undo the work of editing and
restore Rulhière. The minister of foreign affairs was Talleyrand, who had
read the original manuscript back in 1783 and found it too restrained in

its republicanism. Now Napoleon was contemplating the recreation of a Polish state, partly to pressure Russia, which was then fighting in the Third Coalition against France, and Rulhière's commitment to Poland appeared appropriate to the international moment. In 1807 the emperor established the Grandy Duchy of Warsaw, and in Paris Rulhière's *History of the Anarchy of Poland* was published at long last, in four volumes.

France's intellectual preoccupation with Poland in the years of crisis after 1766 was now harnessed to a French imperial presence in Eastern Europe under the aegis of Napoleon. Rulhière, however, was to undergo yet another posthumous twist of fortune, for no sooner did his four volumes appear in 1807 than Napoleon made peace with Russia at Tilsit, a peace that would last until the 1812 invasion of the Grande Armée. Now Tsar Alexander, Catherine's grandson, protested against the publication of Rulhière in France. So in 1808 the national archives undertook to investigate the authenticity of the original manuscript; the director of the archives, in charge of the investigation, was Hauterive, who had admired "picturesque" Bulgaria in 1785, on his way to Moldavia. Then in 1810 the national academy censured Rulhière for his partisanship as a historian; the academy's most voluble critic of the book was the old physiocrat Dupont, who went to Warsaw in 1774, presuming to "the honor of creating a nation by public instruction." Dupont could have been commenting on a whole generation's intellectual engagement with Poland, including his own, when he compared Rulhière's work to "one of those novels so improperly called historical."[118]

"The Republic of the Orient"

In the year before the French Revolution, that dangerous sexual criminal and unusual literary talent the marquis de Sade was a prisoner in the Bastille and at work on an epistolary novel, *Aline and Valcour*. One of the philosophical protagonists, soon after defending the proposition that "incest is a human and divine institution," went on incidentally to propose that Europe be recomposed of "only four republics, designated under the names of the West (*d'Occident*), of the North, of the East (*d'Orient*), and of the South." Here the eighteenth-century conceptual reorientation of the continent, from the north-south to the east-west axes, achieved equilibrium in the unstable imagination of the marquis de Sade, who constituted Eastern Europe as Europe's republic of the Orient:

Russia will form the republic of the Orient; I want her to cede to the Turks, who I send back out of Europe, all the possessions that Petersburg has in Asia. . . . In recompense, I join to her Poland, Tartary, and all that which the Turk leaves in Europe.[119]

The map was rearranged with casual confidence, and even Russia was partitioned to establish a distinct demarcation between Eastern Europe and Asia, between Europe's republic of the Orient and the Orient itself. The consolidation of Eastern Europe was then conceived as Russia's compensation. Such geopolitical fantasies were not so far from those that excited Voltaire in his letters to Catherine, and while Sade was writing in the Bastille, those fantasies were achieving a renewed plausibility. From 1788 Joseph and Catherine were at war with the Ottoman empire once more. The Habsburg army again besieged Belgrade, and the Russian army moved on Moldavia. Diplomats contemplated complex schemes of compensation in which portions of Poland and Ottoman Europe were variously detached and reassigned in the name of a greedy ideal of equilibrium. The international crisis culminated in the final partitions of Poland in 1793 and 1795.

Catherine's Ottoman war initially appeared as an opportunity for Poland to seize its independence, which was undertaken by the Four-Year Sejm convening in 1788. This meant that as the French Revolution exploded in 1789, a simultaneous revolution was under way in Poland, and both produced constitutions in 1791. Stanisław August himself played a leading role in the Polish revolution, and was served by two Italians who linked the revolution to the Enlightenment abroad. Scipione Piattoli, who originally came from Florence to Poland as a children's tutor, ended up participating in the writing of the Polish constitution. Filippo Mazzei, who had served Patrick Henry and Thomas Jefferson in Europe during the American Revolution, now represented Stanisław August and Poland in revolutionary Paris, where he enjoyed the friendship of Lafayette. In 1790, when Stanisław August donated his jewels to the national cause, Marmontel praised his patriotism from France and sent a new edition of *Belisarius*, of which the original was dedicated to Catherine twenty years before. The Polish king replied that praise from Paris reminded him of the words of Alexander the Great: "Oh Athenians, what would one not do to be praised by you!" He insisted that he meant not to compare himself immodestly to Alexander, only to identify Paris with ancient Athens.[120] It was a formula that recognized the hierarchy of nations in Europe, even while France and Poland were both pursuing their respective revolutions.

The French revolutionaries, from the reciprocal perspective, greeted the Polish constitution of May 3, 1791, with qualified enthusiasm and some condescending ambivalence. In fact, Western Europe's most hyperbolical celebrant of the Polish constitution was also the most eloquent ideological enemy of the French Revolution, Edmund Burke. He acclaimed the bloodlessness of Poland's revolution the better to underline his horrified reflections on the revolution in France. Yet he also proclaimed the perspective of Western Europe when he marveled at the Poles, "a People without arts, industry, commerce, or liberty," suddenly producing "the happy wonder" of a peaceful revolution. Meanwhile, the French revolutionaries put the Polish revolution in its place, with special insistence on Poland's backwardness. Camille Desmoulins in 1791 allowed only that "considering the point from which the Polish people departed, one sees that relatively they have made toward liberty a stride as great as ours," while another revolutionary of the Paris commune was pleased to see the French example "imitated at the extremity of Europe." The qualification of relativity was taken for granted in an appeal to Frenchmen: "Poland has just made a revolution, very honorable without doubt for that country, but Messieurs, would you want however such a Constitution?" Revolutionaries in France could also appeal directly to the Poles in the rhetorical manner favored by the Enlightenment, enjoining them for instance to improve upon their revolution by emancipating the peasantry.[121] Jean-Claude-Hippolyte Méhée de la Touche, who received subsidies from Russia, insisted that "France has nothing in common with Poland."[122] Robespierre the Incorruptible, who accepted no subsidies from anyone, ruled out any hierarchical comparison among revolutions when he proclaimed, preposterously, that "the French people appear to have outstripped the rest of the human race by two thousand years."

In 1791, the year of the Polish constitution, public opinion in England was mobilized over the Russian-Turkish war and Russian ambitions in Eastern Europe. William Pitt prepared an ultimatum to Catherine, demanding peace and the status quo in Eastern Europe, threatening to send the English navy to the Black Sea and the Baltic. One London newspaper expressed concern that "Russia will by degrees swallow up every neighbouring state," but the Russian embassy in London countered by sponsoring pamphlets, especially "Serious Enquiries into the Motives and Consequences of the Present Armament against Russia," written in French, then translated into English by John Paradise.[123] Pitt backed off from his ultimatum, and Catherine ended the Turkish war on her own. Then in 1792 she invaded Poland to destroy the constitution and proceed to the second partition of 1793. Voltaire was no longer alive to appreciate it, as he did the first, in correspondence with Catherine, but Grimm, at the age of 70, was still around to write to her in the spirit of obscene banter that she enjoyed. Poland was a "little slut" (*petite égrillarde*) who required "someone to shorten her petticoats, someone to take in her corset, someone even to trim her nails." Such were the metaphors of partition in 1793. In that same year Edmund Burke, in spite of his enthusiasm for the Polish constitution in 1791, resigned himself to the partition by reflecting that "with respect to us, Poland might be, in fact, considered as a country in the moon." Condorcet, also in 1793, recognized a more realistic geography of remote displacement when he wrote a poem on "A Pole Exiled in Siberia."[124]

Poland was utterly partitioned in 1795 and ceased to exist as a state. Yet even as the partitioning powers agreed by treaty that the name of Poland "shall remain suppressed as from the present and forever," the poet's pen of Thomas Campbell was seizing upon the subject and defying the taboo:

> Where barbarous hordes of Scythian mountains roam,
> Truth, Mercy, Freedom, yet shall find a home. . . .
> Oh, bloodiest picture in the book of Time,
> Sarmatia fell, unwept, without a crime.[125]

The Enlightenment had discovered Poland as a part of Eastern Europe, and Romanticism was ready to take up the task of preserving such a precious construction, with all its interesting intimations of ancient Sarmatia, barbarous Scythia, and even the moon. Rousseau had challenged the Poles to preserve Poland in their own hearts, but his own *Considerations*, and the writings of his whole generation with its Polish preoccupations, also inscribed the name of Poland on the intellectual agenda of the Enlightenment.

The coming of the French Revolution ruptured Catherine's relations with the Enlightenment. She was unequivocally hostile to the revolution, regarding it as an international ideological menace, so that in 1791 even an edition of Voltaire was suppressed in St. Petersburg. The philosophe Volney, who wrote about the Ottoman Orient, returned to her an honorary medal once received from Russia, but there was still Grimm to write contemptuously to Volney on her behalf, assuring him that Catherine had already "forgotten your name and your book." [126] Now it was émigré royalists, not enlightened philosophers, who came in crowds to St. Petersburg; twenty years after the visit of Diderot, the Russian capital received the brother of Louis XVI, the count d'Artois, the future Charles X of the Restoration. There was even a plan to establish the émigrés in their own colony on the sea of Azov, twenty years after Voltaire and Catherine fantasized about settling a colony of Swiss watchmakers in just the same place.

Marie Antoinette's favorite portraitist, Elisabeth Vigée-Lebrun, arrived in St. Petersburg in 1795. In her memoirs she invoked the eighteenth-century formulas, writing about "Russia's interior, where our modern civilization has not yet penetrated." Actually, she never saw much of the interior, and even a short excursion outside the capital, with a Russian servant, left her feeling like "Robinson Crusoe and his man Friday." [127] She painted Marie Antoinette from memory in St. Petersburg, but had only just begun to paint Catherine when the tsarina died in 1796. There was still the opportunity to do the portrait of the now stateless Stanisław August, who arrived in St. Petersburg in 1797, a year before his own death. Mme Vigée-Lebrun remembered first hearing of him in Paris many years ago—"through several people who had met him at the home of Mme Geoffrin"—and now she too enjoyed his favor: "Nothing was so touching as to hear him repeat how happy he would have been if I had been in Warsaw while he was still king." She painted him twice, "two large half-length paintings, one in the costume of Henry IV, the other in a velvet coat." As for Stanisław August, he may indeed have been pleased to make the acquaintance of Mme Vigée-Lebrun, but his most precious encounter in St. Petersburg was his pilgrimage to the Hermitage, to visit Voltaire's library.[128] Catherine had bought the library after Voltaire's death in 1778, and had his books shipped to St. Petersburg, where they remain to this day.

In 1801, the first year of the new century, William Cobbett in England published in his newspaper, *The Porcupine*, a series of open letters to the foreign secretary, then Lord Hawkesbury, the future Lord Liverpool. Cobbett's letters denounced the treaty under negotiation at Amiens in that year, by which England concluded peace with Napoleon for the moment. It was the closing of the continent to England and the predomination of Bonaparte that sharpened Cobbett's vision of the contours of Europe, that caused him to look to the distant east for lands that still eluded the Napoleonic hegemony. Yet there especially he saw no international sustenance for England:

What political relations can we have with countries situated beyond the Niemen and the Boristhenes? We maintain a communication with these countries by Riga, much in the same manner that we maintain a communication with China by Canton. It is, then, but too true, that the best half of Europe has been subjugated by France, and that the other half now lies prostrate at her feet.[129]

In this extraordinary passage Cobbett summed up the eighteenth-century construction of Eastern Europe and pointed toward its consequences in the nineteenth and twentieth centuries. The notion of an impossibly distant domain, beyond the Niemen and the Dnieper, was consistent with Burke's telescopic view of Poland, "considered as a country in the moon." The inevitable answer to the question of "what political relations can we have" would be decisively ventured by Napoleon with the invasion of Russia in 1812.

When Cobbett employed the analogy between China and the lands beyond the Niemen and the Dnieper, he drew upon the Enlightenment's repeated readings of Eastern Europe as "the Orient of Europe." Riga, for him, was the point of access, as it was for Diderot on the road to St. Petersburg. In the twentieth century, Riga, as the capital of Latvia, became the station from which the American foreign service, including the young George Kennan, reported on Soviet Russia after the revolution:

The old Petersburg was of course now dead, or largely dead—in any case inaccessible to people from the West. But Riga was still alive. It was one of those cases where the copy had survived the original. To live in Riga was thus in many respects to live in Tsarist Russia. . . . Below us in the rain-drenched harbor could be heard the hooting of switch engines and the clanking of the strings of battered broad-gauged freight cars, as they finished their month-long treks to dockside from God knew where in the vast interior of Russia.[130]

While Kennan and the American foreign service conscientiously preserved a continuity of perspective on Tsarist Russia and the Soviet Union, one may also observe the uncanny continuity of conception from the memoirs of Elisabeth Vigée-Lebrun, where Russia's interior was "where our modern civilization has not yet penetrated," and the memoirs of George Kennan, who mapped that same interior as a domain of only "God knew where."

The crucial distinction in Cobbett was between "the best half of Europe" and "the other half," implicitly identified as "the lands beyond the Niemen and the Boristhenes." The conclusion of the same letter drew a line across the continent that further articulated that division: "Europe, my Lord, is shut against us; from Riga to Trieste we can only penetrate into her countries through France."[131] The line from Riga to Trieste has marked a historic bisection of Europe, again looking backward and forward from Cobbett in 1801. In 1772 Voltaire proclaimed "a new universe created," from Archangel to the Borysthenes," and then in 1773 he saluted Catherine for "the unscrambling of all this chaos," from Gdańsk to the mouth of the Danube. Voltaire's mapping of a domain from the Baltic to the Black Sea was roughly the same as that which Cobbett outlined from the Baltic to the Adriatic. Yet neither was conceivable as a coherent geographical association of lands and peoples before the eighteenth century. Only then was it possible for Rulhière or Ségur to write of "the east of Europe" or "the Orient of Europe," for Sade to devise Europe's "Republic of the Orient." Such was the invention of Eastern Europe. In the twentieth century George Kennan made easy generalizations about "the fuzzy intelligence" found in "the countries east of the Vistula and the Danube."[132] This was exactly the mapping of Voltaire's "chaos," from Gdańsk to the Danube. In 1946 Churchill described an iron curtain "from Stettin in the Baltic to Trieste in the Adriatic," announcing the advent of an epoch in international relations. Yet this mapping was not altogether new, for the line that Churchill sketched was that of Voltaire in 1773, beginning on the Baltic, and that of Cobbett in 1801, ending at Trieste. The iron curtain in the twentieth century descended exactly where the Enlightenment had drawn the border between Western Europe and Eastern Europe, hanging cultural curtains, not of iron, but of subtler stuff.

Chapter Seven

Peopling Eastern Europe,
Part I: Barbarians in Ancient History
and Modern Anthropology

"To Unscramble the Mélange"

The baron de Tott became the most famous foreigner in the Ottoman empire in the eighteenth century, the object of Voltaire's raillery and Munchausen's rivalry, but when Rulhière was researching the Turks and the Tartars he consulted in the archives of the French foreign ministry not only the reports of Tott but also those of Charles de Peyssonnel. In 1755 Peyssonnel went to the Crimea as French consul, the same year that Tott was sent to Constantinople; contemporaries in foreign service, they developed overlapping domains of concern, inasmuch as the Crimea was still politically associated with the Ottoman empire. Yet Tott's special interest was military affairs, and he achieved his international mystique as the consultant for Ottoman artillery, while Peyssonnel pursued a less explosively dramatic expertise. He was more interested in archaeology than artillery, and he used his base in the Crimea to make quiet contributions to the ancient history of Eastern Europe. His first consular concern was the commerce of the Black Sea, and in 1755 he forwarded to the foreign ministry his *Memoir on the Civil, Political, and Military State of Little Tartary.*[1] In 1765, however, Peyssonnel submitted to the Royal Academy of Inscriptions and Belles-Lettres his *Historical and Geographical Observations on the Barbarian Peoples who Inhabited the Banks of the Danube and the Black Sea*, in which his personal experience of the contemporary Crimea was chronologically displaced and geographically extended to explore the ancient history of a considerably broader domain. The first chapter was a geographical introduction to the Danube area, "from all times the rendezvous and receptacle of all the barbarians who have gathered in this region of the earth, to spread from there, not only into the neighboring provinces, but in all of Europe, and even in the most remote cantons of Asia and Africa." Peyssonnel then promised "to unscramble the extreme confusion" created under such circumstances by the confluence of so many barbarians moving in so many directions.[2] The role that he assumed in exploring ancient history and geography thus corresponded to that which Voltaire assigned to Catherine's imperial policy, "unscrambling" chaos.

Peyssonnel identified two crucial vectors of barbarian invasion; there were "Barbares Orientaux," especially the Scythians, moving from east to west, and "Barbares Septentrionaux," especially the Slavs, moving from north to south. He quoted Pliny to insist, taxonomically, that "one must regard as Oriental Scythians all the barbarians who began to hurl themselves toward the Occident under the name of Dacians, Getae, and Sarmatians." Their ultimate origin was "Asiatic Scythia," identified also by the geographical designation of "great Tartary," that is, Central Asia and Siberia. Peyssonnel himself had personal experience of "little Tartary," the Crimea, and the shores of the Black Sea. "In the campaign that I made with the khan of the Tartars in 1758, I had the opportunity to travel across all of that coast," he wrote, and in that region it was possible to discover ethnographical evidence for writing the ancient history of barbarian invasions:

It is in these countries which surround the Black Sea, where one finds the vestiges of the peoples of Colchis and of Asiatic Scythia, the Huns, the Avars, the Alans, the Hungarian Turks, the Bulgars, the Pechenegs, and others who came at different times to make incursions on the shores of the Danube, which had been invaded before them by the Gauls, the Vandals, the Bastarnae, the Goths, the Gepids, the Slavs, the Croats, the Serbians.[3]

Apparently, Peyssonnel was persuaded that the anthropological eye could assist the reconstruction of ancient history from classical sources, when it was a matter of identifying the barbarians of Eastern Europe.

This conviction appears all the more important when one considers that eighteenth-century travelers to Eastern Europe often experienced a similar collapsing of chronology between their contemporary observations and the barbarian background. Twenty years after the publication of Peyssonnel's book, Ségur entered Poland and remarked that "one finds oneself amid hordes of Huns, Scythians, Veneti, Slavs, and Sarmatians." A little further along, in Russia, he found that the peasants "bring to life before your eyes those Scythians, Dacians, Roxolans, Goths, once the terror of the Roman world." One might suppose that Ségur was simply rendering a literary impression of barbarousness by the metonymous association of names, but Peyssonnel obviously considered his observation of "vestiges" to be scientific rather than literary. The juxtaposition of Peyssonnel and Ségur, their analogous discoveries of ancient barbarians in contemporary Eastern Europe, suggests that the line between literary evocation and anthropological observation was not an emphatic one. Eastern Europe was precisely that part of Europe where such vestiges were in evidence, where ancient history met anthropology. The categories of ancient history that identified the barbarians of Eastern Europe, in Peyssonnel and above all in Gibbon, not only corresponded to the impressions of contemporary travelers, but also entered directly into the emerging social science of anthropology, most fundamentally in Herder's discovery of the Slavs. For although the Slavs were only one barbarian people among many in the enumerations of Peyssonnel and Ségur, they were to become the essential ethnographic key to the modern idea of Eastern Europe.

For Peyssonnel the unscrambling of barbarian invasions involved, basically, discovering their respective vectors, as westward-bound Scythians or as southward-bound Slavs. It was the physics of geography in motion, complicating the ethnographic classification of peoples. The Bulgarians, for instance, were "Oriental Scythians" who moved from beyond the Volga to "Pontic Scythia" on the Black Sea. The Huns, however, were "truly Slavonic or Sarmatian Scythians."[4] They came from "European Sarmatia," on the Don, and "one must not confuse them with the Hungarians," who came later from Turkestan. In classifying the Huns, Peyssonnel drew upon ancient sources and contemporary anthropological observation:

The portraits that the poet and historian give us of these peoples, infinitely resemble our Tartars of today, and especially the Nogais, who are extremely ugly and dirty, agile, indefatigable, always on horse. . . . Though one observes between these two nations a perfect resemblance of manners, and though they could have had a common origin in the most remote times, it is necessary to regard them however as two very distinct peoples, since their languages have not the least affinity. The Huns were Slavonic or Sarmatian Scythians, and the Nogais are Tartar and Circassian Scythians.[5]

Here language was the factor that marred the near perfect matching of ancient and contemporary barbarians, though Peyssonnel's methodology clearly encouraged the search for such a fit.

In the chapter on the "First Appearance of the Avars and Slavs or Slavonics on this side of the Danube," Peyssonnel himself admitted frustration at the multitude and diversity of barbarians, wondering "how to be able to unscramble the mélange of these different peoples." By the sixth century the shores of the Danube were littered with "the debris of all the barbarians who had lived in Pannonia," who had become "so confused that it would be quite difficult, even if we lived in those times, to determine precisely which of these peoples were the origin of the Avars."[6] Eastern Europe was already then an ethnographic field of debris, and Peyssonnel, an observer of vestiges in the eighteenth century, projected his own intellectual confusion onto the mingled peoples of the past. His stated purpose of unscrambling in fact implied a domain of scrambled confusion that his own analysis paradoxically dramatized. The Wallachians appeared as especially scrambled: "One must in effect regard these peoples as a mélange of Romans and Greeks, with the Dacians, the Getae, the Gepids, the Jazyges, the Sarmatians, the Saxons, the Goths, the Huns, the Avars, the Slavs, the Pechenegs, the Turks, and all the Oriental and Septentrional barbarians who have successively occupied the land that the Moldavians and Wallachians inhabit today." He himself had visited Wallachia and was "most astonished" to hear a peasant identify it as "the Roman land," that is, Romania.[7] There were no such simple answers in the mélange of Peyssonnel's Eastern Europe.

Eighteenth-century maps of the ancient world were not quite up to Peyssonnel's level of obfuscation; they had to achieve a certain degree of graphic representability. In Robert's *Atlas Universel* of 1757 a map of the Roman empire showed, to the west of "Germania," a broad band of "Germano-Sarmatia," stretching across Eastern Europe from the Baltic to the Black Sea. Farther east was "Sarmatia" proper, in the space of contemporary Russia, and "Parva Scythia" appeared north of the Black Sea. The map of Charlemagne's empire represented peoples as well as places, with the eastern border of the empire occupied by "Sclavi" and "Hunni."[8] D'Anville's *Ancient Geography* of 1771 labeled the area of Eastern Europe as "Sarmatia," with "Scythia" still farther to the east.[9]

Peyssonnel's ancient history was less susceptible to mapping inasmuch as it described a geography in motion, the invasions of diverse barbarians. The fundamental diagram of ethnographic forces was expressed as a vector of eastern barbarians, most generally the Scythians, and later a vector of northern barbarians, most generally the Slavs. The Scythians were discovered everywhere in eighteenth-century Eastern Europe, conditioning its barbarous aspects, ultimately identified with the contemporary Tartars. They were known from their important role in the fourth book of Herodotus, resisting the Persians, sacrificing prisoners of war, drinking the blood of their fallen enemies. François Hartog has argued that, for Herodotus and the Greeks, the Scythians were the embodiment of cultural "otherness," and furthermore that the ambiguities of ancient geography made the Scythians of Herodotus "a people midway between two different spaces, on the frontiers of Asia and Europe."[10] Such a location rendered the Scythians especially convenient for the eighteenth-century construction of Eastern Europe, though they were also employed for other ends, as in Voltaire's tragedy of 1767, *The Scythians*, in which they supposedly represented the citizens of Geneva. Even then, Voltaire could not resist the associations of Eastern Europe when he sent the play to his occasional correspondent in Hungary, Janos Fekete: "A descendant of the Huns wants to see my Scythian drama." Although the identification of the ancient Scythians with the contemporary Tartars was considered quite convincing, the ethnography of the Enlightenment eventually came to recognize the even more essential role of the Slavs in relating the ancient and contemporary aspects of Eastern Europe. The Slavs were reported as one barbarian people among many in the ancient sources, but they were a verifiably extensive language group in the contemporary world, linking different lands of Eastern Europe. Peyssonnel emphasized their significance by prefacing his book with an essay on the origin of the Slavonic language. When Voltaire took an interest in the book upon publication in 1765, it was with the facetiously declared intention of "learning right well the ancient Slavonic language."[11]

The point of Peyssonnel's preface on language was to argue that Slavonic was not native to Adriatic Illyria but was borne by barbarian invasions from beyond the Danube. Those invasions mapped a Slavonic linguistic domain in ancient history, still verifiable in the contemporary world: "In Europe one speaks it in Dalmatia, Liburnia or Croatia, which is the Occidental part of Illyria, in Occidental Macedonia, in Epirus, Bosnia, Serbia, Bulgaria, Russia, Muscovy, Bohemia, Poland, Silesia; it is also alive in several countries of Asia." In all these lands, according to Peyssonnel, one common language was spoken in closely related dialects, though he excepted the Hungarian language from this Slavic domain, relating its roots to Tartar or Turkish, and tracing its origin to Siberia. The linguistic search for the origin of the Slavonic language was again a problem of unscrambling Eastern Europe; there were so many peoples "all included under the general name of Slavs or Slavonics, chasing and succeeding each other," that all were easily "mixed and confused." Peyssonnel proclaimed himself ready to "unscramble the chaos as much as my researches on the Slavonic language may permit."[12] It was an irresistible formula for the eighteenth-century discovery of Eastern Europe, so much so that even though language could and did serve as a key to the scrambled code, Peyssonnel's pursuit of the origin of the Slavonic language placed that subject in a new level of contextual chaos. With a reference to Tacitus, the issue of origin ended in a meaninglessly broad attribution to the ancient Sarmatians: "these Sarmatian nations who by diverse incursions invaded, under the general name of Slavonics, Poland, Russia, Moravia, Hungary, and all the lands where their language is still alive today."[13] The name of Sarmatia, which covered the lands of Eastern Europe in the *Ancient Geography* of d'Anville, also served as an ultimate ethnographic umbrella in Peyssonnel's ancient history of these lands.

Peyssonnel described a linguistic diagram of Eastern Europe, in concentric circles. Hungary and Transylvania were at the center, speaking the language of the Hungarians, "descended from the barbarians of Turkestan." Then came a circle, really a half-circle, of Moldavia and Wallachia, curving around Transylvania, speaking "an idiom of Latin corrupted by the mélange of all the barbarian languages that successively infested that country." The Slavic language formed the last and largest circle, surrounding the others and defining the full extent of Eastern Europe. This diagrammatic deformation of geography by geometry showed how effectively language might serve as the analytical criterion for constructing a coherent domain. Peyssonnel also presented a "New Tableau of the Situation of the Slavonic Peoples," all at once unscrambling the chaos that he himself had painstakingly represented: "It is no longer necessary to pay any attention to the different origin of these peoples, who, in the preceding centuries, have made all the diverse incursions of which I have spoken in sufficient detail; one need no longer consider them except as Slavonics."[14] Apparently, Eastern Europe was in the eye of the beholder, a matter of focus, of attention, of *trompe l'oeil*. Or perhaps, with the advent of the linguistic key, it was more an issue of the ear.

If Peyssonnel appreciated that Eastern Europe could be structured with reference to the Slavonic language, Pierre-Charles Levesque was the first Frenchman fully to appreciate that the mastery of that language was essential to writing the history, ancient or modern, of its domain. His *History of Russia* was published in Paris in 1782, the same year that Rulhière began to give readings from his history of Poland. These contemporary works were the historical masterpieces of the French Enlightenment on Russia and Poland, respectively, and both held the field into the nineteenth century. While Rulhière was finally published in 1807, the year that Napoleon established the Grand Duchy of Warsaw, Levesque went into a new edition in 1800, and then again in 1812, the year of the author's death, the year of the emperor's invasion of Russia. If, however, Rulhière's Poland was essentially the product of research in Paris, Levesque conducted his researches in Russia. He went in 1773, the same year as Diderot, indeed with Diderot's recommendation, and long outlasted the great philosophe, returning to Paris only in 1780. Levesque taught literature in a military school in St. Petersburg while pursuing the work of scholarship that made him the most accomplished French Slavicist of the century. He appreciated his own academic primacy in the preface to the *History of Russia*:

In vain a Frenchman might promise himself to write the history of Russia, while remaining in Paris in his study, or contenting himself with excavating in our most vast libraries. . . . One must go to Russia, there to surrender oneself for several years to a dry and stubborn study, to learn not only modern Russian, but also the ancient Slavonic-Russian dialect, in which all the chronicles are written. . . . That is what I have done.[15]

Such a preparation left Levesque ready not only to write the whole history of Russia, but also to provide an introduction on "The Antiquity of the Slavs." The linguistic domain that Peyssonnel so tortuously identified was endowed with a certain cultural consistency by Levesque in reflections on religious mythology.

Rulhière, in the *Anarchy of Poland*, had little to say about ancient history, but simply registered both Poles and Russians as parts of the same people "who, under the common name of Slovene or Slav, spread twelve centuries ago in all the east of Europe." Levesque, in the *History of Russia*, had more to say, and a more complex conception. He did not identify the Russians as Slavs, but argued rather that as a consequence of language, customs, and ancient sources "they became confused with the Slavs." Furthermore, the Slavs themselves were "confused by the ancients with the Scythians." Levesque saw the Slavs as "coming out of the Orient" and entering into Russia, which was therefore "their first habitation in Europe." Though they may have descended upon the Roman empire as "Septentrional" barbarians, they were nevertheless, according to Levesque, by ultimate origin "Oriental" barbarians. Those who invaded the empire were the ancestors of those who "occupy today Bohemia, Bulgaria, Serbia, Dalmatia, a part of Hungary," even Pomerania and Silesia in Germany, and those who remained in Russia and Poland were divided into tribes: "Lekhs on the shores of the Vistula, Polians on those of the Dnieper, Polotchans on the banks of the Polota which falls into the Dvina, Dregvitches between the Dvina and the Pripet."[16] This was an ancient anthropology of total taxonomical variety, structured according to the geographical landmarks of the region.

"It is generally enough believed," wrote Levesque, "that Peter I, in mounting the throne, saw around him only a desert, peopled by savage animals whom he knew how to make into men."[17] Tracing Russian history back to the prehistoric tribes of the ancient Slavs, Levesque proceeded to narrate the course of Russian history, building to, not beginning with, the reigns of Peter I and Catherine II. In this he sought to enlarge upon the perspective of an older generation of the Enlightenment, that of Voltaire. The power of the conventional perspective was such that Grimm's *Correspondance Littéraire* reviewed Levesque's *History of Russia* with a yawn: "One easily understands that the ancient history of Russia could not be susceptible of great interest; these first times offer only monuments of war and savage manners."[18] In fact, even as historiography opened itself to the earlier history of the lands of Eastern Europe, the paradigm of Peter exercised its fascination even beyond the history of Russia. The *General History of Hungary* by Claude-Louis de Sacy, published in 1780, contemporary with Levesque's *History of Russia*, proceeded "from the first invasion of the Huns to our own days." Setting Hungary and France in opposition, "at the two extremities of Europe," Sacy implicitly accepted a continental polarization between Eastern Europe and Western Europe. It was therefore all the more natural to assert that the reign of Maria Theresa—who died in 1780—constituted for Hungary "the epoch of a revolution resembling that made by Peter the Great in Russia." This "revolution" was really a matter of civilization itself: "The useful arts began to flower in that country; even the sciences spread a beneficent half-light (*demi-jour*)."[19] The evocation of *demi-jour* nicely expressed the intermediary idea of Eastern Europe between the darkness of barbarism and the light of civilization. That conception rendered the ancient history of barbarian incursions, including the Huns and the Slavs as well as the Scythians and Sarmatians, an essential component of the Enlightenment's Eastern Europe.

"The Ancient and Actual State of Moldavia"

Peyssonnel identified Hungary and the Romanian principalities, Wallachia and Moldavia, as linguistically distinct enclaves in his circle diagram of the Slavic domain. Like Peyssonnel in the Crimea in the 1750s, Hauterive in Moldavia in the 1780s explored the significance of language and ancient history for the contemporary condition of the province. From 1785 to 1787 he served officially as French secretary, and unofficially as French consul, to the prince of Moldavia at Jassy, the hospodar, who recognized the sovereignty of the Ottoman sultan. One of his secretarial predecessors there, in the 1770s, was Jean-Louis Carra, the future mesmerist and revolutionary, who wrote a *History of Moldavia and Wallachia*, which began by observing that "France, England, a part of Germany and of Italy, occupy the center of the continent, and from this center go forth the lights that illuminate the other regions of the globe." Moldavia and Wallachia, according to Carra, could even be successfully colonized, because they were not such remote regions of the globe, "because the distance is not so considerable and because one could hope for all the resources of civilized Europe." Transmitting light from Western Europe to Eastern Europe, however, also reciprocally meant receiving news and obtaining knowledge of lands like Moldavia and Wallachia, and Carra clarified the relation of lands and peoples accordingly.

It is not for the barbaric, ignorant peoples to be the first to know us; but it is for us, on the contrary, for us . . . to unravel (*démêler*) the character, the genius, even the physiognomy of contemporary peoples, placed upon this earth as if submitted to our observations and to our critiques. It is for us, finally, to know these same peoples, before they can know themselves, and seek to know us in their turn.[20]

Hauterive composed in 1787, after two years in Jassy, an unpublished *Memoir on the Ancient and Actual State of Moldavia*, addressed in epistolary form to the new phanariot hospodar, Alexander Ypsilanti, "Mon Prince."

As a letter to a prince the memoir was apparently a prescription of enlightened absolutism, and Hauterive promised the hospodar that history could offer him "the light and encouragement of great examples." Yet as soon as Hauterive turned to ancient history and its relevance to the manners of the Moldavian nation, the memoir appeared closer in spirit to Rousseau's *Considerations* than to Voltaire's correspondence.

If I belonged, my prince, to the nation over which you are going to rule, it is for you that I would undertake to become its historian, and I would devote myself above all to raising it before your eyes, to respond to the calumnious prejudices which tend to debase it, as if it were not worthy or capable of receiving the benefits of a happy administration. I would have the courage to publish that of all the peoples who surround us and who glory in an ancient genealogy, we are still the one who preserves in its customs and in its laws the most conformity to those of its founders. . . . We are the only ones who, without forming an integral part of a vast empire, preserve, under the condition of a tribute, our name and our civil forms. . . . We are finally the only ones who keep the laws and the language of the first people of the universe, as titles of a filiation which attests to the noblest origin, some of their customs as national traditions, and finally the precious and ineffaceable traits of the simplicity of those ancient Romans who subdued the universe, and of the Scythians who were not subdued by anyone.[21]

The Frenchman's rhetorical assumption of Moldavian identity ("we are the only ones"), his presumptuous judgment of the nation as "worthy" and "capable," and above all his appreciation of ancient customs as "national traditions" were strikingly suggestive of Rousseau's exhortation to the Poles. In fact, the *Considerations* was published in Paris in 1782, so Hauterive could have read it before leaving for Constantinople in 1784. Rousseau believed that in all of Europe only Poland possessed a glimmering of the ancient spirit of the Greeks and the Romans, that only "national institutions" produced a "national physiognomy" to distinguish the Poles from other peoples, that it was therefore essential to maintain "ancient customs," and that these were to be valued most for "simplicity in manners."[22] Because Eastern Europe as a whole appeared to offer such appropriate material for theoretical improvisation on the subject of national identity, either the Poles or the Moldavians could be made to fit the same intellectual format.

To be sure, Hauterive was far more specifically knowledgeable than Rousseau about the ancient and contemporary history of Eastern Europe.

He presented a detailed catalogue of "the peoples who surround us" in Moldavia, reporting that in ancient times "the Dacians, the Huns, the Goths, the Visigoths, the Ostrogoths, the Avars, the Vandals, and the Comans have passed by here," while in more recent history "the Bulgars, the Hungarians, the Transylvanians, the Cossacks, the Russians, and the Poles have in turn been sovereigns of this land."[23] Almost twenty years before, Voltaire was thrilled to imagine Catherine's armies crossing the Danube and conquering Moldavia; now, resistance to Russian influence was part of Hauterive's mission as an agent of the French foreign ministry. He declared it to be a principal purpose of his memoir to dissuade any Moldavian, and especially the prince, from "the mad hope of being better off in the changing of domination."[24] This was merely a matter of policy, but Hauterive's notable intellectual achievement in the memoir was to formulate the principles of this policy in terms of linguistic affinity and ancient history.

Thus it was that while Peyssonnel was astonished to hear Wallachia identified as "the Roman land," Hauterive embraced the "genealogy," the "filiation," that established Moldavia and Wallachia as Roman lands, today Romania. Their language he recognized as a Roman language, that is, a Romance language, that of "the first people of the universe," while he saw in the Moldavians themselves the "ineffaceable traits" of the ancient Romans—and also of the ancient Scythians! This crossing of the Scythians and the Romans in ancient history to produce the modern Moldavians was the perfect cultural antidote to Russian imperialism, since both Scythians and Romans were emphatically not Slavic. It was also the perfect expression of the eighteenth-century idea of Eastern Europe, locating Moldavia historically between the Western civilization of the Romans and the Oriental barbarism of the Scythians.

Hauterive affirmed "the fraternity of the peoples who, between the Danube, the Dniester, and the Black Sea, as in Italy, speak an idiom truly derived from Latin." He celebrated the Moldavian relation to the Romans, and also, in a Rousseauist vein, praised the Moldavian boyars for an "attachment to ancient manners, a more austere character, and less of a penchant for that European civilization which, when it does not operate in a brusque and total effect, does nothing but add new vices to the old ones."[25] He did not specify whether these ancient manners, which rendered Moldavians resistant to European civilization, were those of the Roman republic or the Scythian horde. In another memorandum, not directly addressed to the hospodar, Hauterive admitted that he himself was put off by a perceived want of European civilization when he arrived in Moldavia in 1785: "The figures at first seemed to me barbarous, the costume absurd, the uniforms ragged, the houses holes of mud, the priests beggarly and hypocritical riffraff, and the language frightful (*épouvantable*). My eyes and my ears began to become accustomed."[26] After his return from Moldavia in 1787, his next diplomatic posting in 1792 was to be the consulate in New York.

The Moldavian language, which Hauterive initially found so "frightful" to the ear, was an important subject in the memoir, and he considered especially the issue of its origin in the ancient world. Though his early report of 1785 spoke of Moldavian as "an idiom truly derived from Latin," the memoir of 1787 presented a more complex linguistic filiation, to some extent anticipating modern academic hypotheses about the origin of Romanian. Rather than a derivation or degeneration from classical Latin, he proposed that Moldavian was "the popular language of the Romans," arguing from the relations between articles and nouns. This perspective on the language, however, also had consequences for locating Moldavia between civilization and barbarism:

> It is still the Roman language, not that of Cicero and the century of Augustus. It dates from much further back. The Moldavian language is that of the soldiers of Romulus; it has preserved the hardness of their manners and all the coarseness of their ways. That alteration which, in the progress of Roman civilization, softened the prosody by gentler accents and more sonorous terminations, the popular language did not experience, or at least the people of the fields did not participate in this circumstance of civilization. They preserved in their idiom the barbarism of the earliest times.[27]

Hauterive thus made Moldavian older than Latin, but of lesser civilization. He argued for language as the most important factor in preserving national identity, since manners, law, and religion might undergo variation with circumstance, but "one cannot constrain a nation to forget a language."[28]

Consistent with his policy of warning against the Russian empire, Hauterive identified the menace to Moldavian as coming from that direction. He worried that the Orthodox Church in Moldavia was employing the Slavonic liturgy, while other Russian influences encouraged more generally the use of the Cyrillic alphabet instead of the Latin for written Moldavian. To demonstrate the inappropriateness of writing Moldavian in Cyrillic, he proposed what seemed to him a preposterous hypothetical case, of writing French in Cyrillic: "If St. Louis had brought back the Slavic alphabet from Palestine and had given it to the French language, we would say not *mort* but *moart.* . . . Our language instead of tending perpetually to soften would have become more and more expressive and hard."[29] Such an appeal was obviously intended less for advising the hospodar of Moldavia than for amusing Hauterive's future fellow members ("our language") of the French Academy of Inscriptions and Belles-Lettres. The memoir, however, remained unpublished until the twentieth century, when it was presented to the Romanian Academy in Bucharest in 1902. When Moldavia and Wallachia joined to form independent Romania in 1859, the Latin alphabet became the standard for written Romanian, but in the Soviet Socialist Republic of Moldavia, the language was written in Cyrillic. Hauterive arrived at a modern appreciation of the interplay of international politics, national identity, and language by considering the case of Moldavia in the context of Eastern Europe.

Hauterive identified Moldavian as the language of "the soldiers of Romulus," and in formulating the connection between language and ethnography, he invoked the soldiers of Trajan, who conquered Dacia at the beginning of the second century. In a literal interpretation of Rousseau's notion of "national physiognomy," Hauterive looked at the people of Moldavia and saw them as the soldiers represented on Trajan's column in Rome:

One still recognizes in them the high stature and robust constitution of Roman soldiers, and when one has seen the traits of the conquerors of the Dacians on the reliefs of the column that was raised in memory of the conquest of Trajan, it is not without pleasure that one meets them again in Moldavia, in the physiognomy of their descendants.[30]

Trajan's column was in fact an important and complex reference for the eighteenth-century discovery of Eastern Europe, a sort of travelers' totem pole. Ségur arrived in Russia in 1785, the same year that Hauterive came to Moldavia. When Ségur gazed upon the Russians, he saw "those Scythians, Dacians, Roxolans, Goths, once the terror of the Roman world," brought to life; they were the "demi-savage figures that one has seen in Rome on the bas-reliefs of Trajan's column," reborn and animated "before your gaze."[31] Ségur, like Hauterive, thought irresistibly of Trajan's column when he traveled in Eastern Europe. Hauterive, urging a national identity on the Moldavians, identified them as the Roman soldiers on the column, soldiers characterized by "the hardness of their manners and all the coarseness of their ways." That was, of course, only half the ancestry that Hauterive assigned to the Moldavians; the other half was Scythian and explicitly barbarian. Ségur, however, regarding the Russians, thought not of the Roman soldiers on Trajan's column but of the barbarian captives, including the Dacians and the Scythians. Ségur and Hauterive expressed complementary visions, perhaps becoming a little confused as they spiraled around the column, following the reliefs to the very top. Were those Roman soldiers or Scythian barbarians? It was in Eastern Europe that such figures came to life, were animated "before your gaze," there where the world of the ancient barbarians met the modern anthropological eye.

"Swarms of Savages"

Gibbon's *Decline and Fall of the Roman Empire* was one of the most influential and enduring literary monuments of the Enlightenment, crystallizing the eighteenth-century perspective not only on the civilization of Rome but also on the barbarians who helped bring about the decline and fall. They descended upon Rome, and later upon Constantinople, Septentrional barbarians and Oriental barbarians, as Peyssonnel classified them, moving across Eastern Europe. Gibbon went to Rome and experienced his inspirational epiphany in 1764, the year before Peyssonnel published his work on the barbarians of the Danube and the Black Sea. Born in 1737, Gibbon was ten years younger than Peyssonnel and was the almost exact contemporary of Levesque, born in 1736. Gibbon began to work seriously on the *Decline and Fall* in the early 1770s, and the sensationally successful first volume appeared in 1776. The next two volumes were published in 1781, when Levesque's *History of Russia* was about to appear in Paris, and Gibbon wrote the last lines of his masterpiece in 1787, when Hauterive composed his memoir on Moldavia. The final volumes of Gibbon were published the next year, in 1788. His scholarly career thus overlapped those of Peyssonnel, Levesque, and Hauterive, and, more significantly, they also overlapped in the geographical terrains of their respective histories. The drama of Gibbon's *Decline and Fall* was focused above all on Rome and Constantinople, but the geographical landmarks and ethnographic inhabitants of Eastern Europe were inevitably included, with increasing prominence in the middle and latter volumes. Unquestionably, this was the most widely read and ultimately influential treatment of Eastern Europe in ancient history.

Gibbon attended to Eastern Europe in the opening pages of his gargantuan history, when he celebrated Trajan's conquest of Dacia and the "absolute submission of the barbarians." Gibbon then mapped the conquered province:

> Its natural boundaries were the Dniester, the Teyss, or Tibiscus, the Lower Danube, and the Euxine Sea. The vestiges of a military road may still be traced from the banks of the Danube to the neighbourhood of Bender, a place famous in modern history, and the actual frontier of the Turkish and Russian empires.[32]

The geographical boundaries suggested that Gibbon here was on Peyssonnel's historical terrain, by the Danube and the Black Sea. Like Hauterive, Gibbon moved easily between "ancient" and "actual" history in Eastern Europe, invoking modern history and contemporary empires. The narrative even implied that perhaps Gibbon himself had followed the vestiges of that Roman road from the Danube to the Dniester, but a footnote attributed that observation to d'Anville, the mapmaker who worked on ancient geography. Gibbon was every bit as much of an armchair traveler as Voltaire when it came to Eastern Europe. In fact, when he acclaimed Bender as "a place famous in modern history," he took for granted that his readers would know about Bender from Voltaire's *Charles XII*. Located on the Dniester, between Moldavia and Tartary, Bender was where Charles

Detail of "Romani Imperii Tabula Geographica," map of the Roman Empire, from Robert's *Atlas Universel*, Paris, 1757; east of "Germania" and the empire, the precise mapping of the names of places gives way to an imprecise mapping of the names of peoples, the tribes of ancient barbarians; these are subsumed under the broad geographical band of "Germano-Sarmatia," printed on the diagonal from northwest to southeast, while farther east there lies the even broader band of "Sarmatia," marking the end of the map; above the Crimean peninsula the atlas attaches the label "Parva Scythia," Little Scythia. (From the Harvard Map Collection, Harvard University.)

camped as the guest of the Tartars after his defeat at Poltava. It was famous even more recently when Catherine's army triumphantly besieged Bender in 1770, and Voltaire cheered from a distance at Ferney. Gibbon's allusions here showed that he possessed the conventional consciousness of the century that discovered Eastern Europe.

In Chapter X, still part of that first volume of 1776, Gibbon followed "The general Irruption of the Barbarians," and this subject took him across the whole area of Eastern Europe. The barbarians in question were the Goths. Gibbon stipulated their Scandinavian origin, though suggesting the possibility of an even more remote origin in "Asiatic Sarmatia." He set the stage for the great "irruption" of the third century by postulating an earlier migration across the Baltic from Sweden—"to the mouth of the Vistula"—before proceeding to his main subject, "the second migration of the Goths from the Baltic to the Euxine." Again Gibbon consulted d'Anville's *Ancient Geography* to set the Goths on a river odyssey, down the Dnieper (the Borysthenes, to him): "The windings of that great stream through the plains of Poland and Russia gave a direction to their line of march."[33] They encountered various peoples whom Gibbon classified as Sarmatian, such as the Jazyges, the Alans, and the Roxolans, until finally the Goths were up against "the Scythian hordes." Thus the migration of the Goths enabled Gibbon to give his readers a tour of the barbarians of Eastern Europe, from the Baltic to the Black Sea.

Interestingly, Gibbon's Goths were shown to follow precisely the course that Voltaire traversed with Charles XII, crossing the Baltic from Sweden, passing through Poland and Russia to the Ukraine and the Crimea. Voltaire exploited this itinerary to represent Eastern Europe in the eighteenth century, Gibbon to represent it in the third century. Voltaire also encountered barbarians, indeed Sarmatians, along the way: "One sees still in the Polish soldiers the character of the ancient Sarmatians." Gibbon described the Ukraine as a prize to tempt any conqueror, ancient or modern: "a country of considerable extent and uncommon fertility, intersected with navigable rivers, which, from either side, discharge themselves into the Borysthenes; and interspersed with large and lofty forests of oaks." In a footnote Gibbon admitted his ahistorical conflation of the ancient and contemporary geography of the Ukraine: "The modern face of the country is a just representation of the ancient, since, in the hands of the Cossacks, it still remains in a state of nature."[34] Voltaire, in the *Essay on Manners*, had been just as casual about projecting the modern Cossacks back into the ancient world:

Their life is entirely similar to that of the ancient Scythians and the Tartars on the shores of the Black Sea. To the north and the east of Europe (*l'orient de l'Europe*), all that part of the world is still rustic: it is the image of those so-called heroic centuries when men, limited to the necessary, pillaged that necessary from their neighbors.[35]

Voltaire and Gibbon both produced reciprocal conflations, between ancient and modern, between modern and ancient, in writing the history of Eastern Europe.

The protagonist of Chapter XXXIV was Attila the Hun, and the Huns, vaguely identified as Scythians, were immediately located with reference to the geography of Eastern Europe: "Their victorious hordes had spread from the Volga to the Danube." Attila himself was described according to racial characteristics, and Gibbon employed contemporary barbarians as a standard of reference: "The portrait of Attila exhibits the genuine deformity of a modern Calmuck; a large head, a swarthy complexion, small deep-seated eyes, a flat nose, a few hairs in the place of a beard, broad shoulders, and a short square body, of nervous strength, though of a disproportioned form." The footnote referred the reader to the *Natural History* of Buffon. The anthropological equation of the ancient Scythian and the "modern Calmuck" was a matching of barbarians. After raising the possibility of human sacrifice, Gibbon outlined more generally the absence of civilization among Attila's Huns. "The Scythian monarch," he observed, "however ignorant of the value of science and philosophy, might perhaps lament that his illiterate subjects were destitute of the art which could perpetuate the memory of his exploits." That art, of course, was Gibbon's own, the art of history. Attila was not even sufficiently alert to the opportunities of civilization to make use of Roman captives "to diffuse through the deserts of Scythia the rudiments of the useful and ornamental arts." Such a notion of diffusion suggested Gibbon's own conviction that civilization could indeed act upon barbarians and stimulate development. Attila, however, making his capital "between the Danube, the Theiss, and the Carpathian hills, in the plains of Upper Hungary," always preserved "the simplicity of his Scythian ancestors."[36] For Gibbon too, as for Peyssonnel and Hauterive, the Scythian factor was indispensable for identifying ethnographically the barbarians of Eastern Europe.

Gibbon's Eastern Europe was most fundamentally formulated in Chapter XLII, which surveyed the "State of the Barbaric World" in the sixth century and introduced the "Tribes and Inroads of the Sclavonians." He began with a dual classification: "The wild people who dwelt or wandered in the plains of Russia, Lithuania, and Poland, might be reduced, in the age of Justinian, under the two great families of the BULGARIANS and the SCLAVONIANS." The former were identified as Tartars—"and it is needless to renew the simple and well-known picture of Tartar manners." The Sclavonians, however, merited more attention, and were explained in terms of language, racial character, and primitive economy.

Their numerous tribes, however distant or adverse, used one common language (it was harsh and irregular), and were known by the resemblance of their form, which deviated from the swarthy Tartar, and approached without attaining the lofty stature and fair complexion of the German. Four thousand six hundred villages were scattered over the provinces of Russia and Poland, and their huts were hastily built of rough timber in a country deficient both in stone and iron. Erected, or rather concealed, in the depth of forests, on the banks of rivers, or the edge of morasses, we may not perhaps, without flattery, compare them to the architecture of the beaver, which they resembled in a double issue, to the land and water, for the escape of the savage inhabitant, an animal less cleanly, less diligent, and less social, than that marvellous quadruped. The fertility of the soil, rather than the labour of the natives, supplied the rustic plenty of the Sclavonians.[37]

That Gibbon found the Slavic language harsh and irregular was no more than conventional; Hauterive entirely agreed. That he thought the Slavs racially inferior to the Germans (less lofty, less fair) was a point that, beginning in the eighteenth century and building to the twentieth, Germans themselves would assert with an ever more strident pretense of science. Yet Gibbon's venture into natural history, his comparison between Slavs and beavers, was very much his own, intended as wit, and the implicit issue was civilization itself. The beavers were celebrated for their architecture, the Slavs disparaged for a want of cleanliness, diligence, and sociability.

On a more generous note Gibbon allowed that the Slavs were "chaste, patient, and hospitable" (without any insinuating remarks about the relative chastity of beavers). Like Levesque, Gibbon recognized a primitive Slavic religion, a god of thunder, a variety of nymphs. Political organization, however, was entirely lacking: "The Sclavonians disdained to obey a despot, a prince, or even a magistrate." His representation of their military manner was the epitome of savagery, for they fought "almost naked," and their weapons were "a bow, a quiver of small poisoned arrows, and a long rope, which they dexterously threw from a distance, and entangled their enemy in a running noose." Still more disturbingly savage was their treatment of prisoners: "Without distinction of rank or age or sex, the captives were impaled or flayed alive, or suspended between four posts and beaten with clubs till they expired, or enclosed in some spacious building and left to perish in the flames." In constructing this imagery of barbaric horror, Gibbon relied upon Procopius, while admitting that the Byzantine historian might have exaggerated.[38] In Gibbon's epic account of the struggle between civilization and barbarism, the latter was at home in Eastern Europe among "the wild people who dwelt or wandered in the plains of Russia, Lithuania, and Poland."

In Chapter L, Gibbon introduced, and discussed at length, Mohammed, Islam, and the Arabs, who were favorably compared with the Scythians.[39] These subjects were of paramount importance in the chapters that followed as well, so that at the beginning of Chapter LV Gibbon excused himself to the reader for any appearance of digression, insisting that "in war, in religion, in science, in their prosperity, and in their decay, the Arabians press themselves on our curiosity." Yet this justification was no more than an introduction to the real subject of the chapter, which was Eastern Europe, whose peoples were pronounced unworthy of comparable curiosity or historical attention:

But the same labour would be unworthily bestowed on the swarms of savages who, between the seventh and the twelfth century, descended from the plains of Scythia, in transient inroad or perpetual emigration. Their names are uncouth, their origins doubtful, their actions obscure, their superstition was blind, their valour brutal, and the uniformity of their public and private lives was neither softened by innocence nor refined by policy. The majesty of the Byzantine throne repelled and survived their disorderly attacks; the greater part of these barbarians has disappeared without leaving any memorial of their existence, and the despicable remnant continues, and may long continue, to groan under the dominion of a foreign tyrant. From the antiquities of, I. *Bulgarians*, II. *Hungarians*, and III. *Russians*, I shall content myself with selecting such facts as yet deserve to be remembered.[40]

Here again Gibbon negatively constructed an idea of civilization by describing its absence among barbarians. Here again ancient disorderliness was translated into contemporary despicability. The political formula by which he readily consigned the peoples of Eastern Europe to foreign tyranny was conventional, but in this case ambiguous. Probably he was referring to the Bulgarians, first on his agenda, who were ruled by the sultan in Constantinople. Yet it was equally true that, when Gibbon was writing this chapter in the 1780s, the Hungarians were ruled by the Habsburgs from Vienna, where Joseph II wielded his scepter in a spirit of rigorous absolutism, while the Russians were governed no less absolutely by a German princess, Catherine II. In any case Gibbon was ready to interpret contemporary subjection to foreign tyranny as the proper comeuppance of swarming savagery in the ancient world.

Gibbon's discussion of the Bulgarians began with the incorrect assertion that they were Slavs by origin. Arguing on the plausible ground that the Bulgarians spoke a Slavic language, he also carelessly included the Wallachians in his enumeration of related peoples:

The unquestionable evidence of language attests the descent of the Bulgarians from the original stock of Sclavonian, or more properly Slavonian, race; and the kindred bands of Servians, Bosnians, Rascians, Croatians, Wallachians, etc. followed either the standard or the example of the leading tribe. From the Euxine to the Adriatic, in the state of captives, or subjects, or allies, or enemies, of the Greek empire, they overspread the land.[41]

Gibbon's analytical vocabulary counted the Slavs as many tribes constituting a single race; his mapping from "the Euxine to the Adriatic" measured the depth of Eastern Europe to its western limit. The source that he cited was a Latin treatise on the origin of the Slavs, by John Christopher de Jordan, published in Vienna in 1745, yet Gibbon questioned the value of that work on account of the author's own origin. "His collections and researches are useful to elucidate the antiquities of Bohemia and the adjacent countries," noted Gibbon of Jordan, "but his plan is narrow, his style barbarous, his criticism shallow, and the Aulic counsellor is not free from the prejudices of a Bohemian." It was Gibbon's own prejudice, and his incorrect identification of the Bulgarians as Slavs by origin, that enabled him to work from the antiquities of Bohemia in writing the history of Bulgaria. At the same time he admitted the influence of Scythia, when he narrated the dramatic defeat of the Byzantine emperor Nicephorus in 811, by the Bulgarian khan Krum, and the employment of the emperor's skull as a gilded goblet. "This savage cup," remarked Gibbon, "was tinctured with the manners of the Scythian wilderness."[42] His odd resort to "tincture," with its connotations of color, suggested the vaguely racial anthropology by which an eighteenth-century historian of the ancient world attempted to express the filiation and diffusion of manners among barbarians.

"When the black swarm of Hungarians first hung over Europe, about nine hundred years after the Christian era," wrote Gibbon, introducing the next nation on his agenda, "they were mistaken by fear and superstition for the Gog and Magog of the Scriptures, the signs and forerunners of the end of the world." Gibbon referred to the Latin works of eighteenth-century Hungarian scholars, that of George Pray published in Vienna in 1775, that of Stephen Katona published in Pest between 1778 and 1781. "Their rational criticism can no longer be amused with a vain pedigree of Attila and the Huns," observed Gibbon, after which he himself did not hesitate to assign the Hungarians an even more vaguely allusive pedigree, ranking them "among the tribes of Scythia." Like the Bulgarians, their migration defined the depth of Eastern Europe, from the Volga to the Danube, and even after they settled in the lands of modern Hungary, their national existence was paralleled by that of "their long-lost brethren" on the Volga, "pagans and savages who still bore the name of Hungarians."[43] Gibbon thus established the intermediary position of Eastern Europe, with its different degrees and varying proportions of civilization and savagery.

While Gibbon referred to the writings of the tenth-century Byzantine emperor Constantine Porphyrogenitus, he was also aware that the "modern learning" of his own century could further refine the classical classification of barbarian peoples. Linguistic learning indicated that "the Hungarian language stands alone, and as it were insulated, among the Sclavonian dialects; but it bears a close and clear affinity to the idioms of the Fennic race, of an obsolete and savage race, which formerly occupied the northern regions of Asia and Europe." Gibbon also referred to contemporary "Tartar evidence," relating Hungarian to the languages of Siberia.[44] When Gibbon

was writing, the eighteenth century had already discovered the basic outline of the modern linguistic appreciation of Hungarian as a Finno-Ugrian
language. This was the fruit of various geographical researches, conducted
in Siberia especially, starting in the reign of Peter. Strahlenberg, Peter's
Swedish prisoner, collected words and compared languages in Siberia in
the 1720s, and the Russian historian Tatishchev was active from around
the same time in similar researches. The German historian of Russia G. F.
Müller compiled lists of words in Siberia in the 1730s; J. E. Fischer, who
followed in the 1740s, created a Siberian dictionary, and explicitly formulated the linguistic relation between Siberia and Hungary. Fischer's work
on the origin of the Hungarians was published in 1770 and was cited by
Gibbon in a footnote.[45] However, as recently as 1765 Jaucourt had reported
in the Encyclopedia, quite mistakenly, that "the language of Hungary is
a dialect of Slavic." Academic uncertainty around this linguistic issue was
aggravated by the general eighteenth-century inclination to confuse and
associate the peoples of Eastern Europe, whether in ancient or in modern
history. For Gibbon linguistic comparison allowed an association of the
modern Hungarians and the Tartars, which paralleled and reinforced his
association of the ancient Hungarians and the Scythians.

Gibbon's image of these barbarians was one of generally picturesque
savagery: "The tents of the Hungarians were of leather, their garments
of fur; they shaved their hair and scarified their faces." Yet in their hands
he placed an item of specifically attributed anthropological origin: "Their
native and deadly weapon was the Tartar bow." The invocation of ancient
Scythia tended to be less precise, more proverbial; for instance, when the
Hungarians went on the rampage, "such was their Scythian speed, that in
a single day a circuit of fifty miles was stripped and consumed." Gibbon
admitted that "their appetite for raw flesh might countenance the popular
tale that they drank the blood and feasted on the hearts of the slain." He
was, however, also capable of discussing sanguinary issues in a less sensational regard, representing blood, not imbibed but inherited, as a factor
in the racial constitution of the Hungarians. "The native race, the Turkish or Fennic blood," wrote Gibbon, "was mingled with new colonies of
Scythian or Sclavonian origin."[46] Here the Slavic and Scythian aspects of
Eastern Europe were located literally in the blood.

Finally, Gibbon addressed the origin of the Russians, "the brethren of
the Swedes and Normans," who crossed the Baltic, like the Goths before
them, "and visited the eastern shores, the silent residence of Fennic and
Sclavonian tribes." The "silence" of these eastern shores was that of peoples
hitherto unheard by ancient history, and Gibbon now awkwardly shifted
the designation of "Russians" from the Scandinavian visitors to the silent
tribes. "The primitive Russians of the lake Ladoga," he wrote, "paid a tribute, the skins of white squirrels, to these strangers, whom they saluted with

the title of *Varangians* or Corsairs." Eventually, the strangers "mingled with the Russians in blood, religion, and language." Like the Finno-Ugrian character of the Hungarian language, the Scandinavian-Varangian origin of the Russians was sufficiently established in eighteenth-century scholarship to satisfy Gibbon. His basic citation was Levesque's history, published in 1782, which offered Gibbon indirectly the evidence of the Russian chronicles. Gibbon also cited Coxe's travels, which appeared in 1784, stimulating general interest in Russia before the final volumes of the *Decline and Fall* were published in 1788.[47] Such was Gibbon's experience of Russia, the vicarious voyage and the fastidious footnote.

As a geographical source he cited d'Anville, *The Empire of Russia, Its Origin and Its Increase*, but he obviously had the cartographer's *Ancient Geography* in mind as well, for Russia was located with reference to "the geography of Scythia," even "the loose and indefinite picture of the Scythian desert." Gibbon followed his Russians down the Dnieper to the Black Sea, mapping a commercial domain across Eastern Europe "from the Baltic to the Euxine, from the mouth of the Oder to the port of Constantinople." The drama of Gibbon's narration lay in the Russian undertakings against Constantinople in the ninth and tenth centuries, and with withering condescension he represented the perspective of the barbarians on Byzantine civilization: "They envied the gifts of nature which their climate denied; they coveted the works of art, which they were too lazy to imitate and too indigent to purchase." Yet the "piratical adventure" that ensued was not merely a matter of ancient history, for "the image of their naval armaments was revived in the last century in the fleets of the Cosacks, which issued from the Borysthenes to navigate the same seas for a similar purpose." Once again the boundary between ancient and modern history collapsed, as seventeenth-century Cossacks embarked in their "canoes" upon the Dnieper and paddled right back into the tenth century. The footnote was even more explicit, citing Beauplan's seventeenth-century *Description of the Ukraine*, commenting that "except the circumstance of fire-arms, we may read old Russians for modern Cosacks." Such a reading was hardly historical, and left Gibbon uninhibited about bringing his ancient history right up to Catherine's reign: "In our own time, a Russian armament, instead of sailing from the Borysthenes, has circumnavigated the continent of Europe."[48] Thus the Russians appeared again at Constantinople, no longer in canoes, of course, yet implicitly unchanged in their ultimate purpose.

The climax of the chapter came with the conversion of Kiev and the Russian renunciation of human sacrifice, while Gibbon concluded with some general reflections on the coming of Christianity to the barbarians of Europe. "The northern and eastern regions of Europe," he wrote, formulating the geographical idea of Eastern Europe, "submitted to a religion more different in theory than in practice from the worship of their native idols." Though Gibbon could not resist such a swipe at Christianity, he did not actually consider the difference between civilization and barbarism to be insignificant:

The admission of the barbarians into the pale of civil and ecclesiastical society delivered Europe from the depredations, by sea and land, of the Normans, the Hungarians, and the Russians, who learned to spare their brethren and cultivate their possessions. The establishment of law and order was promoted by the influence of the clergy; and the rudiments of art and science were introduced into the savage countries of the globe.[49]

Subtly Gibbon modulated from ancient history toward a more modern perspective, for the point of reference here was no longer Rome or Byzantium but Europe. With the emergence of "the Sclavonic and Scandinavian kingdoms," he had no need to check his compass to determine the ultimate geographical orientation of civilization: "They imbibed the free and generous spirit of the European republic, and gradually shared the light of knowledge which arose on the western world."[50]

"So Many Little Wild Peoples"

In 1764, the year that Gibbon went to Rome, Johann Gottfried Herder, then twenty years old, went to Riga to begin a career as a teacher and minister. Riga, along with the province of Livonia, Latvia today, had belonged to the Russian empire since 1710, when Peter the Great obtained it from Sweden at the expense of Charles XII. Nevertheless Riga retained a privileged position of relative autonomy within Peter's empire; dominated by its German middle class, the city continued to enjoy the vestigial privileges of its independent Hanseatic history. Yet in the summer of 1764, before Herder's quiet arrival in the fall, Riga welcomed a far grander visitor, its new empress, Catherine. It was she who would eliminate the autonomy of Livonia in the 1780s, refusing to recognize local limits to her enlightened absolutism, but even thereafter, as Cobbett would testify at the turn of the century, Riga remained especially open to the Baltic, at the edge of Russia but not quite of it. Indeed, the whole Baltic coast until the eastern extremity of St. Petersburg itself constituted a sort of open border to Eastern Europe in the eighteenth century. Herder had come east to Riga along the coast from Königsberg, fresh from an education in the lectures of Kant; in Königsberg he was in Prussia, the subject of Frederick. To the west, on the same coast was Gdańsk in Poland, as Riga was in Russia, yet preserving an analogous urban autonomy. Both Gdańsk and Riga, by virtue of their respective rivers the Vistula and the Dvina, served as points of access into Eastern Europe.

Gibbon left Rome with a vision of its past glory so overwhelming that all the barbarians of Europe would eventually fall into place, located with respect to an unequivocal center of civilization. Herder left Riga in 1769 embarking on a sea voyage that took him along the Baltic and through the English Channel to Nantes in France; from there he later made his way to Paris. His journey thus took him from the edge of Eastern Europe to the very heart of Western Europe. Yet his account, his *Journal of my Voyage in the Year 1769*, was thoroughly preoccupied with the Eastern Europe he was leaving behind, a travel journal that almost moved in the opposite direction from that of the journey itself. Indeed, the first sentence of the journal was an expression of disorientation, confused even in time by the alternate calendar of the Russian empire: "May 23rd/June 3rd, I departed from Riga and on the 25th/5th, I went to sea, to go I don't know where."[51] Herder ended up spending most of the rest of his life in Goethe's Weimar, but he carried with him always the idea of Eastern Europe that was born in Riga and developed in the journal of 1769. Gibbon would assign the barbarians to their peripheral places with the magnificent condescension and occasional irony of a splendid classical stylist. Herder, at sea, seized upon those same barbarians with an eager embrace and stormy enthusiasm in a style that would soon be known as *Sturm und Drang*. The barbarians of ancient history were thrust into the anthropological present, and even into a furiously imaginative future. They would eventually come to rest, twenty years later, in the vast schema of Herder's *Ideas for the Philosophy of the History of Mankind*, in Part IV, Book XVI, Section IV: "Slavic Peoples." For Gibbon the Slavs, considered as a subject of ancient history, were little better than beavers, or perhaps a little worse. For Herder the Slavs were objects of fascination and admiration, whose qualities and character could best be appreciated through the emerging disciplines of anthropology and folklore.

The journal of 1769 was a work of the Baltic, and began with reflections on the North, as witnessed imaginatively from the sea: "The cold North here appears to be the birthplace of sea monsters, as of barbarians, human giants, and the devastators of the world." Herder mingled the terms of ancient history and monstrous mythology, with his mental compass fixed for the moment on north. Yet directional disorientation immediately followed, as he descended further into ancient history: "Was the North or the South, East or West, the *Vagina hominum*?" Herder proposed an answer in the seafaring metaphor of two "streams" of primitive cultural diffusion. One flowed from the Orient into Greece and Italy, bringing "music, art, manners, and science." The other stream went "over the North from Asia into Europe," parallel to his own route from Riga to Nantes, creating an irregular terrain of uneven development.[52] He considered the case of Riga, his point of departure, where he hoped to return someday to establish a national school, "to make the humanly wild Emile of Rousseau into the national child of Livonia." Though he seemed to cherish the wildness of Emile, his program for Livonia was one of civilization:

Everything today must adapt itself to politics; also for me it's necessary, with my plans! What my school could be against luxury and for the improvement of manners! What it would have to be to bring us nearer in language and education to the taste and refinement of our century, and not to remain behind. To emulate (*nachzueifern*) Germany, France, and England! To be for the honor and education of the nobility! What it could hope of Poland, Russia, and Courland![53]

The notions of emulation, of improving manners, of remaining behind, clearly expressed a developmental scale. The geography of development was centered on Riga, which Herder envisioned as a hinge between Germany, France, and England on the one hand, and Poland, Russia, and Courland on the other, between Western Europe and Eastern Europe. His plans for a school in Riga would recognize by emulation the primacy of Western Europe and serve as a beacon of hope to Eastern Europe at the same time. As Herder's ship sailed west on the Baltic, he left Eastern Europe geographically behind him, but resolved that in another sense it should not "remain behind."

"I shipped past Courland, Prussia, Denmark, Sweden, Norway, Jutland, Holland, Scotland, England, the Netherlands, to France," wrote Herder, charting his course across the Baltic. "Here are some political sea dreams (*Seeträume*)." The dream that then unfolded was a product of perspective, for Herder had reached the northwestern coast of Europe and now suddenly looked over his shoulder to see, behind him, the eighteenth century's most spectacular vision of Eastern Europe:

What a view from the West-North of these regions, when one day the spirit of civilization (*Kultur*) will visit them! The Ukraine will become a new Greece: the beautiful heaven of this people, their merry existence, their musical nature, their fruitful land, and so on, will one day awaken: out of so many little wild peoples, as the Greeks were also once, a mannered (*gesittete*) nation will come to be: their borders will stretch out to the Black Sea and from there through the world. Hungary, these nations, and an area of Poland and Russia will be participants in this new civilization (*Kultur*); from the northwest this spirit will go over Europe, which lies in sleep, and make it serviceable (*dienstbar*) according to the spirit. This all lies ahead, and must one day happen; but how? when? through whom?[54]

Such was the scope of Herder's sea dream; he gazed from the Baltic, and his vision reached all the way to the Black Sea, extending over all of Eastern Europe. His associative impulse invented Eastern Europe "out of so many little wild peoples," but also out of the Ukraine, Hungary, Poland, and Russia. Herder imaginatively welded the pieces together into one new "civilization," employing the German concept of *Kultur*. The Ukraine, which for Gibbon remained entirely "in a state of nature," a mere temptation to conquest, was for Herder the seat of that new civilization; its people were "merry" and "musical" and needed only to become "mannered." Here was Eastern Europe as the domain of virtually millenarian prophecy. Yet for all Herder's enthusiasm, his agent of civilization was the spirit of the northwest, or rather the West-North, regarding Eastern Europe from Herder's own perspective at sea, seeking to render it "serviceable."

Finally, almost at the end of his voyage to France, Herder turned his attention to the special case of Russia, the empire in which he had lived as a subject for five years. He reflected, like every other philosophe of the Enlightenment, on Catherine's plans for a legal code, whether it would bring "true civilization" to Russia. "Of what does true civilization consist?" he asked; and then answered, "not just in giving laws, but in forming manners." Having stated this conventional reservation, Herder went on to consider what kinds of laws would suit Russia, and rejected the projects of "lawgiving minds" (*gesetzgeberische Köpfe*) from England, France, or Germany, and likewise the examples of ancient Greece or Rome. A code for Russia would have to find inspiration in the Orient, in order to suit "the character, the multiplicity, and the level (*Stufe*) of the Russian nations." Herder's emphasis on the variation in "level" among the nations of Russia led him to the point of elaborating what was perhaps the century's most analytically conceived scale of development for Eastern Europe. Russia as a whole might exist on a lower level of civilization, but even within Russia Herder insisted on marking "divisions into completely cultivated, half cultivated, and wild regions." These levels he now schematized geographically: "The wild peoples are on the borders: the half-mannered is the country: then, the mannered seacoast. Use (*Gebrauch*) of the Ukraine. Preceding plan here."[55] Herder's cryptic reference to the "use of the Ukraine" seemed to cast a different light on his prophecy of a new civilization there. The designated "plan" was to put the Ukraine to use, to value its "musical nature" but even more its "fruitful land," to render it agriculturally "serviceable" to the political project of integrating Russia's unevenly developed levels.

Not only were "lawgiving minds" from the lands of Western Europe unable to assist Russia, according to Herder, but also those lands ran a risk to their own civilization in undertaking the enterprise: "One of the great peoples in economic trade, for example, England, will stir up another that is wild, and thus be ruined itself—couldn't that one be Russia!" To stir up Russia was even to risk provoking an "inundation of peoples." Herder considered the decline and fall of the Roman empire: "Only Rome and the barbarians—that was different: there it rumbled (*munkelte*) for a long time, as the rabble says: in our time it will have to rumble still longer, but break loose all the more suddenly."[56] The fall of Rome was recast in the contemporary world, indeed forecast for the future, but geographically reoriented so that Western Europe would now await the barbarians, while Eastern Europe was to be the source of the inundation.

The only comparable prophetic utterance in the eighteenth century, equally cryptic, was that of Rousseau in the *Social Contract* seven years before, when he predicted that the Tartars would subjugate Russia to become "its master—and ours." Like Rousseau, Herder was suspicious of civilization, and therefore perhaps readier to believe that it might be overwhelmed by barbarians, little wild peoples, a new civilization. The cultural glory of France was over, thought Herder: "The century of Louis is past; also the Montesquieu's, d'Alembert's, Voltaire's, Rousseau's are past: one lives on the ruins." The ultimate testimony to literary stagnation was the Encyclopedia of Diderot, proof that the French were no longer capable of original work.[57] Yet France was the destination of Herder's voyage, and one last time before he finished his journal, he looked back behind him to face the future of Russia.

"Great Empress!" he exclaimed, addressing her directly, as so many other philosophes did, and like them he did not hesitate to tell her that her work toward a code was simply "wrong" (*unrecht*). She had failed to face up to the nature and consequences of despotism in Russia. "Great Empress! No!" he exclaimed again, and wondered "now where is Montesquieu at his post," and where to find "a second Montesquieu." Konrad Bittner, writing about Herder and Russia, has suggested that Herder envisioned that second Montesquieu, who would suit laws to the Russian spirit, as none other than himself.[58] Indeed, from the venerable Voltaire at Ferney to the young Herder at Riga, in the 1760s almost every philosophe imagined himself as Catherine's correspondent and consultant. Casanova discussed calendar reform with her in St. Petersburg in 1765; in 1767 Lemercier arrived to reform everything else. Herder in 1765 wrote a poem of praise to Catherine, and in 1767 he too received an invitation to give up his teaching in Riga and become a school inspector in St. Petersburg.[59] There was every difference between being invited to Russia as an international celebrity, as Rousseau was in 1766, and being offered a job as a young teacher of promise, as Herder was in 1767. In any event, Herder declined and remained in Riga until 1769, when he left the Russian empire altogether. The missed opportunity of 1767, however, suggests that his fascination with Russia, like that of so many other philosophes, was something he preferred to entertain platonically; indeed, it appeared to achieve maximum intensity when he was on the boat to France.

In 1769 Herder wrote to Riga from Nantes to request books about Russia, including a German edition of Voltaire's *Peter the Great*, and news about Catherine's progress toward a code of laws.[60] His interests, however, were developing away from the politics of Russia toward the anthropology and folklore of the Slavs. Years later, in 1802, the year before his death, Herder momentarily reverted to the Russian fantasies of the previous generation. In a passage of striking similarity to Voltaire's letters and Diderot's interviews, Herder regretted that Peter had chosen to establish his capital at St. Petersburg instead of at Azov. "What a different form Russia might have received!" he sighed. A Russian capital at Azov would have enjoyed "the most beautiful climate, at the mouth of the Don, in the most fortunate middle of the empire, from where the monarch could have used his European and Asiatic provinces like his right and left hand." All this Peter gave up for the chance, from St. Petersburg, "to mix in the littlest trade of little Western Europe ('des kleinen westlichen Europa')."[61] Herder's explicit articulation of "Western Europe" was a matter of geographical and philosophical perspective, as demonstrated by the fact that it appeared so diminutive and insignificant.

"Awakened from Your Long Sluggish Sleep"

Herder's intellectual interests in the 1770s embraced the issues of both language and ancient history. In 1772 he wrote his "Essay on the Origin of Language," and, in the middle of the decade, his studies on the "Oldest Records of the Human Race." His attention to origins and antiquities, however, proceeded in the context of a growing fascination with folklore, marked in 1778 and 1779 by the publication of his collections of folk songs. In this discipline Herder was a founding father, and the relevance of his work went far beyond the folklore of Eastern Europe. Yet, ever since Herder, the peoples of Eastern Europe have been special objects of folkloric attention, even into our own times. In an essay of 1777 Herder saw folk songs as the key to advancing "the map of mankind," a new folkloric geography with an emphasis on backwardness:

All unpolished peoples sing and trade; what they trade they sing, and sing their transactions. Their songs are the archive of the people ("das Archiv des Volks"), the treasury of their science and religion, their theogony and cosmogony, the deeds of their fathers and the events of their history.[62]

Folklore for Herder was the point at which such peoples emerged from the unpolished past into the anthropological present, each bearing its own archive as an ethnographic identification. Who were these peoples? Herder proceeded to locate the frontiers of folklore: "In Europe itself there is still a row of nations in this manner unutilized, undescribed. Ests and Letts, Wends and Slavs, Poles and Russians, Frisians and Prussians."[63] Obviously the work of utilization, of description, with which he challenged his contemporaries was largely to be done in Eastern Europe. Yet the listing was a curious one, inasmuch as it mixed up national and regional, ancient and ethnographic designations. The Slavs did not yet automatically subsume for Herder the Poles and the Russians. Herder's folkloric approach was changing the categories of analysis.

Herder's first collection of folk songs appeared in 1778, the year of Rousseau's death. Herder certainly paid tribute to Rousseau by proposing in

1769 to make Emile the national child of Livonia, and there was an important convergence in their ideas about national culture and national identity. In Rousseau's *Considerations* he prescribed national institutions to Poland, "to form the genius, the character, the tastes, and the manners" of the Poles. He insisted that they conserve "ancient customs" and even "introduce suitable ones that may be proper to the Poles," so that they might consolidate their national identity.[64] Rousseau's interest in ancient customs was consistent with Herder's folkloric concerns, but the proposal for the introduction of new customs (that is, paradoxically uncustomary customs) underlined Rousseau's ulterior purpose of forming a national identity. For Herder a people's identity lay in its folklore, its ancient customs, the historical archive by which it might be studied and identified. Herder's anthropological approach was aimed not at forming the identities of peoples, but at recognizing them and locating them on "the map of mankind." While Rousseau proposed to make the name of Poland nationally indelible, safe in the hearts of the Poles, Herder eliminated the Poles from his academic schema, not long before Poland was eliminated from the map of Europe. By emphasizing issues of language, ancient history, anthropology, and folklore, he discovered the methodological angle of perspective from which Poland seemed to disappear into general Slavdom. Herder's mastery of the "archives" justified his own arbitrary selection of analytical categories.

Herder settled in 1776 in Weimar, one of the rising cultural capitals of Western Europe. His *Ideas for the Philosophy of the History of Mankind* was a product of Weimar in the 1780s, the first part appearing in 1784, and the fourth in 1791. The last volumes of Gibbon appeared in 1788, so the two epic projects overlapped in the writing. They also overlapped in subject, for after the first two parts, in which Herder considered such issues as the earth, the nature of man, the varieties of man, and the origins of language, science, art, and religion, the third part addressed ancient history, especially the Greeks and the Romans. The fourth part then began with the barbarians of ancient history, "the peoples of the northern old world." These were "barbaric and displaced nations," and some "remnants" of them might still be encountered in the mountains or inaccessible areas, "where barely still their old language and some remaining old customs mark their origin." Such were the rare opportunities for the enterprising anthropologist, but more general traces were evident to the cultural observer at home, in Weimar for instance. For the northern barbarians, wherever they went, "brought a Vandal-Gothic-Scythian-Tartar way of life, whose marks (*Merkmale*) Europe now still bears in many respects."[65] Certainly the search for Scythian signs and Tartar traces was fundamental in the eighteenth century for studying the ancient history of Eastern Europe.

In successive sections Herder then discussed, first, Basques, Gaels, and Cimbri; second, Finns, Letts, and Prussians; third, German peoples; and fourth, Slavic peoples. The Hungarians were mentioned along with the Finns, but Herder predicted that, as a consequence of mixing and mingling, the Hungarian language was on the way to extinction. Such a prophecy left Eastern Europe all the more completely the domain of the Slavic peoples, which Herder designated geographically, "from the Don to the Elbe, from the Baltic to the Adriatic." These formulas for defining the region by its rivers had the effect of dissolving its national borders, suggesting for Voltaire in the eighteenth century one all-embracing Russian empire, for Churchill in the twentieth century one monolithic Soviet bloc. For Herder the breaking down of borders produced an ethnically unified area, "the most monstrous region of earth which in Europe *one* Nation for the most part inhabits still today."⁶⁶ When Herder focused on the issue of ethnography, the distinction between ancient and contemporary history conveniently collapsed.

"They loved farming," wrote Herder of the Slavs, imagining them among "flocks and grains," but also recognizing a commercial economy, predicated upon their geographical position. Though he formally classified them among the northern barbarians, Herder's geography unequivocally located them in Eastern Europe, between Europe and Asia: "On the Dnieper they built Kiev, on the Volkhov Novgorod, which soon became blooming commercial towns, since they united the Black Sea and the Baltic, and brought the products of the Orient (*Morgenwelt*) to northern and western Europe." As an economic presence in Germany, the Slavs worked with mines, metals, and mead, "planted fruit trees and in their fashion led a merry, musical life." Herder had celebrated their "musical nature" twenty years before in his journal of 1769; now he himself became the composer of a folk fantasy of the Slavic peoples. "They were benevolent," insisted Herder, "hospitable to the point of prodigality, lovers of territorial freedom, but submissive and obedient, enemies of robbery and plunder." Inevitably they fell victim to subjection and oppression, especially by the Germans, so that "their remnant in Germany resembles what the Spanish made out of the Peruvians."⁶⁷ Herder's vision of the Slavs as the victimized peoples of peace and freedom contrasted with that of Gibbon, published three years before, in which the Slavs appeared with their poisoned arrows, and engaged in impaling, flaying, beating, and burning their prisoners.

The ancient history of the Slavs was evidently a subject that allowed considerable play to the creative imagination in the eighteenth century. In fact, Herder's imagination coursed through the centuries, from ancient history over the present and into the future, to proclaim another extraordinary prophecy:

The wheel of changing time revolves meanwhile incessantly; and since these nations inhabit for the most part the most beautiful region of Europe, when it is fully cultivated and trade is opened there, when there is also nothing else to suppose but that in Europe politics and legislation will and must promote more and more the silent industry and peaceful traffic of peoples with each other, instead of the martial spirit; so also will you too, so deeply sunken, once industrious and happy peoples, finally one day be awakened from your long, sluggish sleep, be freed from your chains of slavery, that you may use as property your beautiful areas from the Adriatic Sea to the Carpathian Mountains, from the Don to the Moldau, and there celebrate your ancient festivals of peaceful industry and trade.[68]

Not the least extraordinary feature of Herder's prophecy was the sudden modulation into the second person plural, from anthropological analysis to direct address, so that he could actually prophesy to the Slavs themselves. The grammatical shift is so abrupt and unsettling that translators have sometimes ignored it and translated *you* as *they*.[69] Just as Voltaire wrote letters to Catherine, and Rousseau addressed his "brave Poles," Herder employed both models, first calling upon the "great empress" in his journal of 1769, then prophesying to all of the Slavic peoples in 1791, in the fourth part of the *Ideas*. This was the ultimate extension of the Enlightenment's philosophical address, embracing all of Eastern Europe in one breath, one *you*, from the Adriatic to the Carpathians, from Peter's fortress at Azov on the Don to the spires of Prague on the Moldau. If in the journal he imagined himself as a second Montesquieu, now he saw himself as a second Rousseau, awakening and liberating the Slavs and restoring them to their ancient festivals.

In 1769 Herder foresaw an upheaval in Eastern Europe, but now that no longer appeared as a menace to civilization in Western Europe. The Slavs would return to their ancient customs and peaceful past, so that the ancient history of the Slavs, preserved in folklore, discovered by anthropology, would also be their destiny in the future. Herder concluded his section on the Slavic peoples by entrusting them to the folklorists, like himself:

Since we have from several regions beautiful and useful contributions to the history of this people, so is it to be wished that also from others their gaps may be completed, the progressively disappearing remains of their usages, songs, and sagas may be collected, and finally a "History of this Race (*Völkerstamm*) as a Whole" may be given, as the picture of mankind requires.[70]

Though Herder had just prophesied a splendid future for the Slavs, based on their ancient ways, he now commissioned the anthropological study of those ways in a tone that implied imminent extinction. The dramatic alternatives of extinction and restoration were confused, their difference dissolved, in the overwhelming intellectual injunction to establish the Slavs on the "map of mankind," in the mind of the Enlightenment.

In some "general reflections" Herder invited his readers to take stock of their own geographical position: "See there, eastward to the right, the monstrous heights which are called Asiatic Tartary." German readers were thus directed to look right over Eastern Europe, an imaginative leap that suddenly rendered the heights of Tartary visible from Weimar. Then Herder asked them to envision the geography of Asia and northern Europe as a "descending plain," from "the Tartar heights westward," and downward to the sea. This almost geometrical expression of geography explained the pressure of the Asiatic "hordes" upon Europe, which was, in a sense, the simple extension of Tartary. Inevitably, as a consequence, "between South Asia and Eastern Europe, between the Asiatic and European North, a kind of community of peoples was joined together, in which also very uncultivated nations took part."[71] While preserving his earlier idea of two streams, here represented as inclined terrains, Herder dramatized the ambiguous intermediary position of Eastern Europe by looking just beyond to the "uncultivated nations" rolling down the plains. Eastern Europe was a profoundly pressured ethnographic frontier.

Herder had outlined a fifth part for the *Ideas*, a continuation into modern history. He never wrote that fifth part, which made the extant whole more emphatically a work of anthropology and ancient history. In his outline for the unwritten continuation, however, he projected a section on "North and East" to discuss Denmark, Sweden, Poland, and Hungary, while Russia was left for a later section, to be discussed together with Africa and the East and West Indies.[72] Modern history would have compelled him to divide the Slavic peoples into separate states, as indicated. In forgoing the fifth part, Herder preserved his vision of an anthropological, ethnographical, folkloric unity, which found its identity among the barbarians of ancient history.

To appreciate its significance and originality, one may consider for contrast the dismissal of Eastern Europe in Kant's *Anthropology* of 1798. Kant, who was Herder's teacher in Königsberg and later Herder's philosophical foe, constructed Eastern Europe as a whole out of its modern components:

Since Russia, which has not yet reached a definite concept of its natural capacities—which lie ready to be developed, and will be required—and Poland—but it no longer exists—and the nationals of European Turkey, that have never been and never will be up to what is requisite for the acquisition of a definite folk character: so the sketching of these can here be appropriately passed over.[73]

Kant's purpose in this passage was to dismiss all of Eastern Europe from consideration, but to do so he had to dismiss each of three parts—Russia, Poland ("it no longer exists"), and European Turkey—individually.

Hegel performed the same operation in his *Lectures on the Philosophy of History*, from his courses in Berlin in the 1820s, but employed as Herder did the conceptual unity of the Slavs. They came up in a lecture on the barbarians of ancient history: "We now find also in the East of Europe ('im Osten von Europa') the great Slavic nation." The equation of Eastern Europe and the Slavs was already axiomatic, though Hegel mentioned the presence of Magyars, Bulgarians, Serbians, and Albanians as "barbaric remnants" of "Asiatic origin." He conceded that the peoples of Eastern Europe played an intermediary role in "the struggle between Christian Europe and non-Christian Asia." Generally, he allowed that "a part of the Slavs were conquered (*erobert*) by western reason," but on the whole his verdict was negative:

Nevertheless this whole mass remains excluded from our consideration, because until now it has not stepped forward as an independent force in the array of the forms of reason. Whether this will happen in the future, does not concern us here; for in history we have to deal with the past.[74]

Hegel's refusal to consider the future of the Slavs was perhaps an allusion to Herder with his prophecies. The divergence between Hegel and Herder, separated by a generation, was striking. Though Hegel fully accepted Herder's analytical categorization of the Slavs, he was not the least bit interested in responding to the latter's call for ongoing folkloric researches into their songs and sagas. Yet Herder, in formulating the Slavs as above all an object of folkloric study, helped to establish the philosophical perspective according to which Hegel would exclude them from historical consideration.

"Manners of the Morlacchi"

Peyssonnel claimed to have found on the Black Sea "vestiges" of Scythian peoples, of Huns, and Avars, and Bulgars. Herder believed that one could find in Europe barbarian "remnants" who preserved their ancient customs. In 1770 an international scientific expedition went to Eastern Europe, setting out from Venice to explore Dalmatia, the Adriatic coast of twentieth-century Yugoslavia. Among its scientific concerns was the anthropological study of the Morlachs, or Morlacchi, a people perceived as a vestige or remnant of ancient barbarism, surviving into eighteenth-century Europe. The terms "Morlach" and "Vlach" were sometimes confusedly applied to describe the same people, scattered throughout southeastern Europe, whose origin and ethnic identity was uncertain, complicated by assorted Slavic and Romanian affiliations. In the eighteenth century the Morlacchi of Dalmatia acquired a distinct mystique of their own as utter barbarians at only the slightest geographical remove from Western Europe, and the expedition of 1770 catapulted them to the heights of celebrity in the decade that followed. The abbé Alberto Fortis, an enlightened Italian priest and scientist, participated in the expedition and published in Venice in 1774 an account of its work, as *Travels into Dalmatia: Concerning General Observations on the Natural History of that Country and the Neighbouring Islands; the Natural Productions, Arts, Manners and Customs of the Inhabitants.* Those last were the Morlacchi, and it was especially Fortis's description of them that made his book a success, quickly translated from the Italian into English, French, and German. The book was dedicated to Lord Bute, the former prime minister of England and a patron of the expedition, and Fortis outlined the cultural geography of his travels when he wrote, "It was Your Lordship's learned Curiosity and Munificence, so well known through the Polite Parts of Europe, that first encouraged me to cross the Adriatick."[75] The "polite parts of Europe" (in the Italian original, *l'Europa colta*) implicitly embraced both Fortis's Italy and Bute's England, but the Adriatic was broached as the border that separated them from less cultivated, less polite parts. On the other side Fortis found the Morlacchi.

Michèle Duchet, in *Anthropology and History in the Century of Enlightenment*, has explored the eighteenth-century origins of modern anthropology. Giuseppe Cocchiara, in his *History of Folklore in Europe*, has argued persuasively for the importance of the eighteenth century, culminating in Herder, for shaping the modern discipline of folklore.[76] Both anthropology and folklore would come clearly into their own as academic disciplines in the nineteenth century, but in the eighteenth century, perhaps especially because their academic contours were as yet uncertainly defined, they both played a role in developing the idea of Eastern Europe. Voltaire, reconceiving history as the history of manners or customs, of *moeurs*, pointed the way from history into anthropology. In his historical *Essay on Manners* he could envision Europe—"from Petersburg to Madrid"—progressing as a whole through modern history, "better peopled, more civilized, richer, more enlightened," but he could also use the standard of *moeurs* to mark the division of Europe, distinguishing "our part of Europe" from lands like Thrace and Tartary.[77]

Attention to the manners of Europe was only more sharply focused by the Enlightenment's engagement with other continents. David Spadafora, in *The Idea of Progress*, has emphasized the importance of the Scottish Enlightenment—including such figures as Adam Ferguson, John Millar, and Lord Kames, as well as David Hume and Adam Smith—for writing about "the progress of human culture" and describing the stages of society from barbarism to civilization. P. J. Marshall and Glyndwr Williams, in *The Great Map of Mankind*, have studied the development of eighteenth-century English perspectives on Asia, America, Africa, and the Pacific. Herder used the expression "the map of mankind" ("Die Karte der Menschheit") in an essay of 1777, and Marshall and Williams took their title and epigraph from Edmund Burke, who used the same expression in the same year:

Now the Great Map of Mankind is unrolld at once; and there is no state or Gradation of barbarism, and no mode of refinement which we have not at the same

"The Vojvoda Pervan of Coccorich, A Noble Young Lady of Coccorich, A Young Lady of the Kotar," from Alberto Fortis, *Travels into Dalmatia*, London, 1778; the discussion of the "Manners of the Morlacchi" was accompanied by folkloric images of men and women in local costume; Fortis claimed to have witnessed in Dalmatia "customs, poetry, music, clothing, and habitations as Tartar as they could be in Siberia," while seeking to dispel the legend of the Morlacchi "as a race of men, fierce, unreasonable, void of humanity, and capable of any crime." (By permission of the Houghton Library, Harvard University.)

instant under our View. The very different Civility of Europe and of China; The barbarism of Tartary, and of arabia. The Savage State of North America, and of New Zealand.[78]

Burke thus emphasized the broadening of perspective and knowledge in his century, which embraced the entire globe. When he later wanted to put Poland out of English consideration he had to relocate it on the moon. The development of an anthropological perspective on Eastern Europe occurred in the context of the Enlightenment's worldwide mapping of civilization and barbarism. The case of Eastern Europe was special because it was part of Europe, not one of the polite parts to be sure, but the barbarian Morlacchi were to be found not in New Zealand, not even in Tartary, but just across the Adriatic Sea.

Fortis was born in Padua in 1741 (three years before Herder) and became a priest as a teenager. He preferred, however, the study of geology to that of theology, and ended up founding an enlightened journal in Venice in 1768, *Europa Letteraria*, "Literary Europe." His original conception of Europe was classically Italian, oriented from south to north. Rome was "the capital of the world," but a "sad capital" for him, an unenthusiastic priest; in his journal he urged Italians not to despise the "inhabitants of the North," who may soon know enough "to despise us" instead. The expedition to Dalmatia in 1770 would unite north and south, Englishmen and Italians, in a common western perspective of scientific study and cultural condescension, aimed eastward. Before that opportunity arrived, Fortis distinguished himself with a geological poem, "On the Cataclysms Suffered by our Planet," and a rather rudely anticlerical satire, the "Letter of a Mountain Priest about the Question of Baptizing Abortions," written in 1769. Fortis left Venice for Dalmatia the following year.[79]

Voltaire, in his *Essay on Manners*, associated Dalmatia with the most remote lands of Eastern Europe, naming "part of Dalmatia, the north of Poland, the banks of the Don, and the fertile country of the Ukraine" as a domain of colonization where people "looked for lands in a new universe and at the limits of the old one." Fortis, whose work on the Morlacchi was also presented as an essay on manners, made the same association of Dalmatia with Eastern Europe.

I saw customs, poetry, music, clothing, and habitations as Tartar as they could be in Siberia. For natural history it is a land of gold, as it is for travelers whom we call cultivated. Besides having these advantages, I took away with me that of babbling (*cinguettar*) now quite tolerably in Slavic.[80]

Like Herder, Fortis too, even from Dalmatia, could see the heights of Tartary hanging over Eastern Europe, in this case exercising a vague anthropological and folkloric influence on customs, poetry, music, and clothing —as witnessed from the perspective that "we call cultivated." He even speculated that "that last inundation of the Tartars," in the age of Genghis Khan, had deposited in Dalmatia Tartars and Kalmucks who were "still distinguishable." The linguistic key, however, the Slavic language of the Morlacchi, placed them more precisely in the context of Eastern Europe. Language was also the guide to ancient history, in which the origin of the Morlacchi was "involved in the darkness of barbarous ages, together with that of many other nations, resembling them so much in customs and language, that they may be taken for one people, dispersed in the vast tracts from the coasts of our sea to the frozen ocean." This was Eastern Europe, ethnographically unified, from the Adriatic Sea to the Arctic Ocean, peopled long ago by "the emigrations of the various tribes of the Slavi, who, under the names of Scythians, Geti, Gaths, Huns, Slavini, Croats, Avari, and Vandals, inundated the Roman provinces." Having measured the unity of Eastern Europe from the Arctic to the Adriatic, Fortis considered its other dimension from the Adriatic to the Black Sea. The barbarian peoples he enumerated were those whose vestiges Peyssonnel found on the Black Sea, and Fortis wondered whether the Morlacchi as well might have come from that region. He supported this speculation with an etymological analysis, reading Morlachs as Mor-Vlachs, that is, Black Vlachs from the Black Sea. He did, however, insist upon the fact that the Morlacchi were not racially black, that they were "as white as the Italians."[81] That such a reassurance seemed necessary suggested that his readers might have assumed otherwise.

The introduction to Fortis's discussion of the Morlacchi was entitled "Manners of the Morlacchi," and he addressed himself to his readers and their presumed familiarity with a dark legend of this people.

You have, no doubt often heard the Morlacchi described as a race of men, fierce, unreasonable, void of humanity, and capable of any crime. The inhabitants of the sea coast of Dalmatia tell many frightful stories about the cruelty of those people, that, induced by the avidity of plunder, they often proceeded to the most atrocious excesses of violence, by fire and sword.[82]

This assumption of familiarity must seem odd to the twentieth-century reader of Fortis, for today there are but few who have ever heard of the Morlacchi at all. Even when Fortis went to Dalmatia in 1770 their legend was probably limited to the coasts of the Adriatic, and his assumption that their name would strike terror into the hearts of his readers was only plausible in the context of the original Italian edition, published in Venice. It was Fortis's work that would make the Morlacchi into a subject of international fascination. Their subsequent fall from fame to obscurity suggests the particular power of Eastern Europe to seize the imagination of Western Europe in the age of Enlightenment, especially when it was a matter of barbarism discovered so close to home.

The legend of the Morlacchi, which Fortis assumed his readers would know, was in its general outlines remarkably similar to Edward Gibbon's defamatory representation, as yet unpublished, of the Slavs in ancient history: a people who "plundered with impunity the cities of Illyricum and Thrace" and murdered their enemies with "wanton and deliberate cruelty." The resemblance is suggestive of that complex convergence between ancient history and modern anthropology that informed the Enlightenment's perspective on barbarism in Eastern Europe. Fortis himself declared his commitment to qualifying his readers' prejudices against the Morlacchi, as "a duty incumbent on me, to write what I personally saw relative to their customs, and inclinations, and thereby to form some apology for that nation."[83] The form of his apology was essentially a work of modern anthropology, outlined as a survey of moral and domestic virtues, friendship and quarrels, talents and arts, superstitions and manners, marriage and childbirth, food and dress, music and dance—and finally funerals. As anthropological as this program may appear, Fortis himself did not use the word "anthropology," which was only just coming into its modern usage as a neologism in the late eighteenth century. The original theological meaning of the word expressed the attribution of human qualities to God, but in 1788 a work entitled *Anthropology, or the General Science of Man*, by Alexandre-César Chavannes, gave the word its modern meaning.[84] With the century's growing interest in savage peoples and the "map of mankind," the name offered a useful designation to an already evolving science.

In his discussion of the "moral and domestic virtues," Fortis admitted that those of the Morlacchi were "different from ours," but, with a Rousseauist twist, he made them out to be actually superior in their "sincerity, trust, and honesty"—of which Italian traders took unscrupulous advantage. The Morlacchi were "naturally hospitable and generous," as Fortis knew from his experience among them as a stranger. Upon leaving one of his hosts, Fortis made a portrait sketch, as a souvenir, "that, in spite of the interposition of sea and mountains, I might have the pleasure of beholding him, at least, in effigy"—but also as an anthropological document to be published in the book. Again in the spirit of Rousseau, Fortis declared that "friendship, that among us is so subject to change on the slightest motives, is lasting among the Morlacchi," even solemnly and sacredly confirmed by "Sclavonian ritual." Fortis appeared to agree with the opinion of "the old Morlacchi, who attribute the depravation of their countrymen to their intercourse with the Italians." He further believed that "wine and strong liquors, of which the nation is beginning to make daily abuse, after our example, will, of course, produce the same bad effects as among us." The civilization of "cultivated Europe," of the "polite parts," was thus conceived as a force for corruption and depravation, acting upon the natural morality of an admirable primitive people. Fortis admitted that the Morlacchi were sometimes terrible and barbarous in their hereditary vendettas, but claimed to have heard that in Albania "the effects of revenge are still more atrocious."[85] If the Morlacchi offered an example of barbarism just across the Adriatic from Venice, the prospect of Albania, further along the coast, promised a picture of even more spectacular barbarism.

"Notwithstanding their excellent disposition to learn every art," wrote Fortis, "the Morlacchi have the most imperfect notions of husbandry, and are very unskillful in the management of their cattle." His discussion of their economic backwardness went hand in hand with a profound conviction that they were eminently teachable and therefore capable of improvement and development. "They have a singular veneration for old customs," he wrote, "and little care has hitherto been taken either to remove their prejudices, or to teach them better methods." Differing here from Rousseau, Fortis appeared unsentimental about "old customs" for their own sake. In fact, Rousseau was writing about Poland at the same time that Fortis was traveling in Dalmatia. "Their ploughs, and other rural utensils, seem to be of the most rude invention," observed Fortis of the Morlacchi, and furthermore, "the taylor's art is confined to ancient and unalterable patterns." In an adumbration of modern folkloric interest, Fortis remarked that "the Morlack women are skilful in works of embroidery and knitting." As for dairy work, the production of cheese and butter "might pass well enough, if they were only done with more cleanliness."[86]

As a man of the Enlightenment Fortis devoted a special section to "the superstition of the Morlacchi," discussing their beliefs in vampires and witches, and narrating such material with enlightened irony:

The women, as may be naturally supposed, are a hundred times more timorous and visionary than the men; and some of them, by frequently hearing themselves called witches, actually believe they are so. The old witches are acquainted with many spells; and one of the most common is to transfer the milk of other people's cows to their own. But they can perform more curious feats than this; and I know a young man, who had his heart taken out by two witches, while he was fast asleep, in order to be roasted and eat by them.[87]

From Fortis's light condescension, one would hardly guess that Western Europe in the previous century had just emerged from the most long-lasting, widespread, and murderous witch hysteria in history, when witch beliefs flourished at every level of society and culture. Fortis appeared comfortable with the idea that such beliefs were at home in Eastern Europe. Interestingly, the Italian historian Carlo Ginzburg has speculated that the folkloric origins of witch beliefs in Europe may be found in Eastern Europe (including Dalmatia in particular), where they were brought by the ancient influences of Scythia and Siberia.[88] These twentieth-century "Eurasian Conjectures" are very much on the model of the Enlightenment's Eastern

Europe, its lands in the lurking eastern shadow of the heights of Tartary and the hordes of Scythia.

Fortis's anticlericalism encouraged him to include the priests of the Morlacchi among the forces of superstition. There were both Roman Catholic and Greek Orthodox churches, and if Fortis had a personal bias toward his own, it was only admitted in the observation that the Catholic churches appeared less dirty. He reported that the priests generally exploited the "silly credulity" of the people, for instance by selling them "superstitious scrolls." Furthermore, in a detail that perfectly matched other eighteenth-century accounts of Eastern Europe, he claimed that the priests actually beat their parishioners, to "correct the bodies of their offending flock with the cudgel."[89] Like Tott in Moldavia and Coxe in Russia, Fortis too discovered corporal discipline as one of the traveler's landmarks in Eastern Europe.

Fortis did not hesitate to apply the word "barbarous" to the Morlacchi, though he might allow for some qualification. The scarlet caps, worn by girls as "a mark of virginity," were described in their elaborate ornamentation with coins, shells, beads, feathers, "all kinds of splendid trumpery"— "to attract and fix the eyes of all who are near them, by the multitude of ornaments, and the noise they make on the least motion of their heads." After fixing the attention of his readers on these Morlacchi virgins, he admitted that "in the variety of those capricious and barbarous ornaments, sometimes a fancy not inelegant is displayed." As for their hair, "they always have medals, beads, or bored coins, in the Tartar or American mode, twisted amongst it." The association of the Morlacchi with the Tartars merely followed the conventional formula for peoples of Eastern Europe; the further correlation of Tartars and American Indians was an additional "twist" by which eighteenth-century anthropology sought to consolidate its idea of barbarism. When a virgin of the Morlacchi was married, the ceremony was "performed amidst the noise of muskets, pistols, barbaric shouts, and acclamations." The consummation of the marriage was announced with a pistol shot. A wedding custom that Fortis found "savage and brutal" involved the groom beating or kicking the bride—"or some piece of similar gallantry"—yet, following his century's wisdom on Eastern Europe, the Italian concluded that "the Morlack women, and perhaps the greatest part of the Dalmatians, the inhabitants of the cities excepted, do not dislike a beating."[90]

Childbirth among the Morlacchi "would be thought very extraordinary among us," Fortis commented, for the woman "frequently delivered in the fields, or on the road, by herself," and then "returns the day after to her usual labour, or to feed her flock." Such physical hardiness appeared only less extraordinary than the acrobatic quality of their nursing: "The prodigious length of the breasts of Morlacchian women is somewhat extraordinary; for it is very certain, that they can give the teat to their children over their shoulders, or under their arms." Fortis did not actually claim to have witnessed this feat. As for singularities of appearance in Morlacchi men, he mentioned that "they shave their heads, leaving only a small tuft behind, like the Poles and Tartars."[91] There is no reason to believe that Fortis was ever in Poland or Tartary, and this association of peoples was again a conventional formula in the construction of Eastern Europe.

The publication of Fortis's *Travels into Dalmatia* in 1774 stirred academic controversy in Italy over the Morlacchi, and there were two prompt and critical counterpublications by Dalmatians who thought they knew the subject better than Fortis did. Pietro Nutrizio Grisogono published *Reflections on the Present State of Dalmatia* in Florence in 1775, and Giovanni Lovrich wrote *Observations on Diverse Pieces of the Travels into Dalmatia of the Signor Abbé Alberto Fortis*, appearing in Venice in 1776. Lovrich considered himself especially expert on "The Customs of the Morlacchi," and challenged Fortis on a number of particular points. For instance, he considered it to be out of the question that Morlacchi women were ever able to nurse their children over the shoulder or under the arm. In a fussier hair-splitting quibble, Lovrich insisted that the tuft of Morlacchi men was not quite like that of Poles and Tartars, but rather a little bit longer. What Lovrich did not challenge was the classificatory distinction between the Morlacchi and the "cultivated, polished nations," from whose perspective the former appeared "strange and barbarous."[92] Fortis took the opportunity to reply to the criticisms of Lovrich in a mock "sermon," published in Modena in 1777.

In addition to academic controversy in Italy, there was also a politically controversial aspect to the publication of Fortis's book in Venice. For though Voltaire might associate Dalmatia with Poland and the Ukraine, and Fortis looked as far afield as Siberia, in fact Dalmatia was governed by Venice as a part of her Adriatic empire. From that perspective, Fortis's revelations of barbarism were suggestive of administrative neglect and therefore embarrassing—the more so when they achieved international celebrity in so many translations. Fortis did not receive the professorship at Padua to which he aspired. One of those who spoke against Fortis in Venice was the poet and dramatist Carlo Gozzi, deeply conservative, hostile to the Enlightenment. His personal artistic cause was the restoration of the commedia dell'arte, and, far from the spirit of scientific anthropology, his plays—such as *King Stag*, *The Snake Woman*, and *Turandot*—were dramatized fairy tales, rich in fabulous, fantastic, and Oriental motifs. Yet his charge against Fortis was inadequate appreciation of the responsibilities of empire: "I do not believe that the abbé Fortis, for whose intellect one must have much esteem, deigned to recall that in order to induce in Venetian Dalmatia and Albania all that good which comes with industry, it would

be necessary to began by spreading little by little, with insistence on custom and on thought, an effective, good morality, which might prepare the
brains, the spirits, and the hearts for reason and obedience."[93]

In 1780 Fortis published in Naples a work *On the Cultivation of the Chest-
nut to be Introduced into Dalmatia.* Rather than pursuing agricultural and
economic progress for the Morlacchi, he hoped to help them find their
way back to the primitive life that he envisioned as their ideal. Cultivating
chestnuts, the Morlacchi farmer might be "removed from the plow that
he does not know how to manage, and restored to the pastoral life that
alone suits his indolence and nomadic origin."[94] In 1784 Fortis turned his
attention to southern Italy, and published *Geographical-Physical Letters on
Calabria and Puglia.* In 1787 he wrote *On Mineral Nitrates,* his scientific
thoughts on chemical fertilizers. Accused of Jacobinism, he left Italy for
France in 1796, and finally achieved official recognition under Napoleon,
whose favor found a place for so many of the eighteenth-century experts
on Eastern Europe. Fortis died in Bologna in 1803, and six years later, in
1809, Napoleon incorporated Dalmatia into the French empire as one of
the provinces of Illyria.

"Music and Poetry, Dances and Diversions"

Fortis's *Travels into Dalmatia* was translated from the Italian into English, French, and German, and his account of the Morlacchi made its most
lasting mark on eighteenth-century intellectual history not in Italy, though
it did stir controversy there, not in England, though Lord Bute sponsored the expedition and was honored in the dedication, and not in France,
though Napoleon was to honor the Italian priest in his last years. The Morlacchi made their most remarkable impact in Germany in the 1770s, and
especially Fortis's account of their folk songs and poetry. Fortis, with his
scientific interest in old customs, stumbled into a folkloric gold mine, the
poetry of the South Slavs.

The Morlacchi have their rustick assemblies, especially in houses where there are
several young women; and in these the memory of ancient national stories is perpetuated. A musician always attends these meetings, and sings the old *pisme* or
songs, accompanying them with an instrument called *guzla,* which has but one
string, composed of many horse hairs. The tune, to which these heroic songs are
sung, is extremely mournful, and monotonous, besides, they bring the sound a
little through the nose, which agrees perfectly well with their instrument.[95]

Fortis himself was apparently bored, even as he made the important discovery of these songs, and his comment on the nasality of the singing
already hinted at his condescension.

Yet those songs have a great effect on the minds of the hearers, who are at pains to
get them by heart; and I have seen some of them sigh, and weep at a passage, which

did not appear to me the least moving. Perhaps the force of the Illyric words, better understood by the Morlacchi, might produce this effect; and perhaps, as seems to me more probable, their artless minds, little stored with ideas, might more readily be affected with any turn of expression that appeared to them extraordinary.⁹⁶

The nature of the songs, and especially the audience's emotional response to them, underlined for Fortis the difference between his own poetic connoisseurship and their "artless minds, little stored with ideas." Though he might not understand the Illyric words as well as the Morlacchi did, Fortis had acquired the ability to "babble" in Slavic, and so he translated into Italian and published some of these songs, with a warning: "Whoever reads, or hears them, must be contented to supply the want of detail, and precision, which the Morlacchi neglect, and which are carefully attended by the civilized nations of Europe."⁹⁷ Ultimately, Fortis interpreted the poetry as evidence of the gulf that separated the civilized nations of Europe from the rest, marking the difference of Eastern Europe.

In 1775 Goethe wrote a poem, which he annotated as "aus dem Morlackischen," from the language of the Morlacchi. Then in 1779, Herder published the second part of his *Volkslieder*, his collection of folk songs. There was nothing from Russia, nothing from Poland, and nothing from the Ukraine in spite of his prophecy, but there were several songs from "Morlackische Geschichte," the history of the Morlacchi. A note explained that these came from the Italian translations of Fortis, and that was presumably Goethe's source as well. For Goethe the Morlacchi offered the pretext for exquisite poetic effects based on Ottoman and Oriental associations:

> Was ist Weisses dort am grünen Walde?
> Ist es Schnee wohl oder sind es Schwäne?
> Wär es Schnee, er wäre weggeschmolzen;
> Wärens Schwäne, wären weggeflogen.
> Ist kein Schnee nicht, es sind keine Schwäne,
> 's ist der Glanz der Zelten Asan Aga.
>
> What is white there in the green woods?
> Is it snow or is it swans?
> If it were snow it would have melted away;
> If it were swans, they would have flown away.
> It is not snow, it is not swans,
> It's the gleam of the tents of Asan Aga.⁹⁸

For Herder on the other hand the Morlacchi were not Orientals but Slavs, and he chose a poem on "Radoslaus," which ended with the coming of a "king of the Slavs." Thus the Morlacchi, studied and publicized by Fortis as virtual barbarians, emerged into the highest sphere of eighteenth-century German culture. Goethe would continue enthusiastic about the poetry of the South Slavs into the nineteenth century, when the Serbian scholar Vuk Karadžić published, in Vienna in 1814, "A Small Collection of

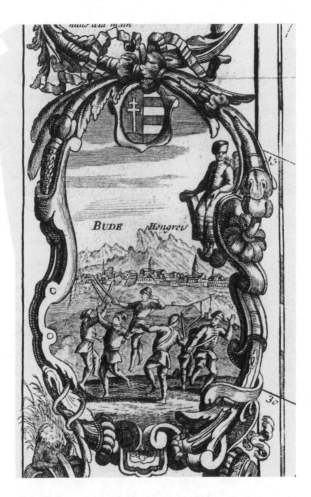

"BUDE, Hongrois," Buda, Hungarian; illustrated in a cameo scene along the border of a map of "Europe divided according to the extent of its principal parts," by L. C. Desnos, published in Paris in 1772 and dedicated to the Dauphin, the future Louis XVI. The geographical "principal parts" of Europe on the map are supplemented by images of Europe's principal peoples around the rim of the map. Hungary is generously, though misleadingly, outlined on the map as an independent geographical entity, including Transylvania, Wallachia, Moldavia, and Bessarabia; the Hungarians are pictured in a folkloric scene, with their warlike reputation in France, from the Rakoczi insurrection at the beginning of the century, here transmuted in an image of dancing with swords. The caption above the image states that the Hungarians "love war and horses and are bold and wild," that "this nation which is so jealous of its liberty is nevertheless under the domination of the Germans and in part under that of the Turks," and that "they have a singular dance, turning and jumping in the air with surprising agility, while striking each other's swords." (From the Harvard Map Collection, Harvard University.)

Slavonic-Serbian Songs of the Common People," attracting the attention of Romantic Europe.[99]

Fortis's appreciation of folklore in Dalmatia in the 1770s, for all its qualifications of condescension, nevertheless showed a clear advance in sensibility over the observations of Boscovich in Bulgaria in the 1760s. He too was a priest and scientist, traveling though "barbarous regions, of various usages and customs." In Bulgaria he witnessed and described a performance of Balkan folk dancing, on a day when "the mud was so high in front of the houses and throughout the village that one could scarcely set foot outside of them." This did not deter the dancers, who "came from the countryside to sing and dance in that mud, if one could call dancing an extremely slow movement that they made, holding each other tight by the arms, and going almost as much backwards as forwards." This account, though fairly careful in its basic description, nevertheless rendered the dancing highly undignified by setting the whole scene in the mud. Boscovich further qualified the event by wondering if one could call it dancing, and the phrase "as much backwards as forwards" hinted at a metaphorical interpretation of the dance according to eighteenth-century ideas about civilization in Eastern Europe. The next day there was music in the mud: "A strong rain came from behind the mountains, and when it ended there came, from the village, people to entertain us with barbarous singing and playing, to earn a tip."[100] In this case there was no description to compare with Fortis's careful account of the folk songs of the Morlacchi. Boscovich in Bulgaria found himself in "barbarous regions" and had no hesitation about dismissing the music he heard as suitably "barbarous singing and playing." The tip was probably not a generous one.

Fortis's account of singing in Dalmatia in the next decade was both more artistically appreciative and more carefully descriptive. "I have translated several heroic songs of the Morlacchi," he wrote, "and some of them appear to me both well conducted and interesting." He compared the Morlacchi songs unfavorably with "the poems of the celebrated Scotch bard, which we have lately had the pleasure of seeing translated into our language," that is, the poems of Ossian. The "discovery" of Ossian in 1762 by James Macpherson was a sensational international event in the history of folklore in the eighteenth century; enthusiasts included both Goethe and Herder, so Fortis, in making Ossian his standard of reference, showed himself versed in and attuned to the folkloric interests of his generation. It was only established in the nineteenth century that the poems of Ossian were not works of Gaelic antiquity but Macpherson's own compositions, a brilliant and profoundly influential hoax. The songs of the Morlacchi were actually of greater antiquity and authenticity, and Fortis, while admiring Ossian more, allowed that "the Morlack poetry is not destitute of merit; and has, at least, the simplicity of Homer's times, and serves to illustrate the manners of the nation."[101]

He described with special vividness the responsive singing of the Morlacchi in the mountains:

A Morlacco travels along the desert mountains singing, especially in the night time, the actions of ancient *Slavi* Kings . . . and if another happens to be travelling on a neighbouring mountain, he repeats the same verse, when the other has sung it, and this alternation continues, as long as they can hear each other. A loud, and long howl, which is an *oh!* barbarously modulated, constantly precedes the verse, the words of which are pronounced rapidly, almost without any modulation, which is all reserved for the last syllable, and ends with another long howl, by way of trill, raised louder and louder, while the breath lasts.[102]

This was reasonably scrupulous folkloric accounting, with attention to subtleties of repetition and modulation. Yet the howls were described as "barbarously modulated," and Fortis's account of Morlacchi dancing, equally attentive to details of form, also suggested the spirit of barbarism:

They dance to the sound of the bag-pipe, and the voices of their singers, a favourite dance, which they call *kolo*, or circle, which soon turns into *skocci-gosi*, that is, high dancing. All the dancers, men and women, taking hold of each other's hands, form a circle, and turn slowly round, to the harsh notes of the instrument. Then the circle changes its form, sometimes into an ellipsis, and sometimes a square, according as the dance becomes more animated; and, at last, transforms itself into the most violent springs and leaps, in which the women also join, and the whole becomes wild confusion. The Morlacchi have an incredible transport for this rude dance, for neither the fatigues of the day, nor a long journey, nor hunger itself can detain them from it, or from continuing several hours, with very little intermission, in such violent exercise.[103]

Here Fortis concluded his section on "Music and Poetry, Dances and Diversions," to begin his next section on "Medical Art among the Morlacchi" with the observation that "it happens frequently enough, that inflammatory fevers are the immediate consequences of these violent dances just mentioned."[104] His introduction of Slavic terminology, and his description of the circle's changing shape was again fine folkloric description, but the order of his own observations collapsed along with the dance itself, as he insisted on emphasizing, confusion, transport, and fever. The "rude dance" was interpreted according to the perceived rudeness of the Morlacchi themselves.

Exactly contemporary with Fortis's research was a map of Europe by L. C. Desnos, printed in Paris in 1772, dedicated to "Monseigneur le Dauphin," two years before the dauphin became Louis XVI. Around the border of the map the peoples of Europe were summed up in several sentences each, and the summaries were accompanied by appropriate pictures. The picture which represented the Hungarians showed men dancing with swords, and the little text mentioned that "they have a singular dance, turning and jumping in the air with surprising agility, while striking each other's swords, which they hold bare in the hand." Gibbon's Hungarians drank blood, plundered with Scythian speed, and wielded the deadly Tartar bow. When the Hungarians, however, were represented in dance with their swords, any savage associations were rendered tame and entertaining, and in this way the folkloric sensibility of the eighteenth century contributed to the mastery of Eastern Europe. The same map of 1772 included the Tartars as one of the peoples of Europe—the "little Tartars" of the Crimea—but they were not yet considered to be tame: "In the invasions that they make among their neighbors, they lead all the men, women, and children into slavery, except for old ones whom they kill, and sell the others to the Turks." The picture showed warriors on horseback amid corpses, captives, and cattle. In 1787, when Ségur went to the Crimea with Catherine, the Tartars, now tamed, would form part of the "magnificent spectacle" staged for the tsarina at Sevastopol.[105]

Fortis's interest in folkloric phenomena in Dalmatia in the early 1770s was matched by that of William Coxe in Russia in the last years of that decade. Coxe traveled in Russia in 1778 and 1779, the very years in which Herder published his *Volkslieder* in Germany, so the Englishman's attention to songs in Russia dated to the most important moment in the Enlightenment's discovery of folklore. Herder wanted Russian songs for his collections, and in October 1778 received a letter from his friend and publisher J. F. Hartknoch, regretting that "collecting folk songs is not easy," and further: "I know what an effort I've made to get Russian ones," to no avail.[106] At just the same time, even as Hartknoch and Herder were giving up, Coxe was hearing those unobtainable folk songs in Russia, and so his account of them, in a certain sense, completed Herder's collection.

Coxe took note of singing on the road from Smolensk to Moscow when he was authorized to commandeer the horses he needed, and ended up also conscripting peasants as coachmen. The peasants drove "by starts and bounds," whip in hand, and "urged their horses forwards by hooting and whistling like cat-calls." Coxe observed that "the intervals of these noises were filled with singing, which is a favourite practice among the Russians, and has been mentioned by most travellers who have visited this country."[107] The song was thus set to the jerking rhythm of unsteady driving on uneven roads. It occurred in the aural context of "hooting and whistling like cat-calls" and perhaps an occasional cracking of the whip, so that singing appeared as part of the peasants' hortatory communication with their animals. This was a just slightly more dignified representation of folklore than that of Boscovich, when he described the Bulgarians dancing in the mud. Coxe's association of singing and hooting was also not far from Fortis's association of singing and howling.

Coxe next discussed singing when he described an excursion from Moscow to the monastery of the Holy Trinity. Again it was an issue of practical travel, this time associated not with driving the animals but rather with beating the peasants themselves to obtain their cooperation. This was the work of "our friend the sergeant," wielding "his cudgel, whose eloquence was more persuasive than the most pathetic remonstrances." Coxe observed that "the boors were certainly accustomed to this species of rhetoric; for they bore it patiently, and with perfect good-humour; and the moment they were seated on the box, began whistling and singing their national songs as usual."[108] In suggesting an intimate relation between corporal discipline and the singing of national songs, Coxe made folklore into an essential aspect of the eighteenth-century traveler's experience of Eastern Europe. In this case the peasants' constitutional adaptation to the cudgel was demonstrated by the fact that they immediately started to sing after being beaten. The folk song itself participated in a dialogue with the "eloquence" and "rhetoric" of the cudgel, making song and stick into complementary expressions of barbarism.

This was no coincidental association for Coxe, but one that came up again on the road from Moscow to St. Petersburg. In this case he began with an account of the cudgel, and then proceeded directly to his most detailed folkloric description of Russian singing.

As I have before remarked, it is absolutely necessary for a foreigner, who wishes to travel with expedition, not only to provide himself with a passport, but also to procure a Russian soldier, who instead of attending to the arguments of the peasants, or waiting for the slow mediation of the post-master, summarily decides the business by the powerful interposition of his cudgel. The boors, quickly silenced by this dumb mode of argumentation, find no difficulty in adjusting their pretensions, and the horses almost instantly make their appearance.

In our route through Russia I was surprised at the propensity of the natives to singing. Even the peasants who acted in the capacity of coachmen and postilions, were no sooner mounted than they began to warble an air, and continued it, without the least intermission, for several hours. But what still more astonished me was, that they performed occasionally in parts; I frequently observed them engaged in a kind of musical dialogue, making reciprocal questions and responses, as if chanting (if I may so express myself) their ordinary conversation. The postilions *sing* from the beginning to the end of a stage; the soldiers *sing* during their march; the country men *sing* amid the most laborious occupations; the public-houses re-echo with their carols; and in a still evening I have frequently heard the air vibrate with the notes of the surrounding villages.[109]

In this extraordinary passage Coxe was quite attentive to the formal nature of singing in Russia, emphasizing its performance in parts, as dialogue. Indeed, he could only comment on issues of form, since, as he failed to remind his readers, he could not understand a word of what he was hearing. What was most remarkable about the structure of his own narration was the abrupt transition, once again, from the subject of corporal discipline to that of popular song. First the peasants had to be "quickly silenced" with the cudgel, and only then could they begin to sing; indeed, by the end of the passage Coxe seemed to hear all of Russia singing. Their song might be a "musical dialogue," but it was strictly with each other, for no dialogue was possible with the travelers, except perhaps through the intermediary of the soldier and his cudgel. Coxe's account of folk music in Russia emphasized at the same time his appreciation and his alienation from the people he encountered on his travels. This was just the way that the evolving discipline of folklore generally mediated the encounter between Western Europe and Eastern Europe.

Fortis concluded his discussion of the Morlacchi, appropriately, with a brief comment on their funerals, but that subject also was colored by the language of his folkloric interest. "The family weeps and howls over the dead," Fortis reported. "The praises of the deceased are sung." From the subject of funerals he made the transition to a general conclusion, summing up what he had described as "the most remarkable customs of a people hitherto little known to the different nations of Europe." In making known those customs, Fortis showed himself to be an eighteenth-century anthropologist, who discovered his subject just across the Adriatic, within the Venetian empire, yet emphatically outside "the Polite Parts of Europe." His work, however, was not only on behalf of science: "I shall think the pains and labour I have taken well bestowed should this account contribute to your entertainment, and that of the public." [110] Remarkable customs could always be construed as entertaining, but with the added element of folkloric description, an account of singing and dancing, the anthropological representation of Eastern Europe became quite literally a work of entertainment. The idea of Eastern Europe as a folkloric domain of song and dance, first elaborated in the age of Enlightenment, has survived into the twentieth century and our own times. The folklore of Eastern Europe may, of course, be approached with sincere appreciation, but such appreciation emerged historically in a climate of complex condescension, at the moment when Eastern Europe was discovered on the geographical frontier between Europe and Asia, on the philosophical frontier between civilization and barbarism, and on the academic frontier between ancient history and modern anthropology.

Chapter Eight

Peopling Eastern Europe,
Part II: The Evidence of Manners
and the Measurements of Race

"Remarkably Negative"

In 1791, the year that Johann Gottfried Herder published the fourth part of his *Ideas*, with his reflections and prophecies about the Slavs, Johann Gottlieb Fichte traveled to Poland. Herder could reasonably have traveled through Poland in 1769 on his way to France, but instead he sailed on the Baltic, barely waving at Poland from the boat as he passed by, to judge from his journal. Much later in life, in 1798, Herder composed a poem in which he construed the partition of Poland as a warning to Germany:

> Look at your neighbor, Poland, how mighty once,
> And how proud! Oh, she kneels, robbed of jewels and honor.[1]

Still later, in 1802, Herder reached way back into the eighteenth century, and into the conventions of the Enlightenment, to write a poem about Stanisław Leszczyński. One verse was addressed to Poland itself—"Woe, unhappy Poland, for you!"—and another to Leszczyński—"But well, Stanislaus, for you!"—proceeding to praise his Herculean labors, rewarded by "an empire of science and art," not Poland but Lorraine.[2] The poem did seem to suggest that Leszczyński was lucky to have lost Poland, that Poland was unworthy of an enlightened monarch.

Yet Herder was also well aware that, for Germans like himself, Poland was a "neighbor," geographically proximate and accessible, not so dramatically remote as it appeared to Mme Geoffrin in Paris. In 1790 the great Goethe made a one-week excursion into Poland, as far as Cracow, recording almost nothing of his impressions but summing up the experience in a letter to Herder: "In these eight days I have seen much that is remarkable, even if it has been for the most part only remarkably negative."³ The next year Fichte, not yet a literary celebrity like Goethe but only an aspiring philosopher, made his trip to Poland to take a job as a private tutor in Warsaw. He was in Poland for a month and recorded his impressions in a diary. Though his experience was also on the whole "remarkably negative," his travel diary has preserved the all-important details that added up to a German's negative construction of Poland in the eighteenth century. Precisely because Poland was so geographically accessible to Germans, in some respects even intimately related to Germany, it was interpreted as alien and backward with all the more intellectual energy. In the case of Fichte this process appears especially interesting as the early, formative experience of a philosopher who would eventually establish himself—in his "Addresses to the German Nation" of 1807 and 1808—as an ideological oracle of modern German nationalism.

Fichte left from Leipzig in Saxony at the end of April and traveled through Silesia, at that time a part of Prussia, on his way to Poland. His diary recorded that for him the experience of Poland began already in Silesia, long before he reached the Polish border. In Silesia he saw "villages worse than the Saxon ones, that already appear very Polish." The correlation of "worse" and "Polish" was clear. The presence of Jews was also notable, and, at the inn, "everything not what it would have been in Saxony." He contemplated the "true Silesian character" and remarked, "One thinks here of a Polish German. God, what a difference!" ("Gott welcher Abstand!") Beyond Breslau, the provincial capital, Fichte broadened his analysis to include issues of economy, ethnography, and language. The landscape was changing; the fields appeared "less cultivated," the people "more Slavic" (*sclavischer*), the language "rougher." Soon he was passing through "true Polish villages, that also have Polish names." The population was mostly Catholic. The language was German, but it was almost incomprehensible to him ("garnicht mehr zu verstehen").⁴ Yet he had not yet passed the political border between Prussia and Poland.

Silesia today is part of Poland. It also belonged to Poland in the Middle Ages, but was ceded to Bohemia in the fourteenth century. Along with Bohemia it fell to the Habsburgs in the sixteenth century, and was seized from them by Frederick the Great in 1740, provoking years of warfare and

lifelong enmity between himself and Maria Theresa. With its mixed popu-
lation, noted by Fichte in 1791, Silesia was divided by plebiscite between
Germany and Poland after World War I, annexed entirely by Hitler in 1939,
then fully restored to Poland in 1945. In the eighteenth century, Silesia's historical connections to Poland and Bohemia cast it in the shadow of Eastern
Europe, even as Frederick triumphantly established Prussian rule. Robert
Arnold, in Vienna at the end of the nineteenth century, wrote a book about
Germany's "Poland literature" (*Polenlitteratur*) in the eighteenth century,
identifying several important points of cultural contact and ambivalent
intimacy between Germany and Poland. There was Silesia, first of all; then
there were the cities of Gdańsk and Thorn on the Vistula, where German
burghers lived under Polish sovereignty, both seized by Frederick in the
partitions of 1772 and 1793, respectively. The historian Wolfgang Wippermann has traced the origins of the idea of a German "Drang nach Osten,"
and found that in the eighteenth century, scholars in Silesia, and also in
Gdańsk, were already writing about Polish medieval history, emphasizing
the importance of medieval German immigration into Poland.[5]

In eighteenth-century Warsaw German editors and publishers were active, bringing Polish literature and scholarship to the attention of Germany
in the "Warschauer Bibliothek" in the 1750s, and the "Polnische Bibliothek"
in the 1780s. In Saxony, Fichte's place of birth, point of departure, and
standard of reference, Poland was of particular, even proprietary, interest.
The year of his birth, 1762, was the penultimate year of the longstanding
dynastic union between Saxony and Poland; the Wettin electors of Saxony
ruled over both lands, from the election of Augustus II to the Polish throne
in 1697 to the death of his son Augustus III in 1763. During this period,
the "Poland literature" of Saxony included the farcical "Letter of a Right
Coarse Polack to One of his own Kind" in 1704, and "Confused Poland"
in 1711, pronouncing that "in this great confused part of the world it's evident that unhappy Poland is the most confused province." Polish magnates
attended the court at Dresden, and the university at Leipzig became a meeting place for Polish and German minds in the age of Enlightenment.[6] So
the summoning of Fichte from Leipzig in 1791 to tutor in Warsaw made
sense as a residual consequence of the contacts between Poland and Saxony
established earlier in the century.

By the time Fichte crossed the border from Prussia into Poland, he had
already experienced an increasing level of Polishness through Silesia, but
the border crossing nevertheless made a powerful impression:

The first village is Ponikowo, German, but a shudder came over me, especially at
the sight of the large dogs running freely around. . . . The dress of the peasants
takes on here already in the first village something wild and neglected.[7]

Poland then was a land of wild dogs and wild people, and furthermore
"full of Jews." Fichte did meet a girl who interested him, "whom I wanted

to study," and he made this observation: "She has completely the exterior of a German-Pole, a fine skin and color, but fleshy." This was clearly a racial study, and while Fichte was studying the girl, her fiancé came along, and "he was not polite." That night there was nothing to eat at the inn, and "bad, bad beer." With that Fichte considered himself "properly installed in Poland."[8]

The next day Fichte made general observations about Polish women. They all had long black hair, and one in particular appeared "so slovenly (*schlumpig*), like all Polish women, so shaped, so inviting, and so dirty." He further observed that they showed "a stronger sex drive than German females." Dirtiness was a recurrent theme, as Fichte described streets "full of straw, garbage, and manure." He observed that the towns "swarm (*wimmeln*) with Jews," and his verdict on Germans in Poland was not fully favorable either: "they are pleasant, reasonable, obliging, and polite, only unclean, just like the national Poles, and almost more so, since in them it is more striking to a German eye." When he got to Warsaw he would pass judgment more decisively on "the coarseness (*Grobheit*) of the Germans in Poland."[9]

Fichte's observations of 1791 were echoed two years later in 1793 in the travel journal of Joachim Christoph Friedrich Schulz, published as the *Journey of a Livonian from Riga to Warsaw*. He was traveling to the Tyrol for a health cure, and made the land voyage from Riga through Poland, which Herder had avoided in 1769 when he sailed over the Baltic. Schulz, who was Fichte's exact contemporary (both of them born in 1762), crossed Poland in the opposite direction, entering from the east, passing from Baltic Courland into Lithuania instead of from Silesia into Poland. When Schulz arrived in the first Lithuanian village, having entered the Commonwealth of Poland and Lithuania, he found "everything is different from a half mile before." The people were Catholic, and spoke a different language, with "their exterior of a completely different character," in dress, appearance, and demeanor. In the next village he observed the preponderance of Jews. They had found in Poland "a kind of fatherland," he observed, noting also their "Oriental formation," and the fact that a crowd of them "swarmed (*wimmelte*) around my wagon," eager to be of service. Schulz was familiar with Coxe's account of Poland, and soon had seen enough to generalize about the villages of Lithuania: "every village is a picture of disorder and ruin." The Lithuanians, like the Jews, presented "a sort of Oriental appearance." Near Bialystock Schulz was intrigued to discover two Saxon families who had come to Poland in the reign of Augustus II and now numbered 44 people, marrying each other so as to exclude "Polish blood," preserving "true Saxon manners and dialect," as well as a level of "neatness and cleanliness" that the German traveler compared favorably to the rest of Lithuania.[10]

Schulz's *Journey of a Livonian* was published in Berlin in 1795–96, then in French translation in 1807, the same year that Rulhière's history was finally published, the year that Napoleon established the Grand Duchy of Warsaw. Schulz was republished in Breslau in 1941, when the Nazis had conquered Poland and reclaimed Silesia; in that year it was hailed as a work on Poland whose relevance "has still not become obsolete, to the present day."[11] In fact, German academic interest in Poland in the twentieth century offered observations that sometimes resembled those of Fichte and Schulz in the eighteenth century. In 1926 Albrecht Penck, professor of geography in Berlin, compared "the tidy German and the frequently wretched Polish villages" in the province of Poznań, marking "the great frontier of civilization." In that same year another nationally minded German geographer, Wilhelm Volz, looked back to the Middle Ages, when "higher German *Kultur* triumphed over primitive Slavdom." Also in 1926 Walter Kuhn, a student of ethnicity and linguistics, went to the Ukraine to study German communities there, administering questionnaires and celebrating "the strength and beauty of the German *Volkstum.*" Kuhn became a professor at the university of Breslau in 1936, and returned to his German communities in the Ukraine in 1939, with the Nazi occupation of Poland, to assist in resettling them in view of their "exceptional racial quality." Kuhn's reports as an academic expert were taken into account as Germans in Eastern Europe were racially evaluated by the SS to determine whether they were fit for repatriation to Germany. Each individual subject was assigned a "racial estimate ranging from 1aM/1 ('very valuable') to 1V 3c (a 'reject')."[12] Such scientific precision was beyond the travelers of the eighteenth century, who nevertheless noted generally the "coarseness" of Germans in Poland, or alternatively the "neatness and cleanliness" of Germans in Lithuania.

"Half-Wildness and Half-Civilization"

The academic issue of race was under discussion in the German Enlightenment. It was one of the issues over which Kant and Herder argued philosophically in the 1780s, with Kant placing the greater emphasis on distinctions of color, dating from his essay "On the Different Races of Men" in 1775. In 1785 Herder published the second part of his *Ideas*, surveying the different peoples of the world, and arguing for the principle that "mankind appears in such different forms upon the earth, but it's overall one and the same human type."[13] Kant promptly responded in the *Berlinische Monatsschrift* and provoked a new entry into the controversy in 1786, "Something More about the Human Races" by Georg Forster, writing from Lithuania. Forster possessed an asset that both Kant and Herder lacked, that is, some experience of the world outside Europe and of other races. Born near Gdańsk in 1754, of a German family in Poland, as a boy in the 1760s

Forster traveled around Russia with his father, who was commissioned by Catherine to study the possibilities for German settlement on the Volga. In 1772, when Forster was eighteen, he and his father joined Captain Cook's second voyage as natural historians, setting out from England for three years of exploration and discovery in the South Pacific. Georg Forster made his name by writing an account of the voyage, published in English and in German. In 1784 the Commission on National Education in Poland invited him to teach at the university of Vilnius, where he stayed until 1787.[14]

Like the physiocrat Dupont de Nemours, who answered the call of the Commission in 1774, Forster was far from pleased with his position in Poland. Like Fichte, who was overcome by a "shudder," Forster too, even after three years at sea with Captain Cook, confessed that he was frightened upon entering Poland:

It was the dilapidation, the filthiness in the moral and physical sense, the half-wildness (*Halbwildheit*) and half-civilization (*Halbkultur*) of the people, the sight of the sandy land everywhere covered with black woods, which went beyond any conceptions I could have formed. I wept in a lonely hour for myself—and then, as I gradually came to myself, for the so deeply sunken people.[15]

The modulation from horror to pity was striking, as was the intermediary level implicit in such notions as *Halbwildheit* and *Halbkultur*, perfectly suitable to the eighteenth century's idea of Eastern Europe. Forster was capable of conventional references to ancient history, to "Slavic and Hunnic barbarians," and, like Gibbon, allowed himself animal imagery in expressing his frustration: "To make bears into men, that pertains neither to the pen nor to the tongue." Forster made the expression "polnische Wirtschaft," Polish economy, a byword for backwardness.[16] It is still used in German today to describe a disorderly household, the domestic economy, but for Forster it also possessed a macroeconomic significance. He was passionately critical of serfdom in Poland, for both moral and economic reasons, without ever losing sight of the fact that Poland was in Europe:

Among all the nations in Europe the Poles alone have taken ignorance and barbarism so far, as to almost extinguish (*vertilgen*) the last trace of brain power (*Denkkraft*) in their serfs; but they themselves bear the hardest punishment for it, partly because the cattle-like (*viehische*) vassal brings them in scarcely the tenth part of the income that the freer, happier, more rational peasant would bring them, partly because they themselves . . . through their impotence have become the mockery and amusement of all their neighbors.[17]

Forster measured barbarism in terms of economic irrationality and the cultural contempt of other nations. He was not far from Frederick's verdict on the Poles as "the last people in Europe."

Writing from Vilnius to a friend, Forster even drew upon his own experience of the South Pacific as a point of reference for describing Poland as an intermediary mishmash:

You would find ample material to laugh at in this mishmash (*Mischmasch*) of Sarmatian or almost New Zealander crudeness and French super-refinement . . . or perhaps also not; for one laughs only about people whose fault it is that they are laughable; not over those who through forms of government, rearing (such should education be called here), example, priests, despotism of mighty neighbors, and an army of French vagabonds and Italian good-for-nothings, become spoiled already from youth, and have no prospect for future betterment before them. The actual people, I mean those millions of cattle in human form, who are here utterly excluded from all privileges of mankind . . . the people is at present through long-habitual slavery truly sunken to a degree of bestiality and insensibility, of indescribable laziness and totally stupid ignorance, from which perhaps even in a century it could not climb to the same level as other European rabbles.[18]

In this representation of backwardness, measured in degrees and levels against other lands of Europe, in centuries of lag time, Forster nevertheless did not include in his list of determining factors that of racial incapacity, and this despite the fact that race was very much on his mind while he lived in Lithuania and formed such harsh judgments of Poland.

In his essay "Something More about the Human Races," Forster did not draw upon any material from his experience of Poland, even though he was living in Vilnius when he wrote it. Indeed, it opened with a wry tribute to the fact that the intellectual controversies of the Enlightenment reached "into the interior of these Sarmatian woods," as he himself sought to ward off "paralysis of the spirit" in the intellectual isolation of Lithuania. He began from the premise that in matters of race, empirical observation was more valuable than a systematic theoretical approach, siding with Herder rather than Kant on the fundamental unity of mankind. Admitting nuances of difference, Forster was most interested in the contrast, not between German and Pole, but between black and white:

The most apelike Negro is so closely related to the white man, that in the crossing of both stocks the designating characteristics of each interweave and amalgamate in blending with each other. The divergence is very small; both men, the black and the white, stand quite near beside each other; and it could not very well be otherwise, unless mankind should pass into ape nature, and the Negro, instead of remaining a man, should become an ape.[19]

Forster believed that climate was a powerful natural determinant of race, which was therefore variable, and he wondered whether "a Negro family, after being displaced to our climate, in a certain series of unmixed generations would have lost its color, and gradually exchanged its apelike formation for the climatic European one."[20]

In conclusion, he passionately regretted that even if the unity of mankind were definitively established, if black men were shown to be "our brothers," the evil of slavery would nevertheless continue. "Where is the bond," he asked, "however strong it may be, that can hinder degenerate Europeans from ruling over their fellow white men as despotically as over the Negro?" Here perhaps, at the very end of his essay, Forster may have been referring to his experience of Poland, where he had observed with horror the harshness of serfdom. His appeal to white people on behalf of blacks even employed the same phrases as his letter on serfdom in Poland:

White man! are you not ashamed, to abuse your power over the weak one, to cast him deep down among the beasts, to want to extinguish (*vertilgen*) even the trace of brain power (*Denkkraft*) in him?[21]

Forster urged the white man to act as a father to the black man, to "develop" in him "the holy spark of reason," to help him "become what you are or can be." Far from caring to distinguish Poles and Germans as distinct races, Forster even applied a bridging theory of development to the perceived gap between blacks and whites. He also understood that white people in Europe, in Poland among other places, were oppressed and abused like black slaves elsewhere, without the pretext of racial difference. Forster's essay clearly indicates that, even though Fichte and Schulz employed certain nuances of racial distinction in their observations on Poles and Lithuanians, the German Enlightenment was still far from achieving a consistent and concerted racial perspective on Poland in particular and Eastern Europe in general.

"The Orangutan of Europe"

Fichte's first impression of Warsaw was far from favorable: "The entrance is like a Polish country town, huts instead of houses, manure on the street." In the center he discerned the same striking contrasts that other eighteenth-century travelers noted; there were "countless churches and palaces, and in between two splendid palaces often a hut which threatened to collapse." On the same street as the Czartoryski palace there were nothing but Jews (*lauter Juden*). His hotel did not improve his opinion of the city: "I had to make my bed myself. I complained, so someone said to me: that is the custom here." He exclaimed, "What an abominable lavatory!" and noted that this hotel was considered "one of the good ones in Warsaw."[22]

Fichte was only in Warsaw for two weeks, so his recorded impressions were neither extensive nor detailed. Schulz, however, presented an extremely comprehensive portrait of the city based not only on his short stay in 1793 but also on months of experience in 1791–92, when he served as a representative of Mitau in Courland (today Jelgava in Latvia) at the

Four-Year Sejm. His account covered Warsaw from architecture, churches, hotels, and hospitals to theater, gambling, picnics, and prostitution. In fact, the vision of eighteenth-century Warsaw was so vivid and complete that after the book was republished in Nazi Germany in 1941, its next edition was in postwar Poland in 1956, when old Warsaw was being painstakingly reconstructed after its utter annihilation by the Nazis in 1944.[23] Like Fichte, Schulz remarked on the contrasts of the city: "So palaces and huts, princes and beggars, form the physical and moral foundation of Warsaw." As for the streets, "when it rains, they appear inundated with garbage, and the arrangements that are made to clean them are not worth mentioning." He warned visitors "not to pay attention to the unclean crowd of Jews," and thus he drew attention to them himself. Schulz also pointed out the prostitutes of the city, explaining that prostitution in Warsaw gave evidence of "the old Polish roughness of manners." He judged that "here the immoral traffic of both sexes is of an extent, a publicity, a variety, and toleration, but also a degree of provocation, costliness, corruption, bound with a mixture of shamelessness and brutality, which perhaps no other great capital of Europe has reached." Schulz located Warsaw culturally and geographically by its "distance from the more refined European lands."[24]

Schulz came to Warsaw to attend the Sejm in September 1791, while Fichte had already come and gone in June, so their stays did not overlap. Yet the Sejm had been in session since 1788, and Fichte appeared oblivious to the fact that he was visiting Warsaw in the middle of a revolution. Only a month before his arrival, on May 3, the Sejm had adopted the constitution that Edmund Burke hailed from afar, but it went unremarked by Fichte in Warsaw, out of either indifference to the politics of Poland or preoccupation with his personal affairs and the abominable lavatory at his hotel. His obliviousness was the more striking for the fact that, just then, all over Germany, there was mounting sympathetic interest in Poland. The *Berlinische Monatsschrift*, which published Kant's essay on race in 1785, which Forster received in Vilnius to stay in touch with the Enlightenment, now praised the Polish constitution in 1791, the more easily for the fact that Poland was temporarily in alliance with Prussia. At the same time, since the constitution made the Saxon Wettins into the hereditary successors of Stanisław August, there was also praise from Saxony for Poland's "very great progress" and "rational enlightenment." Christian Friedrich Schubart, who published in his *Deutsche Chronik* in 1774 a poem on "Polonia" in tears, after the first partition, in 1791 celebrated the constitution in overly optimistic verse: "Rejoice, Polonia, now! your night is forever illuminated." Schubart died that same year, before he could be disappointed in his enthusiastic expectations, but a number of young Germans followed his lead to write poetry on the triumphs and ultimately the tragedies of Poland in the 1790s. These included Johann Daniel Falk, Johann Christian Gretschel,

Aloys Wilhelm Schreiber, and Andreas Georg Rebmann, constituting a revolutionary cohort of German poets, writing about Poland in the 1790s, anticipating the Romantic enthusiasm of the 1830s.[25]

Throughout Germany in 1794, and especially in Vienna, Kościuszko was the hero of the day, his picture was everywhere, and he was celebrated under the interesting orthography of "Kutschiuzky." In a German novel, which appeared in the middle of the decade as *The Peripatetics of the Eighteenth Century*, Jesus and John wandered through Poland, lamenting the downfall of the 1791 constitution. Another German novel called *Scenes from the Polish Revolution* was published in 1797, taking its details of Poland from Schulz's account, but modeling its structure on Louvet's *Loves of the Chevalier de Faublas*.[26] In 1790 the memoirs of Maurice Beniowski were published in French, recounting his adventures, which ranged from Poland to Madagascar, and were then translated into German by none other than Georg Forster. Beniowski soon became the subject of a German drama by August Friedrich Kotzebue in 1795, and a French opera by François-Adrien Boieldieu in 1800.[27]

Ernst Ludwig Posselt in 1796 lamented the partitions, which rendered Poland an "antiquity," which made "the history and geography of Europe a full chapter shorter" and annihilated the state "after so many partitions, that almost every third year made a new map of it necessary." Of course, German opinion was not unanimously sympathetic to Poland, and the mapmakers of Nuremberg, the heirs of Homann, were particularly hasty about hurrying Poland off the map of Europe. Güssefeld's map of 1794 prematurely eliminated Poland in the coloring of countries, though the name was still printed. In his map of 1798 Güssefeld eliminated the name as well.[28]

In 1791, the year of Fichte's journey, there appeared a fictionalized German travel account in which the traveler discovered in Warsaw that "the Poles don't know that men think and feel, and that knowledge elevates man."[29] The possibility of assigning the Poles to a lower "elevation" on the scale of humanity could also be exercised politically during these revolutionary years, and German writers allowed themselves the same liberty with the Hungarians. In 1792, when nationalist sentiment still seemed to menace Habsburg rule in Hungary, an anonymous pamphlet was published in Frankfurt and Leipzig, probably written by Leopold Alois Hoffmann, putting the Hungarians in their place with the rhetorical formulas that subordinated Eastern Europe. The epigraph falsely claimed to come from Rousseau's *Considèrations on the Government of Poland*, in German translation: "I laugh at the unworthy peoples, who, after they have heated up with liquor, presume to speak of freedom." This was hardly Rousseau's perspective on the Poles, and here it was anyway being applied to the Hungarians, as if those two peoples could be interchangeably despised. An unworthy people, the author proposed, "who want to make a claim to civilization (*Kultur*)," who presume to equality with "the most enlightened nations," is comparable to a "puffed-up fool in bourgeois life." Only since Hungary has had the good fortune to be ruled by the Habsburgs, he further insisted, have people begun to distinguish between the words *Ungar* and *Barbar*, Hungarian and barbarian. The Hungarians might claim to be enlightened people (*Aufgeklärten*), but their political unruliness "showed again their old Scythian wildness." They could be merely ranked among "the less cultivated nations" or, in the same paragraph, exposed to all of Europe as "ever wild barbarians, in all their nakedness."[30] The cultural conventions of the eighteenth century, by which Eastern Europe was subordinated to Western Europe, allowed some German writers in the revolutionary decade to dismiss Poland and Hungary as beneath political consideration.

Fichte in Warsaw, in 1791, neither belittled nor approved the revolution that was unfolding around him; he did not appear to notice it. Instead, he was deeply preoccupied with his personal situation, which had taken an unexpected and unfortunate turn. He had come to Warsaw to accept a position as a private tutor in a noble Polish family, and the family, the countess in particular, was not satisfied with him when he presented himself. The problem was that Fichte's French was weak, and she thought this disqualified him as a competent tutor for her son. Fichte recorded a vicious caricature of the countess at the end of his travel diary. There was something "wild" about her gaze, something "coarse" about her tone; she stuttered out of "affectation," used too much makeup, and appeared to be "always drunk." But what could he do? He wrote her a letter, in French of course, explaining that he would never have come to Warsaw if he thought anything more was expected of him than Latin, history, geography, mathematics, and mediocre French. He hoped, however, that she would be generous enough to compensate him for "my wasted time, my broken engagements, and the expenses of my return voyage." If she would do so, he would undertake to introduce her to a French abbé "who knows French perfectly."[31] He had lost his job, his whole reason for coming all the way to Warsaw, and the Polish countess, with her wild eye and coarse tone, dared to condescend culturally to him.

In 1780, ten years before, a scurrilous French pamphlet appeared under the title "The Orangutan of Europe, or the Pole such as he is," advertising itself as "a methodical work which won a prize for natural history in 1779." It was as if Forster's racial speculations about the "apelike Negro" were indeed transposed as parody into a Polish key. With methodical abuse the pamphlet pronounced the Pole to be "the worst, the most contemptible, the vilest, the most hateful, the most dishonorable, the dumbest, the filthiest, the falsest, the most cowardly creation among all the apes." Such exceptional hostility was at first attributed to the pen of Frederick himself, but later the author was identified with greater probability as a certain French officer who had been cashiered from the Polish army.[32] For a foreigner to be fired in Poland was clearly a provocation to furious contempt, and if Fichte's feelings were more muted, it was probably because he turned his trip into a triumph after all. Without wasting any more time in Warsaw, he found a boat to take him down the Vistula to Gdańsk, and from there he traveled along the Baltic to Königsberg. The journey to Warsaw in itself was a failure, so Fichte reconceived his whole voyage; Warsaw was only a short stop on the way to Königsberg and Kant.

Retrospectively, in a letter to a friend, Fichte made his trip to Poland into a trivial and casual episode:

After a crowd of adventures in Silesia and Poland, which for three weeks, mostly after my fashion, I traveled through, I arrived at Warsaw; and the house, for which I was intended, suited me so badly, that I immediately upon my arrival seized an opportunity to break off the engagement. A great suit might almost have ensued; but finally I let myself be paid off with a few dozen well milled ducats, and with them traveled through another stretch of Poland; and went from there to Königsberg— you guess for which man's sake.[33]

Thus explained, the whole journey made sense in a way that anyone could guess. Poland was just something to be traveled through, offering "adventures" but none worth describing; Fichte's disaster in Warsaw was incidental, and, in this version, he himself was settling the countess, breaking off the engagement, letting himself be paid off. Poland disappeared altogether in the letter that Fichte wrote to Kant in Königsberg, introducing himself. He wrote to Kant, of course, not in French but in German: "I came to Königsberg to learn to know better the man, whom all Europe honors, but whom certainly few men in all Europe love so much as I do."[34] He wrote a philosophical essay for Kant's consideration. Kant liked it and helped Fichte get it published in 1792 as "An Attempt at a Critique of all Revelation." So it came about that Fichte established himself as a philosopher, all as a consequence of the trip to Poland, or rather as a consequence of its failure. He had traveled right through Poland to philosophical glory in the eastern outpost of the German Enlightenment. Along the way he had made some incidental, anthropological observations about Poland and Germany, summed up in his own exclamation, "God, what a difference!"

"From Civilization to Incivilization"

In 1769, the year that Herder left Riga and prophesied a new civilization in the Ukraine, Dartmouth College was founded far away in Hanover, New Hampshire. In 1770, the year that Fortis went to Dalmatia to study the customs of the Morlacchi, the new school in New Hampshire was being established as an educational center for attending to America's own so-called savages, the American Indians. Dartmouth's program involved training not anthropologists to study the customs of the Indians, but rather missionaries to convert them to Christianity. In 1772 John Ledyard, a young man from a family of New England Puritans, came to Dartmouth to enter that program, and ended up spending some time among the Iroquois, before dropping out of school. Instead of a missionary, he became a sailor, and ultimately an explorer. In 1776, the year that America declared its independence from England, Ledyard was in England, joining the third and final voyage of Captain Cook. Like Forster on the second voyage, Ledyard had the opportunity to visit New Zealand and Tahiti; the unluckiest destination of the third voyage was Hawaii, where in 1779 Cook was killed on the beach in a violent encounter with the Hawaiians. That expedition had also searched for the elusive Northwest Passage around Canada, traveling through the Bering Strait. Ledyard met Russian fur traders in the Aleutian Islands, and could appreciate the proximity of Siberia and Alaska, of the Russian empire and the continent of North America.[35]

In Paris in 1785 Ledyard sought to set up an expedition to travel through Russia and Siberia and then explore northwestern America. He consulted with Thomas Jefferson, the American minister in Paris, with Friedrich Melchior Grimm, Catherine's cultural agent there, and with John Paul Jones, who was soon to enter Catherine's service. In 1786 he wrote to his cousin in America that it was all arranged: "In about fourteen days I leave Paris for Brussells, Cologne, Vienne, Dresden, Berlin, Varsovie, Petersburg, Moscow, Kamchatka, Sea of Anadivy, Coast of America, from whence if I find any more cities to New York, when I get there I will name them to you."[36] This powerful geographical vision of continuity, passing from Western Europe to Eastern Europe to Asia to America, was to become a subject of reflection for Ledyard as he proceeded, not quite according to plan. He was in St. Petersburg in 1787, invoking the barbarians of ancient history in a letter to Jefferson in Paris: "I can only say that you are in no danger of having the luxurious repose of your charming climates disturbed by a second incursion of either Goth, Vandal, Hun, or Scythian." Not so in St. Petersburg: "We had a Scythian at table that belongs to the royal society of Physicians here." It was a joke, but one that took its humor from the conventional eighteenth-century association of Eastern Europe and ancient Scythia. There in St. Petersburg, Ledyard made contact with Pallas, the German natural historian who explored the Russian empire in Catherine's service, and also with the French ambassador to Russia, none other than Ségur. Ledyard sought their support to obtain Catherine's authorization for his projected journey across her empire.[37] Perhaps he was careless about obtaining that authorization, or perhaps his requests were carelessly handled, since at that moment Catherine and Ségur were about to depart on the great voyage to the Crimea. In any event, whatever authorization Ledyard obtained turned out to be quite inadequate, and for that reason his own journey was to end in farcical disaster.

Siberia was a sensitive subject in eighteenth-century Russia. Mark Bassin has suggested, in his study on "Inventing Siberia," that from the time of Peter, the identity of Russia was sought in the symmetrical division between two moieties, Russia in Europe and Russia in Asia.[38] Much as Western Europe defined its civilization with respect to the semi-Oriental backwardness of Eastern Europe, so Peter's and Catherine's Russia aligned itself with Europe in contrast to a colonial domain of Siberia, fully in Asia. This distinction rendered Siberia a sensitive subject. Catherine was furious when the abbé Chappe d'Auteroche, a French astronomer who went to Siberia in 1761 to witness the transit of Venus, published in 1768 his *Voyage to Siberia*, which cast aspersions generally on civilization in Russia. In fact, the tsarina was angry enough to compose herself, in French, an *Antidote, or Examination of a Bad Book, Superbly Printed*, derisively rebutting Chappe.[39] Perhaps she thought of him when she learned, almost twenty years later, that Ledyard was making his way across Siberia.

Ledyard kept a "Journal of his Travels thro' Siberia, to the Pacific Ocean, in his attempt to circumnambulate the Globe," and he began with the journey from Kazan, on the Volga, to Tobolsk, beyond the Urals. The land in between, he remarked, "which formerly belonged to the Poles, must be poor indeed, if judged of by the wretched appearance of its inhabitants."[40] Like Chappe before him, he was forming a poor impression of Catherine's empire, and somehow he had gotten the inaccurate idea that this land once belonged to Poland. The Commonwealth of Poland and Lithuania did, at its greatest extent, reach beyond the Dnieper, but it never came anywhere near the Volga, let alone the Urals. Obviously Ledyard was aware that a partition of Poland had taken place not too long ago, and that Russia had gained at Poland's expense, but he showed himself quite ignorant of the political geography of Eastern Europe. He was not really interested in contemporary history. As his Siberian journal quickly revealed, he was interested above all in the anthropology of race, from the first sighting of Tartars around Kazan:

The nice Gradation by which I pass from Civilization to Incivilization appears in every thing: their manners, their dress, their Language, and particularly that remarkable and important circumstance of *Colour* which I am now fully convinced originates from natural Causes; and is the effect of external and local circumstances. I think the same of *Feature*. I see here the large mouth, the thick lip, and broad flat nose as well as in Africa.[41]

The notion of the "nice Gradation by which I pass from Civilization to Incivilization" was essential to the Enlightenment's construction of Eastern

Europe, but here Ledyard extended that scale into Siberia, along the Eurasian landmass. The markings on his graded ruler of civilization were those of the itinerary he had sketched in Paris: to Brussels, Cologne, Berlin, Warsaw, St. Petersburg, Moscow, Kamchatka. Herder represented Europe and Asia together, physiographically, as a "descending plain" from the heights of Tartary; in Ledyard's scheme the direction of descent was reversed and rendered purely metaphorical, from west to east, from civilization to incivilization. Manners were first on the list of factors that measured the degree of civilization, but Ledyard added emphasis to the other factors of "Colour" and "Feature," the variables of race. He himself, like Forster, seemed to believe that race was determined by "natural causes," climate and environment. His interest in the possible racial analogy between Tartars and Africans would make Africa his next destination, and it would prove to be even unluckier for him than Siberia.

By the time Ledyard reached the Yenisei River he had divided the "Tartars"—a term that he applied very broadly—into three classes, according to features and complexion: "What I call the third class, are the lighteyed and fair complexioned Tartars which I believe include the Cossacs." In distinguishing Tartars from Europeans, Ledyard devoted meticulous attention to the ears, for "the ears of Calmuc and Mongul Tartars, project uniformly and universally farther from their heads than those of the Europeans." This rather bold generalization followed upon his having actually measured the ears of precisely three individuals, and calculated the statistical average of their respective ear projections. In addition to such careful measurements, Ledyard's fascination with race was manifested in repeated reports on the children of racially mixed marriages. He studied the eyes and hair of "four children descended of a Calmuc man and a Russian woman." Then he considered a woman "whose mother was a Savage near Ischutskoi and her father a Russian," a case that "strengthened my opinion that the difference of Colour in Man is not the effect of any design in the Creator," but more likely "a Work of Nature." Of the Russians he observed that "the Contour of their manners is Asiatic and not European," but in terms of ethnographic descent their filiation was with Europe, especially Eastern Europe. Here measurement played no part, permitting speculation to indulge its fancy: "The Russ proper are descended of the Polanders, Sclavonians, Bohemians, and Hungarians." These were in turn descended from the Greeks, the Greeks from the Egyptians, and the Egyptians from the Chaldeans. As if to confirm this chain of descent, Ledyard made the peculiar observation that "the present Russ Dress is Egyptian."[42] His encounter with Egypt and the Egyptians, two years later, would bring about his sudden and mysterious death.

At Yakutsk Leydard observed people "born half Russ, half Tartar," and thought them "very different & much superior in their Persons to either the Tartars or Russ." He wondered whether racial intermarriage might be the ultimate cause that "originally made the European different from the Tartar or the Negro," the natural cause of "difference among Mankind." He saw "a Man descended of a Yakutee Father and Russian Mother & the son of this Man," which allowed for speculation about the transmission of racial character beyond the first generation. He wrote as one who wished to construct a science of race: "I conclude therefore that after the first descent, the Operations of Nature by Generation have little or no effect upon the Colour, and I remark also that whenever this change in the Colour by generation takes place that the alteration is from the darker to the lighter Colour much oftner than the Reverse." Obsessively, he put together pieces of random racial evidence, seeking to formulate scientific principles from his observations in Siberia. Inevitably, he set his general conclusion along the presumed "gradation" of civilization, from Europe into Asia: "By the same gentle gradation in which I passed from the height of civilized Society at Petersburg to incivilization in Siberia, I passed from the Colour of the fair European to the Copper-coloured Tartar." Race and civilization were thus correlated factors for Ledyard, both following a ruled line that passed from west to east. His hypothesis could be even more broadly formulated: "General Remark is that far the greatest part of mankind compared with European Civilization are uncultivated & that this part of Mankind are darker Coloured than the other part *viz* European. There are no white Savages & few uncivilized people that are not brown or black."[43]

While Ledyard's observations followed his progress across the land mass of Europe and Asia, his speculations wandered away to Africa. The "copper-coloured" Tartars were not black, of course, but when he considered "the form and features of the Face," as opposed to simple color, he made the connection: "I remark that it is not an European Face but very remote from it; it is more an African Countenance." He pursued this comparison feature for feature, noses and nostrils, lips and mouths, eyes and cheekbones. All Tartars looked alike to Ledyard—though in fact he encountered a variety of peoples in Siberia, not all of whom considered themselves Tartars. "I know of no Nation," he observed, "no people on Earth among whom there is such an uniformity of features except the Chinese, the Negroes & the Jews as there is among the Asiatic Tartars." One possible factor in this perceived uniformity was that "they have ever been Savages averse to Civilization, and have therefore never until very lately and now rarely have commixed with other Nations." Instead, "they have ever been more among the Beasts of the forest than among men," a fact that appeared significant to one who believed race was determined by natural, environmental influences. Still, he admitted the limitations of his own scientific knowledge: "I am also ignorant how far a people constantly living with Beasts may operate in changing the features of the Face." This was the frontier of so-called science, and Ledyard knew of an English anatomist who was studying "the Head of a Negro" for resemblances to the monkey: "If I could, I would send him the Head of a Tartar who lives by the Chace and is constantly in the Society of Animals who have high Cheek Bones; & perhaps in his Strictures on this he would also find an Anatomical likeness to the Fox, the Wolf, the Dog, the Bear &c."[44] For the moment, Ledyard could only measure the ears of living specimens, but he envisioned a more radical scientific analysis.

The racial identification of the Tartars had already been considered by the philosophers of the Enlightenment. Louis Buffon's *Natural History*, in the discussion of "Varieties in the Human Species" in 1749, singled out the Tartars as a special case among white men: "There are as many varieties in the race of blacks as in that of whites: the blacks have, like the whites, their Tartars and their Circassians." David Hume's essay of 1748, on "National Characters," was annotated by the author in 1754 with a remark on race that similarly set apart the Tartars. Hume declared himself "apt to suspect" that blacks were "naturally inferior to whites." He thought "there never was a civilized nation of any other complexion than white," and that even "the most rude and barbarous of the whites, such as the ancient GERMANS, the present TARTARS, have still something eminent about them."[45] The Tartars were more usually identified with the ancient Scythians than the ancient Germans, but in any event there was a certain academic consensus at midcentury that at least they were white. Both Buffon and Hume agreed on that, though both singled out the Tartars as an exceptional case. The whiteness of the Tartars was important, not just because of their physiographical connection to Europe on Herder's descending Eurasian plain, but also because some Tartars actually lived in Europe itself, in the Crimea and on the Volga, that is, in Eastern Europe. Ledyard, however, from an American perspective, was prepared to challenge the whiteness of the Tartars. He basically agreed with Hume that all civilized peoples were white, but, finding nothing "eminent" about the Tartars except perhaps their ears, he added the corollary that "there are no white Savages." Ledyard found the solution to this problem in a bold hypothesis, based on his American background.

In the summer of 1787 Ledyard wrote a letter from Siberia to Thomas Jefferson in Paris, excitedly confiding an extraordinary discovery:

I shall never be able, without seeing you in person & perhaps not even then, to inform you how universaly & circumstantialy the Tartars resemble the aborigines of America: they are the same people—the most antient, & most numerous of any other, & had not a small sea divided them, they would all have still been known by the *same name*. The cloak of civilization sits as ill upon them as our American tartars—they have been a long time Tartars & it will be a long time before they are any other kind of people.[46]

The Tartars then were simply American Indians, the Indians just American Tartars, equally alien to civilization, and Ledyard was the perfect person to establish this identity inasmuch as he had personal experience of both peoples. From the first Tartars he encountered at Kazan he saw that their personal ornaments were "but a modification of the *Wampum*." At Lake Baikal, he found that "they have tents or wigwams covered with matting bark or Skins, and are the genuine American wigwam form thus." It was just a matter of terminology, "the Yoort or Hut as we generally call it, or as the American Tartars call it pretty generally Wigwaum." He saw tattoos that reminded him of "the Mohegan tribe in America," and heard of similar markings among "the Peasantry of Moldavia." He speculated on the custom of scalping among the ancient Scythians and the contemporary American Indians, even recalling the Hawaiians, that is, "the Indians at Owhyhee," who "brought a part of Captain Cook's head, yet they had cut off all the Hair." He noted as "very remarkable that both the Asiatic and American Tartars have the same chaste or superstitious notions of Women during the Menstrual Illness."[47] All this anthropological evidence of manners confirmed the racial hypothesis that derived from a perceived uniformity of appearance. The Tartars, American and Asian, might be divided into tribes, "but Nature has set a Barrier to this Distinction & to all Distinction among them that marks them wherever found with the indisputable signature of Tartar: No matter if in Nova Zembla, Mongul in Greenland, or on the banks of the Mississippi, they are the same." They were also all equally alien to civilization, and Ledyard wondered rhetorically whether a Tartar could ever make a watch, or a telescope. "In the United States of America as in Russia," he observed, "we have made our efforts to convert our Tartars to think and act like us, but to what effect?"[48] He himself, in his Dartmouth days, must have contemplated the conversion of the Indians to Christianity, but now, having traveled all over the world, he raised the crucial question of conversion to civilization.

Fortis found in Dalmatia a "Tartar or American mode" of wearing beads and coins in the hair, and even Gibbon appeared implicitly interested in analogies between America and Eastern Europe when he wrote of Hungarian tents, Tartar bows, Russian squirrel skins, and Cossack canoes. It was Ledyard, however, who could testify from direct comparative observation, and further to confirm his anthropological hypothesis about the identity of the Tartars and the Indians, he intended to cross Siberia to Kamchatka and then continue his researches on the Pacific coast of North America. Two hundred miles from the ocean, however, he was suddenly arrested by order of the tsarina and rushed westward all the way back across the Russian empire as a prisoner, to be dumped unceremoniously in Poland. Catherine had returned from the Crimea to learn that Ledyard was poking around Siberia without proper authorization. An American contemporary, proclaiming Ledyard an "eccentric Genius," lamented that "the Caprice of a Woman probably prevented the world from receiving some new and important information that would have been the result of this extraordinary Journey had it been compleated."[49] Ledyard himself indignantly protested his innocence of any offense, as he was transported, altogether against his will, back into Eastern Europe.

The eccentricity of Ledyard's anthropological researches in Siberia, which may have put him under suspicion in St. Petersburg, stood out in contrast to the more obviously innocuous journey to Siberia of the Englishman John Parkinson, five years later. He was a clergyman and traveling companion, accompanying a young gentleman named Bootle on an unconventional "Northern Tour," inasmuch as France was rendered unvisitable by the Terror. Though he might sum up the tour as "northern," Parkinson's travel diary also recorded the distinction between Russia and "western Europe." At court in St. Petersburg he admired the "motley crew" in which "Cossacks, Kirghese and Tartars, intermingled, contributed very much to the oddity of the appearance." He was entertained by Cossack and Russian dances, which seemed to him to "savour" of the "savage and barbarous." Parkinson set out from the capital to see something of the empire, commenting conventionally on "the wretchedness of the roads." Using Coxe as a reference, he recorded leaving Europe for Asia at the Volga, and he entered Siberia at the Urals, proceeding as far as Tobolsk. There he saw a Siberian dance on the occasion of Catherine's birthday.[50] Returning to the Volga, Parkinson met up with Pallas to guide him, and encountered the Kalmucks, remarking that "I never saw countenances in my life which seemed to indicate greater peace of mind, greater Philanthropy, greater contentment than those of the good people here." This was a far cry from Ledyard's style of racial physiognomy. Parkinson took an interest in the Russian sport of goose fighting, thought the local costumes on the Volga "a very agreeable and picturesque sight," and was later "amused" by the Circassians, who performed "a greaty variety of their national dances."[51] Parkinson's conventional appreciation of the picturesque in Eastern Europe, refined perhaps by a more modern sensitivity to folkloric elements, may serve to dramatize by contrast the radically original and sometimes bizarre nature of Ledyard's anthropological researches and speculations.

Even before his arrest, when he still hoped to proceed from Siberia to America, Ledyard knew that eventually he would have to complete his racial research in Africa. In Yakutsk, he imagined himself at the end of his voyages, with a hint of unhappy premonition: "Africa explored, I lay me down and claim a little portion of the Globe I've viewed—may it not be before." His precipitous return from Siberia to Europe, as a prisoner, canceled his plans for North America, for the moment, and set him to contemplating Africa again. On the 4th of July, 1788, he sent a note to Jefferson at the embassy in Paris:

Mr. Ledyard presents his compliments to Mr. Jefferson—he has been imprisoned and banished by the Empress of Russia from her dominions after having almost gained the Pacific Ocean. He is now on his way to Africa to see what he can do with that continent.[52]

Jefferson wrote from Paris in March 1789 to the American ambassador in Spain:

My last accounts from Lediard (another bold countryman of ours) were from Grand Cairo. He was just then plunging into the unknown regions of Africa, probably never to emerge again. If he returns, he has promised me to go to America and penetrate from Kentucky to the Western side of the Continent.[53]

Ledyard, however, was not to explore America or even Africa; Cairo was the end of the road. He died there at the age of 38, and the circumstances of his death suggested that he was not only an "eccentric genius" but perhaps seriously unbalanced as well. Reports of his end reached England from Cairo, and Thomas Paine forwarded them to Thomas Jefferson in Paris. Ledyard was about to leave Cairo when weather delayed his departure, and "Mr. Ledyard took offence at the delay and threw himself into a violent rage with his conductors which deranged something in his system." It ended in the bursting of a blood vessel, and he died in a matter of days.[54] As he returned from Siberia, a prisoner, his fantasies of exploration were already focused on the ill-fated African expedition, but before he could set out for Africa, he had to be transported from Siberia to Europe, and then make his own way from Eastern Europe to Western Europe.

"Between the Eastern and Western World"

Passionately anticipating "the End of my unfortunate Voyage as a Prisoner without a Crime," Ledyard was, at first, thrilled to leave Russia behind him and enter Poland as a free traveler. "O Liberty! O Liberty! how sweet are thy embraces!" he exclaimed. "Having met thee in Poland I shall bless that Country; indeed I believe it wants the blessing of every charitable mind." Ironic condescension thus qualified his enthusiasm from the start, and almost immediately his mind took a turn for the less charitable when he had to lodge in the house of a Jew—"a large dirty house filled with dirt & noise & children." In fact, he found the whole Polish-Russian frontier region "solely inhabited by Jews who are ever nuisances." It was not, however, the numerousness of the Jews, but rather the poverty of the peasantry that persuaded Ledyard to revoke his blessing on Poland. It was "Malice against the Empress of Russia" that made Ledyard "a partizan of the King of Poland, the moment I entered his Dominions," but after three days there he wanted only to "hurry out of the Country." He was horrified at the sight of "not only the poorest Peasantry but the poorest men I ever saw." They were "wretched diminutive and ill formed, ill fed, ill clothed & ill looked." With his passion for measurement he estimated that "5 Feet 2, 4, or 5 Inches is the average height of those I have seen; bandy-legged, splay footed, & knock-kneed."[55] The oppression of the peasants, perceived as slaves, was certainly one of the identifying marks of Eastern Europe for eighteenth-century travelers, but for Ledyard that issue was reconceived in the language of physical anthropology, and pity evidently mingled with repulsion.

Coming straight out of Asia himself, on the way to Western Europe, Ledyard could hardly help registering Poland's intermediary geographical position as he hurried to pass through. Naturally Ledyard interpreted this position anthropologically, so that customs and manners constructed the domain of Eastern Europe:

There is a Melange of Dress here & so of other Customs. The effects of the Geographical situation of its Inhabitants between the Eastern and Western World, this is with difficulty described. The Jews are entirely in the Eastern Stile. . . . The Poles on the other hand (if I include the Ladies, who I am apt to think are the best judges & examples of Dress & Cleanliness) have more of the European than Asiatic about; but both the Dress & Manners of Europe sit ill upon them.[56]

The European clothes and manners that seemed to "sit ill" on the Poles recalled the "cloak of civilization" that to Ledyard's tailoring sensibility sat ill upon the Tartars. In one bold rhetorical sweep he separated Eastern Europe from Western Europe by declaring that "there is a rude, unfinished, capricious fantastic Taste that divides both Poland & Russia from the Genius of Europe."[57] It was of course Ledyard himself, the "eccentric genius" from America, who denied "the Genius of Europe" to Poland and Russia, according to his own taste, and though he could be both capricious and fantastic in his opinions, in this case he was close to the conventional perspective of the Enlightenment. Voltaire distinguished "our part of Europe" as superior "in its manners and in its genius" to the other part, which extended from Thrace to Tartary.

"Today after Dinner I left Vilna whose Environs on the West Side are very pretty," recorded Ledyard in his diary, but he did not linger there, for the "West Side" of Vilnius was by no means western enough.

I quit it gladly for the Godlike Regions of the West. If I had believed from Information I never could have formed any adequate Idea without the little Tour I have made of the inferiority of the Eastern to the Western World & that so vast a difference could be found in the qualities of the Hearts & even the Minds of men.

If cultivation can produce such effects I see nothing romantic in supposing that the Men of the West may become Angels.[58]

The "Genius of Europe" clearly pertained to "the Godlike Regions of the West." With such a powerful directional sense of the contrast between east and west, Ledyard's "little Tour" reveals the anachronism of Parkinson's notion of a "Northern Tour."

Ledyard's vision of the "Men of the West" as angels contrasted sharply with his perception of the Polish peasantry, "the lowest order of People, Slaves, & I cannot bear the sight of one." Whenever he saw a slave he felt the need "to think & act for him, & I have not time to do either." His time was particularly limited, since he was hurrying out of Poland as fast as he could, disparaging it uncharitably as he went:

Charming Weather for the Season. I cannot find any thing that interests me among the Poles; perhaps it is because I am stupid or inattentive, & I wish as good an apology in their Favour might exist, but in my Soul I doubt it.[59]

Naturally it could not be Ledyard's stupidity, so presumably it was theirs; just as it was their capricious taste, and not his, that cut off Poland and Russia from the genius of Europe. Having thus dismissed the Poles, and lumped them with the Russians, it only remained to associate both with the Tartars of Siberia, in accordance with the perceived "inferiority of the Eastern to the Western World." Ledyard's approach was typically anthropological, and he threw in the Jews ("entirely in the Eastern stile") for good measure:

The Custom of the Young Women or Virgins wearing the Hair hanging down & the Married hiding it is very curiously adhered to by the Jews who are tenacious in all their Customs, so that if they had originally been a good People they would now be the best on Earth. The same Custom is also Universal among the Poles, Russians, & Tartars. This is another of those Eastern Customs the offspring of Eastern Jealousy. The Moment a Woman is married among them she becomes marked as we do a Horse we have bought. To hide the Hair is to have it cut off & to have cut off the Ears for the same purpose would not have been more ridiculous. Thus has that inoffensive & endearing part of the human Race been ever Used by Man; in the early & uncivilized parts of Society.[60]

Here Jews, Poles, Russians, and Tartars were bound together anthropologically by "Eastern Customs," which were furthermore judged to be "ridiculous" and "uncivilized," in a comprehensive construction of Eastern Europe. Ledyard's irony about cutting off the ears was curious in view of the fact that he took a special scientific interest in that part of the anatomy, and had once allowed himself to contemplate (in humor, perhaps) sending the head of a Tartar to London for further scientific study.

The continuity and consistency of the "eastern world" came abruptly to an end on the day that Ledyard crossed the border from Poland into Prussia. Ségur had crossed the other way, from Prussia into Poland, three years before, and felt that he had "left Europe entirely." Ledyard now had no doubt that he had at last returned to the "Godlike Regions of the West." He drew upon all his anthropological expertise, and experience as a world traveler, to analyze the curtain that separated Eastern Europe and Western Europe:

The quick Transition I have made of late from Kingdom to Kingdom with a kind of passive attention to their different manners has so habituated me to take notice of every thing I see, & ruminate upon them, that I believe in my heart nothing escapes me; the most delicate traits are familiar to me, & like an old American Indian Hunter I have Eyes & Ears peculiarly adapted to my Situation. . . . In other parts of my Voyage the transition has been so gentle from the different Characters of People different to each other that I sometimes lost the Gradations. . . . There also were others quite abrupt but none of them were so when I compared to the change I mark to day in entering the Dominions of the late King of Prussia.[61]

In a striking transformation of identity, harking back to his Dartmouth days, Ledyard assumed the role of the American Indian Hunter, on the trail of civilization itself. The gentle transition and gradation that he found on that trail was obviously the same as that which he repeatedly invoked when traveling in the other direction, west to east: "the nice Gradation by which I pass from Civilization to Incivilization." Now he was going east to west, passing back to civilization, but the gradation was not as nice, not as gentle, as he had previously experienced it. The passage from Poland to Prussia, the entry into Western Europe was "quite abrupt."

He summed it up in an enumeration of the vices and virtues that constituted the "inferiority of the Eastern to the Western World," the superiority of civilization:

I have within the Space of 3 English Miles leapt the great barrier of Asiatic & European manners; from Servility, Indolence, Filth, Vanity, Dishonesty, Suspicion, Jealousy, Cowardice, Knavery, Reserve, Ignorance, Bassess d'Esprit & I know not what, to everything opposite to it, busy Industry, Frankness, Neatness, well loaded Tables, plain good manners, an obliging attention, Firmness, Intelligence, &, thank God, Cheerfulness & above all Honesty, which I solemnly swear I have not looked full in the Face since I first passed to the Eastward & Northward of the Baltic. Once more welcome Europe to my warmest Embraces.[62]

His earlier sense of a "nice gradation" gave way before his experience of "the great barrier," and he located it with perfect precision. That so many qualities of manners, morality, and economy could be aligned on either side of that barrier, distinguishing the genius of Europe from "everything opposite to it," separating "Asiatic and European manners," was geographically paradoxical. After all, Ledyard had been traveling in Europe ever since he recrossed the Urals, or at least from the Volga, for more than 1,000 miles. It was a paradox that could only be resolved by the idea of Eastern Europe.

This was not ordinary geography, but, in Ledyard's term, "Philosophic Geography," the intellectual expression of the Enlightenment.

I do not know where to fix the Philosophic Geography of the other parts of Europe, but if my Vanity should ever tempt me to do it I should be sure of one spot to fix the foot of my Compass. There is something singularly decisive in the limits here marked by the great Frederick. I wish to God he had been a Tartar; his rich Genius would not have cursed all Asia with the useless Conquests of the half formed Zengis Chan, but would have chased from that ignominious & almost useless quarter of the World with equal address & vigour the baneful Sources of those Vices which have even to this very day retarded the bold & noble advances made by the Sons of Europe to a state of Society only worthy of mankind, & if I dare to subjoin the approbation of God.[63]

Frederick died two years before, in 1786, and in 1788 Ledyard could still conjure his memory and make his "rich Genius" represent the "Genius of Europe." Ledyard invoked Frederick, just as Voltaire had chronicled the adventures of Charles XII, to indulge in fantasies of conquest in Eastern Europe and beyond. For when it turned its attention to Eastern Europe, the genius of Europe was so often a genius of conquest and mastery, and always in the name of the "bold & noble advances" of civilization. When Ségur thought he had left Europe entirely, and when Ledyard, crossing in the other direction, welcomed Europe back to his warmest embraces, they both meant Western Europe. They both discovered Eastern Europe, because they needed it, as the complementary domain whose backwardness illuminated by contrast the Genius of Europe, those Angels of Civilization, in the Godlike Regions of the West.

Conclusion

Inventing Eastern Europe was a project of philosophical and geographical synthesis carried out by the men and women of the Enlightenment. Obviously, the lands of Eastern Europe were not in themselves invented or fictitious; those lands and the people who lived in them were always quite real, and did indeed lie relatively to the east of other lands that lay relatively to the west. The project of invention was not merely a matter of endowing those real lands with invented or mythological attributes, though such endowment certainly flourished in the eighteenth century. The Enlightenment's accounts were not flatly false or fictitious; on the contrary, in an age of increasingly ambitious traveling and more critical observation, those lands were more frequently visited and thoroughly studied than ever before. The work of invention lay in the synthetic association of lands, which drew upon both fact and fiction, to produce the general rubric of Eastern Europe. That rubric represented an aggregation of general and associative observations over a diverse domain of lands and peoples. It is in that sense that Eastern Europe is a cultural construction, an intellectual invention, of the Enlightenment.

To say that the work of association was an act of invention is not to say that there are no interesting resemblances between some of the lands in question; there are also, however, dramatic differences among them. Inventing Eastern Europe meant picking out the resemblances to produce a pattern of relations, and failing to note the differences that marred the pattern. An egregious example was the entry on Hungary in the great Encyclopedia, which codified knowledge according to the Enlightenment's elevated standard of critical science. When enlightened readers referred to the Encyclopedia they learned that "the language of Hungary is a dialect of Slavic," and, in consequence, "therefore it has some relation to the languages of Bohemia, Poland, and Russia." This plain error was not intended to deceive or mislead, and yet it served the purpose of establishing "some relation" among languages and lands. Other sorts of observations might appear less absolutely true or false, but any rubric of resemblance was inevitably a matter of emphasis and priority, the structuring of similarities and differences to produce a particular pattern out of the possible kaleidoscopic combinations.

The map of Europe does not actually allow for the free scope of the kaleidoscope in the reshuffling of its shapes. The points of the compass indicate directional alignments on the map, north and south, east and west, and these binary oppositions were invested with cultural significance, structured by patterns of similarity and difference, and presumptions of precedence and hierarchy. The invention of Eastern Europe was an event in intellectual history that occurred as the Enlightenment invested an overwhelming significance in the alignment of Europe according to east and west, while, correlatively, reducing and revising the significance of the Renaissance alignment according to north and south. Eastern Europe, on the map, came to exist in the analytical eye of the enlightened beholder.

The categories of analysis that framed the map of Eastern Europe revealed the agenda of the Enlightenment in affirming the relatedness of the component lands. Ségur summed up St. Petersburg in a series of binary oppositions, "the age of barbarism and that of civilization, the tenth and the eighteenth centuries, the manners of Asia and those of Europe, coarse Scythians and polished Europeans." By the middle of the nineteenth century the formulas were fixed, and Balzac could characterize all the peoples of Eastern Europe in terms of the binary contrasts "between Europe and Asia, between civilization and barbarism." The cultural framework on which Eastern Europe was constructed was one of paired analytical antitheses, defining a coherent character for diverse lands. If the opposition of Europe and Asia endowed the idea of Eastern Europe with its geographical meaning, that of civilization and barbarism gave it a philosophical meaning of urgent importance to the Enlightenment. Yet these interlocking terms of the definition were not neatly aligned any more than the lands themselves were essentially alike. The Enlightenment, for all its intense Orientalism, was very far from equating absolutely the continent of Asia with the quality of barbarism. These were only overlapping categories of analysis, and the intellectual tensions that emerged from this irregular arrangement of binary oppositions left the artifice of association among lands essentially unstable.

Such instability in the cultural construction of Eastern Europe renders that concept readily susceptible to the intellectual deconstruction of the late twentieth century. The target, however, turns out to be intriguingly elusive. The more one discovers of the tensions and contradictions that went into the invention of Eastern Europe, the more one must also recognize that the Enlightenment itself obviously relished those contradictions as the key to the whole construction. When Ségur entered Poland and felt that he "left Europe entirely," when the prince de Ligne went to the Crimea and wondered if one could ascribe to Europe a land "which resembles it so little," they defined Eastern Europe as a problem of paradox, defying conventions of resemblance and relation. The shifting borders that attended the partitions of Poland and the recessions of the Ottoman empire, even the uncertain and controversial eastern border of Europe itself—the Don, the Volga, the Urals, the Yenisei—did not undermine the idea of Eastern Europe but only enhanced a concept that flourished on its own instability.

Voltaire proposed the "unscrambling of all this chaos," first as an intellectual challenge in writing about Peter, then as a military objective in writing to Catherine, and Peyssonnel similarly sought "to unscramble the mélange" of diverse barbarians in the ancient history of Eastern Europe. Yet both Voltaire and Peyssonnel were themselves such enthusiastic scramblers of the subject that one hesitates to say whether the invention of Eastern Europe was really a matter of scrambling or of unscrambling. In fact, it was both, as the philosophes of the Enlightenment shuffled differences and resemblances over the map of Europe, so that they themselves might seek the key, and pick out the pattern. The idea of Eastern Europe never attained the definitive "otherness" of the Orient, but its parts were made to cohere within a system of related characteristics, imitating the principles of the taxonomic tables of Linnaeus. Yet the stability of such systematic coherence was inevitably undermined by overlapping influences from either side, as surely as the nomadic Tartars migrated across the intercontinental steppe, as surely as the nomadic actresses and opera singers of Paris and Venice migrated to the stages of Warsaw and St. Petersburg.

Eastern Europe is not the subject of this book. The grammar of the title emphasizes that Eastern Europe is considered here above all as an object, that is, the object of an array of intellectual operations practiced upon it by the Enlightenment in Western Europe. As the chapter titles further suggest, inventing was a function of crucial constituent operations: entering, possessing, imagining, mapping, addressing, and peopling Eastern Europe. Each approached its object somewhat differently, but all contributed to the definition and construction of what was at once a geographical domain and a philosophical idea. Entering and possessing Eastern Europe were aspects of the traveler's experience, as a calibrator of borders and transitions, as a witness of beatings and oppressions. If entry and possession are suggestive of sexual mastery—perfectly plausible in the case of Casanova—they also indicate the assumption of intellectual mastery by which Eastern Europe was made to offer itself up to the "gaze" of travelers such as Ségur, to become an object of analysis for the Enlightenment.

Imagining and mapping were not the competing operations of fantasy and science, but were closely related functions; the imagination of Voltaire fed upon geography and ranged over the map, while the cartography of the Enlightenment was deeply influenced by an unscientific imagery of Eastern Europe. Neither were fantasy and travel mutually exclusive modes, when a fictional adventurer like Baron Munchausen declared himself the rival of Tott, and an authentic traveler like the prince de Ligne registered his actual experience as a triumph of the imagination. In general, one could sort the commentators on Eastern Europe into travelers on the spot, and philosophers from afar, but in their writings they encountered each other for the joint adventure of philosophical travel. By the same token, the idea of Eastern Europe possessed both geographical and philosophical components, which Ledyard explicitly linked under concept of "Philosophic Geography." Such intellectual hybridism was hardly unique to the subject of Eastern Europe in the eighteenth century; the philosophical significance of geographical discovery was equally apparent in the Tahiti of Bougainville and Diderot. Yet, the adjacency of Eastern Europe, its relative accessibility compared to the remoteness of the South Pacific, rendered it peculiarly susceptible to a cultural construction that partook of both fact and fantasy.

Geographical adjacency also made Eastern Europe accessible to the posted letters of the Enlightenment, and the forms of epistolary address were essential to the political significance of inventing Eastern Europe. The correspondence between Voltaire and Catherine, or between Mme Geoffrin and Stanisław August, suggests that addressing Eastern Europe permitted philosophy to negotiate from afar its claim and relation to power. From Paris Eastern Europe appeared as an ideal domain for enlightened monarchy, inasmuch as despotism was displaced to a reassuring distance, and the philosophes could contribute their opinions and advice, even, in the case of Diderot, a "plan of civilization." Rousseau's Poland, as opposed to Voltaire's Russia, proposed a political theory of national identity rather than enlightened absolutism, and was framed in direct address to an entire nation instead of a single monarch. The projects of the physiocrats further confirm that Eastern Europe was constructed as an experimental domain that gave free play to the social theories and political reveries of the Enlightenment. Voltaire's Russia was the land where everything remained to be done—even "undone and redone" according to the tactless Lemercier—

while Rousseau's Poland was anyone's game, for "whoever would wish to form a regular plan for the recasting of that government."

Rousseau not only addressed the Poles directly, but also presumed to tell them who they were, to offer them a "national physiognomy." Peopling Eastern Europe was the Enlightenment's ultimate operation of intellectual mastery over this domain, daringly conceived, with dramatic consequences. Focusing on the peoples, more than just mapping the lands, the Enlightenment discovered in Eastern Europe new dimensions and disciplines in social theory, and pioneered the analytical possibilities of modern ethnography, anthropology, folklore, and racial science. In an extraordinary academic twist the conventional discipline of ancient history was made to provide the language and labels for a new anthropology, so that the barbarians of Eastern Europe who battered against the Roman and Byzantine empires were rediscovered, alive and well, in the eighteenth century. The Enlightenment saw Scythians and Sarmatians everywhere in Eastern Europe, and finally the Slavs were identified as the ethnographic key to the entire domain. Gibbon and Herder were writing about the Slavs at roughly the same time, in totally different contexts, and by placing their accounts side by side one may appreciate the crossing of disciplines that put a name to the peoples of Eastern Europe.

If Eastern Europe appears in this book as an intellectual object under construction—entered, possessed, imagined, mapped, addressed, and peopled—then the active subject may be identified from the sources, the travelers and philosophers of the Enlightenment. Yet that subject also was under construction, by its own hand and pen, inasmuch as inventing Eastern Europe was inseparably dependent upon the reciprocal process of inventing Western Europe. They came into focus together as complementary moieties, on the map and in the mind, since observers could hardly define the fundamental difference of Eastern Europe without implicitly formulating the perspective from which they observed. Voltaire took as his standard "our part of Europe," with something special in its manners and its genius; the frank possessive betrayed the personal stake of those voices that spoke of the disjunction of Europe in the eighteenth century. The invention of Eastern Europe was a subtly self-promoting and sometimes overtly self-congratulatory event in intellectual history, whereby Western Europe also identified itself and affirmed its own precedence. The evolving idea of "civilization" was essential to this process, and provided the most important philosophical term of reference for putting Eastern Europe in a position of emphatic subordination. The crucial binary opposition between civilization and barbarism assigned Eastern Europe to an ambiguous space, in a condition of backwardness, on a relative scale of development. Even from within the French Revolution, Desmoulins would only concede that "considering the point from which the Polish people departed, one sees that relatively they have made toward liberty a stride as great as ours."

Such a position of explicit relativity inevitably cut both ways and undermined both constructions, qualifying both the presumed backwardness of Eastern Europe and the assumed superiority of Western Europe. Development and direction were both relative concepts, and it was no more possible to label a land as absolutely backward than to locate it as absolutely eastern. If the physiocrat Dupont de Nemours had to go to Poland to be able to report back to Quesnay that France was "the first nation of our continent," if Ledyard the explorer had to cross Siberia to believe that "the Men of the West may become Angels," it was because the Enlightenment had already applied to France and "the Men of the West" perhaps the most comprehensive corpus of social criticism ever mobilized in an intellectual movement. From Montesquieu's *Persian Letters* to Marat's *Polish Letters*, it was perfectly apparent that the philosophes would allow to their homelands at best a relative edge, and only that in the context of an outpouring of critical reflections. When Salaberry discovered on the road to Constantinople "the more or less of civilization," he was salvaging from the social criticism of the Enlightenment, already in an age of revolution, the only affirmation that remained philosophically plausible. For that reason such an affirmation appeared all the more urgent, and the construction of Eastern Europe was invested with enormous intellectual energy precisely because the complementary construction of Western Europe was so unstable. Even the most dramatic disagreements between the philosophes, for instance between Voltaire and Rousseau, reveal them all the more clearly as participants in the same discourse about Eastern Europe, united in the discursive authority with which they addressed the object of their considerations.

The Enlightenment allowed for contest and contrast in the construction of Eastern Europe, and even insisted on paradox as something essential to its formulation, but such overt instability in the object of discourse served to mask the inherent instability of the compromised subject, engaged in its urgent other project, inventing Western Europe. The Enlightenment put all its most important concerns on the line—literally the geographical line of continental division—to deploy and develop them in the construction of Eastern Europe: the nature of man, the relation of manners and civilization, the aspiration of philosophy to political power. So, by the end of the eighteenth century Eastern Europe and Western Europe faced each other across the map on the mind of the Enlightenment, the data of geography arranged according to the priorities of philosophy, the agenda of philosophy elaborated within the contours of geography.

The idea of Eastern Europe was all the more unstable for the fact that shifting borders repeatedly redefined its political components in the course of eighteenth-century international relations. The territorial turmoil that attended the partitions of Poland and the recessions of the Ottoman empire generated geopolitical uncertainty on one side of the domain, as surely as the purely geographical uncertainty over the border between Asia and Europe ruled out any firm demarcation on the other. If international affairs contributed to the image of Eastern Europe as a domain of geopolitical chaos, of sliding borders and slipping parts, that image in turn created the cultural climate in which those affairs were conceived and reported. Diplomacy, cartography, and philosophy operated in a triangular relation of mutual endorsement, reinforcement, and justification. The connections were even explicit when the philosophical geographer was actually on diplomatic assignment, like Ségur in St. Petersburg or Hauterive in Jassy. More generally, the agenda of international relations shaped the invention of Eastern Europe according to fantasies of influence and domination. One might well argue that all knowledge offers power, that every discourse is implicitly a discourse of domination, but in the case of Eastern Europe, as in that of the Orient, one finds more precise correlations. Voltaire's *Charles XII*, the philosophical foundation for the construction of Eastern Europe, was plainly an account of military conquest. Mme Geoffrin pronounced the Poles "made to be subjugated," while Tott taught his readers "to know the Moldavians" by dramatizing a detailed strategy of corporal discipline. The idea of Eastern Europe was not always a direct stimulant to conquest, but it could sometimes be construed as a subtle invitation. Certainly, in inventing Eastern Europe the Enlightenment created the cultural context for presumptuous projects of power in the eighteenth century, and thereafter.

Voltaire's fantasies of conquest in Eastern Europe focused serially on a Swedish king, a Russian tsar, and a German princess. Although a French army occupied Prague in 1741, on the whole French ambitions in Eastern Europe in the eighteenth century were in pursuit of influence, either in the correspondence of the philosophes, or in the business of diplomatic agents. At the beginning of the nineteenth century, however, France pursued a policy of empire in Eastern Europe, as Napoleon created the "Grand Duchy of Warsaw" in 1807, the "Illyrian Provinces" in 1809, and finally invaded Russia and occupied Moscow in 1812. The political relevance of the Enlightenment's idea of Eastern Europe was quite clear from the controversy that surrounded the posthumous publication of Rulhière's *Anarchy of Poland* in 1807. The intellectual continuity that bound the early nineteenth century to the late eighteenth century was equally apparent in Ségur's memoirs of the 1780s, published only after the fall of Napoleon, for readers who could envision Moscow in flames, the city that a French army had conquered and then abandoned.

To appreciate the importance of the eighteenth-century idea of Eastern Europe for the imperialism of Napoleon, one may consider the account of the Russian campaign recorded by Philippe-Paul de Ségur, the son of Louis-Philippe. Philippe-Paul was a brigadier general and aide-de-camp to Napoleon during the campaign. He recalled that Napoleon, invading

Russia, was reading about the campaigns of Charles XII, suspecting that Voltaire's version was not entirely accurate: "Nevertheless at this critical time the name of Charles XII was constantly on his lips." The younger Ségur spoke for his fellow French soldiers as they stood before Moscow. The formulas in which he summed up their first impressions of the city matched those of his father and the previous generation: "At the sight of this gilded city, this brilliant capital uniting Europe and Asia, this majestic meetingplace of the opulence, the customs, and the arts, of the two fairest divisions of the earth, we stood still in proud contemplation. Our day of glory had come!"[1] Of course, their days of glory in Moscow were numbered.

Ségur's image of Napoleon, watching Moscow burn, assigning the blame to Russian incendiaries, summed up the previous century's construction of Eastern Europe. Napoleon allegedly exclaimed, "What a horrible sight! To do it themselves! All those palaces! What extraordinary resolution! Why, they are Scythians!" Then, on the terrible retreat from Moscow, the French marshals were muttering that Napoleon was defeated in Russia, "like Charles XII in Ukrania," and Napoleon himself, "approaching the country of the Cossacks," was similarly preoccupied. "Poltava!" he exclaimed in despair, according to Ségur.[2] Thus, passing from the memoirs of the father to the son, from the diplomatic service of Louis XVI to the military staff of Napoleon, one may observe the intellectual formulas of the Enlightenment, deployed in the military maneuvers of the next generation.

As for the great adventure in the middle of the nineteenth century, the war against Russia and assault on the Crimea undertaken by France and England under the auspices of Napoleon III and Queen Victoria, that campaign has sometimes been considered as an episode whose eccentricity derived from its outlandishly remote theater of military operations. The Crimea, however, was no whim of the Victorian imagination, Palmerstonian or Tennysonian; it was a land that had been clearly identified as a focus of fantasies and locus of conquest in the 1780s, and descended as an object of geopolitical interest to the statesmen of the 1850s. The imaginative prince de Ligne laid siege to Iphigenie at Tauride, outside Sevastopol, long before the armies of England and France besieged the fortified city. By the Treaty of Paris in 1856, the autonomy of Moldavia, Wallachia, and Serbia was recognized, and the maritime status of the Danube and the Black Sea was regulated. Such a disposition of the issues of Eastern Europe from the distance of Paris fulfilled the fantasies of the philosophes in the previous century. It was they who first constructed a map of Eastern Europe that invited the remote regard of enlightened observers to envision from afar, indeed from Paris, the presumptuous practice of operations, regulations, delimitations, and even annexations. At the Congress of Berlin in 1878 the independence of Serbia and Romania was recognized, as well as the autonomy of Bulgaria, and the Habsburg occupation of Bosnia and

Hercegovina, all involving the readjustment of borders and reassignment of territories.

Diplomatic operations from afar upon the map of Eastern Europe became standard practice in the nineteenth century, and reached their culmination at Versailles after World War I, when the political geography of Eastern Europe was revised and recast from top to bottom. It should be noted that such practice was far from altogether negative in its significance for the lands and peoples it affected, just as the Enlightenment was quite mixed, even divided, in its sympathies and appraisals concerning Eastern Europe. What remained constant was a certain fundamental imbalance in the conception of subject and object, of who operated upon whom, and from what philosophical and geographical perspective. At Versailles, where high ideals and good intentions certainly played their part, that basic imbalance was all the more evident from the dominant role of the "Big Four"—Woodrow Wilson, Lloyd George, Georges Clemenceau, and Vittorio Orlando—taken together with the outright exclusion of Bolshevik Russia.

The dilemma of Russia's exclusion or inclusion dated from long before Bolshevism and was framed philosophically prior to its most important diplomatic ramifications. The Enlightenment's idea of Eastern Europe was based upon neither definitive exclusion nor unqualified inclusion, but rather on the powerful prerogative of formulating that dilemma. The philosophers, geographers, and travelers of the eighteenth century reserved the right to decide for themselves, or to pose the problem and leave it undecided. One of the most influential travel accounts of the nineteenth century, *Russia in 1839*, by the marquis de Custine, was itself deeply influenced by the formulas and prerogatives established in the previous century. Custine seized upon the "contrasts" of St. Petersburg, "where Europe and Asia exhibit themselves to each other in mutual spectacle." With almost erotic fascination he studied "the men of pure Slavonian race," gazing deep into their eyes of "oval Asiatic shape" and detecting the subtlest nuances of expression in "those changing hues, which vary from the green of the serpent, and the grey of the cat, to the black of the gazelle, though the ground colour still remains blue." His gaze was triumphant over their eyes, as Custine warned his readers that "it is here only too easy to be deceived by the appearances of civilization," advising them that with studious attention to manners "you perceive the existence of a real barbarism."[3]

Custine insisted on the absolutely personal prerogative of distinguishing the Russians from himself and his readers: "I do not reproach the Russians for being what they are, what I blame in them is, their pretending to be what we are." He invoked the names of Voltaire and Diderot to formulate the liminal dilemma of a people "spoilt for the savage state, and yet wanting in the requisites of civilization." With perfect aristocratic aplomb he permitted the standard of civilization to make nonsense out of geography, as he located Russia in the context of Eastern Europe: "There is between France and Russia a Chinese wall—the Slavonic language and character. In spite of the notions with which Peter the Great has inspired the Russians, Siberia commences on the Vistula."[4] Almost every basic element of the eighteenth century's invention of Eastern Europe was packed into this nineteenth-century phantasmagoria, whose associations and images followed a kind of dream logic to the conclusion of continental differentiation.

One may observe that Custine's "Chinese wall" of 1839 prefigured the "iron curtain" of 1946 as the barrier between Eastern Europe and Western Europe. The analogy appears particularly important when one considers the amazing comeback of Custine in the age of the Cold War. In 1946 the book promptly appeared in a new edition in France, and in the 1950s it reached the American public with an introduction by Walter Bedell Smith, the postwar U.S. ambassador to the Soviet Union. Smith pronounced *Russia in 1839* to be "political observation so penetrating and timeless that it could be called the best work so far produced about the Soviet Union." Speaking for his embassy staff, he declared that "Custine's letters were the greatest single contribution in helping us to unravel, in part, the mysteries that seem to envelop Russia and the Russians." Furthermore, as ambassador, Smith suggested, "I could have taken many pages verbatim from his journal and, after substituting present-day names and dates for those of a century ago, have sent them to the State Department as my own official reports." This edition was republished as recently as 1987, at the very end of the Cold War, with the recommendation of Zbigniew Brzezinski on the back cover: "No Sovietologist has yet improved on de Custine's insights into the Russian character and the Byzantine nature of the Russian political system."[5] Such comments, even as they ahistorically assert the unchanging character of Russia, establish even more emphatically the unchanging characterization of Russia by foreign observers in fixed formulas. The nineteenth-century insights of Custine, which followed so closely the formulas of the Enlightenment, were recycled, celebrated, and deployed in the age of the Cold War.

Custine transmitted his message more immediately to the later nineteenth century, and his most menacing suggestions entered into a nightmarish mythology of Eastern Europe. In 1769 Herder heard the "rumbling" of "wild peoples in Eastern Europe" and warned against rousing some future demographic "inundation." A century later, in 1871, the French philosopher Ernest Renan recorded his own apocalyptic apprehensions:

The Slav, like the dragon of the Apocalypse, whose tail sweeps along a third of the stars, will one day drag behind him the herds of Central Asia, the ancient clientele of Genghis Khan and Tamerlaine. . . . Imagine what a weight will bear upon the balance of the world on the day when Bohemia, Moravia, Croatia, Serbia, all the Slavic populations of the Ottoman empire, group around the great Muscovite conglomeration.[6]

Such personal feverishness in France over Eastern Europe was matched by a public political climate in England in the 1870s, furiously aroused over the Eastern Question of Russia and the Ottoman empire in the Balkans. Gladstone's engagement on behalf of Bosnia and Bulgaria was met by Disraeli's contrary commitment to the containment of Russia. Gladstone demanded the removal of the Ottomans, "bag and baggage," from Bulgaria as reparation "to the civilization which has been affronted and shamed," while the English ambassador in Constantinople also appealed to "civilization," when he took the opposite view that England's policy need not be deflected just because "some Bashibazuks have murdered some worthless and unfortunate Bulgarians." As for Queen Victoria, she stood with Disraeli and against Russia, declaring that she would not "remain the sovereign of a country that is letting itself down to kiss the feet of the great barbarians," exclaiming, "Oh, if the Queen were a man, she would like to go and give those Russians, whose word one cannot believe, such a beating!"[7] One would almost suppose that Victoria, in her outrage, was influenced by the well-established mythology of Russian barbarism and the efficacy of the knout.

In 1914 William Sloane, professor of history at Columbia in New York, already the author of a biography of Napoleon, published a new book, *The Balkans: A Laboratory of History*. Sloane was a traveler as well as a professor and began with an account of what he had witnessed in the Balkans:

In the matter of civilization it was the past in the present, a social and semipolitical system projected three centuries forward. Wildest Europe was more picturesque and instructive than our own Mid West, because the frontier of its barbarism and civilization is not only densely populated but also, more than that, by Caucasians. Neither the yellow, red, nor black man is anywhere a problem.[8]

The whole vocabulary in which the issues of Eastern Europe were defined was that of the eighteenth century: barbarism and civilization, wildness and the frontier, the picturesque and the instructive, and finally an ingenuous note of surprise that the people were actually white. The professor further warned that with the increasing power of the Balkan states, eventually, "there will be forced upon western Europe some kind of closer union for protection against a hostile invasion of inferior civilization composed of Slavic stock, Greek Catholicism, and Oriental government." Sloane declared southeastern Europe to be not only a laboratory but also an "ethnological museum," and his own discussion of ethnology started, naturally enough, with the Scythians.[9]

The first decades of the twentieth century were exceptionally important for the academic study of Eastern Europe, which yielded in France and England scholarship that was more serious and more sympathetic than that of Sloane, though no less personally engaged, and even more ambitious in its political purposes. Indeed, the professors of the twentieth century rivaled the philosophes of the Enlightenment in their pursuit of influence on the map, entering with fierce partisanship into the controversies among rival states and nations in Eastern Europe during World War I and at Versailles. Ernest Denis of the Sorbonne, author of *Bohemia since the White Mountain* in 1903, was the founding editor in 1917 of *Le Monde Slave*, which aimed to influence France's wartime policy toward the Slavic world. R. W. Seton-Watson, whose prewar publications in London included *Racial Problems in Hungary* in 1908 and *The South Slav Question and the Habsburg Monarchy* in 1911, founded the journal *The New Europe* in 1916 and advised the British delegation at the peace conference in 1919. Harold Nicolson, a member of that diplomatic delegation, wrote that "it was the thought of the new Serbia, the new Greece, the new Bohemia, the new Poland which made our hearts sing hymns at heaven's gate," as a consequence of "long and fervent study of *The New Europe*." Nicolson claimed that he himself "never moved a yard without previous consultation with experts of the authority of Dr. Seton-Watson who was in Paris at the time."[10]

There was much to admire in the academic and political work of these experts, in their dedication to the ideals of national self-determination. Their advocacy in the remaking of the map and the delineation of borders at Versailles, for all the flaws in the final settlement, marked a high point in the modern history of academic engagement with Eastern Europe and academic influence on its geopolitical condition. These professors are the direct academic ancestors of those who now study the subject at the end of the twentieth century. Archibald Cary Coolidge, professor of history at Harvard, conducted inquiries for Woodrow Wilson and Colonel House on Eastern Europe, and Harold Nicolson said of Coolidge that "there were moments when that humane and brilliant man was the sole source of reliable information which the Peace Conference possessed."[11] Coolidge at Harvard was the professor of Robert Kerner; Kerner at Berkeley was the professor of Wayne Vucinich, and Vucinich at Stanford was my own academic adviser.

Between the world wars one may discern the first inklings of intellectual self-consciousness about the forms and phrases of analysis with which Western Europe dominated the discussion of Eastern Europe. At the apex of literature, one might consider Thomas Mann's *The Magic Mountain* of 1924, which looked back to the illness and instability of prewar Europe in the social microcosm of an Alpine sanatorium, including in its restaurant a "good" Russian table and a "bad" Russian table, assorted according to manners. The hero, Hans Castorp, is helpless before the hypnotic power of the "Kirghiz eyes," first of his schoolmate Pribislav Hippe, and then of the sanatorium guest Clavdia Chauchat, from somewhere on the steppe. At the same time Settembrini, the Italian humanist, is suspicious of Clavdia's "Tartar physiognomy," and more generally of the "Parthians and Scythians" at the good and bad Russian tables. Settembrini believes that human progress has taken a directional course, has "conquered more and more territory in Europe itself and was already pressing Asia-wards." He can detect something suspiciously unprogressive and Asiatic even in the cheekbones of Martin Luther: "I should be greatly surprised, if there were not Wendish, Slavic, Sarmatic elements in play there." [12] Thomas Mann himself stands at an author's ironic remove from these forms and sentiments at play in his fiction.

The literature of travel, however, was far more important than fiction to the already venerable tradition of Western Europe's perspective on Eastern Europe; a new self-consciousness about that tradition inevitably found expression in the tale of a traveler. In 1937 Rebecca West went to Yugoslavia, and her epic account of that voyage in *Black Lamb and Grey Falcon* still stands as the twentieth century's most overwhelming attempt to come to terms with what it meant to contemplate Eastern Europe as an intellectual from Western Europe. The Englishwoman in the Balkans was not an unprecedented figure. Lady Mary Wortley Montagu was studying Arabic poetry in Belgrade in 1717, and in 1863 Georgena Muir Mackenzie and Paulina Irby traveled through Bulgaria, Serbia, and Bosnia, bringing their own bathtub, later publishing their *Travels in the Slavonic Provinces of Turkey-in-Europe*. They sought to study "the interior of a half civilised country," citing Gladstone against the Ottomans as enemies of "the progress of civilisation," and cautioning readers that "before attempting to estimate the capabilities of the South Slavonic races, one must fully realise the effects of a Turkish occupation of more than four centuries." In Serbia they looked for "relics testifying that it was once a Christian and civilised land," Byzantine church architecture "amid the savagery of Albanian villages." [13] While these Christian Victorians earnestly hoped that the Slavs would find their way toward the progress and civilization of Western Europe, Rebecca West in the 1930s traveled a similar itinerary in the reciprocal conviction that the ailing civilization of Western Europe urgently needed to nourish itself with the spiritual resources of the Slavs. "Is it so wonderful there?" asked her husband, and she mystically replied, "Well, there is everything there. Except what we have. But that seems very little." He asked whether she meant that England had very little, and she answered, "The whole of the West." The bar of her Belgrade hotel offered a scene "that I might have seen in London or Paris or New York," for the most part: "But in none of those great cities have I seen hotel doors slowly swing open to admit, unhurried and at ease, a peasant holding a black lamb in his arms." She described him lovingly, refusing to surrender to romantic condescension, right down to the last detail, the signature detail that every traveler of the Enlightenment had noted as the badge of backwardness in Eastern Europe: his sheepskin jacket. In the market of Sarajevo, she watched an older woman, apparently full of wit and wisdom, and dubbed her "the Voltaire of this world."[14]

Rebecca West believed that Europe was incomplete without Eastern Europe, and she also knew that this realization came almost too late. In 1937 she already understood the menace of Germany to Eastern Europe, and the German villainess of the book, the detestable Gerda, offers uncompromising objections and obstructions to the author's spiritual pilgrimage: "I do not understand you, you go on saying what a beautiful country this is, and you must know perfectly well that there is no order here, no culture, but only a mish-mash of different peoples who are all quite primitive and low."[15] The epithet of "mish-mash" in Yugoslavia in the 1930s could have come from one of Georg Forster's letters from Lithuania in the 1780s. The slogans of "no order" and "no culture" were about to become the ideological accompaniment to the Nazi conquest of Eastern Europe. By the time Rebecca West was completing her manuscript, back in England in 1941, the Nazis were already bombing both London and Belgrade.

The German assaults on Czechoslovakia and Poland in 1939, followed by the invasions of Yugoslavia and the Soviet Union in 1941, suggest the geopolitical scope of Hitler's policy toward Eastern Europe as a whole, the conquest and occupation of its lands, the enslavement and extermination of its peoples. These aims were not only strategic and economic but also furiously ideological and, at the same time, peculiarly academic in the mobilization of Germany's professorial resources to address and endorse issues of policy in Eastern Europe. Just as English, French, and American professors had their say in the making of the settlement at Versailles, concerning Eastern Europe, so the German professors were called into play for the overturning of that settlement; the conquest of *Ostraum* was endorsed by the scholarship of *Ostforschung*. Albert Brackmann, professor of medieval history, spoke for the academic experts on Eastern Europe when he declared in 1935 that "our scholarly research will be involved wherever it is necessary to support and promote the interest of Germandom." After the outbreak of the war, when he was commissioned to prepare a booklet for the SS on "the destiny of Poland and Eastern Europe," he summed up the historical issues thus: "The German people were the only bearers of civilization in the East, and as the main power in Europe, defended Western civilization and brought it to the uncivilized nations." Such pious invocation of "civilization" on behalf of Nazi policy in Eastern Europe may appear altogether grotesque, but the formulas that Brackmann employed were well established within a long tradition of pronouncements about Eastern Europe. The heritage of the eighteenth century was similarly apparent in another equally distasteful demonstration of academic insight by Otto Reche, an expert on "the anthropological conditions in Poland," who worried in 1939 that even Germans in Eastern Europe were at risk for contamination by the "racial mish-mash, with strong Asiatic elements." Reche sought to present Eastern Europe as a coherent racial domain, noting "the common tendency to shorter and broader shaped heads, of lower and broader facial formation, of prominent cheekbones, primitive nasal formation and of thick, taut hair."[16] Such pointed expert scholarship served to underpin every aspect of German policy toward Eastern Europe during World War II.

It would be tempting to see these particular German experts as the evil end of the road for a certain academic approach to Eastern Europe, but, in fact, professors are survivors, and philosophical formulas are remarkably adaptable. Some of the same old professors who eagerly endorsed the agenda of the Nazis in Eastern Europe resurfaced in the postwar German academy to mouth the same old formulas, far from discredited, and neatly adapted to the ideological specifications of the Cold War. In 1952 the *Zeitschrift für Ostforschung* declared that "the frontiers of two distinct spheres of civilization run straight through Europe."[17] What made the Cold War such an epoch in the intellectual history of the idea of Eastern Europe was not only its capacity for appropriating and applying a discourse that dated back to the Enlightenment, but also its capacity for camouflaging the cultural origins of that idea. Precisely because the Soviet bloc gave the idea of Eastern Europe some substantial geopolitical significance, because Stalin succeeded far better than Catherine in assembling the empire that Voltaire only imagined, it became possible, after World War II, to neglect, forget, and obscure the fact that the division of Europe was also an ongoing work of intellectual artifice and cultural construction. If Churchill's iron curtain of 1946 followed an already established line of continental demarcation, "from Stettin in the Baltic to Trieste in the Adriatic," that line was then passed on to the academic literature on Eastern Europe of the next generation. The most venerable textbook of the postwar period, *A History of the Modern World*, by R. R. Palmer and Joel Colton, first published in 1950 and still highly regarded, introduces a chapter on "The Transformation of Eastern Europe, 1648–1740," with the observation that "for Europe as a whole a real though indefinite line ran along the Elbe and the Bohemian mountains to the head of the Adriatic Sea."[18] This echoing of Churchill offered an implicit justification for the treatment of "Eastern Europe" as a real and coherent subject rather than an anachronistic, artificial rubric, which offered a certain analytical and ideological convenience.

One fascinating literary artifact of the Cold War is a juvenile American text of 1962, entitled *Slavic Peoples*, as if in parodic allusion to Herder's section on "Slawische Völker" in the *Ideas for the Philosophy of History of Mankind*. Junky drawings of people in folk costume seemed to suggest a folkloric lumping of the Slavs, again perhaps in parody of Herder, who envisioned the Slavic celebration of "ancient festivals." The author, Thomas Caldecot Chubb, was sympathetic to his subject, beginning with a chapter called "From the Land of Gog and Magog" and concluding with the question of "What the Slavs Have Done for Us." He asked, "What, for example, has little Pyotr of Russia inherited from his long line of ancestors who have climbed from their primitive marshes? His father manufactures tractors or atomic warheads in the Donets basin or at Novosibirsk beyond the Ural Mountains." [19] In 1962, the year of the Cuban missile crisis, the Russians were being represented in America as people who had climbed out of primitive marshes. Surely, "little Pyotr" was supposed to evoke the image of big Peter, who built his capital on the marshes and brought those marshes into the Enlightenment's mythology of Russia. The relevance of that mythology for the fantasies of the Cold War was also evident in the wisdom of James Bond, in *From Russia with Love*, published in 1957: "I quite agree about the Russians. They simply don't understand the carrot. Only the stick has any effect. Basically they're masochists. They love the knout. That's why they were so happy under Stalin." When the irresistible Tatiana Romanova begs Bond to beat her if she eats too much, he readily agrees, "Certainly I will beat you." [20]

The end of the Cold War has already stimulated serious political and academic reflection on the conceptual division of Europe. Both statesmen and professors have come to recognize that the end of the iron curtain does not promise any easy or immediate reconciliation of the continental moieties, in politics, economics, or culture. What remain still relatively unappreciated are that the conceptual division of Europe dates from long before the Cold War, that the idea of Eastern Europe was originally and fundamentally a work of cultural artifice, and that the intellectual history of two centuries still profoundly influences the perceived pattern of similarities and differences across the continent. In August 1991, with the failure of the coup in the Soviet Union, when Gorbachev returned to Moscow from the Crimea, the front page of the *New York Times* declared the Russians ready "for the mammoth task of civilizing their country." This presumably unconscious quotation from Voltaire's *Peter the Great* strongly suggests the power of old formulas, according to which Russia remains always just about to begin becoming civilized, whether in the eighteenth or the twentieth century. In September the *Neue Zürcher Zeitung* in Switzerland headlined its "Hope for a European Russia," while the *Corriere della Sera* in Italy stated the dilemma even more explicitly, saluting Russia as "A Great Mother Eternal between the Orient and the Occident." The *Boston Phoenix* presented the problem of the professors: "From Red to Crimson: Why Harvard's big thinkers disagree over how to transform the Soviet Union."[21] The eighteenth-century physiocratic enterprise of prescription for Eastern Europe is alive and well in Cambridge, Massachusetts.

In March 1992, the *New York Times* commented, "Looking at the East, Western Europe knows that chaos in the former Soviet bloc will bring a flood of immigrants and refugees." Chaos in Eastern Europe was, of course, a formula favored by Voltaire. The issue of development was dramatized in the *Times* in April with the front-page headline "East Bloc Treading Water in a Sinkhole of Lethargy." An article on "ethnic battles" in May sounded the note of barbarism in an enumeration of peoples, following the form of scrambled ethnography: "The roll call of warring nationalities invokes some forgotten primer on the warring tribes of the Dark Ages— Ossetians, Georgians, Abkhasians, Daghestanis, Azeris, Armenians, Moldovans, Russians, Ukrainians, Gaugauz, Tatars, Tajiks."[22] Even the Russians were relegated to the Dark Ages in that "forgotten primer," whose roll call of warring tribes went on and on. Was it perhaps a page out of Peyssonnel?

Meanwhile, in May 1992, far from the ethnic battles in Eastern Europe, Mikhail Gorbachev came to Fulton, Missouri, to speak where Churchill spoke in 1946, to proclaim the end of the Cold War and draw a rhetorical veil over the iron curtain. Yet the cultural construction of the map of Europe divided the continent long before the Cold War, and that division persists, usually unexamined, mainly misunderstood. Gorbachev himself is one of those who has looked at the iron curtain from the other side and considered its cultural consequences. "We are Europeans," he declared in *Perestroika* in 1987. "The history of Russia is an organic part of the great European history." He too has called the roll call of peoples, but not to invoke the warring tribes of the Dark Ages: "The Russians, Ukrainians, Byelorussians, Moldavians, Lithuanians, Letts, Estonians, Karels and other peoples of our country have all made a sizable contribution to the development of European civilization."[23] With the word "civilization" he threw down the gauntlet and challenged us all to rethink our mental maps of Europe.

"In Western Europe," writes Czesław Miłosz, "it is enough to have come from the largely untraveled territories in the East or North to be regarded as a visitor from Septentrion, about which only one thing is known: it is cold." In his memoir *Rodzinna Europa* (*Native Europe*) he seeks to present himself, a Polish poet from Lithuania, in relation to the continent as a whole: "Undoubtedly I could call Europe my home, but it was a home that refused to acknowledge itself as a whole; instead, as if on the strength of some self-imposed taboo, it classified its population into two categories: members of the family (quarrelsome but respectable) and poor relations."[24] His autobiographical imperative was a wrestling with the refusal of Western Europe to recognize him as a fully enfranchised member of the family, to regard him as more than just a visitor from the cold continental frontier. So he had to tell his story: "If I want to show what a man who comes from the East of Europe is like, what can I do but tell about myself?"

My book is about the intellectuals of Western Europe, inventing Eastern Europe. As Miłosz suggests, the intellectuals of Eastern Europe have had to respond to the imposed images and formulas devised in Western Europe. The intellectual history of that response would be another book, an account of the complex cultural strategies of resistance, appropriation, deference, complicity, and counterattack pursued in the different lands of Eastern Europe. Having written a book with Western Europe as its subject, I would at least like to leave the last word to Eastern Europe. Whose voice is so commanding, what work so overwhelming, as to offer a counterblast to the brilliance, the erudition, the confidence, of the philosophes? It has to be Tolstoy; it has to be *War and Peace*. For what is the subject of *War and Peace* if not the presumptuousness of Western Europe in its invasion of Eastern Europe?

Dramatically embedded in the literary narrative of the invasion is the tension of Tolstoy's relation to the French sources—like the memoir of Philippe-Paul de Ségur, among many others—Tolstoy's dependence upon them to construct the French perspective, and yet his refusal to accept that perspective. He even quotes the French sources, and always ironically, like the labeling of Moscow as an "Asiatic capital," with its churches resembling "Chinese pagodas." In *War and Peace*, Napoleon himself, at the sight of Moscow, exclaims upon "that Asiatic city of the innumerable churches," and then imagines the city as an "Oriental beauty," a maiden he is about to ravish. He calls for a map: "In the clear morning light he gazed from the city to the map, from the map to the city, verifying details, and the certainty of possessing it agitated and awed him." Napoleon's preoccupation with the map, and the implied connection between mapping and possessing, suggest how thoroughly Tolstoy understood the Enlightenment's idea of Eastern Europe. In fact, as Napoleon looked from the map to the city, Tolstoy further demonstrated his ironic appreciation of that idea. He had Napoleon gaze upon Moscow's "ancient monuments of barbarism and despotism" and resolve to teach the Russians "the meaning of true civilization."[25]

In the epilogue of *War and Peace*, as Tolstoy cut through the historical controversy over how to explain the French invasion of Russia, he found his answer in the basic directional arrows of the compass. "The fundamental and essential point of European events at the beginning of the present century," according to Tolstoy, "is the militant mass movement of the European peoples from west to east and then from east to west." Thus he eliminated all the cultural associations attached to "west" and "east," freed them from such weighty burdens as the balance between civilization and barbarism, left only the simple vectors of motion, equal and opposite, reciprocal and reversible. After having discovered such a simple truth of science, he was inevitably ironic about modern history's regard for "the welfare of the French, German, or English people," or even "the welfare and civilization of humanity in general, by which is usually meant the peoples inhabiting a small north-western corner of a large continent."[26] Tolstoy, writing from his own corner of the continent, appreciated the issues of geographical perspective and philosophical presumption that made Europe a matter of east and west.

◆ *Reference Matter* ◆

Notes

Introduction

1. Winston Churchill, "The Iron Curtain," *Blood, Toil, Tears and Sweat: The Speeches of Winston Churchill*, ed. David Cannadine (Boston: Houghton Mifflin, 1989), pp. 303–5.

2. Tacitus, *Germania*, in *The Agricola and the Germania*, trans. H. Mattingly and S. A. Handford (London: Penguin, 1970), p. 114.

3. William Coxe, *Travels into Poland*, from *Travels into Poland, Russia, Sweden, and Denmark: Interspersed with Historical Relations and Political Inquiries* (London, 1785; rpt. New York: Arno Press and New York Times, 1971), preface.

4. Louis-Philippe, comte de Ségur, *Mémoires, souvenirs, et anecdotes, par le comte de Ségur*, vol. I, in *Bibliothèque des mémoires: relatif à l'histoire de France: pendant le 18e siècle*, vol. XIX, ed. M. Fs. Barrière (Paris: Librairie de Firmin Didot Frères, 1859); and John Ledyard, *John Ledyard's Journey Through Russia and Siberia 1787–1788: The Journal and Selected Letters*, ed. Stephen D. Watrous (Madison: Univ. of Wisconsin Press, 1966).

5. Abel Mansuy, *Le Monde slave et les classiques français aux XVIe–XVIIe siècles*, préface de Charles Diehl (Paris: Librairie Ancienne Honoré Champion, 1912), pp. 8, 10.

6. Edward W. Said, *Orientalism* (New York: Vintage Books, 1979), pp. 1–3.

7. Martin Bernal, *Black Athena: The Afroasiatic Roots of Classical Civilization*, vol. I, *The Fabrication of Ancient Greece 1785–1985* (New Brunswick, N.J.: Rutgers Univ. Press, 1987); Federico Chabod, *Storia dell'idea d'Europa* (Bari: Editori Laterza,

1965), pp. 82–121; Denys Hay, *Europe: The Emergence of an Idea* (Edinburgh: Edinburgh Univ. Press, 1968), pp. 117–27; Jean-Baptiste Duroselle, *L'Idée d'Europe dans l'histoire* (Paris: Denoël, 1965), pp. 77–133; see also Janusz Tazbir, "Poland and the Concept of Europe in the Sixteenth-Eighteenth Centuries," *European Studies Review* 7, no. 1 (Jan. 1977): 29–45.

8. Wolfgang Amadeus Mozart, *Briefe*, ed. Horst Wandrey (Zürich: Diogenes, 1982), p. 371.

9. Immanuel Wallerstein, *The Modern World-System: Capitalist Agriculture and the Origins of the European World-Economy in the Sixteenth Century* (New York: Academic Press, 1974), p. 97.

10. Ibid., p. 301.

11. Daniel Chirot, ed., *The Origins of Backwardness in Eastern Europe: Economics and Politics from the Middle Ages Until the Early Twentieth Century* (Berkeley: Univ. of California Press, 1989), pp. 1–15.

12. Harold B. Segel, *Renaissance Culture in Poland: The Rise of Humanism 1470–1543* (Ithaca, N.Y.: Cornell Univ. Press, 1989), p. 13; see also Antoni Mączak, "Progress and Under-Development in the Eyes of Renaissance and Baroque Man," *Studia Historiae Oeconomicae* 9 (1974): 77–94.

13. Mansuy, pp. 32, 56–57.

14. Ibid., pp. 14–15.

15. Jacques Margeret, *The Russian Empire and Grand Duchy of Muscovy: A 17th-Century French Account*, trans. Chester S. L. Dunning (Pittsburgh, Pa.: Univ. of Pittsburgh Press, 1983), pp. 8, 10, 23.

16. John Smith, *Travels and Works of Captain John Smith: President of Virginia, and Admiral of New England, 1580–1631*, ed. Edward Arber, Part II (Edinburgh: John Grant, 1910), pp. 805, 857, 866–68.

17. Adam Olearius, *The Travels of Olearius in Seventeenth-Century Russia*, trans. Samuel H. Baron (Stanford, Calif.: Stanford Univ. Press, 1967), pp. 126–47; see also Walter Leitsch, "Westeuropäische Reiseberichte über den Moskauer Staat," in *Reiseberichte als Quellen europäischer Kulturgeschichte: Aufgaben und Möglichkeiten der historischen Reiseforschung*, ed. Antoni Mączak and Hans Jürgen Teuteberg (Wolfenbüttel: Herzog August Bibliothek, 1982), pp. 153–76.

18. John Milton, *A Brief History of Moscovia: And of Other Less-Known Countries Lying Eastward of Russia as far as Cathay* (London: Blackamore Press, 1929), p. 32.

19. James Boswell, *The Life of Samuel Johnson*, ed. Frank Brady (New York: New American Library, 1968), pp. 236–37.

20. Norbert Elias, *The History of Manners*, trans. Edmund Jephcott (New York: Pantheon Books, 1978), pp. 44–50; Joachim Moras, *Ursprung und Entwicklung des Begriffs der Zivilisation in Frankreich (1756–1830)*, in *Hamburger Studien zu Volkstum und Kultur der Romanen*, vol. 6 (Hamburg: Seminar für romanische Sprachen und Kultur, 1930), pp. 4–8, 32–43, 46–47, 55–57, 63; and Lucien Febvre, "*Civilisation*: Evolution of a Word and a Group of Ideas," *A New Kind of History: From the Writings of Febvre*, ed. Peter Burke, trans. K. Folca (New York: Harper & Row, 1973), pp. 219–57.

21. Ségur, I, pp. 329–30.

22. Honoré de Balzac, *Cousin Bette*, trans. Marion Ayton Crawford (London: Penguin, 1965), pp. 229–30.

23. Larry Wolff, *The Vatican and Poland in the Age of the Partitions: Diplomatic and Cultural Encounters at the Warsaw Nunciature* (New York and Boulder: Columbia Univ. Press, East European Monographs, 1988), p. 178.

24. Timothy Garton Ash, "Does Central Europe Exist?" *The New York Review of Books* (Oct. 9, 1986), republished in *The Uses of Adversity: Essays on the Fate of Central Europe* (New York: Random House, 1989), pp. 179–213; Timothy Garton Ash, "Mitteleuropa?" *Daedalus: Journal of the American Academy of Arts and Sciences* 119, no. 1 (Winter 1990): *Eastern Europe . . . Central Europe . . . Europe*, pp. 1–21; see also Krishan Kumar, "The 1989 Revolutions and the Idea of Europe," *Political Studies* 40 (1992): 439–61; and R. J. W. Evans, "Essay and Reflection: Frontiers and National Identities in Central Europe," *The International History Review* 14, no. 3 (Aug. 1992), pp. 480–502; and Robin Okey, "Central Europe/Eastern Europe: Behind the Definitions," *Past and Present* 137 (Nov. 1992), pp. 102–33; and Iver B. Neumann, "Russia as Central Europe's Constituting Other," *East European Politics and Societies* 7, no. 2 (Spring 1993), pp. 349–69.

25. Mikhail Gorbachev, *Perestroika: New Thinking for Our Country and the World* (1987; New York: Harper & Row, Perennial Library, 1988), pp. 177, 180.

One ◆ Entering Eastern Europe

1. Louis-Philippe, comte de Ségur, *Mémoires, souvenirs, et anecdotes, par le comte de Ségur*, vol. I, in *Bibliothèque des mémoires: relatif à l'histoire de France: pendant le 18e siècle*, vol. XIX, ed. M. Fs. Barrière (Paris: Librairie de Firmin Didot Frères, 1859), pp. 288–89, 293.

2. Ibid., I, p. 293.   3. Ibid., I, p. 300.

4. Ibid.   5. Ibid., I, p. 301.

6. Ibid., I, p. 302.   7. Ibid., I, p. 301.

8. Ibid., I, pp. 316–17.   9. Ibid., I, pp. 329–30.

10. Ibid., I, pp. 332–33.   11. Ibid., I, p. 333.

12. Ibid., I, p. 399.

13. Louis-Philippe, comte de Ségur, *Mémoires, souvenirs, et anecdotes, par le comte de Ségur*, vol. II, in *Bibliothèque des mémoires: relatif à l'histoire de France: pendant le 18e siècle*, vol. XX, ed. M. Fs. Barrière (Paris: Librairie de Firmin Didot Frères, 1859), p. 93.

14. Ibid., II, p. 93.

15. Ségur, I, p. 356.

16. Peter Putnam, ed., *Seven Britons in Imperial Russia 1698–1812* (Princeton, N.J.: Princeton Univ. Press, 1952), pp. 237–41; see also "Coxe, William," *Dictionary of National Biography* (Oxford Univ. Press), Vol. IV, pp. 1346–47.

17. William Edward Mead, *The Grand Tour in the Eighteenth Century* (Boston: Houghton Mifflin, 1914), p. 4.

18. William Coxe, *Travels into Poland*, from *Travels into Poland, Russia, Sweden, and Denmark: Interspersed with Historical Relations and Political Inquiries* (London, 1785; rpt. New York: Arno Press and New York Times, 1971), p. 122.

19. Ibid., p. 125.

20. Ibid., pp. 148–49.

21. Elizabeth Craven, *A Journey Through the Crimea to Constantinople: In a Series*

of Letters from the Right Honourable Elizabeth Lady Craven, to His Serene Highness the Margrave of Brandebourg, Anspach, and Bareith, Written in the Year MDCCLXXXVI (Dublin, 1789; rpt. New York: Arno Press and New York Times, 1970), p. 158.

22. Coxe, *Travels into Poland*, pp. 186–87.

23. Ségur, I, p. 329; Coxe, *Travels into Poland*, p. 150.

24. Coxe, *Travels into Poland*, pp. 191, 197, 199.

25. Ibid., p. 193.   26. Ibid., pp. 142, 188, 201, 205.

27. Ibid., pp. 143–44.   28. Ibid., p. 209.

29. Ibid.   30. Ibid., pp. 209–10.

31. Ibid., p. 205; Coxe, *Travels in Poland and Russia*, from *Travels in Poland, Russia, Sweden, and Denmark*, 5th ed. (London, 1802; rpt. New York: Arno Press and New York Times, 1970), I, p. 251.

32. Coxe, *Travels in Poland and Russia*, I, pp. 255–56, 272; see also Anthony Cross, "British Knowledge of Russian Culture (1698–1801)," *Canadian-American Slavic Studies* 13, no. 4 (Winter 1979): 412–35.

33. Coxe, *Travels in Poland and Russia*, I, pp. 267, 270.

34. Ibid., I, pp. 271–72; II, pp. 68–69.

35. Ibid., I, p. 268.   36. Ibid., I, p. 277.

37. Ibid., I, p. 283.   38. Ibid., I, pp. 283–85.

39. Ibid., I, pp. 287–89.   40. Ibid., I, pp. 306–7.

41. Ibid., II, pp. 66, 69, 70.   42. Ibid., II, pp. 62, 64, 67, 72.

43. Ibid., II, pp. 77, 91–94.   44. Ibid., II, pp. 97–98.

45. Ibid., II, p. 107.   46. Ibid., II, pp. 104, 134.

47. Ibid., II, pp. 121–22.   48. Ibid., II, pp. 140, 156.

49. Lady Mary Wortley Montagu, *The Complete Letters of Lady Mary Wortley Montagu*, ed. Robert Halsband, Vol. I (1708–20) (Oxford: Clarendon Press, 1965), pp. 293–96.

50. Ibid., pp. 295–97.

51. Ibid., p. 297.

52. Gyula Antalffy, *A Thousand Years of Travel in Old Hungary*, trans. Elisabeth Hoch (Hungary: Kner, 1980), p. 220.

53. Lady Mary Wortley Montagu, pp. 297–99.

54. Ibid., pp. 301–3.

55. Ibid., p. 305.

56. Antalffy, pp. 114–18.

57. Lady Mary Wortley Montagu, p. 307.

58. Ibid., pp. 304, 316.   59. Ibid., pp. 313–14, 320.

60. Ibid., pp. 309–10, 312.   61. Ibid., p. 337.

62. "Salaberry," *La Grande Encyclopédie* (Paris: Librairie Larousse, 1886–1902), vol. 29, pp. 326–27; Jean-Louis Carra, *Histoire de la Moldavie et de la Valachie* (Jassy: Société Typographique des Deux-Ponts, 1777), p. xv.

63. Charles-Marie, marquis de Salaberry d'Irumberry, *Voyage à Constantinople, en Italie, et aux îles de l'Archipel, par l'Allemagne et la Hongrie* (Paris: Imprimerie de Crapelet, 1799), pp. 65–66, 69.

64. Ibid., pp. 76, 81.   65. Ibid., pp. 82–83.

66. Antalffy, pp. 189–92.   67. Salaberry, pp. 86, 91–92.

68. Ibid., pp. 97–98.
70. Salaberry, pp. 102–4, 110.
72. Ibid., p. 124.
73. Ibid., pp. 82, 125; Lady Mary Wortley Montagu, p. 340.
74. Salaberry, pp. 134, 138.
75. Salaberry, p. 143.
76. Lady Mary Wortley Montagu, p. 358; Salaberry, p. 145.
77. Salaberry, pp. 214–16.
79. Ibid., pp. 184–86.
81. Ibid., p. 148.

69. Antalffy, pp. 194, 201.
71. Ibid., pp. 100–101.

78. Ibid., p. 167.
80. Ibid., p. 152.

Two ◆ *Possessing Eastern Europe*

1. Giacomo Casanova, *History of My Life*, trans. Willard Trask, Vol. 10 (London: Longman, 1971), p. 99.
2. Casanova, *History of My Life*, pp. 110–12.
3. Casanova, *History of My Life*, pp. 112–13.
4. R. R. Palmer and Joel Colton, "The Transformation of Eastern Europe, 1648–1740," in *A History of the Modern World*, 3rd ed. (New York: Alfred A. Knopf, 1965), p. 174; see also Jerome Blum, "The Rise of Serfdom in Eastern Europe," *American Historical Review* 62, no. 4 (July 1957): 807–36.
5. Casanova, *History of My Life*, pp. 113–14.
6. Voltaire and Catherine, *Correspondence*, in *Documents of Catherine the Great: The Correspondence with Voltaire and the Instruction of 1767*, ed. W. F. Reddaway (1931; New York: Russell & Russell, 1971), p. 159.
7. Casanova, *History of My Life*, p. 135.
8. Ibid., pp. 114–16; Casanova, *The Life and Memoirs of Casanova*, Vol. I, trans. Arthur Machen, ed. George Dunning Gribble (1929; rpt. New York: Da Capo, 1984), p. 320.
9. Casanova, *History of My Life*, pp. 114–15.
10. Ibid., pp. 114–16.
11. Ibid., p. 119.
12. Casanova, *The Life and Memoirs*, p. 138.
13. Casanova, *History of My Life*, p. 120.
14. Ibid., p. 130.
16. Ibid., p. 121.
18. Marquis de Sade, *Juliette*, trans. Austryn Wainhouse (New York: Grove Press, 1968), p. 891.
19. Casanova, *History of My Life*, pp. 124–25.
20. Ibid., p. 125.
22. Ibid., pp. 129–30.
24. Ibid., pp. 138–42.
26. Ibid., p. 133.
28. Ibid., p. 156.
30. Ibid.
32. Ibid., p. 202.

15. Ibid., p. 118.
17. Ibid., pp. 121–22.

21. Ibid., p. 127.
23. Ibid., p. 131.
25. Ibid., p. 132.
27. Ibid., p. 154.
29. Ibid.
31. Ibid., p. 177.
33. Ibid.

34. Louis-Philippe, comte de Ségur, *Mémoires, souvenirs, et anecdotes, par le comte de Ségur*, vol. I, in *Bibliothèque des mémoires: relatif à l'histoire de France: pendant le 18e siècle*, vol. XIX, ed. M. Fs. Barrière (Paris: Librairie de Firmin Didot Frères, 1859), pp. 300, 329.

35. Ibid., I, p. 331.　　　　　　　36. Ibid., I, p. 432.
37. Ibid., I, p. 343.　　　　　　　38. Ibid., I, p. 345.
39. Ibid., I, pp. 338–40.　　　　　40. Ibid., I, pp. 341–43.

41. Louis-Philippe, comte de Ségur, *Mémoires, souvenirs, et anecdotes, par le comte de Ségur*, vol. II, in *Bibliothèque des mémoires: relatif à l'histoire de France: pendant le 18e siècle*, vol. XX, ed. M. Fs. Barrière (Paris: Librairie de Firmin Didot Frères, 1859), pp. 9–10.

42. Ibid., I, pp. 336–37.　　　　　43. Ibid., II, p. 79.
44. Ibid., II, p. 80.　　　　　　　45. Ibid.
46. Ibid., II, pp. 165–68.

47. Samuel Eliot Morison, *John Paul Jones: A Sailor's Biography* (1959; New York: Time Incorporated, 1964), pp. 388–93.

48. Morison, p. 13.

49. Ibid., pp. 406–9; Ségur, II, p. 166.

50. Ségur, II, pp. 170, 178.

51. Bernard Lewis, *The Emergence of Modern Turkey*, 2nd ed. (Oxford: Oxford Univ. Press, 1968), pp. 48–49.

52. François de Tott, *Mémoires du baron de Tott sur les Turcs et les Tartares* (Amsterdam, 1785), "Discours préliminaire," pp. vii–xxi; Tott, "Premiere partie" (I), p. 5.

53. Tott, "Seconde partie" (II), p. 6; see also A. M. F. Verdy du Vernois, *Essais de Géographie, de Politique, et d'Histoire sur les possessions de l'Empereur des Turcs en Europe: pour servir de suite aux Mémoires du Baron de Tott* (London, 1785).

54. Tott, II, p. 11.

55. Ibid., II, pp. 12–13.

56. Ibid., II, pp. 14–15.

57. Lady Mary Wortley Montagu, *The Complete Letters of Lady Mary Wortley Montagu*, ed. Robert Halsband, Vol. I (1708–20) (Oxford: Clarendon Press, 1965), p. 311.

58. Tott, II, p. 17.

59. Ibid., II, pp. 18–20.

60. Ibid., II, pp. 21–23.

61. Elizabeth Craven, *A Journey Through the Crimea to Constantinople: In a Series of Letters from the Right Honourable Elizabeth Lady Craven, to His Serene Highness the Margrave of Brandebourg, Anspach, and Bareith, Written in the Year MDCCLXXXVI* (Dublin, 1789; rpt. New York: Arno Press and New York Times, 1970), pp. 372, 382.

62. William Coxe, *Travels in Poland and Russia*, from *Travels in Poland, Russia, Sweden, and Denmark*, 5th ed. (London, 1802; rpt. New York: Arno Press and New York Times, 1970), I, pp. 389–90.

63. Ibid., I, p. 391.　　　　　　　64. Ibid., I, pp. 392–93.
65. Ibid., I, p. 392.　　　　　　　66. Ibid., II, p. 74.
67. Ibid.　　　　　　　　　　　　68. Ibid., I, p. 390.

69. Gyula Antalffy, *A Thousand Years of Travel in Old Hungary*, trans. Elisabeth Hoch (Hungary: Kner, 1980), pp. 198–201.

70. Charles-Marie, marquis de Salaberry d'Irumberry, *Voyage à Constantinople, en Italie, et aux îles de l'Archipel, par l'Allemagne et la Hongrie* (Paris: Imprimerie de Crapelet, 1799), p. 89.

71. Ibid., p. 95.

72. Coxe, *Travels in Poland and Russia*, III, pp. 116–17; see also Anthony Cross, "The Philanthropist, the Travelling Tutor, and the Empress: British Visitors and Catherine II's Plans for Penal and Medical Reform," in *Russia and the World of the Eighteenth Century*, eds. R. P. Bartlett, A. G. Cross, and Karen Rasmussen (Columbus, Ohio: Slavic Publishers, 1988), pp. 214–28.

73. Coxe, *Travels in Poland and Russia*, III, p. 110.

74. Ibid., III, pp. 110–11.

75. Ibid.

76. Sade, *Juliette*, pp. 882, 885.

77. Joseph Marshall, *Travels Through Germany, Russia, and Poland in the Years 1769 and 1770* (London, 1772; rpt. New York: Arno Press and New York Times, 1971), pp. 126, 167, 243.

78. John Parkinson, *A Tour of Russia, Siberia, and the Crimea, 1792–1794*, ed. William Collier (London: Frank Cass, 1971), p. 11.

79. Marshall, pp. 142, 147, 151.

80. Charles Secondat, baron de Montesquieu, *The Spirit of the Laws*, trans. Thomas Nugent (New York: Hafner, 1949), Vol. I, p. 235; Marshall, p. 143.

81. Marshall, pp. 146, 196.

82. Ibid., p. 188.

83. Ibid., pp. 122, 270–71, 308.

84. Peter Putnam, ed., *Seven Britons in Imperial Russia 1698–1812* (Princeton, N.J.: Princeton Univ. Press, 1952), pp. 125–40; and "Richardson, William," *Dictionary of National Biography* (Oxford Univ. Press), Vol. XVI, p. 1139.

85. William Richardson, *Anecdotes of the Russian Empire: In a Series of Letters Written, a Few Years Ago, from St. Petersburg* (London, 1784; rpt. London: Frank Cass, 1968), pp. 51–54, 203–6.

86. Ibid., pp. 6, 475.

87. Ibid., pp. 68–70, 215, 247.

88. Ibid., pp. 374–75; see also Franco Venturi, "From Scotland to Russia: An Eighteenth-Century Debate on Feudalism," in *Great Britain and Russia in the Eighteenth Century: Contacts and Comparisons*, ed. Anthony Cross (Newtonville, Mass.: Oriental Research Partners, 1979), pp. 2–24.

89. Richardson, p. 193.

90. Ibid., pp. 193–96, 222.

91. Ibid., pp. 39, 417.

92. Ibid., p. 233.

93. Ibid., p. 197.

94. Ibid., p. 199.

95. Ibid., p. 239.

96. Ibid., pp. 240–41.

97. Ibid., pp. 242–43.

98. Ibid., p. 241.

99. Ibid., pp. 244–49.

100. Ibid., pp. 253–54, 453; and David Brion Davis, *The Problem of Slavery in Western Culture* (Ithaca, N.Y.: Cornell Univ. Press, 1966), chapter XIII.

101. Coxe, *Travels in Poland and Russia*, III, p. 133.

102. Ibid., III, p. 135.

103. Ibid., III, pp. 134–35, 152–53.

104. Ibid., III, p. 158.

105. Ibid., III, p. 156.

Three ◆ *Imagining Eastern Europe*

1. Voltaire, *Histoire de Charles XII* (Paris: Garnier-Flammarion, 1968), p. 44; see also Lionel Gossman, "Voltaire's *Charles XII*: History into art," *Studies on Voltaire and the Eighteenth Century*, ed. Theodore Besterman, Vol. XXV (Geneva: Institut et Musée Voltaire, 1963), pp. 691–720; and J. H. Brumfitt, *Voltaire: Historian* (London: Oxford Univ. Press, 1958), pp. 5–25; and Furio Diaz, *Voltaire Storico* (Turin: Giulio Einaudi, 1958), pp. 77–109.

2. Voltaire, *Histoire de Charles XII*, p. 49.

3. Ibid., pp. 53, 68–72.

4. Ibid., pp. 118, 123–24.

5. Ibid., p. 126; Michel Foucault, *The Order of Things: An Archaeology of the Human Sciences* (New York: Vintage Books, 1973), p. 144.

6. Voltaire, *Histoire de Charles XII*, pp. 129–30.

7. Ibid., p. 125.

8. Ibid., pp. 157–58.

9. Ibid., p. 115.

10. Ibid., pp. 202–3; Charles-Marie, marquis de Salaberry d'Irumberry, *Voyage à Constantinople, en Italie, et aux îles de l'Archipel, par l'Allemagne et la Hongrie* (Paris: Imprimerie de Crapelet, 1799), p. 146.

11. Voltaire, *Histoire de Charles XII*, pp. 60, 97, 124, 130; Foucault, *Discipline and Punish: The Birth of the Prison*, trans. Alan Sheridan (New York: Vintage Books, 1979), p. 215.

12. Carolus Linnaeus, *Systema Naturae, 1735: Facsimile of the First Edition*, eds. M. S. J. Engel-Ledeboer and H. Engel (Nieuwkoop: B. de Graaf, 1964), p. 19.

13. Gotthold Ephraim Lessing, "Zeitungsartikel und Rezensionen: Berlinische privilegirte Zeitung, 1751," *Werke*, vol. VII (Hildesheim: Georg Olms Verlag, 1970), pp. 159–60.

14. Gotthold Ephraim Lessing, "Der Horoskop," *Werke*, vol. VIII (Hildesheim: Georg Olms Verlag, 1970), pp. 196–204.

15. Johann Gottfried Herder, *Journal meiner Reise im Jahr 1769*, ed. Katharina Mommsen (Stuttgart: Philipp Reclam, 1976), p. 78.

16. Voltaire, "Le Russe à Paris," in *Oeuvres complètes de Voltaire*, Vol. 10 (Paris, 1878; rpt. Liechtenstein: Kraus Reprint Limited, 1967), pp. 119–31.

17. Jean-Paul Marat, *Polish Letters* (Boston, 1905; rpt. New York: Benjamin Blom, 1971), I, p. 200.

18. Ibid., I, pp. 101, 122–23, 147, 167.

19. Ibid., I, pp. 168, 172, 180, 211.

20. Ibid., II, pp. 1–3.

21. Miss Jane Porter, *Thaddeus of Warsaw: A Tale Founded on Polish Heroism* (New York: A. L. Burt, n.d.), p. ix; Honoré de Balzac, *Cousin Bette*, trans. Marion Ayton Crawford (London: Penguin, 1965), p. 73; George Eliot, *Middlemarch*, ed. W. J. Harvey (London: Penguin, 1965), p. 895; Louisa May Alcott, "My Boys," in *Aunt Jo's Scrapbag*, ed. Helen Martin (Boston: Little, Brown, 1929), p. 326.

22. Marat, *Polish Letters*, I, pp. 106, 114, 181; II, pp. 65, 136–37, 199.

23. Ibid., II, pp. 211–12.

24. Jean-Jacques Rousseau, *The Social Contract*, trans. Maurice Cranston (London: Penguin, 1968), p. 49; Marat, *Polish Letters*, II, p. 213.

25. Rudolf Eric Raspe, *The Travels and Surprising Adventures of Baron Munchausen* (London: Dedalus, 1988), p. 9; "Raspe, Rudolf Eric," *Dictionary of National Biography* (Oxford Univ. Press), Vol. XVI, pp. 744–46; Percy G. Adams, *Travelers and Travel Liars, 1660–1800* (Berkeley: Univ. of California Press, 1962), pp. 216–17.

26. Raspe, pp. 10–13. 27. Ibid., pp. 13, 17.

28. Ibid., pp. 23–24. 29. Ibid., p. 23.

30. Ibid., p. 75; Marquis de Sade, *Juliette*, trans. Austryn Wainhouse (New York: Grove Press, 1968), p. 875.

31. Raspe, p. 29.

32. William Richardson, *Anecdotes of the Russian Empire: In a Series of Letters Written, a Few Years Ago, from St. Petersburg* (London, 1784; rpt. London: Frank Cass, 1968), p. 177.

33. William Coxe, *Travels in Poland and Russia*, from *Travels in Poland, Russia, Sweden, and Denmark*, 5th ed. (London, 1802; rpt. New York: Arno Press and New York Times, 1970), II, pp. 244–45; Raspe, pp. 32–37.

34. Raspe, p. 82. 35. Ibid., pp. 191–92.

36. Ibid., pp. 240–48. 37. Ibid., p. 253.

38. Wolfgang Amadeus Mozart, *Briefe*, ed. Horst Wandrey (Zürich: Diogenes, 1982), pp. 370–71.

39. Paul Nettl, *Mozart in Böhmen*, neubearbeitete und erweiterte Ausgabe von Rudolph Freiherrn von Prochazkas *Mozart in Prag* (Prague: Verlag Neumann, 1938), pp. 96–97.

40. Friedrich Melchior von Grimm, "The Little Prophet of Boehmischbroda," in *Source Readings in Music History: The Classic Era*, ed. Oliver Strunk (New York: Norton, 1965), pp. 60–61.

41. Hester Lynch Piozzi, *Observations and Reflections: Made in the Course of a Journey Through France, Italy, and Germany*, ed. Herbert Barrows (Ann Arbor: Univ. of Michigan Press, 1967), p. 383.

42. Nettl, pp. 57–65.

43. Eduard Mörike, "Mozart on the Way to Prague," trans. Walter and Catherine Alison Philips, in *German Novellas of Realism*, I, ed. Jeffrey L. Sammons (New York: Continuum, 1989), p. 255; Wolfgang Amadeus Mozart, *Mozarts Briefe*, ed. Wilhelm A. Bauer and Otto Erich Deutsch (Frankfurt: Fischer Bücherei, 1960), p. 149.

44. Giacomo Casanova, *Casanova's Icosameron*, trans. Rachel Zurer (New York: Jenna Press, 1986), pp. 20–22.

45. Nettl, p. 158.

46. Lorenzo Da Ponte, *Memorie*, in *Memorie, I libretti mozartiani: Le Nozze di Figaro, Don Giovanni, Così fan tutte* (Milan: Garzanti, 1981), p. 129.

47. Isabel de Madariaga, *Russia in the Age of Catherine the Great* (New Haven, Conn.: Yale Univ. Press, 1981), p. 534; Andrew Steptoe, *The Mozart–Da Ponte Operas: The Cultural and Musical Background to Le Nozze di Figaro, Don Giovanni, and Così fan tutte* (Oxford: Clarendon Press, 1988), p. 39.

48. Nettl, pp. 79–80. 49. Ibid., p. 193.

50. Ibid., pp. 201–2. 51. Ibid., pp. 216–21.

52. Da Ponte, *Memorie*, pp. 168–69. 53. Ibid., pp. 141–42.

54. Nettl, pp. 207–8. 55. Ibid., p. 238.

56. Jean Fabre, *Stanislas-Auguste Poniatowski et l'Europe des Lumières: Etude de Cosmopolitisme* (Paris: Editions Ophrys, 1952), p. 462.

57. Da Ponte, *Così fan tutte*, in *Memorie, I libretti mozartiani: Le Nozze di Figaro, Don Giovanni, Così fan tutte* (Milan: Garzanti, 1981), p. 622.

58. Ibid., p. 680.

59. Ibid., p. 685.

60. Johann Pezzl, *Sketch of Vienna*, in H. C. Robbins Landon, *Mozart and Vienna* (New York: Schirmer, 1991), pp. 65–66.

61. Alexandre-Maurice Blanc de Lanautte, comte d'Hauterive, "Journal inedit d'un voyage: de Constantinople à Jassi, capitale de la Moldavie dans l'hiver de 1785," in *Mémoire sur l'état ancien et actuel de la Moldavie: Présenté à S. A. S. le prince Alexandre Ypsilanti, Hospodar régnant, en 1787, par le comte d'Hauterive* (Bucharest: L'Institut d'arts graphiques Carol Göbl, 1902), p. 286; see also "Hauterive," *La Grande Encyclopédie* (Paris: Librairie Larousse, 1886–1902), vol. 19, pp. 935–36.

62. Hauterive, pp. 301, 305.
63. Ibid., p. 295.
64. Ibid., p. 299.
65. Ibid., pp. 293, 304.
66. Ibid., pp. 302–4.
67. Ibid., p. 305.
68. Ibid., pp. 306–7.
69. Ibid., pp. 307–8.
70. Ibid., pp. 309–10.
71. Ibid., pp. 310–11.
72. Ibid., p. 312.
73. Ibid., pp. 311–13.
74. Ibid., p. 315.
75. Ibid., p. 317.
76. Ibid., p. 318.
77. Ibid., p. 323.
78. Ibid., p. 327.

79. Elizabeth Craven, *A Journey Through the Crimea to Constantinople: In a Series of Letters from the Right Honourable Elizabeth Lady Craven, to His Serene Highness the Margrave of Brandebourg, Anspach, and Bareith, Written in the Year MDCCLXXXVI* (Dublin, 1789; rpt. New York: Arno Press and New York Times, 1970), pp. 361–62; see also "Anspach, Elizabeth," *Dictionary of National Biography* (Oxford Univ. Press), Vol. I, pp. 508–9.

80. Craven, pp. 372, 377, 380.
81. Ibid., pp. 392–96.
82. Ibid., pp. 401–9.
83. Ibid., p. 5.
84. Ibid., pp. 146, 153, 156–57, 161–62.
85. Ibid., pp. 171–72.
86. Ibid., pp. 167–71.
87. Ibid., pp. 168, 174–75.

88. Johann Wolfgang von Goethe, *Italian Journey: 1786–1788*, trans. W. H. Auden and Elizabeth Mayer (San Francisco: North Point Press, 1982), pp. 115–16.

89. Johann Wolfgang von Goethe, *Iphigenia in Tauris*, trans. Charles E. Passage (New York: Frederick Ungar, 1963), pp. 21–22.

90. Craven, pp. 184, 191.
91. Ibid., pp. 194, 200, 205, 214–17.
92. Ibid., p. 225.
93. Ibid., pp. 233–34.
94. Ibid., p. 234.
95. Ibid., p. 247.
96. Ibid., pp. 248–49.
97. Ibid., p. 249.

98. Louis-Philippe, comte de Ségur, *Mémoires, souvenirs, et anecdotes, par le comte de Ségur*, vol. II, in *Bibliothèque des mémoires: relatif à l'histoire de France: pendant le 18e siècle*, vol. XX, ed. M. Fs. Barrière (Paris: Librairie de Firmin Didot Frères, 1859), p. 87.

99. Louis-Philippe, comte de Ségur, *Mémoires, souvenirs, et anecdotes, par le comte de Ségur*, vol. I, in *Bibliothèque des mémoires: relatif à l'histoire de France: pendant le 18e siècle*, vol. XIX, ed. M. Fs. Barrière (Paris: Librairie de Firmin Didot Frères, 1859), pp. 428–29.

100. Ibid., I, p. 425.   101. Ibid., II, pp. 34, 41.

102. Ibid., I, p. 429.   103. Ibid., I, pp. 429–30, 434.

104. Ibid., I, p. 436.   105. Ibid., I, pp. 436–37.

106. Ibid., I, pp. 438–39.   107. Ibid., II, pp. 1–2.

108. Ibid., II, p. 4.   109. Ibid., II, p. 6.

110. Ibid., I, pp. 422–23; II, p. 14.   111. Ibid., II, pp. 13, 30.

112. Charles-Joseph, prince de Ligne, *Correspondance et pensées du prince de Ligne*, in *Bibliothèque des mémoires: relatif à l'histoire de France: pendant le 18e siècle*, vol. XX, ed. M. Fs. Barrière (Paris: Librairie de Firmin Didot Frères, 1859), p. 72.

113. Ségur, II, p. 21.

114. Ibid., II, pp. 30–36.

115. Ibid., II, pp. 32, 41–43; Ligne, p. 69.

116. Ségur, II, p. 44.

117. Ibid., I, p. 423; Ligne, pp. 70–71.

118. Ségur, II, pp. 51, 55; Ligne, p. 75.

119. Ségur, II, p. 47.

120. Ibid., II, p. 54.

121. Ibid., II, pp. 57–58; Goethe, *Italian Journey*, p. 318.

122. Ligne, p. 71; Goethe, *Italian Journey*, p. 324.

123. Ségur, I, p. 374.   124. Ibid., II, p. 60; Ligne, p. 88.

125. Ségur, II, pp. 63–65.   126. Ibid., II, p. 64.

127. Ligne, pp. 73–74.   128. Ibid., p. 92.

129. Ségur, II, pp. 67–70; John T. Alexander, *Catherine the Great: Life and Legend* (Oxford: Oxford Univ. Press, 1989), p. 260.

130. Ligne, pp. 77–81; Goethe, *Italian Journey*, pp. 26, 116, 124.

131. Ligne, p. 82.   132. Ibid., pp. 82–85.

133. Ségur, II, p. 72.   134. Ibid., II, pp. 72–74.

135. Ligne, p. 89.   136. Ségur, II, p. 85.

137. Ibid., II, pp. 96–97.   138. Ibid., II, p. 97.

139. Ligne, p. 86.   140. Ségur, II, p. 88.

141. Ibid., II, p. 90.   142. Ibid., II, pp. 87–89.

Four ◆ *Mapping Eastern Europe*

1. Voltaire, *Histoire de Charles XII* (Paris: Garnier-Flammarion, 1968), p. 113; J. B. Harley, "Maps, Knowledge, and Power," in *The Iconography of Landscape: Essays on the Symbolic Representation, Design and Use of Past Environments*, ed. Denis Cosgrove and Stephen Daniels (Cambridge: Cambridge Univ. Press, 1988), pp. 277–312.

2. Nicolas Sanson, *Nouvelle introduction à la Geographie pour l'usage de Monseigneur le Dauphin: Par laquelle on peut apprendre en peu de temps et avec facilité la Geographie, et la Division de toutes les parties du Monde: les Empires, les Monarchies, Royaumes et Etats qui le composent separement* (Paris: Chez Hubert Jaillot, 1695), p. 25.

3. Leo Bagrow, *History of Cartography*, 2nd ed., ed. R. A. Skelton, trans. D. L. Paisey (Chicago: Precedent Publishing, 1985), pp. 174–75; see also Leo Bagrow, *A History of the Cartography of Russia up to 1600*, ed. Henry W. Castner (Ontario: Walker Press, 1975); and Leo Bagrow, *A History of Russian Cartography up to 1800*, ed. Henry W. Castner (Ontario: Walker Press, 1975).

4. Robert and Robert de Vaugondy, *Atlas Universel*, vol. I (Paris, 1757), p. 22.

5. Dmitri von Mohrenschildt, *Russia in the Intellectual Life of Eighteenth-Century France* (New York: Columbia Univ. Press, 1936), p. 212.

6. William Coxe, *Travels in Poland and Russia*, from *Travels in Poland, Russia, Sweden, and Denmark*, 5th ed. (London, 1802; rpt. New York: Arno Press and New York Times, 1970), III, pp. 210–11.

7. M. S. Anderson, *Britain's Discovery of Russia 1553–1815* (New York: St. Martin's Press, 1958), p. 80.

8. Jean Fabre, *Stanislas-Auguste Poniatowski et l'Europe des Lumières: Etude de Cosmopolitisme* (Paris: Editions Ophrys, 1952), pp. 380, 486, 669, note 62.

9. Fabre, p. 381.

10. Joseph Marshall, *Travels Through Germany, Russia, and Poland in the Years 1769 and 1770* (London, 1772; rpt. New York: Arno Press and New York Times, 1971), pp. 179–80.

11. Marshall, pp. 179, 183.

12. Elizabeth Craven, *A Journey Through the Crimea to Constantinople: In a Series of Letters from the Right Honourable Elizabeth Lady Craven, to His Serene Highness the Margrave of Brandebourg, Anspach, and Bareith, Written in the Year MDCCLXXXVI* (Dublin, 1789; rpt. New York: Arno Press and New York Times, 1970), pp. 249–50, 409.

13. Robert, *Atlas Universel*, p. 30.

14. Ibid., p. 21, 30.

15. Ibid., p. 30; see also François de Dainville, S.J., *Le Langage des Géographes: Termes, Signes, Couleurs des Cartes Anciennes 1500–1800* (Paris: Editions A. et J. Picard, 1964).

16. Robert, *Atlas Universel*, p. 22.

17. Adam Zamoyski, *The Polish Way: A Thousand-Year History of the Poles and Their Culture* (New York: Franklin Watts, 1988), figure 112; Marshall, p. 184.

18. Norman Davies, *God's Playground: A History of Poland*, Vol. I (New York: Columbia Univ. Press, 1984), p. 542.

19. Piotr S. Wandycz, *The United States and Poland* (Cambridge, Mass.: Harvard Univ. Press, 1980), p. 49.

20. Sanson, pp. 3–7.

21. W. H. Parker, "Europe: How Far?" *The Geographical Journal* 126, Part 3 (Sept. 1960): 285.

22. Abel Mansuy, *Le Monde Slave et les Classiques Français aux XVIe–XVIIe siècles*, préface de Charles Diehl (Paris: Librairie Ancienne Honoré Champion, 1912), pp. 10–11; Parker, p. 281.

23. Mansuy, p. 16.

24. Samuel Fiszman, "The Significance of the Polish Renaissance and Baroque for Eastern Slavic Nations," in *The Polish Renaissance in Its European Context*, ed. Samuel Fiszman (Bloomington: Indiana Univ. Press, 1988), pp. 238–42.

25. Mark Bassin, "Russia Between Europe and Asia: The Ideological Construction of Geographical Space," *Slavic Review* 50, no. 1 (Spring 1991); 5–7.

26. Philipp Johann von Strahlenberg, *An Historico-Geographical Description of the North and Eastern Parts of Europe and Asia; But more particularly of Russia, Siberia, and Great Tartary; Both in their Ancient and Modern State: Together with an Entire New Polyglot-Table of the Dialects of 32 Tartarian Nations; As Also, a Large and Accurate Map of those Countries; and variety of Cuts, representing Asiatick-Scythian Antiquities. Written Originally in High German by Mr. Philip John von Strahlenberg, a Swedish Officer, Thirteen Years Captive in those Parts* (London: J. Brotherton, J. Hazard, W. Meadows, T. Cox, T. Astley, S. Austen, L. Gulliver, and C. Corbet, 1738), pp. 16–17.

27. Parker, p. 287.

28. Homann, "Europa," Nürnberg, 1720 (Harvard Univ., Map Collection); Desnos, "L'Europe divisée selon l'étendue de ses principales parties," Paris, 1772 (Harvard).

29. Delisle, "L'Europe," Paris, 1700 (Harvard); Hass, "Europa," Nürnberg, 1743; rpt. 1777 (Harvard).

30. Robert, *Atlas Universel*, p. 21.

31. Voltaire, *Histoire de l'empire de Russie sous Pierre le Grand*, in *Oeuvres complètes de Voltaire*, Vol. 16 (Paris, 1878; rpt. Liechtenstein: Kraus Reprint Limited, 1967), p. 408.

32. Gyula Antalffy, *A Thousand Years of Travel in Old Hungary*, trans. Elisabeth Hoch (Hungary: Kner, 1980), pp. 117–18.

33. Béla Köpeczi, *La France et la Hongrie au début du XVIIIe siècle: Etude d'histoire des relations diplomatiques et d'histoire des idées* (Budapest: Akadémi Kiadó, 1971), pp. 537–38; Antalffy, p. 177.

34. Anderson, p. 62.

35. Strahlenberg, pp. 5–6.

36. Anderson, p. 85; Mohrenschildt, p. 187; Edward Godfrey Cox, *A Reference Guide to the Literature of Travel*, Vol. I (Univ. of Washington Publications in Language and Literature, Volume 9, Nov. 1935; rpt. New York: Greenwood Press, 1969), p. 194.

37. Albert Lortholary, *Le Mirage russe en France au XVIIIe siècle* (Paris: Boivin, 1951), p. 61.

38. Köpeczi, pp. 376, 528.

39. Ibid., pp. 381, 585–86.

40. Ibid., p. 458.

41. Ibid., pp. 455, 464, 470, 473, 481, 485–86.

42. Ibid., pp. 346–49, 546.

43. Ibid., pp. 386, 488.

44. Ibid., p. 593.

45. Moll, "A New Map of Germany, Hungary, Transylvania, and the Suisse," 1712 (Harvard); Zürner, "Europa," 1712 (Harvard); Delisle, "Carte d'Europe," Paris, 1724 (Harvard); De Witt, "Accuratissima Europae," Amsterdam, 1730 (Harvard).

46. Homann, "Europa," Nürnberg, 1720 (Harvard); Homann, "Europa," Nürnberg, 1730 (Harvard); Hass, "Europa," Nürnberg, 1743; rpt. 1777 (Harvard).

47. Nicolas Gueudeville, "Dissertation sur la Hongrie et sur la Boheme," in

Atlas Historique ou Nouvelle Introduction à l'Histoire, à la Chronologie, et à la Geographie Ancienne et Moderne, vol. II, Henri Abraham Châtelain (Amsterdam: Chez l'Honoré & Châtelain, 1720), pp. 71–72.

48. "Carte Ancienne et Moderne: Des Differents Etats et Pays au long du Danube," *Atlas Historique ou Nouvelle Introduction à l'Histoire, à la Chronologie, et à la Geographie Ancienne et Moderne*, vol. II, Henri Abraham Châtelain (Amsterdam: Chez l'Honoré & Châtelain, 1720).

49. "Carte Genealogique des Rois de Hongrie et de Boheme; et l'Abregé du Gouvernement de ces deux Royaumes," *Atlas Historique* (1720).

50. Gueudeville, *Atlas Historique* (1720), p. 83.

51. "Carte du Royaume de Boheme," *Atlas Historique* (1720).

52. "Nouvelle Carte de la Hongrie," *Atlas Historique* (1720).

53. Köpeczi, pp. 522–24.

54. Gueudeville, *Atlas Historique* (1720), pp. 68–71.

55. Karl A. Roider, *Austria's Eastern Question 1700–1790* (Princeton, N.J.: Princeton Univ. Press, 1982), p. 44.

56. Ibid., p. 52.

57. Ibid., p. 57.

58. Voltaire, *Histoire de Charles XII*, pp. 89–90; Theodore Besterman, *Voltaire*, 3rd ed. (Chicago: Univ. of Chicago Press, 1976), p. 640.

59. Jean Fabre, "Stanislas Leszczynski et le mouvement philosophique en France au XVIIIe siècle," in *Utopie et Institutions au XVIIIe siècle: Le Pragmatisme des Lumières*, ed. Pierre Francastel (Paris and the Hague: Mouton, 1963), pp. 25–41; see also Emanuel Rostworowski, "Stanisław Leszczyński et les Lumières à la Polonaise," in *Utopie et Institutions au XVIIIe siècle: Le Pragmatisme des Lumières*, ed. Pierre Francastel (Paris and the Hague: Mouton, 1963), pp. 15–24.

60. Louis de Jaucourt, "Pologne," *Encyclopédie: ou dictionnaire raisonné des sciences, des arts et des métiers*, nouvelle impression en facsimilé de la première édition de 1751–1780 (Stuttgart: Friedrich Frommann Verlag, 1967), vol. XII, p. 931.

61. Robert, *Atlas Universel*, p. 35.

62. Robert de Vaugondy, "A New and Accurate Map of Europe," London, 1770 (Harvard).

63. Roider, pp. 72–73, 80.

64. Anderson, p. 83; Robert, *Atlas Universel*, p. 30.

65. Voltaire, *Histoire de la guerre de 1741* (Paris: Editions Garnier Frères, 1971), p. 33.

66. Ibid., pp. 33–34.

67. Jan Lavicka, "Voltaire et la Bohême," *Studies on Voltaire and the Eighteenth Century*, Vol. 219 (Oxford: Voltaire Foundation, 1983), p. 109.

68. Köpeczi, p. 553.

69. Anderson, pp. 139–40; Voltaire, *Histoire de l'empire de Russie sous Pierre le Grand*, p. 405.

70. Georges Gusdorf, *Les Principes de la pensée au siècle des lumières* (Paris: Payot, 1971), p. 128.

71. Frederick II, King of Prussia, *L'Histoire de mon temps*, in *Oeuvres posthumes de Fréderic II, roi de Prusse*, vol. I (Berlin: Chez Voss, 1788), p. 69.

72. Oliver Goldsmith, *The Citizen of the World*, ed. Austin Dobson (London: J. M. Dent, 1934), chapter LXXXVII, pp. 240–41.

73. James Porter, *Turkey; Its History and Progress: From the Journals and Correspondence of Sir James Porter*, Vol. I (London: Hurst and Blackett, 1854), p. 8.

74. Mrs. James Porter, "Letter from Lady Porter to her sister, Mdlle de Hochepied, at Pera, containing an account of Sir James Porter's journey from Constantinople to London, with two children, Greek nurse and servant, and accompanied by several gentlemen; among others, the learned Jesuit, Father Boscowitz, who has published a detail of this journey," in James Porter, *Turkey; Its History and Progress: From the Journals and Correspondence of Sir James Porter*, Vol. I (London: Hurst and Blackett, 1854), p. 379.

75. Mrs. James Porter, p. 374.

76. "Boscovich," *Dizionario Biografico degli Italiani*, Vol. XIII (Rome, 1971), pp. 221–230.

77. Ruggiero Giuseppe Boscovich, *Giornale di un Viaggio da Costantinopoli in Polonia dell'abate Ruggiero Giuseppe Boscovich* (Milan: Giordano Editore, 1966), p. 5.

78. Ibid., pp. 86, 110.   79. Ibid., pp. 3–4.
80. Ibid., p. 6.   81. Ibid., p. 8.
82. Rocque, "Carte Generale des Postes de l'Europe," 1758 (Harvard).
83. Boscovich, pp. 21–22.   84. Ibid., p. 31.
85. Ibid., p. 34.   86. Ibid., p. 35.
87. Ibid., pp. 37–42, 50.   88. Ibid., pp. 59–62.
89. Ibid., p. 62.   90. Ibid., pp. 69–71.
91. Ibid., pp. 74, 79, 87, 102.   92. Ibid., pp. 72–75, 89–90.
93. Ibid., pp. 90–92, 106–7.   94. Ibid., pp. 125–26.
95. Ibid., pp. 122, 127–28.   96. Ibid., p. 65.
97. Mrs. James Porter, p. 377.   98. Ibid., p. 390.
99. Boscovich, p. 9.

100. Hass, "Europa," Nürnberg, 1743; rpt. 1777 (Harvard); "Le Voyage d'un Danois," 1744 (Harvard).

101. Boscovich, pp. xx, 190–91.

102. Robert Darnton, *The Business of Enlightenment: A Publishing History of the Encyclopédie 1775–1800* (Cambridge, Mass.: Harvard Univ. Press, 1979), p. 8.

103. "Boheme," *Encyclopédie: ou dictionnaire raisonné des sciences, des arts et des métiers*, nouvelle impression en facsimilé de la première édition de 1751–1780 (Stuttgart: Friedrich Frommann Verlag, 1967), Vol. II, p. 294.

104. "Bulgarie," *Encyclopédie*, II, p. 462.

105. John Lough, "Louis, Chevalier de Jaucourt (1704–1780): A Biographical Sketch," *The Encyclopédie in Eighteenth-Century England and Other Studies* (Newcastle upon Tyne: Oriel Press, 1970), pp. 25, 49–51.

106. Louis de Jaucourt, "Hongrie," *Encyclopédie*, VIII, p. 284.
107. Jaucourt, "Hongrie," *Encyclopédie*, VIII, pp. 284–85.
108. Ibid., VIII, p. 285.   109. Ibid.
110. Ibid., VIII, pp. 285–86.   111. Ibid., VIII, p. 286.
112. Jaucourt, "Pologne," *Encyclopédie*, XII, p. 925.
113. Ibid., XII, pp. 928–33.   114. Ibid., XII, pp. 925, 929, 934.

115. Ibid., XII, pp. 930–31.   116. Ibid., XII, p. 931.

117. Coxe, *Travels in Poland and Russia*, III, pp. 369–76.

118. Jaucourt, "Pologne," *Encyclopédie*, XII, pp. 931–34.

119. Jaucourt, "Russie," *Encyclopédie*, XIV, p. 442; Voltaire, *Histoire de l'empire de Russie sous Pierre le Grand*, p. 403.

120. Jaucourt, "Russie," *Encyclopédie*, XIV, p. 443; Voltaire, *Histoire de l'empire de Russie sous Pierre le Grand*, pp. 419–21.

121. Jaucourt, "Russie," *Encyclopédie*, XIV, p. 445.

122. Jaucourt, "Tartares," *Encyclopédie*, XV, p. 926; see also Alan W. Fisher, *The Crimean Tatars* (Stanford, Calif.: Hoover Institution Press, 1978).

123. Sanson, pp. 3–5.

124. Delisle, "L'Europe," Paris, 1700 (Harvard); Zürner, "Europa," 1712 (Harvard).

125. Jaucourt, "Tartares," *Encyclopédie*, XV, p. 920.

126. Ibid., XV, p. 921.

127. Robert de Vaugondy, *Nouvel Atlas Portatif* (Paris: Chez Robert, 1762), maps III, IV.

128. Jaucourt, "Tartares," *Encyclopédie*, XV, pp. 921–23.

129. Ibid., XV, pp. 924–26.

130. Jaucourt, "Europe," *Encyclopédie*, VI, pp. 211–12.

131. Robert de Vaugondy, "Géographie," *Encyclopédie*, VII, pp. 611–12.

Five ◆ *Voltaire's Russia*

1. Voltaire and Catherine, *Correspondence*, in *Documents of Catherine the Great: The Correspondence with Voltaire and the Instruction of 1767*, ed. W. F. Reddaway (1931; New York: Russell & Russell, 1971), pp. 58, 77.

2. Rocque, "Carte Generale des Postes de l'Europe," 1758 (Harvard).

3. Voltaire and Catherine, pp. 79, 124.

4. Ibid., p. 133.   5. Ibid., p. 181.

6. Ibid., p. 186.   7. Ibid., p. 1.

8. Ibid., p. 2; see also David Griffiths, "To Live Forever: Catherine II, Voltaire, and the Pursuit of Immortality," in *Russia and the World of the Eighteenth Century* (Columbus, Ohio: Slavica Publishers, 1988), pp. 446–68; Isabel de Madariaga, *Russia in the Age of Catherine the Great* (New Haven, Conn.: Yale Univ. Press, 1981), pp. 327–42; and John T. Alexander, *Catherine the Great: Life and Legend* (Oxford: Oxford Univ. Press, 1989), pp. 97–142.

9. Carolyn H. Wilberger, *Voltaire's Russia; Window on the East*, in *Studies on Voltaire and the Eighteenth Century*, Vol. CLXIV, ed. Theodore Besterman (Oxford: Voltaire Foundation at the Taylor Institution, 1976), pp. 54, 141.

10. Jean-Jacques Rousseau, *The Social Contract*, trans. Maurice Cranston (London: Penguin, 1968), p. 90.

11. Voltaire, *Histoire de l'empire de Russie sous Pierre le Grand*, in *Oeuvres complètes de Voltaire*, Vol. 16 (Paris, 1878; rpt. Liechtenstein: Kraus Reprint Limited, 1967), pp. 377, 427.

12. Voltaire and Catherine, p. 3.

13. Theodore Besterman, *Voltaire*, 3rd ed. (Chicago: Univ. of Chicago Press, 1976), p. 406.

14. Voltaire and Catherine, pp. 3–6.

15. Ibid., pp. 48, 51.

16. Ibid., pp. 6–7.

17. Albert Lortholary, *Le Mirage russe en France au XVIIIe siècle* (Paris: Boivin, 1951).

18. Lortholary, pp. 74–76; Dmitri von Mohrenschildt, *Russia in the Intellectual Life of Eighteenth-Century France* (New York: Columbia Univ. Press, 1936), pp. 275–80.

19. Wilberger, p. 27.

20. Mohrenschildt, p. 32; Louis de Rouvroy, duc de Saint-Simon, *Memoirs of Louis XIV and his Court and of the Regency*, Vol. III (New York: Collier, 1910), p. 1011.

21. Lortholary, pp. 23–25.

22. Wilberger, p. 76.

23. Voltaire, *Histoire de Charles XII* (Paris: Garnier-Flammarion, 1968), p. 51.

24. Charles Secondat, baron de Montesquieu, *The Spirit of the Laws*, trans. Thomas Nugent (New York: Hafner, 1949), I, p. 299.

25. Montesquieu, I, p. 299.

26. Lortholary, p. 33; Béla Köpeczi, *La France et la Hongrie au début du XVIIIe siècle: Etude d'histoire des relations diplomatiques et d'histoire des idées* (Budapest: Akadémi Kiadó, 1971), pp. 603–4.

27. Wilberger, p. 32.

28. Voltaire, "Anecdotes sur le czar Pierre le Grand," in *Oeuvres complètes de Voltaire*, Vol. 23 (Paris, 1878; rpt. Liechtenstein: Kraus Reprint, 1967), pp. 281–93.

29. Wilberger, pp. 33, 49.   30. Lortholary, p. 48.

31. Wilberger, p. 41.   32. Ibid., p. 43.

33. Ibid., pp. 124–27; Peter Gay, *The Enlightenment: An Interpretation: The Science of Freedom* (New York: W. W. Norton, 1977), p. 67.

34. Wilberger, pp. 52–53.

35. Ibid., pp. 37–38, 54–61.

36. Ibid., pp. 119–20; Voltaire, *Histoire de l'empire de Russie sous Pierre le Grand*, p. 586.

37. Wilberger, pp. 120–22; Voltaire, *Histoire de l'empire de Russie sous Pierre le Grand*, p. 589.

38. Wilberger, p. 46.

39. Ibid., pp. 45–47.

40. Voltaire, *Histoire de l'empire de Russie sous Pierre le Grand*, pp. 408, 415, 427.

41. Ibid., pp. 506–9.

42. Wilberger, pp. 278–79.

43. Voltaire, "Le Russe à Paris," in *Oeuvres complètes de Voltaire*, Vol. 10 (Paris, 1878; rpt. Liechtenstein: Kraus Reprint Limited, 1967), p. 121.

44. Voltaire, *Histoire de l'empire de Russie sous Pierre le Grand*, pp. 456, 468.

45. Voltaire and Catherine, pp. 9–10, 15.

46. Ibid., pp. 15–18.

47. Voltaire, *Histoire de l'empire de Russie sous Pierre le Grand*, p. 408.

48. Voltaire and Catherine, pp. 17–19; Voltaire, *Histoire de l'empire de Russie sous Pierre le Grand*, p. 377.

49. Peter Gay, *Voltaire's Politics: The Poet as Realist*, 2nd ed. (New Haven, Conn.: Yale Univ. Press, 1988), p. 180.

50. Voltaire and Catherine, p. 20. 51. Ibid., p. 23.

52. Ibid., pp. 25–27. 53. Ibid., pp. 28–29.

54. Ibid., pp. 33–34. 55. Ibid., p. 34.

56. Ibid., p. 35. 57. Ibid., pp. 38, 48.

58. Ibid., p. 60. 59. Ibid., pp. 73, 81–83, 90, 97.

60. Ibid., pp. 93, 100–101. 61. Ibid., pp. 117, 123–26.

62. Ibid., pp. 148–50. 63. Ibid., p. 162.

64. Ibid., p. 172. 65. Ibid., pp. 186–87.

66. Karl A. Roider, *Austria's Eastern Question 1700–1790* (Princeton, N.J.: Princeton Univ. Press, 1982), pp. 132, 156–57.

67. Voltaire, *Essai sur les moeurs*, in *Oeuvres complètes de Voltaire*, vol. III (Paris: Chez Furne, 1835), pp. 607–9.

68. Voltaire and Catherine, pp. 84, 187.

69. Ibid., pp. 118–19. 70. Ibid., pp. 138, 149.

71. Ibid., pp. 154–61. 72. Ibid., pp. 161–63.

73. Ibid., p. 171. 74. Ibid., pp. 169, 176, 186.

75. Lortholary, pp. 174–76.

76. Giacomo Casanova, *History of My Life*, trans. Willard Trask, Vol. 10 (London: Longman, 1971), pp. 103, 141–42.

77. Rudolf Eric Raspe, *The Travels and Surprising Adventures of Baron Munchausen* (London: Dedalus, 1988), p. 75.

78. Mohrenschildt, p. 145; Lortholary, pp. 90–91; Alexander, p. 14.

79. Lortholary, pp. 97–98.

80. Mohrenschildt, p. 94.

81. Lortholary, pp. 179–81.

82. Voltaire and Catherine, p. 203; Lortholary, pp. 184–86; Louis-Philippe, comte de Ségur, *Mémoires, souvenirs, et anecdotes, par le comte de Ségur*, vol. I, in *Bibliothèque des mémoires: relatif à l'histoire de France: pendant le 18e siècle*, vol. XIX, ed. M. Fs. Barrière (Paris: Librairie de Firmin Didot Frères, 1859), pp. 442–43.

83. Lortholary, pp. 212–13.

84. Voltaire and Catherine, p. 192; Maurice Tourneux, *Diderot et Catherine II* (Paris: Calmann Lévy, 1899), pp. 75–76.

85. Tourneux, p. 83.

86. Denis Diderot, "Entretiens avec Catherine II" (1773), in *Oeuvres politiques*, ed. Paul Vernière (Paris: Editions Garnier Frères, 1963), pp. 257–58, 326.

87. Diderot, "Entretiens," p. 260; see also Arthur Wilson, "Diderot in Russia, 1773–1774," in *The Eighteenth-Century in Russia*, ed. J. G. Garrard (Oxford: Clarendon Press, 1973), pp. 166–97; and Isabel de Madariaga, "Catherine and the Philosophes," in *Russia and the West in the Eighteenth Century* (Newtonville, Mass.: Oriental Research Partners, 1983), pp. 30–52.

88. Diderot, "Entretiens," pp. 265–66.

89. Mohrenschildt, pp. 257–58.
90. Diderot, "Entretiens," pp. 266–67; Tourneux, p. 492.
91. Mohrenschildt, p. 55.

92. Diderot, "Entretiens," p. 301.   93. Ibid., p. 302.
94. Ibid., pp. 309–10.   95. Lortholary, pp. 217–18.
96. Diderot, "Entretiens," p. 326.   97. Tourneux, p. 472.
98. Ibid., pp. 475–76.   99. Ibid., pp. 477, 481–82.
100. Ibid., p. 482.   101. Ibid., pp. 485–89.
102. Ibid., p. 492.

103. Lortholary, pp. 236, 379, note 146.
104. Ségur, I, pp. 444–45.
105. Diderot, "Observations sur le Nakaz" (1774), in *Oeuvres politiques*, ed. Paul Vernière (Paris: Editions Garnier Frères, 1963), pp. 343–45.
106. Diderot, "Observations," p. 349.

107. Ibid., pp. 350–51.   108. Ibid., p. 351.
109. Voltaire and Catherine, p. 190.   110. Ibid., p. 194.
111. Ibid., p. 195.   112. Ibid., p. 196.
113. Ibid., pp. 198–201.   114. Ibid., pp. 206, 213.

Six ◆ *Rousseau's Poland*

1. William Richardson, *Anecdotes of the Russian Empire: In a Series of Letters Written, a Few Years Ago, from St. Petersburg* (London, 1784; rpt. London: Frank Cass, 1968), pp. 401–3; John T. Alexander, *Catherine the Great: Life and Legend* (Oxford: Oxford Univ. Press, 1989), p. 98.
2. Jean-Jacques Rousseau, *Considerations sur le gouvernement de Pologne*, in *Discours sur l'économie politique, Projet de constitution pour la Corse, Considerations sur le gouvernement de Pologne*, ed. Barbara de Negroni (Paris: Flammarion, 1990), p. 163.

3. Rousseau, p. 163.   4. Ibid.
5. Ibid., pp. 164–65.   6. Ibid., pp. 165–66, 211.
7. Ibid., pp. 170–71.   8. Ibid., p. 171.
9. Ibid., p. 173.   10. Ibid.
11. Ibid., p. 177.

12. Ibid., p. 178; see also Jerzy Michalski, *Rousseau i sarmacki republikanizm* (Warsaw: Panstwowe Wydawnictwo Naukowe, 1977).
13. Jean Starobinski, *Jean-Jacques Rousseau: Transparency and Obstruction*, trans. Arthur Goldhammer (Chicago: Univ. of Chicago Press, 1988), p. 145.
14. Rousseau, p. 261.
15. Marietta Martin, *Une Française à Varsovie en 1766: Madame Geoffrin chez le roi de Pologne Stanislas-Auguste* (Paris: Bibliothèque Polonaise, 1936), pp. 27, 42; Pierre, marquis de Ségur, *Le Royaume de la rue Saint-Honoré: Madame Geoffrin et sa fille* (Paris: Calmann-Lévy, 1897), p. 288.
16. Marie Thérèse Rodet, Madame Geoffrin, and Stanislas-Auguste Poniatowski, *Correspondance inédite du roi Stanislas-Auguste Poniatowski et de Madame Geoffrin* (1764–1777), ed. Charles de Mouy (Paris: E. Plon, 1875), p. 239; Martin, p. 78.

17. G. P. Gooch, "Four French Salons," in *Catherine the Great and Other Studies* (1954; rpt. Hamden, Conn.: Archon Books, 1966), p. 117.

18. Martin, p. 12.

19. Mme Geoffrin and Stanislas-Auguste, pp. 102–3.

20. Ibid., p. 103.   21. Ibid., p. 108.

22. Ibid., pp. 114–15.   23. Martin, p. 27.

24. Mme Geoffrin and Stanislas-Auguste, pp. 115, 137, 140–42.

25. Ségur (Pierre), *Le Royaume*, p. 432; Mme Geoffrin and Stanislas-Auguste, *Correspondance*, p. 131.

26. Ségur (Pierre), *Le Royaume*, pp. 434–36.

27. Ibid., pp. 437–38.

28. Ibid., pp. 442–43.

29. Mme Geoffrin and Stanislas-Auguste, p. 143.

30. Ibid., pp. 147–48.

31. Ibid., p. 150; Ségur (Pierre), *Le Royaume*, p. 235.

32. Mme Geoffrin and Stanislas-Auguste, pp. 151–52.

33. Ibid., p. 153.

34. Ibid., pp. 154–56.

35. Ibid., p. 158.

36. Jean Fabre, *Stanislas-Auguste Poniatowski et l'Europe des Lumières: Etude de Cosmopolitisme* (Paris: Editions Ophrys, 1952), pp. 630–31, note 68; Albert Lortholary, *Le Mirage russe en France au XVIIIe siècle* (Paris: Boivin, 1951), pp. 162–63.

37. Mme Geoffrin and Stanislas-Auguste, pp. 162–63, 167.

38. Ibid., p. 168.

39. Ibid., pp. 112, 167.

40. Ibid., p. 174.

41. Ségur (Pierre), *Le Royaume*, p. 447.

42. Mme Geoffrin and Stanislas-Auguste, pp. 177–78.

43. Ibid., pp. 180, 193.

44. Ibid., pp. 205–7, 223–24; Martin, p. 33.

45. Ségur (Pierre), *Le Royaume*, pp. 264–67, 281.

46. Mme Geoffrin and Stanislas-Auguste, p. 233.

47. Ibid., pp. 239–41.

48. Ségur (Pierre), *Le Royaume*, p. 272.

49. Ibid., p. 273.

50. Jacques Derrida, *Of Grammatology*, trans. Gaytri Chakravorty Spivak (Baltimore: Johns Hopkins, 1976), pp. 118–40.

51. Mme Geoffrin and Stanislas-Auguste, pp. 242–44.

52. Ibid., p. 349.

53. Martin, p. 35.

54. Stanislas-Auguste Poniatowski, *Mémoires du roi Stanislas-Auguste Poniatowski*, vol. I (St. Petersburg: l'Académie Impériale des Sciences, 1914), pp. 567–68.

55. Martin, pp. 53–54; Fabre, p. 305.

56. Ségur (Pierre), *Le Royaume*, pp. 273–74.

57. Ibid., pp. 230, 461.

58. Rousseau, p. 259.

59. Martin, p. 76.
60. Mme Geoffrin and Stanislas-Auguste, p. 250.
61. Ibid., p. 276.   62. Ibid., pp. 265–74, 294.
63. Ibid., pp. 315–16.   64. Ibid., pp. 321, 329.
65. Ibid., p. 355.   66. Ibid., p. 364.
67. Ibid., pp. 365–66.   68. Ibid., pp. 326–27, 336.
69. Ibid., pp. 343–44.   70. Ibid., pp. 359, 382, 387, 432.
71. Ibid., pp. 349, 379–80.   72. Ibid., p. 443.
73. Ibid., pp. 451, 456.   74. Ibid., pp. 464–66.
75. Ibid., pp. 470–71, 475–77.   76. Rousseau, p. 172.

77. Voltaire, *Candide*, trans. John Butt (London: Penguin, 1947), chapter 26; Wanda Dzwigala, "Voltaire's Sources on the Polish Dissident Question," *Studies on Voltaire and the Eighteenth Century*, Vol. 241 (Oxford: Voltaire Foundation, 1986), pp. 191–92; Emanuel Rostworowski, "Républicanisme 'Sarmate' et les Lumières," in *Studies on Voltaire and the Eighteenth Century*, ed. Theodore Besterman, Vol. XXVI (Geneva: Institut et Musée Voltaire, 1963), p. 1417; Fabre, p. 316; see also Stanisław Kot, *Rzeczpospolita Polska w literaturze politycznej Zachodu* (Cracow: Nakladem Krakowskiej Spólki Wydawniczej, 1919); Ryszard W. Woloszynski, "La Pologne vue par l'Europe au XVIIIe siècle," *Acta Poloniae historica* (1965): 22–42; and Woloszynski, *Polska w opiniach francuzów: Rulhière i jego wspólczesni* (Warsaw: Panstwowe Wydawnictwo Naukowe, 1964).

78. Voltaire, "Essai historique et critique sur les dissensions des églises de Pologne" (1767), *Oeuvres de Voltaire: Mélanges Historiques*, vol. II (Paris: P. Pourrat Freres, 1839), pp. 57–60; Fabre, p. 634, note 144.

79. Emanuel Rostworowski, "Voltaire et la Pologne," *Studies on Voltaire and the Eighteenth Century*, ed. Theodore Besterman, Vol. LXII (Geneva: Institut et Musée Voltaire, 1968), p. 114; Fabre, p. 323.

80. Voltaire, "Discours aux confédérés catholiques de Kaminieck en Pologne, par le major Kaiserling, au service du roi de Prusse" (1768), *Oeuvres de Voltaire: Politiques et Législation*, vol. II (Paris: P. Pourrat Freres, 1839), pp. 154, 165–66.

81. Voltaire and Catherine, *Correspondence*, in *Documents of Catherine the Great: The Correspondence with Voltaire and the Instruction of 1767*, ed. W. F. Reddaway (1931; New York: Russell & Russell, 1971), p. 109; Dzwigala, p. 198.

82. Jean-Paul Marat, *Les Aventures du jeune comte Potowski*, ed. Claire Nicolas-Lelièvre (Paris: Renaudot, 1989), pp. 118, 130.

83. Marek Tomaszewski, "L'Univers héroique polonais dans *Les Amours du chevalier de Faublas* et son impact sur l'imaginaire social à la fin due XVIIIe siècle," *Revue de Littérature Comparée*, no. 2 (Apr.–June 1990): 430–31.

84. Voltaire, *Les Lois de Minos*, in *Oeuvres complètes de Voltaire*, vol. 5, *Théâtre* (Paris: Perronneau, 1817), p. 296.

85. Fabre, p. 249.

86. Marat, *Les Aventures*, p. 256; Dzwigala, p. 201; M. Romain-Cornut, *Voltaire: complice et conseiller du partage de la Pologne*, 2nd ed. (Paris: Jacques Lecoffre, 1846), pp. 17–21.

87. Ambroise Jobert, *Magnats polonais et physiocrates français (1767–1774)* (Paris: Librairie Droz, 1941), p. 20.

88. Jobert, pp. 51, 86; Larry Wolff, *The Vatican and Poland in the Age of the Partitions: Diplomatic and Cultural Encounters at the Warsaw Nunciature* (New York and Boulder: Columbia Univ. Press, East European Monographs, 1988), Chapter VII.

89. Jobert, pp. 24–27.

90. Ibid., pp. 27–32.

91. Ibid., pp. 36–38; see also Kasimir Opalek, "Les Physiocrates et leur role dans le renouveau culturel au siècle des Lumières en Pologne," in *Utopie et Institutions au XVIIIe siècle: Le Pragmatisme des Lumières,* ed. Pierre Francastel (Paris and the Hague: Mouton, 1963), pp. 169–84.

92. Jobert, pp. 45–48; Rousseau, p. 220.

93. Jobert, p. 57; Wolff, Chapter V.

94. Jobert, pp. 60–62.   95. Ibid., pp. 64–66.

96. Ibid., pp. 67–71.   97. Ibid., pp. 72–73, 77.

98. Ibid., pp. 79–82.

99. Adam Smith, *The Wealth of Nations* (London: Penguin, 1982), pp. 345–46.

100. Ibid., p. 308.

101. Claude Carloman de Rulhière, *A History or Anecdotes of the Revolution in Russia in the Year 1762* (London, 1797; rpt. New York: Arno Press, and New York Times, 1970), p. 1.

102. Alice Chevalier, *Claude-Carloman de Rulhière, premier historien de la Pologne: sa vie et son oeuvre historique* (Paris: Les Editions Domat-Montchrestien, 1939), pp. 105–14; Ségur (Pierre), *Le Royaume,* pp. 220–24.

103. Rulhière, *Anecdotes of the Revolution in Russia,* pp. viii–xi, 52; Chevalier, pp. 74, 115–16.

104. Chevalier, pp. 43–44.

105. Claude Carloman de Rulhière, *Revolutions de Pologne,* vol. I, ed. Christien Ostrowski (Paris: Librairie de Firmin Didot Frères, 1862), p. 1.

106. Rulhière, *Revolutions de Pologne,* I, pp. 6–7.

107. Chevalier, pp. 121–22.   108. Ibid., pp. 152–54.

109. Ibid.   110. Ibid., p. 155.

111. Ibid., pp. 160–62, 166, 175.   112. Ibid., pp. 233, 330–33.

113. Giacomo Casanova, *Istoria delle Turbolenze della Polonia,* ed. Giacinto Spagnoletti (Naples: Guida Editori, 1974), pp. 100, 447.

114. Casanova, p. 54; Chevalier, p. 250; Fabre, p. 7.

115. Chevalier, pp. 244, 295.   116. Ibid., pp. 168–69, 182–83.

117. Ibid., pp. 372–80.   118. Fabre, p. 571, note 42.

119. Marquis de Sade, *Aline et Valcour,* in *Oeuvres,* ed. Michel Delon, Vol. I (Paris: Gallimard, 1990), pp. 852–53.

120. Fabre, p. 510; see also Emanuel Rostworowski, *Ostatni Król Rzeczypospolitej: geneza i upadek konstytucji 3 maja* (Warsaw: Wiedza Powszechna, 1966).

121. Marcel Handelsman, "La Constitution polonaise du 3 mai 1791 et l'opinion française," in *La Revolution Française,* Vol. LVIII (Paris, 1910), pp. 416, 425, 429, 433.

122. Fabre, pp. 27, 575, note 28.

123. M. S. Anderson, *Britain's Discovery of Russia 1553–1815* (New York: St. Martin's Press, 1958), pp. 165–69.

124. Lortholary, p. 263; Anderson, p. 193; Robert Arnold, *Geschichte der*

Deutschen Polenlitteratur: von den Anfängen bis 1800 (Halle: Max Niemeyer, 1900), p. 168.

125. Thomas Campbell, "Poland," in *English Romantic Writers*, ed. David Perkins (New York: Harcourt, Brace & World, 1967), p. 603.

126. Lortholary, pp. 263–64.

127. Elisabeth Vigée-Lebrun, *The Memoirs of Elisabeth Vigée-Le Brun*, trans. Siân Evans (Bloomington: Indiana Univ. Press, 1989), pp. 161, 189; Dmitri von Mohrenschildt, *Russia in the Intellectual Life of Eighteenth-Century France* (New York: Columbia Univ. Press, 1936), pp. 25–26.

128. Vigée-Lebrun, pp. 208, 366; Fabre, p. 552.

129. William Cobbett, *Letters to the Right Honourable Lord Hawkesbury*, 2nd ed. (London: Cobbett and Morgan, 1802), p. 82.

130. George Kennan, *Memoirs 1925–1950* (New York: Pantheon Books, 1967), pp. 29–30.

131. Cobbett, p. 83.

132. Kennan, p. 26.

Seven ◆ *Barbarians Ancient and Modern*

1. Nicolae Iorga, *Les Voyageurs Français dans l'Orient Européen* (Paris: Boivin, 1928), p. 105.

2. Charles de Peyssonnel, *Observations historiques et géographiques, sur les peuples barbares qui ont habité les bords du Danube & du Pont-Euxin* (Paris: Chez N. M. Tilliard, 1765), pp. 1–2.

3. Ibid., pp. 4–7.   4. Ibid., p. 30.

5. Ibid., p. 39.   6. Ibid., pp. 50–51.

7. Ibid., pp. 194–95.

8. Robert and Robert de Vaugondy, *Atlas Universel*, vol. I (Paris, 1757), maps 4, 12.

9. Jean-Baptiste d'Anville, *A Complete Body of Ancient Geography* (London: Robert Sayer, 1771), maps 1, 3.

10. François Hartog, *The Mirror of Herodotus: The Representation of the Other in the Writing of History*, trans. Janet Lloyd (Berkeley: Univ. of California Press, 1988), p. 30.

11. Albert Lortholary, *Le Mirage russe en France au XVIIIe siècle* (Paris: Boivin, 1951), p. 297, note 87; Albert Gyergyai, "Un correspondant hongrois de Voltaire: le comte Fekete de Galanta," in *Studies on Voltaire and the Eighteenth Century*, vol. 25, ed. Theodore Besterman (Geneva: Institut et Musée Voltaire, 1963), p. 789.

12. Peyssonnel, pp. vii–ix, xv–xvi.

13. Ibid., pp. xxxvi–xl.

14. Ibid., pp. 9–10, 71.

15. Pierre-Charles Levesque, *Histoire de Russie*, vol. I (Hambourg et Brunswick: Chez Pierre-François Fauche, 1800), pp. viii–ix.

16. Claude Carloman de Rulhière, *Revolutions de Pologne*, vol. I, ed. Christien Ostrowski (Paris: Librairie de Firmin Didot Frères, 1862), pp. 1–2; Levesque, I, pp. 1–6.

17. Levesque, I, pp. 55–56.

18. Dmitri von Mohrenschildt, *Russia in the Intellectual Life of Eighteenth-Century France* (New York: Columbia Univ. Press, 1936), p. 227.

19. Claude-Louis de Sacy, *Histoire générale de Hongrie: Depuis la première invasion des Huns, jusqu'à nos jours*, vol. I (Yverdon, 1780), pp. vii, xxxi.

20. Iorga, pp. 104–8; Robert Darnton, *Mesmerism and the End of the Enlightenment in France* (Cambridge, Mass.: Harvard Univ. Press, 1968), pp. 98–100; Jean-Louis Carra, *Historie de la Moldavie et de la Valachie* (Jassy: Société Typographique des Deux-Ponts, 1777), pp. ix, xvi–xvii, 220.

21. Alexandre-Maurice Blanc de Lanautte, comte d'Hauterive, *Mémoire sur l'état ancien et actuel de la Moldavie: présenté à S. A. S. le prince Alexandre Ypsilanti, Hospodar régnant, en 1787, par le comte d'Hauterive* (Bucharest: L'Institut d'arts graphiques Carol Göbl, 1902), pp. 20–22.

22. Jean-Jacques Rousseau, *Considerations sur le gouvernement de Pologne*, in *Discours sur l'économie politique, Projet de constitution pour la Corse, Considerations sur le gouvernement de Pologne*, ed. Barbara de Negroni (Paris: Flammarion, 1990), pp. 170–77.

23. Hauterive, *Mémoire*, pp. 42–44; Hauterive, "La Moldavie en 1785: faisant suite au journal d'un voyage de Constantinople à Jassy," in *Mémoire sur l'état ancien et actuel de la Moldavie: présenté à S. A. S. le prince Alexandre Ypsilanti, Hospodar régnant, en 1787, par le comte d'Hauterive* (Bucharest: L'Institut d'arts graphiques Carol Göbl, 1902), pp. 357–58.

24. Hauterive, *Mémoire*, p. 236.

25. Ibid., p. 176; Hauterive, "La Moldavie," p. 359.

26. Hauterive, "La Moldavie," pp. 331–32.

27. Hauterive, *Mémoire*, pp. 252, 258.

28. Ibid., pp. 264–66.

29. Ibid., pp. 266–70.

30. Ibid., p. 78.

31. Louis-Philippe, comte de Ségur, *Mémoires, souvenirs, et anecdotes, par le comte de Ségur*, vol. I, in *Bibliothèque des mémoires: relatif à l'histoire de France: pendant le 18e siècle*, vol. XIX, ed. M. Fs. Barrière (Paris: Librairie de Firmin Didot Frères, 1859), pp. 329–30.

32. Edward Gibbon, *The Decline and Fall of the Roman Empire* (New York: Modern Library, n.d.), I, p. 6.

33. Gibbon, I, pp. 211–14.

34. Ibid., I, p. 214.

35. Voltaire, *Essai sur les moeurs*, in *Oeuvres complètes de Voltaire*, vol. III (Paris: Chez Furne, 1835), p. 583.

36. Gibbon, II, pp. 245–47, 254, 263.

37. Ibid., II, p. 591.

38. Ibid., II, pp. 591–94.

39. Ibid., III, p. 61.

40. Ibid., III, p. 316.

41. Ibid., III, pp. 317–18.

42. Ibid., III, pp. 318–19, note 8.

43. Ibid., III, pp. 321–22.

44. Ibid., III, pp. 322–23.

45. Ibid., III, pp. 322–23, note 22; Janos Gulya, "Some Eighteenth Century Antecedents of Nineteenth Century Linguistics: The Discovery of Finno-Ugrian,"

Studies in the History of Linguistics: Traditions and Paradigms, ed. Dell Hymes (Bloomington: Indiana Univ. Press, 1974), pp. 260–63.

46. Gibbon, III, pp. 324–26, 329.

47. Ibid., III, pp. 330–31, note 45.

48. Ibid., III, pp. 332–33, 335, note 58, 337.

49. Ibid., III, p. 343.

50. Ibid., III, pp. 343–44; David Spadafora, *The Idea of Progress in Eighteenth-Century Britain* (New Haven, Conn.: Yale Univ. Press, 1990), pp. 223–24; Roy Porter, "Civilization, Barbarism, and Progress" (Chapter 6), *Edward Gibbon: Making History* (London: Weidenfeld and Nicolson, 1988), pp. 135–57.

51. Johann Gottfried Herder, *Journal meiner Reise im Jahr 1769*, ed. Katharina Mommsen (Stuttgart: Philipp Reclam, 1976), p. 7.

52. Ibid., p. 15.　　　　　　　53. Ibid., pp. 38–39.

54. Ibid., pp. 77–78.　　　　　55. Ibid., pp. 80–81.

56. Ibid., p. 90.　　　　　　　57. Ibid., pp. 91–92.

58. Ibid., pp. 101–2; Konrad Bittner, "Die Beurteilung der russischen Politik im 18. Jahrhundert durch Johann Gottfried Herder," in *Im Geiste Herders*, ed. Erich Keyser (Kitzingen am Main: Holzner-Verlag, 1953), p. 47.

59. Robert T. Clark, *Herder: His Life and Thought* (Berkeley: Univ. of California Press, 1955), p. 60.

60. Bittner, pp. 50–51.

61. Ibid., pp. 68–69.

62. Herder, "Von Ähnlichkeit der mittlern englischen und deutschen Dichtkunst," *Herders Werke*, vol. II, ed. Regine Otto (Berlin and Weimar: Aufbau-Verlag, 1982), p. 289.

63. Herder, "Von Ähnlichkeit," p. 290.

64. Rousseau, pp. 171–73.

65. Herder, *Ideen zur Philosophie der Geschichte der Menschheit*, in *Herders Werke*, vol. IV, ed. Regine Otto (Berlin and Weimar: Aufbau-Verlag, 1982), pp. 385–86.

66. Ibid., p. 393.

67. Ibid., pp. 393–95.

68. Ibid., p. 395.

69. Herder, *Outlines of a Philosophy of the History of Man*, trans. T. Churchill (New York: Bergman), pp. 483–84.

70. Herder, *Ideen zur Philosophie der Geschichte*, p. 395.

71. Ibid., pp. 396–97.

72. Ibid., pp. 463–64.

73. Immanuel Kant, "Der Charakter des Volks," *Die Anthropologische Charakteristik*, in *Schriften zur Anthropologie, Geschichtsphilosophie, Politik, und Pädigogik*, 2, *Werkausgabe*, vol. XII (Frankfurt: Suhrkamp Verlag, 1977), p. 670.

74. Georg Wilhelm Friedrich Hegel, *Vorlesungen über die Philosophie der Geschichte*, in *Werke*, 12 (Frankfurt: Suhrkamp Verlag, 1970), p. 422.

75. Alberto Fortis, *Travels into Dalmatia: Containing General Observations on the Natural History of that Country and the Neighbouring Islands; the Natural Productions, Arts, Manners and Customs of the Inhabitants* (London, 1778; rpt. New York: Arno Press and New York Times, 1971), p. iv.

76. Michèle Duchet, *Anthropologie et Histoire au siècle des lumières: Buffon, Voltaire, Rousseau, Helvétius, Diderot* (Paris: François Maspero, 1971); Giuseppe Cocchiara, *The History of Folklore in Europe*, trans. John N. McDaniel (Philadelphia: Institute for the Study of Human Issues, 1981).

77. Voltaire, *Essai sur les moeurs*, pp. 607–9.

78. P. J. Marshall and Glyndwr Williams, *The Great Map of Mankind: British Perceptions of the World in the Age of Enlightenment* (London: J. M. Dent, 1982), epigraph; Spadafora, pp. 253–320.

79. Gianfranco Torcellan, "Profilo di Alberto Fortis," in *Settecento Veneto e altri scritti storici* (Turin: G. Giappichelli, 1969), pp. 273–79.

80. Torcellan, p. 283; Voltaire, *Essai sur les moeurs*, p. 561.

81. Fortis, pp. 45–47.

82. Ibid., p. 44.

83. Gibbon, II, p. 593; Fortis, p. 44.

84. Duchet, p. 12. 85. Fortis, pp. 51–58.

86. Ibid., pp. 60–61. 87. Ibid., pp. 61–62.

88. Carlo Ginzburg, *Ecstasies: Deciphering the Witches' Sabbath*, trans. Raymond Rosenthal (New York: Pantheon Books, 1991), pp. 207–25.

89. Fortis, p. 63.

90. Ibid., pp. 66–67, 70–75.

91. Ibid., pp. 77, 82.

92. Giovanni Lovrich, *Osservazioni di Giovanni Lovrich sopra diversi pezzi del Viaggio in Dalmazia del Signor Abate Alberto Fortis* (Venice: Francesco Sansoni, 1776), pp. 79, 81, 116.

93. Torcellan, p. 288. 94. Ibid., pp. 290–91.

95. Fortis, p. 82. 96. Ibid., p. 83.

97. Ibid.

98. Johann Wolfgang von Goethe, "Klaggesang: von der edlen Frauen des Asan Aga, aus dem Morlackischen," *Sämtliche Werke*, vol. I (Zürich: Artemis Verlag, 1977), p. 301.

99. Stephen Clissold, ed., *A Short History of Yugoslavia* (Cambridge: Cambridge Univ. Press, 1968), p. 119.

100. Ruggiero Giuseppe Boscovich, *Giornale di un Viaggio da Costantinopoli in Polonia dell'abate Ruggiero Giuseppe Boscovich* (Milan: Giordano Editore, 1966), pp. 6, 37–38.

101. Fortis, p. 84; Cocchiara, pp. 135–40.

102. Fortis, p. 85.

103. Ibid., p. 86.

104. Ibid.

105. Desnos, "L'Europe divisée selon l'étendue de ses principales parties," Paris, 1772 (Harvard); Ségur, *Mémoires, souvenirs, et anecdotes, par le comte de Ségur*, vol. II, in *Bibliothèque des mémoires: relatif à l'histoire de France: pendant le 18e siècle*, vol. XX, ed. M. Fs. Barrière (Paris: Librairie de Firmin Didot Frères, 1859), p. 66.

106. Bittner, p. 60.

107. William Coxe, *Travels in Poland and Russia*, from *Travels in Poland, Russia,*

Sweden, and Denmark, 5th ed. (London, 1802; rpt. New York: Arno Press and New York Times, 1970), I, pp. 273–74.

108. Ibid., I, pp. 392–93.

109. Ibid., II, pp. 74–75.

110. Fortis, pp. 88–89.

Eight ◆ *Manners and the Measurements of Race*

1. Robert Arnold, *Geschichte der Deutschen Polenlitteratur: von den Anfängen bis 1800* (Halle: Max Niemeyer, 1900), p. 145.

2. Ibid., p. 52.

3. Ibid., p. 87.

4. Johann Gottlieb Fichte, *Briefwechsel*, vol. I, ed. Hans Schulz (Hildesheim: Georg Olms Verlagsbuchhandlung, 1967), pp. 171–75.

5. Arnold, pp. 8–15, 40–56; Wolfgang Wippermann, *Der 'Deutsche Drang nach Osten': Ideologie und Wirklichkeit eines politischen Schlagwortes* (Darmstadt: Wissenschaftliche Buchgesellschaft, 1981), p. 22.

6. Arnold, pp. 27–29, 31–33, 95–96.   7. Fichte, p. 175.

8. Ibid., p. 176.   9. Ibid., pp. 176–78, 181–83.

10. Joachim Christoph Friedrich Schulz, *Reise nach Warschau: Eine Schilderung aus den Jahren 1791–1793*, ed. Klaus Zernack, in *Polnische Bibliothek* (Frankfurt: Suhrkamp Verlag, 1982), pp. 10–13, 24–25, 32–33.

11. Ibid., pp. 348–49.

12. Michael Burleigh, *Germany Turns Eastwards: A Study of Ostforschung in the Third Reich* (Cambridge: Cambridge Univ. Press, 1988), pp. 26–28, 105–7, 176–79.

13. Johann Gottfried Herder, *Ideen zur Philosophie der Geschichte der Menschheit*, in *Herders Werke*, vol. IV, ed. Regine Otto (Berlin and Weimar: Aufbau-Verlag, 1982), p. 472.

14. Gerhard Steiner, *Georg Forster* (Stuttgart: J. B. Metzlersche Verlagsbuchhandlung, 1977), pp. 8–46.

15. Georg Forster, *Briefe*, in *Werke*, vol. IV, ed. Gerhard Steiner (Frankfurt: Insel Verlag, 1970), p. 320.

16. Arnold, pp. 108–9; Wippermann, p. 21.

17. Arnold, p. 109.

18. Ibid., pp. 113–14.

19. Georg Forster, "Noch etwas über die Menschenrassen," in *Forsters Werke*, vol. I (Berlin and Weimar: Aufbau-Verlag, 1968), pp. 3–4, 16–17.

20. Ibid., pp. 22, 25.   21. Ibid., p. 33.

22. Fichte, pp. 183–84.   23. Schulz, p. 370; Arnold, p. 90.

24. Schulz, pp. 40, 43, 68, 70, 136, 177–78.

25. Arnold, pp. 78, 119–21, 161, 167–77.

26. Ibid., pp. 127, 179–81.

27. Ibid., pp. 190–91.

28. Ibid., p. 161; Güssefeld, "Europa," Nürnberg, 1794 (Harvard); Güssefeld, "Charte von Europa," Nürnberg, 1798 (Harvard).

29. Arnold, p. 113.

30. Leopold Hoffmann, *Grosse Wahrheiten und Beweise in einem kleinen Auszuge aus der ungarischen Geschichte* (Frankfurt and Leipzig, 1792), pp. ii, xi–xii, xvii, xxi, xxv.

31. Fichte, pp. 185–87.   32. Arnold, pp. 63, 144.

33. Fichte, p. 214.   34. Ibid., p. 196.

35. John Ledyard, *John Ledyard's Journey Through Russia and Siberia 1787–1788: The Journal and Selected Letters*, ed. Stephen D. Watrous (Madison: Univ. of Wisconsin Press, 1966), pp. 3–10.

36. Ibid., p. 19.

37. Ibid., pp. 123–24.

38. Mark Bassin, "Inventing Siberia: Visions of the Russian East in the Early Nineteenth Century," *American Historical Review* 26, no. 3 (June 1991): 767–70.

39. Dmitri von Mohrenschildt, *Russia in the Intellectual Life of Eighteenth-Century France* (New York: Columbia Univ. Press, 1936), pp. 112–14; Albert Lortholary, *Le Mirage russe en France au XVIIIe siècle* (Paris: Boivin, 1951), pp. 191–97; Chappe d'Auteroche, *Voyage en Sibérie*, 4 vols. (Paris: Chez Debure, 1768).

40. Ledyard, p. 143.   41. Ibid., p. 144.

42. Ibid., pp. 145, 153, 156–58, 161.   43. Ibid., pp. 174, 177–78.

44. Ibid., pp. 178–80, 193.

45. Michèle Duchet, *Anthropologie et Histoire au siècle des lumières: Buffon, Voltaire, Rousseau, Helvétius, Diderot* (Paris: François Maspero, 1971), p. 258; P. J. Marshall and Glyndwr Williams, *The Great Map of Mankind: British Perceptions of the World in the Age of Enlightenment* (London: J. M. Dent, 1982), p. 246; David Hume, "Of National Characters," in *Essays: Moral, Political, and Literary: By David Hume*, Vol. I, ed. T. H. Green and T. H. Grose (London, 1882; rpt. Scientia Verlag Aalen, 1964), p. 252.

46. Ledyard, p. 127.

47. Ibid., pp. 144, 164, 177, 182, 194–95.

48. Ibid., pp. 145, 180.

49. Ibid., p. 257.

50. John Parkinson, *A Tour of Russia, Siberia and the Crimea 1791–1794*, ed. William Collier (London: Frank Cass, 1971), pp. 56, 63, 66, 98, 109, 118, 138.

51. Ibid., pp. 148, 151, 153, 188.   52. Ledyard, pp. 167, 252–53.

53. Ibid., p. 257.   54. Ibid., pp. 30–31.

55. Ibid., pp. 201–5.   56. Ibid., p. 210.

57. Ibid., p. 211.   58. Ibid., p. 223.

59. Ibid.   60. Ibid., pp. 223–24.

61. Ibid., pp. 227–28.   62. Ibid., p. 228.

63. Ibid., pp. 228–29.

Conclusion

1. Philippe-Paul, comte de Ségur, *Napoleon's Russian Campaign*, trans. J. David Townsend (New York: Time/Life Books, 1965), pp. 43, 97.

2. Ibid., pp. 109, 228–31.

3. Astolphe, marquis de Custine, *Empire of the Czar: A Journey Through Eternal Russia*, trans. anonymous, intro. George Kennan (New York: Doubleday, 1989), pp. 123, 128.

4. Custine, *Empire of the Czar*, pp. 128, 155.

5. Custine, *Journey for Our Time: The Russian Journals of the Marquis de Custine*, trans. Phyllis Penn Kohler, intro. Walter Bedell Smith (Washington, D.C.: Gateway Editions, 1987), pp. 7, 9, 11.

6. Ernst Birke, "Die französische Osteuropa-Politik, 1914–1918," *Zeitschrift für Ostforschung* (1954, Heft 3), p. 322.

7. R. W. Seton-Watson, *Disraeli, Gladstone, and the Eastern Question* (New York: Norton, 1972), pp. 75, 244, 267.

8. William M. Sloane, *The Balkans: A Laboratory of History* (New York: Eaton & Mains, 1914), p. vii.

9. Ibid., pp. viii, 3, 56.

10. Harold Nicolson, *Peacemaking 1919* (New York: Grosset & Dunlap, 1965), pp. 33, 126; see also Hugh and Christopher Seton-Watson, *The Making of a New Europe: R. W. Seton-Watson and the Last Years of Austria-Hungary* (Seattle: Univ. of Washington Press, 1981); and Domenico Caccamo, "Presupposti e obiettivi della storiografia sull'Europa orientale," in *Introduzione alla Storia dell'Europa Orientale* (Rome: La Nuova Italia Scientifica, 1991), pp. 9–21; and Larry Wolff, "French Policy Towards Eastern Europe During the First World War: From *Dragon de l'Apocalypse* to *Cordon Sanitaire*," in *Essays in History: The E. C. Barksdale Student Lectures* (Arlington, Texas: Phi Alpha Theta, Univ. of Texas, 1980), pp. 177–90.

11. Nicolson, p. 27.

12. Thomas Mann, *The Magic Mountain*, trans. H. T. Lowe-Porter (New York: Alfred A. Knopf, 1967), pp. 157, 228, 289, 517.

13. Georgena Muir Mackenzie and Paulina Irby, *Travels in the Slavonic Provinces of Turkey-in-Europe* (London: Bell and Daldy, 1867), pp. xx, xxix, xxx.

14. Rebecca West, *Black Lamb and Grey Falcon: A Journey Through Yugoslavia* (Penguin Books, 1982), pp. 23, 328, 483; see also Larry Wolff, "Rebecca West," *The New York Times Book Review* (Feb. 10, 1991).

15. West, p. 662.

16. Michael Burleigh, *Germany Turns Eastwards: A Study of Ostforschung in the Third Reich* (Cambridge: Cambridge Univ. Press, 1988), pp. 137, 151, 167, 242; see also Larry Wolff, rev. of *Germany Turns Eastwards*, by Michael Burleigh, *Harvard Ukrainian Studies* 15, no. 3/4 (Dec. 1991): 456–59.

17. Burleigh, p. 306.

18. R. R. Palmer and Joel Colton, "The Transformation of Eastern Europe, 1648–1740," in *A History of the Modern World*, 3rd ed. (New York: Alfred A. Knopf, 1965), p. 174.

19. Thomas Caldecot Chubb, *Slavic Peoples* (Cleveland: World Publishing Company, 1962), p. 105.

20. Ian Fleming, *From Russia with Love* (London: Pan Books, 1959), pp. 142, 184.

21. *New York Times*, 22 Aug. 1991, p. 1; *Neue Zürcher Zeitung*, 7/8 Sept. 1991, p. 1; *Corriere della Sera*, 8 Sept. 1991, "Corriere Cultura," p. 5; *Boston Phoenix*, 13 Sept. 1991, Section I, pp. 32–33.

22. *New York Times*, 25 Mar. 1992, p. 1; 8 Apr. 1992, p. 1; 24 May 1992, p. 10.

23. Mikhail Gorbachev, *Perestroika: New Thinking for Our Country and the World* (1987; New York: Harper & Row, Perennial Library, 1988), p. 177.

24. Czesław Miłosz, *Native Realm: A Search for Self-Definition*, trans. Catherine S. Leach (New York: Doubleday, 1968), p. 2.

25. Leo Tolstoy, *War and Peace*, trans. Rosemary Edmonds (Harmondsworth, Eng.: Penguin Books, 1982), pp. 843, 1034.

26. Ibid., pp. 1343–44, 1401.

Index

In this index an "f" after a number indicates a separate reference on the next page, and an "ff" indicates separate references on the next two pages. A continuous discussion over two or more pages is indicated by a span of page numbers, e.g., "pp. 57–58." *Passim* is used for a cluster of references in close but not consecutive sequence.

Library of Congress Cataloging-in-Publication Data

Wolff, Larry.
Inventing Eastern Europe : The Map of Civilization on the Mind of
the Enlightenment / Larry Wolff.
p.   cm.
Includes index.
ISBN 0-8047-2314-1 (alk. paper)
1. Europe, Eastern—Description and travel.   2. Europe, Eastern—
Civilization—18th century.   I. Title.
DJK13.W65   1994
947—dc20
93-32774   CIP

∞ This book is printed on acid-free paper.
It has been typeset in 10/12 Galliard
by Tseng Information Systems, Inc.